FRAUD AND RISK IN COMMERCIAL LAW

This book focuses on contemporary problems related to fraud and risk in commercial law.

It has been said by some that we are in a 'golden age of fraud'. In part this has been caused by globalisation, technological changes and the financialisation of business. This has resulted in the creation of automated linkages with integrated supply chains and the creation of systemic risks, which have been exacerbated by new forms of intangible assets like tokens and their ease of movement. While regulation has ebbed and flowed given the desire of governments to generate economic growth, as well as the distrust of their coercive powers, the courts have sought to strike a balance between considerations such as commercial certainty and fairness.

The book provides an analysis of key contemporary issues on the theme of fraud and risk in commercial law, including: technology and fraud, secondary liability and 'failure to prevent' economic crime, abuse of business entities, insolvency and creditor protection, injunctions and other orders, cross-border issues, the relationship between regulation and private law, and solutions for policy makers.

Fraud and Risk in Commercial Law

Edited by
Paul S Davies
and
Hans Tjio

·HART·
OXFORD · LONDON · NEW YORK · NEW DELHI · SYDNEY

HART PUBLISHING

Bloomsbury Publishing Plc

Kemp House, Chawley Park, Cumnor Hill, Oxford, OX2 9PH, UK

1385 Broadway, New York, NY 10018, USA

29 Earlsfort Terrace, Dublin 2, Ireland

HART PUBLISHING, the Hart/Stag logo, BLOOMSBURY and the Diana logo are trademarks of Bloomsbury Publishing Plc

First published in Great Britain 2024

A catalogue record for this book is available from the British Library.

A catalogue record for this book is available from the Library of Congress.

Library of Congress Control Number: 2024937492

ISBN: HB: 978-1-50997-075-9
ePDF: 978-1-50997-077-3
ePub: 978-1-50997-076-6

Typeset by Compuscript Ltd, Shannon

PREFACE

This book is the second in the series by Hart Publishing on current issues in commercial law. The first, *Intermediaries in Commercial Law*, was published in 2022. This new volume is the product of a conference held at the National University of Singapore that was jointly organised with University College London in June 2023. That conference in turn came about due to concerns about the prevailing levels of fraud and complexity of risk in the world today. In part this has been caused by the usual suspects: globalisation, technological changes and the financialisation of business.

Jim Chanos, the well-known hedge fund manager who is familiar with risk creation and management, termed this the 'Golden Age of Fraud'. He must have been deeply affected by this view, both philosophically and perhaps financially, as he closed his hedge funds on 31 December 2023, having been in operation for almost 40 years.[1]

Across jurisdictions we can see a proliferation of scams of all forms by people intent on exploiting all possible ways to persuade innocent parties to part with their money, property and information. One problem is that there always seem to be new exciting labels, gimmicks or ideas in social and even mainstream media so that there is always a sense of optimism that there is money to be made. This feeds into individuals' fear of missing out. That appears to have played a large part in the recent FTX scandal.[2]

This preface leaves the heavy lifting of discussing what each author says to the first introductory chapter by Senior Judge Andrew Phang SC who lays out the contours of the various topics. These range from the development of technology and its exploitation to the role of private law and risk mitigation. His Honour links these areas to some of the cases on fraud that he encountered in his time on the Bench. Rounding up the general discussion on globalized risk is a chapter by Michael Bridge who looks at the operation of force majeure clauses and the frustration doctrine in terms of risk allocation.

Technology has been both a boon and a bane in the context of fraud and risk. There is the possibility that it can be used to detect fraud and minimize risk, as

[1] See A Gara and J Hughes, 'Short seller Jim Chanos to close his main hedge funds' 18 November 2023. Available at: www.ft.com/content/68d3a4cc-322e-421d-99d9-6657b21f7044.

[2] J Naughton: 'How did Sam Bankman-Fried attract investors? Well, Fomo probably helped' *The Guardian*, 11 November 2023. Available at: www.theguardian.com/commentisfree/2023/nov/11/how-did-sam-bankman-fried-attract-investors-well-fomo-probably-helped#:~:text=50-,Guardian%20 Pick,%2C%20appealed%20to%20lenders'%20greed.

Christopher Bruner discusses in his chapter. In fact, there may be mission critical situations in which management must adopt technology such as artificial intelligence to improve their oversight of possible fraud. However, it is often used in less positive ways and may, in fact, be used to create a further layer of complexity to shield a company from management or director wrongdoing. In this context, Elise Bant advocates for a test of 'systems intentionality' to modernise the test of attribution of corporate responsibility especially in cases of automated fraud.

Technology has also been used to create or attempt to create new forms of wealth and its management. Against the background of the collapse of the crypto trading platform FTX as the dominant story of the past year, Justin Lim examines the position of investors or customers on these platforms given their custodial/contractual relationships. The whole situation is complicated in situations of insolvency and restructuring. But there have been many other scandals involving crypto funds and even the underlying 'property' like stablecoins themselves. Timothy Chan and Kelvin F K Low cast a critical eye on the latest incarnation of the cryptoasset-as-fundraising story, that of blockchain tokenisation, which may represent further attempts by businesses to pursue 'asset-light' strategies where they earn fees from managing tokenised property that are no longer on their own balance sheets. In other words, they become new intermediaries with high transaction costs given the inherent difficulties in accurately recording and legally transferring many forms of sub-divided property.

Although Lord Leggatt in *Philipp v Barclays Bank* rightly suggested that private law and regulation should remain apart where possible,[3] it seems inevitable that there will be gaps in regulatory schemes that need to be filled in relation to liability and enforcement. The importance of private law in the commercial sphere is obviously crucial. For example, in *Grand View PTC v Wong*,[4] the Privy Council considered how the proper purpose rule for trustees could take into account letters of wishes. That case further confirmed the links between fraud and risk in that 'fraud on a power' is not necessarily about actual fraud or an excess of power; rather, it can involve an abuse of power in the sense of taking unnecessary risks beyond what the power was intended for even if 'the trustee may have acted in good faith and genuinely with a view to benefiting the beneficiaries'.[5]

Liability and enforcement in its various guises, including remedies, is discussed in chapters by Yip Man, on the *Mareva* injunction, focusing on the context of crypto fraud and its jurisdictional problems; Magda Raczysnka, who revisits the area of equitable tracing and its sometimes metaphysical presumptions; and William Swadling, who focuses on the power of rescission and how it actually works in law and practice. Tan Cheng Han then looks at third parties that are affected through the lens of agency law and Paul S Davies examines the settlement

[3] [2023] UKSC 25, [2023] 3 WLR 284.
[4] [2022] UKPC 47, [2023] WTLR 149.
[5] ibid [5] (Lord Richards).

of disputes. There is a public interest in encouraging compromises, which again recalls the uneasy but extant relationship between private law and regulation.

This link is further explored in the subsequent chapters on financial fraud, an area where regulation has intervened more than in much of what might be considered to be general commercial law. Yet gaps remain, and private law still has a part to play, even regarding regulated financial institutions. Özlem Gurses discusses how traditional insurance concepts are applicable to modern commodities fraud. Hans Tjio looks at banks and automated push payment fraud on their customers, as well as transactions defrauding creditors in general.

The last chapters in this book are comparative in a wider sense and focus on risk mitigation. Jodi Gardner and Devon Airey start at the institutional level by looking at small microbusinesses and how they are at greater risk today. Such businesses, unlike financial institutions, are more akin to consumers who are victims of fraud but can also be perpetrators or facilitators. There is then a different comparison across jurisdictions as Weiming Tan critically looks at *Caremark* duties in Delaware, which appear to impose oversight responsibilities on directors and/or management in the US, and assesses their suitability for legal transplantation into the United Kingdom. Virginia Harper Ho wraps up by studying the mechanisms used in China to enhance social credit and trust to reduce the risk of fraud. These approaches are not without weaknesses and are open to criticism but provide much food for thought given the challenges we face in combating fraud ex post and managing risk ex ante.

In bringing this project to fruition we are very grateful for the financial support of the EW Barker Centre for Law & Business at the National University of Singapore and the Commercial Law Centre at UCL. The sterling work of Elicia Chia, Ifraim Sofian Faylasuf and Shirley Mak ensured that the conference ran smoothly and the engagement of all those who attended the conference has improved the chapters within this book. Our research assistants, Chua Rui Yuan, Caleb Khoo Rui Biao, Ng Hao Xiang, Glenda Tan Pei Xuan and Tan Yean San, helped to prepare the manuscript and, as ever, the team at Hart Publishing have been a pleasure to work with and have ensured that the publication process has been as smooth as it could possibly be; we are very grateful to Roberta Bassi, Sinead Moloney and Verity Stuart. Paul would also like to thank the Leverhulme Trust for its generous support of his work through a Philip Leverhulme Prize.

Paul S Davies
London

Hans Tjio
Singapore

2024

CONTENTS

LIST OF CONTRIBUTORS

Devon Airey is a barrister at 3 Verulam Buildings.

Elise Bant is Professor of Private Law and Commercial Regulation at the University of Western Australia, a Professorial Fellow at the University of Melbourne and Fellow of the Australian Academy of Law.

Michael Bridge KC (Hon), FBA, Cassel Professor of Commercial Law Emeritus, London School of Economics; Visiting Professor, National University of Singapore.

Christopher M Bruner is the Stembler Family Distinguished Professor in Business Law at the University of Georgia School of Law and a Research Member of the European Corporate Governance Institute.

Timothy Chan is a Sheridan Fellow at the National University of Singapore.

Paul S Davies is Professor of Commercial Law at University College London and a barrister at Essex Court Chambers.

Jodi Gardner is the Brian Coote Chair in Private Law at the University of Auckland and an Adjunct Senior Research Fellow at the Centre for Banking & Finance Law, National University of Singapore.

Özlem Gürses is Professor of Commercial Law at King's College London.

Virginia Harper Ho is Professor of Law at City University of Hong Kong School of Law.

Justin Lim is a Sheridan Fellow at the National University of Singapore.

Kelvin FK Low is Professor of Law at the Faculty of Law, the University of Hong Kong.

Andrew Phang SC is a Senior Judge of the Supreme Court of Singapore and Distinguished Professor of Law at the Yong Pung How School of Law, Singapore Management University.

Magda Raczysnka is Associate Professor of Law at University College London.

William Swadling is Professor of Law at the University of Oxford and a Fellow of Brasenose College.

Tan Cheng-Han SC is Professor of Law and Chief Strategy Officer at the Faculty of Law, National University of Singapore.

Weiming Tan is an Assistant Professor at the Faculty of Law, National University of Singapore.

Hans Tjio is CJ Koh Professor and Director of the EW Barker Centre for Law and Business at the Faculty of Law, National University of Singapore.

Yip Man is Professor and the Associate Dean (Faculty Matters & Research) at the Yong Pung How School of Law, Singapore Management University.

TABLE OF CASES

A

B

C

D

E

F

G

I

J

K

L

M

N

O

P

Q

R

S

T

U

V

W

X

Y

Z

TABLE OF LEGISLATION

England and Wales

Australia

China

France

Germany

Japan

Jersey

New Zealand

Singapore

United States

International Material

1

Negotiating a Brave New World: Fraud and Risk in Modern Commercial Law

ANDREW PHANG*

1. Introduction

We live in a brave new world. Much of what was once the stuff of fiction has now become reality. In particular, we have witnessed technological advances the like of which we would not even have begun to contemplate even at the turn of the second millennium. No one has been exempt – not even this mid-sexagenarian. Now, almost a quarter of a century on, we have to take stock of the double-edged sword that is technology. Indeed, technology has – unfortunately – facilitated fraud in a manner and on a scale that we have never witnessed before.

With technology has come globalisation and internationalisation. The world is a much smaller place. From a physical standpoint, we are often just hours away from each other, notwithstanding being thousands of miles distant. With the Covid-19 pandemic, technology enabled interaction to continue even when physical interaction was precluded.

That we are present here is testimony to the sea changes that I have just mentioned. The present conference is a timely one because it examines, amongst other issues, the legal impact of both globalisation and technology on fraud and risk in commercial law. As already mentioned at the outset, fraud, in particular, has been facilitated in an especially unfortunate manner and it is therefore no surprise that many of the papers in today's conference address this issue in a myriad of various commercial contexts.

However, that is not the end of the matter. It is true that long before the advent of technology, commercial law had already come into being. But it has not stood still and has been developing ever since. For example, company law as we know

* All views expressed are personal views only and do not reflect the views of the Supreme Court of Singapore, the Singapore Management University or the University of Reading. I would like to express my deepest appreciation to Professor Hans Tjio and Professor Paul Davies for their helpful comments and suggestions, as well as to Mr Chua Rui Yuan for his excellent editing of the manuscript. However, all errors remain mine alone.

it has changed quite radically.[1] So has banking and finance law. When I was a student, much of the first part of the banking law course was occupied with learning the legal intricacies surrounding the law of negotiable instruments in general, and that surrounding the writing of cheques in particular. Cheques are, in fact, now being phased out in the Singapore context. The law of insurance has changed as well. While some of this is regulatory in nature, private law needs to fill the gaps as regulation (particularly in the legislative sphere) always lags behind what happens in practice. This, however, has to be done judiciously given the need for judicial restraint. New legal strategies are therefore also required in order to deal with the issues of fraud and risk in commercial law. They are utterly necessary as commercial law provides the legal lifeblood without which the heart of trade and commerce would have come to a standstill. As already alluded to, globalisation and technology are also often (albeit not invariably) inextricably intertwined with such legal analysis as well as strategy even as we attempt to understand fraud and risk in new commercial contexts.

And all this simultaneously impacts the legal *remedies* that may be awarded, which are as (on occasion, more) important than the legal rights from which they flow[2] as are (as we shall see in a moment) the appropriate *legislative responses*.

All that I have said thus far constitutes the backdrop against which this conference takes place. What, then, is the relevance of the specific concepts of fraud and risk in the context of commercial law and which constitute the focus of the present conference?

2. Fraud and Risk in Commercial Law

2.1. Fraud

Let me first turn briefly to the issue of fraud in commercial law. The term 'fraud', however, has many meanings. It may refer to tortious fraud[3] (that might also impact commercial transactions[4]); it can even refer to equitable fraud.[5] Indeed,

[1] See, eg, A Godwin, PW Lee and RT Langford (eds), *Technology and Corporate Law: How Innovation Shapes Corporate Activity* (Cheltenham, Edward Elgar Publishing, 2021).

[2] See, eg, A Phang, 'The Law of Remedies: The Importance of Comparative and Integrated Analysis' (2016) 28 *Singapore Academy of Law Journal* 746.

[3] See, eg, GKY Chan, *The Law of Torts in Singapore*, 2nd edn (Singapore, Academy Publishing, 2016) ch 14, especially paras 14.002–14.031 (on the legal principles relating to tortious deceit in the Singapore context).

[4] See, eg, in the context of the law of contract, P Koh, 'Misrepresentation and Non-Disclosure' in ABL Phang (gen ed), *The Law of Contract in Singapore*, 2nd edn (Singapore, Academy Publishing, 2022) vol 1, ch 11, especially paras 11.165–11.200.

[5] See, eg, A Phang, 'Equitable Fraud: Some Personal Reminiscences and Reflections' (2019) 13 *Journal of Equity* 114. Indeed, as Professor Sheridan himself observed in his seminal work, LA Sheridan, *Fraud in Equity: A Study in English and Irish Law* (London, Pitman & Sons, 1957) 1:

> '… Fraud is infinite in variety; sometimes it is audacious and unblushing; sometimes it pays a sort of homage to virtue, and then it is modest and retiring; it would be honesty itself if it could only

commercial transactions themselves cover a broad range of legal activities that go beyond the more traditional categories. In these broader areas of commercial law, we encounter the issue of fraud in a variety of contexts, albeit more often than not with common underlying threads.

If I might digress for a brief moment, all of us have encountered the concept of fraud at one time or another. As I reminisced in an earlier conference,[6] one encounter as a legal academic with equitable fraud occurred when, by a stroke of good fortune, I managed to obtain a copy of Professor LA Sheridan's seminal book entitled *Fraud in Equity: A Study in English and Irish Law*[7] and also managed, with the kind assistance of a long-serving administrative staff of the Faculty of Law at the National University of Singapore,[8] to get it personalised by Professor Sheridan himself. The book itself came in handy as I was preparing the Welcome Address for that very conference itself.[9] Another encounter with fraud came whilst I was a judge, albeit as a participant in an academic symposium on misleading silence.[10]

I had occasion to deal with the burden of proof in fraud during my first year on the Bench as a trial judge.[11] In that case, I had occasion to consider (as well as apply to the facts) what continues to be a somewhat thorny legal doctrine – not least because it raises both theoretical as well as practical issues, all of which interact with each other. This related to the standard of proof in *civil* proceedings where fraud and/or dishonesty was alleged. Following (and in fact being bound by) the Singapore Court of Appeal decision in *Tang Yoke Kheng v Lek Benedict* ('*Tang Yoke Kheng*'),[12] I held as follows:[13]

> In summary, the standard of proof in civil proceedings where fraud and/or dishonesty is alleged is the civil standard of proof on a balance of probabilities. However, where

afford it. But fraud is fraud all the same; and it is the fraud, not the manner of it, which calls for the interposition of the Court.' In *Stonemets* v. *Head*, in the course of an amusing judgment in the Missouri Supreme Court, Lamm, J., burst into flower to much the same effect: 'Fraud is kaleidoscopic, infinite. Fraud being infinite and taking on protean form at will, were courts to cramp themselves by defining it with a hard and fast definition, their jurisdiction would be cunningly circumvented at once by new schemes beyond the definition. Messieurs, the fraud-feasors, would like nothing half so well as for courts to say they would go thus far, and no further in its pursuit. Accordingly definitions of fraud are of set purpose left general and flexible, and thereto courts match their astuteness against the versatile inventions of fraud-doers.'

[6] This was the 2019 Journal of Equity Annual Conference.

[7] Sheridan (n 5).

[8] The late Mr Young Cheng Wah. Together with Professor Sheridan (who was the first Dean of the Faculty of Law, National University of Singapore (and see A Phang, 'Founding Father and Legal Scholar – The Life and Work of Professor LA Sheridan' [1999] *Singapore Journal of Legal Studies* 335)), they were, in fact, the only two initial staff members of the Department of Law at the then University of Malaya in Singapore (as it was first known; the University of Malaya in Singapore later became the University of Singapore and, subsequently, the National University of Singapore). See also ABL Phang, 'Mr Young Cheng Wah – A Personal Appreciation' (1995) 16 *Singapore Law Review* 23.

[9] Phang (n 5).

[10] And see A Phang, 'Critical Pressure Points in the Regulation of Silence in Misleading Conduct' in E Bant and JM Paterson (eds), *Misleading Silence* (Oxford, Hart Publishing, 2020) ch 2.

[11] See *Chua Kwee Chen v Koh Choon Chin* [2006] SGHC 92, [2006] 3 SLR(R) 469.

[12] *Tang Yoke Kheng v Lek Benedict* [2005] SGCA 27, [2005] 3 SLR(R) 263.

[13] *Chua Kwee Chen* (n 11) [39] (emphasis in original).

> such an allegation is made (as in the present proceedings), *more* evidence is required than would be the situation in an ordinary civil case. Such an inquiry lies, therefore and in the final analysis, in the sphere of practical application (rather than theoretical speculation). In this regard, a distinction ought not, in my view, to be drawn between civil fraud and criminal fraud.

Indeed, in this case, I also attempted to elaborate – in the context of the issue and facts in that case – on the *interaction* (alluded to, in fact, in the above quotation) between theory on the one hand and practice on the other, as follows:[14]

> 22 Indeed, in the practical sphere of *application*, the court is well equipped and able to draw the necessary lines, *regardless* of the specific formula adopted. In the circumstances, and contrary to the proposition set out above (at [20]), it might well make for more *conceptual* clarity if the courts adhere to *just two* standards of proof, *viz*, the civil and criminal standards, respectively – *provided that this will not make a difference to the amount of proof required by the court concerned, especially in situations of fraud where more evidence would be required compared to a normal civil case because of the seriousness inherent in an allegation of fraud.* In this, we find the balance between theory and practice, between concept and application. It is not something which academic theory can capture – not fully, at least. The sphere of practical application is not susceptible of comprehensive theoretical analysis simply because theory tends, by its very nature, towards static frameworks. The sphere of practical application, on the other hand, is dynamic. But it is a dynamism that can run riot and confuse for the future without the framework which theory and its concomitant concepts provide. Hence, both *interact and are integrated* with each other, but *no one can claim superiority or precedence over the other.* The *residuary tension* that results reflects the imperfection and dynamism that constitute a kind of paradox which we live with but can never fully explain.
>
> 23 The position laid down in *Tang Yoke Kheng* seeks, in fact, to combine theory and practice. The court has, quite correctly if I may be permitted to say so, drawn the line at the point where theory would threaten practice. In the final analysis, theory must serve practice in order that justice and fairness is achieved. And justice and fairness is all about *actual* people and events, not flights of academic fancy. Hence, the promulgation of a *third* standard of proof would only serve to confuse the situation where the courts were already always doing what they ought to be doing *in practice* – which is to require more evidence in situations where fraud has been alleged. Indeed, it might be asked: If a third standard of proof is permissible, why not recognise more standards of proof as the facts of each case will obviously vary from each other (see also *PJTV Denson (M) Sdn Bhd v Roxy (Malaysia) Sdn Bhd* [1980] 2 MLJ 136). At this point, in fact, theory pulls us back, ironically perhaps, to legal *terra firma* – simply because the question just posed *conflates* theory with practice. In other words, the framework of the civil and criminal standards of proof, whilst *guiding* lawyers and courts in the sphere of application to the *facts* concerned, is *not the same as the facts themselves.* This, I hope, illustrates the *interactive* nature of theory and practice. When one escapes its 'boundaries', the other reins it in – and *vice versa*.

[14] ibid [22]–[24] (emphasis in original).

24 Indeed, it is, in the final analysis and as already mentioned, the *substance* rather than the form or label which is of the first importance although, as I have been at pains to point out, both theory and practice do interact and it is *this interaction* which constitutes the *substance* of the matter.

Over the course of my tenure as an appellate judge over a period of almost seventeen years, it is not perhaps surprising that I did indeed deal with cases on fraud from time to time (principally in the context of the law of contract[15]). An interesting decision of the Singapore Court of Appeal where an important issue was raised but not definitively decided was *RBC Properties Pte Ltd v Defu Furniture Pte Ltd* ('*RBC Properties*').[16] For the purposes of the present chapter, I am, in fact, referring to one particular aspect of that case – the measure of damages that ought to obtain pursuant to s 2(1) of the Misrepresentation Act[17] (a point which has also since been the subject of a perceptive comment[18]). Although the court did express some provisional views on this particular issue,[19] it is also important to note that, as the issue itself was not argued before the court, the court stated that it would express a conclusive view only when it was next directly in issue before it.[20] What is interesting for the purposes of the present piece is the fact that the provisional view expressed by the court was in fact *at variance with the prevailing case law.* In particular, in the English Court of Appeal decision of *Royscot Trust Ltd v Rogerson* ('*Royscot Trust*'),[21] it was held (disagreeing with the then prevalent academic opinion on this particular issue) that the measure of damages to be awarded under s 2(1) of the Misrepresentation Act ought to be that measure which would have been awarded for *fraudulent misrepresentation or deceit.* This view was subsequently cited with approval by the Singapore High Court in *Ng Buay Hock v Tan Keng Huat.*[22] However, drawing upon, inter alia, the secondary legal literature,[23] the court in the *RBC Properties* case suggested that the approach laid down in the *Royscot Trust* case (as briefly described above) might be *reconsidered.* It should, however, also be noted

[15] See, eg, the Singapore Court of Appeal decisions of *Wishing Star Ltd v Jurong Town Corp* [2008] SGCA 17, [2008] 2 SLR(R) 909 (in relation to the award of damages for fraudulent misrepresentation) and *Wee Chiaw Sek Anna v Ng Li-Ann Genevieve* [2013] SGCA 36, [2013] 3 SLR 801 (in relation to the elements of fraudulent misrepresentation).

[16] *RBC Properties Pte Ltd v Defu Furniture Pte Ltd* [2014] SGCA 62, [2015] 1 SLR 997. I draw here from Phang (n 2) 763–764.

[17] Misrepresentation Act (Cap 390, 1994 Rev Ed) (Singapore).

[18] See T Liau, 'Abolishing the Fiction of Fraud in the Misrepresentation Act' [2015] *LMCLQ* 464.

[19] *RBC Properties* (n 16) [80]–[85].

[20] ibid [85].

[21] *Royscot Trust Ltd v Rogerson* [1991] 2 QB 297 (CA).

[22] *Ng Buay Hock v Tan Keng Huat* [1997] SGHC 58, [1997] 1 SLR(R) 507.

[23] *RBC Properties* (n 16) [83]–[84], citing R Hooley, 'Damages and the Misrepresentation Act 1967' (1991) 107 *LQR* 547; J Cartwright, *Misrepresentation, Mistake and Non-Disclosure*, 3rd edn (London, Sweet & Maxwell, 2012) para 6-64, n 386; I Brown and A Chandler, 'Deceit, Damages and the Misrepresentation Act 1967, s. 2(1)' [1992] *LMCLQ* 40; H G Beale (gen ed), *Chitty on Contracts*, 31st edn (London, Sweet & Maxwell, 2012) para 6-075; as well as E Peel, *Treitel: The Law of Contract*, 13th edn (London, Sweet & Maxwell, 2011) para 9-066.

that the court in the *RBC Properties* case had also noted the approach of two Law Lords in the House of Lords decision in *Smith New Court Securities Ltd v Citibank NA* ('*Smith New Court*'),[24] in particular, that of Lord Steyn who had observed that the *Royscot Trust* case had been subject to 'trenchant academic criticism'.[25] Indeed, the court proceeded to observe thus:[26]

> Although both Lord Steyn and Lord Browne-Wilkinson expressed no conclusive view on *Royscot Trust* in *Smith New Court*, the tenor of their judgments (particularly that of Lord Steyn) suggests that the days of Royscot Trust might be numbered.

The court in the *RBC Properties* case then further observed as follows:[27]

> Indeed, as we have already noted, there is no reason in both logic and principle why a plaintiff should be as well-placed as he would have been had the misrepresentation concerned taken place in a situation of *actual* fraud or deceit since, *ex hypothesi*, the situation is in fact *not* one that pertains to actual fraud or deceit but on the contrary one that *falls short* of it. Further, and consistent with Lord Steyn's observations in *Smith New Court*, it is extremely difficult to see how the moral turpitude entailed under s 2(1) would [be] on the same level as that entailed in a situation of fraudulent misrepresentation or deceit.

This area of private law may have been another indication that fraud always has to be seen in context. Returning to the question of common underlying threads in relation to fraud in commercial law, one such thread is that of technology. Indeed, recent instances of fraud in relation to crypto exchanges, for example, have underscored the need to devise legal solutions to avoid such undesirable consequences for both individuals as well as corporations alike.[28] Indeed, the papers in the second session of this conference (by Professor Kelvin Low and Professor Timothy Chan,[29] Professor Elise Bant,[30] Professor Christopher Bruner[31] and Professor Justin Lim[32]) address contemporary issues that arise in relation to fraud in relation to the exploitation of technology in various commercial contexts.

If I might digress for a moment, the importance of technology is one of the reasons why I have consistently advocated the introduction of a compulsory law and technology course in the law school curriculum. It need only be an introductory course that would therefore be accessible to all law students. It can be done if my own experience as a non-techie is anything to go by. I am pleased to note that the Faculty of Law at the National University of Singapore is in the

[24] *Smith New Court Securities Ltd v Citibank NA* [1997] AC 254 (HL).

[25] ibid 283, citing R Hooley, 'Damages and the Misrepresentation Act 1967' (1991) 107 *LQR* 547.

[26] *RBC Properties* (n 16) [84].

[27] ibid (emphasis in original).

[28] See Justin Lim, Chapter 5 in this volume. Reference may also be made, in the Singapore context, to the General Division of the High Court decision of *CLM v CLN* [2022] 5 SLR 273.

[29] See Chapter 6 in this volume.

[30] See Chapter 4 in this volume.

[31] See Chapter 3 in this volume.

[32] See Chapter 5 in this volume.

process of introducing such a course.[33] This is one of the reasons why I mooted a simple – albeit not simplistic – law and technology book that would be of use to both students as well as the legal profession. That book has since been published,[34] although, in the nature of things, it may need to be updated more frequently than other law textbooks.

Returning to the issue of fraud in commercial law, in order to combat such fraud, the precise *context* is, in my view, of the first importance. It is therefore heartening to note that the present conference does in fact attempt to cover a wide variety of possible contexts. On occasion, in fact, it is imperative to go back to basics. For example, in so far as corporate fraud in a digital age is concerned, Professor Elise Bant attempts to provide us with a principled and practical method for identifying the culpable corporate mind in the face of otherwise complex and diffused organisational structures,[35] whilst Professor Christopher Bruner examines the range of potential risks that must be guarded against as a result of the use of Artificial Intelligence in the corporate sphere (which, on the positive side, generates a multitude of positive operational efficiencies).[36] To take yet another illustration, Professor Kelvin Low and Professor Timothy Chan attempt to dispel what they perceive to be the superficially attractive gloss surrounding tokenisation and bring us back to what they view to be its true nature.[37]

2.2. Risk

Commercial transactions entail – potentially at least – risk. How that risk is to be allocated lies at the heart of many legal doctrines. If only we lived in a perfect world and everyone was an angel. There would be no legal disputes and possibly no need for the law. Unfortunately, that is not the case. The imperfection

[33] In their Message in *TRAIL – Year in Review 2022* (Centre for Technology, Robotics, Artificial Intelligence and the Law, National University Faculty of Law) at https://law.nus.edu.sg/trail/wp-content/uploads/sites/9/2023/01/NUS-TRAIL-Year-in-Review-2022.pdf (accessed 15 May 2023), the Co-Directors of the Centre, Associate Professor Daniel Seng and Professor David Tan, note (albeit with respect to more advanced academic modules) as follows (at 4):

> [W]e will be working on developing and launching a new law and technology module to better equip law students to understand the interface between technology and law. Drawing on the expertise of TRAIL, its Academic Fellows and collaborators from other institutions, students will learn basic Python programming, be familiarised with legal tech apps and platforms and be equipped with design thinking skills so as to better enable them to handle the vicissitudes of a more technologically oriented legal practice.

[34] See S Chesterman, YH Goh and ABL Phang (gen eds), *Law and Technology in Singapore* (Singapore, Academy Publishing, 2021).

[35] See Chapter 4 in this volume.

[36] See Chapter 3 in this volume.

[37] See Chapter 6 in this volume. Reference may also be made to KFK Low and E Mik, 'Pause the Blockchain Legal Revolution' (2020) 69 *ICLQ* 135; KFK Low, 'Confronting Cryptomania: Can Equity Tame the Blockchain?' (2020) 14 *Journal of Equity* 240; and KFK Low, 'The Emperor's New Art: Cryptomania, Art and Property' [2022] *Conveyancer and Property Lawyer* 382.

inherent in the world translates – in the commercial sphere – to a tension. The law of contract best exemplifies this tension. On the one hand, contracts must be observed as parties ought to be kept to their bargain (having freely assessed the actual and potential risks involved before entering into the agreement concerned with each other): that is one concept of fairness. However, at the other end of the business continuum, there may arise situations that result in *undue* injustice to one of the parties and this has given rise to countervailing doctrines such as the vitiating factors to ensure that justice is done: this is another concept of fairness (which must, however, be legitimately constrained lest commerce and business be rendered chaotic and unworkable).[38] One such vitiating factor – fraud – has already been considered earlier. Indeed, as we have also seen, the concept of fraud goes well beyond the law of contract – extending (as noted by the papers in this conference) into areas such as company law,[39] the law of insurance,[40] banking law,[41] the law of trusts,[42] the law relating to Mareva injunctions,[43] cross-border insolvency,[44] as well as microbusiness.[45] It is therefore vital to stem its toxic and even deadly legal effects, and the papers in this conference have gone a long way in furnishing us with the appropriate legal approach as well as weapons to weather this onslaught in a variety of important commercial contexts.

However, there are also situations that do not involve any legal wrongdoing on the part of a party. One example may be seen in the law of contract, when an external catastrophic event that was not within the contemplation of the parties at the time the contract was made occurs in such a manner that the parties themselves may consider themselves discharged from their agreement by operation of law. The doctrine of frustration – which has civil law roots – was developed as a (limited) legal device to achieve justice and fairness between the parties.[46] However, what happens when something as catastrophic as the COVID-19 pandemic occurs? Parties might look immediately to what they had agreed, particularly in the form of *force majeure* clauses which are then subject (under the common law at least) to the principles of contractual interpretation.[47] It may, however, be the case that

[38] See, eg, A Phang, 'Security of Contract and the Pursuit of Fairness' (2016) 16 *Journal of Contract Law* 158.

[39] See Chapters 3 and 4 in this volume.

[40] See Professor Özlem Gürses. Chapter 12 in this volume. See also, by the same author, Ö Gürses, *The Insurance of Commercial Risks: Law and Practice*, 5th edn (London, Sweet & Maxwell, 2017).

[41] See Professor Hans Tjio, Chapter 13 in this volume.

[42] See Professor William Swadling, Chapter 9 in this volume.

[43] See Professor Yip Man, Chapter 7 in this volume.

[44] In the context of crypto-assets, see Professor Justin Lim, Chapter 5 in this volume.

[45] See Ms Devon Airey and Professor Jodi Gardner, Chapter 14 in this volume.

[46] See generally, CH Tham and ZX Tan, 'Frustration' in Phang (n 4) vol 2, ch 19, as well as E Peel, *Frustration and Force Majeure*, 4th edn (London, Sweet & Maxwell, 2022).

[47] Which are themselves still developing. And see generally, YH Goh, *The Interpretation of Contracts in Singapore* (Sweet & Maxwell Asia, 2018) as well as P Koh, YH Goh and ABL Phang, 'Express and Implied Terms' in Phang (n 4) vol 1, ch 6, especially paras 06.049–06.111. Reference may also be made to the Singapore Appellate Division of the High Court decision of *Ser Kim Koi v GTMS Construction Pte Ltd* [2022] SGHC(A) 34 at [81].

in situations such as these, *legislative intervention* might be needed to supplement the existing common law rules. This was indeed the somewhat distant past (in the form of Singapore's Frustrated Contracts Act 1959[48]) as well as the fairly recent past (see the COVID-19 (Temporary Measures) Act 2020, enacted in response to the COVID-19 pandemic[49]). Indeed, the topic of *force majeure* clauses constitutes the first paper by Professor Michael Bridge[50] in the very first session of this conference (which session itself provides us snapshots of the effects of globalisation on risk and fraud in commercial law). As I have already mentioned, the doctrine of frustration in general and *force majeure* clauses, in particular at common law, find almost precise analogues in (and even historical influence from) the civil law. It may be that the civil law adopts a slightly more wait-and-see approach which the COVID-19 provisions here brought in to ameliorate a more rights-based common law approach. There is therefore much that various jurisdictions can learn from each other in this particular regard. Indeed, I have consistently emphasised the importance of comparative analysis, especially in the interconnected world in which we live today. Such analysis is not only important in relation to the development of the common law by the courts (particularly in novel situations) but is also important in ensuring that legal scholarship is rendered more textured.[51]

That the present conference in fact emphasises the importance of comparative analysis is clear from the papers themselves. Indeed, some of the topics dealt with in this conference *necessarily* involve direct comparative analysis[52] or at least deal with material which has the potential for consideration by other jurisdictions either because they deal with a major jurisdiction and/or with multi-jurisdictions (such as, respectively, the papers by Professor Virginia Harper Ho[53] and Professor Weiming Tan[54]).

2.3. Remedies and Responses

As already alluded to earlier, this conference deals not only with rights but also with the relevant remedies (as well as other related responses). In this respect (and not surprisingly), recourse, in the main, to private law is essential. This is

[48] Frustrated Contracts Act 1959 (2020 Rev Ed) (Singapore). This was, not surprisingly, modelled on its UK legislative counterpart.

[49] COVID-19 (Temporary Measures) Act (No 14 of 2020) (Singapore). And see generally, Tham and Tan (n 46) paras 19.215–19.248 (where the learned authors also deal with the relevant common law decisions as well as the Act).

[50] See Chapter 2 in this volume.

[51] See, eg, Phang (n 2) 748–751.

[52] See, eg, Professor Yip Man, Chapter 7 in this volume and Professor Justin Lim, Chapter 5 in this volume.

[53] See Chapter 16 in this volume.

[54] See Chapter 15 in this volume.

illustrated, for example, by the papers by Professor Magda Raczysnka,[55] Professor William Swadling,[56] Professor Paul S Davies,[57] and Professor Tan Cheng-Han.[58] Indeed, in the nature of things, most of the papers do necessarily touch on remedies and/or responses as well.

However, as we have seen in relation to the law relating to frustration and *force majeure*, the appropriate legal response may also lie in the *legislative* sphere.[59] This is further illustrated by Professor Weiming Tan's paper in relation to the corporate governance sphere.[60] At this juncture, it might be apposite to note – on a more general level – that the Singapore courts themselves have, on occasion, indicated the need for legislative reform (particularly when the need is urgent).

One recent example may be found in thc Singapore Court of Appeal decision of *Esben Finance Ltd v Wong Hou-Lianq Neil*.[61] The case itself raised a variety of issues. For present purposes, however, only one issue is pertinent – whether or not claims in unjust enrichment fall within the ambit of section 6 of the Singapore Limitation Act 1959.[62] Put simply, the court held that claims in unjust enrichment did *not* fall within the ambit of the Act.[63] In adopting this approach, it differed from the UK approach which basically holds that such claims, being coincident with quasi-contractual claims, did constitute a cause of action founded on simple contract within the meaning of the UK Limitation Act 1980[64] (the equivalent of s 6 of the Singapore Limitation Act). The court held, first, that the proposition that such claims were based on quasi-contract or an implied contract had clearly been rejected as the law relating to unjust enrichment had developed over the past few decades in both the UK itself as well as in Singapore. Secondly, the court held that a claim in quasi-contract was conceptually different from a contractual claim as the former involved the use of a fiction where there was in fact no contract.[65]

In so far as claims for restitution for wrongs were concerned, the court noted that such claims related only to the remedial response to a civil wrong and the question of whether such claims did indeed fall within the ambit of the Singapore Limitation Act therefore depended on the nature of the underlying wrong.

[55] See Chapter 8 in this volume; See also generally, by the same author, M Raczynska, *The Law of Tracing in Commercial Transactions* (Oxford, Oxford University Press, 2018).

[56] See Chapter 9 in this volume.

[57] See Chapter 11 in this volume.

[58] See Chapter 10 in this volume.

[59] See text to n 49 above.

[60] See Chapter 15 in this volume.

[61] *Esben Finance Ltd v Wong Hou-Lianq Neil* [2022] SGCA(I) 1, [2022] 1 SLR 136.

[62] Limitation Act 1959 (2020 Rev Ed) (Singapore).

[63] I draw liberally here from my essay that was delivered in more abbreviated form as the University of Reading Law School Annual Lecture 2023 on 28 February 2023: see A Phang, 'The Importance of Comparative Common Law – A View from Singapore' [2023] *JBL* 538. The reader is referred to this essay for a discussion of other aspects of the case as well as other leading Singapore decisions in the areas of contract law and the law of torts.

[64] Limitation Act 1980 (Cap 58) (UK).

[65] See generally, *Esben Finance* (n 61) [48], [52] and [57]–[69].

Where, therefore, a claim for restitution for wrongs was founded on a civil wrong for which a limitation period *was* provided pursuant to the aforementioned Act (such as a tort), the limitation period provided under this Act applied.[66]

However, a claim in *unjust enrichment* was *not* founded upon any contract, tort, trust or other ground in equity and such a claim therefore constituted a distinct and new branch of the law of obligations (alongside the law of contract, the law of tort, and the law of equity).[67] The court proceeded to observe that the legislative history of the Singapore Limitation Act indicated that claims in unjust enrichment lay outside the ambit of that Act as the law of restitution and unjust enrichment was a developing branch of the law of obligations and most claims thereunder would not have been in the contemplation of the Legislature at the point of drafting the Singapore Limitation Act and its predecessor legislation. Statutory limitation periods were creatures of statute and it was not the function of the courts to act as 'mini-legislatures' by reading into the Singapore Limitation Act a statutory limitation period for a claim which the Legislature did not intend to impose, given the absence of a sweeping-up or catch-all provision imposing a general limitation period for all other claims not expressly specified in that Act itself. The present situation – and this is the main point for the purposes of the present essay – resulted in an urgent clarion call for *legislative intervention* to provide a time bar for claims in unjust enrichment.[68]

A couple of commentators have observed that the approach of the court in this particular regard 'ought not [to] be overly surprising to a Singaporean audience' and has indeed 'long been in the making'.[69] One commentator has, however, observed that such a holding might potentially open the floodgates of litigation with respect to unjust enrichment claims which arose more than six years ago.[70] However, the learned author did also admit that 'it could be that due to effluxion of time, claimants would face an uphill task as a matter of evidence of proving the relevant unjust factor and the fear of floodgates of claims is exaggerated'.[71] It should also be noted that a future court itself would have the discretion, should the issue be raised, to determine when the effective date of such a clarification in the law should take place.[72]

[66] ibid [70]–[74].

[67] ibid [76]–[78].

[68] ibid [81]–[85].

[69] See R Leow and T Liau, 'A Pyrrhic Victory for Unjust Enrichment in Singapore? *Esben Finance Ltd v Wong Hou-Lianq Neil*' (2023) 86 *MLR* 518, 524–525 (citing the decisions of the Singapore High Court in *MCST No 473 v De Beers Jewellery Pte Ltd* [2001] SGHC 206, [2001] 2 SLR(R) 669 [68]–[79] and the Singapore Court of Appeal in *MCST No 473 v De Beers Jewellery Pte Ltd* [2002] SGCA 13, [2002] 1 SLR(R) 418 [32]).

[70] See HW Tang, 'Limitation Period for Unjust Enrichment Claims, at the Claimant's Expense, Lack of Consent, Illegality, and Vindication of Property Rights: *Esben Finance Ltd and Others v Wong Hou-Lianq Neil*' (2022) 33 *King's Law Journal* 345, 353.

[71] ibid.

[72] Indeed, such a discretion exists even in the context of the scope of the doctrine of prospective overruling: see the Singapore High Court decision of *Public Prosecutor v Hue An Li* [2014] SGHC 171, [2014] 4 SLR 661.

3. Conclusion

This short Introduction cannot do justice to the papers presented in this conference. Indeed, the astute reader would have realised that they are so nuanced that they defy summary as well as categorisation – even in relation to the more limited categories of points that I have raised.[73] They need to read and studied closely. No summary can do them justice. The editors (whose work and effort in selecting and organising the various authors should not be underestimated) and the authors themselves are to be heartily commended for not only adding to the relevant legal literature but also for also educating us and making us reflect further on the various legal issues. As a result, the brave new world that faces us has been rendered that much less daunting.

[73] As evidenced, for example, by there being more than one reference to the same paper in the present chapter.

2

Force Majeure Clauses: Character, Scope and Protection

MICHAEL BRIDGE KC

1. Introduction

This chapter deals with contractual efforts to deal with future uncertainty against the backdrop of the law on contractual frustration. The inflexible and strict character of that law renders it unsuitable to meet the needs of contracting parties facing an uncertain future that may imperil the planned contractual adventure or upset the agreed allocation of commercial risk. The focus here is on sale of goods and charterparty contracts calling for future or protracted performance. Particular attention will be paid to the decision of the courts in *Classic Maritime Inc v Limbungan Makmur Sdn Bhd*.[1]

The existing law on frustration with its narrow forgiveness of non-performance amounts to an invitation to contracting parties to depart from the common law and plan for the future with the aid of *force majeure* clauses. This chapter deals with the following questions. First, do *force majeure* clauses amount in some or all instances to exception clauses with the consequences that flow from such a characterisation? Here we shall see an emergent distinction, not precisely drawn in the past, between a true exception clause and what might be styled a frustration (or cancellation) clause.[2] Secondly, what are the consequences of this distinction in a particular case? The consequences in question concern (a) whether a clause protects an obligor party from liability for non-performance even if the obligor is otherwise unable to perform; and (b) whether, even if the clause does not afford protection to the obligor, its liability in damages might yet be reduced by the impact of untoward future events. In particular, may an obligor, unable to claim the protection of a clause for not being ready and willing to perform on the

[1] [2018] EWHC 2389 (Comm), [2019] 1 Lloyd's Rep 349, reversed in part [2019] EWCA Civ 1102, [2020] 1 Lloyd's Rep 178. On *force majeure* in general, see E Peel (ed), *Treitel: Frustration and Force Majeure*, 4th edn (London, Sweet & Maxwell, 2021) ch 12.

[2] I prefer 'cancellation clause' since 'frustration clause' threatens the inappropriate incorporation of frustration rules.

occasion of the untoward event, plead that that same event reduces or eliminates its liability in damages for non-performance?

An obligor unable to claim the protection of the doctrine of frustration or of a *force majeure* clause commits a breach of contract. If the breach is sufficiently serious for the obligee to terminate, the oblige is both released from further performance and entitled to damages for the harm committed by the breach. Apart from loss arising immediately from the breach, these damages will compensate for the loss of future benefits that would have been earned but for the termination of the contract. A critical question now is whether account should be taken of post-termination matters in settling the recoverable amount. These matters might include events for which neither party had assumed contractual responsibility, such as a natural disaster. They might also include the obligee's own capacity to perform at the future date. This chapter deals only with the first of these matters.[3]

Further questions arising for consideration concern the relationship between *force majeure* clauses and frustration; the application of such clauses to instances where the obligor may opt between two methods of performance; and the drafting of clauses so that they do not too easily permit an obligor to be liberated from further performance.

2. *Force majeure*: Exception Clauses and Frustration Clauses

Prior to *Classic Maritime Inc v Limbungan Makmur Sdn Bhd*,[4] the nature and variety of *force majeure* clauses were underappreciated. That decision brings to the surface the difference between clauses that excuse one or both parties from liability and clauses that cancel the contract. Prior to *Classic Maritime*, concerns about *force majeure* clauses centred on whether they were governed by the Unfair Contract Terms Act 1977. Indeed, for the purpose of the Act, *force majeure* clauses, seemingly of either type, may be subject to one or more of its provisions depending on their type, especially under section 3(2)(b).[5] Given the varying language of the Act and the mixed bag of contractual clauses that it captures, it would appear to have little to say about the existence and nature of any distinction between exception clauses and frustration clauses. The impact of *Classic Maritime* may not yet have been fully felt. *Chitty*, taking the two types of clauses together, states that, whether *force majeure* clauses excuse or cancel, they 'have been said not to be

[3] D Winterton, 'Prioritising Proof over Speculation: Resolving the Prospective Inability Problem in Contract Damages' (2023) 86 *MLR* 843.

[4] [2019] 1 Lloyd's Rep 349, reversed in part [2020] 1 Lloyd's Rep 178, CA.

[5] This concerns 'rendering a contractual performance substantially different from that which was reasonably expected' or 'render[ing] no performance at all'.

exemption clauses'.[6] *Chitty* also states, that 'it is difficult to draw any clear line of demarcation between the two types of clause'.[7]

Apart from what it has to say about the damages liability of an obligor unable to invoke the protection of a *force majeure* clause, *Classic Maritime* shines a bright light on the difference between exception clauses and frustration clauses when excusing non-performance. The contract was one of affreightment for 51 cargoes of iron ore pellets, with shipment to take place in the Brazilian port of Ponta Ubu for carriage to Malaysia. The charterer, Limbungan, was a special purpose vehicle wholly owned by a Malaysian parent, Lion,[8] and the carrier, Classic Maritime, was a Marshall Islands company operating out of Monaco. Limbungan did not have a contract with Lion for the supply of cargoes but instead responded from time to time to the presentation of supplies of iron ore pellets by Lion.[9] Lion in turn had been party to a long-term supply contract, not yet renewed, with a Brazilian mining company, Samarco, apparently to be sourced from the Samarco mine, whose workings were flooded in consequence of a catastrophic burst of the Fundão dam. At the time of the burst, Limbungan was already in default under the contract of affreightment for failing to supply two consignments. Lion's Malaysian buyer had no demand for iron ore pellets because the market for its manufactured steel briquettes had been undercut by dumped Chinese steel. These two consignments, together with a further five falling due after the collapse of the dam, were the subject of the present action by the carrier, for damages for Limbungan's failure to supply seven consignments of iron ore pellets. Our concern is with the five consignments falling due after the dam disaster.

Limbungan sought shelter behind what was styled in the contract an 'exceptions' clause:

> Neither the … owners, nor the charterers … shall be responsible for … failure to supply, load, discharge or deliver the cargo resulting from: act of God … floods … accidents at the mine … or any other causes beyond the owners' [or] charterers' control; always providing that such events directly affect the performance of either party under this charterparty …

Limbungan's contention was that the dam burst caused performance of its obligations to become impossible, and that therefore it did not have to show that, 'but for' the dam burst, it would have performed its loading obligations.[10]

[6] H Beale (ed), *Chitty on Contracts*, 34th edn (London, Sweet & Maxwell, 2022) [28-086], citing *Fairclough, Dodd & Jones Ltd v JH Vantol Ltd* [1957] 1 WLR 136, 143.

[7] ibid.

[8] This guaranteed the performance of Limbungan's obligations.

[9] It had also in the past shipped cargoes from another member of the corporate group. There was a finding that this member was unable to obtain supplies from another mining corporation from a different mine unaffected by the dam disaster. Consequently, if there had been a causal link between the dam burst and the charterer's inability to source cargoes from the Samarco mine, the charterer did not have in fact an alternative opportunity to supply iron ore pellets from another mine: [2019] 1 Lloyd's Rep 349 at [129] and [132]. See further discussion below.

[10] [2020] 1 Lloyd's Rep 178 at [15], CA.

At both first instance and in the Court of Appeal, this clause was treated as what it purported to be, namely an exception clause. It was to be distinguished from a contractual frustration clause cancelling the contract on a stated event. Whereas an exception clause referred to what had already happened and its impact on extant obligations under a contract remaining on foot, a frustration clause looked to the future in providing for the discharge of the contract.[11] Once a clause provided for cancellation, that was it: the ability or not of an obligor otherwise to perform at that time did not come into play.

It was otherwise for an exception clause. The obligor had to be ready and willing to perform at the time of the event in order to claim the protection of the clause. The burden of proving this was on Limbungan,[12] which failed to demonstrate that it had in hand 'arrangements' for the provision of the five cargoes so that its failure to supply cargoes resulted from the flooding of the mine. These did not have to be legally binding[13] but had to be more than a hope of future cargoes following past contractual practice. The market for steel was depressed and, owing to the absence of any demand for iron ore, Limbungan's own supplier, Lion, had not yet renewed its contract with the mine for acquiring the iron ore that Limbungan needed for its contractual shipments.[14] At this point, it should be noted that, even if Limbungan had had a binding contract with its own supplier, if Lion had failed to supply iron ore in breach of contract, that failure to supply should not have been a defence to the shipowner's claim against Limbungan unless the *force majeure* clause embraced Lion's default in quite specific terms.[15] Similarly, a plea of frustration should also fail.[16]

Before turning to the causation issue in more detail, it has to be settled why the causation issue does not present itself in the case of a frustration clause. The prohibition of shipment clause in *Bremer Handelsgesellschaft mbH v Vanden-Avenne Izegem PVBA*[17] stated that in the case of governmental action in the country of the loadport 'preventing fulfilment' of the contract, the contract was to be 'cancelled'. That case involved an extended treatment of the accompanying *force majeure* clause, with the prohibition clause receiving a strikingly brief

[11] [2019] 1 Lloyd's Rep 349 at [81], [2020] 1 Lloyd's Rep 178 at [61], CA.

[12] [2019] 1 Lloyd's Rep 349 at [101].

[13] [2019] 1 Lloyd's Rep 349 at [95], [2020] 1 Lloyd's Rep 178 at [14], CA.

[14] The case is unclear on what would be non-binding 'arrangements'.

[15] *Fyffes Group Ltd v Reefer Express Lines Ltd (The Kriti Rex)* [1996] 2 Lloyd's Rep 171; *Lebeaupin v Richard Crispin and Co* [1920] 2 KB 714. cf *Coastal (Bermuda) Petroleum Ltd v VTT Vulcan Petroleum SA (No 2) (The Marine Star)* [1996] 2 Lloyd's Rep 383, 386–87, CA, where a clause concerning 'any cause beyond sellers … control' excused the seller when non-performance was caused by the seller's own supplier and where the court resisted the argument that liability should be imposed on the seller so that it could be run up the chain to the seller's own supplier.

[16] *CTI Group Inc v Transclear SA (The Mary Nour)* [2008] EWCA Civ 856, [2008] 2 Lloyd's Rep 526; *Atisa SA v Aztec AG* [1983] 2 Lloyd's Rep 579. The unsuccessful defendant should have ensured that it would have a claim over against its own supplier or should have contracted with the claimant on terms excusing its own liability if its supplier failed to perform.

[17] [1978] 2 Lloyd's Rep 109, HL.

treatment.[18] In the House of Lords, Lord Wilberforce, addressing the prohibition clause, asked 'whether the seller must prove that he had the goods ready to ship within the contract period, and a ship to carry them'.[19] Drawing upon an earlier decision of the Court of Appeal,[20] he concluded, without examining the meaning of 'preventing fulfilment', that there was no such need.[21]

At first instance in *Classic Maritime*, Teare J asserted that a causal 'but for' test was not required for frustration at common law, and so, for that reason, should also not be required for a frustration clause.[22] A similar approach was adopted in the Court of Appeal,[23] following the decision in the *Vanden-Avenne* case.[24] Yet it is far from self-evident that a clause providing for cancellation, regardless of whether the event in question would satisfy the demanding test of frustration at common law, should import automatic cancellation as would be the case for frustration at common law.[25] Moreover, it is all very well to say, as was said at both instances, that a frustration clause, in providing for cancellation, speaks to the future of the contract once the event occurs,[26] and that it makes clear provision for contractual cancellation'. It also speaks to the past in requiring the governmental intervention to have prevented fulfilment of the contract. The words 'preventing fulfilment' are words of causation and they do not mean the same as 'of a nature that would or might prevent fulfilment'. They surely require the event to be causally linked to the obligor's non-performance: the contract on its face calls for cancellation only if the events that trigger its application have in fact happened. The stumbling block preventing this surely straightforward conclusion in the case of a frustration clause is the decision of the House of Lords in *Vanden-Avenne*. It is understandable that neither the trial judge nor the Court of Appeal in *Classic Maritime* should have wished to take issue with that decision, especially since they were dealing with a clause characterised as an exception clause, where the causal requirement dispensed with in *Vanden-Avenne* for frustration clauses was reinstated. Even so, the question has to be asked why the language of cancellation should eliminate an obligor's passage through the causal gateway

[18] This chapter deals only with governmental prohibition and its treatment in standard clauses. *Force majeure* clauses, however, can overlap prohibition clauses, hence the recent consolidation by GAFTA of the two clauses into a single prevention of shipment clause.

[19] [1978] 2 Lloyd's Rep 109, 114, HL.

[20] *Tradax Export SA v Andre & Cie SA* [1976] 1 Lloyd's Rep 416, 426: 'If there was an absolute prohibition, the sellers need not in my view prove that they had goods ready to ship.'

[21] Likewise, Viscount Dilhorne who also would have put on the buyer the onus of proving that the seller could have shipped the goods: [1978] 2 Lloyd's Rep 109, 121, HL. Lord Russell at 129 thought it had been established that the seller could have performed had it not been for the embargo.

[22] [2019] 1 Lloyd's Rep 349 at [81].

[23] [2020] 1 Lloyd's Rep 178 at [52], CA.

[24] [1978] 2 Lloyd's Rep 109, HL. See also *Tradax Export SA v Cook Industries Inc* [1982] 1 Lloyd's Rep 385, 391.

[25] For a criticism of automatic cancellation of the contract, see MG Bridge, 'Frustration and Excused Non-Performance' (2021) 137 *LQR* 580.

[26] [2019] 1 Lloyd's Rep 349 at [81], [2020] 1 Lloyd's Rep 178 at [57], CA.

that leads to cancellation.[27] Furthermore, if, apart from the magic language of cancellation, the wording of an exception clause and of a frustration clause are 'in essence the same',[28] the existence of divergent approaches to interpretation is hard to justify, whichever view one takes of any 'but for' requirement that the obligor be ready and willing to perform at the time of the untoward event.

The expression 'frustration clause' may not be an apt one to the extent that it assumes an essential similarity between the clause and the common law doctrine of frustration that in principle needs to be justified. Moreover, if the contract does not itself use the expression, but instead refers to the clause as a *force majeure* clause or something similar, an automatic attachment of the effects of frustration at common law to the clause when it is triggered is even less justifiable. Issues of readiness and willingness to perform prior to the frustrating event do not present themselves when it comes to common law frustration, but does it follow that this should also be the case where the parties have contracted out of the common law doctrine, extending the scope of permissible non-performance, in favour of a clause that does contain causal language? The highly artificial argument that the language of causation in a frustration clause merely invites the assumption that an obligor, but for the event, would have been able to perform the contract is not a satisfactory answer to this question. This approach was expressed in the following way by Donaldson MR, faithful to the decision in *Vanden-Avenne*:[29] 'If shippers or other sellers wish to take the benefit of [the prohibition] clause, they must still prove that the embargo would have prevented fulfilment of the contract on the assumption that they would otherwise have been in a position to fulfil it.' This is an odd way of putting it. It means that, in order to determine whether an event prevented shipment, we have to assume that the event prevented such shipment from taking place. This interpretation of the clause, hardly sufficient to add persuasive strength to the conclusion reached in *Vanden-Avenne*, renders the presence of causal language in the clause otiose. Dispensing altogether with a requirement of readiness and willingness if the clause is a frustration clause, as was the case at both instances in *Classic Maritime*, has the merit of avoiding a test devoid of content.

Returning now to the issue of factual causation, it is clear, particularly in the judgment of the Court of Appeal in *Classic Maritime*, that the resolution of this issue should not turn upon whether a clause could be described as a *force majeure* clause,[30] as a means of breaking out of the distinction between exception and

[27] For an approach that lightens the causal requirement to vanishing point, see Donaldson MR in *Bremer Handelsgesellschaft mbH v Westzucker GmbH* [1981] 2 Lloyd's Rep 130, 135, CA, discussed in the following paragraph.

[28] As argued by counsel for Limbungan: [2019] 1 Lloyd's Rep 349 at [80].

[29] In *Bremer Handelsgesellschaft mbH v Westzucker GmbH* [1981] 2 Lloyd's Rep 130, 135, CA (concerning the prohibition clause in a GAFTA 100 contract), relied upon in *Classic Maritime v Limbungan Makmur Sdn Bhd* [2019] 1 Lloyd's Rep 349 at [77], [2020] 1 Lloyd's Rep 178 at [19], CA.

[30] [2020] 1 Lloyd's Rep 178 at [40], CA. The clause under consideration was not so described in the contract.

frustration clauses, but rather upon the construction of the clause as a whole. This was so even though the clause contained language associated with untoward events of a type not to be found in a conventional exception clause.[31] This approach is consistent in character with the established practice of treating as exception clauses those clauses that either define the scope of a contractual undertaking or exclude liability in the event of a breach of that undertaking.[32] As a matter of construction, the question was whether the charterer's failure to present the five cargoes following the dam burst resulted from that flooding of the Samarco mine. Teare J opted for answering this question in the negative through the eyes of a 'reasonable and realistic businessman'.[33] It is not clear, however, that such an ideal personage would have a cogent response to difficult questions of causation or would have insisted on an event as having only one cause. The Court of Appeal, influenced by language pointing to the effect of an event upon a particular shipment as opposed to shipments in general,[34] came to the same conclusion as Teare J that Limbungan had failed to satisfy the 'but for' test and so was liable in damages. It could not, in the opinion of the court, be said that the failure to supply cargoes 'resulted from' the dam burst.[35] The conclusion is certainly a defensible one but it does not justify the absence of a readiness and willingness requirement in the case of frustration clauses.

3. GAFTA Frustration Clauses

I propose now to track changes made in GAFTA contracts to the language of their prohibition clause,[36] which deals with the effect on a contract of governmental intervention in the export of goods. This clause has been authoritatively treated as a frustration clause, given its cancellation of the contract once the stated conditions have been met.[37] Along with a companion clause concerning *force majeure*, the language of the prohibition clause came under intense scrutiny in the welter of cases that followed the US governmental partial restriction of export when the upper Mississippi valley flooded in 1973. This governmental prohibition went to the physical act of shipment and did not speak to the dealing in paper of intermediate traders, who were not themselves the original shippers. The causal language

[31] ibid at [31]–[32] (viz floods, Acts of God, accidents etc).

[32] B Coote, *Exception Clauses* (London, Sweet & Maxwell, 1964).

[33] [2019] 1 Lloyd's Rep 349 at [73]. See also [2020] 1 Lloyd's Rep 178 at [48], CA. The expression was coined by Kerr J in *Seabridge Shipping Ltd v Antco Shipping Ltd (The Furness Bridge)* [1977] 2 Lloyd's Rep 367.

[34] Other reasons given – the application of the clause to both shipowner and charterer and the coverage in the clause of a wide series of events – would appear to add little force to the court's conclusion.

[35] [2020] 1 Lloyd's Rep 178 at [45], CA.

[36] In recent years, formerly a particular example of *force majeure*, the subject of a separate clause, prohibition has now been merged with *force majeure* to produce a 'Prevention of Shipment' clause.

[37] *Bremer Handelsgesellschaft mbH v Vanden-Avenne Izegem PVBA* [1978] 2 Lloyd's Rep 109, HL.

in the relevant clause has been altered more than once since the events of 1973. This prompts the question, if cancellation requires causal language merely to be assumed to have been satisfied, why have the drafters of this clause been so concerned to deal with causal language in drafts of the clause after the events of 1973? Would a 'reasonable and realistic businessman' of the type involved in the drafting of the prohibition clause regard that causal language as bereft of purpose?

This is the prohibition clause as it stood at the time of the Mississippi floods:

> 21. PROHIBITION. In case of prohibition of export, blockade or hostilities or in case of any executive or legislative act done by or on behalf of the Government of the country of origin or of the territory where the port or ports of shipment named herein is/are situate, *preventing fulfilment*, this Contract or any unfulfilled portion thereof so affected shall be *cancelled* … If required, Sellers must produce proof to justify their claim for cancellation (emphasis added).

In the litigation that followed the floods, intense efforts were made by sellers, not merely to show that the US Department of Agriculture had imposed percentage limits on the quantity of soya to be shipped for export, but also to show that goods were unavailable for performing in full their delivery obligations. The governmental prohibition did not extend to 'loophole' exceptions concerning soya already in the course of loading, or on lighter vessels, or in the loadport ready for loading, or en route to the loadport. This meant that dealings in relation to those goods were not caught by the governmental prohibition and that a seller with access to such goods could not successfully plead the prohibition.

In so far as loophole cargo fell outside the partial prohibition on shipment, sellers with access or potential access to loophole cargo could not avail themselves of the cancellation provision as interpreted by the House of Lords in *Vanden-Avenne*. These sellers were required to show that there was no soya available to them that had not already been appropriated to other contracts. Since this task required them to account for the destination of all loophole cargoes, given that they could not trace back to a single shipper by way of a non-existent string, in the absence of notices of appropriation relating to shipped goods that would have connected parties in string,[38] the burden on sellers can be seen to have been formidable. The clause and the litigation with which it was associated demonstrate a keen preoccupation with establishing a causal link between the event and the unavailability of loophole cargo. This burden was a most exacting one, in contrast with the benevolence shown to sellers in the case of shipments that fell within the governmental prohibition and that now could no longer take place in full. In this latter case, sellers were dispensed from any causal requirement to show themselves ready and willing to perform at the date of the prohibition.

[38] A Canadian court once described the multiplicity of contracts so far not connected with each other in string as 'random dots on a page': *Naber Seed & Grain Co v Prairie Pulse Inc* 2004 SKQB 518 at [7].

A later version of the prohibition clause was produced that covered in more relaxed terms both goods the subject of the prohibition and loophole goods falling outside the prohibition:

> 18. PROHIBITION. In case of prohibition of export, blockade or hostilities or in case of any executive or legislative act done by or on behalf of the Government of the country of origin or of the territory where the port or ports of shipment named herein is/are situate, restricting export, whether partially or otherwise, any such restriction shall be deemed by both parties to apply to this contract and to the extent of such total or partial restriction to prevent fulfilment whether by shipment or by any other means whatsoever and to that extent this contract or any unfulfilled portion thereof shall be cancelled … [I]f required, Sellers must produce proof to justify the cancellation (emphasis added).

This version of the prohibition clause greatly lessened the seller's burden so far as loophole cargo was concerned and also reinforced the interpretative approach in matters of causation adopted by the House of Lords in *Vanden-Avenne*. It was now enough for the seller to point to governmental action that merely restricted export, whereupon language in the clause deemed the restriction both to apply to the particular contract and to prevent fulfilment of that contract.[39] Putting aside the case of loophole cargo, if any clause was designed to underline the position, previously adopted by the courts, that there was no need for a seller to be ready and willing to perform in the run up to cancellation, this was that clause. But the revision still poses the question why the drafters of the prohibition clause sought to express in even more lenient terms a clause that had already been leniently interpreted by the House of Lords. An argument against leniency in general is that it gives a measure of licence to speculative sellers who have taken a short position in the market, so releasing them from the commercial risk of a rising market that they had consciously assumed. Once governmental intervention occurred, they are off the hook in rising market conditions to the extent of that intervention as expressed in general terms.

Contrast that now with the current prevention of shipment clause, incorporating the previous prohibition and *force majeure* clauses:

> 20. PREVENTION OF SHIPMENT. 'Event of Force Majeure' means (a) prohibition of export or other executive or legislative act done by or on behalf of the government of the country of origin or of the territory where the port or ports named herein is/are situate, restricting export, whether partially or otherwise … (emphasis added).

There now follows language giving the buyer an option to cancel after a stated period before leading up to automatic cancellation after a further period:

> Should Sellers' performance of this contract be prevented, whether partially or otherwise, by an Event of Force Majeure, the performance of this contract shall be suspended

[39] But the clause was restrictively interpreted in *Agrokor AG v Tradigrain SA* [2000] 1 Lloyd's Rep 497 to require the seller to show what effect the governmental action had had on its plans.

> for the duration of the Event of Force Majeure … after which, if the Event of Force Majeure has not ceased, any unfulfilled part of the contract shall be automatically cancelled (emphasis added).

This amounts to a doubling back in the direction of the clause in force at the time of the 1973 floods. What is particularly noticeable is the absence of deeming language in this version of the clause. It is hard to know what to make of this deletion. One view is that it merely reverts to the way the earlier version of the clause was judicially interpreted at the time of the 1973 floods. Another view is that a clause, retreating from the language of deemed causation, and returning to the language of actual causation, is in truth demanding that a causal link be shown between the governmental intervention and the seller's non-performance, even though the language of restricting export has been retained, alongside the language of prevention, from the previous draft. Otherwise, what was this exercise all about?

If this is correct, there is now a full-blown requirement, distinct from the availability or not of loophole cargo, that the seller be ready and willing to perform at the time of the governmental intervention. Despite the interpretation of the earlier prohibition clause in *Vanden-Avenne*, and even though the interpretation of such clauses is a question of law, the subsequent iterations of the clause open the door to reconsidering what the drafters meant when they used the language of causation. Even if the interpretation of a clause lacking the context of a factual hinterland can be treated as purely a question of law, an authoritative interpretation of words in a standard form contract should not prevent a reinterpretation of the clause in the light of subsequent drafting events. The approach adopted by Donaldson MR to the interpretation of the prohibition clause current in 1973[40] should therefore no longer apply in the case of the current prevention of shipment clause, given the history of the clause that followed the post-1973 events litigation. Let us not, however, make too much of all of this in the commodities markets. If one accepts a requirement for causation to be satisfied, then, drawing upon the language in *Classic Maritime*, the seller would now have to have in hand 'arrangements' for shipment. It is uncertain how demanding this requirement would be in practice: it might depend upon market conditions. The facility with which an intermediate seller might acquire goods prior to the untoward event might pass for 'arrangements'; alternatively, an agreement of sorts with a supplier might be needed. The word 'arrangements' is flexible to the point of vagueness. It would make commercial sense for the former approach to be adopted. That said, what might pass for 'arrangements' in a commercial world involving commodities such as wheat and soya bought and sold through the medium of paper in highly liquid markets is one thing. Prior to governmental intervention, conditions of supply and demand are likely to have been active. Invoking the notion of 'arrangements' taking the form of a well-grounded expectation that supplies would be forthcoming would still

[40] *Bremer Handelsgesellschaft mbH v Westzucker GmbH* [1981] 2 Lloyd's Rep 130, 135, CA.

mean that cancellation would have to be traced back to the relevant event, but this should not be too demanding. It should nevertheless be stressed that having to demonstrate a causal link between the untoward event and non-performance could have a real impact in markets of the type in *Classic Maritime*, a case that dealt with shipments of iron from a designated mine in depressed market conditions. The supply of iron ore from a particular mine is far from the same thing as the supply of soya from multiple points in the Mississippi river system.

It remains legitimate to ask whether the causal language in frustration clauses should be disregarded as was sanctioned by *Classic Maritime*. If a causal requirement were to be applied equally to frustration and exception clauses, a head-on collision with the decision of the House of Lords in *Vanden-Avenne*[41] could be avoided by concluding that the subsequent fate of the prohibition clause demonstrates the intention of the drafters in a way that was not clearly established when the House of Lords ruled on the matter. If that decision, nevertheless, still commands the interpretation of the language of causation, casting a shadow on contracts of the type dealt with in *Classic Maritime*, the oddity remains of a 'but for' test being required for exception clauses but not for frustration clauses. In view of the close similarity of the language used in both types of clauses, that is hardly acceptable. Does the word 'exception' in the exception clause, or the word 'cancel' in the frustration clause, mandate such a sharply divided approach to the interpretation of these clauses? Do not both clauses amount to the same thing, in the way, for example, that a clause excluding liability and a clause defining the scope of a contractual undertaking do so?[42]

A final point concerning the difference between exception clauses and frustration clauses is this. Suppose in the case of an exception clause that *force majeure* is successfully pleaded and that the event in question completely disables further performance of the contract. What now happens to the contract? If the contract were one of sale governed by the UN Convention on Contracts for the International Sale of Goods, the obligee would be able to treat the excused non-performance as amounting to a fundamental 'breach' so as to 'avoid' the contract (i.e., terminate it). The expression 'non-performance', used in the Uniform Principles of International Commercial Contracts,[43] is greatly to be preferred to the language of fundamental breach since it does not speak to damages liability. In English law, given the absence of cancellation language in the *force majeure* clause and the absence of a breach, the contract would, as a matter of law, seem to be on perpetual life support unless the parties by further agreement either put it to rest or revived it on amended terms. This would in some instances at least take the form of an implied common intention of abandonment.[44]

[41] [1978] 2 Lloyd's Rep 109, HL.

[42] B Coote, *Exception Clauses* (London, Sweet & Maxwell, 1964).

[43] Article 7.3.1.

[44] *Pearl Mill Co Ltd v Ivy Tannery Co Ltd* [1919] 1 KB 78. On abandonment, see MG Bridge, *The Sale of Goods*, 4th edn (Oxford, Oxford University Press, 2019) [6.23]–[6.24].

4. Frustration Clauses and Frustration

The companionship of frustration clauses and the doctrine of frustration was a vital part of the reasoning at both levels in *Classic Maritime*. This prompts the question, what effect does a *force majeure* clause, whether framed as an exception clause or as a frustration clause, have on the operation of the doctrine of frustration. This question breaks down into the following two sub-questions. First, does the presence of a *force majeure* clause displace altogether the operation of the doctrine of frustration? Secondly, if not, would the same result have been reached in *Classic Maritime* if the charterer, Limbungan, had pleaded frustration?

4.1. Availability of General Law?

The first question is concerned with whether an obligor resisting performance is free to choose between the clause and the general law. It is clearly a matter of interpretation whether and to what extent the clause ousts the operation of the doctrine of frustration. Frustration does not operate regardless of the parties' intentions. Contracting parties are free to expand the range of relief, as is common with *force* majeure clauses, or to allocate risk in such a way as to preclude the operation of frustration.[45] Where a *force majeure* clause on its face is evidently designed to expand relief, it is intrinsically unlikely that it might also serve to limit the parsimonious relief offered by the common law doctrine. Such a situation, although unlikely to arise, might have arisen in *Classic Maritime*. To the extent that common law frustration and a *force majeure* clause go hand-in-hand in dealing with an untoward event, it is arguable that an obligor might indifferently claim a defence to non-performance on either basis. By way of comparison, a contract might permit termination for breach, with a defined procedure to bring that about, whilst also permitting termination because a particular term is a promissory condition or its breach in the circumstances goes to the root of the contract. It is inherently more likely that an express termination clause laying down a termination procedure would oust the application of the general law on discharge for breach,[46] than that a *force majeure* clause would oust the application of the general law of frustration. As the rigours of the *contra proferentem* rule abate, it is hard to see good reasons for not enforcing a protocol that the contract on its construction requires to be followed in all cases of termination for breach.

[45] See, eg. *Joseph Constantine Steamship Line Ltd v Imperial Smelting Corp Ltd* [1942] AC 154, 163–164, HL.

[46] Even here, they may be a bias in favour of duality: eg *Npower Direct Ltd v South of Scotland Power Ltd* [2005] EWHC 2123 (Comm).

4.2. Frustration in *Classic Maritime*?

With that in mind, we may turn to the second question to consider whether the charterer, Limbungan, might have fared better if it had pleaded frustration of the contract so far as the five affected shipments were concerned. The first issue that needs to be resolved here concerns the unwieldy nature of frustration with its accompaniment of automatic discharge and inaptness when dealing with instances of partial impossibility, which was the position in *Classic Maritime.* Automatic frustration distorts the law on impossibility of performance[47] and ought not to be extended to frustration clauses that go beyond frustration at common law. Admittedly, 'automatic' cancellation is a feature of some express clauses, such as those dealing with governmental prohibition, but this comes into play only after the expiry of a grace period extending the time of performance in aid of preserving the contract. Certainly, if contracting parties wish to provide for automatic cancellation, that should be their sovereign right. But automatic cancellation, especially if linked to the abandonment of a 'but for' requirement, should not. without good cause. be read into a contract any more readily than automatic discharge would be recognised in the event of a repudiatory breach.[48]

The scope for frustration in *Classic Maritime* calls for a further look at the facts. The contract of affreightment did not require the iron ore to be sourced from the Samarco mine that was flooded when the Fundão dam burst. The question was whether Limbungan might have obtained iron ore from another mine not affected by the dam burst. This.breaks down into two parts: whether Limbungan was bound to seek an alternative source of supply; and if so, whether it was, in fact, disabled from securing alternative iron ore. The first part introduces the subject of alternative means of contractual performance. Depending on the construction of the contract, an obligor might be required to provide alternative performance where more than one possibility exists,[49] or might be taken to have had an option that it was not bound to exercise to perform the contract in a different way.[50] The contract of affreightment in *Classic Maritime* appeared not to protect Limbungan from liability if Limbungan were able to secure supplies from the alternative mine. This issue, nevertheless, would come to life only if Limbungan were able to satisfy the 'but for' test in relation to the Samarco

[47] MG Bridge, 'Frustration and Excused Non-Performance' (2021) 137 *LQR* 580. It gives rise to a degree of awkwardness, eg *Joseph Constantine Steamship Line Ltd v Imperial Smelting Corp Ltd* [1942] AC 154, HL: (1) Frustration 'kills the contract itself and discharges both parties automatically' (at 163); (2) 'Some kinds of impossibility may in some circumstances not discharge the contract at all' (at 164).

[48] E Peel (ed), *Treitel: The Law of Contract*, 15th edn (London, Sweet & Maxwell, 2021) [18-005] (and cases there cited).

[49] *HA Brightman & Co v Bunge y Born Lda Soc* [1924] 2 KB 619, CA (charterers, required to load 'wheat and/or maize and/or rye' but unable to load a full cargo of wheat owing to a railway strike, yet bound to supplement with maize/rye).

[50] *Reardon Smith Line Ltd v Ministry of Agriculture, Fisheries and Food* [1963] AC 691, HL (the 'Vancouver Strikes' case) (charterers with obligation to load wheat did not have to exercise their option to substitute barley or flour at higher freight rates).

mine, which it was unable to do. Making that assumption, however, it was established that Limbungan made no attempt to supply the missing shipments from the other mine. Nevertheless, any such efforts would have been unavailing because the owner of the mine was interested only in long-term supply contracts,[51] a finding that addresses the disablement part of the inquiry.

5. Alternative Performance

A question touched upon in *Classic Maritime* itself concerns when an obligor, having unavailingly pursued one permissible means of performance, is exonerated from seeking performance by alternative means. This question is, in turn, bound up with another. Taking sale as an example for this other question, when is a seller's obligation to deliver, normally strict, diluted to one of due diligence when subsequent circumstances impede performance? This question arises where the seller has a window of opportunity to perform but circumstances drastically narrow that window. Some authority supports converting this strict duty into one of due diligence.[52] Reverting to the first question, other authority holds that, even if both parties contemplate that performance will take place one way, nevertheless the obligor is strictly bound to perform in the alternative way unless able to take shelter in a *force majeure* clause.[53] In *Classic Maritime* itself, however, greater leniency is evident. Limbungan was not under a strict duty to source its cargo from another mine whose refusal to supply the iron ore, except under a long-term supply contract, was treated as an answer to non-performance from that source. In addition, if a contract defines performance in a particular way but grants the performing party an option to perform in a different way, the impossibility of performing the contract in the selected way does not require the performing party to change its option.[54] If, however, the contract envisages performance by more than one means, a duty to perform by alternative means should remain current despite the event disabling one means, subject to the alleviation of the duty as mentioned above.

Consequently, the five shipments that could not have been made out of the Samarco mine would not have been required from the other mine. This conclusion is not readily reconciled with the rule that a contract is not frustrated merely

[51] [2019] 1 Lloyd's Rep 349 at [129].

[52] *Charles H Windschuegl v Alexander Pickering & Co Ltd* (1950) 84 Ll L R 89, 94; *Ross T Smyth & Co (Liverpool) Ltd v WN Lindsay (Leith) Ltd* [1953] 1 WLR 1280, 1284; *Warinco AG v Fritz Mauthner* [1978] 1 Lloyd's Rep 151, 153–54. See also *AV Pound & Co Ltd v MW Hardy & Co Inc* [1956] AC 588, HL, where the FOB buyer was so far advanced in its plans to export to East Germany that it could not be required to alter the destination so that the Portuguese authorities might grant permission for export, even though it was not a requirement of the contract that the seller was bound to ship the goods on a vessel bound for East Germany.

[53] *Seabridge Shipping Ltd v Antco Shipping Ltd (The Furness Bridge)* [1977] 2 Lloyd's Rep 367, 375.

[54] *Reardon Smith Line Ltd v Ministry of Agriculture, Fisheries and Food* [1963] AC 691, HL.

because performance has now become much more onerous,[55] an approach likely to hold also for the interpretation of a *force majeure* clauses.

6. Other Questions

Apart from automatic cancellation, discussed above, other questions are presented by frustration in its relationship to *force majeure* clauses. First, might not Limbungan have been excused on the ground of frustration at common law? A plea of frustration does not require prior readiness and willingness to perform. The exception clause did not rule out the application of frustration. On the facts, there is a credible argument that the contract was frustrated.

6.1. Frustration Clauses and the Law Reform (Frustrated Contracts) Act 1943

A second question concerns the role of the Law Reform (Frustrated) Contracts Act 1943 if there is a frustration clause going beyond the range of frustration at common law. The 1943 Act has been heavily criticised and is rarely applied. It concerns the division of expenses and allocation of benefits where 'a contract … has become impossible of performance or been otherwise frustrated'.[56] These expressions are not defined in the Act. A contractual frustration clause stipulating events giving rise to the cancellation of the contract cannot, on that account only, bring into play the machinery of the 1943 Act, though the parties themselves are at liberty to provide contractually for an outcome identical to that reached by the Act. A contract should be regarded as impossible of performance only if such is the case on the actual facts and not assumed to be so just because the clause is broad enough to encompass what has happened. The contract should not be considered impossible to perform merely because the contract itself provides for cancellation. Similarly, the Act should not apply on its own terms, as it would in the event of frustration, merely because the event in question comes within the scope of the clause, even if the clause were to be styled a 'frustration clause' instead of a 'prevention' or '*force majeure*' or 'prohibition' clause. This question becomes more pertinent if an event falls within the scope of a contractual clause and also would amount to a frustrating event according to a narrower common law test. Section 2(3) requires a court to give effect to a contractual provision applicable in the event of frustration or what would otherwise be frustration but for that clause. The provision seems to be directed at clauses

[55] See, eg, *Brauer & Co (Great Britain) Ltd v James Clark (Brush Materials) Ltd* [1952] 2 All ER 497.
[56] Section 1(1).

preventing the frustration of the contract, not expanding its scope, by allocating the risk of the untoward event on one of the parties. The answer to the above question about the continuing applicability of the common law rule must turn upon whether, as a matter of construction, the intent of the contract was to oust or merely extend the application of that rule. A court, it is submitted, should be slow to conclude that there is an intention to oust the Act if the contract does not contain contrasting provision for the division of expenses and benefits.

6.2. The Damages Question

A third question, which bulked large in *Classic Maritime* itself, concerns the measure of damages recoverable against an obligor who was not ready and willing to perform at the time of the untoward event. The tone of the inquiry can be established at the outset by posing the aim of contract damages when compensating for loss in two different ways. The first and better-known way is to award damages that as near as possible give the obligee the benefit of its contractual expectation: '[I]n giving damages for breach of contract, the party complaining should, so far as it can be done by money, be placed in the same position as he would have been in if the contract had been performed.'[57] In other words, the award takes the obligee over the rainbow to the lost world of contractual fulfilment. The second way was expressed by Lord Blackburn as follows, speaking of wrongs in general: '[I]n settling the sum of money to be given for reparation of damages you should as nearly as possible get at that sum of money which will put the party who has been injured, or who has suffered, in the same position as he would have been in if he had not sustained the wrong for which he is now getting his compensation or reparation.'[58] The first formulation says nothing about what the obligee did do or could have done to earn the contractual expectancy. The second way, when applied to contract claims, opens up the possibility, by bringing into play the obligee's position prior to the wrong, of considering what the obligee had to do to cross the rainbow. The words are capable of taking account of the position the obligee was in at that time as well as the position the obligee would otherwise have had to be in in the future in order to earn its contractual expectancy.

Turning now to the position in *Classic Maritime*, the approach at first instance was to consider the position the shipowner would have been in if Limbungan had had the necessary arrangements in hand and, but for the dam burst, would have been able to provide the five missing shipments. In what the judge at first instance denied was 'an impermissible sleight of hand',[59] he took as his starting point the position of the shipowners if Limbungan had made the necessary arrangements

[57] *Wertheim v Chicoutimi Pulp Co* [1911] AC 301, 307, PC.
[58] *Livingstone v Rawyards Coal Co* (1880) 5 App Cas 25, 39, HL.
[59] [2019] 1 Lloyd's Rep 349 at [146].

for the supply of cargoes at the time when the dam burst. That would have prevented the mine from supplying iron ore to Limbungan's own supplier, which would then have had a knock-on effect on the performance of Limbungan's supply obligation to the shipowner. It was the court's conclusion, therefore, that the shipowner was not entitled to substantial damages. One way of justifying this conclusion would be to say that Limbungan's prior absence of readiness and willingness to perform had been overtaken by the dam burst.[60] The shipowner was bargaining for the supply of iron ore cargo, not for Limbungan's readiness and willingness to perform. Yet, the judge's conclusion sits oddly with its interpretation of the exception clause. If the bursting of the dam could overtake what would otherwise have been the shipowner's due measure of damages, then why did it not overtake Limbungan's prospective breach of contract in not having arrangements in hand for the supply of iron ore cargoes prior to the due dates of shipment? The judge's conclusion, does, however, reflect what in fact the shipowner lost as a result of Limbungan's inability to have in place the necessary arrangements to provide the iron ore cargo. The judge's conclusion on the measure of damages was nevertheless reversed in the Court of Appeal, whose conclusion will be considered below after a review of certain critically important authorities.

The line of authorities referred to above affirm the compensatory principle of damages. In so doing, they reject the notion that damages are to be seen as crystallised at the point of breach, blind to future events, whether they subsequently accrue or remain contingent at the point when the court assesses damages. A convenient starting point is Lord Diplock's judgment in *Gill & Duffus SA v Berger & Co*,[61] where a CIF buyer committed a repudiatory breach, accepted by the seller, when the buyer refused to pay against conforming documents. If the goods had turned out to be non-conforming, which was not the case, then Lord Diplock would have been prepared to offset against the seller's damages claim a counterclaim for damages by the buyer. CIF contracts are odd in this respect. If the goods had been non-conforming, then the breach had already occurred either on shipment or later when the goods on board the carrying vessel were appropriated to the contract, both events occurring before documentary tender. The nature of a CIF contract, with its allocation of commercial risk, does not allow the buyer to raise a complaint about the goods when faced with a conforming documentary tender. The seller's physical breach is, as it were, postponed to the future, coming to life after the completion of the documentary exchange.

[60] cf *Avery v Bowden* (1855) 5 El & Bl 714, 119 ER 647, where a charterer's failure in breach of contract to load in Odessa was later overtaken by the Russian blockade of Constantinople in the Crimean War. See also *Borealis AB v Geogas Trading SA* [2010] EWHC 2789 (Comm) at [44]–[45] (*novus actus interveniens* and events 'obliterating' the prior breach of contract).

[61] [1984] AC 382, HL.

The problem of future consequences erupted in *The Golden Victory*,[62] where a charterer, on a declining freight market, unlawfully repudiated the charter one-third of the way into its seven-year term, the owner then accepting the repudiation. Before damages came to be assessed, a war broke out about two-thirds of the way into the seven-year term, which would have triggered a war clause permitting the charterer to cancel the contract. At this point, damages had not yet been assessed. There was a finding that the charterer would indeed have cancelled the charter had the contract still been on foot at that time. On the question of whether damages should be discounted in the light of this, the House of Lords divided 3-2 in favour of taking the event into account, the majority invoking the so-called *Bwllfa* principle[63] that a court should not close its eyes to what, in fact, has happened between the commission of a wrong and the calculation of damages for that wrong. The majority applied, therefore, the compensatory principle of damages in a pure way. In a somewhat impassioned dissent, the minority invoked the principle of certainty, as well as practical arguments concerning the undesirability of settlements being postponed as the defendant waits hopefully for something to turn up, to justify not waiting for the actual outbreak of war. It also asserted, treating the charter as more of a capital asset than an income stream, that the majority approach ignored the value to the owner of the charter at the point of repudiation.[64] This criticism, in assuming the existence of a guaranteed income stream, nevertheless begged the question.

In a case involving a default clause, where no appreciable difference in approach existed between the awards under such clauses and awards of damages under the Sale of Goods Act, the Supreme Court in *Bunge SA v Nidera NV*[65] unanimously applied the same approach as the majority in *The Golden Victory*. The buyer invoked a prohibition clause prematurely, a few days before an announced export ban was due to take effect. In the event, the ban lasted for the whole of the shipment period and for some time beyond. The seller's damages were appropriately discounted. There was no distinction to be drawn between a one-off contract like a sale of goods contract and a contract calling for protracted performance, like the seven-year charter in *The Golden Victory*. The seller had lost nothing of value. *Bunge* was a case of anticipatory repudiation, whereas *The Golden Victory* concerned a present repudiation for the balance of the seven-year charter. The significance of this emerges as we return to *Classic Maritime*.

[62] *Golden Strait Corp v Nippon Yusen Kubishika Kaisha (The Golden Victory)* [2007] UKHL 12, [2007] 2 AC 353. Followed in *Flame SA v Glory Wealth Pte Ltd (The Glory Wealth)* [2013] EWHC 3153 (Comm), [2014] QB 1080. See also *MDW Holdings Inc v Norvill* [2022] EWCA Civ 883, [2023] 1 All ER 929.

[63] *Bwllfa and Merthyr Dare Steam Collieries Ltd (1891) v Pontypridd Waterworks Co* [1903] AC 426, HL.

[64] cf Lord Mance in the Court of Appeal [2005] EWCA Civ 1190, [2006] 1 WLR 553 at [24]: '[T]he owners were never entitled to absolute confidence that the charter would run for its full 7-year period. They never had an asset which they could bank or sell on that basis.'

[65] [2015] UKSC 1543, [2015] 3 All ER 1082.

In the Court of Appeal in that case, the trial judge's assessment of damages was reversed, the court taking the view that they should be substantial in line with the compensatory principle.[66] The court began with a recital of the expectation measure of damages before discussing and then putting aside *The Golden Victory* and *Bunge SA v Nidera NV*, since taking account of post-breach events should be confined to anticipatory repudiation to the exclusion of actual repudiation.[67] *Bunge* did indeed concern an anticipatory repudiation but *The Golden Victory* did not. The charterer in *The Golden Victory* was repudiating an obligation that had fallen due and would continue to run in the future, hence the court in *Classic Maritime* was reintroducing in a different application the distinction rejected in *Bunge* between a one-shot performance contract and a contract calling for protracted performance. The distinction drawn by the court, moreover, would give claimants an incentive not to accept an anticipatory repudiation but instead to wait until the obligation or obligations fell due. In any case, Limbungan's prospective inability to supply cargoes at the due date was itself an anticipatory repudiation of the contract, even though it did not take the form of a renunciation and had not been accepted by the owner as a repudiatory breach.[68] That said, why should it make a difference that the breach in *Classic Maritime* was an actual and not an anticipatory repudiation if the overriding purpose of a damages award is to effect compensation?

Having made this distinction between present and anticipatory repudiation, the court in *Classic Maritime* went on to conclude that the value to the owner of the charterer's contractual obligation to deliver the five disputed cargoes lay in the freight that it was entitled to charge. The charterer's obligation was to provide cargoes and not to be ready and willing to do so.[69] The shipowner had not received what it had bargained for and Limbungan was not in a position to claim the protection of the exception clause.[70] Moreover, Limbungan had incurred an absolute obligation to provide the five missing cargoes.[71] In focusing on that primary obligation in the way it did, nevertheless, the court paid insufficient attention to what in fact the owner had lost as a result of that breach. One could as easily have said that the value of the charterer's promise to the shipowner in *The Golden Victory* was the stream of charter hire for the seven-year term. The court's emphasis on Limbungan's primary obligation as absolute in nature therefore deflected attention from the extent and scope of the secondary obligation to pay damages. To sum up, in assessing damages in the way that it did, the court drew a distinction between present and anticipatory repudiation that, for

[66] [2020] 1 Lloyd's Rep 178 at [66], CA.

[67] ibid [80]. Followed in *MDW Holdings Inc v Norvill* [2022] EWCA Civ 883, [2023] 1 All ER 929.

[68] See, eg, *Universal Cargo Carriers Ltd v Citati* [1957] 2 QB 401.

[69] [2020] 1 Lloyd's Rep 178 at [81]–[82], CA. This sits uncomfortably with a requirement of readiness and willingness being necessary for the protection of the exception clause.

[70] ibid [81].

[71] ibid [89].

the purposes of the compensation principle, amounted to a distinction without a difference.[72]

7. Conclusion

Classic Maritime highlights issues that need to be resolved, but the Supreme Court refused leave to appeal. There is no good reason for treating causation differently for exception and frustration clauses when it comes to readiness and willingness. The application of the expectation principle of damages, with its compensatory aim, to post-breach events also calls for further consideration.

[72] Similarly critical of the distinction drawn are M Howard and J Knott, 'Force Majeure, Frustration and Exceptions Clauses: Damages in Hindsight' (2020) *LMCLQ* 179, who nevertheless support the conclusion on the measure of damages.

3

Managing Fraud Risk in the Age of AI

CHRISTOPHER M BRUNER*

1. Introduction

Artificial intelligence (AI) applications are widely expected to revolutionise myriad aspects of life, and recent advances are thought to represent the technology industry's 'most important inflection point in decades'. Industry leaders consider emerging AI systems to be 'as important as the introduction of the web browser in the early 1990s' and anticipate that they 'could lead to breakthroughs in areas ranging from drug research to education'.[1] Many, however, including pioneers in their development, have increasingly voiced concerns about the harm that could result – including endemic disinformation, widespread employment redundancy, and even autonomous weapons systems.[2] The extraordinary variance between potential benefits and potential costs has prompted comparisons with atomic energy, in that each might power human progress or annihilate us.[3] Grappling with such powerful technology will undoubtedly require a range of regulatory responses, from public to private law, and from global to local regimes.[4]

Advanced AI systems are likewise expected to impact fundamental aspects of business, including 'all operational as well as internal control matters, from

* For helpful comments and suggestions, thanks to Elise Bant, Paul Davies, Roy Shapira, Hans Tjio, and participants at the Fraud and Risk in Commercial Law Conference. For research assistance, thanks to Amanda Milner.

[1] C Metz, '"The Godfather of A.I." Leaves Google and Warns of Dangers Ahead' *New York Times* (1 May 2023).

[2] ibid (citing Geoffrey Hinton). See also M Caldwell et al., 'AI-Enabled Future Crime' (2020) 9 *Crime Science* 1, 5–6; M E Diamantis, 'Employed Algorithms: A Labor Model of Corporate Liability for AI' (2023) 72 *Duke Law Journal* 797, 799–800; E Hickman and M Petrin, 'Trustworthy AI and Corporate Governance: The EU's Ethics Guidelines for Trustworthy Artificial Intelligence from a Company Law Perspective' (2021) 22 *European Business Organization Law Review* 593, 615–16; R Timperlake, 'Should AI Developers Really Be Our Ethics Gatekeepers?' (*AI Magazine*, 11 December 2021). Available at: https://aimagazine.com/ai-strategy/should-ai-developers-really-be-our-ethics-gatekeepers; D C Vladeck, 'Machines without Principals: Liability Rules and Artificial Intelligence' (2014) 89 *Washington Law Review* 117, 117–21.

[3] Metz (n 1).

[4] S Chesterman, *We, the Robots? Regulating Artificial Intelligence and the Limits of the Law* (Cambridge University Press 2021).

strategy setting to risk management and compliance',[5] prompting similar vacillation between giddy optimism and grave concern for the risks – including fears that sophisticated AI might facilitate commercial fraud. Growing reliance on algorithmic processes to manage increasingly data-driven businesses has already created new AI-based threats, to which businesses must respond with new AI-based defences, and the growing complexity of this landscape has placed a strain on compliance and risk management functions. At the same time, these developments have already exposed shortcomings of conventional legal theories of fraud and manipulation that took shape by reference to human actors, not machines.

This chapter explores current and potential impacts of AI on corporate management of fraud risk in both operational and compliance contexts. Section 2 discusses the nature of AI and explores forms of fraud risk that may arise from these novel and rapidly evolving technologies. Specifically, this section discusses both 'offensive AI' deployed to defraud businesses and 'defensive AI' deployed by businesses in response and assesses how this shifting landscape might impact corporate oversight obligations.

Section 3, then, assesses how increasingly autonomous AI – where the system makes decisions on its own, without direct human involvement – challenges the viability of conventional legal theories of fraud and manipulation. This section discusses the difficulty of applying concepts such as scienter, reliance, and causation to algorithmic processes that lack conventional capacity for intentionality and defy conventional explanation as to how inputs and outputs relate to one another, undermining the capacity of conventional legal theories to deter abusive applications of such technology. This section then presents proposals to reform such legal theories to respond to these doctrinal problems and assesses how such reforms might work in tandem with 'gatekeeper regulation' focused on conditioning incentives of actors thought to be well-positioned to detect and prevent fraud and manipulation. Section 4 briefly concludes.

2. Offensive AI, Defensive AI and Corporate Oversight

This section discusses the nature of AI and then explores forms of fraud risk that may arise from these novel and rapidly evolving technologies. Such efforts may

[5] L Enriques and D A Zetzsche, 'Corporate Technologies and the Tech Nirvana Fallacy' (2020) 72 *Hastings Law Journal* 55, 66. See also I H-Y Chiu and E WK Lim, 'Managing Corporations' Risk in Adopting Artificial Intelligence: A Corporate Responsibility Paradigm' (2021) 20 *Washington University Global Studies Law Review* 347, 352–59; R Feldman and K Stein, 'AI Governance in the Financial Industry' (2022) 27 *Stanford Journal of Law, Business & Finance* 94, 103; G Hertig, *Using Artificial Intelligence for Financial Supervision Purposes* (Singapore-ETH Centre 2021) 4–6; A Kamalnath and U Varottil, 'A Disclosure-Based Approach to Regulating AI in Corporate Governance' (2022) NUS Working Paper 2022/001, 1–2. Available at: https://ssrn.com/abstract=4002876; A Lior, 'Insuring AI: The Role of Insurance in Artificial Intelligence Regulation' (2022) 35 *Harvard Journal of Law & Technology* 467, 476–77.

involve sophisticated deployment of malicious extra-corporate AI applications – 'offensive AI', as the cybersecurity industry describes it. This will, in turn, require responsive corporate efforts in the form of 'defensive AI'. This section describes burgeoning efforts along these lines and their impacts upon corporate compliance and risk management functions, and then analyses their potential doctrinal implications for managerial oversight obligations under corporate law.

2.1. What is AI?

AI involves 'a set of techniques aimed at approximating some aspect of human or animal cognition using machines' – a broad category of technology including a range of methods and degrees of autonomy from human decision-makers. Advanced AI methods include machine learning, involving 'capacity of a system to improve its performance at a task over time', and deep learning, involving 'many-layered structures to extract features from enormous data sets in service of practical tasks requiring pattern recognition'.[6] So-called 'general' AI, approximating human cognitive capacities, remains theoretical[7] and is set aside here. Nevertheless, AI 'has progressed at an astounding clip'[8] and is widely expected to affect all dimensions of business because it can extract useful information from extraordinary volumes of data, far outstripping human processing and analytical capacities.[9]

How such technologies will be deployed and how they will ultimately relate to human decision-makers remain unclear because there are several degrees of autonomy that AI applications might involve. So-called 'assisted AI' has 'either a low level or no autonomy', merely performing defined tasks, whereas 'advisory AI' has 'a heightened level of autonomy' in that it provides 'information and advice' to human decision-makers. By contrast, truly 'autonomous AI' involves machines themselves making decisions, without real-time human involvement.[10] Where a given application falls on this spectrum has a big impact

[6] R Calo, 'Artificial Intelligence Policy: A Primer and Roadmap' (2017) 51 *UC Davis Law Review* 399, 404–05. See also Caldwell et al. (n 2) 3–5; V Ciancaglini et al., *Malicious Uses and Abuses of Artificial Intelligence* (Trend Micro Research 2020) 3–5; I Evtimov et al., 'Is Tricking a Robot Hacking?' (2019) 34 *Berkeley Technology Law Journal* 891, 895; Feldman and Stein (n 5) 101–03; T C King et al., 'Artificial Intelligence Crime: An Interdisciplinary Analysis of Foreseeable Threats and Solutions' (2020) 26 *Science and Engineering Ethics* 89, 91–92; G Marcus, 'Deep Learning: A Critical Appraisal' (2018) 2. Available at: https://arxiv.org/pdf/1801.00631.pdf.

[7] R Abbott and A Sarch, 'Punishing Artificial Intelligence: Legal Fiction or Science Fiction' (2019) 53 *UC Davis Law Review* 323, 331–32. See also C M Bruner, 'Distributed Ledgers, Artificial Intelligence and the Purpose of the Corporation' (2020) 79 *Cambridge Law Journal* 431, 444–46; Calo (n 6) 431–35; Feldman and Stein (n 5) 102–03.

[8] Feldman and Stein (n 5) 102.

[9] See n 5 and accompanying text.

[10] M Petrin, 'Corporate Management in the Age of AI' [2019] *Columbia Business Law Review* 965, 980–83. See also Chiu and Lim (n 5) 352–53.

on associated fraud risks and corporate oversight obligations, as well as the degree to which existing legal theories of fraud and manipulation are prepared to grapple with potential abuses.[11]

Extant literature has explored numerous legal, ethical, and practical challenges arising from human reliance on AI,[12] the most significant of which for understanding the intersection with commercial fraud is the 'black box' problem associated with advanced algorithms that incorporate complex machine learning and deep learning techniques.[13] Such AI is intrinsically opaque in that 'the parameters of neural networks can only be interpreted in terms of their weights within a mathematical geography'. This renders such AI 'black boxes, whose outputs cannot be explained' in conventional terms that directly trace them back to specific inputs.[14] Among other things, this presents fundamental challenges for legal theories of fraud and manipulation hinging on showing causation and a culpable mental state.[15]

2.2. Offensive versus Defensive AI

Although detailed information on use of AI in cyberattacks remains limited, it is increasingly recognised that such 'offensive AI' substantially raises the threat level,[16] both through malicious use of externally generated AI and through attacks upon AI used internally by the targeted business.[17] The advent of offensive AI permits 'targeted attacks at unprecedented speed and scale while avoiding traditional, rule-based detection measures';[18] a recent survey found that over the last year '34.5% of polled executives report that their organizations' accounting

[11] Sections 2.2–2.3 and 3 below.

[12] For background, see Bruner (n 7) 442–46; C M Bruner, 'Artificially Intelligent Boards and the Future of Delaware Corporate Law' (2022) 22 *Journal of Corporate Law Studies* 783, 785.

[13] F Pasquale, *The Black Box Society: The Secret Algorithms that Control Money and Information* (Harvard University Press 2015) 3, 8–9.

[14] J Pontin, 'Greedy, Brittle, Opaque, and Shallow: The Downsides to Deep Learning' (*Wired*, 2 February 2018). Available at: www.wired.com/story/greedy-brittle-opaque-and-shallow-the-downsides-to-deep-learning/. See also Y Bathaee, 'The Artificial Intelligence Black Box and the Failure of Intent and Causation' (2018) 31 *Harvard Journal of Law & Technology* 889, 897–98, 901–06; Chesterman (n 4) 65–66, 79–80, 146–48; Ciancaglini et al. (n 6) 8; Diamantis (n 2) 820–21; Feldman and Stein (n 5) 103–04; E Lim, 'B2B Artificial Intelligence Transactions: A Framework for Assessing Commercial Liability' (2022) 5. Available at https://ssrn.com/abstract=4025415; Marcus (n 6) 10–11.

[15] Section 3 below.

[16] S Goldman, 'Crippling AI Cyberattacks Are Inevitable: 4 Ways Companies Can Prepare' (*VentureBeat*, 16 May 2022). Available at: https://venturebeat.com/ai/crippling-ai-cyberattacks-are-inevitable-4-ways-companies-can-prepare/; B Guembe et al., 'The Emerging Threat of AI-Driven Cyber Attacks: A Review' [2022] 36 *Applied Artificial Intelligence* 1, 2; J Sparapani and L Ruma (eds), *Preparing for AI-Enabled Cyberattacks* (MIT Technology Review Insights 2021) 2. See also Evtimov et al. (n 6) 899–903; A Janofsky, 'AI Could Make Cyberattacks More Dangerous, Harder to Detect' *Wall Street Journal* (13 November 2018). Blockchain technology can also facilitate fraud. See T Chan and KFK Low, Chapter 6 in this volume.

[17] Caldwell et al. (n 2) 5; Ciancaglini et al. (n 6) 5.

[18] Guembe et al. (n 16) 2.

and financial data were targeted by cyber adversaries', while 'nearly half (48.8%) of C-suite and other executives expect the number and size of cyber events … to increase in the year ahead'.[19] The US Federal Trade Commission indicates that 'consumers reported losing nearly $8.8 billion to fraud in 2022, an increase of more than 30 percent over the previous year', much of which resulted from 'fake investing scams and imposter scams'.[20] Meanwhile the broader economic impact of cybercrime is expected to grow exponentially in coming years, harming the global economy to the tune of $600 billion in 2021[21] and 'predicted to hit $8 trillion in 2023 and … $10.5 trillion by 2025'.[22]

AI can increase fraud risks by augmenting fraudsters' traditional methods. In 2019, for example, cybercriminals 'used artificial intelligence-based software to impersonate a chief executive's voice and demand a fraudulent transfer of €220,000' – a vivid instance of 'artificial intelligence being used in hacking'.[23] This represents an advanced form of phishing straightforwardly accomplished using voice impersonation software.[24] More dramatically, 'deepfake videos', in which 'a computer-generated face (often of a real person) is superimposed on someone else', have allowed 'fraudsters [to] make the target person say or do just about anything', and this technique is expected to facilitate frauds in commercial, corporate, investment, and other contexts.[25] Likewise, AI-powered phishing scams can deliver malware, including ransomware. AI is expected to render fake emails 'almost indistinguishable from genuine communications from trusted contacts' and ultimately to 'conduct cyberattacks autonomously, disguising their operations and blending in with regular activity'.[26] AI algorithms are further expected

[19] C Brooks, 'Cybersecurity Trends & Statistics for 2023: More Treachery and Risk Ahead as Attack Surface and Hacker Capabilities Grow' *Forbes* (5 March 2023) (quoting a Deloitte survey).

[20] ibid. See also E Cibula, 'AI Fraud Detection: How Technology Is Modernizing Financial Fraud' (*IT Chronicles*, 21 February 2023). Available at: https://itchronicles.com/artificial-intelligence/ai-fraud-detection-how-technology-is-modernizing-financial-fraud/. See also A Emecheta, 'How Is AI Used in Fraud Detection?' (*AI Time Journal*, 18 April 2023). Available at: www.aitimejournal.com/how-is-ai-used-in-fraud-detection; C Pape, 'AI Has Taken Over Imaginations. It's Also Taking Over Fraud.' *American Banker* (11 January 2023).

[21] A Anand, 'How Is AI Used in Fraud Detection?' (*Analytics Steps*, 21 September 2021). Available at: www.analyticssteps.com/blogs/how-ai-used-fraud-detection (citing McAfee data).

[22] Brooks (n 19) (citing Cybersecurity Ventures estimates).

[23] C Stupp, 'Fraudsters Used AI to Mimic CEO's Voice in Unusual Cybercrime Case' *Wall Street Journal* (30 August 2019). See also Ciancaglini et al. (n 6) 57–58.

[24] A Rajagopal, 'AI Could Escalate New Type of Voice Phishing Cyber Attacks' (*Cyber Security Hub*, 15 July 2019). Available at: www.cshub.com/attacks/articles/ai-could-escalate-new-type-of-voice-phishing-cyber-attacks; Stupp (n 23). See also A Maurushat, A Bello and B Bragg, 'Artificial Intelligence Enabled Cyber Fraud: A Detailed Look into Payment Diversion Fraud and Ransomware' (2019) 15 *Indian Journal of Law and Technology* 261, 265–76 (describing 'payment diversion fraud' techniques).

[25] Y Pashaeva, 'Scammers Are Using Deepfake Videos Now' (*Slate*, 13 September 2021). Available at: https://slate.com/technology/2021/09/deepfake-video-scams.html. See also Caldwell et al. (n 2) 6–7; Ciancaglini et al. (n 6) 52–65.

[26] Sparapani and Ruma (eds) (n 16) 3–5. See also Brooks (n 19); Guembe et al. (n 16) 22; Maurushat, Bello and Bragg (n 24) 276–83; K Wiggers, 'Dear Enterprise IT: Cybercriminals Use AI Too' (*VentureBeat*, 17 June 2021). Available at: https://venturebeat.com/2021/06/17/dear-enterprise-it-cybercriminals-use-ai-too/.

to make it far easier for fraudsters to identify corporate user credentials through faster and more efficient means of testing potential combinations.[27]

At the same time, AI gives rise to entirely new fraud risks, particularly when a company itself employs AI as a core element of its business model. Reflecting the data-intensive nature of machine learning-based AI, 'data poisoning' involves undermining the integrity of the data on which a company's own AI models are built.[28] Such an attack 'aims to modify a model's training set by inserting incorrectly labelled data with the goal of tricking it into making incorrect predictions', which could 'compromise the integrity of the model, generating consistent errors' that the attacker can exploit.[29] Essentially 'any machine learning model that sources third party data for training is vulnerable' and, once data is poisoned in this manner, 'recovering from the attack is so difficult that some developers may not even attempt the fix'.[30] Other techniques for manipulating machine learning models are anticipated, including 'fooling' the system with 'adversarial examples' and seeking to 'compromise the privacy of data contained within the training set'.[31] The growing AI literature continues to identify and assess both existing and potential uses of AI in cybercrime,[32] and it is critical to recognise that such techniques, once developed, are easily replicated – indeed, they may be sold by entrepreneurial fraudsters to others as a pre-packaged illicit business model.[33]

The growing threat of offensive AI naturally prompts businesses to implement 'defensive AI' in response – 'self-learning algorithms that understand normal user, device, and system patterns in an organization and detect unusual activity without relying on historical data'.[34] Unsurprisingly, the need for powerful defensive AI has rapidly gained corporate attention – indeed, '44% of executives are assessing AI-enabled security systems, and 38% are deploying autonomous response technology'.[35] Meanwhile, 'around 80% of executives in the telecommunications industry believe their organization wouldn't be able to respond to

[27] B Chalupski, 'How Fraudsters Use AI to Commit Ecommerce Fraud' (*Merchant Fraud Journal*, 17 September 2019). Available at: www.merchantfraudjournal.com/ai-ecommerce-fraud/. See also V Combs, '3 Ways Criminals Use Artificial Intelligence in Cybersecurity Attacks' (*TechRepublic*, 7 October 2020). Available at: www.techrepublic.com/article/3-ways-criminals-use-artificial-intelligence-in-cybersecurity-attacks/; Guembe et al. (n 16) 22–23; Janofsky (n 16).

[28] Caldwell et al. (n 2) 9; Goldman (n 16).

[29] S Marchal, 'How Data Manipulation Could Be Used to Trick Fraud Detection Algorithms on E-Commerce Sites' (*Help Net Security*, 24 May 2021). Available at: www.helpnetsecurity.com/2021/05/24/fraud-detection-algorithms/. See also Combs (n 27); Guembe et al. (n 16) 26; Evtimov et al. (n 6) 901–02.

[30] Marchal (n 29).

[31] Evtimov et al. (n 6) 900–02.

[32] Ciancaglini et al. (n 6) generally.

[33] Caldwell et al. (n 2) 6. Of course, companies themselves may use AI to commit fraud. Ciancaglini et al. (n 6) 46; Hickman and Petrin (n 2) 617.

[34] Wiggers (n 26). See also Guembe et al. (n 16) 31. Similar dynamics arise in the public sphere. I F Coita, L C Filip and E A Kicska, 'Tax Evasion and Financial Fraud in the Current Digital Context' (2021) 30(1) *Annals of the University of Oradea, Economic Sciences* 187, 188.

[35] Wiggers (n 26) (citing a Darktrace report).

cyberattacks without AI',[36] suggesting that this will loom larger for data-intensive businesses.

Anti-fraud efforts are certainly improving, and there are various AI-based strategies that businesses employ, dovetailing closely with compliance and oversight functions. Machine learning-based AI can be a powerful tool in fraud detection because such systems can review extraordinary numbers of transactions, detect patterns, free up human investigators 'to focus their efforts on the most promising instances', and 'learn from investigators when they evaluate and clear questionable transactions'.[37] Major challenges, however, include maintaining the requisite quantity and quality of data, integrating data siloed by department, preventing harmful biases from contaminating the dataset,[38] and ensuring sufficient explainability.[39] Use of AI for fraud protection inevitably poses complex tradeoffs in terms of false positives v false negatives, fraud detection v customer satisfaction, and accuracy of classification v data privacy.[40] At the same time, it is inherently difficult to keep up 'as cybercriminals look to stay one step ahead of their targets'.[41] This back-and-forth dynamic is aptly described as a 'cat and mouse game',[42] a 'battle of algorithms',[43] and even a 'cyber arms race'.[44]

2.3. Corporate Oversight Obligations

There is growing pressure to devote more resources and managerial attention to such dynamics, arising both from the commercial realities described above and from corporate law. The American Bar Association's *Corporate Director's Handbook* observes that '[a]s businesses and the legal requirements under which they operate become ever more complex … and reliance on technology increases, the stakes

[36] ibid (citing a Statista report). See also Y Bao, G Hilary and B Ke, 'Artificial Intelligence and Fraud Detection' in V Babich, J Birge and G Hilary (eds), *Innovative Technology at the Interface of Finance and Operations* (Springer forthcoming), 1–4. Available at: https://ssrn.com/abstract=3738618; Sparapani and Ruma (eds) (n 16) 5.

[37] Anand (n 21). See also Bao, Hillary and Ke (n 36) 27–28; Cibula (n 20); Emecheta (n 20); L Quest et al., 'The Risks and Benefits of Using AI to Detect Crime' *Harvard Business Review* (9 August 2018).

[38] Bao, Hillary and Ke (n 36) 6–10. See also Chiu and Lim (n 5) 365–68; Quest et al. (n 37).

[39] Bao, Hillary and Ke (n 36) 17.

[40] ibid 13. See also Quest et al. (n 37). Regarding the perils of overreliance on automated systems, consider the UK Post Office's Horizon scandal, in which '[h]undreds of sub-postmasters and postmistresses were wrongly prosecuted after faulty computer software calculated that money was missing from post office branches'. See 'Post Office Scandal Explained: What the Horizon Saga Is All About' (*BBC News*, updated 20 February 2024). Available at: www.bbc.com/news/business-56718036. See also A Wang and D Brown, 'How AI Solutions and Strong Leadership Could Have Avoided the UK's Worst-Ever Miscarriage of Justice' *Forbes* (13 May 2022). On the importance of keeping 'humans in the loop' to 'guard against the risks of algorithmic failures', see H Tjio, P Koh and L P Woan, 'Company Law' in S Chesterman, G Yihan and APB Leong (eds), *Law and Technology in Singapore* (Academy Publishing 2021) para 14.041.

[41] Wiggers (n 26). See also Brooks (n 19); Goldman (n 16); Pape (n 20).

[42] Pape (n 20); Goldman (n 16).

[43] Sparapani and Ruma (eds) (n 16) 2.

[44] Brooks (n 19); Ciancaglini et al. (n 6) 49; King et al. (n 6) 97; Lior (n 5) 523.

involved in effectively managing risk and ensuring legal compliance only increases'.[45] Specifically, the 'increasing prominence of technology in business … has exponentially increased cybersecurity risk for virtually all corporations', raising the significance of 'technology failures and security breaches and increasingly sophisticated cyber-crime schemes' – all of which increase the importance of compliance and risk management.[46] Reflecting these realities, AI is becoming more central to these efforts, assisting human decision-makers in these critical areas.[47]

That the company's operational use of AI would 'deserve the attention of high-level management' certainly 'seems uncontroversial and is consistent with directors' (and other senior managers') existing oversight duties posited by corporate laws'.[48] Large companies active in this space are well aware of the associated risks,[49] and general proposals have been advanced that would involve enhanced disclosures[50] and robust risk management systems.[51]

At the same time, there is growing recognition that 'AI-powered crime-fighting tools could become a requirement for large businesses, in part because there will be no other way to rapidly detect and interpret patterns across billions of pieces of data'.[52] To the extent this becomes the reality for large, data-driven businesses, this could ultimately have significant legal consequences in terms of AI's role in analysis of oversight obligations under corporate law.[53] As I have argued elsewhere, it is conceivable that in Delaware, the principal jurisdiction for incorporation of large publicly traded US businesses,[54] reliance on AI tools in the oversight context could effectively become mandatory.[55] Although Delaware law likely would not countenance outright outsourcing of such core managerial functions to AI-based systems under long-standing statutory requirements and fiduciary duty principles,[56] similarly venerable fiduciary principles require some effort to implement a reasonable compliance monitoring system – and, for at least

[45] Corporate Laws Committee, American Bar Association Business Law Section, *Corporate Director's Guidebook* (7th edn, American Bar Association 2020) 35.

[46] ibid 36.

[47] Bruner (n 12) 800–03.

[48] Hickman and Petrin (n 2) 599.

[49] See, eg, Microsoft Corporation, Annual Report on Form 10-K for the Fiscal Year Ended 30 June 2022, 29. Available at: www.sec.gov/Archives/edgar/data/789019/000156459022026876/msft-10k_20220630.htm (explaining that '[i]ssues in the development and use of AI may result in reputational harm or liability').

[50] Kamalnath and Varottil (n 5).

[51] Chiu and Lim (n 5).

[52] Quest et al. (n 37).

[53] Bruner (n 12) 803–04.

[54] State of Delaware, Division of Corporations, 'Why Businesses Choose Delaware' (*Delaware.gov*). Available at: https://corplaw.delaware.gov/why-businesses-choose-delaware/.

[55] Bruner (n 12) 794–804.

[56] See Delaware Code title 8 s 141(a)–(b) (US) (requiring that each director 'shall be a natural person'). On Delaware's 'duty of non-delegation' regarding matters 'at the heart of the management of the corporation', see *Canal Capital Corp v French*, 1992 WL 159008, *2–*3 (Del Ch 1992). See also *In re Bally's Grand Derivative Litigation*, 1997 WL 305803, *4–*6 (Del Ch 1997); *In re Broadstripe, LLC*, 444 BR 51, 105 (Bankr D Del 2010); *Mills Acquisition Co v MacMillan, Inc*, 559 A2d 1261, 1281 (Del 1989).

some data-intensive businesses, this may not be possible without substantial reliance on AI-based tools.

Although it was long held that implementing a compliance monitoring system would be required only if red flags indicated a potential problem,[57] in his 1996 *Caremark* opinion Chancellor Allen held that the board must 'exercise a good faith judgment that the corporation's information and reporting system is in concept and design adequate to assure the board that appropriate information will come to its attention in a timely manner'.[58] For many years it remained very difficult for shareholders to prevail on a claim that this duty had been breached because *Caremark* further held that 'only a sustained or systematic failure of the board to exercise oversight – such as an utter failure to attempt to assure a reasonable information and reporting system exists – will establish the lack of good faith that is a necessary condition of liability'.[59]

A recent line of cases, however, has opened the door to more robust enforcement of the *Caremark* duty. In *Marchand*, the Supreme Court of Delaware interpreted *Caremark* to require 'a good faith effort to put in place a reasonable system of monitoring and reporting about the corporation's *central compliance risks*', and concluded that for the monoline ice cream company involved in that case, 'food safety was essential and *mission critical*'. On this basis, the plaintiff was found to have adequately 'pled facts supporting a fair inference that no board-level system of monitoring or reporting *on food safety* existed'.[60] The court's focus on 'central compliance risks' has been interpreted by the Court of Chancery as requiring greater judicial scrutiny in this context, particularly where it relates to a 'mission critical' aspect of the business.[61] For example, in *Clovis*, the court interpreted this to mean that in such circumstances 'the board's oversight function must be more rigorously exercised'.[62] In *Boeing*, then, the court similarly found 'airplane safety' to be 'mission critical' to Boeing, and the plaintiffs survived a motion to dismiss based on 'remarkably similar factual allegations' to *Marchand* regarding the board's oversight failures.[63]

[57] *Graham v Allis-Chalmers Manufacturing Co*, 188 A2d 125, 129–31 (Del 1963).

[58] *In re Caremark International Inc Derivative Litigation*, 698 A2d 959, 970 (Del Ch 1996).

[59] ibid 971. Although initially focused on directors, this *Caremark* duty applies to officers as well. *In re McDonald's Corporation Stockholder Derivative Litigation*, 289 A3d 343, 358–69 (Del Ch 2023). For recent analysis of forms of *Caremark* claims, see *Ontario Provincial Council of Carpenters' Pension Trust Fund v Walton*, 2023 WL 3093500, *28–*34 (Del Ch 2023). For comparative analysis, see W Tan, Chapter 15 in this volume.

[60] *Marchand v Barnhill*, 212 A3d 805, 824 (Del 2019) (emphasis added).

[61] The latter is a subset of the former. *In re McDonald's Corporation Stockholder Derivative Litigation*, – A3d –, 2023 WL 2293575, *16–*17 (Del Ch 2023).

[62] *In re Clovis Oncology, Inc Derivative Litigation*, 2019 WL 4850188, *13 (Del Ch 2019). See also *Hughes v Hu*, 2020 WL 1987029, *13–*17 (Del Ch 2020).

[63] *In re Boeing Company Derivative Litigation*, 2021 WL 4059934, *26 (Del Ch 2021). See also R Shapira, 'Mission Critical ESG and the Scope of Director Oversight Duties' [2022] *Columbia Business Law Review* 732, 745–50.

More recent Chancery decisions suggest that cases involving emerging technologies might eventually be interpreted this way. Although the plaintiffs did not meet the pleading burden in either case, in *Sorenson* the court observed that '[c]ybersecurity has increasingly become a central compliance risk deserving of board level monitoring at companies across sectors'.[64] The court elaborated that this 'is an area of consequential risk that spans modern business sectors' and that, 'as the legal and regulatory frameworks governing cybersecurity advance and the risks become manifest, corporate governance must evolve to address them'.[65] Similarly, in *Bingle*, the court stated that 'cybersecurity, for online service providers, is mission critical'.[66] As a subsequent opinion observes of these remarks, they reflect the fact that 'risks evolve over time', and that although 'the relative importance of cybersecurity risk has not yet led to a *Caremark* claim surviving a motion to dismiss … someday it might'.[67]

As I have argued elsewhere,[68] these technological realities and doctrinal trends could lead to a point where reliance upon sophisticated AI for oversight and compliance monitoring is effectively required to comply with Delaware fiduciary duty obligations. As a practical matter the market appears to be moving in this direction, one survey finding that '89 percent of participants … are already on the path to including AI in their compliance platforms'.[69] This presumably reflects the fact that, '[f]or many companies, data is becoming the most valuable asset', and 'governance of these key assets is of strategic importance and needs to be addressed at the board level'.[70] It is increasingly clear that AI represents the only practical way to detect and prevent crime for large businesses,[71] and it would seem to follow that management of data-driven Delaware corporations not deploying AI-based technologies in their compliance systems run a substantial risk of liability – because a court might interpret this as failure to make a good faith effort to implement a system to monitor 'central compliance risks' that are 'mission critical' to the business, breaching the *Caremark* duty.[72]

[64] *Firemen's Retirement System of St Louis v Sorenson*, 2021 WL 4593777, *1 (Del Ch 2021).

[65] ibid *11–*12. This extends the doctrine beyond legal compliance. See Shapira (n 63) 752–56.

[66] *Construction Industry Laborers Pension Fund v Bingle*, 2022 WL 4102492, *1 (Del Ch 2022).

[67] *Ontario Provincial Council of Carpenters' Pension Trust Fund v Walton*, – A3d –, 2023 WL 2904946, *16 (Del Ch 2023).

[68] Bruner (n 12).

[69] D Ackerman, 'AI Compliance Oversight Is Here … and So Are Next-Gen Compliance Officers' (*Corporate Compliance Insights*, 24 November 2020). Available at: www.corporatecomplianceinsights.com/ai-compliance-oversight-next-gen-compliance-officers (reporting results from a NICE Actimize survey). See also L Brotcke, 'Model Risk Management Oversight of Artificial Intelligence and Machine Learning Applications' (2021) 104 *Risk Management Association Journal* 36; Chiu and Lim (n 5) 352; Kamalnath and Varottil (n 5) 1–2.

[70] M Hilb, 'Toward Artificial Intelligence? The Role of Artificial Intelligence in Shaping the Future of Corporate Governance' (2020) 24 *Journal of Management and Governance* 851, 865. See also Timperlake (n 2).

[71] Quest et al. (n 37).

[72] Bruner (n 12) 803–04.

3. Legal Theories of Fraud in the Age of AI

Although offensive AI techniques may give rise to legal uncertainty under anti-hacking statutory regimes,[73] conventional legal theories can grapple with such situations, which by nature are intentionally pursued – a bad human actor simply uses AI as a tool to commit fraud.[74] In the foregoing sorts of cases, the real problems are practical in nature – establishing jurisdiction, coordinating and paying for cross-border investigations, identifying defendants, tracking funds, and so on.[75] Meanwhile, 'many cyber insurance policies do not specifically cover social engineered fraud unless a company's internal network or computer has been compromised'[76] (although insurance markets may develop in response to perceived limitations[77]). In response to such challenges, experts have suggested developing a 'bounty' system to enlist private actors and exploring how other emerging technologies such as blockchain and quantum encryption might mitigate such problems.[78]

Conceptual challenges arise under the law itself, however, when there is not obviously a bad (or even negligent) human actor directly involved in relevant decision-making. This is increasingly the case with autonomous AI incorporating machine learning that allows it to make decisions on its own – or at least to take actions that are more difficult to attribute to the intention of any human associated with the system's use. Such dynamics create significant regulatory and enforcement challenges.[79] In cases involving 'black box' algorithmic decision-making, how do we apply fraud and related concepts that require showing some particular state of mind and providing some account of how particular inputs caused particular outputs?

This section analyses shortcomings of conventional legal theories of fraud and manipulation in such circumstances, assessing the difficulty of applying concepts such as scienter, reliance, and causation to algorithmic processes that lack conventional capacity for intentionality and defy conventional explanation as to how inputs and outputs relate. This discussion concludes with proposals to reform conventional legal theories to respond to these problems.

[73] Evtimov et al. (n 6) 909–13.

[74] Bathaee (n 14) 932–34; Maurushat, Bello and Bragg (n 24) 284–86.

[75] Feldman and Stein (n 5) 122–25; Maurushat, Bello and Bragg (n 24) 286–93. For further discussion of such challenges, see Y Man, Chapter 7 in this volume.

[76] Maurushat, Bello and Bragg (n 24) 293.

[77] Lior (n 5) 476; Section 3.2.3 below.

[78] Maurushat, Bello and Bragg (n 24) 293–94; V A Rotundu, 'Impact of Blockchain Technology: Benefits and Security Risk and Threats' (2022) 26 *Informatica Economica* 37, 41–42. See also Coita, Filip and Kicska (n 34) 189 (similarly discussing how blockchain technology might facilitate tax enforcement).

[79] L N Tournas and D M Bowman, 'AI Insurance: Risk Management 2.0' (December 2021) *IEEE Technology and Society Magazine* 52, 52.

3.1. Autonomous AI and Conventional Legal Theories

Conventional legal theories of fraud and manipulation generally require assessing states of mind for multiple actors and tracing a cause-effect relationship between the misstatement and the loss. For example, according to the US Restatement (Third) of Torts, establishing common law fraud requires that a material misrepresentation be made 'for the purpose of inducing another to act or refrain from acting', and that the economic loss be 'caused by the other's justifiable reliance on the misrepresentation'.[80] The Restatement clarifies that a misrepresentation triggers liability 'only if' the defendant 'knows or believes that it is false', or 'knowingly states or implies' either 'a false level of confidence' or 'a basis for the representation that does not exist'.[81] This requirement, termed 'scienter', may be satisfied by a showing of recklessness, but this still requires showing 'conscious disregard' of the statement's veracity.[82] Similarly, recovery is permitted 'only if' the plaintiff's reliance is 'justifiable', which essentially requires non-recklessness on the plaintiff's part.[83] The plaintiff must further establish that the misrepresentation 'causes the loss', reflecting 'the usual requirement in tort that a defendant's wrong be a factual or "but for" cause of the harm'.[84] Similar requirements as to state of mind apply under related legal theories, notably including contractual defences such as misrepresentation.[85]

Such concepts likewise figure centrally in fraud analysis under specialised areas of law, such as securities regulation.[86] For example, the US Securities Exchange Act of 1934 (Exchange Act) makes it 'unlawful for any person' to 'use or employ, in connection with the purchase or sale of any security … any manipulative or deceptive device or contrivance' in contravention of Securities and Exchange Commission (SEC) rules[87] and, pursuant to this authority, the SEC enacted rule 10b-5, a general anti-fraud rule for securities transactions.[88] The elements of a private 10b-5 suit are 'similar to those required for common law fraud', including a material misstatement, scienter, reliance, and causation.[89] Such concepts are also

[80] *Restatement (Third) of Torts: Liability for Economic Harm*, s 9 (2020) (US).

[81] ibid s 10.

[82] ibid comments a, c.

[83] ibid s 11 and comment d.

[84] ibid and comment a.

[85] See, eg, *Restatement (Second) of Contracts*, ss 159, 162–64, 167 (1981) (US); Uniform Commercial Code s 1-103(b) (US) (preserving common law defences in the sale-of-goods context). See also J M Paterson and E Bant, 'Automated Mistakes: Vitiated Consent and State of Mind Culpability in Algorithmic Contracting' in E Bant (ed), *The Culpable Corporate Mind* (Hart Publishing 2023) 255, 259–63.

[86] Y Yadav, 'The Failure of Liability in Modern Markets' (2016) 102 *Virginia Law Review* 1031, 1050–62.

[87] 15 United States Code s 78j(b).

[88] 17 Code of Federal Regulations s 240.10b-5 (US).

[89] S J Choi and AC Pritchard, *Securities Regulation: Cases and Analysis* (Foundation Press 2019) 273. See also *Halliburton Co v Erica P John Fund, Inc*, 573 US 258, 267 (2014).

operative in the context of market manipulation, where the Exchange Act prohibits various actions '[f]or the purpose of creating a false or misleading appearance of active trading in any security … or a false or misleading appearance with respect to the market for any security'[90] and creates a cause of action for those injured by '[a]ny person who willfully participates' in such actions.[91]

In light of the technological realities discussed above, it is not difficult to perceive how traditional fraud requirements of scienter, reliance, and causation could prove problematic as AI becomes more central to decision-making in commercial, corporate, and investment contexts – particularly to the extent that such technology incorporates machine learning. AI black-box dynamics render it unclear how inputs link up with decision outputs and particular harms, rendering it impracticable for plaintiffs to establish these core fraud elements.[92]

Although case law remains limited, litigation is picking up pace,[93] and in all likelihood such issues will come front-and-centre as the technology further develops. For example, in *Quoine*, Singapore's Court of Appeal had to determine how to apply the contractual defence of unilateral mistake in the context of algorithmic trading.[94] This case 'represents the first time an apex court in the Commonwealth has ruled on the applicability of contractual principles to situations involving automated trading software'.[95] In *Quoine*, the matter was simpler because the software involved was 'deterministic' in that the same inputs would always lead to the same outputs, meaning that the software 'does not have the capacity to develop its own responses to varying conditions'.[96] Accordingly, existing law could be applied by reference to the programmer's own state of mind.[97] The court recognised, however, that future cases will likely challenge existing doctrine:

> [T]he law in relation to … ascertainment of knowledge in cases where computers have replaced human actions … will, no doubt, develop as legal disputes arise as a result of such actions. This will particularly be the case where the computer in question is creating artificial intelligence and could therefore be said to have a mind of its own.[98]

[90] 15 United States Code s 78i(a)(1). This provision does not apply to exempted securities. ibid s 78i(g).

[91] ibid s 78i(f). For additional background see Choi and Pritchard (n 89) 243–46. See also 7 United States Code s 9 (prohibiting fraud and manipulation in the commodities context).

[92] Bathaee (n 14) 890–93, 906–28; Feldman and Stein (n 5) 105–11.

[93] See Ethical Tech Initiatives, George Washington University, 'AI Litigation Database' (updated 10 October 2022). Available at: https://blogs.gwu.edu/law-eti/ai-litigation-database/.

[94] *Quoine Pte Ltd v B2C2 Ltd* [2020] SGCA(I) 02 [4].

[95] V Ooi and K P Soh, 'Rethinking Mistake in the Age of Algorithms: Quoine Pte Ltd v B2C2 Ltd' (2020) 31 *King's Law Journal* 367.

[96] *Quoine* (n 94) [15].

[97] ibid [79], [97]–[99]; J Lee, 'Smart Contracts and the Limits of the "Rule of Code"' (2022) 10 *Journal of International Banking and Financial Law* 692. See also Abbott and Sarch (n 7) 369–70; Diamantis (n 2) 814–15; Vladeck (n 2) 120. For discussion of how a corporation's mental state can be reflected in an automated system, see E Bant, Chapter 4 in this volume. For discussion of the *Quoine* decision's implications regarding property rights in crypto assets, see J Lim, Chapter 5 in this volume.

[98] *Quoine* (n 94) [185] (quoting the lower court).

As this suggests, legal analyses turning on state of mind will likely become more complicated in future cases involving non-deterministic software.[99]

The manipulation context has received considerable attention, not least because automated and high-frequency trading account for '50 to 70% of volume of equities, 60 to 80% in some futures markets, and around 50% in the U.S. Treasury markets'.[100] Clearly a bad actor could intentionally use AI to manipulate such markets,[101] and legal analysis in such cases is relatively straightforward because relevant decisions are traceable to human actors. But what if trading algorithms aimed at some generic maximand – notably, profit – learn to manipulate markets as a means to that end? Both the practical challenges and legal complexities are heightened by the advent of high frequency trading strategies, moving far more quickly and in much more complex patterns than any human could contemplate, let alone execute.[102] Here, again, much turns on the nature and complexity of the algorithms themselves. Legal theories that might remain conceptually unproblematic applied to deterministic algorithms become far more difficult to apply coherently to machine learning models giving rise to black-box dynamics.[103] This problem arises vividly where an AI system using machine learning techniques learns to manipulate markets toward a generic profit-maximisation goal, without direct human involvement in the relevant decision-making,[104] undercutting application of market manipulation rules designed by reference to human mental states.[105]

State of mind requirements are of course 'pervasive' in law,[106] and similar concerns regarding potential for machine learning-based AI systems to learn to engage in illegal conduct arise in other legal contexts, including antitrust law[107]

[99] Chesterman (n 4) 54–57; Lee (n 97); Ooi and Soh (n 95); Paterson and Bant (n 85) 263–69; T Whittaker and D Varney, 'Explainable Machine Learning: How Can You Determine What a Party Knew or Intended When a Decision Was Made By Machine-Learning?' (*Society for Computers and Law*, 11 December 2020). Available at: www.scl.org/articles/12130-explainable-machine-learning-how-can-you-determine-what-a-party-knew-or-intended-when-a-decision-was-made-by-machine-learning. See also Bathaee (n 14) 906–14; *Information Law*, vol 1, s 1:15 (updated September 2022); Vladeck (n 2) 120–22.

[100] Yadav (n 86) 1073. See also Chesterman (n 4) 21; G G Fletcher, 'Deterring Algorithmic Manipulation' (2021) 74 *Vanderbilt Law Review* 259, 286.

[101] Caldwell et al. (n 2) 10; Chesterman (n 4) 29–30; Ciancaglini et al. (n 6) 44.

[102] Chesterman (n 4) 21–25; Fletcher (n 100) 286–89; Pasquale (n 13) 128–31; G Scopino, 'Do Automated Trading Systems Dream of Manipulating the Price of Futures Contracts? Policing Markets for Improper Trading Practices by Algorithmic Robots' (2015) 67 *Florida Law Review* 221, 226–31; Yadav (n 86) 1064–70.

[103] Fletcher (n 100) 289–99; Scopino (n 102) 226–28, 244–45. See also Y Bathaee, 'Artificial Intelligence Opinion Liability' (2020) 35 *Berkeley Technology Law Journal* 113, 138–43; Chesterman (n 4) 88–89; King et al. (n 6) 95.

[104] Fletcher (n 100) 296–99; Scopino (n 102) 228–31. See also Abbott and Sarch (n 7) 331; Bathaee (n 103) 146–48; Feldman and Stein (n 5) 112–13; King et al. (n 6) 97–98.

[105] Fletcher (n 100) 262–64, 281–84; Scopino (n 102) 233–34, 250–52; Yadav (n 86) 1073–77.

[106] M Chatterjee and J C Fromer, 'Common Law for the Age of AI' (2019) 119 *Columbia Law Review* 1887, 1890.

[107] J Cave, 'Can Machines Learn Whether Machines Are Learning to Collude?' (6th International Conference, INSCI 2019, Perpignan, France, 2–5 December 2019) 133, 136–37. See also Chesterman (n 4) 26–28; Bathaee (n 14) 907–08.

and consumer protection law.[108] Such lack of fit between AI decision-making and legal structures turning on human mental states will presumably distort incentives for the worse because ill-fitting regulation is likely to break down in such contexts. Minimally, this creates an incentive to avoid understanding how the algorithm transforms inputs into outputs – in order to preserve deniability.[109] Indeed, this may even create 'a perverse incentive to use an AI model to make decisions in highly regulated environments', precisely because 'the AI functionality cuts off any possible liability'.[110]

3.2. Reconceptualising Fraud in the Age of AI

Although doctrinal problems associated with autonomous AI are receiving greater attention, it remains unclear how best to address those problems. Navigating this landscape requires that we clarify what we mean when we colloquially suggest that machines can 'think', and that we reform state of mind and causation requirements by reference to what we believe is truly at stake. At the same time, it is important to consider how 'gatekeeper' dynamics might constrain autonomous AI, including 'soft' regulation through insurance markets.

3.2.1. How We Think about whether Machines can Think

Evaluating how to apply state of mind requirements in the age of AI requires beginning with a threshold question – whether AI systems actually 'think' in any legally significant sense.[111] Alan Turing evaluated this functionally by reference to whether a machine could fool a human interrogator into believing that the machine is also human.[112] Others have responded that 'symbol manipulation alone is insufficient to provide understanding, which appears to require some biological processes' associated with consciousness.[113] Most agree that such technology 'can in principle replicate the functional properties of human minds', yet it remains unclear whether this is enough for legal structures hinging on state of mind.[114]

Some suggest that we resolve this by analogising to other situations posing similar ontological uncertainties – notably, corporations.[115] The UK Supreme

[108] L E Willis, 'Deception by Design' (2020) 34 *Harvard Journal of Law & Technology* 115, 147–60. Other fields raise similar issues. See Chatterjee and Fromer (n 106) 1897–1903 (discussing whether machines could have requisite 'volition' under copyright law).

[109] King et al. (n 6) 95. See also Feldman and Stein (n 5) 98.

[110] Bathaee (n 103) 148. See also Diamantis (n 2) 825–26.

[111] *Information Law* (n 99).

[112] AM Turing, 'Computing Machinery and Intelligence' (1950) *Mind* 433, 433–36.

[113] *Information Law* (n 99) (summarising such arguments). See also Chatterjee and Fromer (n 106) 1903–05; King et al. (n 6) 102–03.

[114] Chatterjee and Fromer (n 106) 1906–09.

[115] Regarding ontological uncertainties about corporations, see C M Bruner, 'The Enduring Ambivalence of Corporate Law' (2008) 59 *Alabama Law Review* 1385, 1387–90.

Court, for example, has expressed confidence that we are fully equipped to cross this bridge in the technology context, as '[t]he court is well versed in identifying the governing mind of a corporation and, when the need arises, will no doubt be able to do the same for robots'.[116] So perhaps we could treat AI like a corporation, imputing to it the state of mind of humans standing behind it – presumably including developers, owners, and users – and on this basis punish the AI itself.[117] This, however, would require AI personhood, and would raise significant concerns about absolving the natural persons involved with deploying this technology of any responsibility for its consequences, creating bad incentives.[118]

Others are inclined to sidestep the ontological complexities entirely, emphasising that regardless of how we style AI operations, 'humans would have had to make decisions to design AI technology in particular ways and would have had to delegate operations to it'. From this perspective, the regulatory aim should be 'keeping responsibility where it will do the most good: to encourage humans that design and deploy AI technology to anticipate the role of the technology in producing states of affairs'.[119]

3.2.2. Reforming State of Mind and Causation Requirements

How should we address the problems associated with state of mind and causation requirements in the AI context? The most obvious responses would be either to require strict adherence to the existing elements or to dispense with them entirely. A requirement that AI algorithms be 'more transparent and explainable' could reconnect inputs and outputs and thereby eliminate doctrinal problems associated with state of mind and causation requirements. Given the nature of the technology, however, that would effectively be tantamount to prohibiting machine learning-based AI – a step that, given the potential benefits, many remain unwilling to take.[120] This brings us back to the formulation of anti-fraud and anti-manipulation rules themselves, and an approach with increasing support is to relax, or even eliminate, the core requirements impeding their application, which would essentially shift these regimes along the liability spectrum toward strict liability.[121] Going all the way to strict liability, however, prompts concerns

[116] *Warner-Lambert Company LLC v Generics (UK) Ltd* [2018] UKSC 56 [165].

[117] Abbott and Sarch (n 7) 350–60; Chesterman (n 4) 115–17.

[118] Chesterman (n 4) 115, 120–21; King et al. (n 6) 108–09. See also Vladeck (n 2) 124–29, 149–50.

[119] DG Johnson and M Verdicchio, 'AI, Agency and Responsibility: The VW Fraud Case and Beyond' (2019) 34 *AI & Society* 639, 644–46.

[120] Fletcher (n 100) 313–17. See also Bathaee (n 14) 929–31; Bathaee (n 103) 167; Chesterman (n 4) 144–51. Disclosure could, however, be useful as a regulatory strategy – for example, regarding use of bots to incentivise commercial transactions. See B Stricke, 'People v. Robots: A Roadmap for Enforcing California's New Online Bot Disclosure Act' (2020) 22 *Vanderbilt Journal of Entertainment & Technology Law* 839; California Business and Professions Code ss 17940–43 (US).

[121] For discussion of such approaches, see Bathaee (n 14) 937–38; Fletcher (n 100) 318–21; Scopino (n 102) 292–93. See also H Tjio, W W Yee and Y K Hon, *Principles and Practice of Securities Regulations*

regarding potentially excessive risk aversion, particularly as applied to users of this technology, which suggests that careful balancing is required.[122]

Closely related are approaches that impose strict products liability, or something like it – although this would focus liability on producers, thought to be 'in a position to either absorb the costs, or through pricing decisions, to spread the burden of loss widely'. In other words, producers could effectively include an 'insurance premium' in the price 'to offset expected liability costs'.[123] This approach raises its own complexities, however, including whether AI systems are better characterised as products or services.[124]

An alternative approach targets 'corporate accountability for algorithmic harm' on the logic that 'corporations generally design, own and operate the world's most impactful algorithms',[125] treating AI algorithms 'as though they were employees' under existing agency law principles.[126] This approach would focus the analysis on 'whether a corporation claims substantial benefits from the algorithm's operation and exercises substantial control over it',[127] and holds constant state of mind requirements in existing law.[128] With complex machine learning-based AI, however, the agency analogy breaks down on the control issue. Under existing agency law, an employer faces no liability for an employee's 'frolic' beyond the scope of the work contemplated – yet with complex AI, 'the most difficult liability questions will arise when they operate as more than tools or instruments, beyond the control or direction of the user'.[129]

In evaluating potential responses to the doctrinal problems posed by AI, it is important to recall that this is not the first context where traditional approaches to fraud have had to be modified to accommodate market complexities. In particular, relaxing certain fraud elements has been an important regulatory strategy in the capital markets context. In US securities law, for example, private securities fraud suits are expected to supplement public enforcement.[130] To facilitate this, traditional common law requirements have been substantially relaxed to permit such suits to proceed. Under Exchange Act rule 10b-5,[131] the traditional reliance

in Singapore (3rd edn, LexisNexis 2017) para 8.26 (observing the lack of clarity regarding required state of mind for market manipulation in Australia and Singapore).

[122] Chesterman (n 4) 92–93; King et al. (n 6) 95–96; Yadav (n 86) 1082.

[123] Vladeck (n 2) 146–48. See also Bathaee (n 103) 162–65; Chesterman (n 4) 93–94.

[124] Chesterman (n 4) 95. See also Lim (n 14) 11–14 (examining this question with business-to-business contracts).

[125] Diamantis (n 2) 816.

[126] ibid 840–48. See also Bathaee (n 14) 934–35.

[127] Diamantis (n 2) 848. See also *Restatement (Third) of Agency*, s 7.07 (2006) (US).

[128] Diamantis (n 2) 853.

[129] Chesterman (n 4) 89–90. See also *Joel v Morison* [1834] EWHC KB J39 [5]; *Restatement (Third) of Agency*, s 7.07(2) (2006) (US). The agency approach could also disrupt bargained-for risk allocations. See Paterson and Bant (n 85) 267–68 (rejecting the *Quoine* dissent's approach, providing relief where a reasonable trader would have perceived an error, because this 'effectively assimilates the algorithm to a worker or employee' and contradicts the parties' choice 'not to scrutinise each transaction, prioritising speed and predictability instead').

[130] See Choi and Pritchard (n 89) chs 5, 8; Yadav (n 86) 1042–50.

[131] 17 Code of Federal Regulations s 240.10b-5 (US).

requirement has been substantially relaxed[132] by dispensing with it in cases involving material omissions[133] and otherwise by permitting reliance on the integrity of prices in efficient trading markets to substitute for actual reliance – the 'fraud on the market' theory.[134] As the US Supreme Court has emphasised, the point of the fraud on the market theory is to facilitate private suits by avoiding 'an unnecessarily unrealistic evidentiary burden on the Rule 10b-5 plaintiff'.[135]

More dramatically yet, in the primary market context where fraud risks are heightened (because the issuer and/or significant shareholders are themselves selling securities),[136] the cause of action for misrepresentations in the registration statement under section 11 of the Securities Act of 1933 dispenses with most common law fraud elements – the plaintiff need only plead a material misstatement or omission.[137] Critically, this means that defendants 'cannot seek dismissal based on state of mind related pleadings or lack thereof'.[138] Section 11 defendants (other than the issuer) may, however, avoid liability by establishing their non-negligence[139] under situation-specific requirements typically referred to collectively as the 'due diligence' defence.[140]

AI obviously represents a very different legal context, but the foregoing demonstrates the utility of some under-appreciated principles of regulatory design. Section 11 lists specific categories of defendants,[141] which could be applied to categories of actors involved with deploying AI – notably, developers, owners, and users. It then reverses the burden regarding negligence through the due diligence defence,[142] an approach that merits further attention in the AI context. On this approach, the legal issue would become what prudence requires of variously situated actors,[143] and this need not be analysed identically for all. Section 11 itself distinguishes between 'experts' and non-experts, and between those portions of a registration statement made on an expert's authority and those not.[144] Case law has further differentiated among various categories of non-experts through facts-and-circumstances analysis focusing on proximity to relevant activity and

[132] Choi and Pritchard (n 89) 339–40.

[133] *Affiliated Ute Citizens of the State of Utah v United States*, 406 US 128, 153–54 (1972).

[134] *Halliburton Co v Erica P John Fund, Inc*, 573 US 258, 267–69 (2014). The resulting presumption can be rebutted by a 'showing that severs the link between the alleged misrepresentation and either the price received (or paid) by the plaintiff, or his decision to trade at a fair market price'. ibid 269.

[135] ibid 267–68. For discussion of alternative approaches to reliance and causation, see E Bant and J M Paterson, 'Statutory Causation in Cases of Misleading Conduct: Lessons from and for the Common Law' (2017) 24 *Torts Law Journal* 1, 10–17 (contrasting 'but for' and 'a factor' tests).

[136] S J Choi and AC Pritchard, *Securities Regulation: The Essentials* (Aspen Publishers 2008) 256.

[137] 15 United States Code s 77k(a). See also Choi and Pritchard (n 89) 570.

[138] Choi and Pritchard (n 89) 581.

[139] 15 United States Code s 77k(b)–(c).

[140] Choi and Pritchard (n 89) 596.

[141] 15 United States Code s 77k(a).

[142] Choi and Pritchard (n 89) 596–97. The effect of reversing the burden in this way resembles the 'Systems Intentionality' approach as applied in the machine-learning context. See E Bant, Chapter 4 in this volume.

[143] 15 United States Code s 77k(c).

[144] ibid s 77k(b). See also Choi and Pritchard (n 89) 596–97.

access to information.[145] The SEC, then, has endorsed this sliding-scale approach by identifying factors to this effect considered relevant in applying the due diligence defence.[146] Liability exposure is further variegated by tempering default joint-and-several liability with potential to 'recover contribution' and by limiting outside directors' exposure to their 'percentage of responsibility' (where the violation was not 'knowingly committed').[147] Such an approach disincentivises fraud while fostering nuance to distinguish between levels of culpability across a broad range of actors – by placing the onus on those closest to the relevant activity to advocate role-appropriate standards of prudence and argue that their own conduct met them.

To be clear, I do not propose that US regulators simply apply section 11's precise structure directly in the AI context – let alone that other countries do so. In addition to the unique AI dynamics described above, there is enormous variation globally in degrees of regulatory reliance on private litigation in commercial, corporate, and investment contexts, and the United States remains an outlier in this regard.[148] This structure does, however, point toward viable modes of regulatory design that could prove helpful in reforming fraud and manipulation rules in the AI context. Although there has been some recognition in the literature regarding potential benefits of burden reversal,[149] and likewise some recognition that the same standards need not apply to all categories of actors,[150] there is real potential along the foregoing lines that merits further attention in the AI context.

3.2.3. *Gatekeeper Regulation*

Potential reforms to fraud and manipulation rules in the AI context would require close attention to gatekeeper dynamics. Anti-fraud rules and gatekeeper regulation often go hand-in-hand – as in the securities context, where, in addition to relaxing certain fraud elements, a related strategy has been to focus on 'gatekeepers', meaning those thought to be well-positioned to detect and prevent fraud and manipulation.[151] Although, perhaps ironically, this term is often used to refer to

[145] See, eg, *Escott v BarChris Construction Corporation*, 283 F Supp 643, 684–97 (SDNY 1968). Experts face liability only for portions made on their authority and are held to applicable professional standards. Choi and Pritchard (n 89) 607.

[146] 17 Code of Federal Regulations s 230.176 (US).

[147] 15 United States Code ss 77k(f), 78u-4(f).

[148] See, eg, C M Bruner, *Corporate Governance in the Common-Law World: The Political Foundations of Shareholder Power* (Cambridge University Press 2013) 98–101; *Morrison v National Australia Bank Ltd*, 561 US 247, 269–70 (2010) (recognising this in limiting rule 10b-5's extraterritorial reach in private suits).

[149] See, eg, Fletcher (n 100) 318–20; Willis (n 108) 175–76. See also Chesterman (n 4) 183 (observing that the precautionary principle can be understood as 'a reversal of the burden of proof').

[150] See, eg, Bathaee (n 14) 932–38; Lim (n 14) 12, 17–18.

[151] See Choi and Pritchard (n 89) ch 13. See also J C Coffee Jr, *Gatekeepers: The Professions and Corporate Governance* (Oxford University Press 2006) 1–5.

AI itself being deployed as a form of filter by its user,[152] it has also been used in a more regulatory spirit – notably, in connection with AI ethics, where the focus again falls on developers, owners, and users alike.[153] All these actors could be viewed as AI gatekeepers vis-à-vis the public, and anti-fraud regimes like those discussed above could be viewed as indirect forms of gatekeeper regulation along these lines, aiming to condition their incentives to manage risks within their control.[154] Such a strategy would naturally dovetail with more direct regulation of other actors at a structural level.[155]

At the same time, insurers might function as a form of gatekeeper, particularly given the likelihood that new liability structures would generate risk exposures that insurance markets would be called upon to price.[156] Indeed, insurers have been characterised as 'the initial gatekeepers' by default, acting as 'quasi-regulators' where fast-evolving markets create new categories of liability exposure.[157] In a sense, insurance functions as a form of 'soft law', impacting behaviour in that it affects the perceived 'sword' of liability by conditioning availability of a 'shield'.[158] Liability rules force the exposed entity – say, the manufacturer in a strict liability regime – to become a de facto insurer,[159] which can in turn evaluate the risks and rewards of the activity in light of the availability and cost of actual insurance coverage.[160] In this manner, 'insurers literally advise insureds on how to modify their actions in order to avoid losses'.[161]

Although the extent of AI insurance coverage remains unclear,[162] and although AI black-box dynamics complicate insurance premia just as they do tort analysis,[163] the process may ultimately resemble that with other innovations, such as nanotech – where insurers initially encouraged a 'precautionary principle' in response to poorly understood risks and then gradually distinguished different applications of the technology by risk level as more information became available.[164] In this manner, AI insurance may work in tandem with other legal

[152] See, eg, J Weed, 'Résumé-Writing Tips to Help you Get Past the A.I. Gatekeepers' *New York Times* (19 March 2021).

[153] See, eg, M Dand, 'Where Is the Accountability for Techno-Elite Gatekeepers?' (*Medium*, 4 October 2020). Available at: https://miad.medium.com/where-is-the-accountability-for-ai-ethics-gatekeepers-e696b8a80e62; Timperlake (n 2); Verdict, 'Responsible AI and the Need for Ethical Gatekeepers' (*Verdict*, 25 February 2019). Available at: www.verdict.co.uk/responsible-ai-ethical-gatekeepers/.

[154] See Choi and Pritchard (n 89) 939 (suggesting that Securities Act section 11 functions this way).

[155] See Yadav (n 86) 1090–98 (advocating liability for exchanges to promote market oversight).

[156] Lior (n 5) 474–75.

[157] Tournas and Bowman (n 79) 54. See also Chesterman (n 4) 100; Lior (n 5) 472, 511–12.

[158] Tournas and Bowman (n 79) 52–54. See also Lior (n 5) 483–84.

[159] Vladeck (n 2) 146–48.

[160] Lior (n 5) 472, 524–27. See also Bathaee (n 103) 165.

[161] Lior (n 5) 517.

[162] Lim (n 14) 22.

[163] Lior (n 5) 479–81.

[164] Tournas and Bowman (n 79) 54. See also Lior (n 5) 482–87. Outside compliance advisors – aptly considered 'compliance gatekeepers' – may also prove central. See A Eckstein and R Shapira, 'Compliance Gatekeepers' 41 *Yale Journal on Regulation* (forthcoming). Available at: https://ssrn.com/abstract=4419560.

strategies discussed here, complementing the tort regime and informing future regulation.[165]

4. Conclusion

AI technology is revolutionising business, and legal structures designed for human actors may break down as machines take over more and more domains of activity. New technological threats will require new technological responses, new business models and risks will require new forms of corporate oversight, and new forms of AI decision-making will require legal and regulatory strategies to combat fraud and manipulation.

Although the challenges are in many ways novel, the need for creativity and flexibility in the face of technological and economic change is hardly new. Indeed, fruitful models for legal and regulatory adaptation already exist. The challenge will be overcoming inertia and asking the right questions about how those models might be adapted to this new terrain.

[165] Lior (n 5) 483–84, 518.

4

Where's WALL-E? Corporate Fraud in the Digital Age

ELISE BANT*

1. Introduction

Fraud has always been an unwelcome staple of commerce.[1] It comes in many guises, with a correspondingly varied array of legal and equitable doctrines ranged against it: these include deceit, fraudulent misrepresentation, injurious falsehood, unconscionable dealing and various forms of accessorial liability. These general law claims commonly have statutory siblings or close cousins.[2] A shared focus of such doctrines is the state of mind with which the wrongful act was committed. Whether the misconduct is required to be deliberate, knowing, predatory, reckless, wilfully ignorant or some other reprehensible state,[3] the defendant's mindset is key.[4] This greater degree of culpability in turn opens the door to a more generous

* This chapter forms part of my Australian Research Council Future Fellowship project FT190100475 on corporate fraud and attribution: see https://www.uwa.edu.au/schools/research/unravelling-corporate-fraud-re-purposing-ancient-doctrines-for-modern-times. My sincere thanks to Professors Christopher Bruner, Kelvin Low and Hans Tjio for their detailed comments on this chapter, and to all the contributors for their thought-provoking questions and insights. As always, I am indebted to Professor Jeannie Marie Paterson for her formative feedback on this topic, and for her collaboration on the related project, ARC Discovery Project 180100932 concerning misleading and unconscionable conduct, on which this paper builds. All remaining infelicities and errors rest with me.

[1] PM Eggers, *Deceit: The Lie of the Law* (London, Informa, 2009) ch 1.

[2] For example, the various Australian prohibitions on misleading or deceptive conduct, unconscionable conduct and dishonest conduct: see, eg, Competition and Consumer Act 2010 (Cth) sch 2 (ACL), s 18 and ss 20–21, Corporations Act 2001 (Cth) s 1041G, discussed in E Bant, 'Culpable Corporate Minds' (2021) 48 *University of Western Australia Law Review* 352; E Bant and JM Paterson, 'Systems of Misconduct: Corporate Culpability and Statutory Unconscionability' (2021) 15 *Journal of Equity* 63 and below section 2.2.

[3] For example, 'malicious' as in malicious falsehood, also known as injurious falsehood: *Palmer Bruyn & Parker Pty Limited v Parsons* [2001] HCA 69, (2001) 208 CLR 388.

[4] Complex normative standards such as dishonesty and unconscionability commonly require assessment of a defendant's conduct against objective community standards, in light of the defendant's actual knowledge and intention: see Bant, 'Culpable Corporate Minds' (n 2), 364–368, 379–381, discussing *Ivey v Genting Casinos (UK) Ltd* [2017] UKSC 67, [2018] AC 391; *Barton v R* [2020] EWCA Crim 575, [2021] QB 685 and *Peters v R* [1998] HCA 7, (1998) 192 CLR 493, amongst others.

range of remedies than may apply to lesser forms of wrongdoing[5] and, in the regulatory space, to suitably serious statutory orders such as (in some jurisdictions) civil pecuniary penalties, or fines.[6] These sorts of legal doctrines and rules are, in theory, well adapted to express the law's condemnation of the misconduct, to promote general deterrence alongside specific deterrence of repeated misconduct by the wrongdoer, and (where appropriate and available), to effect retribution on the wrongdoer.[7]

However, the rising dominance of increasingly large and complex corporations in the modern marketplace poses serious challenges to the law's effective regulation of commercial fraud. Most attribution rules, whether common law or statutory, search for a relevant individual whose mind counts for that of the corporation.[8] This game of 'Where's Wally'[9] is easily played by modern corporations seeking to minimise or avoid liability.[10] Most simply, information barriers may prevent bad news from rising to Board or managerial levels, thereby keeping the corporation's directing mind and will (and thus the corporation) safely ignorant of even ingrained wrongful, corporate practices.[11] But corporations may also employ more complex structures and processes that dissipate knowledge

[5] On the comparison between deceit and negligence, for example, see *Palmer Bruyn & Parker Pty Limited v Parsons* [2001] HCA 69, (2001) 208 CLR 388, 413 [78] (Gummow J); *Doyle v Olby (Ironmongers) Ltd* [1969] 2 QB 158 (CA), 167 (Lord Denning MR); *Smith New Court Securities Ltd v Citibank NA* [1997] AC 254 (HL), 264–67 (Lord Browne Wilkinson), 283 (Lord Steyn). Conversely, doctrines of 'equitable fraud' such as innocent misrepresentation, arguably not a wrong, yield only restitutionary remedies, a point that has made statutory reforms such as compensation under the Misrepresentation Act 1967 contentious: see generally JM Paterson and E Bant, 'Misrepresentation, Misleading Conduct and Statute through the Lens of Form and Substance' in A Robertson and J Goudkamp (eds), *Form and Substance in Private Law* (Oxford, Hart Publishing, 2019) 403; E Bant, 'Rescission, Restitution and Compensation' in S Degeling and J Varuhas (eds), *Equitable Compensation and Disgorgement* (Oxford, Hart Publishing, 2017) 277 and, on Australia's statutory prohibitions on misleading conduct, below at section 2.2.

[6] JM Paterson and E Bant, 'Intuitive Synthesis and Fidelity to Purpose? Judicial Interpretation of the Discretionary Power to Award Civil Penalties under the Australian Consumer Law' in P Vines and MS Donald (eds), *Statutory Interpretation in Private Law* (Alexandria, Federation Press, 2019) 154.

[7] E Bant and JM Paterson, 'Effecting Deterrence through Proportionate Punishment: An Assessment of General and Statutory Law Principles' in Bant et al (eds), *Punishment and Private Law* (Oxford, Hart Publishing, 2021) 255.

[8] See generally, Australian Law Reform Commission, *Corporate Criminal Responsibility* (Report No 136, 2020) (ALRC Final Report) ch 4; Law Commission of England and Wales, *Corporate Criminal Liability* (Options Paper, 2022) (Law Commission Options Paper) ch 3.

[9] M Handford, *Where's Wally?* (London, Walker Books, 1987).

[10] GR Skupski, 'The Senior Management Mens Rea: Another Stab at a Workable Integration of Organizational Culpability into Corporate Criminal Liability' (2011) 62 *Case Western Reserve Law Review* 263, 288, discussing the use of the American equivalent 'Where's Waldo?' in the Arthur Anderson's obstruction of justice trial, by defence counsel Rusty Hardin.

[11] Striking examples arose in the context of Australia's various, recent casino inquiries: see, eg, State of New South Wales, *Review of The Star Pty Ltd: Inquiry Under Sections 143 and 143A of the Casino Control Act 1992 (NSW)* (Report, 31 August 2022) vol 1, 9 [48], 28 [148], 29 [155]–[156], 256 [271]; Report of the Hon. Patricia Bergin, AO, SC Report of the Inquiry under section 143 of the Casino Control Act 1992 (NSW), dated 1 February 2021 (the Bergin Report) eg, Bergin Report Volume 1 [2.8.10], [2.8.185], [3.2.80], [3.3.281], [3.4.59], [3.4.126] and Volume 2 [4.3.4], [4.5.91], [4.3.13], [4.3.114–115], [4.3.45].

and hence responsibility across corporate groups, between departments and individuals.[12] The consequence is that there may be no single individual employee or agent of the defendant company who is aware of the conduct that constitutes the alleged wrong, let alone a single individual in whom conduct and culpable mental states coalesce. Aggregation or 'collective responsibility' approaches offer a pragmatic, instrumentalist solution to connecting the dots between the diffused knowledge of individuals within a corporation.[13] However, these are subject to legitimate criticism as unprincipled and unable, without further justification or development, to support findings of more complex conceptions of (diffused) intention and dishonesty.[14]

As Law Commissions in Australia and England have accepted, the consequence is that many large corporations are effectively immune from criminal responsibility for egregious and often highly profitable commercial misconduct.[15] The Australian Law Reform Commission has further observed that precisely the same problems plague civil liability doctrines, including those concerned to prevent fraud.[16] A common solution therefore is required.[17]

The challenge is only heightened with increasing integration of automated processes into core business activities,[18] alongside other, more complex new technologies. Even a simple automated payment process may quickly cause an attribution inquiry to degenerate into an ad hoc and unprincipled search for a human (coder, or coding team, or software engineer, or employee who presses a button, or manager of the department in which the software is notionally situated etc) on which to build some foundation for corporate guilt.[19] The danger of scapegoating is real, as is the converse risk that (once again) the corporation

[12] B Fisse, 'Reconstructing Corporate Criminal Law: Deterrence, Retribution, Fault, and Sanctions' (1983) 56 *Southern California Law Review* 1141, 1189.

[13] Compare *United States v Bank of New England, NA*, 821 F 2d 844 (1st Cir 1987); *Commonwealth Bank of Australia v Kojic* [2016] FCAFC 186, (2016) 249 FCR 421, 446 [101], 448–56 [110]–[143] (Edelman J, with whom Allsop CJ generally concurred); *R v HM Coroner for East Kent, ex parte Spooner (Herald of Free Enterprise/Zeebrugge Ferry Disaster)* (1989) 88 Cr App R 10 (QB).

[14] *Kojic*, ibid; ME Diamantis, 'How to Read a Corporation's Mind' in E Bant (ed), *The Culpable Corporate Mind* (Oxford, Hart Publishing, 2023) 209, 214.

[15] Law Commission Options Paper paras 6.34–6.41, para 1.4, ch 6; ALRC Final Report chs 4 and 6.

[16] Australian Law Reform Commission, *Corporate Criminal Responsibility* (Discussion Paper No 87, November 2019) para 1.21; ALRC Final Report paras 1.15, 1.25.

[17] This is also highly appropriate if, as we are told, the state of a corporation's mind is a matter of fact: *Edgington v Fitzmaurice* (1885) 29 Ch D 459 (CA) 483 (Bowen LJ); *Generics (UK) v Warner-Lambert Company LLC* [2018] UKSC 56, [2018] RPC 21 [171] (Lord Briggs).

[18] Automation itself is nothing particularly new: the old vending and ticket machine cases are prime examples: see, eg, *Thornton v Shoe Lane Parking Ltd* [1970] EWCA Civ 2, [1971] QB 163. Indeed, automation is arguably only a step further along the spectrum from the ubiquitous use of 'standard operating procedures', discussed below.

[19] Bant, 'Culpable Corporate Minds' (n 2) 363; JM Paterson and E Bant, 'Automated Mistakes: Vitiated Consent and State of Mind Culpability in Algorithmic Contracting' in Bant (ed), *The Culpable Corporate Mind* (n 14) 255. As S McConnell, *Code Complete*, 2nd edn (Washington, Microsoft Press, 2004) 502 explains, long-running systems are commonly designed in different parts, by different designers, separated across time, geography and versions.

will avoid responsibility behind executive pleas of impersonal 'systems errors'. Commonly, directors will draw attention to the fact (which may well be right) that their employees are individually honest and hardworking, while they (as directors) were personally unaware of the problem generated 'by the system'.[20] The combination is devastating for both traditional and more generous but individualistic attribution approaches. As more sophisticated machine learning and artificial intelligence systems become embedded in corporate business practices, this new game of 'Where's WALL-E'[21] becomes, potentially, wildly unpredictable, unprincipled, and impractical. One of the worst forms of the game seeks to blame a non-sentient corporate tool, the AI, as being 'responsible' for the deploying corporation's wrongdoing.[22] On this narrative, the corporate escape route is assured by shifting corporate irresponsibility to an allegedly new legal entity. Any move in that direction brings with it an array of further, dangerously effective evasive strategies: corporations may plead ignorance of the innately harmful tendencies of 'off the shelf' programmes (the 'black box' problem), blame 'legacy systems' or argue that different computer systems 'did not speak' to one another.[23] In all of these narratives, the corporation presents itself as an unknowing and hence innocent, or mistaken, participant – at worst a bumbling incompetent in the brave new world of new commercial technologies.[24]

If 'the future of fraud is automated'[25] we are indeed in trouble. This prospect has caused leading commentators, reform commissions and legislatures to seek to avoid the problem of corporate attribution entirely, by shifting to strict outcome or performance-based obligations, or duty-based offences. These focus on the outcomes of the corporation's activities and whether they are fit for purpose,[26] or contravene some objective standard of conduct,[27] or fail to prevent

[20] Commonwealth of Australia, *Royal Commission into Misconduct in the Banking, Superannuation and Financial Services Industry* (Final Report, February 2019) vol 1 (FSRC Final Report) 138–139; see https://pursuit.unimelb.edu.au/articles/charging-dead-clients-is-dishonest-really-who-knew. See also www.sbs.com.au/news/article/nab-says-fees-for-no-service-not-dishonest/u838rxy95; www.afr.com/companies/financial-services/banking-royal-commission-where-nab-went-wrong-on-fee-for-no-service-20190205-h1avui; www.afr.com/opinion/cba-the-gold-medallist-of-the-big-five-for-charging-fees-for-no-service-20180418-h0yxvj.

[21] A Stanton (dir), *WALL-E* (Pixar Animation Studios, 2008).

[22] The false narrative of 'algorithmic agents' is discussed critically in Paterson and Bant, 'Automated Mistakes' (n 19) 267.

[23] See, eg, www.investordaily.com.au/markets/40308-banks-blame-legacy-systems-for-advice-failures. See Bruner (Chapter 3 in this volume) on the perverse incentives that may arise.

[24] See further E Bant, 'Corporate Evil: A Story of Systems and Silences' in P Crofts (ed), *Evil Corporations: Law, Culpability and Regulation* (Routledge, 2024) 223.

[25] LE Willis, 'Performance-Based Consumer and Investor Protection: Corporate Responsibility without Blame' in Bant (ed), *The Culpable Corporate Mind* (n 14) 417, 418.

[26] See, eg, Australia's 'consumer guarantee' provisions: ACL (n 2) Part 3.2 Div 1. The new 'Design and Distribution' obligations have a similar underlying principle: see Corporations Act 2001 (Cth), pt 7.8A and discussion in Willis, ibid. 433–434.

[27] Such as Australia's distinction prohibitions on misleading conduct: see below at section 2.2. The support for introduction of a generalised 'unfair trading' prohibition would also fit this category: see below at section 3.4.

a nominated and particularly egregious wrong on the part of an associate of the corporation.[28]

These are all important parts of an effective, pluralistic approach to containing the rogue corporate hydra.[29] But still minds matter, even in strict liability contexts. It makes a difference to regulators' overall enforcement approaches, to defence, remedy, and penalty whether (for example) the contravening conduct was deliberate, knowing or mistaken.[30] It also matters for the expressive power of the law. Thus, in the recent Australian Royal Commission into misconduct in the financial services industry, Commissioner Hayne examined critically the willingness of banking executives to admit extraordinary levels of corporate incompetence rather than suffer the reputational and liability risks that would flow from characterising the impugned misconduct as dishonest.[31] In these cases, the misconduct arose from automated fee deduction systems that had taken clients' money without proper authorisation, often over long periods and in the face of repeated complaint. Consistently with the foregoing, the unlawful takings were characterised by those officers as due to 'legacy systems' and 'administrative errors'.[32] Employees were praised as hardworking and honest, while executives were readily prepared to admit to being asleep at the wheel while the misconduct occurred. This exposed the corporations to forms of liability that were less reputationally damaging than dishonesty-based contraventions.

With Rebecca Faugno, I have similarly criticised elsewhere the view that 'Failure to Prevent' models necessarily involve a lesser form of liability, grounded in organisational negligence.[33] In some cases, the predicate misconduct of the corporate associate, which the defendant corporation 'failed' to prevent, formed a key component of the defendant's own business model.[34] In such contexts, the very language of 'failure to prevent' arguably mischaracterises the nature of the wrong, which in truth smacks of organisational fraud. Consistently, it can lead to unduly favourable liability outcomes, such as through the approval of deferred prosecution agreements and the conditions on which these are agreed.

[28] See, eg, Criminal Finances Act 2017 (UK), Pt 3; Law Commission Options Paper (n 8) ch 8; Crimes Legislation Amendment (Combatting Corporate Crime) Bill 2019 (Cth); J Clough, 'Failure to Prevent Offices: The Solution to Transnational Corporate Criminal Liability' in Bant (ed), *The Culpable Corporate Mind* (n 14) 395. Compare Bruner (Chapter 3 in this volume) on the merits of combining burden reversal and due diligence defences.

[29] F McGaughey, 'Regulatory Pluralism to Tackle Modern Slavery' in Bant (ed), *The Culpable Corporate Mind* (n 14) 441.

[30] E Bant and R Faugno, 'Corporate Culture and Systems Intentionality: An Essential Part of the Regulatory Toolkit' (2024) *Journal of Corporate Law Studies*. See https://doi.org/10.1080/14735970.2023.2292837.

[31] FSRC Final Report (n 20) 138–39.

[32] ibid 139.

[33] Bant and Faugno 'Corporate Culture and Systems Intentionality' (n 30).

[34] See, eg, *Serious Fraud Office v Rolls-Royce plc & anor* [2017] Lloyd's Rep FC 249.

Against this background, a new model of corporate responsibility, entitled 'Systems Intentionality' offers a way through the thicket.[35] On this account, a corporation manifests its state of mind through its de facto systems of conduct, policies and practices. This chapter briefly introduces the model before showing how it might operate in a range of topical scenarios to automated and algorithmic systems of misconduct of varying complexity. The model is shown to be versatile and practical, but also rests on solid theoretical and doctrinal foundations. The aim is to show that it provides an additional and important means of holding corporate actors to account for misconduct carried out through new technologies, which gives greater effect to the expressive, deterrent and, potentially, retributive power of the laws prohibiting fraud.

2. Systems Intentionality

2.1. An Outline of the Model

A very brief outline of Systems Intentionality is adequate for current purposes. As has already been presaged, the model proposes that corporate states of mind are manifested in their adopted and deployed systems of conduct, policies and practices. As I have explained elsewhere:

> A 'system of conduct' is the internal method or organised connection of elements operating to produce the conduct or outcome. It is a plan of procedure, or coherent set of steps that combine in a coordinated way in order to achieve some aim (whether conduct or, additionally, result). A 'practice' involves patterns of behaviour that are habitual or customary in nature. A practice may cross over into a system, where the 'custom' or 'habit' has become an embedded process or method of conduct. Finally, corporate 'policies' partake of the same nature of systems, but can be understood as generally operating at a higher level of generality. These manifest overarching and high-level purposes, beliefs and values. They embody and reveal the overall corporate mindset, which is then instantiated or operationalised through corporate systems at more granular and event- or conduct-specific levels.[36]

[35] In addition to those cited above, see JM Paterson, E Bant and H Cooney, '*Australian Competition and Consumer Commission v Google*: Deterring Misleading Conduct in Digital Privacy Policies' (2021) 26 *Communications Law* 136; E Bant, 'Catching the Corporate Conscience: A New Model of "Systems Intentionality"' [2022] *Lloyds Maritime and Commercial Law Quarterly* 467; E Bant, 'Reforming the Laws of Corporate Attribution: "Systems Intentionality" Draft Statutory Provision' (2022) 39 *Company & Securities Law Journal* 259; E Bant, 'The Culpable Corporate Mind: Taxonomy and Synthesis' (ch 1), 'Systems Intentionality: Theory and Practice' (ch 9), and 'Modelling Corporate States of Mind through Systems Intentionality' (ch 11), all in Bant (ed), *The Culpable Corporate Mind* (n 14).

[36] Bant, 'Modelling' (n 35) 245–46. Just as for natural persons, the analysis leaves room for conflicting mindsets and values within the one legal (corporate) person. I may be a diligent and trustworthy member of my school parent committee while cheating on my taxes: so too corporations may manifest honest and law-abiding traits in one activity or section, and dishonest and predatory mindsets in another, a point expressly recognised in Australia's 'corporate culture' definition, on which the model

The model is simple, intuitive, and applies equally well to natural as to corporate persons. Natural persons routinely use systems of conduct, such as recipes, directions and notations to guide their decision-making and, hence, conduct. These 'extended mind supports' enable the person to achieve their purpose: to make a cake, find a location, or recall how to do something.[37] Similarly, I say, corporations utilise systems of conduct to enable them to achieve their corporate purposes. However, lacking a natural mind, this is in reality the *only* way in which corporations can engage purposefully with and in the real world. Consistently, the law provides core default rules concerning the role of the board of a company, or the shareholders in general meeting, to address the need to create foundational corporate decision-systems. These are required to transform the corporation from a passive shell to an operational legal person. Systems Intentionality arguably is consistent with these default decision-systems,[38] but simply enables identification and assessment of the mental states of corporations manifested through other, more granular and daily systems, policies and practices.

On this approach, systems of conduct are inherently purposive: thus, in ordinary language, systems are 'plans', 'strategies', or 'methods' of proceeding to some end.[39] Further, understood as integrated steps and processes, systems of conduct will often comprise *both* positive and negative, and proactive and reactive, elements.[40] What may look like a primary system (for example, a marketing strategy or fee deduction system) itself necessarily entails the adoption of certain steps *and* omissions of others. It is the coordinated *set* of processes taken as a whole, framed holistically as a system of conduct at a certain level of generality, which constitute intended conduct.[41] This means that the omission of audit and remedial mechanisms, for example, may legitimately be understood as an intrinsic part of a system's overall design. This is a justifiable interpretive approach, given that systems of conduct are generally intended to roll out over time and produce repeated and consistent patterns of behaviour.[42]

builds: see Criminal Code Act 1995 (Cth) Sch 1, s 12.3(6). The question for liability purposes concerns the mindset with which the relevant act occurred: broader issues of character may properly go to (for example) mitigation or prospects of rehabilitation.

[37] ME Diamantis, 'The Extended Corporate Mind: When Corporations Use AI to Break the Law' (2020) 98 *North Carolina Law Review* 893.

[38] Hence consistent, in the main, with Leow's Allocated Powers analysis of corporate decision structures: see R Leow, '*Meridian*, Allocated Powers, and Systems Intentionality Compared' in Bant (ed), *The Culpable Corporate Mind* (n 14) 119.

[39] The detailed treatment by courts of these concepts, often in light of common dictionary meanings, is contained in Bant, 'Systems Intentionality' (n 35): see, eg, *Australian Competition and Consumer Commission v EDirect Pty Ltd* [2012] FCA 1045, (2012) 206 FCR 160 [91] (Reeves J).

[40] B Fisse, 'Reactive Corporate Fault' in Bant (ed), *The Culpable Corporate Mind* (n 14) 139; Bant, 'Taxonomy and Synthesis' (n 35) 3, 5, 19.

[41] Bant, 'Corporate Evil' (n 24). On the necessity to choose a greater or lesser level of generality to obtain the correct 'angle of focus' in identifying and assessing a system of conduct, see Bant, 'Systems Intentionality: Theory and Practice' (n 35) 192, and Bant, 'Taxonomy and Synthesis' (n 35) 5, 19, 23, 31.

[42] Patterns of behaviour may be coincidental and therefore are neutral as to intention, however they may indicate the presence of a causative system of conduct: see Bant, 'Systems Intentionality: Theory and Practice' (n 35) 190–92 and *Australian Securities and Investments Commission v AGM Markets Pty Ltd (in liq) (No 3)* [2020] FCA 208, (2020) 275 FCR 57 [386]–[391] (Beach J).

It follows that, on its face, a system of conduct (being innately a strategy or plan of procedure) is necessarily intended. The evidential onus then lies on the corporation to substantiate any allegation of mistake or accident (for example, through an employee witness admitting to accidental deployment of the system).[43] Further, corporate knowledge of the key features of a system, and the fact of its operation, is implicit in its successful deployment by the corporation. Absent proof of mistake or similar, a corporation cannot sleep-walk a system of conduct.[44] This means that the starting point for any inquiry is that corporations know the nature of the conduct in which they are engaged through those systems. This applies as much for organically developed practices as it does for systems that operationalise 'on the ground' some higher-level corporate policy.

All of this challenges familiar corporate narratives that seek to characterise the corporation as ignorant (and therefore innocent) of its conduct conducted through its own systems. For example, information barriers that prevent responsible officers from actual knowledge of the corporation's misconduct do not necessarily protect the corporation itself from that knowledge. Similarly, scapegoating individuals on the grounds that they have been discovered performing the corporation's own practices no longer operates as an effective diversion of organisational blameworthiness.[45]

Finally, on this approach, any analysis of corporate mindsets starts with the instantiated system of conduct; that is, with identification and characterisation of the de facto adopted and deployed system. Formal corporate policies nonetheless constitute statements or representations of fact regarding the corporate state of mind.[46] It follows that the presence of a significant gap between formal policy, or the textbook 'standard operating procedures' of a company, and the reality of its corporate intentions and knowledge as manifested through its daily systems, policies and practices, can be understood as a form of misleading or, indeed, deceptive conduct.[47]

2.2. Garden-variety Case Examples

This section models the potential of Systems Intentionality to address more traditional circumstances of corporate fraud before turning, in the following Part, to equivalent wrongdoing accomplished through automation and more sophisticated new technologies.

[43] See below at n 90.

[44] FSRC Final Report (n 20) 157: fees for no services were 'part of an established system and were not matters of accident'.

[45] See Bant, 'Catching the Corporate Conscience' (n 35) 484, 492–95; Bant 'Corporate Evil' (n 24).

[46] Above n 17.

[47] See, eg, ACL (n 2), s 18 (prohibition on misleading or deceptive conduct in trade or commerce); *Magill v Magill* [2006] HCA 51, (2006) 226 CLR 551, 567 (Gleeson CJ) 574 (Gummow, Kirby and Crennan JJ) (tort of deceit).

A little background to the main case examples under discussion is salutary. Both involved Australia's leading consumer regulator, the Australian Competition and Consumer Commission (ACCC), bringing proceedings against pharmaceutical giants. The ACCC alleged the defendants had engaged in repeated contraventions of Australia's powerful prohibition on 'misleading or deceptive conduct'.[48] As expressed in its core form, now found in s 18 Australian Consumer Law:

> A person must not, in trade or commerce, engage in conduct that is misleading or deceptive or is likely to mislead or deceive.[49]

Elegant in its simplicity,[50] the hallmark of this prohibition is its strict, outcome-based character. Thus, while deceptive conduct is certainly captured, the prohibition may also be contravened accidentally, or notwithstanding that the defendant believed, on reasonable grounds, that its conduct was truthful.[51] There is no requirement of any intention to mislead on the part of a defendant, nor any other fault element. The contravention lies in the simple fact that the impugned conduct was 'misleading … or likely to mislead'. The omission of any fault element from the prohibition means the common corporate strategies discussed earlier, such as those that diffuse and compartmentalise individual knowledge, and hence responsibility, well below Board level, are significantly less effective. Consistently, the prohibition has given regulators like the ACCC a powerful and flexible tool to address a spectrum of commercial misconduct, including those arising from new technologies.[52]

Yet, notwithstanding its strict character, regulator claims engage both directly and indirectly with questions of defendant culpability in misleading consumers.[53] The indirect influence of fault considerations in regulator action is considerable, including how contravening conduct is framed, whether it attracts administrative,

[48] Although embedded in consumer protection legislation, the prohibition applies to all transactions 'in trade or commerce', regardless of the status of the plaintiff as consumer or trader. It may be enforced by the independent regulator where no person has, actually, been misled and where no loss has been suffered. It also gives rise to a smorgasbord of remedies for consumers seeking redress for loss or damage suffered because of the misleading conduct. It constitutes, accordingly, a powerful commercial norm in the Australian marketplace: see, among others, E Bant and JM Paterson, 'Limitations on Defendant Liability for Misleading or Deceptive Conduct Under Statute: Some Insights from Negligent Misstatement' in K Barker, W Swain and R Grantham (eds), *The Law of Misstatements: 50 Years on from* Hedley Byrne v Heller (London, Hart Publishing, 2015) 159; E Bant and A McCracken, 'Returning to Sample the Remedial "Smorgasbord" for Misleading Conduct' (2022) 49 *University of Western Australia Law Review* 113. The prohibition is reiterated in various forms across many fields: often, for criminal penalty provisions, adopting additional mental requirements: see J Sabbagh, E Bant and JM Paterson, 'Mapping the Law of Misleading Conduct: Challenges in Legislative Design' (2022) 49 *University of Western Australia Law Review* 144.

[49] ACL (n 2), s 18.

[50] *Wingecarribee Shire Council v Lehman Brothers Australia Ltd (in liq)* [2012] FCA 1028, (2012) 301 ALR 1 [947] (Rares J): see also [948] and Sabbagh et al 'Mapping the Law of Misleading Conduct: Challenges in Legislative Design' (n 48).

[51] *Parkdale Customer Built Furniture Pty Ltd v Puxu Pty* Ltd [1982] HCA 44, (1982) 149 CLR 191, 197 (Gibbs CJ).

[52] Paterson, Bant and Cooney, '*Australian Competition and Consumer Commission v Google*' (n 35).

[53] As do private claims for redress: see Bant and Paterson, 'Limitations on Defendant Liability' (n 48).

civil or criminal enforcement strategies and the availability and content of any negotiated outcomes.[54] Further, Australian courts have developed a range of criteria that inform the award of civil (and criminal) pecuniary penalties for contraventions of key statutes, which also apply to certain forms of misleading conduct. These 'French factors'[55] include the state of mind with which a defendant contravened the statutory prohibition, for example, whether the misconduct was deliberate, knowing or mistaken, as well as mixed normative conceptions such as dishonesty and recklessness.[56] The presence or absence of remorse or contrition is another factor.[57] It follows that while regulators may be able to avoid questions of culpability at the liability stages of enforcement litigation, it inexorably affects the penalty phase.

Traditional attribution rules may be expected to influence adversely regulator efforts to characterise defendant misleading conduct as deliberate, knowing or dishonest. Preferring strict liability or negligence-based litigation options might be comprehensible as a considered price for securing baseline corporate liability: a bird in the hand is better than two in the bush, after all. However, this enforcement strategy risks removing a critical, reputational incentive to corporate rehabilitation and good conduct.[58] Further, these enforcement strategies potentially leave a damaging gap between community and legal characterisations of the nature of the misconduct.[59] This is quite apart from the clear impact on the range of penalty and other orders that may be given in response to the misconduct. The chosen pharmaceutical cases powerfully illustrate these subversive tendencies, as well as the corrective potential of a Systems Intentionality approach.

In the first case, Nurofen pain relief products were distinctively packaged, and priced, by reference to claimed differences in pain relief. Thus, products said to 'target' period pain, back pain and the like were branded distinctly, and were more expensive, than the garden-variety, everyday product. Yet the operative ingredients were identical.[60] While individual instances of consumer harm were small (a matter of a few dollars), the profits enjoyed through this repeated misconduct were very great.[61]

[54] Bant, 'Culpable Corporate Minds' (n 2) 361–64.

[55] First articulated in *Trade Practices Commission v CSR Ltd* [1990] FCA 762, (1991) *ATPR* 41-076.

[56] Paterson and Bant, 'Intuitive Synthesis and Fidelity to Purpose?' (n 6).

[57] *Australian Securities and Investments Commission (ASIC) v Westpac Securities Administration Limited, in the matter of Westpac Securities Administration Limited* [2021] FCA 1008, (2021) 156 ACSR 614 [45] (O'Bryan J): see further R Carroll, 'Corporate Contrition' in Bant, *The Culpable Corporate Mind* (n 14) 315.

[58] See, eg, C Parker and VL Nielsen, 'How Much Does It Hurt? How Australian Business Think About the Costs and Gains of Compliance and Noncompliance with the *Trade Practices Act*' (2008) 32 *Melbourne University Law Review* 554.

[59] Bant, 'Culpable Corporate Minds' (n 2) 363.

[60] *Australian Competition and Consumer Commission v Reckitt Benckiser (Australia) Pty Ltd* [2016] FCAFC 181, (2016) 340 ALR 25 [5]–[6] (the Court), increasing on the regulator's appeal the penalty awarded in *Australian Competition and Consumer Commission v Reckitt Benckiser (Australia) Pty Ltd (No 7)* [2016] FCA 424, (2016) 343 ALR 327.

[61] ibid [7] and [43].

Throughout, the corporate offender characterised its conduct as 'innocent' and, hence, in terms of 'deficiencies' and organisational negligence.[62] The ACCC did not allege in pleadings or submissions that the conduct was deliberate or reckless. At first instance, this made a significant difference to penalty.[63] Overruling this approach, the Full Federal Court determined that state of mind was a matter relevant to penalty, whether pleaded or not.[64] In substantially increasing the penalty, the Court observed that the company had engaged in a deliberate marketing strategy apt to influence consumers for its commercial benefit, thereby, at the very least 'courting the risk of contravention'.[65] It also noted that the deliberate persistence with the strategy for five years, in the face of pointed and correct criticism, was inconsistent with any conception of 'innocent' misconduct.[66] While the Court refrained from finding a deceptive state of mind on these facts, Systems Intentionality explains how and why it is possible, and appropriate, to sharpen the Court's observations. On this approach, it becomes open to conclude that the marketing scheme constituted a deceptive ploy, which manifested the corporation's considered and knowing decision to mislead consumers into paying more for an identical product. This would have demanded a more stringent level of penalty and one that took better account of the profits enjoyed from the stratagem.[67]

First, a general intention to engage in the conduct constituting the sales strategy flows from seeing it as a strategy or scheme. As such, it is necessarily purposive: a combination of steps arranged in a certain way, a method or plan of procedure. Further, a finding of a specific intention to mislead is open because the combination of features of the strategy (distinctive packaging, identical active ingredient, and differentiated price based on false distinctive operation) could have no other objective purpose than to trick consumers into paying more for a relevantly identical product. Further, the corporation must be taken to know these critical features (packaging, ingredients, price) of what was, after all, its strategy to sell its product. The corporate intention and knowledge of the falsity of the representation is therefore patent on the face of the corporation's own strategy. Reinforcing this assessment of deliberately misleading conduct, the strategy was maintained over many years, across multiple jurisdictions, and in the face of repeated individual, regulator and public complaint.[68] The corporation's 'reactive corporate fault' to a scheme intended to apply over an extended

[62] ibid [116].

[63] ibid [117].

[64] ibid [78], [96] and [134]–[136].

[65] ibid [136].

[66] ibid [134].

[67] The defendant's profit derived from the breach is a key consideration when considering the level of penalty: *Australian Competition and Consumer Commission v Woolworths Limited* [2016] FCA 44, (2016) ATPR 42-521 [126] (Edelman J). In *ACCC v Reckitt Benckiser (Australia) Pty Ltd (No 7)* (n 60) [64], Edelman J considered that it would be preferable to focus on the revenue earned from breach.

[68] *ACCC v Reckitt Benckiser (Australia) Pty Ltd (No 7)* (n 60) [74]–[84], including reference to www.choice.com.au/shonky-awards/hall-of-shame/shonkys-2010/nurofen.

period is consistent with a deceptive specific intention.[69] Indeed, the failure to audit and remediate the strategy, including in the face of repeated complaint, simply reinforces the level of corporate indifference to its own deliberate wrongdoing. This warrants a very different level of penalty from that which accompanies gross carelessness, recklessness or even deliberate 'courting the risk'.

A relevantly identical marketing strategy was subsequently carried out with the re-branding of Voltaren Osteo Gel.[70] For five years, pharmaceutical companies Novartis and then GlaxoSmithKline misleadingly marketed and sold Osteo Gel as being specifically designed for treating pain and inflammation caused by osteoarthritis, with the implication that it was more effective than their other product, Emulgel. Again, the truth was that both products had the same active ingredients. Consumers were charged significantly more for Osteo Gel than Emulgel. Again, the conduct was hugely profitable.

Through the lens of Systems Intentionality, here, if anything, the intention manifested by the corporate strategy was even more transparent than in the Nurofen case. This is because the Voltaren marketing strategy involved *removing* existing, helpful information about the common osteo-arthritic pain relief properties from the original generic packaging, so that it only appeared on the Osteo Gel product.[71] This choice to remove the information could hardly be accidental, whatever its marketing managers and team members might say, and (indeed) subjectively believe. It was a key aspect of the corporation's rebranding strategy. Taken with the price difference, it seems clear that the *corporate* intention had been knowingly to mislead consumers into paying more for a relevantly identical product. This was conduct that was 'deceptive … or likely to … deceive'.

Notwithstanding, in penalty proceedings the learned judge characterised the conduct as 'negligent', up until publication of the Nurofen liability judgment, after which it was characterised as 'knowingly courting the risk'.[72] Indeed, in one respect, where misleading comparisons were maintained on a website, his Honour considered the misconduct nearer to 'innocent'.[73] In reaching this view, his Honour was influenced by confessions of error on the part of the corporate solicitor, who valiantly took it upon herself to take responsibility for the 'omission' to correct the website.[74]

These cases illustrate both the strengths and limitations of strict liability approaches to corporate responsibility. On the one hand, the corporations were found liable for misleading conduct, notwithstanding their exculpatory narratives

[69] Above n 40.

[70] *Australian Competition and Consumer Commission v GlaxoSmithKline Consumer Healthcare Australia Pty Ltd (No 2)* [2020] FCA 724.

[71] ibid [17].

[72] ibid [45].

[73] ibid [26], [54].

[74] ibid. See further S Derrington and S Walpole, 'Culpable Ships' in Bant (ed), *The Culpable Corporate Mind* (n 14) 351, 357, 371.

of mistake and unintended carelessness. They were subject to significant penalties for that conduct. These results reinforce the core Australian norm against misleading commercial conduct and give effect to the statutory purpose of deterrence, to a degree. Systems Intentionality, however, would arguably enable regulators and courts to recognise the deliberateness and true level of culpability entailed in this conduct. This would invigorate the (largely neglected in practice) prohibition against conduct that is 'deceptive … or likely to deceive', with consequences for penalty and deterrence. In this way, Systems Intentionality may assist to support and complement strict liability approaches to activate the full range of legal doctrines and rules that operate to counteract corporate fraud.

Further, Systems Intentionality is capable of ready application to equivalent scenarios from the online marketplace. Consider, for example, subscription services that have a simple online sign-up process but make it virtually impossible to unsubscribe.[75] Again, it may be impossible and inappropriate to search for a responsible individual who has ordered, signed off on and/or created the subscription process, to determine the corporate intention. It is entirely likely that no-one exists, or can readily be found, who can be the human hook on which to hang corporate responsibility. To undertake the 'Where's Wally' inquiry may be time-consuming, expensive and, ultimately, fruitless. By contrast, through the lens of Systems Intentionality, even a simple comparison of the relative complexity of the two processes, such as the number of steps required, may assist significantly in determining corporate intention. And this is well before engaging in any analysis of the corporate intentionality manifested by more subtle 'dark patterns'[76] or other manipulative strategies. An overly complex 'unsubscribe' process, particularly when contrasted with simple sign-up steps, clearly manifests a corporate intention to deter consumers from unsubscribing, and a willingness to keep them locked into transactions and financial commitments that the consumers (through their effort to unsubscribe) signal that they no longer want or can afford. This corporate strategy, manifested through the website design, may constitute unfair or unconscionable conduct.[77] The knowledge and intention patent on the face of the system may assist courts in both making findings of contravening conduct and in setting penalties commensurate with the corporation's true culpability.

[75] An example of 'forced continuity': see, eg, Consumer Policy Research Centre, *Duped by Design – Manipulative online design: Dark patterns in Australia* (June 2022) 20. See https://cprc.org.au/dupedbydesign/ and ACCC, *Digital Platform Services Inquiry* (Interim Report No 5, September 2022) 64.

[76] These commonly involve user interfaces, the design of which operates to confuse and manipulate consumers into certain action: see, eg, ACCC, *Digital Platforms Inquiry* (Final Report, July 2019) 424–25; ACCC, *Digital Platform Services Inquiry* (Interim Report No 3, October 2021) 57; J Lugeri and L Strahilevitz 'Shining a Light on Dark Patterns' (2021) 13 *Journal of Legal Analysis* 44; Consumer Policy Research Centre, *Duped by Design* (n 75); Paterson, Bant and Cooney, '*Australian Competition and Consumer Commission v Google*' (n 35).

[77] On the necessity of setting the normative expectations or standards for the digital age, see section 3.4 below.

3. Systems Intentionality and Automated Fraud

With this understanding of the model in action, we are now in a position to turn to consider the potential for Systems Intentionality to shed light on corporate fraud in the digital age. Recall, here the potential for traditional attribution rules to hold corporations to account is greatly reduced, because individuals within the corporation may have little or no involvement in, or knowledge of, the workings of automated systems that increasingly underpin core business activities. Further, as we will see, the advent of new technologies opens up a range of ways in which corporations may engage in serious commercial misconduct. Not all of these will necessarily be counteracted through Systems Intentionality alone. However, what the model does provide is a different means of understanding the intentionality manifested through these systems. This may have a helpful effect on regulators' and courts' capacities to bring to bear existing and new doctrinal avenues for redress, to better effect.

3.1. Automated Systems and Mistake

First, it is salient to observe that determinate automated systems perform according to their programmed instructions, with no margin for variation once deployed. That rigidity means that if a corporation's automated program is deployed and operates according to its terms, it constitutes the corporation's intended conduct: there is little margin for deviation or 'error'. The onus will then fall on the corporation to demonstrate how and why the conduct was accidental, or mistaken.[78] Possible contenders for genuine systems errors are where a system deploys in circumstances for which it was not designed, for example because a human mistakenly presses a button, or through some sort of internal malfunction or 'glitch'. Thus, Robert Goff J hypothesised a scenario in which a computer had 'gone mad' and repeatedly paid out in error as an example of corporate mistake.[79]

What are less likely to be relevant are director (or other, potentially relevant employee) pleas of ignorance of the system or its features. Thus, in the Australian case of *Electric Life Pty Ltd v Unison Finance Group Pty Ltd*,[80] a director of the

[78] See further E Bant, 'Corporate Mistake' in J Gardner et al (eds), *Politics, Policy and Private Law* (Hart Publishing, 2024) (forthcoming) and Bant, 'Modelling' (n 35) 248.

[79] *Barclays Bank v WJ Simms Son & Cooke (Southern)* [1980] QB 677, 697. The inevitability of 'glitches' in automated systems underscores the need for appropriate audit and remedial mechanisms, but also acceptance that even well-designed systems displaying a prudent and ethical mindset may themselves be subject to error: see the pellucid explanation of the complexity in K Low and E Mik, 'Pause the Blockchain Legal Revolution' (2020) 69 *International and Comparative Law Quarterly* 135, 172–73 and McConnell, *Code Complete* (n 19) 1277: '[i]ndustry average experience is about 1–25 errors per 1000 lines of code for delivered software'. See section 3.2 for further discussion of errors in coding critical default settings.

[80] *Electric Life Pty Ltd v Unison Finance Group Pty Ltd* [2015] NSWCA 394.

plaintiff corporation put in place an automated payment system with respect to the hire of various goods under a contract with the defendant. The automated system operated, according to its terms, long after the contract had drawn to a close, the goods had been retired from use and, indeed, misplaced, assumed discarded. The corporation's claim for restitution of the post-contractual payments on the grounds of mistake failed. While this result might seem counter-intuitive, Systems Intentionality emphasises that the director's subjective, mistaken belief that the system would end with the contract contradicted the clear terms of the authorised payment system.[81] The director could not, retroactively, change those terms nor claim some retrospective error on behalf of the corporation. Nor was the mindset of the company bookkeeper relevant: he had no authority to change the automated system and, in any event, had no subjective understanding as to its purpose or terms.[82]

On the characterisation most favourable to the plaintiff, the default setting for the automated system was 'keep paying until manual intervention'. But no process existed to trigger that intervention: no reminders, warnings, audit systems or other means other than the chance recollection of the director to check, or another employee to notice and query the payments (as ultimately occurred). Indeed, the omission of any manual oversight of the system, including any audit and remedial mechanisms, arguably also reflected a corporate choice. The fact that this proved unexpectedly costly in the long term did not negate that the fact that it was part of a deliberate corporate decision to automate the process and omit appropriate audit and remedial mechanisms. Misprediction is not mistake,[83] and courts are concerned not to reward undue risk-taking, even where there is an operative mistake.[84] Unsupervised or unaudited automation carries economic risks as well as rewards, which a corporate arguably accepts in its adoption and deployment.[85]

3.2. Default Settings and Corporate Intentionality

It is also helpful to observe that automated systems are not necessarily, or quintessentially, different to other human-based systems of conduct. It is striking that, in many cases, the daily systems of conduct adopted by corporations with respect

[81] ibid [71].

[82] Compare ibid [60]–[61], [72].

[83] P Birks, *An Introduction to the Law of Restitution* (Oxford, Clarendon Press, 1985) 147; *Dextra Bant & Trust Co Ltd v Bank of Jamaica* [2001] UKPC 50, [2002] 1 All ER (Comm) 193 [29].

[84] *Re Griffiths* [2008] EWHC 118 (Ch), [2009] Ch 162, discussed in *Pitt v Holt* [2013] UKSC 26, [2013] 2 AC 108 [98], [113] and J Edelman and E Bant, *Unjust Enrichment* (Oxford, Hart Publishing, 2016) 174–75.

[85] Bant, 'Corporate Mistake' (n 78). Conversely, where appropriate audit and remedial processes are incorporated, the corporation arguably manifests a prudent mindset, even where these are themselves affected by error: see further n 79 above. Systems Intentionality has both inculpatory and exculpatory effect.

to their natural employees operate to remove individual judgement (and thus unpredictability) from the corporation's core activities essential to its purposes. An example is the widespread use of 'standard operating procedures' (SOPs). When embedded into daily practice,[86] these guide, nudge or direct the employees within the system to respond to environmental prompts (eg the receipt of payment to an account, or an invoice, or a customer complaint) in a pre-determined way. That is, the employees' individual choices to act are, effectively, made for them in advance. Indeed, where an employee plays some purely clerical role within a corporate system, cases suggest that what matters is not what the employee subjectively thought, understood or believed in carrying out their role but simply whether their part within the process was carried out in conformity with the system's objective elements or design.[87] These clerical default settings in the corporation's processes are usually made at critical junctures, to ensure the corporation's priorities and interests are protected. The consequence is that these default settings loudly declare the corporation's intentions and values. Nor is it plausible for corporations to deny knowledge of these foundational corporate choices, which underpin the deployed system.

This perspective is readily transferrable to automated systems and their default settings. A range of examples arose in Australia, where Banks admitted deducting unauthorised payments from customers through automated fee deduction systems.[88] In one, a common scenario, the payments were for life insurance. Patent on the face of the fee deduction system, and therefore known to the corporation, were the facts that: (1) the clients were natural persons (who might die and therefore sought insurance); (2) that their circumstances may well change, such as through death; (3) on such changes, deductions would cease to be authorised; (4) the system therefore required audit and adjustment mechanisms, to ensure that the deductions did not, inevitably, result in unlawful takings.[89] Yet, the banks omitted these mechanisms: again, arguably, a matter of corporate choice. Here, the characterisation of the automated default setting most charitable to the defendant was 'keep taking until manual intervention'. Yet there were no, or no working manual, check processes to prevent the system degenerating into unlawful takings. That the design choices of the automated system, including the omitted steps,

[86] An important caveat: Where, by contrast, the formal SOPs vary wildly from the corporation's embedded practices, they are likely to be mere window-dressing, a form of misleading conduct as to the corporation's true intentions and values: see text to n 46 above. This is often found where important questions of corporate compliance are in issue: the formal SOPs may roundly declare a responsible and ethical corporate citizen quite at odds with the reality manifested through its daily practices: see, eg, *Royal Commission into the Casino Operator and Licence* (The Report, October 2021) on Crown's responsible gaming, anti-money laundering (AML) and junket practices. The AML practices are discussed further in Bant, 'Reforming the Laws' (n 35) 274.

[87] Bant, 'Corporate Mistake' (n 78), discussing *Kelly v Solari* (1841) 9 M&W 54; 152 ER 24 and *BP Oil International Ltd v Target Shipping Ltd* [2012] EWHC 1590 (Comm).

[88] These scenarios are discussed further in Bant 'Culpable Corporate Minds' (n 2) 385; Bant, 'Catching the Corporate Conscience' (n 35) 487 and Bant, 'Corporate Evil' (n 24).

[89] FSRC Final Report (n 20) 154–57.

manifested a corporate intention to prefer profits over lawfulness, is reinforced by assessment of the corporate responses to notification of the unlawful takings. By and large, these involved continuing the practice while the corporation 'investigated' the conduct. Again, given that these were 'set and forget' systems, intended to operate over extended periods, it is legitimate to consider the corporate response to notice of problems with it, in assessing the nature of corporate culpability manifested by the objective features of the system, viewed holistically.

As with *Electric Life*, it is arguably neither here nor there for corporate responsibility that individual directors or employees were subjectively unaware of the problem. These were the corporation's own intended actions, and corporate knowledge of the salient facts was inherent in and patent on the face of the system it deployed. The onus lay on the corporation to explain how the system had failed to deploy as designed, so as to warrant a finding of corporate mistake. From this perspective and in the absence of exculpatory evidence the corporate-conscious decision to proceed to roll out an unsupervised system that was guaranteed to cause unlawful takings showed a reckless indifference to the client's rights and, indeed, smacked of dishonest conduct.

In one case, involving penalty proceedings for contraventions arising from automated fee deductions for other forms of financial service, Moshinsky J of the Federal Court accepted a director's evidence that a human coding error had caused the unlawful takings.[90] However, his Honour expressed concern about the paucity of evidence on how the error arose.[91] Systems Intentionality explains why further explanation was appropriate and, indeed, necessary to justify the allegation of corporate mistake. Default settings of an automated system manifest corporate choices and an individual coder is unlikely accidentally or randomly to exercise that kind of substantive discretion, at a critical functional juncture, on behalf of the corporation, unaided by direction or guidance.[92] In any event, as the judge further observed, any human mistake did not explain why there were no audit or remedial systems in place to identify and address the error as the system played out in practice.[93] Here, as we have seen, Systems Intentionality sees the omission of processes patently required for an ethical and lawful system as

[90] *Australian Securities and Investments Commission v AMP Financial Planning Proprietary Limited* [2022] FCA 1115, (2022) 164 ACSR 64 [47] (Moshinsky J).

[91] ibid [52]–[53].

[92] See K Low and E Mik, 'Lost in Translation: Unilateral Mistakes in Automated Contracts' (2020) 136 *Law Quarterly Review* 563, 567–68, distinguishing between the coder's technical task of writing the program and the client's commercial judgment in setting the transactional parameters; see also McConnell *Code Complete* (n 19) 112–13 on the 'myth of stable requirements', when reality requires recurrent consultation with clients to achieve their ends as systems evolve: see ibid (n 19) at 217.

[93] Above n 90 at [54]. McConnell *Code Complete* (n 19) chs 22 and 23 make clear the critical and unavoidable need for testing and debugging with even the most carefully conceived system. See also *Australian Securities and Investments Commission v National Australia Bank Limited (No 2)* [2023] FCA 1118 [3] (Derrington J), where a bank's failure to turn off an automated system wrongly deducting fees while it 'investigated' the problem 'obviously prioritised the preservation of its own commercial position over its duties to its customers'; see also at [100]–[101] concerning the deliberate and cynical mindset revealed by this conduct and at [108], [118] on the question of organisational intention.

manifesting corporate choice and intended conduct. Again, and at the least, the corporation manifested a culpable indifference to the real risk of harms arising from its unmonitored, automated system.

Quoine Pte Ltd v B2C2 Ltd is a case where default settings again were key, this time to determine whether the defendant knowingly took advantage of an alleged mistake made by traders on a cryptocurrency exchange.[94] The plaintiff's exchange platform had lost liquidity, with the result that it was no longer generating market prices. The defendant's trading algorithm was pre-programmed to revert to a 'deep price' in this event. The Singapore Court of Appeal found that there was no evidence to support the view that this deep price was set to take advantage of trader mistakes: on the contrary, it was, evidently, a default mechanism that was designed to protect the defendant should the platform lose liquidity, an event that occurred due to the plaintiff's, not defendant's, fault. In that case, it was possible, fortuitously, to point to the testimony of the individual human coder, whose innocent intentions both represented and exonerated the defendant company's mindset. However, Systems Intentionality explains how the same conclusion was possible from objective assessment of the defendant's algorithm settings, in particular the conditions that triggered application of the deep price.[95]

Finally, the Australian case of *ACCC v Google* provides further illustration of the significance of seeing default settings in terms of corporate choices, which manifest corporate values, preferences and intentions.[96] In that case, the regulator alleged (among other matters) that Google misled consumers who were concerned to control privacy settings over the steps required to protect their location data. In truth, consumers needed to ensure two default settings were switched to 'off [do not collect location data]'. The first, which was readily identifiable, was already switched to 'off'. Another was far less easy to identify and locate, requiring users to navigate a number of screens and bearing no clear labelling to indicate that it hosted the relevant setting. This second default setting was set to 'on [collect data]'. This difference is significant, potentially signalling a corporate preference to harvest data, consistently with its core business model, rather than protect consumers' privacy. It would have been, one would think, a simple matter for Google to have both default settings switched to 'off' from the outset, if it really valued consumers' rights to protect their information and to choose whether to share personal data. On this analysis, it would have been open to the Federal Court to go beyond its finding of misleading conduct,[97] to conclude that Google had

[94] *Quoine Pte Ltd v B2C2 Ltd* [2020] SGCA(I) 2, [2020] 2 SLR 20. This problem arose from the plaintiff's own mistaken failure to update the platform's critical operating system. On the approach advocated here, the plaintiff's inadequate upgrade processes arguably themselves manifested a certain corporate risk-taking: Paterson and Bant, 'Automated Mistakes' (n 19) 255, 264.

[95] Paterson and Bant, 'Automated Mistakes' (n 19) 255, 266, 270–71. See Low and Mik 'Lost in Translation: Unilateral Mistakes in Automated Contracts' (n 92).

[96] *Australian Competition and Consumer Commission v Google LLC (No 2)* [2021] FCA 367, (2021) 391 ALR 346.

[97] The detailed analysis is contained in Paterson, Bant and Cooney '*Australian Competition and Consumer Commission v Google*' (n 35).

acted deliberately to mislead consumers in relation to the second default setting, with a view to its greater profit and, therefore, acted deceptively.

3.3. Ambiguous Systems of Conduct

The previous discussions illustrate how corporate states of mind may be revealed and instantiated through automated systems. Thus, automated systems of conduct manifest general intentions, placing pressure on allegations of corporate mistake. Default settings may also be eloquent to corporate choices at key ethical pressure points, revealing the corporate values, preferences and intentions. In such cases, the key design features or elements of the system will readily manifest the corporate mindset.

In others, however, courts may need to draw on more extensive, contextual evidence to assess or characterise the particular system and through it, corporate intentionality. An example is *Australian Competition and Consumer Commission v Uber BV*,[98] where Uber's pricing estimate algorithm generally significantly overestimated the cost to customers of using taxis affiliated with the Uber ride service. This meant that its UberTaxi fare estimates, displayed on the Uber app, were not representative of the likely fare range and, accordingly, were inherently likely to mislead consumers. On one view, this systemic over-estimation operated to Uber's financial benefit, by providing a disincentive to customers choosing the UberTaxi service that, after all, supported competitor business. Further, Uber did not monitor the functionality of the algorithm to ensure the accuracy of estimates.[99] Consistently, the market for the service declined over time and, on becoming the subject of regulatory proceedings, was discontinued.[100] On this view, the charging system could have been seen as manifesting a deliberate ploy to undermine that competition through misleading conduct.[101]

O'Bryan J considered whether the system operated to suppress demand for taxi services in the context of considering what 'loss or damage' had flowed from the misleading conduct. His Honour noted that the parties had provided no evidence on that question,[102] nor on why suppression of taxi demand would benefit Uber (given that, presumably, other ride options may remain open to customers).[103] This left open an alternative interpretation, or characterisation of the corporate mindset manifested through the system, consistent with Uber's pleaded position: the problem was unintentional and manifested a genuine corporate mistake.

[98] *Australian Competition and Consumer Commission v Uber BV* [2022] FCA 1466.

[99] ibid [57]. O'Bryan J considered that the problem only 'became apparent' to Uber after a related entity received a notice from the regulator at [60].

[100] ibid [60].

[101] On the issue of state of mind, see ibid. [18] and [100]–[101], which adopts an individualistic approach to corporate attribution.

[102] ibid [17].

[103] ibid [108].

By contrast, Uber was found to have corporate knowledge of the existence and likely impact of certain cancellation notices issued to customers, which wrongly warned of cancellation fees when, in fact, these did not apply. His Honour considered that these were likely to benefit Uber, as they would deter some customers from continuing with the cancellation process. However, this finding was supported by evidence of Uber carrying out controlled testing of the effect of similar cancellation notices on customers, and subjective knowledge of this testing on the part of certain senior managers.[104] While his Honour's findings hinged on employees' knowledge, Systems Intentionality would instead focus on the testing systems deployed by the corporation as manifesting patent corporate knowledge of the problem. This approach supports the finding that the corporate decision to continue in any event with the cancellation notice system was knowing and, consequently, highly culpable, but importantly avoids the need to undertake or solve the 'Where's Wally?' puzzle.

3.4. More Complex Scenarios

What, though, of more complex artificial intelligence (AI) systems, such as those that engage 'machine learning' to optimise performance of allocated tasks? In her recent, powerful essay on the topic, Lauren E Willis identifies a range of striking scenarios in the consumer context where AI systems may be programmed to collect and experiment on data to achieve 'micro-targeted, ever-changing digital actions and communications algorithmically optimised for profit'.[105] Unconstrained by natural ethical boundaries, or fear of external sanctions, AI systems have a proven potential to promote unsuitable transactions at the expense of consumers.[106] This is not a matter of some evil AI intention: the algorithm is simply a tool[107] that is coded to harvest and experiment with relevant information to yield the instructed outcome – often, maximum profit. It is, however, a highly effective tool that may gather and experiment with vastly greater data, and try wildly more variable design options, with micro-targeted success, than a human designer. This elevates the risk of harm to new levels, across a greater range and number of transactions.[108]

Where such systems result in harmful transactions, the 'Where's Wally?' question becomes fanciful. It may well be impossible at the outset for relevant responsible officers, employees or agents of the deploying corporation to know what the AI system will identify as relevant factors. That is, after all, part of the attraction of AI: its capacity to identify data combinations that yield more

[104] ibid [104]–[106].

[105] Willis 'Performance-Based Consumer and Investor Protection: Corporate Responsibility without Blame' (n 25) 419.

[106] ibid 420, 422.

[107] Paterson and Bant, 'Automated Mistakes' (n 19) 267.

[108] Willis 'Performance-Based Consumer and Investor Protection: Corporate Responsibility without Blame' (n 25) 419–24.

profitable outcomes than human designers could ever achieve. Indeed, the predatory nature of AI designs may be all but impossible to prove through ex post human analysis: as Willis observes, AI systems may be processing hundreds of data points simultaneously, meaning that it is impossible for human analysts to determine which correlations counted for which transaction. This, in turn, may mean that the central causation question for most liability purposes – whether the conduct caused harm – is unanswerable.[109] Further, the original coders of an algorithm may be wholly unaware of the purpose to which the program will eventually be put: 'off the shelf' algorithms may be employed to ends or in support of businesses that the coders never envisaged.[110] Underscoring the problem, automated systems are increasingly being designed and distributed by other AI systems, not even human coders.[111] The 'black box' problem here seems close to an insuperable barrier to corporate responsibility.

Faced with this reality, Willis urges alternative approaches, such as performance-based obligations, which turn from intention-based regulation to the effects of AI-dependent corporate actions on consumers.[112] As conceded at the outset of this chapter, this makes a lot of sense. Frankly, given the rate of change in technology-driven and -enhanced commercial harm, it is likely that only a pluralistic approach is likely to have any real impact.

However, even here, seeing the intentionality manifested by corporate systems of conduct may be of considerable assistance to regulators, legislators and judges. Consider the case where a corporation deploys a machine learning tool in the marketplace, without incorporating any means to predict, identify, audit or correct harmful outcomes. Even at this very high level of generality, it is possible to characterise the system as manifesting some interesting states of mind, relevant to corporate responsibility. First, the tool's deployment represents (in the absence of evidence to the contrary) a deliberate decision to act. Secondly, the omission of any monitoring or responsive processes itself shapes the nature of the primary (or positive) elements of the machine-learning system: that is, the system is not simply a 'machine-learning system', but an 'uncontrolled machine-learning system'.[113] Thirdly, the omission of any processes by which the primary system's operation can be monitored and corrected itself reflects a corporate choice. We may pause here to note, as does Willis, that it is implausible that it is, somehow, inherently impossible to build in control mechanisms for machine-learning AI.[114] Fourthly, there must be some baseline purpose or goals that direct the machine-learning system: what is it learning to do?[115] In a for-profit entity, it is safe to assume

[109] ibid 423. See further Bruner, Chapter 3 in this volume.
[110] ibid 422.
[111] ibid 419.
[112] ibid 424.
[113] McConnell *Code Complete* (n 19) chs 22 and 23 and above n 93.
[114] Willis 'Performance-Based Consumer and Investor Protection: Corporate Responsibility without Blame' (n 25) 438.
[115] For further examples of culpability manifested through machine-learning design, see Paterson and Bant, 'Automated Mistake' (n 19) 269–71.

(in the absence of evidence to the contrary) that these ends include maximising profit. But if that is the only goal, it means that (again) there has been a corporate choice to pursue profit unconstrained by considerations that would promote legal and ethical conduct.

Viewed in this way, the scenario arguably manifests from the outset a corporate willingness to court the risk of massive non-compliance with the law in the pursuit of profit. From this perspective, it may not be a complete, defensive answer to liability for a corporation to say that there is no proof of individual harm caused by the AI (the causal problem identified earlier). Systems Intentionality throws on to the corporation the onus of showing that its very deployment of an unbounded system is not inherently highly culpable. The corporation can readily do this by proving evidence of appropriately embedded and audited boundaries, going some way to assisting with the information asymmetry that too often confounds regulators seeking to patrol misconduct by corporations deploying new technologies. However, to the extent that it cannot do so, its inability underscores its culpability.

That being said, the ability of Systems Intentionality to hold corporations to account for reckless deployment of AI systems of conduct depends, in significant part, on the willingness of courts to assess its intended and knowing conduct against appropriately stringent, normative standards.[116] Thus, in one Australian case, a judge considered that the defendant corporation's deliberate manipulation of consumer choice through targeted advertising, derived from data harvested through its misleading conduct, was not in itself harmful.[117] Consumers might find targeted advertising helpful, or welcome. On that approach, it may be unlikely that the conduct would contravene that jurisdiction's prohibition on unconscionable conduct, notwithstanding that it constitutes deliberate and knowing exploitation of the fruits of misleading conduct. Unconscionability has tended to be reserved for commercial conduct that shocks the judicial conscience: a high and often conservative bar, that errs in favour of entrepreneurial enterprises.[118] For this reason, among others, calls for the introduction of a prohibition on unfair trading have increased.[119] These seek to re-set the baseline commercial standards that would be applicable in many AI contexts. Such a prohibition would help enormously in finding (for example) that deliberate and knowing manipulation of consumer consent manifested through sophisticated 'dark patterns' was

[116] For a baseline, 'deconstructed' conception of recklessness, see Bant, 'Modelling' (n 35) 235–39.

[117] *Australian Competition and Consumer Commission v Google LLC (No 4)* [2022] FCA 942 [39] (Thawley J). For a powerful analysis to the contrary, see T Cohen, 'Regulating Manipulative Artificial Intelligence' (2023) 20 *SCRIPTed* 203.

[118] JM Paterson, E Bant, N Felstead and E Twomey, 'Beyond the Unwritten Law: The Limits of Statutory Unconscionable Conduct' (2023) 17 *Journal of Equity* 1.

[119] ACCC, *Digital Platform Services Inquiry* (Interim Report No 3, October 2021) 66; ACCC, *Digital Platform Services Inquiry* (Interim Report No 4, April 2022) 5; ACCC, *Digital Platform Services Inquiry* (Interim Report No 5, September 2022) Recommendation 1, p 64; Consumer Policy Research Centre, *Duped by Design* (n 75).

reckless, dishonest, or unconscionable. Systems Intentionality would operate in tandem with that kind of development, as well as others (such as Failure to Prevent offences[120] and responsible officer stipulations) that seek to shift back on to corporations the responsibility for the full lifecycle of products and services, past the point of sale.

4. Conclusion

Systems Intentionality is not some silver bullet that will slay all forms of corporate fraud. However, it does provide a principled and practical means of interrogating corporate culpability in the digital age. In particular, it avoids the increasingly ad hoc and irrelevant search for the human mastermind behind the misconduct. Where there is such a Moriarty, there is no difficulty with seeing her as the apex decision-maker behind the corporate conduct, consistently with the model. However, Systems Intentionality recognises that corporations frequently act through dispersed systems that pre-programme conduct options, in a way that reflects deliberate corporate choices. These make transparent the corporate values and preferences, often at critical legal and ethical junctures. Even where complex machine learning systems are involved, objective assessment of their core features at point of deployment is likely to reveal important insights into corporate intentionality. All of this helps to navigate and, where appropriate, debunk tried-and-tested corporate narratives of mistake and accident. In this light, Systems Intentionality warrants inclusion as an additional weapon in the law's armoury against corporate fraud.

[120] Indeed, Systems Intentionality arguably supports and promotes proper characterisation of corporate culpability in this context: see Bant and Faugno 'Corporate Culture and Systems Intentionality' (n 30) and Bruner, Chapter 3 in this volume.

5

From Customer to Creditor: Consumer Risk and Protection During Central Cryptocurrency Exchange Insolvencies

JUSTIN LIM*

1. Introduction

The collapse of FTX,[1] a centralised cryptocurrency exchange (CEX), was met with surprise by its customers, not only because of the scale of the alleged fraud,[2] but also because customer-turned-creditors had realised that they never had legal ownership of the crypto-tokens[3] that they had 'bought' on the platform.[4] This meant that those crypto-tokens joined FTX's insolvency estate and customers were merely ordinary unsecured creditors awaiting the return of their funds – not the particular crypto-tokens they thought they had owned. The difficulties faced by FTX's customers were also felt by Singaporeans: Liquid, a prominent CEX in Singapore that had been acquired by FTX in February 2022, would also join FTX's Chapter 11 bankruptcy proceedings.[5] The insolvency of crypto businesses has not been uncommon in Singapore. Just four months before the collapse of FTX, Zipmex, another CEX that operated in Singapore, had filed for a moratorium in

* I am especially grateful to Associate Professor Yeo Chuan Seng and my colleagues at the Conference on Fraud and Risk in Commercial Law for their feedback on this chapter.

[1] *In re FTX TRADING LTD., et al* Chapter 11 Case No 22-11068-JTD.

[2] M Sigalos and R Goswami, 'Sam Bankman-Fried ran FTX as a fraud 'from the start', SEC charges' CNBC (13 December 2022). Available at: www.cnbc.com/2022/12/13/sam-bankman-fried-ran-ftx-as-fraud-from-the-start-sec-charges.html.

[3] This chapter uses the UK Law Commission's definition of 'crypto-token' to mean 'a data structure instantiated within a crypto-token system, such that the particular, individuated instance of a data structure takes on a specific, individual function by virtue of the operation of the socio-technical system in which it exists'. See generally Law Commission, *Digital Assets: Consultation paper* (Law Com No 256, 2022) ('UK Digital Assets Consultation Paper') Appendix 4.

[4] T Hals and D Knauth, 'FTX customers file class action to lay claim to dwindling assets' Reuters (28 December 2022). Available at: www.reuters.com/legal/ftx-customers-file-class-action-lay-claim-dwindling-assets-2022-12-28/.

[5] Above n 1 at THIRD AMENDED NOTICE OF FILING OF CHAPTER 11 PETITIONS AND RELATED MOTIONS AND DECLARATIONS.

Singapore in anticipation of a restructuring plan.[6] Similar episodes with Hodlnaut[7] and Vauld[8] have resulted in Singapore branding itself a 'crypto-restructuring hub',[9] making it a prime jurisdiction to discuss the legal issues highlighted by crypto-insolvencies.

The central theme across the issues this chapter discusses is consumer protection. The recent string of CEX insolvencies has revealed that customers of failed CEXs face significant challenges and misunderstandings that may not be adequately addressed by the judicial and regulatory developments in the space. In particular, customers who have purchased or deposited cryptocurrencies with a CEX often find that they do not have any legal rights in the same or equivalent crypto-tokens when a CEX becomes insolvent. In order to understand how such challenges arise, the customer's legal rights in the crypto-token and to a claim against the CEX must be considered.

Firstly, what rights do customers have in the crypto-token they purchase? While scholars[10] and regulators[11] have spilt ink over the extent and nature of crypto-tokens as property, some CEXs have taken the more straightforward approach to deny the customer any property rights altogether. This has led regulators, such as the Monetary Authority of Singapore (MAS), to propose measures such as consumer risk awareness assessments and access restrictions. However, the nature of informed risk in the platform economy and the legal ambiguities in the crypto industry pose challenges to the efficacy of these strategies.

Secondly, how might customers make a claim for the crypto-token against insolvent CEXs? Beyond disputing their interest in the crypto-token, customers may also seek the rescission of the Terms and Conditions (T&Cs) with CEXs if doing so would restore their proprietary right in the crypto-token. Such claims may take the form of claims in misrepresentation or fraud against the CEX.

Whilst customers face challenges in identifying and enforcing their legal rights against an insolvent CEX, regulators must confront how and to what extent customers should be protected through a proprietary rights regime and regulation. To elucidate these challenges, this chapter takes a novel empirical approach by focusing on the existing contractual relationships between customers and CEXs.[12]

[6] *Re Zipmex Co Ltd and other matters* [2022] SGHC 196, [2023] 3 SLR 1333.

[7] *Re Hodlnaut Pte Ltd* [2022] SGHC 209.

[8] Supreme Court of Singapore, 'Information Note on Defi Payments Hearing on 1 August 2022' (27 July 2022). Available at: www.judiciary.gov.sg/news-and-resources/news/news-details/information-note-on-defi-payments-hearing-on-1-august-2022.

[9] B Cher, 'Singapore goes from crypto hub to crypto restructuring hub' *The Business Times* (16 August 2022). Available at: www.businesstimes.com.sg/opinion-features/columns/singapore-goes-crypto-hub-crypto-restructuring-hub.

[10] See, eg, H Liu, L Gullifer and H Chong, 'Client-Intermediary Relations in the Crypto-Asset World' (2021) University of Cambridge Faculty of Law Research Paper No 18/2021.

[11] See UK Digital Assets Consultation Paper (n 3).

[12] Most scholars have thoroughly looked into applications of property law onto crypto-assets. See. eg, K Low, 'Trusts of cryptoassets' in R Nolan, H W Tang and M Yip (eds), *Trusts and Private Wealth Management: Developments and Directions* (Cambridge, Cambridge University Press, 2022); Liu et al (n 10).

Those relationships are especially pertinent since CEXs and industry players often have a say in shaping the regulatory developments that will apply to them.[13] Regulators should thus be careful not to let the cart lead the horse: the sway of industry players should not outweigh regulatory goals such as consumer protection and a 'responsible digital asset ecosystem'.[14] Furthermore, by taking an empirical approach, this chapter also highlights how CEXs may exploit future regulatory gaps to maintain a status quo that disadvantages or misleads its customers. These challenges are not exclusive to Singapore, but rather ones that regulators across all jurisdictions will doubtlessly face.

2. How Do CEXs Fail?

The business models of CEXs and how they collapse should first be explained. At its core, a CEX is a business that facilitates the buying and selling of crypto-tokens.[15] They are not the only way for a consumer to purchase a crypto-token or participate in crypto-related activities, but they have significantly greater scalability that allows them to offer their services at lower costs and better quality over decentralised exchanges (eg increased range of exchange pairs offered).[16] Because the overwhelming majority of crypto-token transactions are facilitated by central exchanges,[17] CEXs will often be the entities responsible for 'on and off-ramping' customers to and from the crypto-market. It would then be impossible to protect consumers without considering the role CEXs play in being the first port of call for consumers entering the crypto-market.

However, CEXs do not operate solely as an exchange platform for crypto-tokens. They have multiple revenue streams ranging from commissions earned on customers' exchanges, to the investment of customers' cryptocurrencies or funds, thereby operating as a hybrid of traditional stock exchanges and banks. However, they are not regulated in the same way as either of these entities in Singapore. Instead, CEXs are regulated as a payment institution under the Payment Services Act 2019 (PSA). In order to carry out any 'digital payment token service', such as facilitating the exchange of cryptocurrencies,[18] CEXs must register for a payment institution licence[19] or fall into one of the PSA's

[13] For example, MAS, *Proposed Regulatory Measures for Digital Payment Token Services* (P008-2022, October 2022) (DPT Consultation Paper) and UK Digital Assets Consultation Paper (n 3).

[14] DPT Consultation Paper (n 13) [2.13].

[15] Payment Services Act 2019 (PSA), Sch 1, Pt 3 defines a 'digital payment token exchange' as a place or facility that offers, or intends to offer, to buy or sell digital payment tokens.

[16] A Barbon and A Ranaldo, 'On the Quality of Cryptocurrency Markets: Centralized Versus Decentralized Exchanges' (2022) Swiss Finance Institute Research Paper No 22-38.

[17] For example, the Corporate Finance Institute, 'Cryptocurrency Exchanges'. See https://corporatefinanceinstitute.com/resources/cryptocurrency/cryptocurrency-exchanges/.

[18] A 'digital payment token service' is defined as any service of dealing in or facilitating the exchange of digital payment tokens: PSA, Sch 1, Pt 3.

[19] PSA, s 6.

exemptions.[20] Significantly, the choice to regulate CEXs in this way distinguishes most digital payment tokens from money (both as fiat currency or e-money), bank deposits, and securities.

The important function and variety of services offered by CEXs have made them prime flashpoints for litigation. Major decisions in common law jurisdictions featuring CEXs as one of the parties include *Quoine Pte Ltd v B2C2 Ltd*[21] (*Quoine*), and *Ruscoe and another v Cryptopia*[22] (*Cryptopia*). In those cases, Quoine and Cryptopia were both CEXs that were parties to litigation that related to the property rights of their customers. CEXs have also been parties to litigation in cases of hacks or fraud as they may be subject to injunctions or other orders – eg ancillary disclosure orders were made against CEXs in order to aid with the tracing of the plaintiff's stolen cryptocurrency assets in *CLM v CLN and others*.[23]

On the issue of their collapse: while no single factor or event can explain why CEXs become insolvent, fraud is a common feature across most. For instance, the collapse of FTX had been triggered by revelations that the 'FTT token' issued by FTX and other company assets had been used as collateral for its sister investment company's trading activities, Alameda Research.[24] While the verdict is not yet in on whether FTX's trading or accounting amounted to fraud, there was, at a minimum, a misleading of investors and customers alike.[25] The collapse of FTX naturally resulted in the impending insolvencies of its subsidiaries and acquired CEX businesses, such as Liquid/Quoine in Singapore. The issue of fraud also persists after their filing of bankruptcy as customers had begun to dispute the ownership of their crypto-tokens.[26]

As the FTX Chapter 11 proceedings have shown, the collapse of a major CEX affects swathes of customers across multiple jurisdictions and in a variety of ways. The ensuing litigation may involve customers disputing the rights they might have in particular crypto-assets,[27] or may require the courts to determine matters of public policy.

A crucial part of such litigation will be the nature of the contract between the CEX and its customers, which will often be in the form of clickwrap T&Cs that customers accept when using the CEX's platform.[28] By virtue of their different

[20] PSA, s 13; see also Payment Services (Exemption for Specified Period) Regulations 2019, reg 7 and PSA, Sch 1, Pt 2.

[21] [2020] SGCA(I) 2, [2020] 2 SLR 20.

[22] [2020] NZHC 728, 22 ITELR 925.

[23] *CLM v CLN and others* [2022] SGHC 46, [2022] 5 SLR 273 [60].

[24] I Allison, 'Divisions in Sam Bankman-Fried's Crypto Empire Blur on His Trading Titan Alameda's Balance Sheet' CoinDesk (2 November 2022). Available at: www.coindesk.com/business/2022/11/02/divisions-in-sam-bankman-frieds-crypto-empire-blur-on-his-trading-titan-alamedas-balance-sheet.

[25] 'FTX founder Sam Bankman-Fried hit with new fraud charges' CBS News (23 February 2023). Available at: www.cbsnews.com/news/ftx-sam-bankman-fried-faces-new-fraud-charges.

[26] See, eg, *In re: Celsius Network LLC et al* Chapter 11 No 22-10964-MG at MEMORANDUM OPINION AND ORDER REGARDING OWNERSHIP OF EARN ACCOUNT ASSETS.

[27] *Onusz v West Realm Shires Inc, et al*, No 22-50513-JTD (Bankr D. Del.) of *In re: FTX Trading et al.* Chapter 11 Case No 22-11068-JTD.

[28] For a discussion on the enforceability of clickwrap contracts, see E Mik, 'Contracts Governing the Use of Websites' (2016) *Singapore Journal of Legal Studies* 70.

business models and interests, T&Cs vary on issues such as customer's rights in the crypto-token and the duties the CEX may owe to the customer. In order to represent this range and the options available to Singaporean consumers, this chapter cites a variety of T&Cs that span from CEXs with offices incorporated in Singapore (Crypto.com, Gemini), CEXs with offices incorporated in Singapore that are undergoing insolvency proceedings (Zipmex, Liquid), and CEXs without offices incorporated in Singapore (Kraken).

3. Why are Customers not Protected During CEX Insolvencies?

3.1. Who is the Customer?

This chapter focuses on Singaporean consumers that are individuals, as opposed to organisations, interested in entering the crypto-market (eg by trading a crypto-token). The size of this group is already significant. In 2021, nearly 16% of Singaporeans participated in the crypto-market.[29] Similarly, the Singaporean market has generally been receptive to crypto-related products despite adverse developments.[30] Importantly, the chapter also refers to consumers without significant capital. This is in line with MAS' proposed consumer access measures that will mainly impact customers that do not qualify as accredited investors under the Securities and Futures Act 2001.[31]

What expectations do Singaporean consumers have before entering the crypto market? On average, Singaporean consumers consider crypto-tokens to be a form of 'investment',[32] which seems to suggest that they expect some level of ownership in the crypto-asset that they are purchasing. Such an expectation would not be unfair, given that most CEXs market a service that allows customers to 'buy' and 'sell' crypto-tokens.[33] Furthermore, the analogy to typical marketplaces or stock exchanges that can be drawn is obvious: customers or investors purchase the offered products and usually gain ownership of what they purchased. To that end, the UK Law Commission had considered how sales and transfers by novation

[29] A Williams, 'Nearly 16% of Singaporeans surveyed currently own cryptocurrency' The Straits Times (25 October 2021). Available at: www.straitstimes.com/business/banking/nearly-16-of-singaporeans-surveyed-currently-own-cryptocurrency.

[30] R Hartung, 'Commentary: Young Singapore investors are still keen on cryptos despite crash. Here's how we can help them' CNA (6 December 2022). Available at: www.channelnewsasia.com/commentary/ftx-crypto-retail-investors-mas-test-risk-assessment-educate-3122441.

[31] DPT Consultation Paper (n 13) [3.2]–[3.12].

[32] See, eg, A Sarkar, 'Singaporean investors' appetite for crypto is key to mainstream adoption – Survey' Cointelegraph (28 April 2022). Available at: https://cointelegraph.com/news/singaporean-investors-appetite-for-crypto-is-key-to-mainstream-adoption-survey.

[33] See, eg, 'Buy crypto at true cost on crypto.com'. Available at: https://crypto.com/; 'Buy Bitcoin on Zipmex'. Available at: zipmex.com/btc/buy.

could offer a useful analogy to transfers of crypto-tokens.[34] They noted that while the analogies were useful, technical differences and diversity in the types of transactions and crypto-tokens made it difficult to apply such analogies wholesale.

The fact that a 'new' crypto-token is usually created in a typical transfer of a crypto-asset has led the UK Jurisdiction Taskforce to suggest that 'there is a closer analogy with a bank payment where no property in the payer's funds passes to the payee; instead new property is created by credit to the payee's account'.[35] It is indeed the case that many CEXs hold themselves out operationally to be like banks, where the CEX only owes a debt to the customer for the notional value of the crypto-token 'purchased'.[36]

One might then argue that consumers are misled as customers of CEXs when they do not gain ownership of their purchased crypto-tokens since crypto-tokens have been held by the courts to be property,[37] and CEXs are advertising a service that allows customers to 'buy' and 'sell' such property, but CEXs had never intended for the customer to have any property rights in the crypto-token. The likelihood of a successful suit for fraud or misrepresentation is considered in Section 3.3 below, but it is worth noting that because advertisements are generally held to be mere invitations to treat,[38] and that the T&Cs customers accept always include non-reliance clauses, the success of such suits is unlikely.[39]

It is thus established that the customer of a CEX should not immediately be thought to be in the same position as an investor on an exchange or a customer of a regular marketplace. But is the customer of a CEX any more sophisticated than the average consumer? The answer is likely no. It is unsurprising that most consumers do not read the T&Cs before accepting them.[40] Even if they did, the average consumer is also unlikely to be able to appreciate its legal jargon.[41] For instance, in the wake of FTX's collapse, a Reddit user had read through the T&Cs of major CEXs in America, but failed to notice the clauses on custody and trust relationships, nor appreciate that the exemption clauses were boilerplate clauses.[42]

The average consumer's lack of legal finesse is understandable, which makes them a prime target for protection by regulation. Regulation would then need to target both the risk posed to consumers because of volatility in the crypto-market,

[34] UK Digital Assets Consultation Paper (n 3) [13.117]–[13.124] and [13.133]–[13.141].

[35] UK Jurisdiction Taskforce, *Legal Statement on Cryptoassets and Smart Contracts* (November 2019) para 45.

[36] See also UK Digital Assets Consultation Paper (n 3) [13.125]–[13.129].

[37] *ByBit Fintech Ltd v Ho Kai Xin and others* [2023] SGHC 199.

[38] *Partridge v Crittenden* [1968] 1 WLR 1204.

[39] Above n 26.

[40] M Patton, 'How to Protect Users' Copyright Rights in the Age of Social Media Platforms and Their Unread Terms of Service' (2020) 53 *University of San Francisco Law Review* 463, 475–76.

[41] The average reading level of T&Cs were found to be that of academic journals: U Benoliel and S Becher, 'The Duty to Read the Unreadable' (2019) 60(8) *Boston College Law Review* 2255. See also A White and C Mansfield, 'Literacy and Contract' (2002) 13 *Stanford Law & Policy Review* 233, 235.

[42] See www.reddit.com/r/CryptoCurrency/comments/1051wnk/today_i_seriously_read_the_terms_and_conditions/.

and that posed by misleading business practices. Indeed, the current marketing and consumer access restrictions focus on the former rather than the latter.[43] For instance, CEXs in Singapore cannot promote their services in public places, nor provide ATM services for customers to withdraw their crypto-tokens as cash.[44] There have also been government initiatives to increase the financial literacy of consumers with respect to crypto-assets,[45] but these do not cover legal issues like crypto-token ownership. While such measures are important, they do not offer the same kinds of protection that typical consumer protection measures will offer by way of securing consumer rights to a particular product or to relief.[46]

As noted, the analogy to consumer protection for the sale of goods is limited in utility given the greater legal ambiguity, technical complexity, and nascent nature of the crypto-market. Recent judicial and regulatory developments have thus begged the question of how and to what extent consumers in the crypto-market ought to be protected.

3.2. What are the Customer's Rights?

The nature of the customer's right in the crypto-token determines the type of claim available to the customer to obtain the crypto-token or its equivalent value. The most pertinent example is how property subjected to a trust does not join the CEX's insolvency estate – which is the case in most jurisdictions such as the US[47] and Singapore.[48] Another relevant consideration is whether the crypto-token has been used as security for a loan arrangement between the CEX and the customer. Depending on the type of security the crypto-token serves as, the customer may have better priority than other creditors to that particular crypto-token. However, whether crypto-tokens can be used as security for a loan is also the subject of debate as most assets used for security must be capable of physical possession (eg pledges) or will require public registration (eg charges and mortgages).[49]

A customer left without their crypto-token during the CEX's ongoing liquidation would thus be in the best position to recover their crypto-token if the CEX had been holding the crypto-token on trust for the customer. As trust property does not join the insolvency estate, the customer would have a proprietary claim to the crypto-token that takes precedence over all other creditors. Where no trust can be found or where the crypto-token had been entrusted to the CEX (eg for the

[43] DPT Consultation Paper (n 13) [2.4].

[44] MAS, Guidelines on Provision of DPT Services to the Public [PS-G02].

[45] MoneySense is a financial literacy educational platform created by the Singapore government. See www.moneysense.gov.sg/crypto-quiz.

[46] See, eg, Consumer Protection (Fair Trading) Act 2003.

[47] 11 US Code § 541(b)(1).

[48] *McEntire v Crossley* [1895] AC 457 at 461.

[49] See UK Digital Assets Consultation Paper (n 3) at [18.18]–[18.43].

CEX's 'Earn' product), customers may argue the crypto-token was security for a secured loan which may allow them better priority over other creditors' claims to the crypto-token. However, as this section will illustrate, such arrangements are few and far between.

Underlying both claims is the issue of the crypto-token as property: namely (1) What property rights may be vested in crypto-assets? and (2) How can such property rights be acquired? The section starts by outlining the current legal position on these issues before comparing how CEX T&Cs could be read in context of the present law and the proposed regulations.

3.2.1. Property Rights and Crypto-Assets

The Singaporean courts have acknowledged that crypto-assets are types of property on numerous occasions. Significantly, the SGHC has held in *ByBit Fintech Ltd v Ho Kai Xin* (*ByBit Fintech*) that cryptocurrencies are indeed a type of property that can be held on constructive trust.[50] The finding that crypto-assets are types of property follows developments in other jurisdictions: the UK has held that crypto-tokens are types of property in *AA v Persons Unknown*[51] and in the UK Jurisdiction Taskforce's statement;[52] the Internal Revenue Service of the US had deemed crypto-tokens to be types of taxable property,[53] and the proprietary nature of crypto-tokens was not in dispute in bankruptcy-related cases like *In re: Celsius Network LLC*.[54]

Indeed, parties in litigation also tend to assume that crypto-assets are types of property – they instead disagree on the types of property arrangements or rights that the crypto-assets in question may attract. One prominent example of this is *Quoine*. There, the SGCA acknowledged that whether Bitcoin was a type of property was not in contention, but made no conclusion as to whether crypto-tokens like Bitcoin were capable of being trust property as there was no intention to form such a trust on the facts of the case.[55] The Singaporean courts' reasoning to find an institutional constructive trust of the crypto-assets in *ByBit Fintech*, but not find an express trust in *Quoine*, is instructive in a few ways.

Firstly, on the issue of trusts of crypto-tokens, the courts will look for the constitutive elements of the trust. For *ByBit Fintech*, it was sufficient that the court found that the assets were stolen to then give rise to the institutional constructive trust.[56] In the case of an express trust, the court will look for the three certainties of intention, subject matter and object. This is well illustrated when contrasting *Quoine* with *Cryptopia*. Unlike the former, the New Zealand High Court found

[50] *ByBit Fintech Ltd* (n 37) [36] and [44].
[51] *AA v Persons Unknown who Demanded Bitcoin on 10th and 11th October 2019 and ors* [2019] EWHC 3556 (Comm), [2020] 4 WLR 35 [59].
[52] Above n 35.
[53] IRS, *Notice 2014-21 Guidance on Virtual Currency* (25 March 2014).
[54] Above n 26.
[55] *Quoine* (n 21) [139]–[149].
[56] *ByBit Fintech Ltd* (n 37) [42].

that Cryptopia did hold crypto-tokens on trust for its customers. Both cases involve a customer bringing a claim for damages against a CEX when the crypto-tokens associated with the customer's account had been transacted contrary to the customer's intentions. The courts in *Quoine* and *Cryptopia* considered similar issues to reach different conclusions on whether there was sufficient certainty of intention to create a trust. Both courts looked to the CEX's conduct with respect to how it held the crypto-tokens and agreed that segregation was a necessary, but not sufficient, condition for a trust of crypto-tokens to be found.[57] In *Quoine*, the sum of customer crypto-token balances did not necessarily match the amount of crypto-tokens that Quoine held in its cold storage wallet.[58] This was not the case in *Cryptopia*, where the balance of crypto-tokens in Cryptopia's hot and cold wallets were supposed to match with the sum of customer's crypto-token balances.[59] Furthermore, the crypto-tokens Quoine held were also intended to fund Quoine's own 'market-making' and lending – business activities that Cryptopia did not engage in.[60]

Secondly, the courts considered the T&Cs that the customer was subject to. In *Cryptopia*, the crypto-tokens were described as 'Your Coin balances', with *Cryptopia* being appointed as the agent holding the coin balances on behalf of the customer.[61] In contrast, the T&Cs in *Quoine* militated against the finding of a trust: clause 9 of Quoine's Risk Disclosure Statement stated that client funds were not held in trust bank arrangements, and that all client funds may be lost on Quoine's insolvency.[62]

Lastly, because the New Zealand High Court found an express trust to be created on the facts of the case, it did not further consider the argument that '[a]n intention to create a trust is not to be inferred "simply because a court thinks it is an appropriate means of protecting or creating an interest".'[63] The presence of a contractual relationship and reliance on 'construction of the relevant text or oral dealings in their context'[64] may suggest that there is little room for the finding of a constructive trust to protect the interest of customers.

In comparing *Quoine* and *Cryptopia*, it is apparent that the T&Cs and business operations of the CEX are highly relevant to determining if the customer has property rights in the crypto-token they 'bought' through the CEX. Where T&Cs are concerned, the next sections will illustrate how CEXs have fool-proofed their T&Cs to avoid the finding of a trust per *Cryptopia*. However, the legal consequences for doing so are not always clear after one frames the T&Cs against the CEX's overall business and regulations that apply.

[57] ibid [145]; *Cryptopia* (n 22), considering *Quoine* (n 21), [162].
[58] *Quoine* (n 21) [146].
[59] *Cryptopia* (n 22) [22] and [174].
[60] ibid [165].
[61] ibid [27].
[62] *Quoine* (n 21) [148]; *Cryptopia* (n 22) [165].
[63] *Cryptopia* (n 22) [162].
[64] *Quoine* (n 21) [144], quoting *Korda v Australian Executor Trustees (SA) Ltd* [2015] HCA 6; (2015) 255 CLR 62 [11].

3.2.2. Do Customers Have Property Rights When Exchanging on CEXs?

Whether the customer has property rights in the crypto-token thus depends on the T&Cs they are subject to, which in turn also depends on what service of the CEX they are using. The first service this chapter considers is the CEX's titular business of allowing a customer to exchange their funds for a crypto-token. This is often marketed as a 'buying' and 'selling' of crypto-tokens even where the CEX does not intend for the customer to gain ownership of the crypto-token. An example of such an arrangement can be found in Zipmex's T&Cs:[65] clause 7.1 states that customers 'grant Zipmex all rights and title to all On-Exchange Assets'; clause 7.2(a)(5) that the customer's rights are 'limited to a contractual obligation for Zipmex to provide an equivalent amount and type of On-Exchange Assets', ie a 'debtor-creditor relationship'. The T&Cs also do not describe the customer's crypto-tokens as 'your On-Exchange Assets', but rather 'the' or 'all On-Exchange Assets'. This leaves customers without a proprietary claim to their tokens in the wake of a CEX's insolvency: eg, Zipmex has informed its customers that they will be creditors pending its restructuring, ie the customers do not have prima facie proprietary claims to the crypto-tokens they purchased.[66]

Similarly, Liquid (which owns Quoine) disclaims that they do not act as trustee or fiduciary for the customer.[67] Furthermore, clause 13.1 continues to state that 'the use of terms such as "account", "account balance", "deposit", "withdraw", "your Digital Assets" or "your Fiat Currencies" and similar (*sic*) does not imply … any form of custody relationship, and such language is used … as terms of convenience'. Although Liquid's T&Cs do not prescribe a legal relationship with the customer like Zipmex's does, it is already clear from the *Quoine* saga that the intended relationship is one of debtor-banker as Quoine manages customer funds like a bank would.[68]

Of course, not all CEXs intend to deny the customer any property rights to the crypto-token. Gemini's User[69] and Custody Agreement[70] affirm that they are holding 'your digital assets' on trust as a fiduciary and custodian. Similarly, but more ambiguously, Kraken's T&Cs affirm that the customer remains the owner

[65] Zipmex, 'Terms and Conditions Effective 30 Mar 2022'. Available at: https://zipmex.com/terms-and-conditions/.

[66] Zipmex, 'Moratorium' at No. 9. Available at: https://zipmex.com/support/moratorium/moratorium/.

[67] Liquid, 'Liquid Terms of Use 2022/07/25' cl 13.1.

[68] *Quoine* (n 21) [146] and [149].

[69] 'We are a fiduciary under § 100 of the New York Banking Law (the 'NYBL') … Digital Assets custodied on your behalf and reflected in the Digital Asset Account of your Gemini Account are not treated as general assets of Gemini': Gemini, 'User Agreement Last updated September 27 2023'. Available at: www.gemini.com/legal/user-agreement.

[70] 'You agree and understand that we will establish a Custody Account in your name … your Assets will be (i) segregated from any and all other assets held by us … The ownership of your Assets will be clearly recorded in our books as belonging to you …': Gemini, 'Custody Agreement Last updated July 31 2023'. Available at: www.gemini.com/legal/custody-agreement.

of their digital assets,[71] but does not explicitly indicate whether they are holding those assets on trust. That the customer remains the 'owner' of the crypto-token should strongly suggest that the assets are held on trust by Kraken for its customers.

The T&Cs highlighted demonstrate how CEXs can rely on ambiguity to the customer's disadvantage – reinforcing the idea that even if customers do read the T&Cs, they may not appreciate its legal repercussions. For instance, neither Liquid nor Kraken explicitly describe their legal relationship with the customer, obfuscating the finding of a trust or its precise terms.

3.2.3. Do Customers Have Property Rights in 'Earn' Arrangements?

The second CEX service considered is the 'Earn' product that CEXs offer: a common product that allows customers to earn a yield if the customer lends to or 'locks' crypto-tokens[72] with the CEX such that the customer is no longer able to transact or use the crypto-token. Such products are usually ambiguous as to the nature of the transfer of crypto-tokens to the CEX and as to how the yield is being generated (eg through staking, decentralised finance investments, or further lending).[73]

The legal consequences of such arrangements are also unclear for several reasons. Firstly, is it possible to lend crypto-tokens or to use them as security? Where lending is concerned, consumers likely think that a crypto-token is 'loaned' the same way one might loan physical property. Indeed, this was implicit in the UK Law Commission's analysis that, in spite of crypto-assets' incorporeality, variance in control and a state change would be sufficient to evidence a derivative transfer of title through lending.[74] However, as Low and Chan rightly point out, crypto-tokens are 'not suitable for non-fungible loans since, like money, they can only be enjoyed through alienation'.[75] Thus, while crypto-assets themselves might attract proprietary features, their use in a crypto-loan complicates the matter. Bank loans do not generate or retain any property rights for lenders over the specific monies loaned. Furthermore, the SGHC has also deemed that stablecoins, ie crypto-tokens pegged to fiat currencies, were not 'money' for the purposes of a winding-up application.[76] The proprietary consequences and precise legal arrangement are thus not obvious when a customer 'loans' a crypto-token to the CEX.

[71] Kraken, 'Terms of Service Last Updated June 19 2023' cl 6.7.1. Available at: www.kraken.com/legal.

[72] See, eg, Zipmex's 'ZipUp+' offers customers a yield in exchange for 'locking' or 'depositing' their crypto-tokens with the programme. Available at: https://zipmex.com/earn/.

[73] No such information is provided on Liquid's blog post explaining the 'Liquid Earn' product when it was offered. Available at: https://blog.liquid.com/liquid-earn.

[74] UK Digital Assets Consultation Paper (n 3) [13.17]–[13.22].

[75] K Low and T Chan, 'The Implications of CeFi and DeFi in Bankruptcy: A Hot Take on Celsius' (28 April 2023). Available at: https://blogs.law.ox.ac.uk/oblb/blog-post/2023/04/implications-cefi-and-defi-bankruptcy-hot-take-celsius.

[76] *Algorand Foundation Ltd v Three Arrows Capital Pte Ltd* (HC/CWU 246/2022, unreported).

Next, the use of crypto-tokens as security proved to be more difficult as common types of security like mortgages and charges were dependent on public registers, while others like pledges only applied to assets in possession.[77] These challenges are also felt in the Singaporean context where, in general, mortgages and charges must be registered for creditors to retain their interest against the company's liquidator,[78] and assets pledged must be capable of physical possession.[79] The potential inability for crypto-tokens to serve as security may pose problems for the enforceability of the T&Cs and the nature of the customer's claim to the crypto-token in insolvency proceedings.

Secondly, because some CEXs do not even grant their customers any ownership rights in the crypto-token, what exactly *is* being transferred or authorised when the customer agrees to the T&Cs? For instance, Zipmex's 'ZipUp+' T&Cs indicate that the customer 'may transfer any Digital Assets supported by ZipUp+' but reiterates that the relationship between Zipmex and customer is that of creditor and debtor.[80] While the T&Cs do describe the digital assets as 'your digital assets' in the 'Disclosure of Risks', it is not clear that the crypto-tokens deposited under the ZipUp+ programme will solely comprise of the customer's own crypto-tokens (previously stored outside of Zipmex) since crypto-tokens exchanged on Zipmex do not belong to the customer.[81] At the same time, the crypto-tokens deposited in the program are described as a 'Principal',[82] which suggests that the arrangement is intended to be a loan. It is thus possible that the customer is loaning Zipmex a sum of money, represented by Zipmex's obligations to pay the customer the equivalent value and type of crypto-tokens in their amount, in exchange for earning a fixed yield. But this may be problematic because an exchange of a loan for a fixed yield resembles a debt security arrangement and would be regulated under the Securities and Futures Act 2001.[83] This would involve additional disclosure or regulatory requirements[84] which CEXs typically would not have fulfilled. It would also be unusual for a debt security to be offered without a trustee holding or agent managing the collected principal.

If such a loan is not a debt security, it may still fall foul of section 4A of the Banking Act 1970. The section restricts deposit-taking businesses, defining 'deposit' in s 4B(4) to mean 'a sum of money paid on terms under which it will be repaid, with or without interest or a premium … and which are not referable to the

[77] Above n 49. See also T Chan and K Low, 'DeFi Common Sense: Crypto-backed Lending in *Janesh s/o Rajkumar v Unknown Person ('CHEFPIERRE')*' (2023) 86(5) *Modern Law Review* 1278, 1289–1290.

[78] Companies Act 1967, s 131.

[79] See, eg, *State Bank of India Singapore v Rainforest Trading Ltd and another* [2011] SGHC 182, [2011] 4 SLR 699 [78].

[80] See 'Transfer' and 'Our Rights' in Zipmex, 'ZipUp+ Terms and Conditions – Global (Effective 30 Mar 2022)'. Available at: https://zipmex.com/earn-terms-conditions/.

[81] See section 3.2.2.

[82] Above n 80 at 'Zipmex Earn Plans'.

[83] Securities and Futures Act 2001 (SFA), s 2; See also MAS, *Guidelines on the Product Highlights Sheet for Offers of Debt Securities, Hybrid Instruments and Equity Securities [SFA 13-G13]*.

[84] See, eg, Obligations to issue a prospectus: SFA, s 240.

provision of property or services or to the giving of security'. That loans 'referable to the provision of property' are excepted might mean Earn arrangements are not 'deposits' under the Banking Act since the arrangement refers to the customer's crypto-tokens. But it is doubtful that CEXs can have their cake and eat it too. How can the loan be simultaneously referable to property but involve none of the customer-lender's property at all?

Clearly, the nature of the customer's rights and the language of the contract make a straightforward interpretation of the arrangement difficult. This issue is similarly present in other T&Cs like Liquid Earn's, which refers to customers '[subscribing] a supported Digital Asset' rather than transferring property or assigning a right.[85] However not all CEXs rely on ambiguous legal arrangements for their Earn products. Kraken allows the customer to retain ownership of the crypto-tokens after they have been allocated to the staking service.[86] As explained earlier, Kraken and Gemini are CEXs that grant the customer property rights in the crypto-tokens they purchase. Kraken's arrangement thus resembles a lease or loan of crypto-tokens since the customer is allowing the CEX subordinate property rights to use their crypto-tokens. Alternatively, the arrangement also resembles an instruction by the customer as beneficiary to the property for the trustee holder to use the property in a certain way.

Kraken's arrangement guarantees that, upon insolvency, the crypto-tokens allocated to the Earn product are not part of the insolvency estate. The same cannot be said of more ambiguous T&Cs like Zipmex and Liquid's. As discussed earlier, customers of Zipmex and Liquid have no proprietary rights in the crypto-tokens exchanged on the CEX. However, the use of language like 'transfer' in Earn T&Cs like ZipUp+'s suggest that the customer did have some proprietary right over the crypto-token to indicate how the crypto-token should be held or used. This results in a strange outcome where the customer that exposes the crypto-tokens in their account to greater risk by signing up for an Earn product seems more likely to have a proprietary right, while the customer that only uses the CEX as an exchange does not. However, this debacle may be irrelevant since both ZipUp+ and Liquid Earn disclosed that the customer is at risk of losing all the assets should the CEX become insolvent.[87] As *Quoine* has shown, this suggests that no assets were held on trust since the crypto-tokens would join the insolvency estate.[88]

[85] Liquid, 'Liquid Terms of Use (Effective date: 19 April 2021)' cls 12.1–12.2. Available at: https://quoine-prod.s3.amazonaws.com/uploads/policy_document/term_document/252/Liquid_Terms_of_Use_Quoine_Pte_Ltd_2021.04.19.pdf. Note that Liquid no longer offered this product in their new T&Cs (above n 67).

[86] 'You retain ownership of the Supported Tokens and such Supported Tokens shall remain property of you when staked under the terms of this Addendum.' (above n 71, Annex C cl 1.2).

[87] Above n 80, 'YOU ACCEPT THE RISK OF … UP TO AND INCLUDING THE TOTAL AMOUNT OF DIGITAL ASSETS THAT YOU SUBSCRIBE TO VIA ZIPUP+'; Above n 85, 'YOU ACCEPT THE RISK OF LOSS ASSOCIATED WITH THE LOSS OF YOUR DIGITAL.'

[88] Above n 62.

The failure to properly characterise the nature of crypto-tokens as property, and subsequently the CEX's legal arrangement of Earn products, paints a picture of a legal Wild West. The mechanisms described often envision some transfer of property by the customer in order to earn a regular yield in order to avoid coming into the ambit of banking regulations. Yet the customer often has no proprietary rights nor interest in the crypto-token they are 'transferring'. A straightforward application of basic property law (*nemo dat quod non habet*)[89] may suggest that no transaction occurred per the contract since any transfer of property by the customer would have been impossible (an effective rescission). The result would be that the customer's crypto-tokens ought to remain in their account and were treated to have not been allocated to the Earn product. This means that the customer who 'loses' all their crypto-tokens in the Earn product as a result of the CEX's insolvency would return to being a creditor for the value of the crypto-tokens originally stored in their account.

The legal Wild West does not only include this proprietary paradox. Some T&Cs go so far as to suggest arrangements liable to recharacterisation. For instance, Gemini Earn[90] offers customers the opportunity to earn a yield by making an unsecured loan[91] of the crypto-token they beneficially own to a third party,[92] with Gemini acting as the agent. An unsecured loan of money is a one where the lender may only have a claim to the value of the loan rather than a proprietary claim on any security.[93] However, a loan of property generally means the borrower of property gets a property right subordinate to the lender's such that the lender may rely on their superior proprietary right or any relevant contractual right to reclaim possession or unburdened title to the property.[94] The nature of the borrower's subordinate property rights seems contrary to Gemini's disclosure that the borrowed property may be entirely lost and hence unreturnable[95] – such a power to destroy the property would render the lender's superior property right useless. Effectively, the customer in such an arrangement would have relinquished all proprietary rights, and by extension a claim to the property in the CEX's insolvency. If so, it may be better to describe the arrangement as a sale of the customer's crypto-tokens to the CEX in exchange for regular interest payments and an equivalent token to be delivered at a later date.

[89] One cannot give what one does not have, eg *Skelwith (Leisure) Ltd v Armstrong* [2015] EWHC 2830 (Ch), [2016] Ch 345 [54].

[90] 'Gemini Earn Program Terms and Authorization Agreement (Last updated: 14 December 2022)'. Available at: www.gemini.com/legal/gemini-earn-program-terms-and-authorization-agreement#section-1-program-risks.

[91] ibid cl 3, 'All lending by you through our Program will be on an unsecured basis.'

[92] Genesis Global Capital is the only 'Approved Borrower' as of writing. It is noted that Genesis Global Capital is owned by Digital Currency Group, which also owns Gemini. This chapter does not consider whether Gemini is validly acting as agent for the customer and not as co-principal with Genesis Global Capital.

[93] M Bridge, *Personal Property Law*, 4th edn (Oxford, Oxford University Press, 2015) 269.

[94] An exercise of priority in property rights, see, eg, *United Overseas Bank Ltd v Homely Bath Services & Trading Pte Ltd and another* [2019] SGHCR 3.

[95] Above n 88, clause 1.

Given the novel, ambiguous, and confusing nature of these T&Cs, it seems impossible for a customer to appreciate the risks to their assets when the precise legal mechanisms and risks of Earn arrangements cannot be identified. Singaporean regulators may thus be correct in seeking to eliminate such products altogether – these issues are discussed in section 4.1.

3.3. Can Customers Sue Insolvent CEXs to Rescind T&Cs?

If the customer had a property right in the crypto-token prior to the use of the CEX's service, then rescission would mean the crypto-token is returned to the customer and any funds or tokens the customer received in exchange should be returned to the CEX. Rescission is a remedy a party can elect for when the contract is void. It is generally available for fraudulent misrepresentation or where an innocent misrepresentation 'was such as that there is a complete difference in substance between the thing bargained for and that obtained, so as to constitute a failure of consideration'.[96] Such misrepresentation may be found where CEXs market their services to customers as a means to 'buy', 'sell', or 'deposit' crypto-tokens when in actuality no property rights over crypto-tokens as property passes to the customer. Of course, the courts would have to determine if it is indeed a false representation when a CEX claims it is selling a customer a crypto-token with no intention of awarding the customer any property rights in it.

Where the viability of suing an insolvent or fraudulent CEX is concerned, it is not necessary that the original or exact crypto-token be returned since transfers of crypto-tokens themselves involve novation of a new token,[97] and an analogy with shares reveals that 'identical' shares or tokens can be bought to effect rescission where the original ones were sold off.[98] Given this, it is important to note that the insolvent CEX must have sufficient funds or crypto-tokens for rescission to be possible.[99]

Rescission, rather than damages,[100] might thus be an attractive remedy for customers since an award of damages against an insolvent CEX may just be bad debt for the customer as damages do not have special priority in insolvency proceedings.[101] But not all customers would have a meaningful claim in rescission:

[96] *Larpin, Christian Alfred and another v Kaikhushru Shiavax Nargolwala and another* [2022] SGHC(I) 4, [2022] 4 SLR 83 [20], quoting *Lord Gilbert Kennedy v The Panama, New Zealand, and Australian Royal Mail Co (Limited)* (1867) LR 2 QB 580 at 580.

[97] Above n 35.

[98] *Smith New Court Securities Ltd v Scrimgeour Vickers* [1996] UKHL 3, [1997] AC 254.

[99] For instance, FTX was estimated to have $1.2B cash reserves in the wake of its insolvency. E Gkritsi, 'Sam Bankman-Fried's Crumbling FTX Empire Holds $1.2B Cash Reserves' Coindesk (22 November 2022). Available at: www.coindesk.com/business/2022/11/22/sam-bankman-frieds-crumbling-ftx-empire-holds-12b-cash-reserves/.

[100] The court may order damages in lieu of rescission under the Misrepresentation Act 1967, s 2(2).

[101] IRDA, s 203. The power to rescind also survives insolvency proceedings a company may face: *Re Eastgate* [1905] 1 KB 465.

the customer would first need to have a proprietary interest in a crypto-token prior to the transaction with the CEX that deprived them of that interest. In addition, rescission must not be barred. This makes rescission difficult for most customers who only used CEXs as an exchange. As they must first have funded their transactions on the CEX with crypto-tokens they originally owned.[102] Secondly, rescission would generally be barred where mutual restitution is impossible, particularly in the case of services.[103] This would mean that rescission is likely barred for the exchanges made on CEXs since the T&Cs provide for a service that allows customers to exchange cash for crypto-tokens at any time, rather than act as individual contracts for the exchanges of those tokens.

On the other hand, the T&Cs for Earn products can likely be rescinded. While such T&Cs may be ambiguous as to the particular legal arrangement between the customer and CEX,[104] Earn arrangements may resemble products more than services as there is a particular exchange that the parties contract for. Furthermore, notwithstanding adverse events, it is intended that the CEX holds or maintains the allocated crypto-tokens such that the customer can withdraw the tokens back into their regular account. Rescission of this arrangement would thus be straightforward since the CEX merely returns the crypto-tokens it was supposed to hold back to the customer, who should originally have a proprietary interest in those tokens. This is unlike the CEX's exchange service where the crypto-tokens the customer transfers to the CEX may be dissipated after an exchange is made and the exchange T&Cs provide for a service that allows the customer to make several of such transactions across an indefinite period of time.

The rescission of Earn T&Cs constitutes a revesting of legal title in the customer. Generally, it is not necessary to rely on the court to revest legal title through rescission – simply giving notice to the company is sufficient.[105] Where fraud is found, giving notice may not even be required.[106] However, expecting customers to successfully rescind their contracts against insolvent CEXs seems unrealistic when an insolvent CEX continues to hold the customer's crypto-tokens as part of the insolvency estate, and is also likely to dispute the customer's claim in misrepresentation.

3.3.1. *Enforceability of Non-Reliance Clauses in T&Cs*

While this chapter does not conclude on the likelihood of success for a consumer's contractual claims against a CEX succeeding, it is worth highlighting the

[102] It is noted that it is not uncommon for customers to do so by purchasing stablecoins from a stablecoins issuer, then transferring those stablecoins over to the CEX.

[103] *Boyd & Forrest v Glasgow & South Western Railway* [1915] UKHL 205; [1915] AC 526.

[104] See s 3.2.3.

[105] *Abram Steamship Co Ltd v Westville Shipping Co Ltd* [1923] AC 773. See also Swadling, Chapter 9 in this volume.

[106] *Car and Universal Finance v Caldwell* [1965] 1 QB 525.

issues relating to the enforceability of non-reliance clauses in T&Cs[107] to appreciate the types of risk or protection that the law currently offers consumers. Such clauses operate to exclude a CEX's representations, usually in marketing, as to a consumer's ability to 'buy' crypto-tokens or 'deposit' their crypto-tokens with the CEX. Similar non-reliance terms were held to be effective in a bank-client relationship by the Hong Kong High Court in *DBS Bank (Hong Kong) Ltd v Sit Pan Jit*.[108] There, it was held that 'the basis for upholding or striking down a contractual provision was not so much whether the parties were commercial or non-commercial, sophisticated or unsophisticated, of equal or unequal bargaining power, but rather that the provision was one which both parties were aware of and freely agreed'. However, a consumer's informed consent is not necessarily assumed in all situations involving clickwrap T&Cs. The English High Court in *Green v Petfre (Gibraltar) Ltd (t/a Betfred)* found that an online casino platform's T&C's boilerplate exclusion clauses were not incorporated into the contract as they were ambiguous and were not, given their 'onerous and unusual' nature, adequately raised to the consumer's attention.[109]

Furthermore, CEX T&Cs would also be subject to legislation under the Misrepresentation Act 1967 and the Unfair Contract Terms Act 1977 (UCTA). Section 3 of the former subjects clauses that exclude liability or remedies for misrepresentation to the standard of reasonableness in the UCTA. Similarly, s 3 of the latter provides that a contracting party cannot, on their standard terms or when dealing with a consumer, claim to be entitled to render 'a contractual performance substantially different from that which was reasonably expected of him' except insofar as the term is reasonable.[110]

Informed consent and reasonableness are thus two important considerations to keep in mind when determining if boilerplate non-reliance clauses are enforceable. The latter poses some challenges as what is 'reasonable' would be influenced by existing and proposed regulations. As a starting point, UCTA, s 11 defines 'reasonableness' to mean a 'fair and reasonable [term] to be included having regard to the circumstances which were, or ought reasonably to have been, known to or in the contemplation of the parties when the contract was made'. Customers do not accept the CEX T&Cs in a vacuum: CEXs must disclose the risks of dealing in digital payment tokens to its customers before they can deal

[107] Cl 20.3 of Crypto.com's Exchange Terms of Service and cl 6.2 of their Crypto Earn Terms and Conditions both state: '[W]e disclaim all other representations or warranties, express or implied, made to you, your Affiliates or any other person, including any warranties regarding title, non-infringement, timeliness, quality, suitability, merchantability, fitness for a particular purpose or otherwise (regardless of any course of dealing, custom or usage of trade) of any service or any good provided under these Terms.'

[108] [2015] HKEC 548 (unreported).

[109] Notably, the court reached this conclusion without relying on the Consumer Rights Act 2015: *Green v Petfre (Gibraltar) Ltd (t/a Betfred)* [2021] EWHC 842 (QB) at [150]–[172].

[110] UCTA provisions on exclusion clauses were found to apply to non-reliance clauses if they had the effect of excluding liability for misrepresentation altogether: *First Tower Trustees Ltd v CDS (Superstores International) Limited* [2018] EWCA Civ 1396, [2019] 1 WLR 637.

with them.[111] The disclosure includes a disclaimer that the customer is liable to lose all their money, and that they should not transact if they are unfamiliar with the crypto-token. CEXs can thus argue that both the substance of particular clauses and circumstances of contracting are reasonable since it is already disclaimed to the customer that they are at risk of losing their money (and by extension, their property).[112] It would then be immaterial whether the customer loses their crypto-tokens as a result of the T&C's clauses denying their ownership rights or by virtue of its non-reliance clauses effectively denying liability for misrepresentation. Furthermore, it is also currently accepted industry practice that CEXs do not necessarily have to give their customers property rights in their tokens,[113] nor do CEXs or web platforms generally inform users of their rights and remedies.

This returns us to the issue of informed consent, which has been a point of debate in scholarship since the advent of big data[114] and will be further discussed below in context of the proposed regulations. It is sufficient to note here that consumer protection legislation and case law do not provide clear answers as to whether non-reliance clauses in clickwrap T&Cs should be enforceable.

4. How Can We Better Protect Customers of CEXs?

In order to build a 'responsible digital asset ecosystem' for crypto-businesses and customers,[115] MAS has proposed new regulations to tackle the challenges to consumer protection highlighted in this chapter. Notably, MAS does not regulate in a vacuum and its proposed measures do not go as far as to conclude on the nature of crypto-assets as property. Much of the questions of whether crypto-assets can be considered incorporeal property, whether they also serve as money for particular purposes, or whether they can be subject to a trust, have been dealt with by the courts. The object of regulation by MAS is then the activities of crypto-asset businesses. One might contrast this to the approach in civilian jurisdictions where the types of incorporeal property are more clearly delineated, and where it is more common practice for regulators or the government to shoehorn crypto-assets into particular types of property. For instance, bitcoin was characterised as *meuble incorporel* (incorporeal movable property) by the French *Conseil d'État* in 2018.[116] In contrast, it may be inappropriate for regulators in Singapore to determine the precise features of crypto-assets as property given the looser categories of property

[111] MAS, *PSN08 Notice on Disclosures and Communications* at Annex A1-A4.

[112] That is, it is 'fair and reasonable to allow reliance' on the notice: UCTA, s 11(3).

[113] As noted in the UK Digital Assets Consultation Paper (n 3) [16.44].

[114] M Karanicolas, 'Too Long; Didn't Read: Finding Meaning in Platforms' Terms of Service Agreements' (2021) 51 *University of Toledo Law Review* 1.

[115] Above n 14.

[116] See generally K Low and M Hara, 'Cryptoassets and Property', in S Erp & K Zimmermann (eds), *Edward Elgar Research Handbook on EU Property Law* (forthcoming).

in the common law. This then puts industry-level regulation into scrutiny as they are the main, and perhaps only, means by which Singaporean customers of CEXs are protected.

4.1. Are MAS's Proposed Regulations Effective?

MAS has proposed a host of regulations that limit the type of business and marketing activities that CEXs can engage in. With respect to the customer's property rights in the crypto-token, MAS proposed that Digital Payment Token Service Providers segregate customer assets from the company's assets, and ensure that customer assets are held for the benefit of the customer.[117] This directly addresses the issue where customers may be misled into thinking they had ownership of the crypto-token, since CEXs will now be required to hold such tokens on trust for the customer.

However, it may still be plausible for CEXs to argue that because the customer was never the owner of the crypto-token that was exchanged, that they do not fall into the category of 'cash and digital payment tokens belonging to customers'.[118] For instance, Crypto.com's T&Cs explicitly indicate that the customer's 'rights in relation to any On-Exchange Assets are limited to a contractual obligation for crypto.com to provide an equivalent amount and type of On-Exchange Assets'.[119]

To some extent, the risk of 'purchasing' a crypto-token without gaining ownership of it may be mitigated by the proposed disclosure rules which will require CEXs to provide written disclosures as to 'the consequences for the customers' assets if the [CEX] becomes insolvent'.[120] But this may result in a similar situation with existing T&Cs and disclosure rules where the customer is unmotivated and ill-equipped to comprehend the T&Cs.

The likely inadequacy of disclosure rules makes the business practice of limiting the customer's rights to a contractual one to the equivalent value of the crypto-token worth revisiting for the regulators and the courts. With respect to the former, the MAS has proposed restrictions on the types of business activities that digital payment token service providers may engage in (eg restrictions on lending or using customer assets as security[121]), but it does not go so far as to require CEXs to grant customers ownership of the crypto-tokens they purchase. Indeed, there are no marketing restrictions that stop a CEX from offering a customer to 'buy' and 'sell' crypto-tokens without granting them legal ownership of the crypto-token.

[117] MAS, *Consultation Paper on Proposed Amendments to the Payment Services Regulations* (P007, July 2023) ('MAS Proposed Amendments') [4.2]–[4.5].
[118] DPT Consultation Paper (n 13) [4.5].
[119] Crypto.com, 'Exchange Terms and Conditions (14 Feb 2023)' cl 5.2.
[120] MAS Proposed Amendments (n 117) [4.7].
[121] DPT Consultation Paper (n 13) [4.12]–[4.14].

How might the proposed regulations be relevant for the courts? Should the regulations come into effect, they may influence any discussion on the certainty of intention necessary to find a trust since failing to do so would render the CEX regulatorily noncompliant.[122] It is then up to the courts to reject the argument that the CEX did not intend for the crypto-tokens purchased by customers to be 'customer assets'.[123] They could do so by taking a broad interpretation of 'customer assets' or by relying on the representations made by the CEX in marketing when interpreting the T&Cs.[124] While much of this will depend on the exact wording of the implemented regulations, it is clear that the proposed regulations in their present state do not guarantee that customers of CEXs will always have a proprietary interest in the assets they purchase on the CEX.

Separately, MAS's had also explicitly referenced products that 'offer attractive yields for customers that hold DPTs' with the CEXs where the yield is earned through 'staking or lending activities'.[125] It had also cited how the 'collapse of a number of cryptocurrency trading platforms, where a few had conducted staking or lending activities, had led to significant consumer harm', making clear the significant frequency and risk posed to customers of Earn-type products. In response, MAS has proposed a restriction on mortgaging, charging, pledging, or hypothecating retail customer crypto-tokens.

MAS's approach is not as entity-specific as the US, where the Securities and Exchanges Commission has cracked down on particular CEXs offering staking services.[126] At the very minimum, MAS's proposed rule would resolve the earlier question on the enforceability of Earn T&Cs where the crypto-tokens were used as security. However, the generality of the proposed restriction may be defeated by industry practices. Notably, most Earn products do not entail the explicit 'lending and staking of retail customer assets'.[127] Furthermore, CEXs like Liquid and Zipmex can comfortably argue that the customer never had any proprietary interest in the crypto-tokens (where the customer does not merely transfer previously owned tokens) and thus such tokens did not constitute 'customer assets' – although it is noted that this would require the proposed rule on holding customer assets on trust to be ineffective.

However, it might be possible for regulators like MAS to issue clarification as to how certain types of arrangements, transactions, or products will be regarded.

[122] See discussion on *Quoine* and *Cryptopia* in section 3.2.1.

[123] However, it is noted that arguing that the business was intentionally noncompliant may be desirable for CEXs in a dispute between a customer and a CEX in liquidation.

[124] Notwithstanding the precise effect of various non-reliance clauses, this was a consideration by the NZHC in *Cryptopia* (n 22) [176]–[178].

[125] DPT Consultation Paper (n 13) [4.12].

[126] US SEC, 'Kraken to Discontinue Unregistered Offer and Sale of Crypto Asset Staking-As-A-Service Program and Pay $30 Million to Settle SEC Charges' (9 February 2023). Available at: www.sec.gov/news/press-release/2023-25.

[127] MAS, *Response to Public Consultation on Proposed Regulatory Measures for Digital Payment Token Services (Part 1)*, [3.12].

For instance, MAS in 2022 had changed its position in its 'Payment Services Act FAQs' to regard stablecoins as digital payment tokens rather than e-money.[128] To address the legal ambiguity in CEX T&Cs, MAS could issue guidance stating that all Earn arrangements would be regarded as ones that use customer assets as security. However, this would still face difficulties as CEXs may rebrand and reframe their Earn products altogether. For instance, the product could be restructured as a sale of customer crypto-tokens where the regular yield paid to customers acts as an interest payment for delayed payment of the equivalent token.

The legal ambiguity surrounding the characteristics of crypto-assets as property thus offers two challenges for regulators. Firstly, because the law is unclear in this regard, it is possible for CEXs to frame legal arrangements in a way such that regulations will not apply. Secondly, regulators must decide to what extent they can and should protect consumers from high-risk products or services. MAS may be incurring excessive costs in monitoring and enforcement should it be committed to stamping out products and services it deems as harmful. It is thus not unreasonable to expect consumers to accept some of the risks assuming consumers are aware of both their legal arrangements with CEXs, as well as the rules to which CEXs are subject.

The problem then seems to be the extent to which consumers are aware of these regulations and legal arrangements in the first place. It is already mandatory for CEXs to disclose the risks of losing all digital payment tokens to customers;[129] the proposed regulations also suggest greater risk disclosures and obtaining explicit consent.[130] However, as mentioned, such disclosures may fail by design because the product itself is riddled with legal ambiguities that consumers cannot meaningfully appreciate. Regulators like MAS may thus have to bear some additional cost by regulating at the entity level (eg through the licensing regime under the PSA) to work more closely with CEXs to ensure their business practices are aligned with the regulatory goals.

Nonetheless, MAS' proposed regulations will likely set new industry standards that might impact civil actions against CEXs. For instance, the courts might more readily hold that non-reliance clauses or particular business practices are unreasonable per UCTA, s 3 or that they must be separately brought to the customer's attention. However, that the courts can fill in regulatory gaps in this way should not be taken for granted. Because Singaporean consumers are relatively non-litigious,[131] such an opportunity to fill the gap may not even arise.

[128] MAS, *Frequently Asked Questions (FAQs) on the Payment Services Act (PS ACT)*, Question 23.

[129] Above n 111.

[130] For example, non-retail customers should receive 'clear risk disclosure document and [the DPTSP must] obtain the customer's explicit consent': DPT Consultation Paper (n 13) [4.14].

[131] Contrast the lack of litigation from Singaporean consumers in the wake of multiple CEX insolvencies (notwithstanding the moratoriums) with that of the quick collective action by US consumers: see above n 26.

5. Conclusion

Singaporean regulators have an enormous responsibility to ensure that customers are protected in the event of CEX insolvencies. Ex ante insolvency, the regulator can determine the type of legal relationship between the customer, CEX, and the crypto-token as property. The challenges here are not unique to the crypto industry: businesses regularly exploit regulatory gaps or ambiguities for their own benefit.[132] Ex post insolvency, the regulations will be relevant in how the courts determine what is a reasonable clause or a relevant public policy consideration in individual creditor actions and insolvency proceedings respectively. Regulators can also facilitate settlements between the CEX and its customers to ensure the customers' interests are protected prior to the CEX's distribution of assets.

These challenges are not confined to Singapore's regulatory environment. Legal ambiguities and regulatory caution have led to global shortcomings in customer protection in the wake of CEX insolvencies. Singapore's proposed measures take an important step by defining the type of crypto industry it wishes to build by directly restricting undesirable business practices. But as present CEX T&Cs have shown, regulation alone cannot shield customers from harm. Indeed, business practices that exploit the ambiguity of the law, resulting in disproportionate consumer harm, may require stronger regulatory action that eliminates such practices altogether. How the courts treat consumer risk and how regulators will ensure customer protection ex post adversity is worthy of further attention.

[132] For example, in the automobile industry, Y Konishi and S Managi, 'Do Regulatory Loopholes Distort Technical Change? Evidence From New Vehicle Launches under the Japanese Fuel Economy Regulation' (2020) 104 *Journal of Environmental Management* 102377.

6

Blockchain Tokenisation: 'NFTy' Trick or Griftonomics?

TIMOTHY CHAN AND KELVIN FK LOW

1. Introduction

The term 'tokenisation' became something of a buzzword in late 2021 and early 2022 amidst massive blockchain hype. While that hysteria was significantly dampened over late 2022's long and harsh 'crypto winter',[1] 2023 saw a discernible resurgence of interest in blockchain projects. Hong Kong, in particular, pivoted to a crypto-friendly stance,[2] with significant institutional players expressing interest in entering the crypto market there.[3] Interest in 'tokenisation' is again on the rise.[4]

The term 'tokenisation' within crypto generally refers to the process of 'digitally representing assets or items of value through a smart contract on a blockchain'.[5] Proponents contend that the assets that can be thus 'represented' include not only intangible asset classes which have traditionally been securitised (such as mortgages and other receivables) but also high-value *physical* assets, such as land and chattels like wine and art. The tokenisation of the former asset class is relatively

[1] Pak Yiu, D Loh and F Regalado, '"Crypto winter" to "ice age"? What 2023 holds for digital assets' (Nikkei, 30 December 2022). Available at: www.asia.nikkei.com/Business/Business-Spotlight/Crypto-winter-to-ice-age-What-2023-holds-for-digital-assets.

[2] C Mellow, 'Hong Kong Is Now Courting Crypto. What's Behind the Switch' (Barron's, 11 April 2023). Available at: www.barrons.com/articles/hong-kong-crypto-bitcoin-3be92a76.

[3] D Wee, 'DBS Plans to Apply for License to Offer Crypto in HK' (Bloomberg, 13 February 2023). Available at: www.bloomberg.com/news/articles/2023-02-13/dbs-plans-to-apply-for-license-to-offer-crypto-to-hk-customers.

[4] See most recently Citigroup, 'Money, Tokens, and Games: Blockchain's Next Billion Users and Trillions in Value' (30 March 2023). Available at: www.icg.citi.com/icghome/what-we-think/citigps/insights/money-tokens-and-games. See also, eg, W McCurdy, 'BlackRock CEO Says, "Next Generation for Markets" Is Tokenization' (Yahoo Finance, 1 Dec 2022). Available at: www.finance.yahoo.com/news/blackrock-ceo-says-next-generation-120411520.html; Boston Consulting Group, 'Relevance of on-chain asset tokenization in "crypto winter"' (August 2022). Available at: www.documents.addx.co/relevance_of_onchain_asset_tokenization_in_crypto_winter.pdf.

[5] Monetary Authority of Singapore, 'MAS Partners the Industry to Pilot Use Cases in Digital Assets' (Media Releases, 31 May 2022). Available at: www.mas.gov.sg/news/media-releases/2022/mas-partners-the-industry-to-pilot-use-cases-in-digital-assets.

unproblematic since dematerialisation has already allowed the widespread and efficient trading of securities through intermediaries. Although we do not often speak of them as tokenisation systems, effectively any ledger or register system recording assets entails tokenisation since the ledger or registry entry essentially 'represents' the underlying asset, albeit without the farfetched and impractical consequences that tokenisation proponents assume follow. It is therefore the latter claim about the tokenisation of physical assets that is often presented as revolutionary. It is said to have the potential to lower barriers to investment, improve transparency and security, increase liquidity, and facilitate trade.[6] Such statements emanate not only from industry players who are naturally interested in promulgating the purported advantages of such technology to boost profits but also unfortunately from regulators such as HM Land Registry[7] and the Monetary Authority of Singapore ('MAS').[8] The impression given to the public, therefore, is that the tokenisation of physical assets is not only legally effective but also holds the promise of a revolutionary new medium of investment for the future.

2. The Rise of Blockchain Tokenisation

'Tokenisation' means 'different things to different people'.[9] While commonly associated with the blockchain movement in today's headlines, the term in fact originated in data security, where it refers to the 'process of replacing actual sensitive data elements with non-sensitive data elements that have no exploitable value for data security purposes'[10] using various encryption procedures.[11] An example of such tokenisation is Visa's security technology known as 'Visa Token Service', which 'replaces 16-digit Visa account numbers with a token that only Visa can unlock'. Tokenisation in this context enables 'frictionless, card-free payments'

[6] See, eg, MAS, ibid; B Vagadia, *Digital Disruption* (Cham, Springer, 2020), 159; R Ramakrishnan and BE Raj, 'The World of NFTs (Non-Fungible Tokens): The Future of Blockchain and Asset Ownership' in AB Mnaouer and LC Fourati (eds), *Enabling Blockchain Technology for Secure Networking and Communications* (Pennsylvania, IGI Global, 2021) 99; Schindlers Attorneys, 'Tokenisation of Property' (29 September 2021). Available at: www.schindlers.co.za/news/tokenisation-of-property/; Baker Tilly, 'What to know about real estate tokenization' (17 March 2022). Available at: www.bakertilly.com/insights/what-know-about-real-estate-tokenization.

[7] HM Land Registry, 'HM Land Registry to explore the benefits of blockchain' (1 October 2018). Available at: www.gov.uk/government/news/hm-land-registry-to-explore-the-benefits-of-blockchain.

[8] Monetary Authority of Singapore, 'MAS Partners the Industry to Pilot Use Cases in Digital Assets' (n 5).

[9] C Kerrigan, 'Tokenisation in the Real Estate Industry' (2020) 3 *JIBFL* 198.

[10] See T Winston et al, 'How to use tokenization to improve data security and reduce audit scope' (AWS Security Blog, 25 Jan 2022). Available at: www.aws.amazon.com/blogs/security/how-to-use-tokenization-to-improve-data-security-and-reduce-audit-scope/; KFK Low, 'The Emperor's New Art: Cryptomania, Art & Property' (2022) 86 *Conveyancer and Property Lawyer* 378.

[11] See, eg, F Betül Durak et al, 'FAST: Secure and High-Performance Format-Preserving Encryption and Tokenization' in M Tibouchi and HX Wang (eds), *Advances in Cryptology – ASIACRYPT 2021* (Cham, Springer, 2021) 465.

without exposing the sensitive card number which could create vulnerability to fraud.[12] This helps to facilitate e-commerce significantly.

With the advent of blockchain technology, the term 'tokenisation' took on a radically different meaning. The Ethereum blockchain was designed to allow entire programs to be coded onto the blockchain.[13] It became possible to create second-level token systems operating atop the Ethereum blockchain,[14] envisioned by Vitalik Buterin (the founder of the Ethereum blockchain) to have applications 'ranging from sub-currencies representing assets such as USD or gold to company stocks' to 'individual tokens representing smart property'.[15] This architecture made possible the first tokenisation craze in the form of the initial coin offering, or 'ICO', arguably a blatant feint to avoid securities regulation.[16] Project developers created blockchain 'tokens' associated either with some interest in the future governance of the project or future utility,[17] which were offered to investors and typically backed only by a 'white paper' containing a 'general description of the project to be executed and the benefits and disruption that project can bring to the table'.[18] At the outset, it was thought that ICOs fell in a regulatory grey area and therefore offered a flexible approach to corporate fundraising[19] attracting tremendous interest[20] as a result of regulatory arbitrage. But the under-regulation of the ICO sector brought with it significant risks since ICOs were often issued without proper prospectus disclosure and featured little or no corporate governance mechanisms.[21] Interest in ICOs waned drastically from 2019, attributed in part to a 2017 SEC ruling that the DAO's ICO was a security offering, eliminating much of the desired flexibility (or regulatory arbitrage) that had attracted issuers to this business model,[22] and in part to the revelation that a large proportion of ICO launches were outright scams.[23]

[12] See M Saini, 'Visa tokens overtake payments giant's physical cards in circulation' (Reuters, 24 August 2022) at www.reuters.com/business/finance/visa-tokens-overtake-payments-giants-physical-cards-circulation-2022-08-24/#sq_h5j2z0srzk.

[13] See H Arslanian, *The Book of Crypto – The Complete Guide to Understanding Bitcoin, Cryptocurrencies and Digital Assets* (Cham, Springer, 2022) 95; Ethereum Developer Resources, 'Smart Contract Languages' (updated 2 September 2022). Available at: www.ethereum.org/en/developers/docs/smart-contracts/languages/.

[14] See Etherscan, 'Navigating the ERC-20 Token Standard' (Information Center, updated May 2022) Available at: www.info.etherscan.com/erc-20-fungible-token-standard/.

[15] V Buterin, 'Ethereum: A Next-Generation Smart Contract and Decentralized Application Platform' (2014). Available at: www.ethereum.org/en/whitepaper/.

[16] cf L Shin, *The Cryptopians: Idealism, Greed, Lies, and the Making of the First Big Cryptocurrency Craze* (New York: Public Affairs, 2022) 35, 69–72.

[17] See A Gurrea-Martínez and N Remolina, 'The Law and Finance of Initial Coin Offerings' in C Brummer (ed), *Cryptoassets: Legal, Regulatory, and Monetary Perspectives* (Oxford, Oxford University Press, 2019) 120.

[18] Ibid 125.

[19] See K Yeung, 'Regulation by Blockchain: The Emerging Battle for Supremacy between the Code *of* Law and Code *as* Law' (2019) 82 *MLR* 207, 226–30.

[20] R Rau, R Wardrop and L Zingales (eds), *The Palgrave Handbook of Technological Finance* (Palgrave MacMillan, 2021), 175.

[21] Gurrea-Martínez and Remolina, 'The Law and Finance of Initial Coin Offerings' (n 17).

[22] Rau et al, *The Palgrave Handbook of Technological Finance* (n 20), 178.

[23] R Rajbhandari, *A Book About Blockchain: How Companies Can Adopt Public Blockchain to Leap Into the Future* (New York, Business Expert Press, 2021) 1.

But blockchain tokenisation evolved in the wake of the ICO crash through the emergence of the non-fungible token ('NFT') bubble of 2021 and early 2022, with NFTs from the 'Bored Ape Yacht Club' ('BAYC') collection famously reaching a record high price of some $3.4 million in September 2021.[24] NFTs, like ICO tokens, are issued on blockchains with smart contract functionality such as Ethereum, but are christened 'non-fungible' because they are designed to be unique, in that they are serialised and often linked to an image, either on the blockchain itself or via an IPFS link.[25] Here, the term 'fungible' is used loosely and simply means 'interchangeable' rather than bearing its legal definition.[26] Some NFTs purported to offer membership perks to holder communities,[27] while others offered the promise of future utility in blockchain games.[28] Given that many of these use-cases function identically to securities, they have naturally drawn interest from regulators like the US Securities Exchange Commission, and litigation is ongoing.[29]

Beyond such nebulous use-cases, one key theme of the NFT movement is the claim that 'anything can be tokenised'. It is said that NFTs make it possible to 'tokenise things like art, collectibles, even real estate'[30] because, '[a]s NFTs are essentially deeds, one day you could buy a car or home using ETH and receive the deed as an NFT in return'.[31] Tokenisation in this form (which we refer to as 'blockchain tokenisation') refers to the 'process of converting the value of a tangible or an intangible asset (any tradable object) into a digital form (i.e., the token) that can be algorithmically generated, digitally represented, and traded over a blockchain network'.[32] Central to this claim is the idea that the trading of a digital token will be effective to 'transfer the ownership of the physical asset from the seller to the buyer'.[33] As mentioned above, proponents of this technology claim that tokenisation will lower barriers to investment, improve transparency and security, increase liquidity, and facilitate trade.[34] The extent of the optimism surrounding blockchain

[24] R Perper, 'Rare Bored Ape Yacht Club NFT Sells for Record $3.4 Million USD' (Hypebeast, 26 October 2021). Available at: www.hypebeast.com/2021/10/bored-ape-yacht-club-nft-3-4-million-record-sothebys-metaverse.

[25] See Low, 'The Emperor's New Art', n 10.

[26] R Goode, 'Are Intangible Assets Fungible?' [2003] *Lloyd's Maritime and Commercial Law Quarterly* 379.

[27] D van Boom, 'How Bored Ape Yacht Club NFTs Became $400K Status Symbols' (CNet, 28 April 2022). Available at: www.cnet.com/culture/internet/how-bored-ape-yacht-club-nfts-became-400k-status-symbols/.

[28] See Yuga Labs, 'Otherside' at https://otherside.xyz/.

[29] See B van Voris, A Versprille and C Dolmetsch, 'Ripple Ruling on Crypto Rejected by Federal Judge in Terra Case' (Bloomberg, 31 July 2023). Available at: www.bloomberg.com/news/articles/2023-07-31/ripple-ruling-on-crypto-rejected-by-federal-judge-in-terra-case; A Versprille, 'SEC's Crypto Dragnet Widens to NFTs in Case with Media Firm' (Bloomberg, 29 August 2023). Available at: www.bloomberg.com/news/articles/2023-08-28/sec-expands-crypto-dragnet-to-nfts-with-case-against-media-firm.

[30] Ethereum.org, 'Non-fungible tokens (NFT)' (updated 18 October 2022). Available at: www.ethereum.org/en/nft/.

[31] Ibid.

[32] MC Lacity and H Treiblmaier (eds), *Blockchains and the Token Economy* (Cham, Springer, 2022) 158.

[33] G Ferrara et al, 'Physical Assets Tokenization for Blockchain Market' in D Camacho et al (eds), *Intelligent Distributed Computing XIV* (Cham, Springer, 2022) 274.

[34] See n 6 above.

tokenisation is demonstrated in a report by the Boston Consulting Group forecasting that the tokenisation of global illiquid assets will be a '$16 trillion business opportunity' by 2030.[35] More recently, despite dampened expectations following the crypto crash of 2022, Citigroup in a March 2023 report estimated the value of the tokenisation market to be $4 to $5 trillion by 2030.[36]

In view of these widespread claims of tokenisation's revolutionary potential, it is unsurprising to find that various attempts have been made to implement the tokenisation and fractionalisation of exogenous physical assets. Yet, none have achieved mainstream adoption. Real estate, in particular, has always been of key interest to the tokenisation movement,[37] but early initiatives to develop blockchain registries in countries such as Honduras and Sweden came to nought.[38] In England, from March 2019, HM Land Registry conducted a prototype 'digital transfer' via a blockchain transaction,[39] but as of 2022, there was no concrete role for blockchain tokenisation in the Land Registry's latest strategy documents.[40] More recent applications of tokenisation in this context are self-evidently securities, such as SDAX's recently reported offering of a tokenised residential development in Melbourne[41] and Kasa's 'digital asset-backed securities', which are intended to be launched in Singapore.[42] Similarly, Roofstock's attempts to tokenise rental homes in the United States involve the interposition of incorporated companies to hold title to those properties.[43]

Attempts have also been made to tokenise unique chattels, such as paintings, wine, whisky[44] and diamonds. Relying on crypto-friendly legislation, a Swiss company called Sygnum Bank AG in 2021 tokenised Picasso's *Fillette au beret* as

[35] Boston Consulting Group, (n 4).

[36] Citigroup, (n 4), 4.

[37] Kerrigan, 'Tokenisation in the Real Estate Industry' (n 9); O Konashevych, 'General Concept of Real Estate Tokenization on Blockchain' (2020) 9(1) *European Property Law Journal* 21.

[38] See R Thomas and C Huang, 'Blockchain, the Borg Collective and Digitalisation of Land Registries' (2017) 1 *Conveyancer and Property Lawyer* 14; A Proskurovska and S Dörry, 'The Blockchain Challenge for Sweden's Housing and Mortgage Markets' (2022) 54(8) *Economy and Space* 1569.

[39] L Tombs 'Could blockchain be the future of the property market? (HM Land Registry, 24 May 2019). Available at: www.hmlandregistry.blog.gov.uk/2019/05/24/could-blockchain-be-the-future-of-the-property-market/.

[40] HM Land Registry, 'HM Land Registry Strategy 2022+' (31 August 2022). Available at: www. at www.gov.uk/government/publications/hm-land-registry-strategy-2022/hm-land-registry-strategy-2022#who-we-are; HM Land Registry, 'Business Plan 2022–2025' (31 August 2022). Available at: www.assets.publishing.service.gov.uk/government/uploads/system/uploads/attachment_data/file/1101703/HMLR_Business_Plan_2022_to_2025.pdf.

[41] B Cher, 'SDAX Financial raises S$24m in Series B round led by Straits Trading and PSA' (Business Times, 21 December 2021). Available at: www.businesstimes.com.sg/garage/sdax-financial-raises-s24m-in-series-b-round-led-by-straits-trading-and-psa.

[42] T Tay, 'Kasa gets ready to launch fractional investing of Singapore properties' (EdgeProp Singapore, 22 April 2022). Available at: www.edgeprop.sg/property-news/kasa-gets-ready-launch-fractional-investing-singapore-properties.

[43] B Liu, 'Roofstock Sells Alabama Rental Property Via NFT' (Blockworks, 4 February 2023). Available at: www.blockworks.co/news/roofstock-sells-property-via-nft.

[44] See C Dolghier, 'Zilliqa Tokenises Rare Single-Malt Scotch Whisky Casks, Now Available to Accredited Investors on Hg Exchange' (The Tokenizer, 21 January 2021). Available at: www.thetokenizer.io/2021/01/21/zilliqa-tokenises-rare-single-malt-scotch-whisky-casks-now-available-to-accredited-investors-on-hg-exchange/.

well as a bottle of Chateau Latour 2012,[45] and Liechtenstein-based VP Bank is developing custodial tokenisation services for artwork and other physical assets.[46] Surprisingly, the fact that the tokenisation process for art (which necessarily involves the reproduction of the painting in digital form)[47] in these cases likely amounts to a breach of copyright has received little attention.[48] In the US, Icecap Diamonds offers tokenised diamonds for sale, claiming that '[i]f you buy the token you own the diamond'.[49] But in Commonwealth jurisdictions such as England, attempts to tokenise artwork have thus far required the interposition of a trust structure using an independent professional trustee as an intermediary.[50]

3. Legal Risks in Asset Tokenisation

It is striking that, despite the numerous benefits claimed by proponents of asset tokenisation, no projects to date have achieved mainstream adoption. Tokenisation evangelists generally assume that property interests in exogenous assets can be passed effectively via blockchain transactions. Naturally, the claimed benefits can only be reaped if that is true. But to what extent do institutions and investors participating in tokenisation structures run the legal risk of transactions failing to allocate title in the intended manner?

3.1. Assets Subject to Registration Regimes

At the outset, it is clear that in the case of property subject to a registration regime, such as land and shares, tokenisation will be ineffective to transfer title to the extent of non-registration in the relevant register. Blockchain transactions cannot of themselves effect discrete physical operations in the real world, such

[45] M L Rivers, 'The Art of Tokenization: How A Picasso Painted Itself onto the Blockchain' (Forbes Digital Assets, 27 April 2022). Available at: www.forbes.com/sites/martinrivers/2022/04/27/the-art-of-tokenization-how-a-picasso-painted-itself-onto-the-blockchain/?sh=37414c877290.

[46] See Tatler Singapore, 'Asset appreciation: VP Bank is transforming the investment landscape with tokenisation' (31 December 2022). Available at: www.tatlerasia.com/power-purpose/wealth/asset-appreciation-vp-bank-is-transforming-the-investment-landscape-with-tokenisation; E Reguerra, 'Liechtenstein's VP Bank taps Metaco to expand custody and tokenization services' (Cointelegraph, 4 April 2023). Available at: www.cointelegraph.com/news/liechtenstein-s-vp-bank-taps-metaco-to-expand-custody-and-tokenization-services.

[47] See Low, 'The Emperor's New Art' (n 10).

[48] A Chinese court reportedly decided that the reproduction of a painting in the form of an NFT amounted to copyright infringement: see P Culjkovic, 'NFTs and the copyright dilemma' (Lexology, 23 September 2022). Available at: www.lexology.com/library/detail.aspx?g=83b86e8b-5a92-40b9-9326-fa3840f9c110.

[49] Icecap, 'Terms & Conditions Governing Icecap Diamond Tokens' (25 July 2022). Available at: www.icecap.diamonds/terms/.

[50] See Wassielawyer, 'The NFT-linked Trust' (20 February 2022). Available at: www.cryptoconsigliere.substack.com/p/the-nft-linked-trust?r=18x1cq&utm_campaign=post&utm_medium=web&s=r (the author identifies himself as a 'London Finance Lawyer').

as register entries on a land register.[51] So the claim that land can be straightforwardly tokenised and reduced to an NFT, in the absence of significant reform of land registration regimes,[52] is simply misguided. Although examples exist, most entail smoke and mirrors: a Manhattan landowner claimed to have listed an office building 'as an NFT' for 15,000 ETH. Yet, the description of the NFT purported only to give the purchaser 'exclusive rights to acquire the building'; it caveated that '[d]ue to the nature of real estate sales, the sale of the NFT does not warrant the completion of the real estate transaction, or reflect the transfer of the deed or title. The traditional real estate process must still be complete (*sic*)'.[53] The interposition of the NFT served no purpose other than hype. And registered land is not the only asset to which such restrictions apply – legal title to certificated shares passes only upon registration.[54] Of course, while legal interests in registered assets cannot pass automatically with the sale of a blockchain token, it may be possible to effect tokenisation through a trust. It suffices here to note that the use of a trust structure makes the tokenisation process functionally indistinguishable from existing modes of securitisation, save that the interposition of the blockchain introduces various risks instead of creating efficiencies, as we discuss in the penultimate section.

A further obstacle to the tokenisation of registered property is that such property is often also subject to additional restrictions on property ownership. For example, the fractionalisation of real estate beyond four owners is not possible at law in England since what is contemplated is the creation of multiple legal tenancies in common, which has not been possible since 1926.[55] Under Singapore law, although there is no objection to the creation of a legal tenancy-in-common, there are multiple restrictions on the ownership of property which apply to residential property[56] and public housing[57] and which may prohibit foreigners from becoming owners or co-owners of such property.

3.2. Chattels

In relation to valuable chattels, the position is complex. In the analysis below, we seek to demonstrate that, as the law stands, there are grave doubts about the viability of passing title to a chattel via a crypto-token transaction and that attempts to

[51] See, eg, RM Garcia-Teruel and H Simón-Moreno, 'The Digital Tokenization of Property Rights. A Comparative Perspective' (2021) 41 *Computer Law & Security Review* 105543.

[52] And such reform may be far from desirable: see, eg, V Ooi, KP Soh, and J Soh, 'Blockchain Land Transfers: Technology, Promises and Perils' (2022) 45 *Computer Law & Security Review* 105672.

[53] Opensea, 'One Eleven | 109–111 West 24th Street, NYC'. Available at: www.opensea.io/assets/ethereum/0x495f947276749ce646f68ac8c248420045cb7b5e/101384670028251040624379703957067301496215794066136880463632652255105021640705.

[54] *Ireland v Hart* [1902] 1 Ch 522; *J Sainsbury Plc v O'Connor (Inspector of Taxes)* [1991] 1 WLR 963, 977.

[55] Law of Property Act 1925, s 36(2).

[56] Residential Property Act 1976 (Cap 274, 2020 Rev Ed) (Sing).

[57] Housing and Development Act 1959 (Cap 129, 2020 Rev Ed) (Sing).

bypass these legal obstacles through law reform or the devices of equity will not remove the need for an intermediary.

At law, the passing of title to chattels outside of a sale of goods generally requires either delivery or deed.[58] The transaction of a crypto-token clearly will not constitute physical delivery: as was said in the context of smart contracts: 'the "smart contract" will not move trucks or build houses.'[59] It is also hard to see how such a transaction could constitute constructive delivery. For example, if the chattel were held on bailment in a warehouse, some acknowledgement by the bailee would be required for an effective attornment.[60] As to passing of title by deed, such a transaction would not constitute a deed under English law, contrary to widespread misconception among crypto-enthusiasts,[61] given the statutory requirements of attestation[62] and delivery (of the deed).[63] Attestation in this context requires that witnesses be 'present',[64] which (at least in the context of wills) traditionally involved the witnesses being in the 'visual presence' of the person executing the document.[65] 'Delivery' refers not to physical delivery but rather an 'act done so as to evince an intention to be bound',[66] which must be separate from the mere execution of the deed by signature.[67] At common law, while there was no requirement of attestation, deeds must be executed in 'paper or parchment', 'sealed', and delivered.[68] In the absence of statutory reform, therefore, the mere execution of a blockchain transaction is unlikely to constitute a deed.

Where the Sale of Goods Act applies, the general rule is modified such that property passes when intended to pass.[69] It has often been assumed that the Act would apply to the sale of a tokenised chattel.[70] But this overlooks the crucial question of whether the transfer of a co-ownership interest, including a fractional interest, is a 'sale' for the purposes of the Act. A fractional interest in specific

[58] *Cochrane v Moore* (1890) 25 QBD 57; M Bridge, L Gullifer, KFK Low and G McMeel (eds), *The Law of Personal Property*, 3rd edn (London, Sweet & Maxwell, 2022) para 29-001.

[59] KFK Low and E Mik, 'Pause the Blockchain Legal Revolution' (2020) 69 ICLQ 135, 170.

[60] Bridge et al (n 58), para 12-003; Sale of Goods Act 1979, s 29(4).

[61] See text accompanying n 31.

[62] Law of Property (Miscellaneous Provisions) Act 1989, s 1(3)(a).

[63] ibid s 1(3)(b).

[64] See n 62 above.

[65] See, eg, A Learmonth et al, *Williams, Mortimer and Sunnucks on Executors, Administrators and Probate*, 21st edn (London, Sweet & Maxwell, 2018) para 9-20. Note that regulations were passed during the COVID-19 pandemic to include 'presence by means of videoconference or other visual transmission' in the context of wills, but no equivalent proviso has been made in the context of deeds. See the Wills Act 1837, s 9(2) as amended by the Wills Act 1837 (Electronic Communications) (Amendment) (Coronavirus) Order 2020 (SI 2020/952).

[66] *Vincent v Premo Enterprises (Voucher Sales) Ltd* [1969] 2 QB 609, 619; DEC Yale, 'The Delivery of a Deed' (1970) 28(1) CLJ 52.

[67] *Bibby Financial Services Ltd v Magson* [2011] EWHC 2495 (QB), [335].

[68] Note that the requirement of signature did not exist at common law: see HW Tang and KFK Low, *Tan Sook Yee's Principles of Singapore Land Law*, 4th edn (Singapore, LexisNexis, 2019) at 264. The requirement of 'sealing' has recently been affirmed in *Lim Zhipeng v Seow Suat Thin* [2020] 2 SLR 1151; it is unclear whether a seal can be affixed electronically.

[69] Sale of Goods Act 1979, s 17.

[70] H Liu, 'Digital Assets: The Mystery of the "Link"' (2022) 3 *JIBFL* 161, 165.

goods would indeed qualify as 'goods' for the purposes of the Sale of Goods Act.[71] However, given that tokens will typically be purchased using cryptoassets such as Bitcoin and Ethereum, there is serious reason to doubt that the requirement of a 'money consideration called the price' will be satisfied. Notably, a 'clear and liquidated financial advantage accruing to the seller', such as the forgiveness of indebtedness, is not sufficient.[72] A suggestion that 'open source' digital currencies like Bitcoin ought to qualify as money for this purpose[73] rests upon a questionable analogy between cryptoassets like Bitcoin and trading checks, which in *Davies v Customs and Excise Commissioners*[74] were accepted to be 'money consideration' such that there was a sale for the purpose of levying value added tax. The problem is that the trading checks tendered by the buyers in *Davies* represented a claim against the issuing company denominated in fiat currency.[75] They were, therefore, no different from bank cheques or banker's drafts, which are treated as money for the purposes of the definition of 'sale': '[t]he instrument itself may not be money but it is the means by which the seller obtains money'.[76] Such forms of payment are not analogous to cryptoassets such as Bitcoin and Ethereum, which do not represent a claim against an issuer denominated in fiat.[77] Given the current prevalence of the state theory of money over the societary view in many jurisdictions,[78] cryptoassets like Bitcoin and Ethereum are unlikely to qualify as 'money consideration' for the purposes of the Sale of Goods Act 1979. That conclusion is consistent with prevailing views that cryptoassets do not constitute 'currency'[79] and with a recent Singapore decision holding that a USDC 'debt' did not constitute a money debt for the purposes of a statutory demand in insolvency proceedings.[80]

[71] Section 61(1) contains a definition of 'goods'.

[72] M Bridge, *The Sale of Goods*, 4th edn (Oxford: Oxford University Press, 2020), para 2.28; cf *VFS Financial Services Ltd v JF Plant Tyres Ltd* [2013] 1 WLR 2987 at [14].

[73] Bridge, *The Sale of Goods*, ibid, para 2.30.

[74] *Davies v Customs and Excise Commissioners* [1975] 1 WLR 204.

[75] ibid 205.

[76] Bridge (n 72), para 2.28.

[77] Note that other cryptoassets such as USDC, a 'stablecoin', carry a limited right to redemption for fiat currency against an issuer, which may be regarded as a separate chose in action apart from the crypto-token itself: see *ByBit Fintech Limited v Ho Kai Xin* [2023] SGHC 199, [39]. This analysis does not hold for Bitcoin and Ethereum.

[78] See, eg, KFK Low and Y-C Wu, 'The Characterization of Cryptocurrencies in East Asia' in D Fox and S Green (eds), *Cryptocurrencies in Public and Private Law* (Oxford, Oxford University Press, 2019) para 8.02; see also S Green, 'It's Virtually Money' in D Fox and S Green (eds), *Cryptocurrencies in Public and Private Law* (Oxford, Oxford University Press, 2019) paras 2.26–2.43.

[79] See, eg, *B2C2 Ltd v Quoine Pte Ltd* [2019] 4 SLR 17, [142] ('not legal tender in the sense of being a regulated currency issued by a government'); D Fox, 'Cryptocurrencies in the Common Law of Property' in D Fox and S Green (eds), *Cryptocurrencies in Public and Private Law* (Oxford, Oxford University Press, 2019) para 6.61; KFK Low and E Teo, 'Legal Risks of Owning Cryptocurrencies' in D Lee and R Deng (eds), *Handbook of Blockchain, Digital Finance, and Inclusion: Cryptocurrency, FinTech, InsurTech, and Regulation* (London, Academic Press, 2017) 241.

[80] *Algorand Foundation Ltd v Three Arrows Capital Pte Ltd* (HC/CWU 246/2022, unreported); see D Chan, 'Crypto Debt Not Money Debt for Purposes of Statutory Demand, Singapore High Court Rules (WongPartnership, May 2023). Available at: www.wongpartnership.com/upload/medias/KnowledgeInsight/document/18683/CaseWatch_CryptoDebtNotMoneyDebtForPurposesofStatutoryDemand_SingaporeHighCourtRules.PDF. See also *Loh Cheng Lee Aaron v Hodlnaut Pte Ltd* [2023] SGHC

If a transaction involving a token sale in exchange for a cryptoasset consideration is not a sale of goods, it is then likely to be characterised as a barter contract. It has on occasion been suggested that the rules of title transfer under the Sale of Goods Act might apply by analogy.[81] *Koppel v Koppel*[82] provides an example of such reasoning, where the Court of Appeal suggested that the property rules in the Sale of Goods Act applied to any 'document evidencing a transaction for consideration', in that case a contract for the transfer of chattels in consideration for housekeeping and other services. But in *Flynn v Mackin & Mahon*[83] it was held that s 18 of the Sale of Goods Act did not apply to a contract of barter, and elsewhere *Koppel v Koppel* has been suggested to have been decided *per incuriam*.[84] Even if a reasonable case for an analogy can be made, it is not safe to assume that a token sale purporting to pass property in a chattel will be saved by the Sale of Goods Act.

Even if it is possible to pass legal title to chattels via a blockchain transaction (either via the Sale of Goods Act or the generous approach in *Koppel v Koppel*), two important commercial obstacles remain. First, a co-owner cannot be precluded from selling their interest without selling the token.[85] This has been termed the requirement of a 'negative link':[86] in order for asset tokenisation to work, a token transaction must not only be effective to transfer title in the asset (a 'positive' link) but must be the *only way* to transfer title in the asset. The issue this raises is obvious: if it is possible to transfer title in the asset independently of the token, then a subsequent purchaser of the token has no way of ascertaining whether the seller of the token still has good title to the asset, and it is not possible to achieve commercially workable fractionalisation through blockchain tokenisation. The *numerus clausus* principle prevents attempts to circumvent this difficulty through contract: 'incidents of a novel kind' cannot be 'devised and attached to property at the fancy or caprice of any owner'.[87] While it has been suggested that this difficulty might be circumvented by amendment to the Sale of Goods Act,[88] it is far from clear whether such a crypto-friendly amendment is desirable.[89]

323, where the Singapore High Court treated debts denominated in cryptoassets as unliquidated debts for the purposes of a winding up application. The judge expressly stated that 'nothing in [his] decision suggests that cryptocurrency should be treated as money in the general sense' and observed, in any event, that he 'd[id] not find that there has been any acceptance in any major commercial jurisdiction of cryptocurrency as being equivalent to a daily medium of exchange' (at [13]).

[81] *Cochrane v Moore* (n 58), per Lord Esher MR (*obiter*); S Zogg, *Effects of Mistake and Other Defects on the Passage of Legal Title* (Cambridge, Intersentia, 2019) 58; Bridge (n 72), para 3.05. See also R Stevens, *The Laws of Restitution* (Oxford, Oxford University Press, 2023) 195.

[82] *Koppel v Koppel* [1966] 1 WLR 802 at 811 per Harman LJ.

[83] *Flynn v Mackin & Mahon* [1974] IR 101.

[84] C Twigg-Flesner, R Canavan and H MacQueen, *Atiyah and Adams' Sale of Goods*, 13th edn (Edinburgh, Pearson, 2016) 31.

[85] See L Gullifer and D Fox, *Response: Digital assets Call for evidence* (30 July 2021). Available at: www.s3-eu-west-2.amazonaws.com/lawcom-prod-storage-11jsxou24uy7q/uploads/2022/10/Digital-assets-call-for-evidence-responses.pdf, at 27–28; Liu (n 70).

[86] Liu (n 70).

[87] *Keppell v Bailey* (1834) 2 My & K 517.

[88] Liu (n 70), 165.

[89] See the penultimate section below.

Second, even such an amendment would not resolve another commercial impediment to tokenisation, at least on a peer-to-peer level: the seller-in-possession exception to the *nemo dat* rule. Even if it is possible for a buyer to be confident in acquiring property rights to an exogenous asset via an on-chain transaction, the buyer runs the risk of the seller, whilst remaining in possession of the asset, fraudulently reselling the goods to a third party.[90] This is a crucial problem for the notion of peer-to-peer asset tokenisation because any such system makes it incredibly easy for sellers to commit fraud. Should Alice purchase from Bob a bottle of Château Lafite via a token transaction, on Bob's promise to thereafter deliver the bottle to her order, Alice runs the risk that Bob will happily turn around and re-sell the bottle to Carol, who, assuming she takes in good faith and without notice of the sale of Alice, will take free of Alice's interest. One may say that the risk exists in every sale of goods involving a prepayment. But bearing in mind the cryptoverse's obsession with pseudonymity, Alice will have far greater difficulty tracking Bob down and pursuing legal action than the typical defrauded purchaser. Importantly, it is challenging to justify overcoming this difficulty by amending the SGA to disapply the *nemo dat* exceptions in the tokenised asset context, as Liu has suggested.[91] Liu recognises that such situations involve the rights of innocent third parties, who cannot be expected to investigate title.[92] But this is not merely, as Liu suggests, a matter of security of title which can be 'balanced' against the 'need' to 'maintain the integrity of the blockchain as a register'. The *nemo dat* exceptions were incrementally developed at common law[93] and represent a carefully calibrated balance between dynamic and static security that avoids imposing excessive transactional costs on purchasers. How can the seller-in-possession exception be abolished *only* in the context of tokenised goods? Nor is it even practical. Carving out such an exception-to-the-exception would require *all* purchasers of chattels to investigate whether the chattel in question had previously been tokenised (presumably against *all* blockchains), and radically unbalance the law governing the sale of chattels.[94]

3.3. Invoking the Flexibility of Equity

The above discussion demonstrates extensive difficulties with the claim that land and valuable chattels can be straightforwardly tokenised and transferred at law. Barring significant legislative overhaul, proponents of tokenisation should retreat from the claim that *legal* interests can be tokenised and focus on the tokenisation of *equitable* interests.

[90] Sale of Goods Act 1979, s 24.
[91] See Liu (n 70).
[92] ibid.
[93] Bridge et al (n 58), para 31-002.
[94] See TW Merrill and HE Smith, 'Optimal Standardization in the Law of Property: The *Numerus Clausus* Principle' (2000) 110 *Yale Law Journal* 1.

Given the flexibility of the English trust, it seems likely that it is possible to structure blockchain transactions to transfer an equitable interest in land or chattels. Admittedly, the position is not entirely straightforward in view of s 53(1)(c) of the Law of Property Act (which requires a disposition of an equitable interest to be in 'signed writing').[95] But, regardless of whether the transaction of a tokenised interest is a 'disposition', electronic signatures have been held to satisfy statutory references to 'signed writing' for the purposes of s 4 of the Statute of Frauds[96] and s 6(d) of Singapore's Civil Law Act.[97] In the context of s 53(1)(c), the English Court of Appeal in *Hudson v Hathaway* has recently held that subscribing one's name to an email amounts to a sufficient 'signature'.[98] Whilst the extension of this principle to digital signatures of cryptoasset transactions specifically has not yet been tested, the English Law Commission, despite originally proposing reform to clarify the scope and application of s 53(1)(c) in relation to equitable interests in cryptoassets,[99] in its Final Report considered the law sufficiently clear that a digital signature would satisfy the statutory requirement under s 53(1)(c),[100] though oddly without citing *Hudson v Hathaway*. To the extent that *Hudson v Hathaway*, and perhaps future cases, clarifies the position with respect to compliance with s 53(1)(c), it is important to note that such clarification applies also to the existing market for dematerialised securities, which is far larger and more established than that for interests tokenised on blockchains.[101] In Singapore, s 8 of the Electronic Transactions Act 2010 expressly provides for the validity of electronic signatures without excluding dispositions of equitable interests.[102] Finally, it bears stressing that the potential efficacy of an electronic signature so far as compliance with formalities is concerned is unrelated to the question of whether a forged (or unauthorised) electronic signature is likewise effective.[103]

3.4. The Insurmountable Legal Limits to Blockchain Tokenisation

What becomes clear is first that whether or not asset tokenisation is effective to achieve its purported effect is, contrary to popular perception, heavily dependent

[95] The equivalent in Singapore being s 7(2) of the Civil Law Act 1909 (Cap 43, 2020 Rev Ed).

[96] *WS Tankship II BV v Kwangju Bank Ltd* [2011] EWHC 3103 (Comm); *J Pereira Fernandes SA v Mehta* [2006] 2 All ER 891.

[97] *SM Integrated Transware Pte Ltd v Schenker Singapore (Pte) Ltd* [2005] 2 SLR(R) 651; *Joseph Mathew v Singh Chiranjeev* [2010] 1 SLR 338.

[98] *Hudson v Hathway* [2023] 3 All ER 718, [67].

[99] See the Law Commission, *Consultation Paper on Digital Assets* (Law Com No 256, 2022) paras 17.36–17.57.

[100] Law Commission, *Digital Assets: Final Report* (Law Com No 412, 2023) paras 7.75–7.76, endorsing the views of the UK Jurisdiction Task Force, *Legal statement on the issuance and transfer of digital securities under English private law* (2023), paras 119–32.

[101] See the Law Commission, 'Intermediated securities: who owns your shares? A scoping paper' (11 November 2020) paras 7.41–7.63.

[102] Electronic Transactions Act 2010 (Cap 88, 2020 Rev Ed), s 4 read with the First Schedule.

[103] Law Commission, *Electronic execution of documents* (Law Com No 386, 2019) paras 2.33–2.36.

on the type of asset in question, as well as the way the tokenisation framework is structured. This is a trap for unwary investors. Any claim that a linked token transfer is effective to convey a legal interest in land or chattels should be presently viewed with circumspection and even where a trust structure is used, some doubt remains. Perhaps this legal uncertainty is giving pause to even the most forward-looking institutions who might otherwise have proposed blockchain tokenisation projects. And, as we have shown, intermediary interposition remains essential: more circumspect commentators suggest that '[a] trusted caretaker, curator, or other conventional intermediary is required to uphold the tokenized ownership claims that are stored on the distributed ledger and registered to an investor's digital wallet address',[104] and a recent article suggesting a process architecture to support asset tokenisation proposed using a trusted warehousing intermediary.[105] From the consumer perspective, the presence of intermediaries may make tokenisation structures less appealing: one remembers the risk of intermediary misfeasance that gave rise to the litigation in cases such as *Re Goldcorp Exchange Ltd.*[106] Depending on the structure proposed by the intermediary, purchasers of tokenised assets may receive nothing more than the equivalent of a warehouse receipt or delivery warrant conferring no interest in property.[107] And so far crypto intermediaries have given little cause for confidence.[108]

4. A Cost–Benefit Analysis of Tokenisation

The previous section demonstrated the extensive risks attaching to blockchain tokenisation as the law currently stands. Equally significantly, it demonstrated that no amount of legislative reform can enable the peer-to-peer trading of interests in exogenous assets – such reform can at most reduce existing recharacterisation risks and therefore facilitate tokenisation within structures featuring a trusted intermediary such as a custodian or trustee.

What this means is that blockchain tokenisation really achieves just two things and, even then, only through the use of trusted intermediaries: the fractionalisation of interests and the provision of liquidity. So limited, tokenisation is far less groundbreaking than it has been made to appear. In fact, the fractionalisation of physical assets is nothing new. Fractionalisation has been possible at law for centuries and is commonly seen in the syndicated ownership of racehorses.[109]

[104] Lacity and Treiblmaier, *Blockchains and the Token Economy* (n 32), 221.

[105] G Ferrara et al, 'Physical Assets Tokenization for Blockchain Market' (n 33), 278.

[106] [1995] 1 AC 74. Depending on how the transaction is structured, certainty of subject-matter might not be necessary (see Goode's seminal article in 'Are Intangible Assets Fungible' [2003] LMCLQ 379).

[107] See *Dublin City Distillery Ltd v Doherty* [1914] AC 823.

[108] See, eg, Lim, Chapter 5 in this volume, who explores the lack of consumer protection available in respect of another type of crypto intermediaries (exchanges).

[109] See, eg, Equivend, 'First Time Racehorse Ownership FAQs'. Available at: www.equivend.co.uk/racing/1st-time-owners-buying-shares-in-a-racehorse/. See also Twigg-Flesner et al, *Atiyah and Adams' Sale of Goods* (n 84), 276.

In *Marson v Short*, Park J entertained 'no doubt that, in a general sense, a sale of a share in a horse falls within the exception of the statute applicable to sales of goods, wares, or merchandizes',[110] and in *Ellis v Leader* a half share in a colt devolved as property by will.[111] Today, the British Horseracing Authority defines syndication as an arrangement where members 'share the ownership [of] the horse'.[112] Fractional ownership is of course possible not only in relation to racehorses, and commonly features in relation to other valuable chattels such as ships.[113] Apart from direct fractional ownership, it is also possible to fractionalise interests through the medium of a company, as often done in the United States,[114] or a trust. As for the second purported achievement of blockchain tokenisation, liquidity can be created in relation to any type of asset through existing methods of securitisation. While the assets securitised are often receivables, theoretically 'any kind of asset can be securitised':[115] it is possible to securitise commercial real estate and stands of timber[116] and even the entirety of a business through whole business securitisation.[117] We also have market intermediaries such as broker-dealers, which provide the general public easy access to over-the-counter derivative trading of a wide range of commodities from gold to oil.[118] The idea of fractionalising the ownership of physical assets and providing liquidity is far from revolutionary in itself.

There is nothing stopping intermediaries today (provided they are sufficiently trustworthy) from offering services by which they undertake to custody high-value assets, list fractional interests on a bespoke exchange, and allow them to be traded. Such a business model can easily be executed using traditional accounting processes. The true question is whether the use of blockchain technology for accounting and settlement offers any advantages over existing methods, to the extent that it ought to be facilitated by significant legislative overhaul.

4.1. The Fable of Improved Security

Given the hype in the popular media surrounding cryptoassets, it is unsurprising that one of the purported advantages of blockchain tokenisation is the promise

[110] *Marson v Short* (1835) 132 ER 47, 49.
[111] *Ellis v Leader* [1949] Ch 99.
[112] See the British Horseracing Authority, 'Syndicate Code of Conduct' (March 2021). Available at: www.media.britishhorseracing.com/bha/rules/Ownership/Syndicate_CoC.pdf.
[113] Bridge et al (n 58), para 2-037.
[114] Where shares in a racehorse would be issued through a holding company and considered securities in some jurisdictions: see S Dhue, 'Owning a racehorse in the Belmont Stakes is more attainable as fractional ownership platforms grow' (CNBC, 5 June 2021). Available at: www.cnbc.com/2021/06/05/belmont-stakes-investing-in-a-racehorse-is-more-attainable.html.
[115] P Wood, *Project Finance, Securitisations, Subordinated Debt*, 3rd edn (London, Sweet & Maxwell, 2019), para 6-010.
[116] ibid para 6-011.
[117] H Beale et al, *The Law of Security and Title-Based Financing*, 3rd edn (Oxford, Oxford University Press, 2018), para 2.28.
[118] Which creates its own risks: see, eg, H Dempsey, 'LME finds bags of stones instead of nickel in metal warehouse' (*Financial Times*, 18 March 2023). Available at: www.ft.com/content/a8c4d8d5-7c81-4c54-a90a-9f3f60d1bdd2.

of improved security, a veneer which perhaps stems from the supposedly 'immutable' blockchain married with the origins of tokenisation in data security. The Royal Institute of Chartered Surveyors, for example, suggests, therefore, that the '[b]lockchain is considered secure and, if used in transactions across the real-estate market, could significantly reduce the instance of property fraud'.[119] Elsewhere, it is suggested that tokenisation offers 'unparalleled security, as the distributed nature of its ledger inherently better prevents any forms of forgery or record tampering'[120] and 'aids in preventing fraud and may be able to prevent erroneous payments'.[121] But the idea that blockchains provide improved security is unfortunately nothing more than a myth. Blockchain technology is focused on ledger security, not systemic security. The fact that an intermediary uses a blockchain does not say anything about the trustworthiness of the intermediary itself.

More crucially, the end user is always the weakest link: the 'vast majority of land title frauds today target the end user rather than the registry'.[122] A customer seeking to trade interests in a Picasso will be equally vulnerable to phishing whether the intermediary uses blockchain technology or traditional record-keeping methods. In fact, blockchain technology in itself falls *short* of modern payment services standards. The EU Payment Services Directive[123] ('PSD2') generally mandates Strong Customer Authentication,[124] defined as 'an authentication based on the use of two or more elements categorised as knowledge (something only the user knows), possession (something only the user possesses) and inherence (something the user is)'.[125] This accounts for most of the two-factor authentication technologies we are familiar with today. In contrast, blockchain security relies wholly on the private key, which is a single point of failure. Public key cryptography was developed in the 1970s[126] but never deployed for end users to self-custody until the advent of blockchains for a reason: its unsuitability for such a purpose. When tokens are traded through regulated exchanges, such exchanges may have implemented two-factor authentication in compliance with PSD2. But to the extent that asset tokenisation is envisaged to allow direct, peer-to-peer trading of asset-backed tokens on the blockchain, the security of end users is significantly diminished. Multisigs (short for multi-signature) solve the single point of failure problem but exacerbate the self-custody issue since the end user now has to self-custody multiple signatures. Fraud risk is exacerbated by the fact that blockchain projects have often proven to be the province of fraudsters. Reports indicate that more than

[119] Royal Institute of Chartered Surveyors, 'Blockchain and tokenisation in the property sector' (News & opinion, 5 April 2019). Available at: www.rics.org/asean/news-insight/future-of-surveying/data-technology/blockchain-and-tokenisation-in-the-property-sector/.

[120] Tatler Singapore 'Asset appreciation: VP Bank is transforming the investment landscape with tokenisation' (n 46).

[121] Schindlers Attorneys, 'Tokenisation of Property' (n 6).

[122] Low and Mik, 'Pause the Blockchain Legal Revolution' (n 59), 159.

[123] Directive (EU) 2015/2366 of the European Parliament and of the Council on payment services in the internal market [2015] OJ L337/335.

[124] Article 97 (save for excluded transactions).

[125] Article 4(30).

[126] W Diffie and ME Hellman, 'New Directions in Cryptography' (1976) 22 *IEEE Trans Inf Theory* 644.

$100 million worth of NFTs have been misappropriated since July 2021.[127] While such fraud is often perpetuated by tried-and-tested methods such as phishing[128] and social media impersonation,[129] blockchain technology grants fraudsters a wider range of tools to ply their trade. For example, the so-called 'Trojan horse NFT' is programmed to 'create a booby-trapped token: if the user accepts it, it can immediately drain their account'.[130] Admittedly, such programs do not of themselves enable fraud; it is still necessary to deceive the end user into accepting the program, which is likely to take place through a phishing or impersonation attack. However, these programs supercharge the ability of fraudsters to automatically empty victims' accounts. The point is that blockchain 'immutability' is not designed to prevent fraud on end-users. It is designed to prevent ex post modifications of the ledger – registry fraud – which is incredibly rare.

It is hard to see how there is a gain in efficiency from using a blockchain ledger instead of traditional record-keeping methods. Should there be a real need to prevent tampering with the record, this can be done by mandating and, if necessary, encrypting regular backups. Using blockchain ledgers for record-keeping purposes in fact exposes intermediaries to a plethora of new risks. For example, while it is generally thought that an attacker must take over more than 50 per cent of the nodes to gain control of the network in a proof-of-work system, it has been shown that it is sometimes possible to undermine the blockchain with just 25 per cent of the nodes.[131] Nor is the 51 per cent attack so daunting if a blockchain only has a small number of nodes, as the Axie Infinity hack vividly demonstrated.[132] Permissioned systems that use a permissioned Byzantine fault-tolerance consensus algorithm are only secure until one-third of their nodes are compromised.[133] And in the event of fraud, the blockchain's tamper resistance makes it incredibly difficult to carry out rectification when this is, in fact, desirable (either as a response to fraud, as with the Bangladeshi Central Bank heist of 2016,[134] or simply due to inadvertent internal errors). In short, not only does blockchain immutability not protect end

[127] A Hern, 'More than $100m worth of NFTs stolen since July 2021, data shows' (The Guardian, 24 August 2022). Available at: www.theguardian.com/technology/2022/aug/24/nfts-stolen-non-fungible-tokens-criminals-scam-cryptocurrency.

[128] J Crawley, 'OpenSea Says Phishing Attack Impacted 17 Users' (CoinDesk, 21 February 2022). Available at: www.coindesk.com/business/2022/02/21/opensea-says-phishing-attack-impacted-17-users/.

[129] J Coghlan, 'Targeted phishing scam nets $438K in crypto and NFTs from hacked Beeple account' (CoinTelegraph, 23 May 2022). Available at: cointelegraph.com/news/targeted-phishing-scam-nets-428k-in-crypto-and-nfts-from-hacked-beeple-account.

[130] A Hern, 'More than $100m worth of NFTs stolen since July 2021, data shows' (The Guardian, 24 August 2022). Available at: www.theguardian.com/technology/2022/aug/24/nfts-stolen-non-fungible-tokens-criminals-scam-cryptocurrency.

[131] Low and Mik, n 59, 157.

[132] Where US$625 million was lost after hackers gained access to 5 out of 9 nodes: see A Robertson and C Faife, 'A hacker stole $625 million from the blockchain behind NFT game Axie Infinity' (The Verge, 30 March 2022). Available at: www.theverge.com/2022/3/29/23001620/sky-mavis-axie-infinity-ronin-blockchain-validation-defi-hack-nft.

[133] KFK Low, 'Confronting Cryptomania: Can Equity Tame the Blockchain?' (2020) 14 *Journal of Equity* 240, 250.

[134] See Low and Teo, 'Legal Risks of Owning Cryptocurrencies' (n 79), 225.

users from the real-world frauds that are actually commonplace, it also hinders the law's first line of defence to ameliorate such frauds.

4.2. Fractionalisation and Liquidity

The second advantage that blockchain tokenisation commonly claims to offer is increased liquidity, both through fractionalisation and through the possibility of trading through decentralised exchanges.[135] It is said that this will benefit both investors, through increased freedom of choice, and sellers, through the so-called 'liquidity premium'.[136] But fractionalisation may not always be desirable for its own sake, as it creates problems of management. Condominium[137] owners are often reluctant to contribute for repairs,[138] a problem exacerbated when interests of investors and owners diverge. Disputes of this nature cannot be resolved purely by majoritarian rule, which explains why legislation is required to govern strata management and the British Horseracing Authority deems it necessary to regulate the syndication of racehorses for the protection of participants.[139]

Even where fractionalisation is commercially sensible, it does not follow that it will always achieve liquidity benefits. As we have pointed out, it has always been possible for intermediaries to allow the trading of fractional interests. Does anyone really believe that just because an intermediary uses blockchain technology for its back-end processes, a thriving market of investors will appear, eager to invest in a Picasso painting or Birkin bag? In existing examples of intermediated tokenisation using private blockchains, take-up rates have been low. In 2021, Swiss-based Sygnum fractionalised a Picasso and a bottle of Chateau Latour 2012 into 1,000 tokens each. But trading volumes have been low, with only 19 trades for the Picasso and none for the Chateau Latour in all of 2022 and 2023[140] – hardly inspiring.

A tokenisation proponent may suggest that the low volume is because these tokens are tradable only on Sygnum's in-house trading venue, rather than on larger

[135] Tatler Singapore (n 46); M Ozair, 'What Tokenization Is and How It Can Unlock Illiquid and Opaque Markets' (Nasdaq.com, 6 March 2023). Available at: www.nasdaq.com/articles/what-tokenization-is-and-how-it-can-unlock-illiquid-and-opaque-markets?amp; D Jocham, 'Tokenization – Potentials, Challenges and Use Cases in the Financial Industry Environment' (CC Ecosystems News, 14 February 2023). Available at: www.ccecosystems.news/en/tokenization-potentials-challenges-and-use-cases-in-the-financial-industry-environment/.

[136] Deloitte Tax & Consulting, 'The Tokenization of Assets is Disrupting the Financial Industry. Are You Ready?' (2018) 19 *Inside Magazine* 62. Available at: www2.deloitte.com/content/dam/Deloitte/lu/Documents/about-deloitte/Inside/lu-inside19-full.pdf. See also R Bala, 'Tokenization of Assets' in D Tran, M Thai and B Krishnamachari (eds), *Handbook on Blockchain* (Cham, Springer, 2022) 585.

[137] The origin of which term is, in fact, the Latin for 'co-ownership': see A Christudason, 'Subdivided Buildings – Developments in Australia, Singapore and England' (1996) 45 *ICLQ* 343.

[138] See N Crooks, 'Florida to Tackle Condo Reform After Surfside Building Collapse' (Bloomberg, 25 May 2022). Available at: www.bloomberg.com/news/articles/2022-05-24/florida-to-tackle-condo-insurance-reform-after-surfside-collapse#xj4y7vzkg.

[139] British Horseracing Authority, 'Syndicate Code of Conduct' (n 112), 3.

[140] See Sygnum, 'SygnEx'. Available at: www.sygnum.com/sygnex/.

NFT platforms like Opensea, where they would be accessible to larger numbers of investors (or speculators). Even if this is true, participation in a market like OpenSea brings with it a multitude of problems. In the first place, OpenSea charges a significant transaction fee of 2.5 per cent[141] which, during the NFT boom of 2021 and 2022, led OpenSea to achieve a valuation of more than $13 billion.[142] Yet, OpenSea's customer support is notoriously poor[143] and has been the subject of huge data leaks.[144] Its smart contracts are known to have been exploited by fraudsters, leading to the hacks of valuable NFTs.[145] Institutional intermediaries therefore are hardly likely to be thrilled by the prospect of working together with such trading platforms. Moreover, OpenSea only provides support for tokens traded on established chains, such as Ethereum, Polygon, and Solana.[146] The liquidity benefits (if any) associated with decentralised trading will therefore not be available to tokens issued on private permissioned blockchains.

4.3. Efficiency and Speed of Clearing

The third and final claim which will be debunked here is that replacing existing intermediated securities trading infrastructure with blockchain technology will reduce latency[147] and allow 'speedier deal execution and lower transaction fees'.[148] A recent research bulletin published by the Bank for International Settlements claims that, '[b]y moving assets recorded on separated traditional ledgers to a common programmable platform, tokenisation could unlock benefits through greater automation, including faster, cheaper and more convenient transactions'.[149] And the Law Commission's report on Smart Legal Contracts found that '[a]lmost all consultees said that smart legal contracts may increase efficiency and lower

[141] OpenSea.io, 'What are OpenSea's fees?'. Available at: www.support.opensea.io/hc/en-us/articles/14068991090067-What-are-OpenSea-s-fees-.

[142] BBC.com, 'NFT marketplace OpenSea valued at more than $13bn' (6 January 2022). Available at: www.bbc.com/news/technology-59880739.

[143] A Lusina, 'As Theft Thrives, Artists Say OpenSea Does Little to Protect Copyrights' (PetaPixel, 20 December 2021). Available at: www.petapixel.com/2021/12/20/as-theft-thrives-artists-say-opensea-does-little-to-protect-copyrights/; R Nayyar, 'NFTs Tank on OpenSea as Crypto Winter Continues' (Hyperallergic, 8 September 2022). Available at: www.hyperallergic.com/759136/nfts-tank-on-opensea-as-crypto-winter-continues/.

[144] E Curryer, 'NFT giant OpenSea admits data breach and warns of phishing attacks' (Techinformed, 4 July 2022). Available at: www.techinformed.com/nft-giant-opensea-admits-data-breach-and-warns-of-phishing-attacks/.

[145] M Clark, 'OpenSea fixes vulnerabilities that could let hackers steal crypto with malicious NFTs' (The Verge, 13 October 2021). Available at: www.theverge.com/2021/10/13/22723092/opensea-nft-vulnerability-gift-security-researchers-wallet-hack.

[146] Opensea.io, 'Which blockchains are compatible with OpenSea?' Available at: www.support.opensea.io/hc/en-us/articles/4404027708051-Which-blockchains-are-compatible-with-OpenSea-.

[147] C Twemlow, 'Why are Securities Held in Intermediated Form?' in L Gullifer and J Payne, *Intermediation and Beyond* (Oxford, Hart Publishing, 2019), 105.

[148] Bala, 'Tokenization of Assets' (n 136), 585.

[149] I Aldasoro et al, 'The tokenisation continuum' (BIS Bulletin No 72, 11 April 2023). Available at: www.bis.org/publ/bisbull72.htm.

transaction costs because they can be performed automatically without the need for human intervention'.[150]

It is often assumed that this is a good thing. 'Imagine,' Fairfield writes, 'a database for deeds to land that would permit anyone to transmit land ownership to anyone else with the bump of a smartphone'.[151] He suggests that in NFT adoption, 'science is doing the hard work of turning science fiction into reality'.[152] But it is not at all clear that Fairfield's vision is a utopia. On the contrary, given the significance of land transactions, one wonders how fraud will be prevented and/or reversed. It has often been pointed out that formalities serve a cautionary function.[153] But beyond this, faster, immutable transactions hinder fraud detection and are more difficult to reverse. An obsession with speed and convenience plays straight into the hands of fraudsters and gives law enforcement less time to catch up. As already observed above, rectification (today one of the law's leading defences against fraud) is neutered. To the extent that Fairfield depicts a utopia, it may be a utopia for fraudsters.

In any event, the claim that tokenisation promotes efficiency is open to doubt. Where the relevant tokens are deployed on busy permissionless chains, the entire token system becomes subject to network fees and delays on those chains.[154] In May 2022, Yuga Labs (of notorious Bored Ape Yacht Club fame) launched an offering of 'virtual land' which 'crashed Ethereum' for three hours. Competing buyers were bidding ever-higher prices for miners to confirm their transactions, putting so much stress on the entire Ethereum blockchain that 'crypto traders were unable to buy, sell or send coins for hours'.[155] Crucially, this affected not only parties involved in the Yuga offering but anyone desiring to transact on Ethereum, as one user discovered when quoted $1,700 in network fees to send a transaction worth $100.[156] Such problems are not confined to permissionless chains. In an episode said to '[raise] questions of a mismatch between the promises and reality of the technology that underpins cryptocurrencies',[157] ASX Ltd, the operator of the Australian Stock Exchange, has wholly abandoned attempts to replace its aging clearing software (known as 'CHESS') with a new blockchain-based solution.[158] One reason for its

[150] *Smart Legal Contracts: Advice to Government* (Law Com No 401, 2021) para 2.105.

[151] J Fairfield, 'Tokenized: The Law of Non-Fungible Tokens and Unique Digital Property' (2022) 97 *Indiana Law Journal* 1261.

[152] ibid.

[153] Low and Mik, n 59, 160; B McFarlane, *The Structure of Property Law* (Oxford, Hart Publishing, 2008), 104–10.

[154] See Ethereum Developer Resources, 'Gas and Fees' (updated 12 September 2022). Available at: www.ethereum.org/en/developers/docs/gas/.

[155] D van Boom, 'How Bored Ape Yacht Club Broke Ethereum' (CNet, 3 May 2022). Available at: www.cnet.com/personal-finance/crypto/how-bored-ape-yacht-club-broke-ethereum.

[156] ibid.

[157] B Kaye, 'Australian stock exchange says software overhaul won't involve blockchain' (Reuters, 19 May 2023). Available at: www.reuters.com/markets/australian-stock-exchange-says-software-overhaul-wont-involve-blockchain-2023-05-19/.

[158] This came after the failure of a seven-year, A$250 million project: see B Kaye, 'Australian stock exchange's blockchain failure burns market trust' (Reuters, 20 December 2022). Available at: www.reuters.com/markets/australian-stock-exchanges-blockchain-failure-burns-market-trust-2022-12-20/.

failure was that 'by seeking to replicate all CHESS functions on a single system, ASX risked undermining an advantage of blockchain, which was to reduce contact points that slow processing'.[159] Other attempts to develop permissioned chains have not fared better. The Tradelens collaboration between Maersk and IBM was shut down, citing a lack of 'commercial viability',[160] literally months before the British Government celebrated its enactment of the Electronic Trade Documents Act 2023. There is also little interest in the US Depository Trust & Clearing Corporation's 'Project Ion' blockchain-based prototype settlement platform.[161]

4.4. Forks: The Unique Problem of the Blockchain

Far from promoting security, liquidity and efficiency, applications of blockchain technology to date have only served to create new vulnerabilities. We have already mentioned that fraud is rife in the cryptoverse. However, beyond individual instances of fraud, attempts to tokenise physical assets on the blockchain will create a new systemic problem of blockchain forks.

Forks are a well-known problem. Random forks occur constantly on proof-of-work chains and are usually regarded as being of little consequence, since they generally resolve themselves when the longest blockchain is identified through majority consensus.[162] But even random forks are 'less difficult to ignore for asset classes which are actively traded on a consistent basis such as securities',[163] since the precise entitlement of any party must be capable of determination at any given point in time. Hard forks (such as the forks which gave rise to the Ethereum Classic and Bitcoin Cash chains)[164] are even more problematic. They may result in legitimate transactions becoming undone, such that 'some innocent parties may have suffered losses which was not compensated'.[165] These problems are compounded when the token in question is linked to an underlying exogenous asset. After all, 'a fork in a blockchain land registry does not create a duplicate Blackacre Classic'.[166] The problem is a serious one and raises questions about the commercial usability of asset-backed tokens on permissionless chains. When such a chain forks, users

[159] ibid.

[160] L Cecere, 'Tradelens Discontinues Operations. Why You Should Care.' (Forbes, 5 December 2022). Available at: www.forbes.com/sites/loracecere/2022/12/05/tradelens-discontinues-operations-why-you-should-care/?sh=414598324cec.

[161] W Wong, 'Cloud trumps blockchain: DTCC's TIW goes live, and no one's choosing the DLT option' (Waters Technology, 9 March 2023). Available at: www.waterstechnology.com/emerging-technologies/7950677/cloud-trumps-blockchain-dtccs-tiw-goes-live-and-no-ones-choosing-the-dlt-option. There is also no specific timeline for when Project Ion is intended to replace the current system: see Y Yang and A Irrera, 'Clearinghouse's blockchain-based settlement system goes live' (Bloomberg, 22 August 2022). Available at: www.bloomberg.com/professional/blog/clearinghouses-blockchain-based-settlement-system-goes-live/.

[162] See A Summers, *Understanding Blockchain and Cryptocurrencies* (Oxford, CRC Press, 2022) ch 4.

[163] Low and Mik (n 59), 163.

[164] ibid 164.

[165] ibid.

[166] ibid.

will be able to transact their tokens on two different chains – who is to decide which offshoot authoritatively represents title to the asset? If the consequence is that neither token can safely be accepted as transferring title to the asset, then the entire tokenisation structure is flawed from the outset. This problem can be addressed by using permissioned blockchains, but it is not entirely clear what advantages such a structure holds over a centralised ledger with backups.

5. Conclusion

This chapter pushes back against a resurgent tokenisation mania. First, blockchain tokenisation of physical assets is impracticable on a peer-to-peer basis and faces obstacles that cannot be resolved even through legislative intervention. Second, tokenisation via intermediaries is nothing revolutionary in and of itself and has indeed been done for centuries. Third, the oft-touted benefits of tokenisation, namely security, liquidity and efficiency, are no more than myths, and the use of blockchains for accounting and settlement in fact creates idiosyncratic risks.

In the ultimate analysis, the widely touted potential of blockchain asset tokenisation seems no more than smoke and mirrors. In fact, the extreme hype has helped grifters scam investors caught up in the fear of missing out. 'Rug pull' scams are extremely common[167] and have already led to prosecutions in the US.[168] For example, a project called Realux claimed to be developing a system of digital tokens backed by real estate investments, but in February 2022 the project team dumped 70 million tokens on the market and disappeared.[169]

With all these difficulties, why are established institutions far and wide jumping on the tokenisation bandwagon? Considering the lack of a genuine use-case for blockchain technology that offers clear and tangible benefits over existing systems, it appears that much of the interest in the technology at present is either due to the 'fear of missing out' or simply a marketing gimmick. The belief seems to be that 'if we tokenise an asset, people will want to buy it'. But that is completely illogical, unless the intention is to participate in a financial bubble. Yet, that belief is driving ongoing messaging to retail investors from established financial institutions and regulators alike. Given the abject lack of benefits that blockchain tokenisation offers, the latest wave of tokenisation must be recognised for what it ultimately is – nothing more than a grifter's paradise.

[167] See, eg, EJ Beyer, 'The Biggest Rug Pulls in NFT History' (NFTNow, 7 July 2022). Available at: www.nftnow.com/features/the-biggest-rug-pulls-in-nft-history/.

[168] A Robertson, 'Two men arrested for $1.1 million NFT 'rug pull' scam' (The Verge, 25 March 2022). Available at: www.theverge.com/2022/3/24/22995107/us-arrest-charges-crypto-nft-rug-pull-frosties-ethan-nguyen-andre-llacuna.

[169] O Faridi, 'Crypto Scam: Realux, a Real Estate and Tokenization Project, Takes Investors' Funds, Then Quickly Takes Down Website and Disappears' (Crowdfund Insider, 3 February 2022). Available at: www.crowdfundinsider.com/2022/02/186497-crypto-scam-realux-a-real-estate-and-tokenization-project-takes-investors-funds-then-quickly-takes-down-website-and-disappears/.

7

The Mareva Injunction and Crytpo Fraud

MAN YIP

1. Introduction

In *Mercedes Benz AG v Leiduck*, Lord Nicholls began his famous dissenting speech by highlighting the risk and fraud which a *Mareva* injunction (also commonly known as a freezing order in many jurisdictions) ought to address:[1]

> The first defendant's argument comes to this: his assets are in Hong Kong, so the Monaco court cannot reach them; he is in Monaco, so the Hong Kong court cannot reach him. That cannot be right. This is not acceptable today. A person operating internationally cannot so easily defeat the judicial process. There is not a black hole into which a defendant can escape out of sight and become unreachable.

Without a *Mareva* injunction, there is always a risk that any victory on the substantive merits would be rendered hollow in practice by the absence of assets against which the judgment may be enforced. Indeed, it is in cases concerning fraud that the risk of a nugatory judgment is most amplified because the defendant would have the propensity to engage in dishonest practices. Alarmingly, nearly 30 years after *Mercedez Benz*, the 'black hole' has enlarged because fraudsters can easily hide behind complex corporate structures and the anonymity of cyberspace.[2]

This chapter focuses on the use of *Mareva* injunction in the fight against crypto fraud. Britain's fraud reporting agency reported that crypto fraud loss in the UK 'increased more than 40 per cent over the past year, surpassing 300 million for the first time'.[3] The proliferation of crypto fraud has brought to the fore a new set of challenges for national courts that operate on procedural rules rooted in some notion of territoriality. Jurisdictions that embrace cryptoassets, such as the UK and

[1] [1996] AC 284, 305.

[2] It has been reported that the COVID-19 pandemic triggered widespread cyber fraud: see A Kantor, 'Coronavirus triggers epidemic of cyber fraud' Financial Times (15 April 2021). Available at: www.ft.com/content/30553ae9-cdfd-483c-a1ef-c04e3135f9da.

[3] S Venkataramakrishnan, 'UK crypto fraud losses jump 40%' Financial Times (25 May 2023). Available at: www.ft.com/content/88602223-004b-4e27-b9eb-c45e1f850f9f.

Singapore, have also readily embraced its civil weaponry – of which the *Mareva* injunction is one – to help fraud victims trace and recover lost assets and claim personal relief.[4] Vigorous legal protection is crucial to boosting market confidence.[5]

In crypto fraud cases, commencing a substantive cause of action in the forum – whether it will lead to a judgment on the merits in the forum ultimately – is key to the claimant's litigation strategy. Crucially, the role of a worldwide *Mareva* injunction in cross-border crypto fraud litigation must be examined in connection with other supporting or complementary orders, most notably, the proprietary injunction and the information disclosure orders. Through a careful review of recent English and Singapore cases, this chapter identifies the gaps, uncertainties, and constraints within the existing civil litigation framework and proposes areas where reform would be necessary.

The discussion unfolds in three main parts that follow this Introduction. By way of background, Section 2 sets out the requirements for obtaining *Mareva* relief and the modern rationale for courts awarding this form of interim order. Section 3 paints the context against which *Mareva* relief is sought in crypto fraud cases, by identifying the practical difficulties – namely, anonymity of defendants and the difficulty of tracing cryptoassets across jurisdictions[6] – which a claimant faces and the litigation strategy that he/she would adopt to overcome these difficulties. The discussion explains the utility of each of the common orders sought by the claimant. Section IV turns to analyse recent English and Singapore judgments issued on the basis of ex parte hearings which demonstrate a clear judicial practice in both jurisdictions to assist the victim of fraud. However, various points of law have been made hastily in these urgent applications that behove more comprehensive review. The analysis also points to areas that could benefit from further reflection and legal reform.

2. Background: Legal Requirements and Rationale

2.1. Legal Requirements

A *Mareva* injunction is an *in personam* order directed against a defendant to prohibit it from dissipating assets, usually before a judgment has been made,

[4] For a practical discussion of the system flaws and vulnerabilities of blockchain, see B Sookman, 'Blockchain Vulnerabilities and Civil Remedies to Recover Stolen Assets' (2022) 2 *International Journal of Blockchain Law* 25.

[5] It is common for victims to first report the fraud/theft to regulatory and law enforcement agencies. The criminal investigation route falls outside the scope of the chapter.

[6] In *Danisz v Persons Unknown* [2022] EWHC 280 (QB), [2022] All ER (D) 107 (Jan), the English High Court noted that transactions involving cryptocurrencies are such that 'at the click of a mouse, an asset can be dissipated'. In *CLM v CLN* [2022] SGHC 46, [2022] 5 SLR 273 [54], the General Division of the Singapore High Court expressed similar sentiments: cryptocurrencies 'are susceptible to being transferred by the click of a button, through digital wallets that may be completely anonymous and untraceable to the owner, and can be easily dissipated and hidden in cyberspace'.

although it is also possible for courts to award a post-judgment *Mareva* injunction. To maintain an element of surprise which is necessary for the injunction to work effectively, a *Mareva* injunction is usually awarded without giving notice to the defendant.[7] In other words, the application is made ex parte where the defendant is not notified and would thus not be present for the hearing. A defendant who breaches the order is in contempt of court.

Before legislative intervention, and after the landmark ruling in *The Siskina*,[8] it was thought that the injunction applicant is required to satisfy the court that: (1) there is an accrued cause of action before the forum court; (2) there is a good arguable case on the merits of its claim; (3) the forum court must have personal jurisdiction over the defendant; and (4) there is a real risk of dissipation of assets to frustrate the enforcement of an anticipated court judgment. Further, a *Mareva* injunction will only be granted where it is just and convenient to do so, and this discretional element is typically captured by the test of 'balance of convenience'. The 'balance of convenience' test requires the court to consider whether the applicant wound suffer more harm in not obtaining the injunction as compared with the detriment suffered by the respondent if the injunction were awarded. Where a claimant applies for a worldwide *Mareva* injunction, the same requirements apply but 'the threshold of necessity will likely be more exacting'.[9]

A little bit more needs to be said about the requirement of an accrued cause of action before the forum court. It is undisputed that the *Mareva* injunction does not enforce substantive rights. Owing to traditional perception of territoriality, it was once thought that the *Mareva* injunction existed to prevent the frustration of the enforcement of the forum court's judgment. For this reason, in *The Siskina*, Lord Diplock said:[10]

> A right to obtain an interlocutory injunction is not a cause of action. It cannot stand on its own. It is dependent upon there being a pre-existing cause of action against the defendant arising out of an invasion actual or threatened by him, of a legal or equitable right of the plaintiff for the enforcement of which the defendant is amenable to the jurisdiction of the court. The right to obtain an interlocutory injunction is merely ancillary and incidental to the pre-existing cause of action.

The rigidity of the *Siskina* requirement of an accrued cause of action within the jurisdiction, which was upheld by the English courts[11] and other common law

[7] For this reason, full and frank disclosure of all relevant facts is required.

[8] *Siskina (Owners of cargo lately laden on board) v Distos Cia Naviera SA* [1979] AC 210.

[9] *Bouvier, Yves Charles Edgar v Accent Delight International Ltd* [2015] SGCA 45, [2015] 5 SLR 558 [36]. Under Singapore law, there is the further consideration as to whether the defendant has sufficient assets in Singapore to satisfy the anticipated judgment: the fewer the assets in Singapore, the greater the necessity to take protective measures outside Singapore (*Guan Chong Cocoa Manufacturer Sdn Bhd v Pratiwi Shipping SA* [2002] SGCA 45, [2003] 1 SLR(R) 157 [29]).

[10] Above n 8 at 256. Lord Diplock's analysis of the 'power' issue was regarded as obiter dictum by the majority in *Broad Idea International Ltd v Convoy Collateral Ltd* [2021] UKPC 24, [2022] 2 WLR 703 [22].

[11] See, eg, *Veracruz Transportation Inc v VC Shipping Co Ltd* [1992] 1 Lloyd's Rep 353 (CA); *Zucker v Tyndall Holdings plc* [1992] 1 WLR 1127 (CA); *Fourie v Le Roux* [2007] UKHL 1, [2007] 1 WLR 320 (HL).

courts that accepted the authority of *The Siskina*, caused some degree of disquiet. In a powerful dissent in *Mercedes Benz AG*, Lord Nicholls stressed the need for flexibility:[12]

> As circumstances in the world change, so must the situations in which the courts may properly exercise their jurisdiction to grant injunctions. The exercise of the jurisdiction must be principled, but the criterion is injustice. Injustice is to be viewed and decided in the light of today's conditions and standards, not those of yester-year.

In England and Wales, Hong Kong and Singapore, the legislature has intervened to empower the courts to award a 'free-standing' *Mareva* injunction in support of foreign litigation. The abolition of the accrued cause of action requirement where litigation takes place or will take place elsewhere also led to the amendment of jurisdictional gateways for service out of jurisdiction to enable service on a defendant who is based overseas. Whilst England and Wales[13] and Hong Kong[14] chose to insert a new gateway to their respective existing lists to cater for a claim for a 'free-standing' *Mareva* injunction, Singapore opted to go with an open-ended approach to establishing sufficient connection with Singapore. But even this more progressive reform, proceeding from an ambition to become the hub for international disputes,[15] may not be sufficient in the context of using interim injunctions to fight crypto fraud, as I shall explain in Section 4.

2.2. The Enforcement Principle

A modern rationalisation of *Mareva* relief by an apex court was offered in the majority judgment delivered by Lord Leggatt in *Broad Idea International Ltd v Convoy Collateral Ltd*.[16] In that case, the Judicial Board upheld the lower court's decision to set aside the *Mareva* injunction against the second defendant on the basis that the BVI court had no personal jurisdiction over him. Consequently, the *Mareva* injunction against the first respondent, a non-cause of action defendant alleged to be a 'money box' for the second defendant, was also discharged.

The value of Lord Leggatt's decision, however, lies in his analysis of the jurisprudential basis of the *Mareva* relief.[17] He explained that once it is clear that the 'essential purpose' of *Mareva* relief is to facilitate the enforcement of a judgment,

[12] Above n 1 at 308. See further L Collins, 'The *Siskina* again: an opportunity missed' (1996) 112 *LQR* 8.

[13] See Practice Direction 6B para 3.1(5).

[14] See Rules of the High Court (Cap 4, section 54), Ord 11, r 1(1)(oc).

[15] See A Chong and M Yip, *Singapore Private International Law: Commercial Issues and Practice* (Oxford, Oxford University Press, 2023) ch 3.

[16] Above n 10.

[17] Davies forcefully argues that this part of the analysis should be considered as part of the *ratio* because it constitutes a necessary step in the majority's reasoning: P Davies, 'Freezing Orders: Casting Off the Shackles of *The Siskina*?' in B McFarlane and S Elliott (eds), *Equity Today: 150 Years after the Judicature Reforms* (Oxford, Hart Publishing, 2023) 230.

'it is apparent' that there is no link between the court's power to grant the relief and the existence of substantive proceedings before the court.[18] This vindicates prevailing sentiments and is not a profound, transformative restatement of the law. But it does provide an authoritative anchor for greater liberalisation of the rules which support the award of a *Mareva* injunction in modern cross-border litigation. Crucially, neither *The Siskina* nor *Broad Idea* concerned crypto fraud which presents its unique set of challenges. It is to the special context of crypto fraud that we turn.

3. Context: Anonymity, Traceability and Litigation Strategy

3.1. Practical Difficulties

There are three common kinds of crypto fraud. First, the misappropriation of cryptoassets owned by the claimant by a defendant whom the claimant knew.[19] Even though the defendant is known to the claimant, the misappropriated cryptoassets are usually very quickly transferred onward to other persons located outside the jurisdiction.

Second, the payment of cryptocurrencies to anonymous persons as ransom for cyber extortion.[20] Practitioners observe that 'payments in cryptocurrencies have become the ransom of choice because the absence of KYC checks and the lack of regulatory oversight means that the identity of the holders of the funds can often be difficult to determine'.[21]

Third, the misappropriation of the claimant's cryptoassets by an anonymous wrongdoer[22] or a wrongdoer whose true identity is unknown to the claimant.[23] The wrongdoer might have hacked into the claimant's cryptoasset account/wallet or fraudulently induced the claimant to transfer over its cryptoassets. Unlike the first scenario, the claimant does not even know who the primary wrongdoer is or where it is located.

The common problem in all three scenarios described above is that the cryptoassets were either misappropriated by and/or transferred onward to persons

[18] *Broad Idea* (n 10), [90].

[19] See, eg, *Nico Constantijn Antonius Samara v Stive Jean Paul Dan* [2018] HKCFI 1022, [2018] HKCU 1643 (the claimant had entered into an agreement with the defendant); *CLM v CLN* [2022] SGHC 46, [2022] 5 SLR 273 (the defendants were the claimant's acquaintances).

[20] See, eg, *AA v Persons Unknown* [2019] EWHC 3556 (Comm), [2020] 4 WLR 35; *AAA plc v Persons Unknown* [2021] EWHC 2529 (QB). Both cases concerned the application for a proprietary injunction but in *AAA plc*, the claimant invoked the court's powers pre-emptively to avoid payment.

[21] J Rogerson and W Obree, '*AAA plc & ors v Persons Unknown*: Cyber Activism or Blackmail?' White & Case (3 November 2021). Available at: www.whitecase.com/insight-alert/aaa-plc-ors-v-persons-unknown-cyber-activism-or-blackmail.

[22] See, eg, *LMN v Bitflyer Holdings Inc* [2022] EWHC 2954 (Comm), [2023] 2 All ER (Comm) 411; *Osbourne v Persons Unknown* [2022] EWHC 1021 (Comm) (this case concerned the theft of NFTs).

[23] See, eg, *Ion Science Ltd v Persons Unknown* (Unreported, 21 December 2020).

whose identity and location are unknown. Specialist investigators are required to trace the whereabouts of the cryptoassets[24] but this would only generally reveal that the cryptoassets (or a portion) are now stored in a wallet or cryptoasset account controlled or administered by known persons who may be innocent of wrongdoing.[25] Indeed, the claimant must act quickly in enlisting the help of an investigator because cybercriminals are known to move the cryptoassets around very quickly and employ various techniques, including placing cryptoassets in a 'tumbler'[26] and 'peeling',[27] to hide the assets. In *Fetch.ai Ltd v Persons Unknown*,[28] it was alleged that persons unknown gained access to the first claimant's Binance accounts which held various cryptocurrencies. It was further alleged that within a very short period of time, through 'simple expedient' trading of the first claimant's cryptocurrencies at 'massive undervalues', the cryptoassets were moved out of the first claimant's accounts to third party accounts that were 'inferentially operated by or on behalf' of the fraudsters, thereby causing loss to the first claimant in excess of USD 2.6 million.[29] In *CLM v CLN*, the General Division of the Singapore High Court noted that the first defendants had 'dissipated the stolen assets through a series of digital wallets that appear to have been created solely for the purpose of frustrating the plaintiff's tracing and recovery efforts, and which had either no or negligible transactions other than the deposit and withdrawal of the Stolen Cryptocurrency Assets'.[30]

Armed with merely the evidence of a fraud having occurred and the information provided by the investigator, a claimant considering a civil action must expeditiously start a substantive action in court and apply for a suite of interlocutory orders. The substantive action is not quite the point of the claimant's asset recovery strategy at this stage; the interlocutory orders are. Therefore, the action should be commenced in the court of a jurisdiction which has the power to grant such relief. These orders enhance the prospects of preserving the claimant's cryptoassets or their traceable substitutes; preserving the assets of potential defendants who have received or wrongfully dealt with the cryptoassets (whether they remained in that defendant's hands) and may be located anywhere in the world; and obtaining information in relation to the identity of the potential defendants and non-defendants against whom legal actions may be brought and *Mareva*/proprietary injunctions may be addressed. The substantive action in the forum is a hook on which to hang the application of the interlocutory orders. Upon successfully identifying the defendants, it may well be that the claimant needs to take its claim elsewhere.

[24] For a lay discussion on how these investigators trace the cryptoassets, see *LMN v Bitflyer* (n 22) [7]–[10].

[25] See, eg, *Ion Science* (n 23) [10].

[26] Above n 21.

[27] Sookman (n 4) 34.

[28] *Fetch.ai Ltd v Persons Unknown* [2021] EWHC 2254 (Comm), 24 ITELR 566.

[29] ibid [3].

[30] *CLM v CLN* (n 19) [54].

The difficulties confronting a victim of crypto fraud are aptly summarised by Pelling QC J in *Osbourne v Persons Unknown, Ozone*, a judgment concerning an application for a Bankers Trust order against a US company:[31]

> The difficulty about this is that the claimant has no knowledge of where the persons unknown are located, and it is clear that Ozone is an American corporation, with, as far as I can see from the evidence, no connection whatsoever to the English jurisdiction. In those circumstances the issues which arise are whether or not a good cause of action has been demonstrated by the claimant against the persons unknown, and secondly, if and to the extent such a cause of action has been demonstrated, whether she is able to demonstrate that it is appropriate for an order to be made permitting the service of proceedings against persons unknown out of the jurisdiction wherever they might be located, in circumstances where, if I make an information as against the second defendant, the information, if provided, will enable the location of the persons unknown and possibly their identity to become known.

3.2. Dealing with Unknowns

Although *Osbourne* did not concern an application for the *Mareva* injunction, similar difficulties confront a claimant who is applying for one. Importantly, because of the unknowns, a claimant of cryptoasset fraud would rarely ever just apply for a *Mareva* injunction. It is common to also apply for a proprietary injunction to freeze assets that belong to the claimant. The *Mareva* injunction, in contrast, is an order to freeze assets belonging to the defendant. Therefore, the *Mareva* injunction is considered more intrusive than the proprietary injunction. On the other hand, the proprietary injunction would require the claimant to show that the cryptoassets are the claimant's property and it is in this context that the question as to whether cryptoassets are properly 'property' usually arises.[32] The cases demonstrate that the claimant would generally rely on an institutional constructive trust arising pursuant to fraud[33] or theft[34] to show that the misappropriate assets (if still traceable) remain their property.[35] Both types of injunctions are commonly sought

[31] *Osbourne* (n 22) [11]–[12].

[32] *AA v Persons Unknown* (n 20) (concerning Bitcoin); *CLM v CLN* (n 19) [5] (concerning Bitcoin and Ethereum); *Janesh s/o Rajkumar v Unknown Person ("CHEFPIERRE")* [2022] SGHC 264, [2023] 3 SLR 1191 (concerning NFTs). The common law courts have generally answered this question in the affirmative. See further R Goode, 'What is Property?' (2023) 139 *LQR* 1.

[33] *Westdeutsche v Landesbank Girozentrale v London Borough of Islington* [1996] AC 669, 716 (Lord Browne-Wilkinson).

[34] *CLM v CLN* (n 19) [53]. The conceptual basis of a stolen asset constructive trust, derived from Lord Browne-Wilkinson's judgment in *Westdeutsche* [1996] AC 669, 716, has been questioned: *Shalson v Russo* [2004] EWHC 1637 (Ch), [2005] Ch 281 [110]. See also *Bailey v Angove's Pty Ltd* [2016] UKSC 47, [2016] 1 WLR 3179 [30]. In the context of an ex parte hearing and having regard to the standard of proof ('a serious issue to be tried' on the merits'), the court is unlikely to engage in any detailed analysis of the law.

[35] *Fetch.ai* (n 28).

by the claimant because at this stage, it does not know what has happened to the lost cryptoassets – for example, they may have been dissipated or the claimant's title may have been overreached in subsequent transactions.[36] These cases also potentially involve the application of foreign laws that cannot be readily determined. Other causes of action that are conventionally relied upon by the claimant include unjust enrichment,[37] breach of confidence,[38] and various torts.[39]

Further, as some or all of the defendants are persons unknown, it cannot be assumed that they are within the jurisdiction. Hence, the claimant will usually apply for a worldwide *Mareva* injunction and the orders will need to be served out of the jurisdiction on the basis that some or all the defendants are potentially located overseas.[40] The worldwide order ensures 'to the best that can be achieved' for a victim of fraud in enabling any court judgment that to have 'real effect'.[41]

The English and Singapore courts allow orders to be made against persons unknown, as long as the description of these persons is sufficiently certain to identify the persons who fall within the description and those who fall outside of it, and is not overly wide.[42] To help determine the identities of the persons unknown, *Bankers Trust* and *Norwich Pharmacal* orders are also sought from the court to compel known third parties to disclose information relating to the identity of wallet owners or account holders. For instance, a cryptocurrency exchange or an NFT peer-to-peer marketplace may be required by the order to disclose information of the account holder whose account now holds the lost cryptoassets.[43] The claimant would usually make the case that the exchange or marketplace has collected know your client and anti-money laundering information, thereby putting it in a position to provide information relevant to the identification of the individuals behind the accounts of relevant transactions.[44] A *Bankers Trust* order is ordered only where a proprietary claim is made. Where personal claims

[36] *Piroozzadeh v Persons Unknown* [2023] EWHC 1024 (Ch) [8], [25]–[26].

[37] *CLM v CLN* (n 19) [53].

[38] *Fetch.ai* (n 28) [9]–[10]. The court accepted that the private key, which is required to operate the account, constituted confidential information.

[39] For example, the tort of deceit, the tort of misuse of private information and unlawful means conspiracy. See *Ion Science* (n 23).

[40] ibid [12].

[41] Fetch.ai (n 28) [3].

[42] *Ion Science* (n 23) [11]; Fetch.ai (n 28) [5]–[7]; *CLM v CLN* (n 19) [32] and [35] (pursuant to the predecessor procedural regime under Rules of Court 2014); *Janesh* (n 32) [41] (pursuant to Rules of Court 2021 regime, and concerning an application of a proprietary injunction in a case of lost NFTs).

[43] Effectiveness of the order is one of the factors that the court will consider. In *Osbourne* (n 22) [53]–[55], the court noted that the *Bankers Trust* disclosure order was to be made against a US company with no presence in England and Wales which necessarily meant that the ability of an English court to enforce the order is 'limited'. The court ultimately granted the order, adopting an approach consistent with earlier cases and operating on 'the assumption that Ozone would wish to cooperate with the English Courts for the purposes of supplying information which enables the proceeds of fraud to be traced …'

[44] See, eg, *LMN v Bitflyer* (n 22) [10]. The English High Court highlights that 'many exchanges use different companies to contract in different jurisdictions and thus the relevant entity might depend on where the natural person associated with a target address is located'.

are pursued, whether solely or in addition to a proprietary claim, the claimant will have to apply for a *Norwich Pharmacal* order.[45]

There is no guarantee that the orders granted would not be futile, in view of the potential difficulty in tracing the assets,[46] as well as identifying and locating the potential defendants. But this is the best that a victim could do. And it would only be the well-resourced claimants who are likely to be able to pursue claims against persons unknown. Having set out a claimant's litigation strategy and how the *Mareva* injunction fits into the scheme of things, we now turn to review how courts deal with the requirements for worldwide Mareva relief against persons unknown in Section 4.

4. Gaps, Constraints and Reforms

4.1. Preliminary Observations

Four preliminary points need to be borne in mind when we examine these cases. First, in an interlocutory hearing, the standard of proof required is lower than proof on a balance of probabilities required for a trial on the merits because not all the evidence is available at this stage of proceedings. Second, in an ex parte hearing, it does not take very much to convince the court because the defendant is not present to argue to the contrary. Indeed, in cases of crypto fraud, notification is generally not given to defendants and the hearing is held in private, so as not to alert the fraudsters to avoid dissipation of the lost assets. Third, in cases involving persons unknown, there is little known of the defendant which the court could take judicial notice of in deciding if the threshold for granting the orders has been met.[47] In other words, very little stands in the way of a victim of fraud to obtain the interlocutory orders required. Fourth, a number of the requirements for an award of *Mareva* relief – for example, permission to serve out of jurisdiction for establishing personal jurisdiction over the defendant, alternative service, balance of convenience – are equally applicable to the other orders commonly sought together with the *Mareva* injunction and may be decided on the same factual factors. The failure of one requirement may spell doom for the application for another type of order. Also, for this reason, some of the cases discussed below concern other types of interim relief granted in cases of crypto fraud.

[45] *Osbourne* (n 22) [33].

[46] See *Piroozzadeh* (n 36) [33] (concerning a proprietary injunction). The court observed that freezing the cryptoassets in the case could not be achieved in practice because of the pooling structure applied by the eighth defendant (an exchange). The injunction against the eighth defendant discharged on the basis that the claimant did not make a 'fair representation' of the facts and legal consequences.

[47] This is a higher standard than 'a serious issue to be tried on the merits' which is applicable for the less intrusive proprietary injunction.

Before we turn to the requirements that merit closer scrutiny, we can quickly deal with the ones that are straightforward. First, as explained above, the claimant in cases of crypto fraud would generally bring an accrued cause of action in the jurisdiction. Second, demonstrating a good arguable case on the merits presents no difficulty and is usually satisfied on showing some evidence of fraud or misappropriation.[48] Third, the requirement of a real risk of dissipation is also usually satisfied on the same evidence.[49] Finally, courts generally consider it just and convenient to grant a worldwide *Mareva* injunction. As many of these cases are 'hot pursuit' cases and involve wrongdoers and recipients who are persons unknown, courts act swiftly to assist, as the worldwide freezing order is a necessary (or the only) means by which the claimant could have realistic prospects of recovering the lost assets or their value.[50] Even in cases that are not considered 'hot pursuit' because the fraud took place some time ago, the court's sympathy would naturally lie with the claimant. In *Ion Science*, the English High Court said that a worldwide freezing injunction is ordered 'to assist the victims of what appears to have been a significant and prolonged cyber fraud'.[51] Other reasons have more to do with the nature of the cryptoassets – for example, that they could be quickly transferred across jurisdictions and disappear without a trace.[52]

We turn now to consider the more problematic requirements, as well as where the law has not done enough or in fact constitutes a hindrance.

4.2. Personal Jurisdiction Over the Defendant (Service Out)

Whether in England and Wales or Singapore, generally, a claimant of crypto fraud must obtain permission to serve out of jurisdiction.[53] Both English law and Singapore law adopt broadly similar requirements for service out of jurisdiction, even though the precise approach and terminology differ somewhat after the recent procedural reform in Singapore which came into force on 1 April 2022. Under English law, the claimant must show that: (a) there is a good arguable case that its claim falls within one of the jurisdictional gateways set out in CPR PD 6B; (b) a serious issue to be tried on the merits of the claim; and (c) England is the appropriate forum for the trial of the dispute.[54]

[48] *CLM v CLN* (n 19) [53].

[49] See, eg, *CLM v CLN* (n 19) [54].

[50] *Danisz* (n 6).

[51] *Ion Science* (n 23) [18].

[52] *Danisz* (n 6).

[53] Under the Singapore procedural regime, the Rules of Court 2021 (applicable to proceedings commenced on or after 1 April 2022), Ord 8, r 1(3), the court's approval for service out is not required if it is 'allowed under a contract between the parties'. As a majority of the crypto fraud cases involve fraudsters and third parties unknown to the victim, this provision is of infrequent relevance.

[54] *Ion Science* (n 23) [12].

Under Singapore law, the claimant must show that the court 'has the jurisdiction'[55] or is 'the appropriate court to hear the action'.[56] It is likely that claims brought by a victim of cyrpto fraud will come within the purview of the second limb: 'the appropriate court to hear the action'. Formal guidance on whether the Singapore court is 'the appropriate court' can be found in paragraph 63 of the Supreme Court Practice Directions 2021 which essentially retains the requirements for service out of jurisdiction under the predecessor version of the Rules of Court and which broadly corresponds to the English approach. Paragraph 63(2) states that the Singapore court is 'the appropriate court to hear the action' if: (a) there is a good arguable case that there is a sufficient nexus to Singapore; (b) Singapore is the *forum conveniens*; and (c) there is a serious issue to be tried on the merits of the claim. Differing from the English approach on jurisdictional gateways (which are recognised bases of connection), paragraph 63(3) of the Supreme Court Practice Directions 2021 sets out a *non-exhaustive list of factors* (that have some equivalent or similar provisions under CPR PD 6B gateways). That Singapore law now adopts a non-exhaustive list of factors to the inquiry on sufficient connection with Singapore is a significant paradigm shift from the previous regime on service out of jurisdiction.[57] It signals that Singapore courts are at liberty to recognise new situations (beyond the list) where it would be appropriate to serve out of jurisdiction. Indeed, the legislative intent behind the reform is two-fold:[58]

> 'This makes it unnecessary for a claimant to scrutinise the long list of permissible cases set out in the existing Rules in the hope of fitting into one or more descriptions. It also avoids the possibility that a particular category of cases which could and should be heard in Singapore is actually not in the list.

4.2.1. *Jurisdictional Gateway/Sufficient Connection*

The recently reformed Singapore approach to establishing a sufficient connection to the forum is sufficiently flexible to enable the Singapore High Court to grant approval to serve out on new grounds without undergoing arduous legislative amendment. Nor is the Singapore court obliged to treat the paragraph 63 examples as quasi-statutory rules that need to be restrictively interpreted or to resolve any doubts in favour of the defendant.

[55] This ground for service out applies presumably where there is an exclusive choice of court agreement within the meaning of the Choice of Court Agreement Act 2016 designating a Singapore court as the chosen court and approval would be granted as a matter of course. See Chong and Yip, (n 15) para 3.72.

[56] Rules of Court 2021, O 8, r 1(1).

[57] See further Chong and Yip (n 15) paras 3.74–3.75.

[58] Civil Justice Commission Report (29 December 2017), Chapter 6. Available at: www.mlaw.gov.sg/files/news/press-releases/2018/10/Annex C Civil Justice Commission Report.pdf. See also Public Consultation on Civil Justice Reforms: *Recommendations of the Civil Justice Review Committee and Civil Justice Commission* (26 October 2018), paras 52–53. Available at: www.mlaw.gov.sg/files/news/press-releases/2018/10/Annex%20A%20Public%20consultation%20paper%20on%20civil%20justice%20reforms.pdf.

Turning to the English approach, the problem with the jurisdictional gateway approach is that there is a *fixed* list and the degree of flexibility is limited and dependent on the width of interpretation, as well as the operation of paragraph (4A) which allows a further claim to piggyback on the permission to serve out in respect of a claim falling within paragraphs (1A), (2), (6)–(16A) or (19)–(23). In the context of crypto fraud where assets are moved across wallets/accounts swiftly and many parties are involved in the chain of cross-border transfers, whether a particular gateway could be relied upon to serve out on defendants who are subsequent transferees holding accounts in foreign exchanges depends on the interpretation of the wording. To illustrate, in respect of CPR PD 6B paragraphs 3.1(11) and (15)(b), it is not clear whether this gateway is applicable if the property is no longer within jurisdiction at the time of the application for permission to serve outside England or at the time when the cause of action against that particular transferee accrued.[59] In respect of CPF PD 6B paragraph 3.1(15)(a), it is unclear which acts or events must occur within the jurisdiction to bring the gateway into play.[60]

Pertinently, as the UK Law Commission acknowledged, 'because digital assets are intangible and often distributed, their geographical location can be hard to pinpoint'.[61] Fitting claims concerning digital assets within a jurisdictional regime built on the idea of geographical location (whether within or outside the jurisdiction) creates legal uncertainty. In *Cheong Jun Yoong v Three Arrows Capital Ltd*, the General Division of the Singapore High Court, in deciding the question of sufficient connection under the Rules of Court 2021 and specifically whether the claim concerned property situated in Singapore,[62] held that the *situs* of cryptoassets is where the person who has *control* of the cryptoassets is resident.[63] The problem of 'location' of cryptoassets arises also in the natural forum inquiry.

4.2.2. Natural Forum

As to the requirement of the court being the appropriate court or *forum conveniens* to hear the action, both English and Singapore courts apply the *Spiliada* principles.[64] The *Spiliada* test entails a two-stage inquiry: first, the consideration of general connecting factors to identify the forum with the most real and substantial connections with the dispute; and second, the consideration if substantial justice may be obtained in the *prima facie* natural forum identified in the first stage. The

[59] *Osbourne v Persons Unknown* [2023] EWHC 39 (KB) [31]–[38] (Lavender J); *Osbourne v Persons Unknown* [2023] EWHC 340 (KB) [33]–[35]. Whether a cryptoasset is sited in England and Wales in itself is a complex question – see discussion below on *lex situs*.

[60] ibid. [37] (Lavender J); ibid. [36]–[38].

[61] See https://lawcom.gov.uk/law-commission-review-to-examine-how-private-international-law-can-apply-to-digital-assets-and-other-emerging-technology/.

[62] See Supreme Court Practice Directions 2021, para 63(3)(i).

[63] [2024] SGHC 21. This is the first Singapore decision on the location of cryptoassets.

[64] The common law principles of ad hoc jurisdiction allocation were enunciated by the House of Lords in *Spiliada Maritime Corp v Cansulex Ltd* [1987] AC 460.

exercise is discretionary and comparative in nature. Whilst the test identifies the *prima facie* natural forum, practically speaking, the forum court's concern is whether to stay the action before it or allow it to proceed in the interests of the parties and the ends of justice.[65] It does not determine if the foreign natural forum will hear the case, or direct parties to commence proceedings in the foreign court.

In crypto fraud cases which involve defendants who are persons unknown, both English and Singapore courts have used claimant-sided and claimant-biased factors to decide that the forum court is the natural forum. Of course, the court cannot be faulted for not considering defendant-sided factors because it has no information concerning the unknown persons.[66] In *Fetch.ai*, for instance, the English court determined that England is the natural forum on the basis that the claimant's business had been carried on exclusively in England and Wales, the subject matter of the dispute (ie the cryptocurrencies) are under English law to be treated as located in England and that the losses are sustained in England and Wales.[67] In *Ion Science*, Butcher J came to the same conclusion on the basis that the claimants were domiciled in England and Wales; the funds were transferred from England and Wales; the bitcoin are or certainly were located in England and Wales; the claimant's documents were in English and its witnesses were based in England.[68]

The steps in reasoning merit closer scrutiny. The claimant's location, the location of its witnesses and the language of its documents are clearly claimant-sided factors. Then we have the claimant-biased factors which are factors clearly or discreetly tilted towards the claimant. In *Fetch.ai*, losses are considered sustained in England and Wales because 'the assets of which the applicants have been deprived were property located in England'.[69] The assets are located in England because English courts[70] generally follow Butcher J's decision in *Ion Science* which held that the '*lex situs* of a cryptoasset is the place where the person or company who owns it is domiciled'.[71] However, Butcher J had decided on the *lex situs* of the cryptoasset in an urgent ex parte hearing and based on Andrew Dickinson's academic writing:[72]

> … The second of those aspects is on the basis that the lex situs of a cryptoasset is the place where the person or company who owns it is domiciled. That is an analysis which is supported by Professor Andrew Dickinson in his book *Cryptocurrencies in Public and Private Law* at para. 5.108. There is apparently no decided case in relation to the lex situs for a cryptoasset. Nevertheless, I am satisfied that there is at least a serious issue to be tried that that is the correct analysis.

[65] ibid. 476 (Lord Goff).
[66] *Osbourne* (n 22) [30] (an application for a proprietary injunction and a Bankers Trust order).
[67] Above n 28 [18].
[68] *Ion Science* (n 23) [16].
[69] *Fetch.ai* (n 28) [19].
[70] ibid. [14]; *Danisz* (n 6); *Osbourne* (n 22) [16].
[71] *Ion Science* (n 23) [13].
[72] ibid.

An implication flowing from the use of claimant-sided and claimant-biased connections in determining the natural forum is that the court of the claimant's domicile will generally be the natural forum at the ex parte stage, enabling that court to come to the aid of the claimant. From a policy perspective of ensuring access to practical justice for a victim of cryptoasset fraud, this outcome is desirable and accords certainty and convenience to the victim. The question is whether this is how we should arrive at the outcome. Two points need to be addressed head on.

First, the determination of the *lex situs* of a cryptoasset has yet to be properly decided by a higher court. Importantly, for the purpose of formulating a choice of law rule for cryptocurrency, Dickinson does not think there is a need to ascribe a notional *situs* to cryptocurrency.[73] This is because the *situs* for intangible property is artificial. Instead, Dickinson says that the choice of law rule can be 'straightforwardly, and appropriately' framed as a rule to govern 'the proprietary effects outside the cryptocurrency system of a transaction relating to cryptocurrency'.[74] The attribution of the *lex situs* rule (as being the place where the person or company who owns it is domiciled) to Dickinson is therefore curious to say the least. The repeated reference to *Ion Science* does not make this an authoritative statement of the law,[75] although there is always a danger that it may be perceived as such. With Dickinson's proposal clarified, and on the assumption that it is accepted as the choice of law rule for proprietary effects outside the cryptocurrency system of a cryptoasset transaction, the law of the place of the country where the participant resides or carries on business at the relevant time is relevant in the natural forum exercise as the governing law of proprietary issues. If the court is minded to introduce a *situs* for cryptoassets, it is policy-motivated to enable the courts of the country of the claimant's domicile to take jurisdiction. If this is the real motivation, the better way of achieving the outcome is to make express provision in the jurisdictional rules – a step that requires legislative intervention.

Second, the natural forum inquiry in the English cases is hardly natural. The inquiry needs to be tailored to suit the circumstances of cryptoasset fraud involving persons unknown claims. The natural forum inquiry is only meaningful where the dispute can be pursued in more than one forum so as to enable a comparison to be made between the forum court and the alternative foreign forum (generally argued by the defendants). In *Ion Science*, Butcher J acknowledged that 'in a case of a persons unknown claim it is obviously difficulty to identify another forum'.[76] In *Janesh s/o Rajkumar v Unknown Person*

[73] A Dickinson, 'Cryptocurrencies and The Conflict of Laws' in D Fox and S Green (eds), *Cryptocurrencies in Public and Private Law* (Oxford, Oxford University Press, 2019) para 109.

[74] ibid.

[75] In the context of a jurisdictional application, the court should refrain from 'deciding controversial points of law in a developing area on assumed or hypothetical facts': see *Tulip Trading Ltd v Bitcoin Association For BSV* [2023] EWCA Civ 83, [2023] 4 WLR 16 [15] (Birss LJ).

[76] *Ion Science* (n 23) [16].

('CHEFPIERRE'), the General Division of the Singapore High Court, in granting approval to serve out of Singapore in an application for a proprietary injunction, conceded the difficulties it faced:[77]

> 'In the present case, I was satisfied that the court had the jurisdiction to hear the present application. While the decentralised nature of blockchains may pose difficulties when it comes to establishing jurisdiction, to my mind, there had to be a court which had the jurisdiction to hear the dispute. In the present case, based on the available facts before me, that court was the Singapore court. The primary connecting factor was the fact that the claimant was located in Singapore, and carried on his business here.'

I propose to draw a lesson from the 'single forum' cases in anti-suit injunction applications to help us better understand the requirement of 'natural forum' in the specific context of an application for a worldwide *Mareva* injunction against persons unknown. Where anti-suit injunctions are concerned, a case is labelled a 'single forum' case if the action can only be brought in a foreign forum and no action could be maintained in the forum court.[78] Hence, the forum court could not have been the natural forum for the dispute. Nevertheless, the natural forum requirement in the context of anti-suit injunction is to show that there is a *sufficient connection* between the claim and the forum to justify the forum issuing an intrusive interim order. In other words, showing that the forum court is the natural forum for the claim is merely one way of demonstrating a sufficient connection. In 'single forum' cases, exceptionally and consistently with international comity, an anti-suit injunction could be granted by an English court 'in circumstances where the relevant transaction was overwhelmingly English in character'.[79]

Turning to the crypto fraud cases involving person unknown claims, in the interest of observing international comity, the forum court should only intervene to award an intrusive order where there is a sufficient connection between the application and the forum court and it is necessary to do so. A key difference between the anti-suit injunction context and the *Mareva* injunction context under consideration here is that an action can be pursued in the forum in the latter scenario. This should mean that no exceptionality is required to justify the grant of permission to serve out of jurisdiction, if it could be shown that the claims, at the stage of application, are sufficiently (instead of over-whelmingly) connected with the forum. My re-analysis avoids the artificiality of saying the forum court is the natural forum. Instead, it directs focus on the forum court being really the one to provide the much-needed relief and is in this sense a 'single forum'. Even if the matter proceeds to an inter partes hearing and it then turns out that the claim ought to proceed in a foreign forum, the 'single forum' analysis provides principled justification to sustain the *Mareva* injunction. My re-analysis is consistent with the Singapore court's approach in *Janesh* discussed above.

[77] Above n 32 at [30].
[78] See, eg, *Midland Bank v Laker Airways* [1986] QB 689.
[79] *Airbus Industrie GIE v Patel* [1999] 1 AC 119 (HL), 138.

4.3. Alternative Service and the Hague Service Convention

The UK is a Contracting Party to the Convention on the Service Abroad of Judicial and Extrajudicial Documents in Civil or Commercial Matters (the 'Hague Service Convention').[80] Singapore deposited its instrument of accession on 16 May 2023 and the Convention entered into force for Singapore on 1 December 2023. It is generally accepted that the Hague Service Convention operates on a 'non-mandatory but exclusive' model.[81] Relevantly, whilst the instrument purports to provide legal certainty through the application of a harmonised set of rules for the service of judicial and extrajudicial documents overseas (ie through the Central Authority designated by each Contracting Party), it potentially constitutes a hindrance where crypto fraud is concerned if one of the parties sought to be served is located in a Hague Convention state. This is because it may take weeks or months to effect service through the Hague Service Convention machinery. Where interim relief is concerned, expeditious service is crucial. The more effective means of service would be through electronic means – including email, Twitter, by NFT (by way of non-fungible token airdrop) sent to the relevant wallets,[82] etc – which both English and Singapore courts have ordered as alternative service.[83]

The Hague Service Convention does not apply in cases where the address of the person sought to be served is unknown.[84] However, where the respondents' addresses are known and they are located in Hague Service Convention states, English courts will grant alternative service only if there are special circumstances for departing from the service regime under the Convention.[85] In *Russian Commercial Bank (Cyprus) Ltd v Khoroshilov*, the English High Court considered that there were special circumstances in the case justifying departure from the Hague Service Convention machinery:

> '… the evidence was that communications from the Russian Courts had gone unanswered, and that the best efforts of the Russian law enforcement agencies had failed to locate Mr Khoroshilov. Further the arrest warrant would mean that obeying a summons would expose him to the risk of being arrested. These are plainly unusual and special circumstances'.

In *Fetch.ai*, a crypto fraud case, the English High Court observed:[86]

> 'There is, however, an increasing body of case law in which various judges of the Commercial Court have held in various terms that orders which involve either

[80] See www.hcch.net/en/instruments/conventions/full-text/?cid=17.

[81] C Bernasconia and L Thébault (eds), *Practical Handbook on the Operation of the Service Convention* (The Hague, Wilson & Lafleur, 2006) [24]–[41].

[82] *Osbourne v Persons Unknown* [2023] EWHC 39 (KB) (first case in which service by NFT to the relevant wallets as sole means of service was authorised by an English court).

[83] In Singapore, alternative service is known as substituted service.

[84] Hague Service Convention, Art 1.

[85] *Russian Commercial Bank (Cyprus) Ltd v Khoroshilov* [2020] EWHC 1164 (Comm) [97]. Cockerill J clarified that the test of CPR 6.15 (alternative service) is 'good reason' but in the context of the Hague Convention, 'there will only be good reason if there are special circumstances'.

[86] Above n 28 at [46].

> prohibitory injunctions or mandatory orders (including, in particular, freezing orders and the like) should be served by alternative means if that is the only means by which the orders can be drawn speedily to the attention of the respondent concerned because, if the alternative is service by a means which will take weeks and perhaps months to satisfy, then the orders which are made and the reasons for the making of those orders will be defeated. In the circumstances, I am entirely satisfied that it is appropriate to make an alternative service order in respect of the order made against the second respondent.'

The same sentiments were expressed by the English High Court in *Osbourne* which had taken into account that 'there is at least a possibility' that the persons unknown are located in Hague Service Convention states.[87] There appears to be judicial practice in the Commercial Court of authorising alternative service in cases involving interim relief nearly as a matter of course, thereby bypassing the Hague Service Convention obstacle.

It is unclear how Singapore law will deal with alternative service (known as substituted service) where the person sought to be served is located in a Hague Service Convention state. Interestingly, under the current version of Rules of Court 2021, there is no provision for substituted service for service outside Singapore. It is hoped that the Singapore legislature could give some thought to the need for alternative service in cases involving cross-border crypto fraud and how that ought to shape the amendments to the Rules of Court 2021. Perhaps, the more pertinent point is that international treaties that aim to promote harmonised rules and cross-border collaboration should be drafted or amended to accommodate the impact technology has on the service of judicial documents.[88]

4.4. A Balanced Approach: Persons Unknown Who are Innocent of Wrongdoing and 'Newcomers'?

The eagerness of the courts to assist the victim of crypto fraud should be tempered by the countervailing concern to protect the interests of innocent persons whose identities are not yet known at the point of application. The undertaking to pay damages on the part of the claimant may not always be sufficient. In *Fetch.ai*, the English High Court identified three categories of persons unknown: (a) those

[87] Above n 22 at [31].

[88] Interestingly, during the COVID-19 pandemic, various Contracting States had suspended service of process of process through their designated Central Authorities, rendering service through the Hague Service Convention machinery impracticable. See *Australian Information Commission v Facebook Inc* [2020] FCA 531, (2020) 144 ACSR 88. In this case, the Australian court ordered substituted service even though Ireland's High Court and postal services remained operative on the basis that 'it is impracticable to do so in the rapidly changing and evolving environment caused by the current pandemic; the present situation may have changed by the time service in the relevant way would be sought to be effected'.

who are directly involved in the fraud; (b) those who received assets without having paid a full price of them; and (c) innocent receivers 'who have no reasonable grounds for thinking that what has happened in their account belongs to the claimant'.[89] In that case, the claimant sought both a proprietary injunction as well as a worldwide *Mareva* injunction. To protect the innocent receivers, the court restricted the scope of proprietary relief to 'those assets which the third categories of persons unknown either knew, or ought reasonably to have known, belong to the claimant or did not belong to them'.[90]

Further, the worldwide *Mareva* injunction should include appropriate limiting provisions. Two important terms established in English authorities for the modern *Mareva* injunction would be relevant. First, that the order does not operate upon the assets directly or third parties (such as banks) holding the assets; their effectiveness depend on their recognition and enforcement by the courts of the relevant country.[91] Second, it does not prevent foreign banks, which have presence in England and therefore subject to the English court's jurisdiction, from complying with 'what they reasonably believe to be their obligations, contractual or otherwise, under the laws and obligations of the country or state in which those assets are situated or under the proper law of the account in question or any orders of the courts in that country or state'.[92]

An indirect means of protecting persons unknown who may be innocent of wrongdoing is to encourage claimants to hold fire on persons unknown until information in relation to these parties is obtained from respondents to information disclosure orders. The introduction of a new basis for service out of jurisdiction in respect of an application for information disclosure orders could help claimants to direct more consideration to breaking down their cross-border litigation strategy into phases, starting with obtaining more information to help them decide on next steps. The information obtained from the respondents of information disclosure orders would also give the court a more complete picture as to who are the likely addressees of the injunctions. Claimants may be incentivised to adopt such an approach to reduce upstream costs. English law has already introduced such a jurisdictional gateway in CPR PD 6B para 3.1(25) in October 2022 to cater for a claim or application information disclosure orders against non-parties, provided that the claim or application is made for the purpose that proceedings have already commenced in England or which, subject to the content of the information disclosed, are intended to be commenced in England. This gateway was successfully invoked in *LMN v Bitflyer Holdings Inc*.[93]

Finally, English courts have decided, in the traditional contexts of protests and encampment, that prohibitory injunctions against persons unknown can be

[89] *Fetch.ai* (n 28) [7].
[90] ibid.
[91] *Babanaft International Co SA v Bassatne* [1990] Ch 13.
[92] *Baltic Shipping Co v Translink Shipping Ltd and Translink Pacific Shipping Ltd* [1995] 1 Lloyd's Rep 673.
[93] Above n 22.

granted against 'newcomers' – that is, persons who are caught by the injunction not at the time the order was issued but by reason of their conduct subsequent to the issuance of the order.[94] In *MBR Acres Ltd v McGivern*,[95] the English High Court highlighted various uncertainties concerning the operation of injunctions against persons unknown where a 'newcomer' is concerned. First, there are inconsistent authorities as to whether to be captured by the injunction as a 'newcomer', the person must have *knowingly* breached the terms of the order. Second, if the 'newcomer' is automatically captured as a defendant to the order, what are the procedural implications in practice: for example, does the claimant need to formally confirm that it is pursuing a claim against the 'newcomer' and if it chooses not to, whether it needs to discontinue the claim? These questions have been pejoratively described by the High Court as consequences arising from 'moving civil litigation … into the uncertain territory of prohibitions by injunction that are potentially binding on the whole world'.[96] They highlight the important but overlooked inquiry as to the proper jurisprudential basis of unknown persons orders and the need to delineate their boundaries. In principle, there is no reason why the 'newcomer' concept does not apply in respect of other interim orders against persons unknown. In the context of crypto fraud, there may be persons who become subsequent transferees of the cryptoassets. The same questions would undoubtedly arise. Indeed, in *Wolverhampton City Council v London Gypsies and Travellers*, the UK Supreme Court, in affirming the court's powers to grant 'newcomer' injunctions, has observed that the proliferation of online wrongs and the ability of perpetrators to hide behind the veil of anonymity 'has made the availability of injunctions against unidentified persons an increasingly significant question'.[97]

5. Supporting Overseas Litigation?

The current legislative provision for a 'free-standing' *Mareva* injunction may not assist a victim of crypto fraud at the stage of proceedings where the defendants are persons unknown. This is because the provisions are worded in such a way that an action before a foreign court has been commenced or is to be commenced.[98] Where the defendants are persons unknown, their identities and whereabouts are unknown and it is therefore not possible to identify the foreign court before which an action will be commenced. How is the court to decide whether it would be

[94] *Barking and Dagenham London Borough Council v Persons Unknown* [2022] EWCA Civ 13, [2023] QB 295.

[95] [2022] EWHC 2072 (QB).

[96] ibid [74].

[97] [2023] UKSC 47 [3].

[98] See Civil Jurisdiction and Judgments Act 1982, s 25 (as amended by Civil Jurisdiction and Judgments Act 1982 (Interim Relief) Order 1997 (SI 1997/302); Civil Law Act 1909, s 4(10A).

'expedient' (in the case of the English framework) or 'just or convenient' (in the case of the Singapore framework) to grant the order? There is no certainty that the potential defendants have assets in the forum such that a foreign judgment will likely be enforced locally.[99]

It may be asked whether there is scope for awarding a 'free-standing' worldwide *Mareva* injunction against persons unknown in anticipation of an action being commenced in a court at some point. It may be argued that this does not require too great a leap in legal reform because there is already existing legislative provision for a 'free-standing' *Mareva* injunction to support (existing or impending) overseas litigation and the courts readily grant worldwide *Mareva* injunction against persons unknown in cases of crypto fraud albeit there were substantive claims commenced before the forum court in these cases. If the 'enforcement principle' enunciated by Lord Leggatt in *Broad Idea* is to be taken seriously and more broadly, what is stopping countries from enacting laws to provide for a 'free-standing' worldwide *Mareva* injunction against persons unknown? There are two main objections: first, whether such an injunction is necessary; and secondly, whether such an injunction offends international comity. Turning first to the question of necessity, if a claimant is domiciled in England, current English decisions demonstrate that there is no difficulty for a claimant to bring an action in English court and obtain the necessary interim relief with permission to serve out of jurisdiction. One possible scenario where such a novel form of *Mareva* injunction may be required is where the victim is domiciled in a jurisdiction where the domestic courts have no power to grant a *Mareva* injunction (or similar relief) and the circumstances of the fraud are unconnected with the forum. If such are the facts, this brings us to the second objection – why should the forum court come to the aid of this victim? Instead of being a 'constructive player in international litigation',[100] the forum court may be accused of being an 'international busybody'.[101] Interestingly, in *RI International Pte Ltd v Lonstroff AG*, the Singapore High Court suggested by way of obiter that a permanent anti-suit injunction to support foreign international arbitrations may be granted where 'strong reasons' are shown – one instance would be 'where the forum in which the arbitration is to take place does not provide effective interim measures in support of arbitration'.[102]

[99] Civil Law Act 1909, s 4(10C)(b). See also TM Yeo, *Commercial Conflict of Laws* (Singapore, Academy Publishing, 2023) para 07.071.

[100] According to the Ministry of Law of Singapore, the legislative reform to confer a power on the Singapore courts to issue a 'free-standing' *Mareva* injunction in support of overseas litigation is to 'enhance Singapore's standing as a constructive player in international litigation and support our efforts to promote Singapore as a leading dispute resolution hub'. See www.mlaw.gov.sg/news/press-releases/2021-07-26-legislative-amendments-for-future-ready-courts.

[101] This was Singapore's general justification for not issuing an anti-suit injunction in support of foreign court or arbitral proceedings: see *People's Insurance Co Ltd v Akai Pty Ltd* [1997] SGHC 165, [1997] 2 SLR(R) 291 [12]. The 'busybody' criticism would be particularly forceful if the foreign forum in which the substantive claim is commenced has strong objection to such types of interim relief or does not welcome 'intervention' by another court.

[102] [2014] SGHC 69, [2014] 3 SLR 166 [55].

It is often said that cross-border judicial assistance and collaboration are best achieved through bilateral or multilateral treaties but such efforts (especially where multilateral treaties are concerned) are arduous, protracted and their laudable aims are often thwarted or distorted by political motivations. Hence, our laws may therefore continue to lag behind technological developments even when consensus is reached and is implemented across the Contracting States.

6. Conclusion

The UK Law Commission announced the launch of the 'Digital assets: which law, which court?' project in 2022, which will culminate in the publication of a public proposal paper in the second half of 2023.[103] This project is meant to support technological innovation in the UK to help promote the wider goal of economic growth. Singapore is also going big on 'digital assets innovation' which the nation considers 'an important enabler' that can potentially transform 'financial markets, cross-border payments, settlements, capital markets'.[104] The hoped-for innovation will certainly generate new forms of cyber fraud and challenges for victims to claim relief. Strengthening legal protection and ensuring our laws do not fall behind the pace of technological advancement are crucial. The *Mareva* injunction and other interim reliefs are undoubtedly part of the picture. Through an analysis of the litigation context of cryptoasset fraud and the identification of gaps and constraints in current law, this paper hopes to contribute to the grander project of reshaping private international rules to combat new forms of commercial fraud.

[103] See www.lawcom.gov.uk/law-commission-review-to-examine-how-private-international-law-can-apply-to-digital-assets-and-other-emerging-technology/.

[104] J Lau, 'Singapore is open to innovation in digital assets, but not crypto speculation: DPM Wong' The Straits Times (17 November 2022). See www.straitstimes.com/singapore/singapore-is-open-to-innovation-in-digital-assets-but-not-crypto-speculation-dpm-wong.

8

Subordination of the Wrongdoer in Tracing Claims

MAGDA RACZYNSKA

1. Introduction

Claims contingent on tracing ('tracing claims') are an important form of civil redress for fraud in common law jurisdictions, although their relevance is not limited to fraud. The doctrine of tracing enables a person whose asset was misappropriated to identify in the hands of the wrongdoer, or a third party, another asset[1] ('traceable proceeds'). Its purpose is to facilitate a proprietary claim[2] with respect to the traceable proceeds or a personal claim against a defendant who knowingly received them.[3] It is important to acknowledge at the outset that the law of tracing is in a state of flux, with a number of issues relating to the doctrine's scope, operation and basis poised between the core debates of private law[4] such as those about the meaning and extent of property rights, the interaction between common law and equity, or the availability of unjust enrichment.[5] This chapter considers only one aspect of the law of tracing that remains unsettled and proposes how

[1] In this chapter, the term 'asset' is understood broadly as something capable of being assumed (held, controlled) by others in exchange for something else: see *National Provincial Bank Ltd v Hastings Car Mart Ltd* [1965] AC 1175, 1247–48 (Lord Wilberforce). It is used interchangeably with the term 'property'. See M Raczynska, *The Law of Tracing in Commercial Transactions* (Oxford, Oxford University Press, 2018) [1.08]–[1.12]. See, too, L Smith, *The Law of Tracing* (Oxford, Clarendon Press, 1997) 49–50.

[2] One important advantage of a proprietary claim, which hardly seems worth stating, is the protection in the defendant's insolvency as the claimant has a power to demand that the liquidator or administrator should set the asset aside from the insolvent's estate, which is otherwise distributed *pari passu* among the creditors.

[3] The analysis here focuses on tracing when the claimant is interested in proprietary claims.

[4] P Sales, 'The Future of Tracing: Practical and Conceptual Issues' (2017) 25 *Restitution Law Review* 183, 183.

[5] See R Stevens, *The Laws of Restitution* (Oxford, Oxford University Press, 2023) for the most comprehensive and sustained critique of the law of unjust enrichment. Note, in particular, the analysis of tracing at 243–51.

the law should develop. It focuses on misappropriation of assets held on trust,[6] which is the paradigm case when tracing is available. In those cases, the claimant is typically a beneficiary under an express trust or a constructive trust that arises in response to a fraudulent misrepresentation. Nevertheless, the issues discussed here will be of relevance to tracing beyond the trust context.[7]

The problem discussed in this chapter relates to tracing in and out of a mixed fund containing the wrongdoer's (trustee's) own money and misappropriated trust money. The issue is whether the claimant (beneficiary) is entitled to elect what asset to trace into in a way that is most favourable to her (to 'cherry-pick'). Special attention shall be paid to mixed bank accounts given the ubiquity of this form of asset. The following examples provide an illustration of the type of scenario considered in this chapter.

Example 8.1

T is a trustee of a trust for a beneficiary, B. In breach of trust, T pays £10,000 of trust money into her own personal bank account, which immediately before this payment had a balance of £30,000. T then makes various transfers from her (now mixed) account: she first spends £10,000 on nursery fees and energy bills, and later transfers a further £10,000 to pay for a painting. The balance in the account is now £20,000; it never falls below £10,000. The painting has doubled in value.

Example 8.2

The facts are as in Example 8.1, but T then transfers the remaining balance in the account (£20,000) to pay her solicitor for his services. The solicitor is not a bona fide purchaser as he knows about the breaches of trust.

In Example 8.1, can B trace into the painting or is B limited to tracing into the account balance? In Example 8.2, can B elect between tracing into the painting and the payment to the solicitor?

Authorities do not provide a clear answer, and are inconsistent.[8] In *Shalson v Russo* Rimer J said, obiter, that a party seeking to trace could choose to proceed either against the mixed fund or against an asset acquired with money drawn from that fund since it would be unjust to leave the wrongdoing trustee 'with all the

[6] The paradigm scenario considered here is misappropriation by a trustee of an express trust, but the same issues arise where assets are misappropriated by a trustee of a constructive or resulting trust. The analysis of the issues presented in this chapter is the same irrespective of the type of trust.

[7] It is far from uncontroversial when tracing is available.

[8] C Mitchell, P Mitchell, and S Watterson, *Goff & Jones on Unjust Enrichment*, 10th edn (London, Sweet & Maxwell, 2022) [7-53].

cherries and the victim with nothing'.[9] Some willingness to accept (or at least not immediately to reject) cherry-picking can further be gauged from *Lapome v Kent*,[10] although the strike-out action in that case did not require the judge to decide to what extent the claimant could cherry-pick. By contrast, in *Turner v Jacob*, Patten J held that 'where the trustee maintains in the account an amount equal to the remaining trust fund, the beneficiary's right to trace is limited to that fund'.[11] This approach has gained some support in *ED&F Man v Come Harvest.*[12] The two lines of cases render diametrically different results. In Example 8.1 above, B would be able to elect between the mixed fund and the more valuable investment under the approach in *Shalson* but would be limited to the mixed account under *Turner*. In Example 8.2, the issues are complicated by the fact that there is a payment to a third party, not an investment. *Shalson* does not address this, but it is possible to apply the cherry-picking rule against non-bona fide third parties on the basis that such a party should not stand in a better position than the wrongdoing trustee. Nevertheless, cherry-picking in such circumstances was rejected in *ED&F Man*, in which Calver J followed *Turner.* The judge held that the claimant could not elect to trace into a payment to a third party who is not a bona fide purchaser on the grounds that targeting a particular recipient of a mixed fund, out of many possible recipients, would be arbitrary.[13]

The aim of this chapter is to show that Rimer J's obiter in *Shalson* is preferable as a matter of principle and policy. The relevant principle that grounds the beneficiary's entitlement to elect which traceable proceeds to claim is the subordination of the wrongdoer's interests to those of a beneficiary. This is not a new proposition, but this chapter contributes new thinking about the nature of the relevant wrongdoing. In cases of withdrawals from mixtures, the wrongdoing is more complex than previously assumed. It consists not only of the breach of trust (or similar other custodial duty) but also creation of an uncertainty about whose money is withdrawn from the mixed fund.[14] This nuance is collapsed in the *Turner v Jacob* line of cases. The policy argument is that wrongdoers should not have a say which profits from their wrongs to keep. This is narrower than the argument sometimes raised that wrongdoers should not profit from their wrongs. These points also shine light on the limits of cherry-picking.

The chapter structure is as follows. Section 2 shows, contrary to some views expressed in the literature, that tracing is a proprietary process in the sense that it is premised on identification of assets (things or rights) in relation to which a proprietary claim is made. It also addresses how tracing through mixed accounts works. Section 3 looks at the way in which courts approach uncertainty in relation to mixed funds. It argues that in cases of mixed funds, courts have generally shown considerable sensitivity to the issue of uncertain contributions into the mixtures

[9] *Shalson v Russo* [2003] EWHC 1637 (Ch), [2005] Ch 281 [144].
[10] *Lapome Ltd v Kemp* [2023] EWHC 1564 (Ch).
[11] *Turner v Jacob* [2006] EWHC 1317 (Ch) [102].
[12] *ED&F Man Capital Markets v Come Harvest Holdings Ltd* [2022] EWHC 229 (Comm).
[13] ibid [684].
[14] I am very grateful to Irit Samet for discussions that helped me crystallise my thoughts on this point.

and have applied rules of attribution (not merely evidential presumptions) to deal with this uncertainty. The emerging principle is one of subordination of interests of the wrongdoer. Section 4 identifies some policy considerations underpinning cherry-picking and identifies limits to the rule. Section 5 concludes.

2. Tracing as a Proprietary Process

One view of tracing is that it is based on the no-profit rule in fiduciary relations, namely that the fiduciary must account for the profit made in the breach of fiduciary duty.[15] I shall call it the 'no-profits model of tracing'. The principal's proprietary claim over such profits is based on a declaration[16] of a constructive trust over those profits on the basis that a fiduciary 'cannot in good conscience assert his own beneficial interest … as against some other person of whose rights he is aware'.[17]

There are some difficulties with using disgorgements of profits to model tracing. First, it does not reflect the law. Courts do not refer to the no-profit rule as a justification for tracing claims.[18] On the no-profits model of tracing, there would also be no issue with cherry-picking as the fiduciary would hold all gains made in breach of fiduciary duty on constructive trust for the principal, possibly subject to an equitable allowance for the fiduciary's skill and effort.[19] The claimant would have all the cherries. This is evidently not the law, as the discussion in the introduction to this chapter illustrates: even on the more claimant-friendly approach under *Shalson*, the claimant must elect between the different assets, into which she can trace, so she does not have a right to all profits. On the no-profits view of tracing the claimant would obtain a windfall. Secondly, the recognition of a constructive trust over profits taken in breach of fiduciary duty continues to be controversial. While English law is clear that a court will declare a constructive trust over bribes and secret commissions,[20] it is unclear on what basis constructive trusts should be

[15] S Williston, 'The Right to Follow Trust Property when Confused with Other Property' (1888) 1 *Harvard Law Review* 28, 29; D Whayman, 'Obligation and Property in Tracing Claims' [2018] *Conveyancer and Property Lawyer* 157, 158–60, 164.

[16] Note the term Whayman, 'Obligation and Property in Tracing Claims' (n 15) 158 uses is 'imposed' constructive trust, but this must be in a loose sense since English law does not recognise remedial constructive trusts: eg *Re Goldcorp Exchange Ltd* [1995] 1 AC 74 (PC) 104 (Lord Mustill), *Re D&D Wines International Ltd (in liquidation)* [2016] UKSC 47, [2016] 1 WLR 3179 [27]–[28] (Lord Sumption), *Aquila Advisory Ltd v Faichney* [2021] UKSC 49, [2021] 1 WLR 5666 [88] (Lord Stephens). This is by contrast to other Commonwealth jurisdictions – see, eg, in Australia: *Grimaldi v Chameleon Mining (No 2)* [2012] FCAFC 6, (2012) 200 FCR 296, and Canada: *LAC Minerals Ltd v International Corona Resources Ltd* [1989] 2 SCR 574.

[17] *Re D&D Wines* (n 16) [28] (Lord Sumption) (noting *Nesté Oy v Lloyds Bank Plc* [1983] 2 Lloyd's Rep 658).

[18] Note that D Whayman, 'Lapome Ltd v Kemp: *More Questions than Answers Regarding Tracing into Mixtures*' (2024) 140 *LQR* 6, 9 refers to *Re Hallett's Estate* (1880) 13 Ch D 696 as based on account of profit but this is not what the case decided. It might perhaps be argued that it was important in *Hallett's Estate* that the fiduciary is disabled from taking the benefit of the remaining mixed fund, but this was not based on the solicitor's liability for account of profits as a fiduciary. See section 3 below.

[19] *Boardman v Phipps* [1967] 2 AC 46 (HL) but see *Guinness plc v Saunders* [1990] 2 AC 663 (HL).

[20] See, eg, *FHR European Ventures LLP v Cedar Capital Partners LLC* [2014] UKSC 45, [2015] AC 250.

recognised, and whether in relation to profits in other contexts.[21] Thirdly, a model of tracing based on the no-profit rule in fiduciary relations would be difficult to apply outside fiduciary relationships[22] and tracing should not be limited to fiduciary relationships.[23] However, even if a fiduciary relationship is a pre-requisite to tracing (in equity), it does not follow that the basis of a claim to assets that constitute traceable proceeds should be the no-profit rule. Finally, the availability of tracing, on this obligational no-profit model would likely be much more limited than it is at present, given that commercial contracts often exclude or limit the existence of a fiduciary relationship.[24]

A preferable view is that tracing protects proprietary interests in assets when they are held by a person who is under a duty to hold, or administer assets for another, but disposes of the property in an unauthorised way. As a proprietary process, identification of the new (traceable) asset is the core of the exercise. In an often-cited passage Lord Millett said obiter:

> Tracing is … neither a claim nor a remedy. It is merely the process by which a claimant demonstrates what has happened to his property, identifies its proceeds and the persons who have handled or received them, and justifies his claim that the proceeds can properly be regarded as representing his property.[25]

The purpose of identifying assets is so that a claimant can show that an interest she had in an asset has become represented by an interest in a different asset.[26]

[21] The principle was not explained in the leading case of *FHR European Ventures* (n 20). See S Worthington, 'Four Questions on Fiduciaries' (2018) 32 *Trust Law International* 22. Favouring the recognition of a constructive trust was P Millett, 'Proprietary Restitution' in S Degeling and J Edelman (eds), *Equity in Commercial Law* (Sydney, Law Book Co, 2005), ch 12; P Millett, 'Bribes and Secret Commissions Again' (2012) 71 *CLJ* 583. See also Lord Hodge, 'Property Law, Fiduciary Obligations and the Constructive Trust' in F McCarthy, J Chalmers and S Bogle (eds), *Essays in Conveyancing and Property Law in Honour of Professor Robert Rennie* (Cambridge, Open Book Publishers, 2015) 97.

[22] See the very exceptional circumstances in *Attorney-General v Blake* [2001] 1 AC 268.

[23] *Foskett v McKeown* [2001] AC 102, 128 (Lord Millett); Smith, *The Law of Tracing* (n 1); A Televantos, 'Losing the Fiduciary Requirement for Equitable Tracing Claims' (2017) 133 *LQR* 492 (showing that tracing in equity by a legal owner was historically possible); A Nair, *Claims to Traceable Proceeds. Laws, Equity, and the Control of Assets* (Oxford, Oxford University Press, 2018) [6.20]; Raczynska, *The Law of Tracing in Commercial Transactions* (n 1) [1.46]–[1.53], [6.17]–[6.22]; M Hafeez-Baig and J English, *The Law of Tracing* (Alexandria, The Federation Press, 2021) [5-65]–[5.114]. See, too, AJ Oakley, 'The Prerequisites of an Equitable Tracing Claim' (1975) 28 *Current Legal Problems* 64, 65 fn 11.

[24] I am very grateful to Georgia Quenby for this point.

[25] *Foskett v McKeown* (n 23) 128, cited in, eg, *Relfo Ltd (in liq) v Varsani* [2012] EWHC 2168 (Ch) [72] (Sales J), affirmed [2014] EWCA Civ 360, [2015] 1 BCLC 14; *Roadchef (Employee Benefits Trustees) Ltd v Hill* [2014] EWHC 109 (Ch); *Glenn v Watson* [2018] EWHC 2016 (Ch) [540] (Nugee J); *Kahrmann v Harrison-Morgan* [2019] EWCA Civ 2094; *National Bank Trust v Yurov* [2020] EWHC 1779 (Comm) [30] (Cockerill J); *Amarjeet Singh Dhir v Flutter Entertainment Plc* [2021] EWHC 1510 (QB) [182]; *Re Smith* [2021] EWHC 1272 (Comm) [125]; *Shovlin v Site Civils and Surfacing Ltd* [2022] EWHC 3198 (Ch), [2023] 2 BCLC 527 [44]. The passage was also adopted in Australia – see, eg, *Evans v European Bank Ltd* [2004] NSWCA 82, 7 ITELR 19 [155] (Spigelman CJ) (Handley and Santow JJA agreeing); *Westpac Banking Corporation v The Bell Group Ltd (in liq) (No 3)* [2012] WASCA 157, (2012) 270 FLR 1 [2568] (Drummond AJA). See, too, *Boscawen v Bajwa* [1996] 1 WLR 328 (CA) 334 (Millett LJ with whom Waite and Stuart-Smith LJJ agreed), cited in *Menelaou v Bank of Cyprus plc* [2015] UKSC 66, [2016] AC 176 [124] (Lord Carnwath).

[26] *Shalson v Russo* (n 9) [102] (Rimer J).

Identification is important for the simple reason that proprietary claims require identification of specific things or specific rights for the claim to relate to them.[27]

The process of identifying assets as traceable proceeds continues to be debated. The orthodox view is that tracing is about identifying value inherent in an asset.[28] However, the concept of tracing value from one asset to another is problematic.[29] In particular, an exchange of one asset (worth £100) for another (worth £50) does not preclude the exercise of tracing. A better approach to the process of tracing is to focus on the defendant's exercise of powers of disposition of the defendant's interest (rights) in an asset. The defendant can exercise a power to dispose of her interest (rights) in an asset in a way which is either authorised or unauthorised.[30] If authorised, the parties' agreement (or terms on which the power to dispose is granted) determines whether the claimant has an interest in the proceeds of the exercise of the power.[31] Tracing has no role to play in authorised dispositions. Tracing is about an unauthorised exercise of the defendant's power to dispose of her interest (rights) in an asset.[32] What the claimant traces into is the proceeds of the unauthorised exercise of the power of disposition over an asset. As long as the proceeds of the exercise of the disposition power constitute a specific asset (such as a specific right), the claimant can trace into them and to make a proprietary claim to them. For example, where the trustee spends trust money to purchase a car, the exercise of the trustee's power to dispose of the money results in an acquisition of the trustee's rights in a car because the power to dispose of the money was exercised in a contract to purchase a car.

Hafeez-Baig and English argued, similarly to what I said in *The Law of Tracing in Commercial Transactions*, on which this account is based, that tracing is about an unauthorised use of a person's rights.[33] However, their focus is on a specific purpose for which the initial rights are used: to acquire or create new rights.[34] This seems narrower than the idea of identifying a specific asset (eg a right) as proceeds of the exercise of a power to dispose of the initial asset I suggested in *The Law of Tracing*. In many situations, because of the way in which a transaction work, a new right is acquired or created because the initial right is disposed of, so the two approaches look similar. However, my approach leaves open the possibility that a transaction might involve an exercise of a power to dispose of an interest (right) without the disponor acquiring a new right, for example where the outcome of the disposition of one right is a variation of the subject matter of (eg an accretion to)

[27] *Re Goldcorp* (n 16) 89–90 (Lord Mustill).

[28] See *Foskett v McKeown* (n 23) 128 (Lord Millett); *Relfo v Varsani* (n 25) [60] (Arden LJ); *Ultraframe v Fielding* [2005] EWHC 1638 (Ch) [1472] (Lewison J); *Federal Republic of Brazil v Durant International Corp* [2015] UKPC 35, [2016] AC 297 [32]; *Southage Pty Ltd v Vescovi* [2014] VSC 141 [44]–[50] Macauley J.

[29] T Cutts, 'Tracing, Value and Transactions' (2016) 79 *MLR* 381. See, too, Raczynska (n 1) [3.11]–[3.12].

[30] Raczynska (n 1) [1.54] and chs 4, 5 and 6.

[31] ibid chs 4 and 5.

[32] ibid [3.12]. Similarly, see Hafeez-Baig and English, *The Law of Tracing* (n 23) [1.47]–[1.51].

[33] Hafeez-Baig and English (n 23) [1.47]–[1.51].

[34] ibid.

the disponor's other existing right. The difference can be seen with reference to mixed bank account transfers.

Consider the following example. In breach of trust, a trustee pays £10,000 of trust money into her own personal bank account which immediately before this payment had a balance of £30,000. It is clear that that the beneficiary can trace into the mixed account. One difficulty is that it looks like there is no loss or acquisition of right.[35] This is because of the way in which transfers in and out of bank accounts are understood. Edelman and Bant argued that when a payment is made into a bank account, there is no substitution or exchange of a right against the bank.[36] The only thing that changes is the value of the debt that the bank owes to its customer. This presents an issue for Hafeez-Baig and English since rights are used without creation of new rights. They address it by drawing attention[37] to an alternative conception of transfers into bank accounts that involves extinguishment of a right against the bank when new money is paid in, and replacement with a new right.[38] On the understanding of tracing advanced here, there would be no need for the second conception of transfers in and out of bank accounts. This is not because value is traced but rather because the subject matter of the right against the bank, following the payment (ie in the example given here, the right to the balance of £40,000), is varied in the sense that the content of the bank's duty changes (a duty to pay £30,000 becomes a duty to pay a different sum, £40,000). All the while, the right of the customer against the bank to be paid an amount of money represented by the bank balance does not change. A right to be paid £40,000 is clearly more valuable than a right to be paid £30,000 and it enlarges the purchasing power of the right-holder. The reason the claimant-beneficiary can trace into the mixed account is because the trustee's right against her bank is a specific right that constitutes the proceeds of the trustee's unauthorised disposition. The fact that the trustee did not acquire a new right with the unauthorised use of the initial right does not matter; it matters that she holds a specific right whose content reflects an increased duty of the bank to pay. The trustee's right against her bank to be paid is varied in the sense that the content of her right against her bank is now to be paid more than was the case immediately before the transfer. When the claimant traces into a mixed account held by the defendant, the claimant is tracing into the defendant's right against her bank, the subject matter of which right has been varied, as if through an accretion. In practical terms, the purchasing power represented by the trust asset pre-misappropriation is combined with the purchasing power of trustee's own assets.

[35] See T Cutts, 'Dummy Asset Tracing' (2019) 135 *LQR* 140, noting also another difficulty, namely that even if a substitution could be identified, it is not a substitution by the wrongdoer as there is no transfer of rights in the context of bank accounts. On the analysis suggested here, this problem does not arise because the asset traced into need not be a new right acquired through transfer but could be an existing right that has been varied through the exercise of the power to dispose of the initial asset (right).

[36] J Edelman and E Bant, *Unjust Enrichment*, 2nd edn (Oxford, Hart Publishing, 2016) 106.

[37] Hafeez-Baig and English (n 23) [1.59]–[1.62].

[38] *Commissioner of the Australian Federal Police v Tjongosutiono* [2018] NSWSC 48, (2018) 329 FLR 103 [159] (Adams J); D Fox, *Property Rights in Money* (Oxford, Oxford University Press, 2008) [5.05]. See also Cutts, 'Dummy Asset Tracing' (n 35) 144 (noting that either conception is plausible).

Before we move to the next section, a word should be said about common law and equitable rules of tracing. It is often said it is illogical to distinguish between common law and equitable rules of tracing.[39] Yet, judges continue to identify differences between common law and equitable tracing,[40] for example that common law tracing cannot take place though mixed accounts.[41] More fundamentally, rather than unifying the rules of tracing at common law and in equity, concerns are raised whether tracing at common law is at all justified.[42] Either way, it is still appropriate as a matter of authority, to talk about tracing in equity (as opposed to simply 'tracing'), certainly where mixed accounts are concerned, which is the focus of this chapter.

3. Dealing with Uncertainty in Mixed Funds

In section 2, it was established that tracing is a process of identifying assets through an unauthorised exercise of a power to dispose of an interest (interest) in the initial asset. A trustee's misappropriation of trust fund is an unauthorised disposition of the trustee's power over the trust asset, which could be, eg, a right against a bank if trust money is held in a bank account. When a trustee pays misappropriated trust funds into her own account that is in credit, the beneficiary can trace into the mixed account by identifying an accretion to the trustee's right against the bank (a right to demand bank payment of a greater sum than prior to the exercise of the power). When money is withdrawn from such an account, the account holder's right against the bank is varied (diminished) in the sense that she can now demand payment of an amount which is smaller than immediately prior to the withdrawal. Any accretion to or diminution of the account holder's right against her bank means there is a change of the extent to which the account holder (trustee) can exercise a power to acquire or create interests in assets. In short, payments into and out of the account alter the extent to which the trustee can exercise her purchasing power. Where the account is mixed, and has been drawn on, it is uncertain whether the purchasing power represented by the remaining balance in the account is to be attributed to the trustee's own money or the trust funds. However, determining the extent to which an unauthorised use of the claimant's asset is represented by the

[39] See *Foskett v McKeown* (n 23) 128 (Lord Millett) and see 113 (Lord Steyn), approving of an explanation by P Birks, 'The Necessity of a Unitary Law of Tracing' in R Cranston (ed), *Making Commercial Law: Essays in Honour of Roy Goode* (Oxford, Clarendon Press, 1997) 243, 257–58. See, too, P Birks, 'On Taking Seriously the Difference between Tracing and Claiming' (1997) 11 *Trust Law International* 2. See, too, N Andrews and J Beatson, '"Common Law Tracing": Springboard or Swansong' (1997) 113 *LQR* 21 (suggesting the need to create a single set of rules in tracing with common terminology).

[40] *Shalson v Russo* (n 9) [103]–[104] (Rimer J); *London Allied Holdings Ltd v Lee* [2007] EWHC 2061 (Ch) [256]–[257] (Etherton J); *FHR European Ventures* (n 20) [44].

[41] *Trustee of the Property of FC Jones & Sons (A Firm) v Jones* [1997] Ch 159; *Barros Mattos Junior v MacDaniels Ltd* [2005] EWHC 1323 (Ch) [135] (Lawrence Collins QC).

[42] S Worthington, 'The Myth of Common Law Tracing' in C Mitchell and S Watterson (eds) *The World of Maritime and Commercial Law: Essays in Honour of Francis Rose* (Oxford, Hart Publishing, 2020) 309; Hafeez-Baig and English (n 23) ch 3; Edelman and Bant, *Unjust Enrichment* (n 36) ch 5.

defendant's right (against her bank) after the subject matter of the defendant's right has been varied, first through an accretion, then by diminution (through a withdrawal) is not a matter that can be established through facts and evidence because we are dealing with rights, not observable facts. What is needed is a rule of attribution. This section looks at the various fault-based rules that resolve uncertainties against the wrongdoer creating the mixtures.

3.1. Evidential Presumptions

One way to solve a problem of tracing into an account containing a mixture of the wrongdoer's and innocent party's funds is to give the entire mixed fund to the innocent party, with a view to punishing the wrongdoer, without any regard to evidence as to how much the wrongdoer contributed. Such an approach to non-consensual (unauthorised) mixtures was set out, initially, in *Lupton v White.*[43] Lord Eldon LC in *Lupton* articulated what he referred to as 'the great principle, familiar both at law and in equity' that,

> if a man, having undertaken to keep the property of another distinct, mixes it with his own, the whole must both at law and in equity be taken to be the property of the other, until the former puts the subject under such circumstances, that it may be distinguished as satisfactorily, as it might have been before that unauthorized mixture upon his part.[44]

In effect, the principle is about the extent to which a wrongdoer loses her property right. It operates harshly, to expropriate the wrongdoer, where she mixes her property with those of the another without their consent and is not able to identify her part in the mixture. Writing in the mid-eighteenth century, Blackstone thought the rule had long been established,[45] and said its purpose was 'to guard against fraud',[46] although as *Lupton* itself shows, it was not necessary to show that fraud actually occurred.[47] The rule seems to be aimed at both punishing and discouraging wrongful mixtures.[48] *Lupton* concerned what seemed to have been a bailment[49]

[43] *Lupton v White* (1808) 15 Ves Jun 432.

[44] ibid 436–37.

[45] See *In the King's Bench (anonymous)* (sub nom *Stock v Stock)* (1594) Poph 37, 38, and *Warde v Aeyre* (1615) 2 Bulst 323, both cited in W Blackstone, *Commentaries on the Laws of England* ('*Blackstone's Commentaries*') (London 1756–60) Book 2, 405.

[46] *Blackstone's Commentaries* (n 45) 405 (referring to the 'case of confusion of goods .... [where] one willfully [*sic*] intermixes his money, corn, or hay, with that of another man, without his approbation or knowledge, or casts gold in like manner into another's melting pot or crucible').

[47] In *Lupton*, the defendant, whose lead mine adjoined the claimant's mine, undertook to keep a distinct account of the ore which he would take from the claimant's mine. He then mixed the ore to prevent identification, and kept poor accounts, but there was no fraud: *Lupton* (n 43) 437.

[48] *Indian Oil Corporation Ltd v Greenstone Shipping SA (Panama) (The Ypatianna)* [1988] QB 345, 369.

[49] The report does not state clearly that the defendant was a bailee, but refers to agents and bailiffs, all of whom are stewards, ie parties under a duty to administer and apply property for a principal and to account to the principal. It is clear that the defendant in *Lupton* was a steward in that sense as he was in control of claimant's ore, mixed with own ore, as it was being excavated, and was under a duty to account to the claimant for his (claimant's) ore.

of goods, but the principle expressed in *Lupton* has been applied to trustees[50] and agents,[51] and to mixtures of money.[52]

The principle in *Lupton v White* has been limited considerably in the context of unauthorised mixtures of goods, so that a wrongdoer does not lose their property right as easily.[53] In *Indian Oil Corporation Ltd v Greenstone Shipping*,[54] a ship owner wrongfully mixed own oil with claimant's oil. It was impossible to separate the oil, so the claimant argued that it owned the entire mixture pursuant to *Lupton v White*. Staughton J rejected this argument, and held that:

> [in cases of wrongful mixtures of goods] which are of substantially the same nature and quality and they cannot in practice be separated, the mixture is held in common and [the innocent contributor] is entitled to receive out of it a quantity equal to that of his goods which went into the mixture, any doubt as to that quantity being resolved in favour of the [innocent contributor].[55]

Thus, an innocent contributor does not obtain ownership of the entire mixture simply because they did not consent to mixing, and the contribution of the wrongdoer cannot be identified and separated. Staughton J said that an unauthorised mixture of goods belongs to the innocent party only where it is 'totally *unknown how much* of the innocent party's goods *went into* the mixture (emphasis added)'.[56]

Following *Indian Oil*, the penal rule in *Lupton v White* survives but applies in more limited circumstances, which are important for us to understand. Staughton J identified two reasons why the penal rule is needed, which in turn further dictate the circumstances in which the rule applies in addition to the one just stated. One is that giving the ownership of the whole unauthorised mixture to the innocent party might be the only justice that can be done on the facts.[57] The second is where

[50] *Frith v Cartland* (1865) 2 Hem & M 417, 420; 71 ER 525, 526 (Page Wood V-C): 'if a man mixes trust funds with his own, the whole will be treated as the trust property, except so far as he may be able to distinguish what is his own'; *Re Hallett's Estate; Knatchbull v Hallett* (1880) 13 Ch D 696, 719; *Re Tilley's Will Trusts* [1967] Ch 1179, 1183 (Ungoed-Thomas J): 'if a trustee mixes trust assets with his own, the onus is on the trustee to distinguish the separate assets, and to the extent that he fails to do so they belong to the trust'; *Southern Cross Commodities Property Ltd v Martin* 1991 SLT 83, 85 (Lord Milligan) (Scots law); *Batt v Boswell* [2022] EWHC 649 (Ch) [104].

[51] *Lupton v White* (n 43); *Cook v Addison* (1869) LR 7 Eq 466, 470 (Sir John Stuart V-C): 'It is a well-established doctrine in this court, that if a trustee or agent mixes and confuses the property which he holds in a fiduciary character with his own property, so as that they cannot be separated with perfect accuracy, he is liable for the whole.'

[52] See, eg, *Frith v Cartland* (n 50).

[53] See Raczynska (n 1) [2.40] and the literature cited there.

[54] *Indian Oil Corporation* (n 48).

[55] ibid 370–71.

[56] ibid 369.

[57] ibid 368–69, referring to *Lupton v White* (n 43) 440 (Lord Eldon LC), and *Sandeman & Sons v Tyzack and Branfoot Steamship Co Ltd* [1913] AC 680, 695 (Lord Moulton) (referring to situations 'where complete justice was impracticable of attainment').

a wrongdoer destroyed or impaired the evidence through which it can be shown how much an innocent party contributed to the mixture.[58]

In this second guise, the rule is about penalising the wrongdoer where the wrongdoer *caused* evidential uncertainty, meaning that the uncertainty is a direct consequence of the wrongdoer's behaviour. This is generally expressed as an evidential presumption against the wrongdoer,[59] but – as argued in this chapter – the rule could be expressed more generally, as a presumption against the wrongdoer triggered by other forms of uncertainty caused by the wrongdoer, not necessarily evidential uncertainty.

The presumption against the wrongdoer is generally invoked in connection with resolving evidential uncertainty of the kind known from *Armory v Delamirie*.[60] In *Armory*, a jeweller refused to produce a jewel that a chimney sweep boy found and brought it to him, and returned only a ring with an empty socket. The court held that the evidential uncertainty was to be resolved against the wrongdoer. The jury was directed to find that the stone was of the highest possible value that would fit the socket unless the jeweller proved otherwise by returning the jewel. Such evidential presumption against the wrongdoer serves the purpose of protecting against fraud[61] and applies in a wide range of contexts. For example, in *Gray v Haig* the court held that an agent, who makes it impossible to ascertain how much profit he made on a transaction dealing with the goods of the principal, will be disallowed commission which, otherwise, he would be contractually entitled to.[62] In *Lupton* itself Lord Eldon LC relied on *Armory v Delamirie* in which a presumption was used to resolve an evidential (factual) uncertainty.

Evidential presumptions against the wrongdoer, on the conventional view, are thought to resolve problems with tracing into mixed accounts from which withdrawals were made. However, determining to whom the balance in an account belongs, or to whom a withdrawal belongs, is a matter of rights and not a fact that can be established by evidence. Therefore, approaching issues of mixed bank accounts by applying *evidential* presumptions is not appropriate. Consider the following example.

[58] *Indian Oil Corporation* (n 48) 369 (Staughton J): 'if the wrongdoer has destroyed or impaired the evidence by which the innocent party could show how much he has lost, the wrongdoer must suffer from the resulting uncertainty.'

[59] If the wrongdoer does not directly cause the evidential uncertainty (eg refuses to produce evidence in their control), but merely behaves wrongfully, the presumption against the wrongdoer does not apply: see *Sudha Natrajan v The Bank of East Asia Ltd* [2016] SGCA 66, [2017] 1 SLR 141 (Court of Appeal of Singapore) [63] (Sundaresh Menon CJ). Note, however, that under English law at least, a court might rule against the wrongdoer even if she did not directly cause evidential uncertainty if it finds that it must cut a 'Gordian knot' and this is the only justice that can be done on the facts: see immediately above.

[60] *Armory v Delamirie* (1722) 1 Str 505. This should come as no surprise since Lord Eldon LC himself relied on *Armory v Delamirie*: see *Lupton* (n 43) 439, as did Staughton J in *Indian Oil Corporation* (n 48) 369.

[61] *Indian Oil Corporation* (n 48) 369 and text to nn 66-68 below.

[62] *Gray v Haig* (1855) 20 Beav 219, 235; 52 ER 587, 593 (Sir John Romilly MR) (saying clearly that the principle he expresses is found in *Lupton* (n 43)).

Example 8.3

Assume A holds £200 for B in a client account with Bank X. Without authority from B, A transfers that amount into his (A's) bank account with Bank Y, which account has a balance of £300 (A's own money).

A's right against Bank Y is initially to be paid £300. When B's money is transferred into it, A's right is to be paid £500, but the right against Y (to be paid) does not change. Similarly, the bank's (Y's) obligation towards A does not change: the obligation is still to pay; an amount owed under the obligation changes, but it does not make it a new payment obligation.[63] In such a scenario it is not evidentially uncertain whose money contributed what portion to the balance of £500: A's contribution was £300 while B's was £200.

Consider now the following:

Example 8.4

Facts as in the example above. A then withdraws £100 from A's account with Y Bank, so the balance is reduced to £400.

Whose money is withdrawn? It is sometimes said that the issue can be resolved by applying an evidential presumption against the wrongdoer of the kind that existed in *Armory v Delamirie*. Such a view is mistaken – to some extent at least. It is true that A's conduct (paying B's money, without B's consent, into an account containing A's money) creates an 'uncertainty' in the sense that we do not know whose money is withdrawn. However, it is not an *evidential* uncertainty because we are not dealing with wrongdoer obscuring objectively observable (knowable) facts, as was the case in *Armory v Delamirie*. Determining whose money contributes to A's bank balance requires a rule of attribution[64] which is not based

[63] If it were otherwise, a part payment of debt would, by virtue of a mere reduction of the amount owed, create a new debt (and a correlated new right in favour of the obligee for the amount reflecting the balance owed), which is not the case. The point should be self-evident, but if an explanation was needed, consider, for example a situation where an obligation under a loan agreement secured by a mortgage is partly repaid. If the obligation to repay the loan under the loan agreement was extinguished and replaced with a new obligation each time the borrower pays down the loan, this would require creation and execution of a new mortgage (which would be rather inconvenient, and not what happens in practice), at least in cases where the mortgage was expressed to secure the discharge of a particular obligation.

[64] I distinguish between evidential presumptions and rules of attribution because evidential presumptions are about burden of proof, not allocation of entitlements, or at least not directly so. That said, an application of an evidential presumption impacts where entitlements lie, so in that sense evidential presumptions can be seen as rules of attribution in a broader sense, although not one I adopt here.

on evidence but, for instance, fault. The penal rule in *Lupton v White*, in its pre-*Indian Oil* version, is an example of a far-reaching fault-based rule of attribution.[65] It is possible for a legal system to adopt a harsh rule against wrongdoers that favours the innocent party and penalises the wrongdoer, if that were thought to be desirable, but it makes no sense to call such a rule an 'evidential presumption against a wrongdoer' where no amount of evidence can rebut it.[66] It would be helpful if courts articulated more clearly the content of, and the rationale behind, the rules they apply when deciding whether a claimant can trace into or out of a mixed account.

The lack of clear rules of attribution between wrongdoers and innocent parties has led to some creative interpretations of what 'presumption against wrongdoer' might mean. The phrase 'presumption against a wrongdoer' is liable to be understood to mean that interests of the wrongdoer are totally subordinated to those of the innocent party. If taken to a logical conclusion – would result in drastic and penal consequences. Such a rule is not the law. The case of *Serious Fraud Office v Lexi Holdings plc*[67] serves as a good illustration of the problem and shows that the court has not fallen into the trap of 'presuming everything against the wrongder'. In that case, Lexi (in administration) was a victim of fraud committed by, among others, M. Lexi paid M £625,000 into two accounts, each of which already contained M's own money. Lexi argued it had elected an equitable charge over traceable proceeds, securing M's liability to repay the money. The question was which assets were subject to the charge. The counsel for Lexi's administrator argued that equitable charge extended to all of M's assets, even his matrimonial home purchased a decade before, because the misappropriated funds were connected with all of wrongdoer's assets by the application of an evidential presumption against the wrongdoer. The wrongdoer failed to explain what had become with the £625,000 and, the argument went, he did not rebut the presumption.[68] The Court of Appeal rightly rejected this as 'completely unrealistic'.[69] The misappropriated money was paid into M's accounts, and only the mixed accounts were subject to equitable charge.

It was said so far that no 'evidential' uncertainty arises by the mere fact that funds are mixed in an account and that withdrawals are made from it. This does not mean, however, that evidential uncertainty can never arise in the context of mixed accounts. *Sinclair Investments v Versailles Trade Finance Ltd*[70] is an example of a case where the extent to which the misappropriated money survived in a mixed account was evidentially uncertain because the order of events could not be established on the evidence. In that case a fraud was orchestrated such that

[65] See discussion earlier.

[66] Whayman (n 15) 165–66. See also Stevens, *The Laws of Restitution* (n 5) 248 (noting that rights, unlike physical things, cannot be mixed together).

[67] *Director of the Serious Fraud Office v Lexi Holdings plc* [2008] EWCA Crim 1443, [2009] QB 376.

[68] ibid [52].

[69] ibid [53].

[70] *Sinclair Investments (UK) Ltd v Versailles Trade Finance Ltd* [2011] EWCA Civ 347, [2012] Ch 453.

money was misdirected in a set of complex transactions, referred to as 'cross-firing arrangements'. The issue was whether the complexity of the arrangements made it impossible to trace through them into surviving assets because the money was paid into a 'maelstrom' account and effectively disappeared into an evidential 'black hole'. Lord Neuberger MR held that tracing into the 'maelstrom' mixed account continued to be possible, and that 'the onus should be on the fiduciary to establish that part, and what part, of the mixed fund is his property'.[71]

3.2. The Good Man of Equity

It was said earlier that the use of evidential presumptions in the context of mixed accounts is not workable. One possible candidate for an alternative rule of attribution is the 'good man of Equity' principle, as it applied in *Re Hallett's Estate*.[72] It is useful to set the case out in detail.

Re Hallett's Estate concerned Hallett, a solicitor, who held some bonds (worth £2,442) for his client, Cotterill. Without any authority from his client, Hallett sold them and paid the proceeds into his own bank account. He then paid into his account other sums, and made some withdrawals for his own purposes, leaving a balance of £3,000. When Hallett died, his estate was insolvent. The question was whether Cotterill could trace into the remaining balance in the mixed account. The Court of Appeal held that she could, so that the withdrawn amount was attributed to the solicitor's own money.

The majority of the Court of Appeal disapplied the rule in *Clayton's* case, which attributes the earliest withdrawals from the account to the earliest payments into the account.[73] Jessel MR said that the rule in *Clayton's* case was a rule of convenience that did not to apply if there was evidence of contrary intention or circumstances gave rise to a different 'presumption of law'.[74] The 'presumption of law', which Sir George Jessel MR thought applied on the facts of *Re Hallett's Estate* was that the trustee was deemed to behave rightfully vis-à-vis the beneficiaries. He explained it in the following way:

> … nothing can be better settled, either in our own law, or, I suppose, the law of all civilised countries, than this, that where a man does an act which may be rightfully performed, he cannot say that that act was intentionally and in fact done wrongly.

[71] ibid [138].

[72] *Re Hallett's Estate* (n 50).

[73] *Clayton's case* (1815–16) 1 Mer 572. For application of the rule in the case of mixed funds to which trust money was contributed, see *Pennell v Deffell* (1853) 4 De GM & G 372, 43 ER 551; *Hancock v Smith* (1889) 41 Ch D 459 (CA).

[74] *Re Hallett's Estate* (n 50), 728 (Jessel MR) and 738–39 (Baggallay LJ), cited with approval in *Cory Bros & Co Ltd v Turkish Steamship Mecca, The Mecca* [1897] AC 286, 295–96, and in *Equity Trust (Jersey) Ltd v Halabi* [2022] UKPC 36, [2023] AC 877 [203] (Lord Richards and Sir Nicholas Patten, with whom Lord Stephens agreed, and Lord Reed, Lord Briggs, Lady Arden and Lady Rose agreed in this part). See, too, *Re Diplock* [1948] Ch 465, 554: '[the rule applied in *Clayton's* case] is really a rule of convenience based upon so-called presumed intention'.

> A man who has a right of entry cannot say he committed a trespass in entering ... That is the universal law. When we come to apply that principle to the case of a trustee who has blended trust moneys with his own, it seems to me perfectly plain that he cannot be heard to say that he took away the trust money when he had a right to take away his own money. The simplest case put is the mingling of trust moneys in a bag with money of the trustee's own. Suppose he has a hundred sovereigns in a bag, and he adds to them another hundred sovereigns of his own, so that they are commingled in such a way that they cannot be distinguished, and the next day he draws out for his own purposes £100, is it tolerable for anybody to allege that what he drew out was the first £100, the trust money, and that he misappropriated it, and left his own £100 in the bag? It is obvious he must have taken away that which he had a right to take away, his own £100.[75]

Jessel MR refers to the idea that the trustee, as a 'good man of Equity', is disabled from committing a wrong.[76] What this refers to is the way in which the remedial consequences arise when a steward, ie a person under a duty to hold, administer or apply property for another, disposes of the property in an unauthorised way. The paradigm example of a steward is a trustee of an express trust.[77] A beneficiary for whom a trustee holds property is entitled as of right to an account of the trustee's dealings with the property.[78] Where property is shown to be missing in accounts, the beneficiary can elect to falsify the account, which makes the misapplied assets appear in the account, and the trustee is then ordered to bring the reality in line with the accounts by producing the property *in specie*, or paying a sum based on the value of the property at the time the account is taken. The logic of this approach is that the trustee is held to account as if she acted in accordance with the terms of the trust,[79] ie as she was disabled *ab initio* from committing a breach of trust. The same logic is sometimes thought to underpin disgorgement of gains obtained in breach of fiduciary duty[80] and compensation for breach of fiduciary duty. There is much debate whether this logic reflects, and should reflect, the law governing liability for breaches of trusts and of fiduciary duty, but this is not of relevance for present purposes. The key question here is about the extent to which the analysis based on a disability from committing a wrong can help resolve the tracing questions posed in this chapter.

[75] *Re Hallett's Estate* (n 50) 727. See also 743 (Baggallay LJ).

[76] See *Turner v Jacob* (n 11) [100]: 'The trustee is effectively disabled from asserting that the money withdrawn from the account was trust money if the expenditure can be attributed to his own funds in the account.'

[77] Express trustees are prominent examples of stewards. A steward is a person who is under a duty to hold, administer and apply property for the benefit of another. Cases do not generally use the term 'stewardship', but the concept is useful in separating duties a person is under with respect to dealing with another's property from other (eg fiduciary) duties: see C Mitchell, 'Stewardship of Property and Liability to Account' [2014] *Conveyancer and Property Lawyer* 214, especially 214 and 221.

[78] *Doss v Doss* (1843) 3 Moo Ind App 175 (PC) 196–197, 18 ER 464.

[79] *Williams v Central Bank of Nigeria* [2014] UKSC 10, [2014] AC 1189 [13] (Lord Sumption). *cf* liability of the trustee based on compensation for loss in *Target Holdings Ltd v Redferns (A Firm)* [1996] AC 421 and *AIB Group (UK) plc v Mark Redler & Co Solicitors* [2014] UKSC 58, [2015] AC 1503.

[80] See, eg, P Millett, 'Bribes and Secret Commissions' (1993) *Restitution Law Review* 7, 20. For a criticism of the 'good man of Equity' logic in this context, see eg A Mackley, 'A Challenge to the Utility and Distinctiveness of the Good Man Theory of Equity' (2021) 27 *Trusts & Trustees* 376.

In the context of withdrawals from a mixed fund, Jessel MR states that the trustee's wrongdoing is the drawing on the account (or coins out of a bag) that contains trust money ('he cannot be heard to say that he took away the trust money' in the passage above). On his view, the trustee obligation is performed if the withdrawal from the account is of trustee's own money ('when he had a right to take away his own money'). There are several difficulties with this analysis. One is that the analysis is based on the presumed intention of the trustee to do the right thing when, in reality, given that the trustee has already misappropriated trust money and created an uncertainty as to whose money survives in the account, the opposite is true.[81]

Another problem is coherence. The 'good man of Equity' analysis applies selectively to trustee's obligations, as the trustee is treated as having performed some of its obligations but not others. In *Hallett's Estate* itself, Hallett had neither the authority from his client to sell the bonds nor to pay the proceeds into his own account. It is odd to make the trustee liable on the basis that the trustee behaved properly in relation to the withdrawal from the mixed account but not in relation to the initial wrongs. A possible response is that the trustee is seen as having performed the initial obligation of not selling the trust property (the bonds) and is simply substitutively performing that obligation by holding what is left in the mixed account on trust for the beneficiary. This does not, however, accord with the analysis in *Hallett's Estate* where the claim to the balance of a mixed account is based on trustee's performance of an obligation not to withdraw money from the mixed account, rather than the obligation not to sell trust asset in the first place.

A further difficulty with the explanation based on the idea that the trustee is disabled from committing a wrong is that it does not work in the context of tracing into profitable investments out of a mixed fund. For the 'good man of Equity' explanation to work in this scenario, we would need to be able to say that the trustee cannot invest own money if she can rightfully invest trust money. This, in turn, is premised on the trustee having a power to invest in the first place.[82] Not every trustee (or fiduciary, or a steward) has a power to invest trust money: for example, Hallett in *Hallett's Estate* did not. Therefore, where a trustee has no power to invest, tracing into profitable investments would require double deeming: (i) that the trustee has the power to invest, and (ii) that the trustee is disabled from exercising that power wrongfully (ie deeming that the trustee invested profitably money drawn from the mixed fund). The reasoning in *Re Hallett's Estate* does not support such analysis: it does not generally permit tracing into investments out of mixed accounts.[83] In a case such as *Re Oatway*,[84] its application would lead to injustice.[85]

[81] For this criticism, see *Re French Caledonia Travel Service Pty Ltd* [2003] NSWSC 1008, [2003] 59 NSWLR 361 [64] (Campbell J).

[82] Performance of an obligation in relation to a power makes no sense unless the obligor has the power in the first place.

[83] This is probably why the rule in *re Hallett's Estate* is sometimes expressed in terms of a presumption that the trustee's money is withdrawn first.

[84] *Re Oatway* [1903] 2 Ch 356 and see below.

[85] *Primeau v Granfield* (1911) 184 F 480 (US District Court for the Southern District of New York) 484–85 (Learned Hand J).

3.3. Power to Elect as Subordination of the Wrongdoer's Interests

In *Re Oatway*,[86] a solicitor Oatway paid £3,000 of misappropriated trust money together with £4,000 of his own money into his bank account, the balance of which was about £75. He then made some relatively small payments in and out of the account. His account balance was £6,600 when he paid out of that account £2,100 to purchase some shares. He dissipated the balance. When he died, being insolvent, the shares were worth £2,400, and were the only relevant asset. The solicitor's executrix argued that at the time the trustee purchased the shares there was sufficient money in the account for the trustee to make good the breach of the trust, and so the shares belonged to the estate. The beneficiaries argued that they were entitled to the shares as the money was spent from the mixed account on an investment which was still in the hands of the trustee.

Joyce J held that the purchase of shares could not have been made with the trustee's own money. He drew attention to three rules. First, he said that where a trustee wrongfully mixes own money with trust money, the issue is not evidential uncertainty, as the trustee is able to show how much they contributed to the mixture. In such cases (where it was possible to state what portion of mixture the trustee contributed), the trustee 'is still entitled to claim his proper quantity, but subject to the quantity of the other proprietor being first made good out of the whole mass'.[87] Second, he noted that trust money can be traced into investments, even where the price is paid partly with trust money and partly with trustee's own money. Third, he observed that in *Re Hallett's Estate* the beneficiary could choose to trace into the balance in a mixed bank account, and was not limited to tracing into a withdrawal from the account.[88]

It is not clear how Joyce J thought the three rules operated alongside one another to produce the result that the claimant could trace into investments out of a mixed fund ('the investment rule'), but it is reasonably clear that he did not think he was laying down an exception to the existing line of cases. In a critical passage, Joyce J said:

> It is, in my opinion, ... clear that when any of the money drawn out [of a mixed account containing trustee's own and trust money] has been invested, and the investment remains in the name or under the control of the trustee, the rest of the balance having been afterwards dissipated by him, he cannot maintain that the investment which remains represents his own money alone, and that what has been spent and can no longer be traced and recovered was the money belonging to the trust. In other words,

[86] *Re Oatway* (n 84).

[87] ibid. 359, citing *Stephen's Commentaries on the Laws of England*, 12th edn (1895), vol 2, 21–22. Interestingly, it seems that Joyce J did not think this followed from *Lupton v White* (n 43), which – he seemed to have thought – 'applied only to cases where the compound [ie mixture] is such as to render it impossible to apportion the respective shares of the parties' (at 359).

[88] *Re Oatway* (n 84) 360.

> when the private money of the trustee and that which he held in a fiduciary capacity have been mixed in the same banking account, from which various payments have from time to time been made, then, in order to determine to whom any remaining balance or any investment that may have been paid for out of the account ought to be deemed to belong, the trustee must be debited with all the sums that have been withdrawn and applied to his own use so as to be no longer recoverable, and the trust money in like manner be debited with any sums taken out and duly invested in the names of the proper trustees.[89]

Put simply, Joyce J must have thought that an innocent contributor must be 'made good' out of the mixed fund before the trustee can take his portion out of it, and understood mixed fund to include any investment in the hands of the trustee. However, the passage does not make clear in what circumstances the innocent contributor is to be 'made good'. There are two possible interpretations. The first sentence of the quoted passage suggests that the rule applies where the investment out the mixed fund remains in the hands of the trustee, and the balance has been dissipated. By contrast, the second sentence might suggest a broader interpretation of the rule, which applies where there is an investment paid for out of a mixed account, irrespective of the balance having been dissipated ('to determine to whom any remaining balance or any investment'), and irrespective of whether the trustee holds the investment (since there is no reference to the investment being held by the trustee). This follows from the sentence structure, which expresses the objective of the exercise broadly – as identifying either 'any remaining balance or any investment' – while referring to dissipation of assets not as a limitation on the scope of the exercise but as one possible set of circumstances in which the exercise can be conducted. It is not immediately obvious which of the two interpretations is correct, but the latter interpretation is at the very least plausible. The use of '[i]n other words' linking the two sentences suggests that Joyce J did not think he was saying anything different in the second sentence, so logically, the first sentence could have been an example of the broader rule articulated in the second sentence.

The fact that Joyce J thought that investments could have been made out of a mixed fund, and could have been traced into, suggests that he perceived the trustee's wrongdoing to encompass withdrawals, or at least dispositions that make it uncertain whose money was spent on the investment. Such a trustee does not 'have a say' about any part of the mixed fund or withdrawal until duly made investments have been attributed to the claimant's money. Such a subordination of the wrongdoer's interest (and the corresponding claimant's right to choose what to trace into) is not surprising because, on the view suggested in this chapter, the trustee caused the uncertainty as to whose money was spent on the investment. In other words, the interests of the wrongdoing trustee are subordinated to those of the beneficiary because the purchasing power, through the exercise of which the trustee acquired the investment, was itself acquired as direct consequence of the trustee's unauthorised exercise of the power of disposition (or 'purchasing'

[89] ibid 360–61.

power) over the trust fund, combined with the power of disposition (or 'purchasing' power) over his own money. The direct consequence of combined disposition ('purchasing') powers is that it is now uncertain whether the investment was acquired because it was purchased with trust money or trustee's own money. The subordination here is not penal in the sense that the trustee does not lose his interest in the mixed fund merely by virtue of the wrongdoing, but it means the trustee is not the one to first decide whose money is invested in a particular asset or whose money is withdrawn.

A useful explanation of Joyce J's statement in *Re Oatway*, just discussed, is found in *Re French Caledonia Travel Service*, where Campbell J said that 'the defaulting trustee cannot assert an unqualified title to the mixed fund until … beneficiaries have had their respective trust funds restored'.[90]

Trustee's qualified title to the mixed fund means that the trustee is not free to dispose of any part of the mixed fund free from an interest of the beneficiary. In *Re Oatway*, counsel for the executrix argued in that the investment in the shares was made at a time when the solicitor's own share of the bank balance was sufficient to pay the full price of the shares, which – the counsel's argument went – entitled the solicitor to withdraw that sum and to apply it for his own purposes. Joyce J rejected this argument, saying that the solicitor was never entitled to withdraw that sum 'free from the charge in favour of the trust, unless or until the trust money paid into the account had been first restored, and the trust fund reinstated'.[91]

The qualification of the trustee's title to the mixed fund is best explained as a 'notional charge', meaning a power to elect to assert a charge over the mixed fund that would secure the performance of the trustee's duty to reconstitute the trust fund. In other words, it is not a charge until the beneficiary says it is. The power to assert a charge covers the mixed fund[92] to the extent that the trust money continues to contribute to the balance in that fund, and so contributes to the purchasing power of the fund, ie subject to the lowest intermediate balance rule.[93] When the beneficiary elects to accept an investment or to reject it, she also elects between assertion of a charge or a proportionate co-ownership share over the investment, a mixed fund or a withdrawal from the account.[94]

[90] *Re French Caledonia Travel Service* (n 81) [86] (Campbell J) and see also Campbell J at [83].

[91] *Re Oatway* (n 84) 361.

[92] *Re French Caledonia Travel Service* (n 81) [153] (Campbell J) the beneficiary's equitable title in the mixed asset has been explained as arising because it would be 'unconscionable for the holder of the mixed asset to deny the beneficiary an equitable title in the mixed asset, until such time as those obligations of conscience have been discharged'.

[93] *James Roscoe (Bolton) Ltd v Winder* [1915] 1 Ch 62 and see *Re French Caledonia Travel Service* (n 81) [175] (Campbell J) (referring to the rule as fundamental to a principled approach to tracing).

[94] See *Primeau v Granfield* (1911) 184 F 480 (US District Court for the Southern District of New York) 484-485 (Learned Hand J): If to … [the] rule [in *Re Hallett's* that the trustee is presumed to have intended to withdraw his own money first] be added the qualification that if the first withdrawals be invested in losing ventures, then the beneficiary is to have a lien, if he likes, till he uses up that whole investment, and then may elect to fall back for the balance upon the original mixed account from which the withdrawal was made, there is no objection, but it is a very clumsy way of saying that he may elect to accept the investment if he likes, or to reject it'. See, too, *Brady v Stapleton* [1952] 88 CLR 322, 336; *Scott v Scott* [1963] HCA 65, (1963) 109 CLR 649, 664; *Boscawen v Bajwa* (n 25).

A beneficiary's notional charge over the mixed fund operates as an encumbrance over the trustee's title to it. The trustee has no authority to dispose of any part of the mixed fund without encumbrance. At the same time, the lack of authority to dispose of the mixed fund free from the charge does not disable the trustee from exercising the power to dispose of any part of the mixed fund. If the trustee withdraws a sum of money from a (notionally charged) mixed account, and purchases an investment with that money, she does so without authority from the beneficiary. Since the trustee's power of investment was subject to the beneficiary's notional charge (ie power of election), the investment acquired through the exercise of such a power also becomes subject to the beneficiary's power to elect. This explains why a beneficiary can claim profitable investments in the hands of the trustee.[95] It also explains why the beneficiary can claim an investment even if the value of the mixed fund has never fallen below the value of the misappropriated property. That said, this last point requires an explanation in light of subsequent authority.

3.4. Is *Turner v Jacob* a Limitation on Subordination?

In *Turner v Jacob*, Jacob was entitled beneficially under a resulting trust to £10k that was paid into Turner's account and mixed with other funds. Out of that mixed account, money was withdrawn to partly fund the purchase of two properties: Merry Acres in 1997, and Clarkfield in 2002. Jacob argued that her money was not used to purchase Merry Acres but did contribute to Clarkfield. Patten J rejected this argument and held that Jacob's charge (lien) was limited to the mixed fund since the mixed account remained in credit above £10k throughout the purchase of both properties. He said:

> It seems to me that in a case (such as the present) where the trustee maintains in the account an amount equal to the remaining trust fund, the beneficiary's right to trace is limited to that fund. It is not open to the beneficiary to assert a lien against an investment made using monies out of the mixed account unless the sum expended is of such a size that it must have included trust monies or the balance remaining in the account after the investment is then expended so as to become untraceable.[96]

If Patten J is correct, the ratio of *Re Oatway*[97] only applies where: (i) the money paid out of the mixed fund has been invested by the trustee; (ii) the investment remains under the control of the trustee, and (iii) the rest of the balance in the mixed fund has been dissipated.

[95] It is not necessary, therefore, to root tracing in the existence of a fiduciary relationship and the no-profit rule. For an argument that tracing requires a fiduciary relationship, see Whayman (n 15) 157. For a convincing rejection of the need to require a fiduciary relationship in tracing claims, see Televantos, 'Losing the Fiduciary Requirement for Equitable Tracing Claims' (n 23), and see, too, *Foskett v McKeown* (n 23) (Lord Millett). In many situations in practice, fiduciary relationships are excluded by contract, which is another reason why a requirement of a fiduciary relationship in the context of tracing is unfortunate. See earlier, n 24.

[96] *Turner v* Jacob (n 11) [102].

[97] *Re Oatway* (n 84).

There are some difficulties with this approach. First, while it is arguable that Patten J's interpretation of *Re Oatway* is closer to what the case actually decided,[98] it is far from clear that it so did, and a broader interpretation, ie one without the limitations (ii) and (iii) is preferable.[99]

Secondly, neither *Shalson v Russo*[100] nor *Foskett v McKeown*[101] was cited to Patten J,[102] and they might have given him a reason to reach a different outcome.[103] Rimer J said obiter in *Shalson v Russo* that giving the claimant choice what to trace into avoids the injustice of leaving the wrongdoing trustee 'with all the cherries and the victim with nothing'.[104] While *Foskett v McKeown* did not decide the point that Patten J was asked to consider, the fact that the important decision of the appellate court was not cited weakens the authority of *Turner*.

Thirdly, Patten J's approach generates uncertainty because the notional charge that secures trustee's duty to reinstate the trust fund, which Joyce J spoke about in *Re Oatway*, encumbers investments only if the mixed fund is dissipated. Thus, dissipation of one asset (mixed fund) dictates whether a charge can be found over another asset (an investment). In other words, whether the investment can be traced into depends on whether another asset (the mixed fund) has been dissipated. It also means that an asset which is initially unencumbered, might become encumbered some time after it has been acquired by a trustee, and after the trustee created further rights, eg security rights, over the investment, which in turn is liable to generate priority conflicts in relation to that asset. These problems are avoided if the notional charge applies over an investment from the moment the trustee acquires it. Patten J's approach is, therefore, more complex than one which gives the beneficiary a notional charge over all mixed funds, any investments and withdrawals from the start.

Authorities since *Shalson* are not uniform in supporting (or rejecting) cherry-picking. In *ED & F Man*,[105] the less claimant-friendly approach was preferred. In that case, a question arose whether the claimant could elect to trace into a withdrawal that was in the hands of a third party. The judge said it could not because of a concern that this would lead to the claimant 'bringing proprietary claims against different third-party recipients in … an arbitrary manner [ie to allow to cherry-pick between third party recipients]'.[106] This seems like an odd qualm to have; proprietary claims are necessarily effective against indefinite number of

[98] J Hudson, B McFarlane, C Mitchell (eds), *Hayton, McFarlane and Mitchell on Equity and Trusts*, 15th edn (London, Sweet & Maxwell, 2022) para [15-029].

[99] See earlier, section 3.3.

[100] Above n 9.

[101] Above n 23.

[102] As noted in *Lapome Ltd v Kemp* (n 10) [19], [32]. Master Brightwell also notes that *Foskett v McKeown* (n 23) 132 (Lord Millett) was not referred to in *Turner v Jacob* (n 11) but the dictum he refers to need not support cherry-picking.

[103] *Lapome Ltd v Kemp* (n 10) [19], [32] (a point made in relation to *Foskett v McKeown* (n 23)).

[104] *Shalson v Russo* (n 9) [144].

[105] *ED&F Man* (n 12).

[106] ibid [684] (Calver J).

third parties, and there is nothing arbitrary about the fact that a claimant might have a claim against one or some of third parties. The third party in question who obtained a payment from the trustee was a non-bona fide purchaser. It also seems very odd that a non-bona fide purchaser would in effect be able to raise a defence against the beneficiary; such third-party defendants do not normally stand in a better position than the trustee was. A different approach was possibly preferred by the court in *Lapome v Kemp.*[107] Master Brightwell did not express a view on the desirability of cherry-picking[108] but noted that cherry-picking was generally favoured in the literature.[109]

The view preferred in this chapter is that a beneficiary can trace into an investment even if she could still trace into a mixed fund. A beneficiary can also cherry-pick between investments made from a mixed fund. A reason for this is that the trustee must not withdraw any sum from the mixed fund free from the notional charge in favour of the trust, unless or until the trust money paid into the account had been first restored, and the trust fund reinstated. The claimant can then choose in relation to which investments, withdrawals or mixed fund she asserts a charge or a proportionate co-ownership share, and she can do so in a way that is most favourable to her. This is because the wrongdoing of the trustee, consisting in the misappropriation of the trust assets, and creation of an uncertainty as to whose money is withdrawn, invested, or left into the account, is a reason to subordinate the interests of the wrongdoer to those of the claimant – until the claimant had a chance to decide what she traces into. To put it more formally, the trustee by mixing trust money with own money combines the power of disposition represented by different assets. The term 'power of disposition' is not particularly intuitive, so it can also be expressed more intuitively, as a 'purchasing power', remembering that purchase of an investment is only one possible form of disposition. The withdrawals or investments out of the mixed account create an uncertainty as to the extent to which the withdrawals or investments result from the exercise of the purchasing power attributable to trust money or trustee's own money.

4. Policy and Limits of Subordination

When debating what a particular rule should be, it is useful to consider the impact of the rule on the society, and on the law generally. A rule which gives the beneficiary an election between the most profitable investments functions as a

[107] *Lapome Ltd v Kemp* (n 10).

[108] ibid [37].

[109] ibid [19]–[24] citing Mitchell, Mitchell and Watterson, Goff & Jones on Unjust Enrichment (n 8) [7-53], P Matthews, C Mitchell, J Harris and S Agnew, Underhill and Hayton *Law of Trusts and Trustees*, 20th edn (London, LexisNexis, 2022) [94.28], J Glister and J Lee, Hanbury and Martin: *Modern Equity*, 22nd edn (London, Sweet & Maxwell, 2021) [26-021], M Bridge, L Gullifer, G McMeel and K Low, T*he Law of Personal Property*, 3rd edn (London, Sweet & Maxwell, 2021) [32-047], and noting at [25] the more cautious view in L Tucker, N Le Poidevin and J Brightwell, Lewin on Trusts, 20th edn (London, Sweet & Maxwell 2019).

disincentive to the wrongdoers minded to misappropriate, mix and use a claimant's money. The cherry-picking rule does not aim to strip the wrongdoers of all the profits, and so it is not intended to ensure that wrongdoers do not profit from their wrongs. Rather, its purpose is to ensure that wrongdoers do not have a say which profits from their wrongs they can keep as theirs. It is up to the claimant to decide first which assets acquired with the mixed fund to trace into, and to claim. A concern might be raised that a cherry-picking rule increases the chances of the claimant asserting a proprietary claim against valuable assets in the hands of third parties, which prejudices third parties. Against this, it should be remembered that third parties can raise defences against the claimants such as the bona fide purchaser rule, such that worthy third parties are already protected. Another concern about adopting a cherry-picking rule is the possible negative impact on (unsecured, ie ordinary) creditors of defendants (whether wrongdoing trustees or third parties), as they risk going unpaid.[110] This argument, however, only tells us that the balance of interests between creditors and beneficiaries is difficult to strike. It does not tell us whose interests should prevail. From a policy perspective, protection from fraud is a good reason to allow cherry-picking, and so to favour beneficiaries over creditors, where the wrongdoers create uncertainty as to whose assets they dealt with.[111] But it is also important that such protection of beneficiaries operates within some limits, and these are provided by the rigours of the tracing framework set out here.

There are two important limitations of the principle that the interests of the wrongdoer are subordinated to those of the beneficiary when the beneficiary comes to choose what to trace into when a mixed fund is involved. The first limitation is a result of the fact that tracing is a proprietary process and aims to identify the extent to which the claimant's asset (traceable proceeds) survives in the hands of the defendant. Once trust money is withdrawn from an account, the subsequent deposits into the same account are not presumed to have been intended to replace the spent trust money; the presumption against the wrongdoer does not operate generally but only where the wrongdoer (eg a trustee who misappropriated trust money) created an uncertainty over whose money he dealt with. Therefore, the tracing claim to the account is limited to the balance immediately prior to the deposit of the trustee's own money (the so-called 'lowest intermediate balance' rule).[112]

The second is that the claimant, prior to selecting which asset is most advantageous to trace into, has what Joyce J in *Re Oatway* described as a 'notional charge' over the mixed fund.[113] Such a charge exists until the beneficiary exercises an election. It is suggested that the position of the beneficiary when asserting a claim contingent on tracing into and out of a mixed account is best described as a power

[110] The difficulty of balancing the interests of the beneficiary and ordinary creditors was noted by F Maitland, *Equity. A Course of Lectures* (Cambridge, Cambridge University Press, 2nd rev edn, 1936, repr 1969) 220.

[111] For a different view, see R Calnan, *Proprietary Rights and Insolvency* (Oxford, Oxford University Press, 2nd edn, 2016) para [8.181].

[112] *James Roscoe v Winder* (n 93).

[113] See section 3.3.

in rem, whose exercise brings into existence a trust over selected assets ('cherries'). Therefore, a bona fide purchaser of an equitable interest in an asset subject to a 'notional charge' can raise a defence against the claimant beneficiary if the purchaser acquires the equitable interest without notice of the beneficiary's power. This will help strike a balance between the interests of different innocent parties: beneficiaries whose trust fund has been misappropriated on the one hand, and innocent parties unaware that they may be acquiring assets encumbered with interests of others.

5. Conclusion

It is clear that when a trustee misappropriates trust funds and pays the proceeds into own bank account, which is in credit immediately prior to that payment, the principal (beneficiary) can trace into that (mixed) bank account. The beneficiary can then elect whether to claim a co-ownership share in the account or a charge over it to secure the trustee duty to reconstitute the trust. Particular problems arise where the trustee withdraws money from the mixed account in order to purchase assets (makes investments) or pays third parties. In such cases, it is unclear whose money (the trustee's own money or the trust money) was withdrawn and invested or paid away because the trustee's power to acquire or create new rights (eg investments), to confer rights on others (eg through payment), or to vary existing own rights (the right against own bank) is acquired partly through own assets (rights) and partly through an unauthorised disposition of the trust fund.

The price for creating this uncertainty ought to be borne by the person who breached the trust (misappropriated trust assets) and who created the uncertainty. This is not an evidential uncertainty, and the language of evidential presumptions against the wrongdoer is not helpful. Rather, it is an uncertainty as to the extent to which the withdrawals or investments result from the exercise of the purchasing power attributable to trust money or trustee's own money in the mixed account. To resolve this uncertainty, rules of attribution are needed. The law gives the innocent party a right to assert her claim first and a choice over which assets to assert it. The corollary is that the wrongdoer's interests are subordinated to those of the claimant. This means the claimant ought to be able to cherry-pick (to elect) which assets to trace into in a way that is most favourable to her, within the confines of the law of tracing being a proprietary process, namely subject to the lowest intermediate balance rule.

The story about cherry-picking in the context of claims contingent on tracing is a story about how the law deals with uncertainties. It tells us that it might be appropriate to attribute the problem of uncertainty to the person who created it, especially where such a person also wronged the claimant. Yet, it also highlights the importance of drawing precise limits of such attribution and sounds a note of caution against imputing to the same person other problems that might arise along the way.

9

The Proprietary Consequences of Fraud

WILLIAM SWADLING

1. Introduction

Suppose A is fraudulently induced to transfer rights to B.[1] B, for example, knocks on A's door falsely representing that they are collecting for charity; in truth, they believe that charity begins at home. If A hands over a £50 note, they will obviously have claims for compensatory damages against B in the tort of deceit and, alternatively, to be paid the value of their performance in unjust enrichment.[2] Both are necessarily personal claims. But what are the 'proprietary' consequences of the handing over of the note?[3] Does A's right pass to B? If so, does B immediately hold that right on trust for A? Alternatively, can A revest the right in themselves by unilaterally rescinding the transfer or obtaining an order of the court to that effect? Similar questions arise in reverse, where A is fraudulently induced to take a transfer of rights from B. B, for example, may have sold a title to a fake Picasso painting to A, and A is now seeking to recover the purchase price.

The position is confused but seems to be this. The right will pass despite the fraud, though there is supposedly authority to the effect that this is not always the case. If the right does pass, then it is said that A can, in the limited circumstance that the right was transferred pursuant to a contract of sale of goods, unilaterally rescind the contract, thereby revesting the right in themselves. Otherwise, some cases say that B is an immediate trustee for A, though others say there is no immediate trust, but that A has a 'right' or 'power' to rescind, the exercise of which will turn B into a trustee for A. There is doubt whether this can be done unilaterally or requires an order of the court. Once done, however, the trust backdates to the point of transfer, though stripped of most of its content.

[1] At common law, fraud means a misrepresentation which the representor knows to be false, or one made recklessly as to whether it is true or false: *Derry v Peek* (1889) 14 App Cas 337.

[2] Where A's performance is made pursuant to a contract, A will in the same proceedings have to obtain an order rescinding the contract: *Clarke v Dickson* (1858) El Bl & El 148.

[3] The word 'proprietary' is used loosely to include the raising by operation of law of a trust, orders for reconveyance or nullity, and other specific relief.

The object of this chapter is to challenge almost all of this thinking. It will argue that fraud never prevents the right passing, either at law or in equity. It will also argue that there is no ability on the part of A unilaterally to revest the right, and that B is never a trustee for A, either at the point of receipt or on rescission, whether rescission is done unilaterally or pursuant to a court order. There is instead a power in the court of equity, analogous to its power to issues orders for specific performance of a contract and specific delivery up of converted chattels, to order specific reconveyance in the case of fraudulently induced transfers. This jurisdiction is not, however, confined to fraud. Transfers obtained by spontaneous mistake, innocent misrepresentation, duress, undue influence and breach of fiduciary duty can also be ordered to be reversed.

The chapter is divided into eight sections. After this introduction, Section 2 examines the effect of fraud on the transfer. It will be seen that this never prevents the right passing. Section 3 looks at the availability of specific restitution in equity through the so-called 'equity to rescind'. It will be shown to be generally available, though subject to certain conditions or 'bars'. Section 4 looks at arguments for an immediate trust and finds them wanting. Section 5 considers the possibility of the victim of fraud unilaterally rescinding the transfer and obtaining a retransfer of the right. In the limited circumstances where it is available, the reasoning is shown to be deficient. Section 6 asks whether A can turn B into a trustee of the right without the aid of the court, and concludes that they cannot, while Section 7 asks whether the making of a court order for reconveyance creates a backdated trust, also concluding that it does not. Section 8 concludes that the only 'proprietary' consequence of fraud is that A can seek an order for specific restitution from the court.

2. Was there the Transfer/Creation of a Right?

It is undoubtedly the case that rights pass or are created despite their transfer or creation being induced by fraud. In *Feret v Hill*,[4] the defendant titleholder to land was fraudulently induced to grant a lease to the claimant, who had represented he would use the premises as a perfumery when all along he intended it as a common brothel. The defendant ejected the claimant, who sued for wrongful ejectment. Fraud notwithstanding, the court allowed the claim, holding that there had been the grant of a valid lease. Jervis CJ said that the defendant intended and in fact did grant the claimant a lease and delivered possession of the premises to him. What was there to avoid that or divest the claimant of the lease? Though the defendant's motive for granting the lease was fraudulently induced, it did not affect the grant itself, the essential elements of which were present. The claimant's misrepresentation of the proposed use was 'as to something altogether collateral to the contract.'[5]

[4] (1854) 15 CB 207.

[5] ibid 223–24. Maule, Cresswell and Crowder JJ gave similar reasons for allowing the claim.

Thus, the question will be whether, despite the fraud, the conditions for the transfer or creation of the right were satisfied. These will, of course, differ according to the nature of the right in question, but provided they are met, the right will either pass or be created. Cases concerned with titles to goods further illustrate this proposition. In *R v Prince*,[6] a wife forged and cashed in a bank a cheque for £900 on her husband's account, the clerk handing her nine £100 notes. Her lover, to whom she gave one note, was acquitted of handling stolen goods. Title to the notes had passed to the wife despite the clerk's fraudulently induced mistake. In *Clough v London and North Western Railway*,[7] a contract for the sale of titles to pianos was induced by a down-payment of £68 and a fraudulent misrepresentation that the purchaser intended to pay the balance. Mellor J, giving the judgment of the Court of Exchequer Chamber,[8] held that 'The fact that the contract was induced by fraud did not … prevent the property from passing.'[9]

The reason why the right passes despite the fraud, as *Feret v Hill* makes clear, is that, provided all the elements of a valid conveyance are present, there is no super-added requirement that the transfer be not fraudulently induced. The same is true for transfers caused by other forms of mistake, and of duress, undue influence, and breach of fiduciary duty.

In the cases so far discussed, no difference was drawn between a transfer made pursuant to a contract of sale, as in *Clough v London and North Western Railway*, or one outside such contract, as in *R v Prince*. However, there is sometimes said to be an exception in cases of sales of titles to goods where the fraud is such as to invalidate the contract of sale.[10] Here, title is said not to pass.[11] The reason seemingly is that the contract is the conveyance, so that, if void, there is no conveyance. This view is, however, mistaken.[12]

The proposition is supposedly demonstrated by the decision of the House of Lords in *Cundy v Lindsay*.[13] A rogue called Blenkarn ordered handkerchiefs on credit from Lindsay. Blenkarn signed his name to make it look like 'Blenkiron & Co', 'a well-known and solvent house',[14] taking premises at 37 Wood St, Cheapside, the same street from which Blenkiron & Co traded. Lindsay knew about the respectable firm, thought the order came from them, and was accordingly prepared to grant credit. The goods were despatched to 'Blenkiron & Co, 37 Wood

[6] (1865–72) 1 CCR 150.
[7] (1871) LR 7 Ex Ch 26.
[8] Which also included Byles, Blackburn, and Lush JJ.
[9] (1871) LR 7 Ex 26, 34.
[10] This would be contrary to *Stocks v Wilson* [1913] 2 KB 235 where, despite the contract being invalidated by the Infants Relief Act 1874, title was held to pass.
[11] This was, for example, the view of Lords Nicholls and Millett in *Shogun Finance Ltd v Hudson* [2004] 1 AC 919.
[12] See the very helpful discussion in R H Stevens, 'Objectivity, Mistake and the Parol Evidence Rule' in A S Burrows and E Peel (eds), *Contract Terms* (Oxford University Press, 2007), ch 6.
[13] (1878) 3 App Cas 459.
[14] ibid 465 (Lord Cairns LC).

St, Cheapside'. Blenkarn took possession of the goods but never paid for them, selling his title on to Cundy, who purchased in good faith. Cundy was sued by Lindsay in conversion. Liability turned on whether Lindsay's title had passed to Blenkarn and in turn to Cundy. The House of Lords held that it had not, so that Cundy was indeed liable.

Lord Cairns LC formulated the question thus: 'Was there any contract which, with regard to the goods in question in this case, had passed the property in the goods from the Messrs Lindsay to Alfred Blenkarn?' He said: 'If the property in the goods in question passed, it could only pass by way of contract; there is nothing else which could have passed the property.' There was, however, no contract. Cundy intended to deal with Blenkiron & Co, not Blenkarn. Since there was no contract, there could be no passing of title to the goods; it was, he said, 'Idle … to speak of property passing'.[15]

The reasoning is difficult, for it is not clear that the contract is the conveyance in cases of sales of goods. The later Sale of Goods Act 1979, replacing the 1893 Act which codified the common law, speaks instead of the 'intent' of the parties to the contract as the conveyance, which intent is to be found, not only in the express terms of the contract, but in the 'conduct of the parties and the circumstances of the case'.[16] The result in *Cundy* can be defended, however, for if the contract of sale was void, this would not then be an occasion on which the intent of the parties could pass title; we would be thrown back on the general rule that title only passes by deed or delivery,[17] neither of which, as we will see, were present.

The two other speeches in *Cundy v Lindsay* were more equivocal. Lord Hatherley said that no goods were delivered to anyone except for the purpose of transferring property to Blenkiron & Co. There was no sale, just an obtaining by false pretences, and therefore, no delivery of goods with intent to pass property to Blenkarn.[18] Likewise, for Lord Penzance, there was no contract and delivery between the parties. All their letters, although received and answered by Blenkarn, were addressed to Blenkiron & Co, and intended for that firm only. The goods were not delivered to Blenkarn, only to Blenkiron & Co, though at the wrong address.[19]

Cundy v Lindsay is not, therefore, a case of a fraudulent misrepresentation preventing property passing; the reason the property did not pass was because the requirements of a valid delivery were not met. Thus, the presence of fraud does not per se invalidate a grant of rights; the question instead is whether the requirements for a valid grant are present.

[15] (1878) 3 App Cas 459, 466.
[16] Sale of Goods Act 1979, s 17(2).
[17] *Cochrane v Moore* (1890) 24 QBD 57.
[18] (1878) 3 App Cas 459, 468.
[19] ibid 472.

3. The 'Equity to Rescind'

In *Feret v Hill*, Maule J said that the defendant landlord's 'proper remedy' was 'in a court of equity'.[20] What he meant by this was that the defendant should have petitioned the court of equity for an order that the tenant surrender the lease and in the meantime for an injunction restraining them suing at law for wrongful ejectment or enforcing any legal judgment.[21] Then, but only then, could the defendant lawfully eject the plaintiff. This 'proper remedy' is known as the 'Equity to Rescind'.

3.1. Content

The order granted by the court in such cases is a form of specific relief, similar to specific performance, though an order to unwind a transaction rather than to perform it. It was described extra-judicially by Sir Peter Millett as an order for 'specific unperformance'.[22]

Examples of such specific relief, which are again not confined to cases of fraud, are legion. In *Clark v Malpas*,[23] a title to land had been conveyed pursuant to a contract of sale which was grossly unfair, the vendor being poor and illiterate. At first instance, the Master of the Rolls declared the conveyance void, directed it to be cancelled, but refused to direct a reconveyance on the ground that it was unnecessary. Selwyn[24] and Jessel[25] for the plaintiff argued on appeal that this course was 'against the previous understanding of the profession, and it is important that it should be determined what is the correct form.'[26] It was held that the proper form of decree was not to declare the deed void, but to direct it to be set aside and order a reconveyance. Knight-Bruce LJ said that 'in the declaration that the conveyance is void the word void is too strong an expression, for the deed is not legally but only equitably void'.[27] He therefore ordered the defendant to reconvey. Turner LJ held that the decree instead be framed as an 'order in the usual way that it be set aside and that the Defendant do reconvey the property'.[28]

[20] (1854) 15 CB 207, 226.

[21] See the form of relief in both *Williams v Bayley* (1866) LR 1 HL 200 and *Cooper v Phibbs* (1867) LR 2 HL 149 (below). Any injunction would also bind the defendant's trustee in bankruptcy, who simply steps into the defendant's shoes in this regard: *Re Eastgate* [1905] 1 KB 465.

[22] Sir Peter Millett, 'Restitution and Constructive Trusts' (1998) 114 LQR 399, 416.

[23] (1862) 4 De GF & J 401.

[24] Later a Lord Justice of Appeal in Chancery.

[25] Later a Master of the Rolls.

[26] (1862) 4 De GF & J 401, 403.

[27] ibid 405. We will see that the language of 'equitably void' is false (text to n 51).

[28] ibid D O'Sullivan, S Elliott & R Zakrzewski, *The Law of Rescission*, 3rd edn (Oxford University Press, 2023), [3.52], maintain that this represented a change in the law, but the arguments of counsel show this to be wrong.

In *Broun v Kennedy*, a title to land was conveyed as a gift to the plaintiff's legal adviser. The plaintiff later brought an action in equity praying 'that the indenture ... might be declared void, and might be delivered up and cancelled', for an injunction, and other relief. Romilly MR ordered that the deed be delivered up to be cancelled and that the defendant 'reconvey the reversion'.[29]

We also see the grant of orders for 'specific unperformance' in two well-known decisions of the House of Lords. In *Williams v Bayley*,[30] a father agreed to pay his son's criminally incurred debts and granted security for such promise under threat of the son's prosecution. When the son absconded, the father successfully filed a bill for a declaration that the two agreements and the securities thereby created were obtained by the defendant by improper pressure, for delivery up of the securities, and for an injunction restraining the defendants from proceeding at law. In *Cooper v Phibbs*,[31] a case of the spontaneously induced mistaken taking of a lease of a profit, a petition was successfully filed in the Court of Chancery in Ireland for an order 'that the agreement ... might be delivered up to be cancelled, and the Defendant ... perpetually restrained from suing upon the same'.[32]

Three other well-known decisions are *Tate v Williamson*,[33] *Allcard v Skinner*,[34] and *Newbigging v Adam*.[35] In *Tate v Williamson*, an undue influence case involving a sale and purchase of a title to land, Page-Wood VC granted a declaration that the sale agreement be set aside, that the conveyance made in pursuance of that agreement stand only as security for the purchase moneys paid, and that, on their repayment, the defendant reconvey the title to the vendor.[36] In *Allcard v Skinner*, the relief sought was 'a declaration that the Plaintiff was induced to make over the property by the undue influence of the Defendant Skinner and repayment of the moneys and re-transfers of the railway stock'. Lindley LJ described the defendant's 'equitable title' as 'imperfect by reason of the influence',[37] and would have granted the order but for the claimant's subsequent laches and acquiescence. Cotton LJ, dissenting, held that she could recover 'on the ground that it was property the beneficial interest in which she had never effectually parted with'.[38] Because in his view this gave rise to an immediate trust, he disagreed that the claim was barred by laches.[39] However, consistently with what was said in *Clark v Malpas*, also an equity case, Lindley LJ said that the conveyance was voidable, not void[40] In *Newbigging v Adam*, a contract to become a partner in a business was set aside

[29] (1863) 33 Beav 133, 154. His decision was affirmed by the Lords Justices: (1862) 4 De GJ & S 217.
[30] (1866) LR 1 HL 200.
[31] (1867) LR 2 HL 149.
[32] ibid 153–4.
[33] (1865–66) LR 1 Eq 528.
[34] (1887) 36 Ch D 145.
[35] (1886) 34 Ch D 582.
[36] His decree was upheld by Lord Chelmsford LC: (1866–67) LR 2 Ch App 55.
[37] (1887) 36 Ch D 145, 185.
[38] ibid 172.
[39] ibid 175.
[40] ibid 186. Bowen LJ also held that the claim was barred by laches and acquiescence.

on the ground of innocent misrepresentation. The decree was that the defendants were liable to repay the amount paid by the plaintiff with interest at four per cent per annum after deducting sums drawn out by the plaintiff with interest, and that the defendant should indemnify the plaintiff against all debts of the partnership to which he had become liable.[41]

Finally, an example from the twentieth century is *O'Sullivan v MAM*,[42] where various contracts were entered into as a result of undue influence. The court ordered the agreements be set aside, an account of the profits be made by the defendants subject to an allowance for reasonable remuneration for their services, the reconveyance of copyrights, and the delivery up of certain master-tapes.

There are three important points to note about the orders just described. First, the remedy is clearly that of the court. Just as there is no ability in a claimant to order a contracting party to perform and invoke the contempt jurisdiction of equity if the order is disobeyed, so too is there no possibility of the 'equity to rescind' being exercisable by claimants alone. To attract the sanction of the court for non-performance, there must first be an order of the court. Second, as *Clark v Malpas* demonstrates, the order of the court is not self-executing. Just as an order that the defendant perform a contract does not *ipso facto* mean that the contract is performed, so too an order for 'specific unperformance' will not by itself revest the rights in the claimant: there needs to be a retransfer by the defendant.[43] That is so even if the claimant, as in *Broun v Kennedy*,[44] is granted a declaration of invalidity. Third, the orders made are often both complex and conditional, as witness those in *Cooper v Phibbs*, *Tate v Williamson* and *Newbigging v Adam*, with fine adjustments being made between the rights of the parties, backed by the coercive powers of the court.

3.2. Nomenclature

The 'equity to rescind', therefore, is nothing more than the issuance of a court order for specific restitution. In this sense, it is no different from a claimant seeking any other order from the court, for example, that the defendant pay the claimant damages for a breach of contract or the commission of a tort, to pay an amount of money representing the defendant's unjust enrichment, to perform a contract, or to deliver up land or converted goods.

The ability of the claimant to seek an order of 'specific unperformance' is, however, often described in terms of them exercising an 'election'[45] or

[41] (1886) 34 Ch D 582, 585.

[42] [1985] QB 428.

[43] *O'Sullivan* (n 28), citing *Leech v Leech* (1674) 2 Ch Rep 100; *Lady Hudson's Case* (1704) 2 Eq Cas Abr 52; *Clavering v Clavering* (1704) Prec Chan 235; *Harrison v Owen* (1738) 1 Atk 520; *Re Way's Trust* (1864) 2 De G & J 365.

[44] (1863) 33 Beav 133.

[45] This is the language of Mellor J in *Clough v London and Northwestern Railway* (1871) LR 7 Ex Ch 26, 34 and Lord Hatherley LC in *Reese River Silver Mining Co Ltd v Smith* (1869–70) LR 4 HL 64, 74.

'choice'[46] to rescind the transfer. This is a misnomer. An election properly-so-called requires a claimant to choose *at trial* between inconsistent remedies, such as loss or gain for a wrong,[47] or between an order for compensatory damages for breach of contract or specific performance.[48] By contrast, in cases of fraudulently induced transfers, no such choice is being made. The victim of the fraud simply has the option of going to court and obtaining an order to rescind the transfer, ie, an order that the defendant reconvey, just as they have the option of suing for damages in the tort of deceit or for a money remedy in unjust enrichment. We would never describe these last as involving the exercise of an 'election', though the claimant always has the 'choice' not to sue at all. We should equally eschew this language where the 'equity to rescind' is concerned. As will be seen, it leads to confusion.

Equally inaccurate is the description of the ability to petition the court as a 'right to rescind'. We see this language in many cases, for example, in the speech of Lord Blackburn in *Erlanger v New Sombrero Phosphate Co.*[49] However, it is not a right, at least in the Hohfeldian sense of a claim-right,[50] because there is no correlative duty on anyone. Indeed, until a court order is made, it will be the claimant who is subject to duties, as witness the landlord's duty in *Feret v Hill* not to interfere with his tenant's right to exclusive possession of the premises. Only when the court orders a reconveyance can there said to be any duty on the defendant; even then, the duty is arguably owed to the court, not to the claimant.

Likewise, the 'equity to rescind' is not a 'power', though it was also described as such by Lord Blackburn in almost the same breath as when describing it as a right. It is not a power in any Hohfeldian-sense because it does not give the claimant the ability unilaterally to alter the legal position of another. Just as we would not describe a tort victim seeking an order from a court that the tortfeasor pay compensatory damages as exercising a 'power', nor should we see the exercise of the 'equity to rescind' as such. Once again, it is nothing more than an application to the court for specific as opposed to monetary relief.

Finally, the language of voidability is unhelpful,[51] for it gives the impression that the order of the court itself avoids the transfer. However, we know this is untrue. As the cases demonstrate, though courts often grant declarations of invalidity, the order is not self-executing: it does not invalidate the transfer; some further act is necessary. Of course, any exercise by the defendant of rights in the meantime may be restrained by injunction, but that only proves the point. In this sense, therefore, 'voidable' can only mean valid but liable to be ordered to be reversed.

[46] '[T]he innocent party is given a choice as to whether to apply to set aside a voidable contract or to affirm it and to continue to be bound by it': *Flowers v Chief Land Registrar* [2018] UKUT 145 (TCC), [26] (Morgan J).

[47] As in *Neilson v Betts* (1871) LR 5 HL 1 (patent infringement); *United Australia Ltd v Barclay's Bank Ltd* [1941] AC 1 (conversion); *Island Records Ltd v Tring* [1995] 3 All ER 444 (breach of copyright); *Tang Man Sit v Capacious Investments Ltd* [1996] 1 AC 514 (breach of trust).

[48] *Johnson v Agnew* [1980] AC 367, 392 (Lord Wilberforce).

[49] (1878) 3 App Cas 1218, 1278.

[50] W N Hohfeld, *Some Fundamental Legal Conceptions as Applied in Judicial Reasoning* (1913–14) 23 *Yale LJ* 16, 30–32.

[51] As, eg, in *Clark v Malpas* (1862) 4 De GF & J 401 and *Allcard v Skinner* (1887) 36 Ch D 145.

3.3. Conditionality of the 'Equity to Rescind'

The making by the court of orders for 'specific unperformance' are conditional on the claimant giving back to the defendant any benefits received. *Clarke v Dickson*[52] was a case involving the sale of shares induced by a fraudulent misrepresentation. The purchaser sought to set the contract aside and obtain an order for the repayment of the purchase price. It was held that the plaintiff's only option was a claim for damages for deceit. The order was refused because the partnership in which the shares had originally been purchased had since been incorporated, making *restitutio in integrum* impossible. As Crompton J colourfully said, 'If you are fraudulently induced to buy a cake you may return it and get back the price; but you cannot both eat your cake and return your cake.'[53]

We see the conditionality of orders to rescind in *Maguire v Makaronis*,[54] where a solicitor procured a loan contract and grant of security through a breach of fiduciary duty. The borrowers defaulted on the loan but resisted a claim for possession by counterclaiming for the transaction to be set aside. Both the primary judge and a majority of the Victorian Court of Appeal granted the relief sought by the borrowers, though with no requirement that they repay the amounts outstanding on the loan. The High Court of Australia held that relief should have been conditioned on repayment of the loan, otherwise the borrowers would have been 'left with the fruits of the transaction of which they complain, whereas their equity was to have the whole transaction rescinded and, so far as possible, the parties remitted to their original position.'[55] Other decisions illustrating this conditionality are the undue influence cases of *Stump v Gaby*[56] and *Gresley v Mousley*,[57] discussed below.

In this respect, the so-called 'equity to rescind' operates no differently to claims for specific performance of a contract or delivery up of converted goods. Just as not all contracts will be ordered to be specifically enforced and not all converted goods ordered to be delivered up, so too will not all tainted transfers of rights be ordered to be reversed.

3.4. Exigibility of the 'Equity to Rescind'

The victim of fraud obviously cannot obtain an order for a retransfer of rights against the immediate transferee where the right in question has in the meantime passed to a third party. It is, however, possible to bring a claim for specific relief against such third party, provided they did not give value in exchange in good

[52] (1858) El Bl & El 148.
[53] ibid p 152.
[54] (1997) 188 CLR 449.
[55] ibid 475 (Brennan CJ, Gaudron, McHugh and Gummow JJ). Kirby J gave a separate judgment but agreed with this part of the majority's reasoning.
[56] (1852) 2 De G M & G 623.
[57] (1859) 4 De G & J 78.

faith and without notice of the reason for rescission. As Lord Westbury said in *Phillips v Phillips*:

> [W]here there are circumstances that give rise to an equity as distinguished from an equitable estate – as for example, an equity to set aside a deed for fraud, or to correct it for mistake – and the purchaser under the instrument maintains the plea of purchase for valuable consideration without notice, the Court will not interfere.[58]

His lordship does not here distinguish between subsequent purchasers of legal and equitable rights.[59] In this sense, therefore, the 'equity to rescind' does not operate against third parties in the same way as do interests such as equities of redemption, restrictive covenants over land, and interests of beneficiaries of trusts, all of which bind purchasers for value without notice of equitable rights, being postponed only as against those taking *legal* rights.[60] It is for this reason that the 'equity to rescind' is, unhelpfully, described as a 'mere equity', as opposed to an 'equitable interest'. That it behaves differently should not be at all surprising, for it is not a right or power at all, merely the ability to petition a court for specific relief; what is surprising is that it has any third-party effect at all.

3.5. Loss of the 'Equity to Rescind'

Not every claim for an order for specific performance of a contract will succeed. The claim might fail for various reasons, including the fact that the contract is for personal services, that damages are an adequate remedy, it would require constant supervision by the court, laches and acquiescence, or that the order would cause undue hardship. We might call such factors 'bars' to specific performance. In the same way, though the elements of claim for an order of 'specific unperformance' may be made out, it might still fail for various reasons. These 'bars to rescission' are fourfold: affirmation; the intervention of third-party rights; laches; and (as already seen) the impossibility of counter-restitution.[61]

3.5.1. *Affirmation*

Affirmation of the transfer or contract pursuant to which the rights were granted entails the loss of the 'equity to rescind'. While affirmation will be rare in cases

[58] *Phillips v Phillips* (1862) 4 De G F & J 208.

[59] A Reilly, 'What were Lord Westbury's Intentions in *Phillips v Phillips*? Bona Fide Purchase of an Equitable Interest' [2021] CLJ 156.

[60] *Pilcher v Rawlins* (1872) LR 7 Ch App 259.

[61] A fifth bar, that there no could be no rescission in the case of an executed conveyance involving an innocent misrepresentation, laid down in *Seddon v North Eastern Salt Co* [1905] 1 Ch 326 and *Angel v Jay* [1911] 1 KB 666, was abrogated by s 1(b) of the Misrepresentation Act 1967, which provides that 'a person may rescind a contract, notwithstanding that it has been performed, if he would otherwise have been entitled to rescind without alleging fraud'.

of fraud, there are examples. In *Re Hop and Malt Exchange and Warehouse Co*,[62] the claimant was induced to take shares in a company on the faith of fraudulent misrepresentations contained in the prospectus. He subsequently instructed his broker to sell the shares. Lord Romilly MR held that he had thereby affirmed the contract and refused an application for an order that the company remove him from the share register.

3.5.2. *Third-party Rights have Intervened*

The intervention of third-party rights will also mean the court refusing to order relief. In *Oakes v Turquand*,[63] the House of Lords held that a shareholder could no longer rescind a contract to take shares on the ground of fraudulent misrepresentation once the company had gone into insolvency since that would prejudice the rights of the company's creditors. Similarly, in *Society of Lloyd's v Leighs*,[64] the Court of Appeal held that a contract between a Lloyd's Name and certain Lloyd's companies authorising the companies to make settlements on behalf of the Name could not be rescinded for fraudulent misrepresentation because rescission would affect third parties with whom settlements had been made.

3.5.3. *Laches*

There is a general defence in equity of laches, whereby undue delay prejudicial to the defendant bars any claim. As seen, the claim by the nun in *Allcard v Skinner* for an order to rescind a transfer of shares to the Lady Superior on the ground of undue influence was barred because she brought it more than five years after leaving the sisterhood. Unlike statutory periods of limitation, there is no fixed point at which laches takes effect but necessitates an exercise of judgment by the court.

3.5.4. *Impossibility of Counter-Restitution*

We saw that an order for 'specific unperformance' was conditional on the claimant making counter-restitution to the defendant. It follows that where counter-restitution is impossible, no order will issue. Thus, in *Boyd & Forrest v Glasgow & South Western Ry Co*,[65] a contract for the construction of a railway was completely performed before an action was brought to rescind it on the ground of innocent misrepresentation as to the nature of the strata in which the work was to be done, which allegedly made the work performed totally different from that contracted for, and for which the contractor then claimed to be paid on the basis of a *quantum*

[62] (1866) LR 1 Eq 483.
[63] (1867) LR 2 HL 325.
[64] [1997] CLC 1398.
[65] 1915 SC (HL) 20.

meruit. One ground on which the claim failed was the impossibility of *restitutio in integrum*: the land could not be restored to its condition prior to the construction of the railway.

Two points, however, should be noted. First, there need not always be counter-restitution *in specie*: the court can where appropriate order money payments *in lieu*.[66] Second, courts are reluctant to find impossibility of counter-restitution in cases of fraudulent misrepresentation. According to Lord Wright in *Spence v Crawford*, 'the court will be more drastic in exercising its discretionary powers in a case of fraud than in a case of innocent misrepresentation'.[67]

4. Is the Transferred Right Held on an Immediate Trust?

Having seen that the right will pass despite the presence of fraud so long only as the elements required for the transfer are present, but that courts of equity are sometimes willing, via the 'equity to rescind', to make orders for 'specific unperformance', the question arises whether a trust of the right arises immediately on receipt. There are some cases which say, or supposedly say, that it does.[68] There seem to be four arguments for an immediate trust: that A has 'an equitable estate' following the transfer; that fraud causes A's equitable title/beneficial interest not to pass to B; that B's conscience is affected; and, finally, that a trust arises simply because of the fraud. None, however, are convincing.

4.1. A has 'An Equitable Estate'

Following the transfer of the right to B, A is sometimes said to obtain 'an equitable estate', the presence of which means that B holds the right on trust for A.[69] However, this 'equitable estate' turns out to be nothing more than the 'equity to rescind', not an interest under a trust.

In *Stump v Gaby*,[70] a case of undue influence, Ayliffe White was, during his life, in very embarrassed circumstances, and in prison or under arrest for debt. His solicitor, Gaby, took advantage of the situation and obtained from White a

[66] *Erlanger v New Sombrero Phosphate Co* (1878) 3 App Cas 1218.

[67] *Spence v Crawford* [1939] 3 All ER 271, 288.

[68] According to R Chambers, *Resulting Trusts*, (Oxford, Clarendon Press, 1987) 86, 'whenever a provider of property to another is entitled to rescind a transaction … and thereby recover any portion of that property, the recipient holds the recoverable property on a resulting trust for the provider from the moment the right of rescission … first arises'.

[69] See, eg, Taylor J in *Latec Investments Ltd v Hotel Terrigal Pty Ltd* (1965) 113 CLR 265, 284, discussed below, text to nn 81–83.

[70] (1852) 2 De G M & G 623.

deed of assignment of his interest in land for a wholly inadequate consideration. White died soon after and his heir at law sought a declaration that the conveyance was null and void and that possession of the premises be given up to the plaintiff, together with all deeds and muniments of title relating thereto. One question was whether White's ability to petition the court came to an end on his death. Lord St Leonards LC held that it did not, that White remained an owner, subject to repayment of the money to the purchaser. He therefore had a devisable 'equitable estate'.[71] However, what the court did not say was that White was the beneficiary of a trust. Notwithstanding the language of his remaining 'the owner' and having 'an equitable estate', the only issue was whether the 'equity to rescind' came to an end on his death.

Also said to be in favour of an immediate trust is *Gresley v Mousley*,[72] another case of a purchase by solicitor from his client at an under-value. The client brought a bill in equity to set aside the sale, praying that the conveyance be declared fraudulent and allowed to stand only as a security for what, if anything, was due from him and for consequential relief. One issue was whether a successor in title of the now deceased client could maintain the suit. It was held that he could. Knight-Bruce LJ simply said the court was bound by *Stump v Gaby*, which in any case was rightly decided.[73] Turner LJ also relied on *Stump v Gaby*, saying that the decree of the court did not 'create a wholly new right' but 'proceeds upon a pre-existing right. The mere circumstance of an estate not being recoverable otherwise than by action or suit clearly does not prevent it from being devisable.'[74] Unfortunately, there is no discussion of the nature of this 'pre-existing right', which once again can only be the 'equity to rescind'.

A third decision, *Melbourne Banking Corpn v Brougham (No 2)*,[75] involved the release of an equity of redemption to a mortgagee because of an allegedly fraudulent misrepresentation. There was found to be no misrepresentation. A subsidiary question was whether, if the release was voidable, an 'equity to set it aside' passed to the respondent under a general conveyance from the mortgagor's successor or whether it had to be specifically assigned. Lord Selbourne LC held that a general conveyance was enough. Once again, however, the court did not say there was a trust.

More difficult is *Re Garnett*,[76] involving a release by residuary legatees of their rights under their uncle's will. In earlier proceedings, the release was ordered to be set aside because made without independent advice and in ignorance of the value of the rights. The question now was whether those rights were caught by a covenant to settle future property. As a matter of construction of the covenant, the Court of Appeal held they were not. As Lopes LJ explained: '"future" can only mean

[71] ibid 630.
[72] (1859) 4 De G & J 78.
[73] ibid p 89.
[74] (1859) 4 De G & J 78, 92–3.
[75] (1882) 7 App Cas 307.
[76] (1886) 33 Ch D 300.

one thing – the exclusion of property which was originally the wife's at the time of the settlement.'[77] However, there are statements to the effect that, even if this were not so, the rights would not be caught. Cotton LJ said: 'The setting aside of the release did not give them any new right, but merely had the effect of removing that which, if it had stood, would have been a bar and have prevented their previously existing right ….'[78] Lindley LJ said that 'setting aside a release confers no new title', it instead removed 'an impediment to the enjoyment of a pre-existing title. The lady did not acquire a title when the release was set aside. She always was entitled notwithstanding the release.'[79] No authority, however, was cited, and the point is *obiter*. Moreover, it is inconsistent with Lindley LJ's own later statement in *Allcard v Skinner*, discussed above, that 'Gifts liable to be set aside by the Court on the ground of undue influence have always been treated as voidable and not void.'[80]

The point was directly addressed by the High Court of Australia in *Latec Investments Ltd v Hotel Terrigal Pty Ltd*,[81] where a sale of a title to land was made by a mortgagee to its wholly owned subsidiary. The mortgagor sought and was granted an order setting the sale aside on the ground of equitable fraud. However, in the meantime, the subsidiary had granted an equitable charge over the title to an innocent third party. Was the third party chargee bound? It argued that the mortgagor only had an 'equity' to have the sale set aside, not an equitable interest, and that this 'equity' was not binding on a good faith purchaser for value, not only of a legal interest, but, as here, of an equitable one. The court agreed. Kitto J said that the mortgagor had only 'an equity', not an equitable interest,[82] while Menzies J said that *Stump v Gaby* only described the result of a successful suit for rescission, not an immediate trust.[83]

An immediate trust was also rejected by Brennan J *in Daly v Sydney Stock Exchange Ltd*,[84] involving the non-disclosure by a firm of stockbrokers to its client that it was in a parlous financial state. An employee of the firm had advised the client to lend it money, which money was lost on the firm's insolvency. There being a fiduciary relationship between the stockbrokers and their client, the latter had 'an equity to rescind', meaning he could petition the court for an order setting aside the contract of loan. Rescission, however, had never been sought. For the purposes of a statutory compensation scheme, it had to be decided whether the loan monies were paid to the stockbrokers 'as trustees'. The High Court held that the scheme only applied to express rather than constructive trusts. Brennan J went on to say there could not even be a constructive trust as the contract of loan had not been

[77] ibid 307; see also 304 (Cotton LJ); 306 (Lindley LJ).
[78] ibid 303.
[79] ibid 300, 306.
[80] (1887) 36 Ch D 145, 186.
[81] (1965) 113 CLR 265.
[82] ibid 278. As we will see (text to nn 139–148), the orthodoxy is that a trust arises on rescission, backdated to the date of transfer.
[83] (1965) 113 CLR 265, 291. Taylor J held that there was a fully-fledged equitable interest before rescission but that, for different reasons, it did not bind the equitable chargee.
[84] (1985–86) 160 CLR 371.

rescinded.[85] There was no immediate trust, only the possibility of one coming into existence on rescission.[86]

The approach of Brennan J has been followed in England and Wales. In *Lonrho plc v Al-Fayed (No 2)*,[87] the claimant alleged that it was fraudulently induced to sell a parcel of shares to the defendant. This meant, it argued, that it was entitled to rescind the sale and that the defendant, from the start, held the shares for it on trust, with the result that they were subject to various fiduciary obligations and, on the facts alleged, acted in breach of such obligations. The claim was dismissed by Millett J, holding the argument to be 'misconceived'. Though it might be the case that on election to set aside the transfer 'the beneficial interest in the property will be treated as having remained vested in [the plaintiff] throughout, at least to the extent necessary to support any tracing claim', the notion of an immediate trust was inconsistent with the contract and conveyance being valid until set aside.[88]

In *Bristol and West Building Society v Mothew*,[89] a solicitor negligently misrepresented to a mortgagee that his mortgagor client would have no other loans secured on the title. In fact, to the knowledge of the solicitor, the mortgagor intended to grant a second charge to another lender to secure a small indebtedness. The loan monies were paid to the solicitor, who handed them to the mortgagor. Chadwick J held that the loan monies were held on an immediate constructive trust because of the solicitor's misrepresentation, with the consequence that the solicitor committed a breach of trust in paying them over to the mortgagor. The Court of Appeal disagreed. Millett LJ (as he now was) held that though the misrepresentation meant that the transaction could be avoided in equity, it was not void.[90]

Thus, the notion of an immediate trust is inconsistent with the rule that the transfer of rights is valid, even though the court of equity might later order it to be reversed. Such a conclusion is also consistent with the rule encountered above that the 'equity to rescind' does not behave with respect to third parties in the same way as the interest of a beneficiary of a trust, that it is defeasible, not only by equity's darling, but also by a purchaser for value without notice of an equitable interest.[91]

4.2. Equitable or Beneficial Interest does Not Pass

As seen, the right in question will be transferred despite its being induced by a fraudulent misrepresentation so long only as the requirements for a transfer are met. Some cases say, however, that A retains an 'equitable' or 'beneficial' interest in the 'property', which retention causes B to hold the right on immediate trust for A.

[85] ibid 389–90.
[86] Whether this should in fact be so is discussed below, text to nn 139–148.
[87] [1992] 1 WLR 1.
[88] ibid 12.
[89] [1998] Ch 1.
[90] ibid 22.
[91] Above, text to nn 58–60.

We saw this thinking in Cotton LJ's dissent in *Allcard v Skinner*,[92] though it was rejected by the majority. The same thinking, however, appears in the spontaneous mistake case of *Chase Manhattan v Israel-British Bank*, where Goulding J held that 'a person who pays money to another under a factual mistake retains an equitable property in it.'[93] The notion that the transferor retains an 'equitable' or 'beneficial' interest is, however, flawed.

First, and most obviously, A has no 'equitable' or 'beneficial' interest to retain. It was for this reason that *Chase Manhattan* was rightly disapproved by Lord Browne-Wilkinson in *Westdeutsche Landesbank Girozentrale v Islington LBC*, with Goulding J's reasoning described as 'fallacious'.[94] Lord Browne-Wilkinson said that 'a person solely entitled to the full beneficial ownership of money or property, both at law and in equity, does not enjoy an equitable interest in that property. The legal title carries with it all rights.'[95] That must be right. Although A may hold the right 'beneficially' before the transfer, he does not hold with respect to it a separate 'beneficial interest'. 'Beneficial', in other words, is an adverb, not an adjective, describing a way in which rights are held, not a type of right. Moreover, if it really were the case that a right-holder had to have 'the beneficial interest' to retain, a trustee who was the victim of fraud, who could not be said to have 'the beneficial interest', would be unable to sue.

Second, even if there were such a right, we still need an explanation why it does not pass. If the fraud is 'altogether collateral' to the passing of the underlying right, why is it not equally collateral to the transfer of the equitable/beneficial interest? Unfortunately, no case attempts to explain its retention. Indeed, they do not even explain what is necessary for it to pass in the first place, perhaps because there can be no such requirement.

4.3. Transferee's Conscience is Affected

A third argument for a trust is that because equity is a 'court of conscience', trusts arise whenever a right-holder's 'conscience', whatever that might mean, is affected, and that a person who fraudulently induces a transfer to himself of a right is such a person because of his knowledge of the transferor's mistake. We see this thinking in Lord Browne-Wilkinson's speech in *Westdeutsche*, where he said that the result in *Chase Manhattan* could be justified on the basis that the bank retained the money after learning of the payor's mistake.[96]

This reasoning does not work. First, the notion that 'equity is a court of conscience' expresses nothing more than the relationship between law and equity,

[92] (1887) 36 Ch D 145.
[93] [1981] Ch 105, 119.
[94] [1996] AC 669, 706.
[95] ibid.
[96] [1996] AC 669, 715.

between competing legal systems. It describes the fact that courts of equity do not sit on appeal from common law courts, do not overturn common law judgments, but instead direct defendants not to enforce their common law rights. As Lord Hardwicke explained almost three centuries ago:

> Though this court cannot set aside a judgment of a common law court obtained against conscience, yet will it decree the party to acknowledge satisfaction on that judgment, though he has received nothing; because obtained where nothing was due. So it cannot set aside a fine for being obtained by fraud and imposition … yet, on a conveyance so obtained, this court never sent the plaintiff to the Common Bench to set it aside, but considers the person obtaining the estate, even by fine, as a trustee, and decrees him to reconvey on the general ground of laying hold of the ill-conscience of the party, to make him do what is necessary to restore matters as before.[97]

Thus, the phrase 'equity is a court of conscience' describes not a liability rule but an aspect of equitable legal method.

Second, it is not clear how the fact that the recipient's knowledge of the mistake is relevant. Knowledge will certainly not convey to the defendant the fact that they now have the duties of a trustee, which is what Lord Browne-Wilkinson was concerned about when rejecting the notion that there could be a trust absent knowledge.[98] The best it can show, assuming the transferee was not an avid readers of the law reports, was that they now knew they were liable to be ordered to repay/retransfer. Not surprisingly, Lord Browne-Wilkinson's proposition was doubted extra-judicially by Sir Peter Millett: 'By itself notice of the existence of a ground of restitution is obviously insufficient to found a proprietary remedy; it is merely notice of a personal right to an account and payment.'[99]

4.4. Immediate Trust Simply because it is Fraud

The final 'argument' for an immediate trust is simply that they arise in cases of fraudulently induced transfers. This notion again comes from *Westdeutsche Landesbank Girozentrale v Islington LBC*, where Lord Browne-Wilkinson said that coins which were stolen were traceable in equity because held by the thief on trust, and though it was:

> … difficult to find clear authority for the proposition, when property is obtained by fraud equity imposes a constructive trust on the fraudulent recipient: the property is recoverable and traceable in equity. Thus, an infant who has obtained property by fraud is bound in equity to restore it: *Stocks v Wilson* [1913] 2 KB 235, 244; *R Leslie Ltd v Sheill* [1914] 3 KB 607. Moneys stolen from a bank account can be traced in equity: *Bankers*

[97] *Barnesley v Powell* (1749) 1 Ves Snr 284, 289. See also F W Maitland, *Equity* (Cambridge University Press, 1909), 9.

[98] [1996] AC 669, 709.

[99] See n 22, 413.

Trust Co v Shapiral [1980] 1 WLR 1274, 1282C-E: see also *McCormick v. Grogan* (1869) LR 4 HL 82, 97.[100]

There are a number of problems with this statement.

First, the authorities cited, as Rimer J noted in *Shalson v Russo*,[101] do not support the proposition. The most obvious is *McCormick v Grogan*, a case concerning secret trusts, where the alleged 'fraud' was not any deceit but simply the reliance in litigation on statutory rules barring the admission of certain types of evidence of alleged declarations of trust.[102] Second, Lord Browne-Wilkinson illegitimately jumps from theft of a physical thing (coins) to the fraudulently induced transfer of a right. Although both constitute crimes,[103] they are, from a civil law perspective, radically different: title passes in the case of the latter, though not the former.[104] Indeed, even in the case of the former, a trust seems impossible to envisage in terms of subject-matter. Thus, the fact that a transfer was fraudulently induced cannot, ipso facto, turn the transferee into a trustee.

5. Can the Transferor Unilaterally Revest the Right?

We have seen that A has an 'equity to rescind', ie, the ability to petition the court of equity for an order of 'specific unperformance'. The question then is whether A can additionally effect a retransfer of the right themselves, without the aid of either the court or the defendant. According to *Feret v Hill*,[105] the clear answer is that they cannot: only the court of equity has the power to make an order that the lease be surrendered and injunct the lessee from suing at law; only the court of equity can impose sanctions for non-compliance. As we saw, the right in question was created, the elements of a valid grant being present.

However, it is sometimes thought that an exception exists where titles to goods are transferred pursuant to fraudulently induced contracts of sale. Thus, in *Car and Universal Finance Ltd v Caldwell*,[106] a fraudulently induced vendor of a title to a car was able unilaterally to revest the title in himself, so causing a successor in title to the fraudster to commit the tort of conversion.

How does this work? Although the 'equity to rescind', as its name implies, is only available from a court of equity, and, like orders for specific performance and delivery up, dependent on an order of that court, the common law in the mid-nineteenth century did two radical things. First, it allowed rescission of a contract of sale in cases of deceit (and possibly duress). Second, it held that this could be effected by the defrauded party unilaterally. That no court order was

[100] [1996] AC 669, 715–16.
[101] [2005] Ch 281, [106]–[127].
[102] *Blackwell v Blackwell* [1929] AC 318.
[103] Theft Act 1968, s 1; Fraud Act 2006, ss 14 & 15.
[104] A difference noted by the Court of Appeal in *Twinsectra Ltd v Yardley* [1999] Lloyd's Rep Bank 438.
[105] (1854) 15 CB 207 (above, text to nn 4–5).
[106] [1965] 1 QB 525.

necessary is, however, immediately difficult. How are we to know whether there has been any affirmation, whether third party rights have intervened, or whether orders for counter-restitution need be made? Moreover, if they do need to be made, who is to make them? Indeed, who is to judge whether counter-restitution is even possible?

Not surprisingly, authority for the notion that title can be revested at law and without a court order is weak. The point has previously been addressed at length,[107] but, essentially, it was invented by Parke B in the mid-nineteenth century in *Load v Green*.[108] In that it was based on previous authority which does not support it and is inconsistent with principle, it should no longer be followed.[109]

However, even assuming that rescission at law can be effected unilaterally, it is not clear how this causes the right to revest, with the point being merely assumed in the case-law.[110] As seen, it does not happen with the making of an order pursuant to the 'equity to rescind', which is simply an 'order' that it be done, not the reversal of the transfer itself, even where there is granted a declaration of invalidity. Moreover, the doctrine is odd in that it is confined to the passing of titles of goods pursuant to contracts of sale; it does not apply to transfers of any other rights. Though several explanations have been proffered, none work.

5.1. Titles to Goods can Revest without Formality

John Cartwright explains the revesting of the right on the ground that titles to goods can revest 'without further formality', whereas rights such as shares or titles to land need a formal act of reconveyance.[111] This, however, assumes the point which needs to be proved.

5.2. Goods can be 'Recaptured'

Janet O'Sullivan suggests that the reason titles to goods operate differently to other rights is that goods can be 'recaptured'.[112] However, land can be 'recaptured', yet there is no automatic revesting, as *Feret v Hill* illustrates. Moreover, there is no 'recapture' of goods in many of the leading cases, including *Car & Universal Finance* itself. Further, such 'recapture' will only be lawful where an injunction has

[107] W Swadling, 'Property, Rescission, and the Common Law' (2005) 121 LQR 123, 142–52.
[108] (1846) 15 M & W 216.
[109] An argument accepted extra-judicially by Lord Millett in 'Proprietary Restitution', in S Degeling and J Edelman, *Equity in Commercial Law* (2005), 309, 320, fn 31.
[110] See, eg, *Load v Green* (1846) M & W 216, 221 (Parke B); *Car & Universal Finance Ltd v Caldwell* [1965] 1 QB 525; *Newtons of Wembley Ltd v Williams* [1965] 1 QB 560, 571 (Sellers LJ).
[111] J Cartwright, *Misrepresentation, Mistake and Non-Disclosure* (6th edn, 2022) [4.11]. It might be asked why 'delivery' or 'contract' are not rules of formality. Delivery is certainly described as a 'formal act' by McCardie J in *Armstrong v Jackson* [1917] 2 KB 822, 825.
[112] J O'Sullivan, 'Rescission as a Self-Help Remedy: A Critical Analysis' (2000) 59 CLJ 509, 529.

been granted against the right-holder. Otherwise, as *Feret v Hill* demonstrates, any 'recapture' will be tortious. The argument again assumes what it sets out to prove.

5.3. Contract is the Conveyance

A third explanation for rescission of the contract effecting a revesting of title is that the contract is the conveyance and that that contract, because of the rescission, has now gone. However, it is once again unclear that the contract really is the conveyance. As seen, the Sale of Goods Act 1979 provides that the passage of title is determined by the intent of the parties to the contract of sale, and that such intent is to be found not only in the express terms of the contract but also from 'the conduct of the parties and the circumstances of the case'.[113] Moreover, even if the contract did express the parties' intent as to the passing of title, so that no outside factors were involved, the avoidance of the contract cannot negate the fact that the relevant intent was present and effected the transfer. As seen, even an order made by a court of equity for specific unperformance is not self-executing: the defendant still needs to execute a retransfer or deliver up the relevant documents. How, then, is it that a victim of fraud can go further and effect a retransfer of the rights themselves?

5.4. Transferor can Withdraw Consent

It has been said that because transfers of rights are conditional upon the transferor's consent, the law gives the transferor a power in cases of fraudulently induced transfers to revoke their consent, and it is this revocation of consent, which happens on the exercise of the power, which effects the revesting of the right.[114] Thus, Elise Bant writes:

> Transfers of property, just like contracts, are conditional on the transferor's intention – in the case of transfers, the transferor must intend to pass title. Where the transferor's intention to transfer was impaired (by any legal or equitable vitiating factor), the transfer is effective to give the defendant the full legal beneficial title to the asset. But the transfer is voidable at the instance of the transferor. A claimant to such a vitiated transfer is entitled to revoke her consent to the transfer of title and obtain a proprietary interest in the asset. This analysis both explains and justifies the availability of proprietary restitution in cases of vitiated consent transfers.[115]

The same view had earlier been expressed by Birke Häcker who, on the assumption that some transfers of title were void, said:

> [W]here title does pass, it need not do so unimpeachably. Less fundamental defects of consent may allow the transferor to avoid the conveyance and thereby to 'pull back' his

[113] Above, text to n 16.
[114] Though we will deal with this for the moment at common law, advocates of this approach claim that it explains both common law and equitable rescission.
[115] Elise Bant, 'Reconsidering the Role of Election in Rescission' (2012) OJLS 467, 480.

> former title. .... Yet not all impairments of consent warrant this response. Historically, the common law has limited its intervention to cases in which consent was procured by fraud or duress, leaving equity to deal with other instances where a defect of consent was regarded as relevant.[116]

There are several problems with this thinking.

First, it is circular to say, as does Häcker, that the right need not pass 'unimpeachably'. That is certainly true if there is a power to revest the right, but it is hardly an explanation why such power exists in the first place.

Second, no explanation is proffered as to why the transferor is given the power to revoke their consent. Other litigants must put their complaints before a court. Why are these people being singled out for special treatment? Why should they not have to litigate like everyone else?

Third, no explanation is given why this power to withdraw consent is limited at common law to cases of fraud and (possibly) duress. Why are cases of innocent misrepresentation or even spontaneous mistake not ones where the transferor's consent to the transfer can be withdrawn? Both also involve defects of consent recognised at common law such that they generate personal claims in unjust enrichment. Indeed, why does the 'power' to withdraw consent not avail a transferor in all cases of unjust enrichment recognised by the common law, including failure of basis and under the so-called *Woolwich*[117] principle? It might be objected that such cases do not involve defective consents, but why should that matter? All transfers require consent, and although there will have been a defect in consent in both the fraud and duress cases, it will not have been such as to prevent the right passing and so is irrelevant. If the arguments of Bant and Häcker are correct, there is no reason why the transferor should not withdraw their consent in every unjust enrichment case. Yet we know this is not true. The argument, therefore, proves too much.

Fourth, even in cases of fraud and duress, why is withdrawal of consent only available at law with respect to titles to goods conveyed pursuant to contracts of sale? Why not titles to goods conveyed pursuant to a gift? And titles to land? And shares? And intellectual property rights? The explanations of Bant and Häcker would seem to be nothing more than *ex post facto* rationalisations of the existing law. It does not, as Bant claims, both explain and justify the law.

Finally, we would not describe cases like *Kelly v Solari*,[118] where a claim was made for repayment of a mistaken payment, as involving revocations of consent. They are instead claims for an order from the court that the defendant pay the claimant a sum of money. Had a claim been brought in equity in *Feret v Hill* for an order that the defendant surrender the lease, it would have been no different, save that the claim would be for specific rather than monetary relief. We should likewise eschew the language of 'revocation of consent' in such cases.

[116] Birke Häcker, 'Proprietary Restitution After Impaired Consent Transfers: A Generalised Power Model' [2009] CLJ 324, 330; see also 344, 355, 357.

[117] *Woolwich Equitable Building Society v Inland Revenue Commissioners* [1993] AC 70.

[118] (1841) 9 M & W 54.

6. Can A Turn B into a Trustee without the Aid of the Court?

It is undoubtedly the case that A can petition the court of equity for an order that the transferee re-transfer the right; this is the so-called 'equity to rescind'. As will be seen, once such order is made, B is said to be a trustee for A, such trust backdating to the point of transfer. However, a prior question is whether A can generate a trust for themselves without going to court. Can they unilaterally rescind the transfer 'in equity', thereby turning B into a trustee?

6.1. Why Rescission in Equity?

The orthodoxy, as seen, is that, though there is an Hohfeldian power at law to rescind a contract for the sale of goods for fraudulent misrepresentation and (possibly) duress, that is the limit of common law rescission. Events such as innocent misrepresentation, spontaneous mistake, undue influence, and breach of fiduciary duty do not give rise to this 'power' at law. Moreover, even a fraudulently induced conveyance of a title to land or one brought about by duress cannot be rescinded at law. In all these cases, transferors must resort to Equity.

6.2. Unilateral Rescission in Equity?

The question, then, is how the transferor effects rescission in Equity. The position seen so far is that though the transferor has an 'equity to rescind', this is not an Hohfeldian power, merely the ability to petition the court for an order of 'specific unperformance' and consequential relief. On that basis, there can be no such thing as unilateral rescission in equity, just as there is no such thing as unilateral orders for specific performance of a contract or for delivery up of converted goods. However, it is sometimes said that rescission in equity (not just at law) is the act of the party themselves. If so, then something fundamental has happened to the 'equity to rescind'. It no longer comprises the ability to seek a remedy from a court but a true Hohfeldian power, and we have moved from the realm of procedure to that of substance.

However, it is difficult once again to see how it can be a power properly-so-called.[119] The same issues as were discussed in relation to common law rescission apply here, namely, how the 'bars' to rescission can apply without an adjudication and orders made by a court. For instance, the 'equity to rescind' is conditional upon the claimant making counter-restitution. Absent a court order, how is it possible to

[119] See generally, J O'Sullivan (n 112).

know whether counter-restitution is needed and the form it should take? Likewise, how are issues such as the laches and acquiescence to be adjudged? Do we leave it to the claimant to make such decisions?

Not surprisingly, there is no shortage of dicta to the effect that it is the court which does the rescinding, not the transferor. Thus, Lord Blackburn in *Erlanger v New Sombrero Phosphate Co*, after referring to the common law remedy of damages, said:

> But a court of equity could not give damages, and, unless it can rescind the contract, can give no relief. And on the other hand, it can take accounts of profits, and make allowance for deterioration. And I think the practice has always been for a court of equity to give this relief whenever, by the exercise of its powers, it can do what is practically just, though it cannot restore the parties precisely to the state they were in before the contract.[120]

These words make no sense when we see the transferor as themselves effecting rescission; talk throughout of 'the court' shows that this is a remedy of the court.

In the same vein, we saw Lord Wright's description of the remedy in *Spence v Crawford*[121] as being within the discretion of the court. Talking of Lord Blackburn's *dictum* cited immediately above, he said:

> … Lord Blackburn is careful not to seek to tie the hands of the court by attempting to form any rigid rules. The court must fix its eyes on the goal of doing 'what is practically just.' How that goal may be reached must depend on the circumstances of the case, but the court will be more drastic in exercising its discretionary powers in a case of fraud than in a case of innocent misrepresentation.[122]

Lord Wright also spoke of courts going 'a long way in ordering restitution if the substantial identity of the subject-matter of the contract remains,' ordering 'rescission and mutual restitution in certain cases,' and doing their best to 'unravel the complexities of any particular case, which may in some cases involve adjustments on both sides.'[123] Again, none of this is consistent with the notion that it is the claimant rather than the court which effects rescission.

The decision of the High Court of Australia in *Alati v Kruger*,[124] which is often cited as authority for the view that rescission in equity is the act of the transferor, is in fact a good illustration of the opposite proposition. Although the majority cite the decision of the House of Lords in *Reese River Silver Mining Co v Smith*[125] to say it is the 'act of the party', that case turned on a peculiarity of the statutory scheme in question. Moreover, the point was not in issue in *Alati*. Furthermore, there were difficult questions concerning the plaintiff's ability to make *restitutio in integrum*. It was held that though this might have barred any claim to rescind at law, it was:

[120] (1878) 3 App Cas 1218, 1278.
[121] [1939] 3 All ER 271, 288; above, text to n 67.
[122] Ibid 289.
[123] ibid.
[124] (1955) 94 CLR 216.
[125] (1869–70) LR 4 HL 64, 73.

> … necessary here to apply the doctrines of equity, and equity has always regarded as valid the disaffirmance of a contract induced by fraud where the situation is such that, by the exercise of its powers, as for example the power to take accounts of profits and to direct inquiries as to allowances proper to be made for deterioration, it can do what is practically just and thereby replace the parties substantially, even though not precisely, in statu quo.[126]

Such a statement is once again inconsistent with rescission being the act of claimants themselves. Moreover, it is not enough, as the High Court asserts, to say that:

> The function of a court in which proceedings are taken is to adjudicate upon the validity of the purported disaffirmance as an act avoiding the transaction ab initio, and, if it is valid, to give effect to it and make appropriate consequential orders.[127]

Any process of adjudication and the making of consequential orders gives the lie to the notion of equitable rescission as the act of the party.

So far as English authority is concerned, it has been argued that the point is concluded in favour of rescission being an act of the party by the decision of House of Lords in *Abram Steamship Co Ltd v Westville Shipping Co Ltd.*[128] Whilst it is true that Lord Atkinson there said, in a minority speech, that rescission was the act of the party, the authorities on which he relied, *Hunt v Silk*[129] and *Blackburn v Smith,*[130] do not support that proposition, for both are simple breach of contract cases, not ones involving rescission. The confusion is probably explained by the fact that, at that time, 'rescission' was used to describe both termination for breach and rescission properly-co-called,[131] and termination for breach can undoubtedly be brought about by the act of the party not in breach.[132] Moreover, in the earlier decision of *Boyd & Forrest v The Glasgow & South Western Rlwy Co*, the same judge spoke unequivocally of the 'Court of Equity' setting aside contracts.[133]

More recently, in a case where a settlement was sought to be set aside on the ground of unilateral mistake, *Pitt v Holt*,[134] a seven-member United Kingdom Supreme Court held that the 'equitable jurisdiction to set aside a voluntary disposition on the ground of mistake was exercisable whenever there was a causative mistake which was so grave that it would be unconscionable to refuse relief'.[135] This once again makes clear that the ultimate decision lies with the court, that

[126] (1955) 94 CLR 216, 223.
[127] ibid 224.
[128] [1923] AC 773. The argument is that of S Elliott, 'The Basic Structure of Rescission' in B McFarlane and & S Elliott, *Equity Today: 150 Years After the Judicature Reforms* (Hart Publishing, 2023), ch 9.
[129] (1804) 5 East 449.
[130] (1848) 2 Ex 783.
[131] Clarity was only achieved in the late 1970s, with the decisions of the House of Lords in *Johnson v Agnew* [1980] AC 367 and in *Photo Production Ltd v Securicor Transport Ltd* [1980] AC 827.
[132] The confusion is noted in *Mann v Paterson Constructions Pty Ltd* [2019] HCA 32 and the decision of the Privy Council in *Lodder v Slowey* [1904] AC 442 said to be wrongly made as a result.
[133] 1915 SC (HL) 20, 30. Above, text to n 65.
[134] [2013] UKSC 26.
[135] ibid [128].

it must be unconscionable *for the court* to refuse relief. Indeed, in relation to the related appeal in *Futter v Futter*, the Supreme Court indicated that relief on the ground of mistake, had it been claimed, would probably have been refused on the ground that it involved an artificial tax avoidance scheme,[136] a conclusion totally at odds with rescission being the act of the party.

A possible explanation for the confusion is the compressed language often used in the case-law. When it is said that the claimant can rescind, this is an unfortunate contraction of the phrase 'the claimant can petition the court for an order of rescission'. The phenomenon is encountered elsewhere. One example concerns falsification and surcharge of accounts in equity. In *Libertarian Investments Ltd v Hall*, Lord Millett NPJ said that if an account disclosed an unauthorised investment, 'the plaintiff may falsify it', and that if the account is shown to be defective, 'the plaintiff can surcharge' it.[137] However, both statements were immediately followed by words indicating that this involved asking the court to do the things in question, which is precisely what should be the understanding here.

Finally, even those who argue that rescission in equity is the act of the party, generally admit that this is done by the issuance of court proceedings, which only makes the point.

7. Does the Making of a Court Order Create a Backdated Trust?

We now reach the final issue. Having seen that rescission in equity means nothing more than the court ordering the unwinding of the transaction on both sides and perhaps the granting of declarations of invalidity and injunctive relief preventing the transferee exercising the right or enforcing any judgment obtained consequent upon it, the orthodoxy is that, on the making of such orders, the transferee holds the rights in question on trust for the transferor, which trust backdates to the point of transfer. How then does this backdated trust arise?

Before answering this question, we should notice that it is not really a trust. In the already discussed case of *Bristol and West BS v Mothew*, Millett LJ refused to allow such backdating to generate claims for breach of trust, saying that in the earlier case of *El Ajou* he spoke in such terms only to avoid the long-criticised rule that a fiduciary relationship need be present for equitable tracing.[138]

As to why this 'trust' arises, the typical reasoning is that the 'equitable' or 'beneficial title', terms which are used interchangeably, revests when the court order is made. Thus, in *Alati v Kruger* it was said that 'a rescission which the common law

[136] ibid [135]. A recent example of relief being refused on these grounds is the decision of the Court of Appeal in *Bhaur v Equity First Trustees (Nevis) Ltd* [2023] EWCA Civ 534.

[137] *Libertarian Investments Ltd v Hall* [2014] 1 HKC 368, [168], [170].

[138] [1998] 1 Ch 1, 22. Above, text to n 89.

courts would not accept as valid cannot of its own force revest the legal title to property which had passed, but if a court of equity would treat it as effectual the equitable title to such property revests upon the rescission.'[139] The same thinking can be found in English cases. Thus, in *El Ajou v Dollar Land Holdings plc (No 1)*, Millett J (as he then was) spoke of victims of fraud being 'entitled to rescind the transaction and revest the equitable title to the purchase money in themselves …'[140] In *Bristol and West Building Society v Mothew*, the now Millett LJ said: 'The right to rescind for misrepresentation is an equity. Until it is exercised the beneficial interest in any property transferred in reliance on the representation remains vested in the transferee,'[141] with the implication that on rescission this 'beneficial interest' revests, while in *Shalson v Rosso*, Rimer J said that on rescission 'the beneficial title which passed to the representor … revests in the representee'.[142]

We encountered the same thinking when examining the question whether there could be a trust before rescission.[143] It was seen as flawed, for the simple reason that the transferor has no 'beneficial' or 'equitable' title before the transfer; such title could not therefore pass to the transferee. It is equally the case that it cannot repass. Moreover, even if it passed, we still lack an explanation why it revests in the transferor on the making of court orders for rescission.

One explanation might be that the effect of rescission in equity is to avoid the transaction so far as equity, though not the law, is concerned. As seen, judges are prone to describe the transfer as not altogether void but voidable, albeit in equity.[144] On this view, the court of equity on rescission treats the transfer as avoided, meaning it was never made, so that in the eyes of equity, the right never left the transferor. Of course, the reality is different: the right is in the transferee. To resolve this conflict as to the location of the right, the transferee will hold the right on trust for the transferor.

The problem is that this is not how trusts work. As Maitland noted over a century ago, trusts do not involve conflicts as to the location of rights.[145] Moreover, the transaction is not 'voidable' at all. What instead happens is that the court orders specific relief. The thinking seems to be that if the transfer is not void, but that specific relief is ordered, it must mean that the transfer has thereby been avoided. But this does not follow. Though often granted, there is no need for courts to make declarations of invalidity. Indeed, how can such declarations be made when all the elements necessary for the transfer were present? If there really were different requirements of validity in equity, the transfer would have been void in equity from the start. Yet we know that is not the case. The language of voidability seems only to express the idea that the transferee is liable to be ordered to reconvey.

[139] (1955) 94 CLR 216, 224.
[140] [1993] 3 All ER 717, 733. Of course, it is not the claimants themselves who rescind, but the court.
[141] [1998] Ch 1, 22–23.
[142] [2005] Ch 281, [122].
[143] Text to nn 92–95.
[144] Eg, Lindley LJ in *Allcard v Skinner* (1887) 36 Ch D 145, 186.
[145] Maitland (n 97) pp 17–18.

Another argument for a trust would be, by analogy with situations where orders for specific performance of a contract of sale can be granted, that equity looks upon as done that which ought to be done, and it is this which gives rise to the trust. It could be said that once the order to retransfer is made, equity fictitiously treats it as having been performed. However, the argument is already weak in the context of specific performance of contracts of sale;[146] it is equally weak here. Moreover, it cannot explain the backdating of the trust. Indeed, in the context of the so-called 'trust' generated by the availability of specific performance, many judges doubt whether it is a trust at all.[147] The same scepticism should apply here.

8. Conclusion

We saw that fraud does not prevent the transfer or grant of rights to the fraudster: the fact that the transaction was fraudulently induced is 'altogether collateral.' We also saw that it is a mistake to think that the House of Lords in *Cundy v Lindsay* held that there could be no transfer in the case of a contract of sale of goods void as being fraudulently induced. The reason why title did not there pass was because the essential elements of a valid conveyance by delivery were not present; fraud had nothing to do with it.

We also saw the impossibility of victims of fraud unilaterally rescinding grants of rights and thereby revesting rights, and that the exceptional case of a transfer of titles to goods made pursuant to fraudulently induced contracts could not be supported; cases such as *Car and Universal Finance Ltd v Caldwell* were demonstrated to be wrongly decided. Nor is it possible for the victim of fraud unilaterally to rescind in equity and thereby turn the fraudster into a trustee; arguments that self-help rescission in equity was possible were shown to be misconceived. Finally, arguments as to a backdated trust arising on court-ordered rescission were seen as unconvincing.

Victims of fraud have, and only have, an 'equity to rescind', the ability to bring a claim in equity to rescind the transaction, seeking orders from the court for reconveyance of the right and injuncting the fraudster from relying on the right in the meantime. The language of 'election', 'power', and 'right' are all misnomers and apt to mislead. There is only the possibility of the grant of court orders for specific relief, which operate in the same way as orders for specific performance of

[146] W Swadling, 'The Vendor-Purchaser Constructive Trust' in S Degeling and J Edelman (eds), *Equity in Commercial Law* (Lawbook Co., 2005), ch 18; W Swadling, 'The Mischief of Maxims' in B McFarlane and S Elliott, *Equity Today: 150 Years after the Judicature Act Reforms* (Hart Publishing, 2023), ch 5, 94–99.

[147] *Knox v Gye* (1871–72) LR 5 HL 656, 675–6 (Lord Westbury); *Rayner v Preston* (1881) 18 Ch D 1, 6 (Cotton LJ), 11 (Brett LJ); *Berkley v Poulett* [1977] 1 EGLR 86, 93 (Stamp LJ); *Kern Corpn Ltd v Walter Reid Trading Pty Ltd* (1987) 163 CLR 164, 192 (Deane J); *Southern Pacific Mortgages v Scott* [2015] AC 385, [63] (Lord Collins of Mapesbury).

contracts or delivery up of converted goods. That is, or at least should be, the sole extent of the 'proprietary' consequences of fraud.

One so-far neglected question is whether courts award this remedy too liberally. We saw Lord Millett describe it as a form of 'specific unperformance'. Drawing an analogy with specific performance of contracts, he questioned whether such orders should be confined to 'land or other property of special value to the transferor.'[148] He was right so to do. The issue is lost sight of when thinking in terms of trusts arising on rescission, leading to the thought that the claimant is then simply exercising their power under *Saunders v Vautier*[149] to collapse the 'trust'.[150] Of course, *Saunders v Vautier* applies to all trusts, regardless of subject-matter. But it is a false analogy. We do not make this mistake with specific performance and should not do so with specific 'unperformance'.

[148] See n 22, 416.
[149] (1841) 4 Beav 115.
[150] See, eg, Häcker (n 116) at 346.

10

Agency Law and the Protection of Third Parties (and Principals) – Whither the Balance?

TAN CHENG-HAN

1. Introduction

The classic definition of the legal relationship of principal and agent is that of a fiduciary relationship which arises when a principal manifests assent (or consent) to the agent that the agent shall act on the principal's behalf and subject to the principal's control so as to affect the principal's legal relations with third parties, and the agent manifests assent so to act.[1] Where the agent has acted within the scope of the principal's assent, the agent is said to have actual authority to act.[2] It is this authority from the principal, which may arise expressly from what the principal said or by implication, that gives the agent the power to affect the principal's legal position vis-à-vis third parties. It recognises the autonomy of the principal to alter her legal position whether through acts performed personally or through an intermediary who has been vested with the requisite authority. This consensual power to affect the principal's legal position is a feature of agency that distinguishes agents in a legal sense from most intermediaries. It has therefore been suggested that the irreducible core of 'real' agency probably only consists of the 'internal' aspect of consent/assent between principal and agent and the external aspect of the agent's power to affect the principal's legal position (power-liability).[3] The element of a fiduciary relationship is simply the default position that can be departed from expressly or by implication.[4]

[1] American Law Institute, *Restatement of the Law Third, Agency* ('*Restatement, Third*') (Minnesota, American Law Institute Publishers, 2007) §1.01; P Watts and FMB Reynolds, *Bowstead and Reynolds on Agency*, 22nd edn (London, Sweet & Maxwell, 2021) [1-001].

[2] Watts and Reynolds, ibid.

[3] Wee Meng-Seng and Tan Cheng-Han, 'The Agency of Liquidators and Receivers' in D Busch and L Macgregor (eds), *The Unauthorised Agent: Perspectives from European and Comparative Law* (Cambridge: Cambridge University Press, 2009) 8.40.

[4] *McWilliam v Norton Finance (UK) Ltd* [2015] EWCA Civ 186, [2015] 1 All ER (Comm) 1026 [40]; *UBS AG* v *Kommunale Wasserwerke Leipzig GmbH* [2017] EWCA Civ 1567, [2017] 2 CLC 584 [92]

As the starting point for agency at law to arise is the mutual consent of the principal and agent, it is unsurprising that many agency doctrines link to this internal aspect. One of the first questions in determining if the principal-agent relationship has been formed is to ask what words or acts have taken place that will be construed objectively as amounting to the requisite mutual assent. The existence of any agreement between the principal and agent that the latter may act for the former, and the scope of such mutual assent, are matters 'to be ascertained by applying ordinary principles of construction of contracts, including any proper implications from the express words used, the usages of the trade, or the course of business between the parties'.[5] The agreement between the principal and agent may be contractual, in which event the normal rules of contract law will apply, or the agreement may not amount to an enforceable contract, perhaps because the agreement lacked consideration or the agent lacked capacity to contract. If there is no enforceable contract, this does not preclude the agent from having authority if an objective interpretation of the words and acts used indicates the existence of mutual assent. The agent cannot, however, be sued for breach of contract if the agent had agreed to perform an act on behalf of the principal but chose not to exercise such authority. Where the internal dimension of agency exists and the agent has acted for the principal within the scope of the agent's authority, this leads to the external aspect of agency taking effect, usually by the formation of a contractual relationship between the principal and third party to which the agent is not normally a party.[6]

The doctrine of ratification also links to the internal aspect of agency. The doctrine of ratification arises where, at the time the agent purported to act for the principal, the agent did not have the authority to do so. Prima facie, therefore, neither the principal nor the third party have any legal relationship to the other arising out of the agent's act. What ratification does is that it allows the principal to clothe the agent retrospectively with the requisite authority such that the agent is treated as having actual authority from the outset.[7] It is 'akin to an assent by the

where the court agreed with the submission that 'the existence of a fiduciary duty was by no means an essential characteristic of agency'; *Tonny Permana v One Tree Capital Management Pte Ltd* [2021] 5 SLR 477 [94] (affirmed by the Appellate Division of the High Court in *Tonny Permana v One Tree Capital Management Pte Ltd* [2021] 2 SLR 1103 although the Appellate Division disagreed that the fiduciary duty owed by the agent had been displaced contractually).

[5] *Freeman & Lockyer v Buckhurst Park (Properties) Mangal Ltd* [1964] 2 QB 480 (CA), 502; and see also *Tonny Permana* ibid. [103].

[6] It is also a matter of interpretation whether the agent's acts were performed on behalf of the principal or in the agent's personal capacity; see, eg, *Bridges & Salmon Ltd v The Swan* [1968] 1 Lloyd's Rep 5 where the owner of a fishing vessel hired the vessel to JD Rodger Ltd, which was to be responsible for its maintenance and repair. The owner of the vessel, Mr JD Rodger, gave orders for repairs to the vessel on JD Rodger Ltd notepaper and signed 'J Rodger, Director'. When the company could not pay, the repairers sued the owner directly. Taking all the facts into consideration including previous course of dealings, the court found that the owner had contracted on behalf of JD Rodger Ltd. Nevertheless, the owner was found liable for the repairs as Brandon J was of the view that it would be natural for the repairers to assume that the owner would accept personal liability for repairs that benefitted the owner unless the owner made the contrary clear beyond doubt. This case is an example of a person contracting both as agent as well as in his personal capacity.

[7] *Restatement, Third* (n 1) §4.01.

principal to the transaction entered into by the unauthorised agent by adopting the agent's otherwise unauthorised acts'.[8] Since the agent is treated as having been authorised at the time the transaction was entered into, both the principal and third party can sue or be sued on the contract.[9]

In *Keighley, Maxsted & Co v Durant*, Lord Macnaghten referred to the doctrine as a 'remarkable exception' to the general principle that a person can only enforce contracts to which she is a party.[10] The doctrine is therefore regarded by some as anomalous. It has been said that the doctrine creates a fiction that does not conform to the rules of contract since it can be performed unilaterally by the principal and without any communication to the third party.[11] Nevertheless, ratification is consistent with the core of agency to the extent that the agent objectively acted for the principal, the third party had knowledge of this and was willing to enter into such a transaction, and the principal ultimately consented to what the agent did. The only difference is the timing of the consent that in a typical case takes place prior to the transaction. One advantage of ratification is that it resolves any dispute over whether the agent had the requisite authority. A principal that is desirous of the transaction, notwithstanding the agent's lack of authority or possible lack of authority, can put the matter beyond doubt. Lord Macnaghten therefore referred to it as 'a wholesome and convenient fiction'.[12]

Another oft-criticised agency doctrine relates to undisclosed principals. Essentially, this doctrine allows a principal to intervene on a contract entered into by an agent even though the agent contracted with the third party as a principal. If the agent did so within the scope of the agent's authority, the principal can subsequently reveal herself and enforce the contract notwithstanding that the third party thought she was only contracting with the agent and no one else. On the face of it this seems to offend general principles of contract law relating to the formation of contracts.[13] Yet the undisclosed agency doctrine conforms to the internal aspect of agency. As Lord Lindley said in *Keighley, Maxsted & Co v Durant*:[14]

> The explanation of the doctrine that an undisclosed principal can sue and be sued on a contract made in the name of another person with his authority is, that the contract

[8] *Cavenagh Investment Pte Ltd v Kaushik Rajiv* [2013] 2 SLR 543 [31].

[9] A principal may also ratify an agent's wrongdoing (see *Wilson v Tumman* (1843) 6 Man & G 236, 242–43) though this is understandably rare.

[10] [1901] AC 240, 247.

[11] For example, see *Restatement of the Law Second, Agency* (Minnesota, American Law Institute, 1958) ('*Restatement, Second*') §82, comment d; WA Seavey, 'The Rationale of Agency' (1920) *Yale LJ* 859, 886–87; R Powell, *The Law of Agency*, 2nd edn (London, Pitman 1961) 120. Although communication of the fact of ratification is not necessary, if the transaction is challenged the principal will have to adduce evidence that an act amounting to ratification did take place, eg the principal had informed the agent that the former was adopting what the latter did.

[12] *Keighley, Maxsted & Co v Durant* (n 10) 247.

[13] ibid 256, 261 and generally see also F Pollock, 'Notes' (1887) 3 LQR 358, 359; JB Ames, 'Undisclosed Principal – His Rights and Liabilities' (1909) 18 *Yale LJ* 443; FR Mecham, 'The Liability of an Undisclosed Principal' (1910) 23 *Harv L Rev* 513, 515; GE Dal Pont, *Law of Agency*, 4th edn (Australia, LexisNexis, 2020) [19.33].

[14] ibid 261.

> is in truth, although not in form, that of the undisclosed principal himself. Both the principal and the authority exist when the contract is made; and the person who makes it for him is only the instrument by which the principal acts. In allowing him to sue and be sued upon it, effect is given, so far as he is concerned, to what is true in fact, although that truth may not have been known to the other contracting party.

In addition, it is usually a matter of indifference to the third party whether there is an undisclosed principal or not and, if there is, it is commercially convenient that the principal should be able to sue and be sued.[15]

While the internal aspect of agency is key to the development of important principles within the law of agency, another aspect of the law that does not receive as much explicit attention relates to the importance of protecting third parties (and to a lesser extent, the principal) from the risks of dealing with intermediaries. The interposition of intermediaries compared to direct contracting raises risks of a mismatch between the intentions and objectives of the principal and the intermediary, in this case the agent. While the imposition of fiduciary obligations plays a prophylactic role in disincentivising an agent from neglecting the principal's interests,[16] it will not address fully instances where the agent has misunderstood the principal's instructions, or where the agent knowingly acts without authority because the agent, dealing with the practical realities of the transaction and perhaps unable to reach the principal in a timely manner, believes that the agreement entered into benefits the principal. Doctrines such as ratification and undisclosed agency also increase the inherent risks faced by third parties dealing with agents. A large body of agency law therefore seeks to strike a balance between facilitating commercial transactions while ensuring that third parties (and principals) are not unduly prejudiced. The rest of this chapter discusses the balance that the law seeks in the areas of warranty of authority, apparent authority, ratification, and undisclosed agency, after which it concludes.

2. Warranty of Authority

There are two principal means by which the law protects third parties from the risk of unauthorised acts of an agent. One is the doctrine of warranty of authority. Where an agent enters into a contract on behalf of a principal, the agent represents that she has the authority to do so and the law deems the agent to have warranted this to the third party. The consideration moving from the third party for this contractual promise is the act of the third party in entering into the contract. Should the agent not, in fact, have the authority to do what the agent did, the third party may claim against the agent for damages for breach of contract even if the agent acted in good faith under a mistake as to the scope of her authority.

[15] ibid 261–62 and see also *Teheran-Europe Co Ltd v S T Belton (Tractors) Ltd* [1968] 2 QB 545, 555.

[16] The role of fiduciary duties in reducing the risks to principals of using agents will not be discussed in this chapter.

The underlying purpose behind warranty of authority is the law's desire to protect the third party who has relied on the agent's assertion of authority unless the agent has made it clear that she makes no such representation or the true facts are known to the third party.[17] A third party who has entered into a contract on the faith of an agent's representation should, in principle, be entitled to look to such agent for losses suffered if the agent did not have authority and the third party is unable to obtain the benefits of the contract. This is efficient risk allocation because as between the agent and third party, the former is in a superior position to ascertain the scope of her authority.

Yet, the cause of action for breach of warranty of authority is a product of history and if it were to arise for the first time today it is arguable that the law may develop differently. This is because the tort of misrepresentation today accommodates both fraudulent and non-fraudulent misrepresentations, when in the past liability would only arise in respect of fraudulent misrepresentations under the tort of deceit such that a third party who acted on the faith of an agent's representation as to authority would have had no remedy where the representation was made negligently. Breach of warranty of authority was developed to provide a remedy where none existed previously.[18] It has been observed that today the law relating to the warranty of authority covers virtually the same field as liability in the tort of misrepresentation, where that misrepresentation relates to an agent's authority. It is said this is an anachronism because the contractual nature of the claim yields different outcomes for what would normally be a negligent statement that would ordinarily be dealt with under tort law.[19] Breach of contract usually leads to strict liability, there being no necessity as with negligent statements to establish a duty of care; the defence of contributory negligence is not available; and the mode of assessing damages is different between contract and tort. Imposing strict liability on agents who may have acted without fault[20] and not taking account of the contributory negligence of third parties do not appear to optimally balance the risks between them.

As an aside, in New Zealand the courts have ruled out the existence of a duty of care in cases involving warranty of authority.[21] The first reason given was that even assuming the relationship between the agent and third party was of sufficient proximity, and there was a careless representation of authority and reliance, the court should not allow new liabilities in negligence where adequate remedies already exist in contract or equity. As the cause of action for breach of warranty provided an adequate remedy, there was no policy reason for imposing an additional liability in tort. The court was also concerned that to allow a claim in tort opened up the

[17] Watts and Reynolds (n 1) [9-060].

[18] ibid [9-061]; *Chu Said Thong v Vision Law LLC* [2014] 4 SLR 375 [270].

[19] *Chu Said Thong* ibid [266]–[270].

[20] The example commonly given is of the agent who at the time of contracting could not reasonably have known that her principal had passed away suddenly thereby terminating the agent's authority.

[21] *Kavanagh v Continental Shelf (No 46) Ltd* [1993] 2 NZLR 648.

prospect of vicarious liability for principals. The second reason was that allowing such a claim in tort undermined the policies underlying the New Zealand Public Bodies Contracts Act. The courts in Singapore have arrived at a different conclusion and allowed both a claim for breach of warranty of authority and negligent misstatement to be pleaded as alternative causes of action.[22] It is suggested this is the better position as the common law generally recognises that claims in tort and contract can co-exist.[23]

Where a claim in contract and tort can be made, the defence of contributory negligence is available where a defendant's liability in contract is the same as what such defendant's liability would have been in tort. In other words, where contractual liability co-exists with a tortious duty of care, such defence may be asserted[24] and it has been held in Singapore that contributory negligence can be relied on in a claim for breach of warranty of authority where the representation as to authority was made negligently.[25] If correct, this removes one of the differences between a claim for breach of warranty and a claim founded on negligent misstatement. It is not clear, however, if *Fong Maun Yee*, which purported to follow English law but in fact extended it, will be adopted elsewhere as a claim for breach of warranty is strict and not based on negligence unlike a contractual duty to take care. As such, an agent's liability for breach of such warranty is not the same as a claim in tort for negligent misrepresentation even if they can arise on the same set of facts.[26]

3. Apparent Authority

This discussion of warranty of authority provides a useful segue to apparent authority that is the other important mode by which the law provides a measure of protection for third parties who have dealt with an unauthorised agent. It is not always the case that, ratification aside, a third party cannot sue the principal on an unauthorised agreement entered into by an agent. Where a third party can, in effect, enforce an agreement even though the agent acted beyond the scope of her authority, the third party will, at most, be entitled to nominal damages from the agent for breach of warranty because the agent's lack of authority will not have caused the third party any real loss. This is so even if the principal becomes insolvent and the third party cannot effectively enforce any judgment against the principal because the agent only warrants that she had authority to enter into the contract and not its

[22] *Fong Maun Yee v Yoong Weng Ho Robert* [1997] 1 SLR(R) 751; and see also *Chu Said Thong* (n 18) [199].

[23] *Forsikringsaktieselskapet Vesta v Butcher* [1989] 1 AC 852 (Court of Appeal); *Jet Holding Ltd v Cooper Cameron (Singapore) Pte Ltd* [2006] 3 SLR(R) 769; and see also *Barclays Bank PLC v Fairclough Building Ltd* [1995] 1 QB 214.

[24] ibid.

[25] *Fong Maun Yee* (n 22) [55].

[26] *Barclays Bank PLC v Fairclough Building Ltd* (n 23) 230; *B v IVF Hammersmith Ltd* [2018] 2 WLR 1223 [285]; *Chu Said Thong* (n 18) [230].

performance. The situation is no different from that of a principal being in breach of a contract entered into within authority and who, being impecunious, cannot perform the contract or compensate the third party for breach.

The doctrine of apparent authority allows a third party to enforce a contract against the principal despite the agent's lack of authority to enter into the transaction. The underlying basis is the law's desire to protect the legitimate expectations of a third party who has acted reasonably. Nevertheless, the law does not penalise a principal simply because her agent has asserted more authority than was conferred. Any such rule is excessive and reduces the incentive for third parties to exercise some measure of care. The doctrine therefore arises because of an act of the principal who has expressly or by implication represented to the third party (or allowed another person to do so on the principal's behalf) that the agent has a certain authority and the third party reasonably relying on the faith of such representation entered into a contract with the agent.[27] When this happens, English common law states that the principal is estopped from denying the agent's authority as it would be inequitable to allow the principal to assert the true facts when the principal was the person who had misled the third party.[28] While the agent may not have been authorised, responsibility is placed fairly on the principal to the extent that the principal's acts were the catalyst for the third party's belief and the third party had reasonably acted on such belief. Once again, the law accords with efficient risk allocation because the principal is in the best position to convey what the agent's authority is and it would be unrealistic to expect a third party to question a principal further if the principal has objectively represented to the third party that the agent has a particular scope of authority. In addition, absent a fair means of holding principals responsible where their acts have misled a third party, third parties would have no choice but to deal directly with principals including at a minimum obtaining a principal's confirmation of the agent's authority prior to each transaction which may diminish some of the convenience that agents offer in commercial transactions.

One issue that has arisen is whether the type of representation capable of giving rise to apparent authority is wider than that required typically for estoppel by representation. It has been said that in addition to cases that can be said to be something like a genuine representation by the principal of the agent's authority,[29] there are other cases where the representation is only of a very general nature that arises from the principal putting the agent in a specific position carrying with it

[27] Apparent authority can also arise outside of contract, eg whether an agent had apparent authority in relation to a misstatement made by such agent.

[28] *Freeman & Lockyer v Buckhurst Park (Properties) Mangal Ltd* (n 5) 503 and generally, see Tan Cheng-Han, 'Estoppel in the Law of Agency' (2020) 136 LQR 315. In the United States the basis for apparent authority is the objective theory of agency, which is based on the interpretation of the expressions and conduct of the principal that objectively demonstrates the scope of the principal's assent to the agent acting for the principal, see *Restatement, Second* (n 11) §8, comment d and *Restatement, Third* (n 1) §2.03, comment c.

[29] Such as a statement in writing or made orally, or by a course of dealing.

a usual authority such as a managing director of a company or where a person engages a solicitor. In the latter category of cases, the notion of representation is more tenuous and the connection of the principal's liability with estoppel more difficult to maintain.[30] In addition, the authority that the third party is entitled to infer in such cases is that which would normally be implied between principal and agent and it is of this that the court receives evidence. The third party need not testify as to the third party's knowledge and the third party may be ignorant of what authority would be implied in such instances.[31] A second way in which apparent authority may not conform with common law estoppel by representation is that the detriment incurred by the third party may be very small. Simply entering into the contract on the faith of the principal's representation can give rise to apparent authority.[32] These issues raise the question whether the protection offered to third parties by the doctrine of apparent authority is overbroad.

Dealing with the second issue first, it is unsurprising that there is a sufficient detriment simply by the third party entering into the contract. This is in the nature of the representation, namely that the agent has the requisite authority to act on the principal's behalf in relation to the contract in question. Furthermore, the third party may well have incurred a 'detriment' in a more literal way by foregoing another course of action including other contractual opportunities that the third party could have entered into and which no longer exist or exist under less favourable conditions.[33] It will often be the case that the lack of authority only arises as an issue sometime after the contract was entered into, perhaps even months later where circumstances have changed.

The first issue is clearly the more important[34] and difficult one. Putting things in perspective though, the specific positions in which a person placed will generally have significant apparent authority in relation to the conduct of business are few. Within firms, only two positions typically have this status. They are partners and managing directors/Chief Executive Officers (CEO).[35] With partnerships, section 5 of the Partnership Act of 1890 states expressly that every partner is an agent of the firm and his other partners for the purpose of the business of the partnership and the acts of every partner who does any act for carrying on in the usual way business of the kind carried on by the firm bind the firm and his partners, unless the partner so acting has in fact no authority to act for the firm in the particular matter, and the person with whom he is dealing either knows that he has no

[30] Watts and Reynolds (n 1) [8-014].
[31] ibid.
[32] ibid [8-027].
[33] For example, see *Kelly v Fraser* [2012] UKPC 25; [2013] 1 AC 450 [17].
[34] ibid.
[35] Another corporate officer who may have apparent authority by virtue of her position is the company secretary. Such officer is often responsible for the administration of a company and her usual duties include maintaining and updating the company's records, administering and attending meetings of directors and shareholders and preparing the minutes of such meetings. A company secretary may therefore have apparent authority to attest to the validity of minutes of meetings and resolutions passed therein (see *Kelly v Fraser* ibid [13]).

authority, or does not know or believe him to be a partner. This is unremarkable. Partners are co-owners of the enterprise who usually have authority to act for the partnership in relation to the firm's business and therefore even if such authority was curtailed, a partner would have apparent authority save for those who knew about the restriction or were unaware that the person was a partner.

Within corporations, the managing director or its preferred nomenclature today, the CEO, is usually the most senior executive within the entity. Corporations are artificial entities that can only act through human individuals. The starting point for determining the authority of any person acting for the corporation lies in legislation relating to companies and the corporate constitution. In the UK, the Companies Act 2006 does not stipulate that directors are to be appointed by shareholders. This is a matter left to the articles of association and, where the current UK model articles for private companies limited by shares are adopted, this gives the power of appointment both to the shareholders in general meeting by way of an ordinary resolution and to the board of directors.[36] When directors have been appointed, the UK model articles state that directors are responsible for the management of the company's business, for which they may exercise all the powers of the company.[37] In general, corporations in the UK and Singapore vest the power of management in the board of directors.

Where directors have been appointed, they may, if the legislation or corporate constitution allows, collectively agree to delegate any of the powers conferred on them. Such delegation may be to a committee or an individual.[38] As it is unrealistic to expect the entire board to be involved in every decision made or transaction entered into, given also that not all board members are necessarily employed by the company, a significant amount of the board's power is delegated. The senior executive that is typically appointed by the board will usually be the subject of a wide delegation of the board's powers. This may be reflected in the duties and responsibilities set out in the employment contract or it may be implied by the position held. It will not infrequently be a combination of both. Traditionally, the designation used for this position is managing director. Thus in the former UK 'Table A – Regulations for management of a (private) company limited by shares' that served as a model constitution, regulation 84 provided that 'the directors may appoint one or more of their number to the office of managing director or to any other executive office under the company and may enter into an agreement or arrangement with any director for his employment by the company or for

[36] Article 17. In Singapore the default position at section 149B of the Companies Act 1967 (unless the corporate constitution provides otherwise) is that a company may appoint a director by ordinary resolution passed at a general meeting.

[37] Article 3 of the UK model articles for private companies limited by shares. In Singapore, section 157A of the Companies Act 1967 provides that the business of a company is to be managed by or under the direction or supervision of the directors who may exercise all the powers of the company except any power that the Act or the corporate constitution requires the company to exercise in general meeting.

[38] Article 5 of the UK model articles for private companies limited by shares. In Singapore this is the default position under section 157A of the Companies Act 1967, which refers to the company being managed under the direction or supervision of the board.

the provision by him of any services outside the scope of the ordinary duties of a director'. A similar provision still exists in Singapore.[39] In addition, the Singapore model constitution provides that the directors 'may entrust to and confer upon a managing director any of the powers exercisable by them upon such terms and conditions and with such restrictions as they think fit, and either collaterally with or to the exclusion of their own powers, and may from time to time revoke, withdraw, alter, or vary all or any of those powers'.[40]

Given companies must act through human individuals, and that the board almost inevitably delegates its power to others, in particular the managing director (or CEO) who has executive oversight of the company including its day-to-day operations, it is rational for the law to recognise that the managing director will generally have wide actual authority in relation to a company's affairs (including authorising others to act for the company since the managing director herself will often need to delegate tasks to others). Third parties transacting with a company would not expect the entire board to be involved in negotiations or to be present when agreement is reached. Accordingly, where a board has curtailed what would usually be the expected authority of a managing director, as regards third parties who are unaware of such a restriction the law regards the appointment to such position as a sufficient representation of authority. Given the seniority of the position and the long-established role of managing directors, to regard appointment to the position as a sufficient representation in itself is reasonable without the need for individuals to prove actual knowledge of what authority such an officer would normally have. Instead, the burden is placed on the principal to prove that the third party did not believe that the managing director had authority to act in the manner that she did. Without such a starting point, all unauthorised transactions involving a managing director would be unenforceable and the only safe course would be to obtain a board resolution confirming the managing director's authority. In a different age this may have led to lengthy delays before transactions could be concluded, perhaps precluding the transaction altogether to minimise business uncertainty especially in fast moving markets. Even today, such a requirement may be inconvenient in some instances. The present legal position facilitates commercial transactions as the risk of unauthorised transactions being unenforceable is diminished.

Such apparent authority that arises generally by way of appointment to the most senior executive position of a company by whatever name called would extend to having apparent authority to make representations as to the authority of subordinate executives or others acting for the company. No such authority exists generally for other corporate officers including the Chairperson of the board (or indeed any other director) even though the managing director is answerable to the board led by the Chair. For example, it has also been held that the 'branch manager' of an insurance company did not have apparent authority to make

[39] Model constitution for a private company limited by shares, reg 95.
[40] ibid reg 97.

representations as to the authority of a unit manager within the branch[41] and that a 'finance manager' of a listed company had no apparent authority to authorise the taking of loan facilities.[42] This is not to say that apparent authority cannot arise in relation to other officers of the company but the representation will usually be of a more traditional kind such as where there has been a course of dealings with the knowledge of the board.[43]

It is suggested that this may be the explanation for *First Energy (UK) Ltd v Hungarian International Bank Ltd.*[44] In that case the parties had proceeded on the basis that the defendant bank's senior manager had no actual authority to authorise a facility and no representation to the contrary had been made by anyone else on behalf of the bank. Nevertheless it was held that, by virtue of his position, the senior manager was clothed with apparent authority to communicate that head office approval had been given for interim financing through hire purchase agreements. There has been some academic unease over this because it is clear that an agent cannot make representations as to her own authority. Accordingly, absent exceptional circumstances, finding that an agent without actual or apparent authority to enter into a transaction may have apparent authority to represent that the transaction has been authorised, thereby binding the company, comes close to allowing self-authorising agents.[45] While the basis for the existence of apparent authority was the position of the senior manager,[46] it is suggested that the decision may be explicable by the fact that there had been a previous ad hoc financing arrangement through a hire-purchase agreement dated 18 April 1990. The dispute arose in relation to three later projects where, on 2 August 1990, the senior manager sent three hire-purchase agreements to the plaintiff. The duly completed hire-purchase agreements were returned to the bank. To the extent that the later hire-purchase agreements like the first hire-purchase agreement took place against the backdrop of negotiations about outstanding matters affecting a long-term relationship under a facility agreement yet to come into force, the conclusion of the interim solution under the first agreement (and not the senior manager's position per se) may have set the stage for the senior manager to have apparent authority in relation to subsequent interim arrangements.

A more obvious case involving apparent authority to convey the principal's approval is *Kelly v Fraser* involving a representation by the head of the company's employee benefits division that the defendant's transfer of funds into the staff pension plan had been accepted.[47] The head, who had been delegated power to

[41] *British Bank of the Middle East v Sun Life Assurance Co of Canada (UK) Ltd* [1983] 2 Lloyd's Rep 9.

[42] *Skandinaviska Enskilda Banken AB (Publ) v Asia Pacific Breweries (Singapore) Pte Ltd* [2011] 3 SLR 540.

[43] Watts and Reynolds (n 1) [8-014].

[44] [1993] 2 Lloyd's Rep 194.

[45] Tan Cheng Han, *The Law of Agency*, 2nd edn (Singapore, Academy Publishing, 2017) [05.051]–[05.053].

[46] *First Energy (UK) Ltd v Hungarian International Bank Ltd* (n 44) 204, 207 and see also *Kelly v Fraser* (n 33) [14].

[47] ibid.

conduct the day-to-day administration of the plan by the trustees of the plan, did not have authority to approve any such transfer. However, without the knowledge of the trustees, he communicated with the defendant that the transferred sum had been credited into the plan. The Privy Council held that he had apparent authority to do so and the defendant had relied detrimentally on the representation. The trustees were not in the habit of communicating directly with beneficiaries and had delegated this and other administrative tasks to the relevant department of which the head was the senior officer. The head of the department having actual authority to communicate with contributories, including what decisions had been made by the trustees, it followed that absent any fact that should have placed the defendant on notice, he was entitled to believe that the head's communications to him were accurate.

Certain outside agents of the company may also by virtue of their professional positions have a usual actual authority that if limited by the principal may nevertheless still give rise to apparent authority to those who did not know of the limitation. The solicitor is one such agent as solicitors usually have authority to enter into settlements on behalf of their clients that translates into apparent authority if actual authority has been withdrawn or its scope misunderstood.[48] Again, these are likely to be very special cases and in the case of solicitors the rationale appears to be based on the public policy of facilitating the settlement of disputes.[49]

To summarise, notwithstanding the criticism that the idea of estoppel has been stretched beyond what is conventional, the doctrine operates fairly in the circumstances save that insofar as *First Energy* focused on the position of the agent as justification for the agent having apparent authority to communicate the principal's approval of the transaction, this risks over-protecting the third party. That estoppel doctrine generally strikes the right balance can be seen from the US approach to apparent authority which proceeds on the basis that where the circumstances objectively give rise to the appearance of authority, the courts are not concerned with the subjective intentions of the principal and agent but with the objective interpretation of the facts as they stand. The analogy is drawn with the manner in which contract formation takes place.[50] This is an acceptable way to approach apparent authority and it is unlikely that outcomes will be materially different on either approach as the case law now stands.

4. Ratification

If apparent authority is premised on estoppel, under English common law a principal cannot rely on apparent authority to hold the third party to the unauthorised contract. This is because estoppel cannot be the basis for a cause of action but

[48] *Waugh v HB Clifford & Sons Ltd* [1982] 2 WLR 679.
[49] ibid 691.
[50] See the basis for apparent authority in the United States (n 28).

only as a 'defence' to another party's claim or assertion. In the case of third parties who sue on the contract, the cause of action is for breach of contract and estoppel simply operates as a defence to the principal's assertion that the agent was not authorised even if the principal can prove this.

Accordingly, if a principal wishes to rely on an agent's unauthorised act, the principal must adopt such act through what has been referred to above as ratification. Although the doctrine can lead to the creation of a contractual relationship where none would have existed, there can also be instances where the principal's instructions may have been ambiguous and it is not altogether clear whether the agent acted within authority or not. The doctrine of ratification allows any doubt to be resolved which is beneficial to commercial certainty and reduces the need for parties to litigate. To the extent also that the third party was willing to enter into the transaction knowing that the agent was acting for a principal, there is little injustice in holding the third party to this if the principal ratifies the transaction, particularly if the third party can withdraw from the contract prior to ratification.

This is an important caveat because a third party that cannot withdraw even after knowing of the agent's lack of authority may be in danger of being held to hostage if the agent did not have apparent authority. The contract would be unenforceable against the principal while the principal would retain the discretion to adopt the contract depending on whether market conditions made it favourable for the principal to do so.[51] Yet somewhat inexplicably, English law as it presently stands effectively denies the third party the right to withdraw prior to ratification. In *Bolton Partners v Lambert*[52] the third party purported to withdraw his offer that had been accepted by the managing director of the principal though the managing director did not have the authority to do so. After the withdrawal, the principal ratified the managing director's acceptance. The court held that as ratification operated retrospectively, authority was conferred on the agent from the outset and the withdrawal was therefore ineffective.

This is a curious decision. While ratification operates retrospectively, this ought to be on the assumption that there is an arrangement still open to the principal to adopt. Where the third party has already withdrawn from a contract that had not been properly formed because the agent was unauthorised, no agreement remains for any ratification to have effect. Given that the concept of retrospective consent is a fiction, and the courts have shown reluctance in extending it to undisclosed agency,[53] it is at least arguable that there was no need to apply the fiction to a situation where no seeming contractual relationship subsisted. In an earlier case to which *Bolton Partners* did not refer, two of the three judges took the view that

[51] Although if a principal knows that her agent did not act within authority and does nothing, the circumstances may be such that, notwithstanding the principal's inaction, an estoppel arises against the principal so as to preclude the principal from denying that ratification had taken place as silence or inaction can amount to a representation, see Tan Cheng-Han, 'Estoppel in the Law of Agency' (n 28) 327.

[52] (1889) 41 Ch D 295.

[53] *Keighley, Maxsted & Co v Durant* (n 10).

ratification was ineffective after the third-party's withdrawal.[54] The effect of *Bolton Partners* is that it potentially places the third party in the invidious position of not knowing whether she will be bound by the as yet unformed contract and therefore subject to the whims of the market.[55]

A better balance is struck in civilian jurisdictions such as Germany and China. In the German Civil Code (BGB),[56] section 178 states that until a contract is ratified, 'the other party is entitled to revoke it, unless he knew of the lack of power of agency when he entered into the contract'. The revocation may also be declared to the agent. Where the third party knew of the agent's lack of authority, it can rely on section 177 of the BGB. This allows a third party to require the principal to make a declaration as to whether it will ratify the contract. Where this is done, the principal must ratify within two weeks of the receipt of the demand. If the principal does not do so, the principal is considered to have refused to ratify.

The position is similar under the People's Republic of China's General Principles of Civil Law (GPCL).[57] The first paragraph of article 171 of the GPCL provides, inter alia, that an act of agency taken 'without the power of agency … shall not take effect on the principal unless such act is retroactively recognized by the principal'. The second paragraph goes on to say that, pending recognition, a bona fide third party shall have the right to revoke the act in question by notice. The reference to 'bona fide third party' probably means third parties who did not know that the agent was unauthorised.[58] A third party may in any event 'urge a principal to retroactively recognize an act of the principal's agent within one month after the principal receives a notice of such an act'. Should the principal not respond, this will be 'deemed as a refusal of recognition'.

These approaches are more sensible than the common law one represented by *Bolton Partners*. They allow a third party who was unaware of the agent's lack of authority to withdraw at will prior to ratification or to give the principal a fixed time within which to decide whether to ratify. Where the third party knew that the agent was unauthorised but decided to take the risk of entering into the contract, the third party cannot withdraw unilaterally but must first give the principal time to decide whether to ratify. *Restatement, Third* does not accept the position in *Bolton Partners*[59] and it has also been criticised judicially. In *Fleming v Bank of New Zealand*,[60] the Privy Council reserved the right to reconsider it should it become necessary to do so. Interestingly, Lord Lindley, who delivered the Privy

[54] *Kidderminster Corp v Hardwick* (1873) LR 9 Exch 13 and see also *Walter v James* (1871) LR 6 Exch 124.

[55] Where the agent had apparent authority no such issue arises but this can often be uncertain.

[56] 'German Civil Code BGB' (Federal Office of Justice). Available at: www.gesetze-im-internet.de/englisch_bgb/englisch_bgb.html.

[57] 'General Provisions of the Civil Law of the People's Republic of China' (The National People's Congress of the People's Republic of China, 15 March 2017). Available at: www.npc.gov.cn/englishnpc/lawsoftheprc/202001/c983fc8d3782438fa775a9d67d6e82d8.shtml.

[58] See Tan Cheng-Han and Kelry C.F. Loi, 'Unauthorised Agency in Chinese Law' (2013) 30 *JCL* 214, 220–221.

[59] *Restatement, Third* (n 1) §4.05.

[60] [1900] 1 AC 577.

Council's judgment and was one of the judges in *Bolton Partners*, said that *Bolton Partners* 'presents difficulties'.[61]

As a result of the risk imbalance caused by such an approach, English law has had to develop measures to mitigate the risk to third parties of finding themselves potentially unable to enforce an agreement together with the uncertainty of whether subsequent ratification at the discretion of the principal will leave them with a legal obligation to fulfil. One rule recognised in *Bolton Partners* is that ratification cannot undo proprietary rights that have vested in another party prior to ratification because the third party sold the goods in question to such party and property has passed.[62] Nevertheless, it has been suggested that while such party's proprietary rights will not be affected, it does not necessarily mean that the third party is not in breach of contract should ratification take place.[63] Other exceptions to the extreme retrospectivity of *Bolton Partners* are that when an act is required to be done by a certain time, it cannot be ratified after such time;[64] and ratification must take place within a reasonable time.[65] Although they appear to stand as separate rules, it has been suggested that the former can be subsumed under the latter.[66]

Although on the face of it the common law position does not appear to have the convenience found in some civilian jurisdictions of being able to give the principal notice to ratify such that not doing so within a specific time will be taken as refusal, it is suggested that the requirement that ratification must take place within a reasonable time can accommodate this. If a third party realises that the agent was unauthorised and asks the principal to decide whether she wishes to ratify within a specified reasonable time period – in general a period of two weeks seems reasonable – it should not be open to the principal to attempt ratification after the period has expired. As long as a reasonable period has been given to the principal to decide, commercial certainty favours allowing the third party to move on.

Such a safeguard is only relevant to a third party who happens to discover that the agent was not authorised. Accordingly, there is no safeguard for ignorant third parties who find themselves in less favourable market conditions where a principal has chosen *not* to ratify an unauthorised act and is not estopped from denying this. This is a risk inherent in the use of agents and absent apparent authority, the third party can only look to the agent for breach of the agent's warranty of authority.

[61] ibid 587. See also the dissenting judgment of Isaacs J in *Davison v Vickery's Motors Ltd* (1925) 37 CLR 1 and Younger LJ's remark in *Reynolds v Atherton* (1921) 125 LT 690, 698.

[62] *Bolton Partners* (n 52) 307 and see also *Bird v Brown* (1850) 4 Exch 786.

[63] Tan Cheng-Han, 'The Principle in *Bird v Brown* Revisited' (2001) 117 *LQR* 626, 631–32.

[64] *Dibbins v Dibbins* [1896] 2 Ch 348; *Presentaciones Musicales SA v Secunda* [1994] Ch 271, 279.

[65] *Metropolitan Asylums Board v Kingham & Sons* (1890) 6 TLR 217, 218; *Re Portuguese Consolidated Copper Mines, Ltd* (1890) 45 ChD 16, 31, 34; *Celthene Pty Ltd v W K J Hauliers Pty Ltd* [1981] 1 NSWLR 606, 615; *Life Savers (Australasia) Ltd v Frigmobile Pty Ltd* [1983] 1 NSWLR 431, 438; *Trident General Insurance Co Ltd v McNiece Bros Pty Ltd* (1987) 8 NSWLR 270, 282; affirmed (1987) 165 CLR 107; *Hughes v NM Superannuation Pty Ltd* (1993) 29 NSWLR 653, 665.

[66] Tan (n 63) 636–39.

5. Undisclosed Agency

A risk that exists at common law is that a third party may deal with an agent believing the agent to be acting as principal when the agent is in fact acting for a principal. In civilian jurisdictions, the third party's obligations are only to the agent as the contracting party and it is for the agent to account to her principal under such agreement as may exist between them.

The common law position is different as the doctrine of undisclosed agency allows a principal to intervene on her agent's contract as long as the agent acted within actual authority[67] notwithstanding the fact that the agent was acting as principal vis-à-vis the third party and the principal is not, on the face of it, a party to such contract. The doctrine has been criticised as anomalous since it offends the concept of privity of contract.[68] The introduction of an unknown party also potentially exposes the third party to certain risks. On the whole, however, the common law deals with these risks well enough.

One risk is that the identity of the contracting party was important to the third party. In such circumstances, in the unlikely situation that the contracting party was an agent for a principal, it would be unfair to the third party if the principal could intervene given that the third party only wanted to contract with the contracting party as principal, perhaps because of some special skill or characteristic of the contracting party. In such circumstances, it is useful to recall the words of Diplock LJ in *Teheran-Europe Co Ltd v S.T. Belton (Tractors) Ltd*:[69]

> '... a person may enter into a contract through an agent whom he has actually authorised to enter into the contract on his behalf or whom he has led the other party to believe he has so authorised. But we are concerned here only with actual authority. Where an agent has such actual authority and enters into a contract with another party intending to do so on behalf of his principal, it matters not whether he discloses to the other party the identity of his principal, or even that he is contracting on behalf of a principal at all, if the other party is willing or leads the agent to believe that he is willing to treat as a party to the contract anyone on whose behalf the agent may have been authorised to contract. In the case of an ordinary commercial contract such willingness of the other party may be assumed by the agent unless either the other party manifests his unwillingness or there are other circumstances which should lead the agent to realise that the other party was not so willing'.

In other words, the ability of an undisclosed principal to intervene is, despite criticism of the doctrine, premised on the contractual notion of a consensus *ad idem*. The undisclosed principal and agent obviously intend that the contract should be one to which the principal has rights and obligations should the principal wish to intervene or the agent reveals the existence of the principal. At the same time, the law assumes that in cases of ordinary commercial contracts, the third party

[67] An undisclosed principal is not allowed to ratify, see *Keighley, Maxsted & Co v Durant* (n 10).
[68] ibid 261; *Siu Yin Kwan v Eastern Insurance Co Ltd* [1994] 2 AC 199, 207.
[69] See n 15 above, 212.

is willing to contract both with the agent and any other person that the agent has actual authority to act on behalf of. Accordingly, where the identity of the agent (acting as principal) is important to the third party, the principal cannot intervene as any acceptance of the offer as between the agent and third party was intended only to be between these parties and does not encompass any undisclosed principal the agent was acting for.[70]

Another way in which the identity of the agent (as principal) may be said to be important to the third party is where the third party was prepared to enter into a contract save with the party that the agent was acting for, perhaps because of a previous bad experience or the principal is a business rival. Here the agent's identity is not important for any special reason but as an indicator that the agent is simply not a particular person. The position is less clear on this issue though the observations of Diplock LJ in *Teheran-Europe* above[71] and the case of *Said v Butt*[72] may provide some support.[73] In *Said v Butt*, the plaintiff, who was a theatre critic, wanted to be present on the opening night of a play. He had been critical of the staff of the theatre and knew that he was unlikely to be given a ticket in his name as two previous applications had been rejected. As such, he procured a friend to obtain a ticket for him but when he showed up he was turned away. His claim for breach of contract was dismissed on the basis that the 'personal element was strikingly present'.[74]

Said v Butt may, however, be understood simply as an instance where, because of the importance of opening night, the identify of those allowed to attend was important. Although McCardie J said that it is 'scarcely likely' for the management of the theatre to have chosen persons antagonistic to them, he also pointed out that 'the management only disposes of first night tickets for the stalls and dress circle to those whom it selects'.[75] Other cases have allowed undisclosed principals to intervene notwithstanding the third parties' assertion that they would not have contracted with such principal or would have done so on different terms.[76] Such position may be preferable because it affords more commercial certainty as to the enforceability of such agreements instead of providing third parties with a possible way of avoiding it should they have second thoughts, and in any event as a 'principal' herself to the agreement there would generally be nothing to prevent the agent from assigning the benefit of the contract to the principal.[77] A third party who feels strongly against contracting with a particular individual may specifically enquire as to this[78] and if there is a false answer the third party can rely on the

[70] See also *Greer v Downs Supply Co* [1927] 2 KB 28, 35; *Boulton v Jones* (1857) 2 H & N 564, 566.
[71] See n 15 above.
[72] [1920] 3 KB 497.
[73] See also E Peel, *Treitel's Law of Contract*, 15th edn (London, Sweet & Maxwell, 2020) [16-069].
[74] See n 72, 503.
[75] ibid 501–502 and see also the reference to *Smith v Wheatcroft* (1878) 9 Ch D 223, 230.
[76] *Dyster v Randall & Sons* [1926] Ch 932; *Williams v Bulat* [1992] 2 Qd R 566; *Alrich Development Pte Ltd v Rafiq Jumabhoy* [1995] 2 SLR(R) 340.
[77] *Nash v Dix* (1898) 78 LT 445.
[78] *Alrich Development Pte Ltd v Rafiq Jumabhoy* (n 76).

misrepresentation to rescind the contract.[79] The third party may also attempt to prohibit any assignment (or sale) to a particular party that the third party would not have wished to contract with. As the third-party's interest here is not to deal only with a particular individual but rather that the agreement is not with another specific person, it is suggested the better position is to put the onus on the third party to protect herself explicitly.[80]

Another risk for third parties is the potential deprivation of rights they may have against the agent if the principal intervenes since in general a right against one party may not be asserted against another. In the case of undisclosed agency, notwithstanding the intervention of the principal, the third party may as against such principal assert 'any defences or equities which without notice may exist against the agent'.[81] Thus where an agent is indebted to the third party such that the third party is entitled to set off such debt against any monetary obligation under the contract with the agent, the intervention of an undisclosed principal will be subject to such right of set-off if the right arose prior to the discovery of the principal's existence.[82]

One risk that it is suggested the common law has not satisfactorily dealt with is where payment to the agent has taken place prior to the discovery of the undisclosed principal and the agent has not in turn transmitted such payment to the relevant party. In disclosed agency cases, principals and third parties must usually make payment to each other since the agent is typically not a party to the contract and 'falls away' after the contract is formed unless either the principal or third party has made a representation to the other that payment should be made through the agent. Taking first the simpler situation where payment has been made by the third party to the agent, this should be a complete discharge of the third party's obligation to make such payment given that the agent is the only contracting party known to the third party. It must be implicit in undisclosed agency that until the principal reveals her existence, she intends the agent to do all such acts as are necessary under the contract including the receipt of any payments due. This is the position adopted in *Restatement, Third*.[83]

The position is less clear where the undisclosed principal has made payment to the agent. As the principal's existence is unknown and the agent may need to be put in funds to be able to make any payments due to the third party, it may be thought that where the principal has done so prior to her existence becoming known, this operates as a discharge for such payments made within a reasonable time prior to their due date. This is not unfair to the third party who has seemingly contracted only with the agent and was therefore satisfied to look to the credit of the agent. Such a position was taken in *Armstrong v Stokes*.[84] A different perspective was expressed

[79] *Archer v Stone* (1898) 78 LT 34.

[80] See also R Munday, *Agency: Law and Principles*, 4th edn (Oxford, Oxford University Press, 2022) [10.57].

[81] *Gilbert Browning v Provincial Insurance Co of Canada* (1873) LR 5 PC 263, 272.

[82] ibid; *Siu Yin Kwan v Eastern Insurance Co Ltd* [1994] 2 AC 199, 207.

[83] *Restatement, Third* (n 1) §6.07, comment d.

[84] (1872) LR 7 QB 598.

in dicta in *Irvine & Co v Watson & Sons*, a case involving disclosed agency, where Bramwell LJ referred to *Armstrong v Stokes* as 'a very remarkable case'[85] and Brett LJ said that if the case arose again the court reserved the right to reconsider it.[86]

While *Restatement, Third* accepts that payment by the third party will discharge it from further liability, it takes a different view for payments made by the undisclosed principal to the agent. Such principal has the right to expect performance from the third party and, in turn, has a duty of performance to the third party that is not discharged by payment to the agent. A principal can make her existence known to the third party after the contract has been entered into without sacrificing the benefits of contracting through an agent without disclosing the principal's existence.[87] This, however, does not give consideration to circumstances where the principal envisages continuing transactions or similar transactions with other third parties and does not wish others to know that the principal is active in the market in question.[88] Moreover, the third party was happy to transact with the agent as principal and therefore to look to the credit of the agent. Any subsequent discovery of the existence of a principal gives the third party a windfall in the sense of another person the third party may have recourse to in the event of breach while the third-party's obligations remain the same. It is hard to see that the third party is under any real disadvantage if, while undisclosed, the principal makes payment to the agent in the sense of putting the agent in funds to pay the third party, provided the time for such payments was near.[89] If the principal puts her agents in funds for payments due months or years in advance, the principal then takes the credit risk of her agent and the third party should not be prejudiced for payments that have not fallen due from the time the third party discovers the existence of the principal. It is suggested that this draws the right balance between the interests of the principal and third party.

6. Conclusion

An important role the law plays is to maintain an optimal balance between the rights of individuals and groups. By so doing, the law contributes to a functioning and harmonious society. But it is not straightforward for the law to get the balance right because societies' and judges' perspectives will often be limited. It is not easy to see the full extent of the issue or the consequences of a particular approach. As such, the law must always be able to self-correct through the legislature or case law. The law of agency is one example of this ability to do so.

[85] (1880) 5 QBD 414, 417.

[86] ibid 420–21.

[87] *Restatement, Third* (n 1) §6.07, comment d.

[88] As in *Senor v Bangor Mills, Inc*, 211 F 2d 685 (3rd Cir, 1954).

[89] Academic commentators are divided on this issue. Watts and Reynolds (n 1) [8-105] tentatively support the position taken in this chapter while Peel (n 73) [16-074] and Munday (n 80) [10.77] take the opposite view.

11

Compromise Agreements

PAUL S DAVIES*

As Lord Burrows remarked in *Times Travel (UK) Ltd v Pakistan International Airline Corp*, 'The vast majority of commercial disputes do not go to trial and are not expected to do so'.[1] There is a significant public policy which encourages settlement agreements.[2] But such contracts frequently lead to significant disputes in practice, and merit further consideration by commentators. The desire to promote settlement should not distort fundamental principles of contract law.

In *Mionis v Democratic Press SA* Sharp LJ observed that:[3]

> Settlement does not only serve the private interests of the litigants, but the administration of justice and the public interest more generally, by freeing court resources for other cases. The law therefore encourages and facilitates the mutual resolution of disputes by various means, for very sound reasons of public policy; and there is obviously an important public interest in the finality of settlement.

This important statement deserves scrutiny. For example, it is not always clear that settlement does 'serve the private interests of the litigants' – settlement may greatly favour one party over the other. In addition, the parties are bargaining 'in the shadow of the law',[4] which perhaps gives the law reason to ensure that the shadow

* I am grateful for helpful comments from Ben Cartwright, Charles Mitchell, Christopher Monaghan, Nick McBride, and Ros Phelps, as well as audiences at UCL, Cambridge and NUS where previous versions of this chapter were presented. I am also very thankful for the generous support of the Leverhulme Trust through a Philip Leverhulme Prize. The usual disclaimers apply.

[1] [2021] UKSC 40, [2023] AC 101, [51]. Even when cases are listed for full Commercial Court trials, most settle: 'out of 136 full Commercial Court trials listed thus, 56 were heard, denoting a settlement rate at around 59' (Business and Property Courts, *The Commercial Court Report 2022–2022*, [6.2.3]. Available at: www.judiciary.uk/wpcontent/uploads/2023/04/14.244_JO_Commercial_Court_Report_WEB.pdf. The equivalent figure for the previous year was 67%: Business and Property Courts, The Commercial Court Report 2020–2021, [6.2.3]. Available at: www.judiciary.uk/wp-content/uploads/2022/02/14.50_Commercial_Court_Annual_Report_2020_21_WEB.pdf.

[2] *Finzi v Jamaican Redevelopment Foundation Inc* [2023] UKPC 29, [64] (Lord Leggatt); *Marino v FM Capital Partners Ltd* [2020] EWCA Civ 245, [2021] QB 1 [70] (Sir Jack Beatson); *Kings Security Systems Ltd v King* [2020] EWHC 2996 (Ch) [59]–[62] (Miles J). An important goal of contract law is to minimise conflicts: P MacMahon, 'Conflict and Contract Law' (2018) 38 *OJLS* 270.

[3] [2017] EWCA Civ 1194, [2018] QB 662 [89].

[4] See also R Mnookin and L Kornhauser, 'Bargaining in the Shadow of the Law: The Case of Divorce' (1979) 88 *Yale LJ* 950.

it has cast over the negotiations by encouraging settlement is not unfairly exploited by one party. As a result, it sometimes appears that courts are more willing to unwind settlement contracts based on misrepresentation or duress, for example, than is the case for other commercial contracts.[5] Whole books have been devoted to compromise agreements,[6] but it is suggested that the view that compromise agreements should be treated differently from any other type of contract should be approached with scepticism.

This chapter takes a broad approach to compromise, or settlement, agreements.[7] Section 1 outlines why the law encourages compromise generally, and Section 2 considers the pressure this places upon some fundamental contract law doctrines. Confines of space mean that the discussion in this section is limited to consideration, interpretation, misrepresentation and duress. It is suggested that in these areas in particular the general principles of contract law have sometimes been distorted in the context of compromise agreements, and that courts should guard against any such tendency. Section 3 analyses how compromise agreements might affect third parties, especially other (potential) defendants. The law in this area is needlessly complex and can, surprisingly, operate as a disincentive to compromise. That should be avoided. Focusing on whether a settlement between two parties was intended to relieve a third party of liability would both improve and simplify the law. Section 4 concludes.

1. Encouraging Compromises

The law has many levers it can pull in order to encourage compromise. For example, parties are encouraged to make realistic offers to settle under Part 36 of the Civil Procedure Rules, and a failure by one party to 'beat' such a settlement offer can have serious cost consequences.[8] Settlement negotiations are further encouraged by protecting 'without prejudice' negotiations. The 'without prejudice' rule generally prevents statements made in a genuine attempt to settle an existing dispute from being put before the court as evidence of admissions against the interests of

[5] See sections 2.3 and 2.4 below.

[6] Most notably D Foskett, *Foskett on Compromise* 9th edn (Sweet & Maxwell, 2019).

[7] This includes implied settlements: N Andrews, 'Mistaken Settlement of Disputable Claims' [1989] *LMCLQ* 431; HW Tang, 'Settlement Agreements as Defences to Unjust Enrichment Claims' [2008] *RLR* 63. Mutual releases are generally contractual since each release provides consideration for the other, but unilateral releases must be made by deed to be enforceable.

[8] In *Smith v Trafford Housing Trust* [2012] EWHC 3320 (Ch) [13] Briggs J thought it 'the salutary purpose of Part 36, in promoting compromise and the avoidance of unnecessary expenditure of costs and court time …' This was cited with approval by Newey LJ in *Adams v Options UK Personal Pensions LLP* [2021] EWCA Civ 1188, in which the Court of Appeal made it clear that Part 36 offers can potentially leave more to be resolved than contractual offers; see too '*Calderbank* offers': *Calderbank v Calderbank* [1976] Fam 93.

the party which made them. As David Richards LJ observed in *Berkeley Square Holdings Ltd v Lancer Property Asset Management Ltd*:[9]

> The existence of the 'without prejudice' rule, and the policy reasons for it, are well-known and well-established. In Rush & Tompkins Limited v GLC [1989] AC 1280, Lord Griffiths, with whom the other members of the House of Lords agreed, approved Oliver J's statement in *Cutts v Head* [1984] Ch 290 at 306:
>
> > That the rule rests, at least in part, upon public policy is clear from many authorities, and the convenient starting point of the inquiry is the nature of the underlying policy. It is that parties should be encouraged as far as possible to settle their disputes without resort to litigation and should not be discouraged by the knowledge that anything that is said in the course of such negotiations (and that includes, of course, as much the failure to reply to an offer as an actual reply) may be used to their prejudice in the course of the proceedings. They should … be encouraged fully and frankly to put their cards on the table … The public policy justification, in truth, essentially rests on the desirability of preventing statements or offers made in the course of negotiations for settlement being brought before the court of trial as admissions on the question of liability.

More generally, the overriding objective of the Civil Procedural Rules is for the court to deal with cases justly and at proportionate cost; cases should be dealt with expeditiously, fairly, and in a cost-efficient manner.[10] The CPR expressly imposes a duty on the court actively to manage cases to help the parties to settle the whole or part of a case,[11] and to encourage or facilitate the use of alternative dispute resolution mechanisms.[12] The push to encourage parties to settle is so strong that steps are increasingly taken to funnel parties into alternative dispute resolution mechanisms, and in particular mediation.[13] This is apparent even in the commercial context, and in cases in which permission to appeal to the Court of Appeal is obtained. Litigants whose contractual claims are worth less than £500,000 and who refuse to mediate 'may be required to justify to the Court of Appeal their decision not to attempt mediation at subsequent court hearings'.[14] By promoting mediation it appears that *any* settlement is to be desired, rather than only one which reflects the merits of the dispute; after all, the aim of mediation is 'just settlement' rather than 'a settlement which is just'.[15]

[9] [2021] EWCA Civ 551, [2021] 1 WLR 4877, [23]. See too *Oceanbulk Shipping and Trading SA v TMT Asia Ltd* [2010] UKSC 44, [2011] 1 AC 662, [41] (Lord Clarke); *A & A Mechanical Contractors and Company Ltd v Petroleum Company of Trinidad and Tobago* [2022] UKPC 39.

[10] CPR 1.1. For the encouragement of settlements in the tripartite context, see, eg, that settlements are also encouraged in arrangements involving three parties: see *Biggin & Co Ltd v Permanite Ltd* [1951] 2 KB 314.

[11] CPR 1.4(2)(f).

[12] CPR 1.4(2)(e).

[13] See *Dunnett v Railtrack Plc* [2002] EWCA Civ 303, [2002] 1 WLR 2434; *Cable & Wireless Plc v IBM United Kingdom Ltd* [2002] EWHC 2059, [2002] CLC 1319.

[14] Available at: www.cedr.com/commercial/mediationschemes/courtofappeal/.

[15] H Genn, *Judging Civil Justice* (CUP, 2009) 117. See too Sir G Vos, 'The Future for Dispute Resolution: Horizon Scanning' (Sir Brian Neill Lecture, March 2022). Available at: www.judiciary.uk/speech-by-the-master-of-the-rolls-the-future-for-dispute-resolution-horizon-scanning.

Significant steps have therefore been taken to incentivise settlement, but there remain concerns that settlements may be unfair and are not always to be encouraged.[16] Inequality of bargaining power and various external pressures might lead the weaker party into an unnecessary and unfavourable settlement; it is well understood that the expense of litigation and difficulties in financing the trial process may lead to 'low-ball' offers from the stronger party which the weaker party feels bound to accept.[17] Yet a third-party judge may be able to lessen the impact of some of the distributional inequalities that can be exacerbated in compromise negotiations.

In addition, unlike many settlements, a decision of a court is public and can help to clarify the law. This might suggest that litigation should be promoted more strongly over settlement. But that seems inappropriate in England and Wales. Systems requiring and promoting recourse to a third-party judge might be more popular where litigation is relatively simple and cheap. In this jurisdiction, however, litigation tends to be more complex and expensive, and it would be far too onerous to demand that parties litigate their disputes.[18] Settlement is often necessary.[19] The judicial system could not otherwise cope with the deluge of cases with which it would be presented.[20] 'One should also keep in mind the fact that legal processes, however refined, are incorrigibly flawed by the fallibility of witnesses, advocates and judges'.[21]

Nevertheless, concerns about the contents of any compromise agreement have led some courts to scrutinise such settlements very closely.[22] This is understandable, but it is important not to lose sight of the fact that a compromise agreement is a contract, and the general principles of contract law must be applied. Where parties freely entered into a settlement, conscious that that may ultimately turn out to be a good or bad deal, courts should be very wary about rescuing a party from a bad bargain.[23]

[16] See O Fiss, 'Against Settlement' (1984) 93 *Yale LJ* 1073. See too S Shiffrin, 'Remedial Clauses: The Overprivatization of Private Law' (2016) 67 *Hastings Law Journal* 407.

[17] See Sir Geoffrey Vos, 'Mediated Interventions within the Court Dispute Resolution Process' (GEMME lecture, October 2021). Available at: www.judiciary.uk/wp-content/uploads/2021/10/Master-of-the-Rolls-GEMME-Mediated-interventions-within-the-Court-Dispute-Resolution-Process.pdf and 'The Relationship between Formal and Informal Justice' (Hull University, March 2021). Available at: www.judiciary.uk/wp-content/uploads/2021/03/MoR-Hull-Uni-260321.pdf.

[18] See *Guest v Guest* [2022] UKSC 27, [2022] 3 WLR 911, [252] (Lord Leggatt).

[19] For example, in the employment context, one of the purposes of the Enterprise and Regulatory Reform Act 2013 was to encourage the settlement of disputes and the reduction in claims and hearings before the Employment Tribunal; section 23 provides that the terms 'compromise agreement' and 'compromise contract' be replaced with 'settlement agreement', apparently on the basis that 'settlement' is a better description of what the parties are doing and there may have been hesitancy by an employee to enter into an agreement where they were seen to be compromising.

[20] *Jameson v Central Electricity Generating Board* [2000] 1 AC 455, 474 (Lord Hope). Note too that compromise agreements fall outside the scope of UCTA: *Tudor Grange Holdings Ltd v Citibank N.A.* [1992] Ch. 53. Cf. *Binder v Alachouzos* [1972] 2 QB 151, 158 (Lord Denning MR): 'If the court is satisfied that the terms are fair and reasonable, then the compromise should be held binding.'

[21] N Andrews, 'Mistaken Settlement of Disputable Claims' [1989] *LMCLQ* 431, 434.

[22] For discussion of the jurisdiction of the court to refuse to accept undertakings given to the court as part of a settlement, see *Smith v Backhouse* [2023] EWCA Civ 874.

[23] P Davies, 'Bad Bargains' [2019] CLP 253.

It may be that slightly different considerations arise in the context of group litigation, with lawyers for some representative groups acting on a no-win no-fee basis. That is because, where collective proceedings proceed on an 'opt-out' basis, damages are awarded in respect of the whole class. Yet it is inevitable that a large number of class members who did not 'opt-out' will not claim their entitlement if the claim is successful; a significant proportion of the damages fund invariably remains unclaimed.[24] The unclaimed monies would not go to the class members who have come forward, but rather to charity.[25] This can have a distorting effect upon compromise negotiations: defendants are often keen to settle in order to avoid the risk of having to pay out large sums of money that would inevitably go to charity,[26] knowing a much lower financial figure would satisfy the known members of the class amongst whom settlement monies would be distributed. And claimant lawyers may be incentivised to settle to protect the payment of their fees.[27] Such compromise agreements are likely to require the sanction of the court, notably under so-called 'Tomlin orders'[28] and the court may be anxious to ensure that the settlement itself is fair. But the usual pressures to settle mean that it will be a rare case where a court would interfere with the bargain reached by the parties.

2. Pressure on Contract Doctrines

As Marcus Smith J has recently reiterated in *Elston v King*, compromise agreements 'are contracts like any other'.[29] That suggests the usual doctrines of contract law should be applied in the ordinary way. Yet an analysis of some fundamental topics in contract law indicates that principles are sometimes bent to fit the context of compromise.

In *Elston v King*, Marcus Smith J continued:[30]

> The difference between a compromise agreement and other contracts is that – unlike with other contracts – the parties reach a consensus ad idem in relation to a matter on which they disagree. The nature of that disagreement will, of course, vary from case-to-case, but oftentimes, the parties' individual expectations, and so the compromise, will be informed by their individual assessment of what a court might do were the matter to be litigated. Inevitably, this involves reaching a view not on what the facts are or what

[24] *O'Higgins v Barclays* [2022] CAT 16, [2022] *Bus LR* 1334, [88].

[25] Competition Act 1998, s 47C.

[26] See, too, *Mastercard Inc v Merricks* [2020] UKSC 51, [2021] 3 All ER 285 (Lord Sales and Lord Leggatt).

[27] Especially where they have agreed a Conditional Fee Arrangement, as was the case, for example, in *O'Higgins v Barclays* [2022] CAT 16, [2022] *Bus LR* 1334.

[28] But even here the principles applied are essentially contractual: proceedings under CPR Pt 36 'may well create a contract and probably does so in the vast majority of cases': *Orton v Collins* [2007] EWHC 803 (Ch), [2007] 1 WLR 2953.

[29] [2020] EWHC 55 (Ch) [18].

[30] ibid [18]–[19] (emphasis in original; footnotes omitted).

> the law is, but on how the court (often a particular court) will determine certain factual and/or legal questions.
>
> It is the overtness of such disagreements which as a matter of fact, if not as a matter of law, renders compromises different to other contracts. Not only is there a public interest in the finality of litigation but, more importantly for present purposes, the parties will be approaching the compromise not from a common perspective but actually from a divergent one. It is precisely this divergence which the compromise resolves, not by determining it (that is for the court, which ex hypothesi is not involved as an arbiter of the divergence, if there is a compromise) but by reaching an accommodation which both sides find acceptable.

It is true that when concluding compromise agreements one party may well have greater knowledge of relevant factors and details than the other. This gives rise to 'information asymmetries'. Such asymmetries are not unusual when entering into any type of contract, but may be heightened in the context of settlements since the chances of success in litigation depend on what the other party knows and does not know, and how they would have played their hand had it come to litigation.[31] As a result, it may be that settlements resemble 'credence goods' – in other words, goods whose quality the purchaser can only observe with difficulty even after purchase. From an economic point of view, it might appear efficient for courts to intervene in private ordering more readily than in the case of other types of contract to ensure that a market for credence goods does not develop 'lemon characteristics'[32] where the information asymmetry is so great that all contracts become distorted. But courts are ill-equipped to carry out such a regulatory role. The common law does not even intervene to control monopolies.[33] The orthodox approach is to accept that information asymmetries exist in all contracts, to a greater or lesser extent, but that this does not affect their enforceability or the contract law doctrines which apply.

2.1. Consideration

Consideration is often readily found to support compromise agreements. This is well illustrated by *Cook v Wright*.[34] Commissioners responsible for executing a local Act wrongly believed the defendant to be liable to pay certain charges. The defendant denied liability but, when threatened with legal proceedings, agreed to pay a reduced sum in three instalments by promissory notes. Even though it was later admitted that he had never been liable to pay the charges, he was held

[31] And what may be disclosed: see, eg, Civil Procedure Rules, Practice Direction 57AD.

[32] G Akerlof, 'The Market for Lemons: Quality Uncertainty and the Market Mechanism' (1970) 84 *Quarterly Journal of Economics* 488.

[33] *Times Travel (UK) Ltd v Pakistan International Airline Corp* [2021] UKSC 40, [2023] AC 101 [26], [52] (Lord Hodge).

[34] (1861) 1 B & S 559.

liable on the notes which had been given in consideration of the Commissioners' refraining from bringing the action which they thought to be a proper claim.

More recent decisions continue to highlight 'the public policy in favour of holding people to their commercial bargains'.[35] In *Simantob v Shavleyan*,[36] it was held that giving up an argument that a clause to pay $1,000 per day in interest was a penalty clause did constitute good consideration, even though that argument had previously been rejected in an application for summary judgment. It did not matter that the claim was probably unlikely to succeed.

Apparent relaxations in the requirement for consideration in the context of variations of an existing agreement[37] further suggest that it should not be difficult to find consideration to support a compromise agreement. Yet it has also been said that refraining from doing what one has no right to do cannot be sufficient consideration, and that abandonment of a claim which the claimant knows to be invalid cannot be of any value in the eyes of the law and therefore is not sufficient consideration.[38]

This focus upon what the claimant knows continues to be applied in determining whether a compromise agreement is supported by consideration. For example, in *CFL Finance Limited v Laser Trust* the Court of Appeal had to consider when, if ever, the Consumer Credit Act 1974 ('the CCA') applies to agreements settling litigation. Section 8(1) states: 'A consumer credit agreement is an agreement between an individual ('the debtor') and any other person ('the creditor') by which the creditor provides the debtor with credit of any amount.' For this provision to apply, there must be a debt. The court held that in some circumstances the existence of a debt will be clear, such that providing for future payment under a settlement agreement will confer 'credit' under the CCA.[39] Newey LJ said:[40]

> There is room for argument as to quite where the dividing line is between a debt (in relation to which the CCA could apply) and a mere claim (to which it could not). One possibility is that a debt should be considered to exist when the only defence advanced is clearly invalid in law. Arguably, Parliament might be expected to have had in mind a purely objective test of that kind when enacting the CCA. On the other hand, there is also, to my mind, a case for saying that it is enough to prevent the CCA from applying to a settlement agreement that the debtor believed a defence he was advancing to have substance. Such an approach could be said to reflect the desirability of upholding bona fide compromises.

[35] *Simantob v Shavleyan* [2019] EWCA Civ 1105, [50].

[36] [2019] EWCA Civ 1105.

[37] Eg *Williams v Roffey Bros* [1991] 1 QB 1; *MWB Business Exchange Centres Ltd v Rock Advertising Ltd* [2018] UKSC 24, [2019] AC 119, [18] (Lord Sumption); this shift is more pronounced in New Zealand: *Antons Trawling Co Ltd v Smith* [2003] 2 NZLR 23.

[38] *Wade v Simeon* (1846) 2 CB 548. See too *Times Travel* [2021] UKSC 40, [116] (Lord Burrows).

[39] Section 9(1) provides that '"credit" includes a cash loan, and any other form of financial accommodation'.

[40] [2021] EWCA Civ 228, [2021] 4 All ER 717, [51]; see too [58] (David Richards LJ).

Nevertheless, an emphasis upon the knowledge of the claimant is unusual when assessing consideration more generally. Even in the context of compromise agreements, it has been doubted whether the claimant's knowledge should really matter. In *Pitt v PHH Asset Management Ltd*,[41] Peter Gibson LJ said that the claimant's refraining from seeking an injunction was a benefit to the defendant which amounted to an element in the consideration, even though the claimant's claim was bound to fail and had only 'nuisance value'.

McKendrick has observed that in this area the law strikes an 'uneasy compromise' between the view that giving up any sort of claim should constitute good consideration, and the contrary approach that a worthless claim should always be valueless in the eye of the law.[42] That reflects a tension between competing public policies: one favours the promotion of settlement, the other seeks to discourage parties from threatening to pursue claims which are known to be hopeless. It is suggested that the principles regarding what constitutes sufficient consideration should not be distorted by an ill-defined desire to avoid frivolous claims. It would be better to recognise that giving up a claim constitutes consideration, but where the claim given up is known to be bad then that will not support a binding contract for reasons of public policy.[43] An analogy with malicious prosecution seems potentially helpful in this context. In order to establish malicious prosecution, it must be shown that that the claimant had no reasonable or probable cause for bringing the claim, and was acting maliciously, in particular by abusing the process of the court.[44] It may be that the public policy that underpins malicious prosecution outweighs that which encourages settlement, but this can be accepted without undermining well-established general principles concerning consideration.

2.2. Interpretation

Parties are sensibly encouraged to settle their disputes using the clearest language possible, since this should make the interpretation of their agreement straightforward.[45] Attempts to carve out special rules of interpretation for compromise agreements should be treated with caution: the same principles should

[41] [1993] 4 All ER 961, 966. See too *Foskett on Compromise* (n 6) [3-10]–[3-21].

[42] E McKendrick, *Contract Law: Text, Cases and Materials* 10th edn (OUP, 2022) 152.

[43] As Tindal CJ said in *Wade v Simeon* (1846) 2 CB 548 at 564: 'It is almost *contra bonos mores* and certainly contrary to the principles of natural justice that a man should institute proceedings against another when he is conscious that he has no good cause of action.' It has been pointed out that 'If compromises of such claims were upheld, improper pressure might be brought to bear on persons who "owed" void debts': WE Peel, *Treitel on The Law of Contract* 15th edn (Sweet & Maxwell, 2020) [3-038].

[44] *Willers v Joyce* [2016] UKSC 43; [2018] AC 779.

[45] *Arnold v Britton* [2015] UKSC 36, [2015] AC 1619; *Wood v Capita Insurance Services Ltd* [2017] UKSC 24, [2017] AC 1173.

apply to all contracts.[46] The focus is invariably upon what the parties objectively intended, the best evidence of which is found in their written agreement.[47]

Nevertheless, references to special principles in the context of compromise are not uncommon. For example, it sometimes said that there is a 'starting point presumption' that the parties intended a clean break and to resolve all matters between them.[48] But there is no reason for such a presumption, and it must be rejected.[49] Whilst it may be desirable for parties to settle their dispute in its totality,[50] that might not be possible, and it is not for the courts to insist on an all-or-nothing approach: the scope of the settlement depends entirely upon what the parties have agreed.

Interpreting a particular compromise agreement can be difficult – just as it can be for any contract. Instances of 'hard cases' are commonplace. One example is the leading decision of the House of Lords in *Bank of Credit and Commerce International SA v Ali*.[51] A bank made a number of employees redundant. The parties entered into a settlement agreement, under which the bank paid substantial sums of money 'in full and final settlement of all or any claims … of whatsoever nature that exist or may exist' against the bank. The bank subsequently went into insolvent liquidation, and it transpired that it had conducted its business in a corrupt and fraudulent manner. At the time when the settlement agreements were concluded, it was not thought possible for the employees to claim 'stigma damages' to reflect the difficulties they faced in finding new employment as a result of having worked for such an employer, but this understanding of the law was later rejected by the House of Lords.[52] Following that decision, some of the former employees argued that claims for 'stigma damages' could not have been released since they were unknown at the time the settlement agreement was reached.

[46] *Bank of Credit and Commerce International SA v Ali* [2001] UKHL 8; [2002] 1 AC 25, [8] (Lord Bingham), [26] (Lord Nicholls), [37]–[42] (Lord Hoffmann). See too *Schofield v Smith* [2022] EWCA Civ 824, [2023] 1 All ER 480, [19]–[21] (Newey LJ); *Maranello Rosso Ltd v Lohomij BV* [2022] EWCA Civ 1667, [58]–[60] (Phillips LJ); *Adaptive Spectrum and Signal Alignment Inc v British Telecommunications PLC* [2023] EWCA Civ 451, [17]–[20] (Birss LJ).

[47] The construction of oral contracts raises slightly different issues, beyond the scope of this chapter, since that is a question of fact rather than law: *Carmichael v National Power plc* [1999] 1 WLR 2042, 2048–49 (Lord Hoffmann); *Thorner v Major* [2009] UKHL 18, [2009] 1 WLR 776, [82] (Lord Neuberger); *Barton v Morris* [2023] UKSC 3; [2023] 2 WLR 269 (Lord Leggatt).

[48] See, eg, *Starlight Shipping Co v Allianz Marine and Aviation Versicherungs AG (No 3)* [2014] EWHC 3068 (Comm), [2015] 2 All ER (Comm) 747, [52]–[54] (Flaux J); N Andrews, 'Mistaken Settlement of Disputable Claims' [1989] LMCLQ 431, 444.

[49] *Global Display Solutions Ltd v NCR Financial Solutions Group Ltd* [2021] EWHC 1119 (Comm), [322]–[327] (Jacobs J).

[50] As HHJ Tindal laconically observed, 'some settlements are more welcome than others': *Moradi v Home Office* [2022] EWHC 3125 (KB) [2]. But it may be worth encouraging even partial settlements: JJ Prescott, and Kathryn E Spier, 'A Comprehensive Theory of Civil Settlement' (2016) 91 *NYULR* 59.

[51] [2001] UKHL 8, [2002] 1 AC 25.

[52] *Mahmud v Bank of Credit and Commerce International SA* [1998] AC 20.

That argument succeeded in the House of Lords. Their Lordships considered that the context of the agreement clearly led to the conclusion that uncontemplated claims were not released. However, Lord Hoffmann powerfully dissented. This is particularly noteworthy given the emphasis Lord Hoffmann generally placed upon contextual factors which could prompt the court to depart from more 'literal' meanings of contractual language.[53] But in *Ali* Lord Hoffmann considered that there was no reason to depart from the clear meaning of the words chosen, especially since the bank had made a substantial extra payment (of £2,700) which went beyond any uncontested claims: the parties intended to release their claims in full.[54] It is suggested that Lord Hoffmann's approach better aligns with general principles of contractual interpretation.

In *Ali*, there are problematic suggestions that a 'cautionary principle', 'contemplation limb', and 'sharp practice principle' may apply to compromise agreements. All should be treated with scepticism. As regards the first, Lord Bingham said that 'in the absence of clear language, the court will be very slow to infer that a party intended to surrender rights and claims of which he was unaware and could not have been aware'.[55] That received a lukewarm reception from the other members of the House of Lords,[56] and subsequent decisions have not needed to grapple with the boundaries of 'any cautionary principle that applies'.[57] Its basis is obscure and detracts from the fundamental exercise of interpretation with which a court must engage. It would be better now to shift away from any attempts to delineate the contours of the 'cautionary principle'.

Instead, courts might focus upon another tricky aspect of *Ali*: the 'contemplation limb'. Whilst the usual principles of interpretation operate to determine what claims have been compromised, the addition of the contemplation limb means that matters the parties had not subjectively contemplated (or, equivalently, realised or knew) they were releasing may not in fact be released.[58] This is very difficult to reconcile with the general objective approach of English law which pays little attention to the subjective motives of contracting parties. 'As there are no special principles of construction applicable to releases, the private knowledge held by one party to a release but not by the other parties is irrelevant to the interpretation of the release.'[59] There can be no rule of law that claims which were uncontemplated are not covered by a general release.[60] It must be possible to release all potential claims, whether contemplated or not. Everything hinges upon the interpretation of the particular agreement.

[53] *Investors Compensation Scheme Ltd v West Bromwich Building Society* [1997] UKHL 28, [1998] 1 WLR 896; *Chartbrook Ltd v Persimmon Homes Ltd* [2009] UKHL 38, [2009] 1 AC 1101.

[54] [2001] UKHL 8, [42].

[55] ibid [10], [17].

[56] Lord Nicholls observed that it 'cannot be pressed too far': [2001] UKHL 8, [28].

[57] *Maranello Rosso Ltd v Lohomij BV* [2022] EWCA Civ 1667, [59] (Phillips LJ); at first instance HHJ Keyser QC had emphasised that it is 'not a rule of law': [2021] EWHC 2452 (Ch), [91].

[58] *Ali* [2001] UKHL 8, [19] (Lord Bingham), [28], [35] (Lord Nicholls), [41]–[50] (Lord Hoffmann).

[59] *Maranello Rosso* [2021] EWHC 2452 (Ch), [91] (HHJ Keyser QC).

[60] See *Bell v Lever Bros Ltd* [1931] UKHL 2, [1932] AC 161.

In an excellent article, Whayman has explained that the 'contemplation limb' from *Ali* rests upon difficult historical bases, such that its retention does not fit easily within modern contract doctrine.[61] Whayman sensibly concludes that its continued existence is sui generis, but more controversially argues that it serves a pragmatic purpose in avoiding too harsh results. Yet doctrines without secure foundations rarely prosper. Any basis of 'equitable construction' is decidedly shaky.[62] Compromise agreements are contracts like any other and sticking to the familiar exercise of interpretation would help to ensure certainty and predictability, which is especially important in the context of compromises of commercial disputes: the very reason why parties enter settlements is to achieve a clear and final resolution.[63]

A crucial point in *Ali* seems to have been that neither party could have been aware of the possibility that the employee might have had a claim for stigma damages. If the employer had been aware of this possibility, it is far from certain that the employee would have succeeded on the issue of construction. However, in *Ali*, Lord Nicholls did consider the further possibility that 'the party to whom the release was given knew that the other party had or might have a claim [beyond the one he thought he was releasing] and knew also that the other party was ignorant of this'.[64] His Lordship considered that 'seeking and taking a general release in such a case, without disclosing the existence of the claim or possible claim, could be unacceptable sharp practice' and that '[t]he law would be defective if it did not provide a remedy' in such circumstances.[65]

This reliance upon 'sharp practice' is also difficult to explain.[66] At first instance in *Maranello Rosso Ltd v Lohomij BV* HHJ Keyser QC commented that this principle was 'arguable' since it 'was considered obiter in *BCCI v Ali* and was addressed only by Lord Nicholls and Lord Hoffmann'.[67] However, on the facts of *Maranello Rosso*, no 'sharp practice' of the defendants could possibly be established[68] and, in the Court of Appeal, Phillips LJ indicated that it is difficult to see what role any principle of sharp practice could have in the context of fraudulent claims: 'where a release is construed as covering unknown claims in fraud, dishonesty and conspiracy relating to a defined subject matter (as in this case), such construction entails a finding that the parties mutually intended to settle such claims. That would seem

[61] D Whayman, 'The Modern Rule of Releases' [2021] *LS* 493.

[62] It was roundly rejected in *Ali* (see eg [2001] UKHL 8, [17] (Lord Bingham), [24] (Lord Nicholls), [44]ff (Lord Hoffmann), [79] (Lord Clyde) but compare the approach still taken in Australia: *Grant v John Grant & Sons Pty Ltd* (1954) 91 CLR 112; [1954] HCA 23; M Leeming, 'Marshalling Securities and Construing Releases in Equity' (2019) 93 *ALJ* 626. See *Lyall v Edwards* (1861) 6 H&N 337.

[63] Whayman [2021] LS 493, 494: 'The parties, having compromised uncertain claims, ought not to be afflicted by uncertainty thereafter. It would defeat the very point of compromising.'

[64] *Ali* [2001] UKHL 8, [32].

[65] ibid; see too [70]–[71] (Lord Hoffmann).

[66] But perhaps important to understanding the outcome in *Ali*, since, following *Bell v Lever Bros Ltd* [1932] AC 161, the mistake made was not sufficiently fundamental to set aside the contract: D Sheehan, 'Unconscionability and Mistake in the Court of Appeal' [2001] *JBL* 107.

[67] [2021] EWHC 2452 (Ch), [91].

[68] [2022] EWCA Civ 1667, [66].

to leave little scope for a finding that one of the parties was guilty of sharp practice in relation to the existence of such a claim'.[69] This approach is sensible.

Introducing a notion of 'sharp practice' effectively imposes an obligation of disclosure when entering into a compromise agreement. This is unusual, but perhaps chimes well with the recent refusal of Zacaroli J to decide, on an application for summary judgment, that a settlement agreement entered into with the Revenue was not a contract of the utmost good faith. His Lordship held that 'the category of contracts that are of the "utmost good faith" kind is not closed'.[70]

Nevertheless – in the commercial context, at least[71] – the better view is that compromise agreements are not of the utmost good faith and do not require full disclosure of all potential claims.[72] For example, in *Clarion Ltd v National Provident Institution* Rimer J robustly said:[73]

> The compromise of litigation is a contractual exercise in which it is the commonest thing for each side to be aware of facts and matters of which it either knows or at least suspects the other side is ignorant. If each side knew all that the other side knew then either no or only a very different compromise would be reached. In the negotiation of such compromises the parties must be careful not to make any misrepresentations. But there is in my view no general duty imposed upon them in the nature of a duty of disclosure. The negotiations are in the nature of an arm's length commercial bargain. Each party has to look after his own interests and neither owes a duty of care to the other.

This approach should be adopted even where the dispute being compromised relates to an insurance contract, which itself is a contract of utmost good faith:[74] the parties must bear the risks of imperfect knowledge at the time of settlement.

[69] ibid [67].

[70] *The Commissioners for Her Majesty's Revenue and Customs v IGE USA Investments Ltd* [2020] EWHC 2121 (Ch), [2020] STC 2091, [146]. In *Binder v Alachouzos* [1972] 2 QB 151, all three members of the Court of Appeal (Lord Denning MR, Phillimore and Roskill LJJ) placed some weight on the fact that the compromise agreement was entered into in good faith.

[71] In the family sphere, Thorpe LJ once remarked: 'When the misfortune of a contested probate action falls on a family, the pressures and stresses are, in many respects, similar to those that afflict a family torn by contested proceedings following the dissolution of a marriage. In my judgment, the negotiation of compromise of such proceedings, whether in the Family Division or the Chancery Division, must be characterised by candour and not jeopardised by side deals, concealed from one or more of the negotiating parties. In other words, I would hold that there was a duty of full and frank disclosure of facts and circumstances relevant to the weighing of a proposal for the formation of the compromise': *Marshall v Marshall* (unreported, Court of Appeal, 8 October 1998). But even here the better view is that settlements are not contracts of the utmost good faith: *Clarion Ltd v National Provident Institution* [2000] 1 WLR 1888, 1905 (Rimer J). In a similar vein, older cases concerning infant beneficiaries under a will or trust sometimes held that settlements were agreements of the utmost good faith since the Court of Chancery insisted on full disclosure (eg *Gibbons v Caunt* (1799) 4 Ves 849; *Brooke v Mostyn* (1864) 2 De GJ & S 373; *Gordon v Gordon* (1821) 3 Swans 400; *Goymour v Pigge* (1844) 13 LJ Ch 322) but those cases should now be treated with caution: *Foskett on Compromise* (n 6)[4-38]. See too *Wales v Wadham* [1977] 1 WLR 199, 216 (Tudor Evans J).

[72] *Turner v Green* [1895] 2 Ch 205, 208 (Chitty J); *Bell v Lever Bros Ltd* [1932] AC 161, 227–28 (Lord Atkin), 231–32 (Lord Thankerton); *Silver Queen Maritime Ltd v Persia Petroleum Services plc* [2010] EWHC 2867 (QB), [130] (Lindblom J).

[73] [2000] 1 WLR 1888, 1905.

[74] *Baghbadrani v Commercial Union Assurance Co Plc* [2000] Lloyd's Rep IR 94, 118–19 (HHJ Gibbs QC).

Accepting the 'sharp practice' strand of thinking risks disrupting the usual bargaining process through which compromise agreements – like any other type of contract – are made, with the result that parties can be less confident that their agreement will simply be enforced by the courts. The law would be more certain, and on a surer footing, if the 'sharp practice' principle were to be jettisoned.

Ali is a difficult decision, which has made it hard to be confident about the scope of general releases in particular. Although each individual agreement must be construed in its own context,[75] the reluctance simply to apply the usual principles of interpretation has produced unnecessary and undesirable uncertainty. In *Maranello Rosso*, the Court of Appeal pointed out that parties could exclude claims from general releases if they wish;[76] where no such exclusions are apparent, then the broad, general language may be interpreted widely in accordance with its most natural meaning, especially where the 'language, in a professionally drafted document, was fully considered and of a "high order"'.[77]

2.3. Misrepresentation

It has been argued that the public policy in favour of holding parties to settlement agreements is sufficiently strong that such contracts should not be susceptible to rescission on the ground of misrepresentation.[78] That goes too far: a settlement agreement is a species of contract which can be rescinded like any other contract. However, in *Kyle Bay Ltd (t/a Astons Nightclub) v Underwriters*, Jonathan Hirst QC sensibly warned that '[t]he Court should guard against misrepresentation being used – or rather abused – as an improper means of re-opening a compromise agreement'.[79] Unfortunately, the decision in *Zurich Insurance Co plc v Hayward*[80] appears to make it easier to set aside a settlement agreement on the basis of misrepresentation, since the Supreme Court held that even if the representee was not mistaken about the truth of the representation, a contract might still be rescinded for misrepresentation.[81]

[75] It has sometimes been said that general releases do not cover claims in fraud (see eg *MAN Nutzfahrzeuge AG v Freightliner Ltd* [2005] EWHC 2347 (Comm); *Satyam Computer Services v Upaid Systems Limited* [2008] EWCA (Civ) 487; [2008] 2 All ER (Comm) 465) but it is important to note that this is not a general rule: *Maranello Rosso Ltd v Lohomij BV* [2022] EWCA Civ 1667; *Elite Property Holdings Ltd v Barclays Bank plc* [2019] EWCA Civ 204; *Tchenguiz v Grant Thornton UK LLP* [2016] EWHC 865 (Comm); [2016] EWHC 3727 (Comm); *Marsden v Barclays Bank* [2016] EWHC 1601 (QB); [2016] 2 Lloyd's Rep 420.

[76] [2022] EWCA Civ 1667, [59].

[77] ibid. [46]. See too *O'Higgins v Barclays* [2022] CAT 16, [2022] Bus LR 1334, [326]; *Yukos Hydrocarbons Investments Limited v Georgiades* [2020] EWHC 173 (Comm), [226] (Moulder J).

[78] See, eg, *Kyle Bay Ltd (t/a Astons Nightclub) v Underwriters* [2006] EWHC 607 (Comm), [2006] Lloyd's Rep IR 718, [45] (Jonathan Hirst QC).

[79] [2006] EWHC 607 (Comm), [47].

[80] [2016] UKSC 48, [2017] AC 142.

[81] P Davies and W Day, 'A Mistaken Turn in the Law of Misrepresentation' [2019] *LMCLQ* 390; K Loi, 'Pre-Contractual Misrepresentations: Mistaken Belief Induced by Mis-Statements' [2017] *JBL* 598.

Mr Hayward injured his back in a work accident. His employer admitted liability, but Hayward overstated his injuries and sought a large damages award of over £400,000. Zurich Insurance – the employer's insurer – correctly believed Hayward to be exaggerating the consequences of the accident. In particular, it obtained a video of Hayward, post-injury, engaged in heavy lifting inconsistent with his apparent condition. The video called into question Hayward's case on the quantum of damages. Nevertheless, after further negotiations, Zurich Insurance decided to settle for around £135,000.

Some time later, Hayward's neighbours came forward with evidence that Hayward had grossly and intentionally inflated the value of his claim, which was, in reality, around £15,000. That encouraged the insurer to reopen the case. Hayward argued that the settlement agreement could not be rescinded for misrepresentation because Zurich Insurance had never believed his exaggerations. Even though the insurer did not believe Hayward and merely thought there was a possibility that the judge at trial would accept his claims,[82] the Supreme Court was satisfied that the exaggerations regarding Hayward's injuries had caused the insurer to settle for £135,000 rather than closer to £15,000. The settlement could therefore be rescinded even though the misrepresentation had not been believed by the insurer.

Lord Clarke found it 'difficult to envisage any circumstances in which mere suspicion that a claim was fraudulent would preclude unravelling a settlement when fraud is subsequently established'.[83] His Lordship left open the question of whether a claim in misrepresentation could succeed even where the representee was not merely suspicious but knew of the falsity of the statement made.[84] Lord Clarke thought that the facts of *Zurich* did not require him to answer that question as the insurer had not known the true extent of Hayward's embellishments.[85] This is unconvincing: the case did require an answer to that question, since the insurer believed that Hayward was lying.[86] To say that the insurer did not know the extent of Hayward's lies is a distinction without a difference.

Zurich makes it especially difficult to settle claims of fraud conclusively: all that a settling party need now show to reopen the litigation, when it feels that it has improved its case, is that the other side overstated the strength of their case in some way and that such statement influenced the settlement sum originally agreed. This is a very low hurdle. Unsurprisingly, the insurance industry has warmly welcomed *Zurich*:[87] because a settlement can be undone with relative ease, settling now presents little risk that can backfire on insurers – or indeed anyone else who ends up regretting a settlement.[88]

[82] [2016] UKSC 48, [19], [32] (Lord Clarke), [71] (Lord Toulson).
[83] [2016] UKSC 48, [48].
[84] ibid [43]–[45].
[85] ibid [44].
[86] *Zurich Insurance Co plc v Hayward* (6 September 2013) [2.6] (HHJ Moloney QC).
[87] P Rawlings and J Lowry, 'Insurance Fraud and the Role of Civil Law' (2016) 79 MLR 525, 537.
[88] See *Pitt v Holt* [2013] UKSC 26; [2013] 2 AC 108.

Lindeman has argued that *Zurich* should be welcomed as it encourages a key aim of the Civil Procedure Rules – namely, early settlement[89] – because a settlement can now be set aside at a later date if evidence emerges that the other side misrepresented their case.[90] Lindeman may be right that *Zurich* promotes early settlement, but it does so at the cost of settlement being a mechanism for effectively ending disputes with finality.[91] As Underhill LJ pointed out in the Court of Appeal: 'there is a wider principle at stake, that parties who settle claims with their eyes wide open should not be entitled to revive them only because better evidence comes along later'.[92] The principles underpinning misrepresentation should apply in the same manner to compromise agreements as to any other type of contract. The approach adopted in *Zurich* is inappropriate both as regards compromise agreements and commercial contracts more generally. Lord Leggatt has recently branded it 'problematic'[93] and emphasised that in *Zurich* 'the question did not arise whether it is or may be an abuse of process to bring an action seeking to prove fraud by evidence which the claimant already had at the time of the settlement'.[94] It may be that there was an abuse in *Zurich* itself; after all, 'allegations of fraud are not to be regarded as some kind of open sesame which have only to be uttered to enable a party to engage in a new round of litigation of disputes that have been compromised or decided'.[95]

2.4. Duress

Settlement agreements – like all contracts – may also be set aside for duress. Similar to misrepresentation, there may be a temptation to loosen the requirements of duress in the context of settlement agreements, since this might further encourage parties to enter into such contracts. Yet again, though, that approach comes at the expense of certainty and finality, which are important factors that encourage parties to agree settlements. A good recent example of this tension can be found in the decision of the Supreme Court in *Times Travel (UK) Ltd v Pakistan International Airlines Corporation*.[96]

[89] There is some suggestion that *Zurich* may be limited to three-party situations, where the claimant enters into a contract with the defendant, influenced by the risk that a third-party will believe and act on the defendant's misrepresentation: *Holyoake v Candy* [2017] EWHC 3397 (Ch) [390]–[393] (Nugee J); *School Facility Management Ltd v Governing Body of Christ the King College* [2020] EWHC 1118 (Comm), [2020] PTSR 1913 [400]–[401] (Foxton J).

[90] K Lindeman, 'Unravelling Settlements Made With "Eyes Wide Open"' [2017] CJQ 273, 278–79.

[91] See *Roocroft v Ball* [2016] EWCA Civ 1009, [2017] 1 WLR 1137 [71] (King LJ).

[92] [2015] EWCA Civ 327, [25]. For broader discussion, see eg E Bant, 'Unravelling Fraud in the Wake of *Hayward v Zurich Insurance*' [2019] LMCLQ 91.

[93] *Finzi v Jamaican Redevelopment Foundation Inc* [2023] UKPC 29, [66].

[94] ibid.

[95] ibid [76].

[96] [2021] UKSC 40, [2023] AC 101.

Times Travel is a travel agent whose business focused on selling airline tickets to the British Pakistani community. The defendant, as the flag carrier of Pakistan, offered the only direct flights between the UK and Pakistan. It changed the way it calculated the commission due to its travel agents and demanded that the claimant sign new agreements under which it would give up its contractual rights to commission that had already accrued. If these new agreements were not signed, the claimant would not be allowed to sell the defendant's tickets at all. This, inevitably, would have put the claimant out of business. However, the threat was not in itself unlawful: the defendant could choose with whom it wished to contract.

Remarkably, at first instance, Warren J held that the agreements could be set aside on the basis of lawful act duress.[97] That conclusion was firmly rejected by both the Court of Appeal[98] and Supreme Court. Lord Hodge observed that:[99]

> commercial organisations may enter into a dispute or commence litigation without an informed idea of their legal rights or any intention of seeking judicial resolution but with the aim of reaching a settlement of the dispute on better terms than are currently on offer. The vast majority of commercial disputes do not go to trial and are not expected to do so. Each organisation may have to reach its own view as to its entitlements and resolve the dispute accordingly.

It is suggested that a party should be able to threaten not to renew a contract or not to enter into a contract without this being considered to represent illegitimate pressure for the purposes of duress.[100] This is especially important between commercial actors who operate on the basis that they are entitled to act in a self-interested manner. Parties have a choice whether to contract on given terms: one party may drive a hard bargain, but if it is ultimately not as good as what the other side hoped for, then that party must make a final choice whether to agree to the deal or simply walk away. If the contract is concluded, it should not be held to be voidable for duress where the other side threatened to do something it was entitled to do.

Nevertheless, following *Times Travel*, it appears that lawful act duress might arise 'where the defendant, having exposed himself to a civil claim by the claimant, for example, for damages for breach of contract, deliberately manoeuvres the claimant into a position of vulnerability by means which the law regards as illegitimate and thereby forces the claimant to waive his claim'.[101] This clearly marks out compromise agreements as susceptible to lawful act duress, even though contracts

[97] [2017] EWHC 1367 (Ch).

[98] [2019] EWCA Civ 828, [2020] Ch 98.

[99] [2021] UKSC 40, [51].

[100] See, eg, Commonwealth authorities such as *Smith v William Charlick Ltd* (1924) 34 CLR 38; *Morton Construction v City of Hamilton* (1961) 31 DLR (2d) 323. Cf *Crescendo Management Pty Ltd v Westpac Banking Corporation* (1988) 19 NSWLR 40.

[101] [2021] UKSC 40, [4] (Lord Hodge); see similarly [112] (Lord Burrows). Their Lordships also gave the example of blackmail as an example of lawful act duress, but, although common, this is unconvincing: the threat made in instances of blackmail is itself unlawful when combined with the demand for (typically) money (see, eg, [2019] EWCA Civ 828, [53] (David Richards LJ)).

which arise where there is no pre-existing relationship between the parties will not be set aside for the same reason. Yet parties should be held to their compromise agreements in the same way as any other contract. Admittedly, the scope for setting aside settlement agreements based on lawful act duress remains very narrow, but the boundaries of this doctrine remain frustratingly vague. It may be that *Times Travel* will prompt parties to argue lawful act duress[102] more regularly, which could destabilise some (settlement) agreements, but it is to be hoped that such litigation will not be encouraged and, in time, the door will be shut more firmly on the possibility of lawful act duress.[103] Judges should focus squarely upon whether the defendant's threats were unlawful; they are not well-equipped to 'be the arbiters of what is socially unacceptable and attach legal consequences to such conduct'.[104]

3. Third Parties

The focus of much discussion concerning compromise agreements is upon relatively straightforward two-party scenarios. But (commercial) reality is often more complicated and there may be more than one potential defendant.[105] This can increase the difficulty of settling disputes and the jurisprudence in this area often does not appear to encourage compromise. Indeed, judges have lamented that the law can be a 'trap for the unwary'.[106]

Most problematically, the law appears to state that settling with one joint tortfeasor will, presumptively, mean that the claimant will not be able to bring a claim against other joint tortfeasors.[107] This approach has long been criticised; Glanville Williams noted that the '[r]easons given for this rule are technical, and even fictitious'.[108] It is most unlikely to reflect the parties' intentions. The claimant may have chosen

[102] Perhaps unconscionability too: see, eg, N Enonchong, 'The Modern English Doctrine of Unconscionability' [2018] JCL 211.

[103] See also R Ahdar, 'Contract Doctrine, Predictability and the Nebulous Exception' [2014] CLJ 39.

[104] J Beatson, *The Use and Abuse of Unjust Enrichment* (OUP, 1991) 129. See too *Ukraine v Law Debenture Trust Corp Plc* [2023] UKSC 11, [2023] 2 WLR 699, [141], [161].

[105] A different problem arises in the context of subrogation: insurers often protect themselves by inserting clauses into their policies which state that the insured owes a duty to ensure that all rights against third parties are properly preserved, prohibiting them from compromising or releasing claims against third parties: see C Mitchell, P Mitchell and S Watterson, *Goff & Jones on Unjust Enrichment* 10th edn (Sweet & Maxwell, 2022) [21-107]ff.

[106] *Watts v Lord Aldington* [1999] L&TR 578, 595 (Steyn LJ); see too *Jameson v Central Electricity Generating Board* [2000] 1 AC 455, 468 (Lord Lloyd).

[107] *Brown v Wootton* (1604) Cro Jac 73; *Brinsmead v Harrison* (1872) LR 7 CP 547; *Bryanston Finance Ltd v de Vries* [1975] QB 703, 721 (Lord Denning MR) and 730 (Lord Diplock); *Jameson v Central Electricity Generating Board* [2000] 1 AC 455, 473 (Lord Hope). See too *Morris v Wentworth-Stanley* [1999] QB 1004. Similar principles can apply to joint contractors: *Deanplan Ltd v Mahmoud* [1993] Ch 151.

[108] G Williams, *Joint Torts and Contributory Negligence* (Stevens & Sons, 1951) 44. See too *Watts v Lord Aldington* [1999] L&TR 578, 594–95 (Steyn LJ); *Jameson v Central Electricity Generating Board* [1998] QB 323, 336–37, where Auld LJ optimistically said that the rule as to joint tortfeasors is 'in retreat'.

to settle with one particular defendant for a number of reasons; for example, it may be that the defendant is impecunious or on the brink of insolvency, and the figure reached in the settlement was all that that defendant could afford.[109] In such circumstances, a claimant would be surprised to learn that settling with such a defendant for a sum far below the value of the claim could prevent the balance being sought from another defendant. As Lord Bingham put it in *Heaton v AXA Equity and Law Life Assurance Society plc*, '[w]hile it is just that A should be precluded from recovering substantial damages against C in a case where he has accepted a sum representing the full measure of his estimated loss [from B], it is unjust that A should be so precluded where he has not'.[110]

The basis of this approach appears to be that there is only one wrong in instances of joint tortfeasance, unlike other areas where separate wrongs may have been committed by concurrent tortfeasors, so releasing one joint tortfeasor releases them all. This is itself controversial.[111] Old authorities relied upon for this proposition are largely unconvincing.[112] Where judgment has been given against one defendant, statute has now intervened to ensure that that no longer precludes an action being taken against another.[113] But where the settlement is not embodied in a consent order or judgment, the common law continues to apply and to maintain a blunt approach which is a 'juridical relic'[114] and can lead to unanticipated results. Even for those aware of the problem, 'it is a potential disincentive to entering into bona fide and reasonable compromises'.[115] After all, a contract between the claimant and a settling defendant should not generally[116] affect the claimant's rights against a third party, even if that party is joint tortfeasor.[117]

That the law remains in such a plainly unsatisfactory state is surprising, especially given the considerable importance placed by the courts upon compromise, and the frequency with which parties must grapple with these issues. Courts have developed a number of techniques to try to circumvent the problems which arise, for instance by construing the agreement as a personal covenant not to sue that particular defendant rather than a release,[118] or by somehow insisting that a release of one joint tortfeasor does not preclude the possibility of pursuing other

[109] Other reasons given by Lord Bingham in *Heaton v AXA Equity and Law Life Assurance Society plc* [2002] UKHL 15, [2002] 2 AC 329, [5] include that the defendant may be uninsured, and that the claimant may be in urgent need of funds, eg to finance other litigation.

[110] [2002] UKHL 15, [2002] 2 AC 329, [5].

[111] P Davies, *Accessory Liability* (Hart, 2015) 263.

[112] G Williams, *Joint Torts and Contributory Negligence* (London, Stevens & Sons, 1951) 44.

[113] Civil Liability (Contribution) Act 1978 s 3; see previously Law Reform (Married Women and Tortfeasors) Act 1935 s 6.

[114] *Watts v Lord Aldington* [1999] L & TR 578, 598 (Simon Brown LJ).

[115] ibid 595 (Steyn LJ).

[116] See Contracts (Rights of Third Parties) Act 1999; *Schofield v Smith* [2022] EWCA Civ 824, [2023] 1 All ER 480.

[117] *Watts v Lord Aldington* [1999] L & TR 578, 594 (Steyn LJ): 'As far as the unreleased tortfeasor is concerned the settlement between the plaintiff and the released tortfeasor is *res inter alios acta*.'.

[118] *Duck v Mayeu* [1892] 2 QB 511; *Gladman Commercial Properties v Fisher Hargreaves Proctor* [2013] EWCA Civ 1466, [2014] PNLR 11, [23] (Briggs LJ).

joint tortfeasors if such 'right' is expressly or impliedly reserved at the time of making the settlement.[119] These measures have led some judges to seek solace in the fact that well-advised parties are able to draft their agreement such that a right to pursue other defendants can be expressly reserved,[120] but that clearly does not assist those without such resources. Nor does it address the fundamental issues of principle which indicate that the law has taken a wrong turn in its development.

Even where defendants are concurrent wrongdoers rather than joint tortfeasors, the law is 'more complex than it should be',[121] which can discourage compromise. There remain difficulties about how the sum received by the claimant from the first, settling defendant is to be treated.[122] The House of Lords in *Jameson v Central Electricity Generating Board* adopted what appeared to be a far too rigid approach in insisting that 'the effect of the compromise is to fix the amount of his claim',[123] but in *Heaton v AXA Equity and Law Life Assurance Society plc* their Lordships quickly revisited the issue and explained that whether a sum reached under a compromise agreement should be taken to fix the full measure of the claimant's loss is simply a question of interpretation.[124] Focusing upon the (objective) intentions of the settling parties would help to resolve many of the difficulties which plague this area of the law.[125]

Of course, tricky issues arise where there is an overlap between claims which are available against both defendants and other claims which are only available against defendants separately. There can be no precise rules about how much of any settlement is to be attributed to one claim rather than another. Nevertheless, in *Marino v FM Capital Partners Ltd* the Court of Appeal provided helpful and authoritative guidance.[126] That case concerned FM Capital Partners Ltd ('FMCP'), which

[119] *Gladman Commercial Properties v Fisher Hargreaves Proctor & Ors* [2013] EWCA Civ 1466, [2014] PNLR 11, [24] (Briggs LJ); *Watts v Lord Aldington* [1999] L&TR 578. For an interesting recent illustration see *Biscoe v Milner* [2021] EWHC 763 (Ch); see too *Latham Machinery Ltd v Dior Heavylift BV* [2022] EWHC 525 (Comm).

[120] *Gladman Commercial Properties v Fisher Hargreaves Proctor & Ors* [2013] EWCA Civ 1466, [2014] PNLR 11, [84]-[85] (Longmore LJ). In *O'Higgins v Barclays* [2022] CAT 16 [326] (albeit in a different context) the majority observed that 'Of course, all courts in this jurisdiction welcome and encourage settlement: but the best settlements arise between litigants of equal litigation 'heft', and that (of course) includes the funding available for the litigation.'

[121] *Foskett on Compromise* (n 6)[6-37].

[122] *Townsend v Stone Toms & Partners* (1984) 27 BLR 26; W Courtney, 'Settlements Following Breach of Contract' [2013] LMCLQ 158.

[123] [2000] 1 AC 455, 474 (Lord Hope); see also 482 (Lord Clyde).

[124] [2002] UKHL 15, [2002] 2 AC 329, 336–37 (Lord Bingham). See too *Vanden Recycling Ltd v Bevin Tumulty* [2017] EWCA Civ 354; [2017] CP Rep 33; *Officeserve Technologies Ltd (In Liquidation) v Annabel's (Berkeley Square) Ltd* [2018] EWHC 2168 (Ch), [2019] Ch 103. It is also worth noting that if the settling defendant wishes to protect itself against any further possible claims from another defendant seeking contribution, then it may seek an enforceable undertaking from the claimant not to pursue any claim against any other party relating to the subject-matter of the compromise, or obtain an indemnity from the claimant against any liability which may be incurred relating to the subject matter of the compromise: *Heaton* [2002] 2 AC 329, 337.

[125] eg *Watts v Lord Aldington* [1999] L & TR 578.

[126] [2020] EWCA Civ 245, [2021] QB 1.

managed investments on behalf of a Libyan sovereign wealth fund. Mr Marino was the director and CEO of FMCP and Mr Bessot was also a director and the CIO of FMCP. FMCP purchased structured financial products from Bank Julius Baer & Co, and Mr Ohmura was an employee of that bank. During that time, Mr Marino, Mr Bessot and Mr Ohmura each received substantial 'introductory commissions' from Bank Baer, and FMCP brought claims for US$83 million against those individuals for dishonest assistance, bribery and breach of fiduciary duty.

Mr Bessot settled all FMCP's claims against him for US$2.8 million. The question for the Court of Appeal was whether, and if so how much, credit should be given by FMCP to Mr Marino for the sums FMCP received from Mr Bessot. FMCP was prepared to give credit to Mr Marino of 17% of the recoveries from Mr Bessot. Mr Marino argued it should have given credit of 100% or alternatively 80%. The Court of Appeal held that the claimant should be able to 'choose how to allocate recoveries from the other defendants, subject only to the threshold of the allocation not being "obviously unsustainable"',[127] at least in circumstances where the judge is not in a position to assess the strength of the settled claims.[128] Beatson LJ said:[129]

> It is also important to remember the policy considerations favouring the encouragement of compromise even where the claim is unfounded and worthless: see Callisher v Bischoffsheim (1870) 5 QB 449, 452. Those policy considerations would be undermined if a claimant who makes a settlement with one of the defendants, in part to save the cost of proving the case against that defendant, has to give credit to the other defendant for the sum paid under the settlement, unless he or she is able to prove the nature of the case against the defendant who settled. I accept [counsel's] submission that that would be a significant disincentive to settlement, and also that it would also be inconsistent with the way settlements are dealt with in relation to contributions between co-defendants by section 1(4) of the Civil Liability (Contribution) Act 1978.

It is perhaps significant that *FM Marino* concerned bribery, and the law in this area is notoriously difficult. But the leading English authorities indicate that settling with either the recipient or provider of a bribe will not prevent a claimant from pursuing the other defendant. In *The Mayor, Alderman, and Burgesses of the Borough of Salford v Lever*,[130] the claimants were proprietors of gasworks, and the defendant was a coal merchant who submitted tenders for the supply of coal. The defendant had previously agreed to pay to the claimants' manager a bribe of 1*s* per ton, and consequently increased the prices in his tenders by 1*s* per ton. The claimants' manager advised the claimant to accept the defendant's tender. The claimants later discovered that their manager had committed such corrupt acts and entered into an agreement with him that he would assist them in bringing claims against various contractors, including the defendant, and that he would guarantee that at least 10,000*l* would be recovered by depositing at a bank securities worth 10,000*l*.

[127] ibid [73].
[128] ibid [64]–[69].
[129] ibid [70].
[130] [1891] 1 QB 168 (CA).

The claimants subsequently sued the defendant. The defendant argued that it was a joint wrongdoer with the manager, and that as a result the agreement between the claimants and the manager – together with the deposit of the securities – amounted to a discharge of the manager and thereby also a discharge of the defendant.

The Court of Appeal rejected the defendant's argument. The defendant and the manager were not jointly liable for a single wrong. The payer of the bribe and recipient of the bribe are liable for two distinct wrongs, even if the liability of the briber is dependent upon the primary wrong committed by the bribee. As Lord Esher MR remarked, the fraud of the agent was 'separate and distinct' from that of the briber.[131] This led his Lordship to conclude that the briber 'was bound to pay back the extra price which he had received, and he could not absolve himself or diminish the damages by reason of the principal having recovered from the agent the bribe which he had received'.[132] Lindley LJ was similarly forthright, expressing the view that 'it does not lie in the mouth of the defendant, who is a wrongdoer, to say that his liability to account to the corporation for the money received by him is to be determined by the circumstance whether they have already recovered from [the manager] Hunter the money received by him'.[133]

In taking this approach, the court in *Salford v Lever* followed the earlier decision of the Court of Appeal in *Bagnall v Carlton*.[134] In that case, the principal brought an action against the briber for rescission of the transaction entered into as a result of the bribery and a separate action against the agent for recovery of the bribe. The action against the briber was compromised on the basis that the briber paid a sum of money to the principal and the contract remained on foot. The court was clear that this did not affect the principal's cause of action against his agent. James LJ said that this claim 'was, in truth, a totally distinct and separate' claim from that against the briber.[135] As far as the agent was concerned, the settlement with the briber was *res inter alios acta*.

4. Conclusion

It is important to encourage compromise agreements but not at the expense of the application of fundamental contract law principles. There is no need for special

[131] [1891] 1 QB 168, 176.
[132] ibid 177.
[133] ibid 180.
[134] (1877) LR 6 ChD 371. Admittedly, the (Malaysian) decision of the Privy Council in *Mahesan v Malaysia Government Officers' Co-Operative Housing Society Ltd* [1979] AC 374 is sometimes thought to depart from *Salford v Lever* but, properly analysed, that case is different since it involved seeking two different remedies against the same defendant, whereas in *Lever* distinct claims were brought against two separate defendants: see, eg, D Whayman, 'Liability for Bribes and Secret Commissions at Common Law: Obsolete, Unnecessary and Probably a Fusion Fallacy' [2022] Conv 184, 193–94; P Davies 'Bribery' in P Davies and J Penner (eds) *Equity, Trusts and Commerce* (Hart, 2017) 248–49.
[135] ibid 399; see, too, Baggallay LJ at 404.

rules of interpretation, or a more generous approach to misrepresentation,[136] just because the contract at issue settled a (potential) dispute. Orthodox contractual doctrines should apply. Moreover, '[t]here can be no doubt that the rule relating to releases has worked badly'[137] when considering the impact a release might have upon possible claims against third parties: the traditional approach can operate as a serious disincentive to compromise. A rigid distinction between a release and covenant not to sue is no longer appropriate, for example. Standard principles of construction should be applied to determine the meaning and effect of a compromise agreement, and whether settling with one defendant releases another defendant from liability.

[136] Or to mistake: see, eg, *Brennan v Bolt Burden* [2004] EWCA Civ 1017, [2005] QB 303; *Elston v King* [2020] EWHC 55 (Ch), [18]–[20] (Marcus Smith J).

[137] G Williams, *Joint Torts and Contributory Negligence* (Stevens & Sons, 1951) 137.

12

Insurance of Commodities Fraud

ÖZLEM GÜRSES

1. Introduction

Unless otherwise expressly agreed, cargo insurance policies provide cover only for physical loss of or damage (PLOD) to the cargo. Typically, PLOD to the cargo might be suffered through leakage or when it has perished. A cargo owner who is expecting his purchase to be delivered would insure the cargo against the transit risks. Such risks may be listed in the contract, or the cover might be agreed on an 'all-risks' basis. In either case the policy would include some exclusions from the insurance cover. The eventualities that might cause financial loss to the assured are not limited to those that cause material alteration to the insured cargo. Court cases have demonstrated that third-party fraud which involves selling a non-existent cargo to a buyer is not an uncommon event.

On the other hand, only a small number of the cases in which the assured claimed the loss occurred due to such fraud were concluded in the assured's favour. One might question if this is a coincidence, or did the policy wordings in those cases commonly not provide cover for the loss claimed, or is the law somewhat insurer friendly? This chapter aims to demonstrate the complexities involved in insurance claims for – which may be called as – 'paper loss'. The courts do not deny the possibility of insuring against such losses, but the insurance market appears to struggle to find the most appropriate wording to enable this.

2. Commodities Fraud

The trade industry is ever-reliant on document-based processes that are vulnerable to fraud. In its report in 2022, the Association of Certified Fraud Examiners (ACFE) assessed 2,000 cases of fraud affecting organisations in 133 countries and 23 industries.[1] Creating, altering, and destroying physical and electronic

[1] 'Occupational Fraud 2022: A Report to the Nations' (*Association of Certified Fraud Examiners*, 2022). See acfepublic.s3.us-west-2.amazonaws.com/2022+Report+to+the+Nations.pdf.

documents and withholding physical documents were identified in this report as top concealment methods used by fraudsters.

Documentary fraud frequently causes losses not only to the traders but also the financial institutions and insurers. For instance, the final six weeks of 1963 witnessed a commodities market scandal named as 'the great salad oil mystery' or 'salad oil swindle'.[2] The amount lost was estimated to be at least US $180m and involved dozens of banks, import-export firms, commodity houses, insurance companies and a warehousing subsidiary of the American Express Company. Allied Crude, the keystone company of Mr D, used warehouse receipts for oil supposedly in storage and borrowed money from banks and various brokers based on these receipts.[3] In reality, the ships' tanks contained only water, with a few feet of salad oil floating on top to trick inspectors. When inspectors audited Allied's facilities, the company transferred the same oil stock from tank to tank to fool the inspectors while entertaining them during lunch.

The scale of the loss experienced due to the Qingdao fraud was much larger. Through financial crimes spanning an 18-month period from November 2012 to May 2014 CJ's firm raised US$1.78bn in funds using either fake warehouse receipts or fake certificates for aluminium ingots, alumina and refined copper at the eastern Chinese ports of Qingdao and Penglai. They also raised US$520.8m in loans, letters of credit and bank acceptance bills from 13 banks by repeatedly using the same cargoes as pledged collateral.[4]

Slightly different to the cases above, in *Engelhart CTP (US) LLC v Lloyd's Syndicate 1221 for the 2014 Year of Account*[5] copper ingots allegedly shipped to the assured had never existed. Similarly, in *Fuerst Day Lawson Ltd v Orion Insurance Co Ltd*[6] whilst the assured was expecting a cargo of essential oils from Indonesia, what was delivered was water with slight traces of an essential oil on the surface. In *Coven SpA v Hong Kong Chinese Insurance Co*[7] whilst the assured's documents confirmed shipment of 2,787.209 mt broad beans, the actual amount was 2,401.581 mt.

Whether the assured could recover from the insurer would be determined by the interpretation of the policy wording. A contract of insurance is construed like any other commercial document.[8] In interpreting a contractual document, the function of the court is to give effect to the intentions of the parties, and the test is

[2] *Scarburgh Co v American Manufacturers Mutual Insurance* 107 Misc 2d 772 (NY Sup Ct 1979). Scarburgh was the holder for value of an excess of $23 million of fraudulently issued and subsequently worthless warehouse receipts taken as collateral security in vegetable oil financing transactions with Allied.

[3] 'The Vanishing Salad Oil: A $100 Million Mystery' The New York Times (New York, 6 January 1964).

[4] E Wragg, 'Qingdao Fraud Probe Ends with Jail Term' (*Global Trade Review*, 10 December 2018). Available at: www.gtreview.com/news/asia/qingdao-fraud-probe-ends-with-jail-term.

[5] [2018] 2 Lloyd's Rep 24.

[6] [1980] 1 Lloyd's Rep 656.

[7] [1999] CLC 223.

[8] RM Merkin (ed), *Colinvaux's Law of Insurance*, 13th edn (London, Sweet & Maxwell, 2023) [3-005]; J Birds et al (eds), *MacGillivray on Insurance Law*, 15th edn (London, Sweet & Maxwell, 2023) [11-001].

purely objective.[9] The parties' intention is to be gathered from the wording chosen to express their agreement in the policy itself and from the wording of any other documents incorporated in it.[10] A cargo insurance policy is likely to incorporate a standard wording. In *Sunport Shipping Ltd v Tryg Baltica International (UK) Ltd (The Kleovoulos of Rhodes)*,[11] Clarke LJ stated:

> Where a contract has been professionally drawn, as in the case of the Institute Clauses, the draftsman is certain to have in mind decisions of the courts on earlier editions of the clause. Such decisions are part of the context or background circumstances against which the particular contract falls to be construed. If the draftsman chooses to adopt the same words as previously construed by the courts, it seems to me to be likely that, other things being equal, he intends that the words should continue to have the same meaning.

The above seems to be overwhelmingly the guidance for the courts in the interpretation of the cargo insurance policies discussed in this chapter. On the other hand, as acknowledged by Mr Salter QC who was sitting as the deputy High Court judge in *TKC London Limited v Allianz Insurance Plc*:[12]

> There is something of an air of unreality about applying this principle to a standard form commercial policy sold by a major insurer to (amongst others) many SMEs such as TKC. Those small business customers are unlikely to have read (or to have anyone readily available on the staff of their business who has read) MacGillivray on Insurance Law, or any of the other textbooks or authorities to which I have been referred. They are therefore likely to look to the words of the Policy itself, in their ordinary business meaning, to discover what their insurance covers, rather than to the body of learning to which I have been referred. Nevertheless, where this principle applies (for example, in relation to the meaning to be given to technical expression such as 'inherent vice'), it serves the useful commercial purpose of providing legal certainty.

The assureds would argue in the cases mentioned above that their intention was to be covered for their economic loss, whether it is pure or it followed a PLOD to the cargo. The insurer would argue that their intention was not to insure against a loss other than PLOD. The courts' interpretation of the policy wordings in the cases referred to above found a mismatch between the cover provided by the insurance contract and the nature of the assured's loss, namely what caused it. The courts have drawn a clear distinction between physical loss of or damage to cargo and paper loss, namely pure economic loss. The parties, according to the courts, cannot have intended to insure goods which never existed.[13] A paper loss, although loss

[9] The court cases that articulated the rules of contractual construction will not be listed here. As Lord Hodge said in *Wood v Capita Insurance Services Ltd* [2017] UKSC 24 [9], the legal profession has sufficient judicial statements of that nature. See also *Trillium (Prime) Property GP Ltd v Elmfield Road Ltd* [2018] EWCA Civ 1556; *TKC London Limited v Allianz Insurance Plc* [2020] Lloyd's Rep IR 631 [101].

[10] Birds, *MacGillivray on Insurance Law* (n 8) [11-001].

[11] [2003] 1 Lloyd's Rep 138 [28].

[12] [2020] Lloyd's Rep IR 631 [105].

[13] *Coven SpA v Hong Kong Chinese Insurance Co* [1999] CLC 223, 227.

to the assured, is not a PLOD to the cargo. If parties to an insurance contract wish to insure against economic loss where the goods never existed, they would have to do so in clear terms.[14]

Did the assured contemplate at the outset of the contract that their policies would not compensate for the loss suffered due to the fraud that they were exposed to? The answer can only be speculative although the tendency would be to say 'no'. The objective interpretation of the policy wording, however, decided otherwise. It appears to be a difficult task to find a balance between the two competing interests.

3. Material Alteration to the Subject Matter Insured

For the insurer to be liable under the insurance contract, the assured's loss must fall within the insuring clause, namely, it must have been caused by one of the risks insured against.[15] If the cause of the loss was not insured, or was excluded in the insurance contract, the insurer will not be liable to compensate it.

A typical cargo insurance policy would incorporate a standard wording, such as Institute Cargo Clauses (ICC) 2009 (A) whereby the insurers agree to indemnify the assured against 'all risks of loss of or damage to the subject-matter insured except as excluded under the policy'.[16] Similarly, the American Institute Cargo Clauses insure against 'All Risks of physical loss or damage from any external cause'.[17] ICC 2009 (B) and (C) address a more limited cover as they list the risks insured against preceding the wording of 'loss of or damage to the subject-matter insured reasonably attributable to'.[18]

The meaning of the words 'damage' and 'loss' are crucial in determining the scope of the insuring clauses. The ordinary meaning of the words 'loss' and 'damage' requires physical, namely, material, alteration of the subject matter insured.[19] In the context of 'all-risks' policies, the courts' view has been consistent that they apply only to physical loss and damage, and not pure economic loss.[20]

[14] ibid.

[15] The Marine Insurance Act 1906 (MIA 1906), s 55(1). See also J Gilman et al (eds), *Arnould: Law of Marine Insurance and Average*, 20th edn (London, Sweet & Maxwell, 2023) ch 22; Birds (n 8) ch 19; M Song, *Causation in Insurance Contract Law*, 1st edn (Oxford, Informa Law from Routledge, 2014); O Gurses, 'The Proximate Causes of Loss' in R Thomas (ed), *Modern Law of Marine Insurance*, vol 5 (Oxford, Informa Law from Routledge, 2023).

[16] ICC (A) 2009, cl 1.

[17] The American Institute Cargo Clauses 2004 All Risks, cl 1.

[18] ICC (C) 2009, cl 1.

[19] *Moore v Evans* [1918] AC 185, 198.

[20] *Fuerst Day Lawson Ltd v Orion Insurance Co Ltd* [1980] 1 Lloyd's Rep 656; *Engelhart CTP (US) LLC v Lloyd's Syndicate 1221 for the 2014 Year of Account* [2018] 2 Lloyd's Rep 24.

A loss to the assured and a loss to the insured property are two distinct concepts. For instance, loss of market of the insured goods without physical loss or damage falls under the former only.[21] In *Cator v Great Western Insurance Co of New York*,[22] it was held that a suspicion of loss, in the absence of proof does not suffice to show the damage. The assured's cargo of tea was loaded in consecutively marked packages. Some of those packages had to be marked 'damaged' due to sea water entry. The sequence of the packaging numbers had therefore been broken which raised the suspicion that the rest of the packages could also have been damaged. The assured's loss of profit as a result of such suspicion was not damage to the goods.

Similarly, in *Kraal v The Earthquake Commission*,[23] the loss was to the assured only. K's house, which survived with no damage after the two major earthquakes in 2011, was facing rocks on a steep hill. The house was declared as dangerous because of widespread rockfalls that had fallen in its vicinity. Approaching or entering the house was prohibited by the authorities under the civil defence emergency powers. K made a claim against the Earthquake Commission (EQC), as well as the insurer, Allianz. Under the Earthquake Commission Act 1993, ss 2 and 18, the EQC would be liable for 'any physical loss or damage to the property' occurred as the direct result of a natural disaster. Similarly, the Allianz policy covered 'accidental physical loss or damage'.

The court defined the word 'damage' as broad as including physical, as well as reputational or other non-physical harm.[24] However, the word 'physical' imposed a restricted meaning as it indicated something material or tangible as opposed to mental or spiritual, concerning the structure and materials of the property.[25]

In view of the court the word 'loss' was broad enough to cover 'deprivation of a thing'.[26] However, the wording was 'loss or damage to the property'. The preposition 'to' related to what is reached, approached or touched.' If the house had become inaccessible because it was trapped beneath a landslide in circumstances where recovery was unreasonable or unlikely, then the homeowners would have been deprived of their house because something physical had occurred directly to the materials or structure of the house. K's loss, however, was a loss to K, not to the house.

[21] See, eg, the assured lost the use of the jewellery in trade during WWI: *Moore v Evans* [1918] AC 185, 192,193; the cargo whose delivery delayed lost its market value: *Masefield AG v Amlin Corporate Member Ltd* [2011] Lloyd's Rep IR 338.

[22] (1872–73) LR 8 CP 552.

[23] [2015] NZCA 13.

[24] [2015] NZCA 13 [35].

[25] Authorities are consistent on this point. See, eg: *Merlin v British Nuclear Fuels Plc* [1990] 2 QB 557; *Blue Circle Industries Plc v Ministry of Defence* [1999] Ch 289; *Losinjska Plovidba v Transco Overseas Ltd (The Orjula)* [1995] 2 Lloyd's Rep 395.

[26] [2015] NZCA 13 [38].

4. Non-existent Cargo

In *Engelhart CTP (US) LLC v Lloyd's Syndicate 1221 for the 2014 Year of Account*,[27] the claimant bought 9000 mt of copper ingots on CIF China terms from World Gold International Ltd and then sold the cargo to receivers in China, Shing Fu (HK) Metal Co Ltd. Bills of lading were issued in respect of a cargo of 1,967.898 mt of copper ingots, said to be shipped in 102 containers from New York. Some containers were leaking when they arrived in Hong Kong for transhipment to China. All the containers were opened in the presence of cargo surveyors. The bills of lading, packing lists and quality certificates were fraudulent, no copper ingots were shipped in the containers, no such cargo ever existed. The claimant was unaware of the fraud at the time of shipment. One of the key issues[28] was the interpretation of the insuring clause under the 'Marine Cargo and Storage Insurance' title. The insurer agreed to provide cover against 'all risks of physical loss of or damage to the subject matter insured from any external cause'. Having cited the well-known authorities on the principles of contractual construction,[29] Sir Ross Cranston took the purpose of all-risks marine cargo insurance as his starting point: to cover loss of or damage to property. Where no cargo of copper ingots shipped due to their non-existence, the buyer's loss could not be characterised as a physical loss of goods. Something must exist to be physically lost.

Sir Cranston's judgment followed a number of authorities. In *Fuerst Day Lawson Ltd v Orion Insurance Co Ltd*,[30] Fuerst Day purchased a cargo of essential oils from an Indonesian firm. The cargo was found on discharge to contain water with slight traces of an essential oil on the surface. Orion issued a policy insuring 'essential oils in steel or iron drums on steamer and/or steamers and/or conveyances or any other method of transportation from "anywhere to anywhere", lost or not lost, against all-risks'. This large-scale fraud, according to the evidence, attracted considerable publicity in the Indonesian press and appeared to have been investigated thoroughly by the Indonesian police. The claimants had conducted very satisfactory business transactions for many years with the perpetrator of the fraud.

The assured argued that water was substituted for oil after the drums had passed through the customs' examination. However, no satisfactory explanation as to how the substitution could have been made was put forward. Mocatta J had therefore no difficulty in dismissing the possibility of the alleged substitutions. When loaded with either water or oil the drums were heavy weighing between 190–220 kilos.

[27] [2018] 2 Lloyd's Rep 24.

[28] The other two matters were the assured's insurable interest and the fraudulent documentation clause, both of which are discussed below under the relevant headings.

[29] *Rainy Sky SA v Kookmin Bank* [2011] UKSC 50; *Arnold v Britton* [2015] UKSC 36; *Impact Funding Solutions Ltd v Barrington Support Services Ltd (formerly Lawyers at Work Ltd)* [2016] UKSC 57.

[30] [1980] 1 Lloyd's Rep 656.

Nearly all were loaded on deck and no fewer than seven ocean-going vessels, belonging to three different owners, carried, in parcels between them, the 1121 drums containing water. The judge held that all risks cover applies only to physical loss and damage, which requires proof of physical loss of or damage to a cargo. On the balance of probabilities, the evidence was not sufficient to establish that the oil in drums the claimant had agreed to buy from Farmaport ever started on their transit from a warehouse. Rather, it was possible that the drums, from the outset, only contained water with a thin film of essential oils for deception purposes.

Naturally, what the insurer agrees is to compensate the assured's financial loss. However, such financial loss depends on the damage to the goods. When the parties' intention is to insure 'pure' economic loss, that must be stated expressly. Where the subject matter insured is the 'successful completion of the voyage', it is arguable that when the voyage is lost due to a risk insured against, although the goods were left undamaged, the assured may recover for the economic loss suffered. Importantly, the assured is required to abandon the cargo to the insurer. There may be nothing to abandon in some cases, for instance, the cargo might have been captured and its recovery might be unlikely, however, the cargo must exist before its capture. When the subject matter insured becomes a constructive total loss for the loss of the voyage under ss 60 (1) and 60(2)(i) MIA 1906 the assured may recover for a total loss although the subject matter insured was not destroyed.[31] In all these cases the loss is not purely economic.

5. Fortuity

One of the fundamental principles of indemnity insurance is that the purpose of the policy is to secure an indemnity against accidents.[32] The word 'fortuitous' expresses ill luck, something which could not be foreseen.[33] It follows that something 'intentional' or 'inevitable' will be excluded from the insurance cover.[34] The loss is fortuitous when a third party's fraud causes the loss. In an all-risks policy, such a fraud would be covered if the fraud results in PLOD to the cargo.

In the context of content shortage, the shortage must have occurred because of a PLOD to the cargo. Unless otherwise stated in the policy, a mere arithmetic error will not be regarded as a fortuitous incident against which the insurer agreed to

[31] *Mitchell v Edie* (1787) 1 Term Rep 608; *Barker v Blakes* (1808) 9 East 283; *Falkner v Ritchie* (1814) 2 M & S 290. Some strong objections to compensation upon a lost voyage were expressed in *Pole v Fitzgerald* (1750) Willes 641. However, in *Pole* the main reason for the decisions appears to be 'insurable interest'.

[32] *The Xantho* (1887) 12 App Cas 503, 509; *Hamilton, Fraser & Co v Pandorf & Co* (1887) 12 App Cas 518, 524, Lord Halsbury; *Sheehan v Lloyds Names Munich Re Syndicate Ltd* [2017] FCA 1340 [56].

[33] *Samuel v Dumas* [1924] AC 431, 448, Viscount Cave.

[34] *Hodgson v Malcolm* (1806) 2 Bos & PNR 336, 340, Chambre J; *Versloot Dredging BV v HDI Gerling Industrie Versicherung* AG [2013] 2 Lloyd's Rep 131 [32]; *Samuel v Dumas* [1924] AC 431, 457.

provide indemnity.[35] In *Coven SpA v Hong Kong Chinese Insurance Co*,[36] the assured attempted to overcome this principle with a definition it suggested for 'shortage of content'. Accordingly, 'shortage' meant shortage on outturn as compared to the subject matter insured as described in the policy. The Bill of Lading described the cargo as 3,000 bags of Chinese broad beans in bulk said to weigh 2,787.209 mt. The cargo discharged was 2,401.581 mt. The assured also differentiated 'shortage' from 'loss' in that the former looked to how much there ought to be, whereas the word 'loss' looked to how much there was to start with. Thus, there may be (and was here) a shortage (i.e. a deficiency compared to what ought to have been delivered) even if some of the goods never existed in the first place. From the assured's point of view, a shortage caused by measurement error (a paper shortage) was just as much a shortage as any other. The assured paid a price for goods which it never received and paid a premium to insure those goods against a shortage in weight which was calculated by reference to the quantity declared.

The court, however, described the circumstance as a measurement error which was not insured under the policy 'covering all risks of loss and damage to the subject matter insured including shortage in weight but subject to an excess of one per cent of the whole shipment'. Clarke LJ said the expression 'loss … including shortage of weight' was one type of loss. What was covered was a loss of or shortage in weight as against the weight which the goods had when the adventure began. It did not mean that there was to be cover for shortage in weight which was not a physical loss. That appeared from the word 'including'.

In *Englehart* the insurer agreed to provide cover for 'shortage of contents (meaning thereby the difference between the number of packages as per shippers … invoice … and the count of packages removed therefrom by the Assured … at time of container emptying) notwithstanding that seals may appear intact'.

The judge dismissed the assured's contention that this clause supported its claim. The words 'notwithstanding that seals may appear intact' meant that even though the seals appeared to be intact, it was still open to the assured to establish under the clause that there was a shortage in the form of a physical loss.

6. Fraudulent Document Clause

The standard policy wordings vary from time to time considering the market developments and needs for insurance and how they can be accommodated by the insurers. In *Chemical Bank v Affiliated FM Ins Co*,[37] a 'special' clause which did not appear in many other cases mentioned above enabled a recovery for the loss caused by purported shipments of non-existent coffee. Although the policy described 'Goods Insured' as 'all lawful goods and merchandises consisting

[35] *Phoenix Insurance Co v De Monchy* (1929) 34 Ll L Rep 201.
[36] [1999] CLC 223.
[37] 815 F Supp 115, 118 (SDNY 1993).

principally of coffee', a 'Special Condition' was held to be broad enough to provide a more extensive cover than PLOD only. The clause provided that: 'This policy covers loss or damage occasioned through the acceptance by the Assured and/or their agents or shippers of fraudulent Bills of Lading and/or shipping receipts and/or messenger receipts.'

Different formulations of the fraudulent document clause are in use, and the wording is not always as generous as in *Chemical Bank* above which was distinguished in *Centennial Ins Co v Lithotech Sales, LLC.*[38] The policy in *Centennial* insured 'new and refurbished printing presses' against 'all risks of physical loss or damage from any external cause'. The insurance cover was provided for 'loss of or damage to *the property* insured occasioned through the acceptance by the Insured or Insured's agent or customers or consignees or others of Fraudulent Bills of Lading or Shipping Receipts' (emphasis added).

The assured argued that the press it received was severely worn, rusted and fire-damaged, and the bill of lading was drafted inaccurately with the specific intent to deceive. The clause clearly restricted the coverage to direct losses to the insured property requiring the assured to show that (1) the insured property was lost or damaged; (2) the bill of lading was fraudulent; and (3) the loss or damage was caused by the fraudulent bill's acceptance. The court found no evidence that this damage occurred because of any inaccuracies much less any fraud in the bill of lading. The deficiencies in the press pre-existed the issuance of the bill of lading.

The policy in *Englehart*, in which none of the interpretive attempts of the assured was persuasive enough to confirm the policy coverage, had a clause worded similarly. It covered 'physical loss of or damage to goods and/or merchandise insured hereunder through the acceptance by the Assured and/or Shippers of fraudulent documents of title'. Not surprisingly, this clause did not alter the 'all-risks' policy whose scope was limited to PLOD to the subject matter insured. The claimant's losses were economic losses due to the acceptance of fraudulent documents in the expectation that they represented physical goods.

Fraudulent documents clause was inserted in the cargo insurance policies in the aftermath of the salad oil swindle.[39] The acronym FBOL was used to express 'fraudulent bills of lading' where the policy provided cover for 'loss or damage occasioned through the acceptance by the assured and/or their agents or shippers of fraudulent Bills of Lading'. However, a circular by the Joint Cargo Committee, dated 14 January 1983, advised the underwriters in London not to agree to include FBOL clause in their contract. The committee found it undesirable, potentially very dangerous and one which was strongly deprecated by the Joint cargo Committee. The circular added that such cover could have the effect of

[38] 187 F Supp 2d 214 (DNJ 2001).

[39] See J Dunt, 'To What Extent Should Marine Cargo Insurance be Construed to Include Cover for Financial Loss?' ch 6 in *Research Handbook on Marine Insurance Law*, O Gurses (ed) (Cheltenham, Edward Elgar, 2024); *Scarburgh Co v American Manufacturers Mutual Insurance* 107 Misc 2d 772 (NY Sup Ct 1979).

committing underwriters to financial losses unrelated to any maritime perils and where no cargo of any nature exists.[40] As seen above, many fraudulent document clauses provide very restricted cover by requiring PLOD caused by acceptance of a document as such leading to the conclusion that having a fraudulent document clause adds nothing to the 'all-risks' cover if both require PLOD for the assured to recover.

As recently confirmed in *Chubb Insurance Singapore Ltd v Sizer Metals Pte Ltd*,[41] a theft of existing cargo is a fortuity and will be covered under an 'all-risks' policy. If such theft occurred through issuance of fraudulent documents,[42] that would also be covered under an all-risks policy in the absence of a fraudulent document clause.[43] Where a fraudulent document clause requires PLOD to the cargo, it makes no difference to an 'all-risks' policy. However, where the policy lists every insured risk individually, a fraudulent document clause will be an addition to the risks insured against. Instead of having a special clause, 'PLOD caused by acceptance of a fraudulent document' could be added to the risks insured against. The theft here would not be a pure economic loss given the existence of the cargo stolen. Depending on the interpretation of the whole policy, the absence of the PLOD wording may mean that a pure economic loss caused by accepting a fraudulent document falls under the insurance cover. Perhaps for that reason, the parties prefer to add a special fraudulent documents clause, including PLOD in its detailed wording.

The market conditions influence the parties' bargaining power and therefore the policy terms. It was observed in around 2017 that, in the soft market environment, the insurers agreed to waive the assureds' breach of the duty of fair presentation of the risk. Similarly, in *ABN Amro Bank v Royal & Sun Alliance*,[44] Jacob J noted that the insurers agreed to insure non-physical loss or damage at a time when there was overcapacity, with underwriters straining to attract and retain business. In *ABN Amro*, the fraudulent documentation clause added to the policy because of the widely known Qingdao fraud provided:

> 17.2
>
> If as a result of a Document being stolen, lost and/or misappropriated and such document is fraudulently converted such that the Insured suffers physical loss of the related subject matter insured, or the impairment of its interests in the subject matter insured, such a loss shall be recoverable hereunder.

[40] *Chemical Bank v Affiliated FM Ins Co*, 815 F Supp 115, 118 (SDNY 1993).

[41] [2023] SGHC(A) 17.

[42] *Australia & New Zealand Bank Ltd v Colonial & Eagle Wharves Ltd* [1960] 2 Lloyd's Rep 241 the goods were obtained by their importer through fraudulent documents. McNair J rejected the insurer's argument that no physical damage has been suffered by the goods.

[43] J Dunt, 'Can Marine Cargo Insurance Provide Cover for Non-existent Goods?' (2018) *LMCLQ* 465, 470.

[44] [2021] EWHC 442 (Comm). The case was appealed but the signing down issue was not discussed on appeal: [2021] EWCA Civ 1789.

> 17.3
>
> The Insured is indemnified by the Underwriters for the direct financial loss suffered by the Insured including by reason of the impairment of the Insured's interest in the subject matter insured arising by reason of the Insured, either in good faith during the period and in the ordinary course of business acting or relying upon or being supplied with a 'counterfeit document' of 'fraudulently altered document' (as defined below).

Jacob J was persuaded that 'impairment of its interests in the subject matter insured' reflected insurance of non-PLOD risks. Dunt, however, disagrees that the insurable interest covered by a marine cargo policy in the usual form, is property, that is, goods or merchandise.[45] As Clause 17.2 only applies to 'physical loss' or where the 'subject matter insured' is 'impaired', the normal construction, in light of the authorities, is that there must be existing cargo.[46] The wording of Clause 17.3 is, however, not confined to physical loss as it covers 'direct financial loss suffered by reason of the impairment of the Insured's interest in the subject matter insured'.

7. Misappropriation

'Misappropriation' where expressly stated as one of the risks insured against, would include circumstances of where the cargo was delivered to third parties in the absence of the assured's knowledge. The existence of the cargo at the outset is, once again, essential. In *Glencore International AG v Alpina Insurance Co Ltd*,[47] MTI had operated a floating oil storage facility and bunker supply business using a number of vessels anchored in the waters off Fujairah. A number of different oil companies, including Glencore, entered into agreements with MTI under which they delivered oil products to MTI for storage; in some cases, they also sold oil held in store to MTI for use in its bunker supply business. MTI collapsed in February 1998 and thereafter Glencore discovered that the quantity of oil held in the floating storage facility was far smaller than ought to have been the case. During 1997 and the early weeks of 1998 MTI misappropriated large quantities of oil that it was holding in store for Glencore. Some cargoes carried under bills of lading made out to the order of Glencore were diverted by MTI to other destinations without authority. The judge rejected the argument that Glencore was seeking to recover from the insurer in respect of a 'credit risk'. Once Glencore suffered loss by misappropriation, it was not possible for the goods to be returned to Glencore by MTI either by paying damages or by paying the price of the goods themselves. There was a loss in transit when the cargoes were wrongfully diverted and did not enter the storage facility.

[45] Dunt (n 39). See also *Quadra Commodities SA v XL insurance Company SE* [2022] EWHC 431 Comm [64]–[65].
[46] Dunt (n 39).
[47] [2004] 1 Lloyd's Rep 111.

In its report in April 2023, Deutsche Bank once again underlined the importance of physical checks.[48] This included vessel tracking, whereby the bank checks where the cargo being financed is currently located, where it is coming from and where it is going. The report suggested that within the commodity space, Deutsche Bank – or a reputable third-party surveyor – also visit warehouses to confirm that the cargo is stored there. However, as observed in *Quadra Commodities SA v XL Insurance Co SE*,[49] such steps, although seen as precautions, would not suffice to stop the fraudsters, or catch them before it is too late.

The assured in *Quadra* was defrauded by the sellers in Ukraine who issued multiple versions of warehouse receipts for the same parcel of goods. The scheme was known as the 'Agroinvestgroup Fraud', which affected the Ukrainian agribusiness, and came to light in early 2019. Quadra made a number of purchases of Ukrainian corn from Agri Finance on Delivered at Terminal (DAT) sea trade port, Ukraine at the buyer's option, Incoterms-2010. The title of ownership for the commodity was transferred from the seller to the buyer at the moment when the commodity was accepted at the place of delivery.

Quadra instructed an inspection company called Bastico Ukraine Ltd (Bastico) to conduct monthly stock monitoring services at each of the Zaplazsky, Bilgorod and Izmail Elevators for which Quadra had been issued warehouse receipts. This entailed an inspection of the Elevator's documents and a visual inspection of the stock present. Reports issued by Bastico confirmed that corn was stored at the Elevators. About two weeks after these reports were issued, on 30 January 2019, Bastico inspectors attended each of the three Elevators to inspect their documents and conduct a visual assessment and measurement of the stock present. Access to each of the Elevators was denied. Around 15 February 2019, Quadra's lawyers were unable to enter the grounds, and found the warehouses sealed by the Ukrainian security services. In March 2019, Quadra commenced legal proceedings before the Odessa Commercial Court for delivery of the cargo. Agri Finance was placed into liquidation and dissolved.

Upon Quadra's claim, the cargo insurers argued that they insured PLOD to the cargo whereas the loss claimed was purely financial. As different to many other cases mentioned in this chapter, the court was satisfied from the warehouse receipts that the goods that Bastico inspected had been stored at the Elevators. Although they were sold at least 18 times to different buyers, their physical existence at a time in the Elevators was sufficient to hold that they were misappropriated which was one of the risks insured against.[50] It was integral, in the view of the court, that in a fraud as such, there should have been grain in the warehouses to enable their inspection on behalf of traders. This gave rise to an actual

[48] 'Fighting Trade-related Fraud' (*flow*, 19 April 2023) flow.db.com/trade-finance/fighting-trade-related-fraud.

[49] [2023] EWCA Civ 432.

[50] [2022] EWHC 431 (Comm); approved by the Court of Appeal [2023] EWCA Civ 432.

total loss in respect of the cargoes, in that Quadra had been irretrievably deprived of them at the time of the commencement of these proceedings in May 2020.[51]

The fraudulent document clause requiring PLOD through the acceptance by the assured of fraudulent documents was included in the policy. The trial judge held in *Quadra*[52] that if there had been no relevant goods before Quadra received the warehouse receipts, they were not lost by acceptance of those receipts. If there had been relevant goods, the acceptance of the receipts could not be said to have caused their physical loss.[53]

8. Insurable Interest

The difficulties faced by the assured who claims against the insurer for an economic loss in the absence of a cargo may include an argument challenging the assured's insurable interest in the non-existent cargo. In *Coven SpA v Hong Kong Chinese Insurance Co*,[54] Clarke LJ stated: 'A further point which militates against Coven's claim is that it is difficult, if not impossible, to see how the insured could have an insurable interest in the subject matter of the insurance within the meaning of cl. 11.1 of the Institute Clauses[55] in respect of the 385.6 mt of beans which never existed.'

The MIA 1906, s 6(1) states: 'The assured must be interested in the subject-matter insured at the time of the loss though he need not be interested when the insurance is effected.' At the time of the loss, the assured must prove the loss and its amount. The issue, therefore, could be approached from two related angles: insurable interest and the principle of indemnity.

The principle of indemnity is, in the words of Bowen LJ:[56] 'Only those can recover who have an insurable interest, and they can recover only to the extent to which that insurable interest is damaged by the loss.'

There is no precise definition of insurable interest[57] although it has been required statutorily since 1745.[58] The MIA 1906, s 5(2) states:

> In particular a person is interested in a marine adventure where he stands in any legal or equitable relation to the adventure or to any insurable property at risk therein, in

[51] ibid [112].

[52] ibid. This point was not appealed in [2023] EWCA Civ 432.

[53] [2022] EWHC 431 (Comm) [119].

[54] *Coven SpA v Hong Kong Chinese Insurance Co* [1999] CLC 223, 227.

[55] Cl 11.1 of the Institute Commodity Trade Clauses (A) provided: 'In order to recover under this insurance the Assured must have an insurable interest in the subject-matter insured at the time of the loss.' ICC 2009 (A) has cl 11.1 the wording of which is identical.

[56] *Castellain v Preston* (1883) 11 QBD 380, 397.

[57] *Quadra Commodities SA v XL Insurance Co SE* [2022] EWHC 431 (Comm) [54].

[58] Marine Insurance Act 1745 19 Geo 2 c 37. The Marine Insurance Act 1906 repealed the 1745 Act and replaced the insurable interest requirement under its s 5. For a thorough assessment of insurable interest, see F Arnould-Dwyer, *Insurable Interest and the Law*, 1st edn (Oxford, Routledge, 2020).

> consequence of which he may benefit by the safety or due arrival of insurable property, or may be prejudiced by its loss, or by damage thereto, or by the detention thereof, or may incur liability in respect thereof.

The above is not exhaustive,[59] rather it is general guidance indicating what to look for to find if the assured has an insurable interest in the subject matter insured. The interest may be proprietary, but it does not have to be. The MIA 1906, s 5(2) expresses a broad concept of insurable interest.[60] A mortgagee can insure its interest (the loan) in the mortgaged ship, a tenant may insure the property rented, a bailee may insure its interest in the goods which is under its care.

The courts have found it difficult to provide a definition which will match all situations.[61] However, they have identified some elements to guide through an exercise to confirm insurable interest that:[62]

(i) the assured may benefit by the safety or due arrival of the insured property or be prejudiced by its loss or damage or detention, or in respect of which he may incur a liability;
(ii) the assured stands in a legal or equitable relation to the adventure or to any insurable interest in such adventure; and
(iii) the benefit, prejudice or incurring of liability must arise in consequence of the legal or equitable relation of the assured to the property or adventure.

The assured's insurable interest is inevitably linked with the subject matter insured. Therefore, the scope of the insuring clause can be fundamental to approve the assured's interest in it. If the subject matter insured is the goods, and the goods never existed, there will be neither a loss of the subject matter insured, nor a time for the loss to attach.

The courts also unanimously of the view that in confirming insurable interest the context and the terms of a policy with which the court is concerned will be all-important.[63] It follows that whether a policy embraces the insurable interest intended to be covered is a question of construction. *Wilson v Jones*[64] is a typical example of the significance of the insuring clause on this matter. In this case a joint-stock company undertook the project that would lay down a line of cable

[59] *Quadra Commodities SA v XL Insurance Co SE* [2022] EWHC 431 (Comm) [56], [2023] EWCA Civ 432.

[60] See, eg *Hepburn v A Tomlinson (Hauliers) Ltd* [1966] AC 451, 477 and 481, Lord Pearce; *O'Kane v Jones (The Martin P)* [2004] 1 Lloyd's Rep 389, 419; *Commonwealth v Imperial* (1977) 69 DLR (3d) 558; *Petrofina* (UK) *Ltd v Magnaload Ltd* [1984] QB 127; *National Oilwell* [1993] 2 Lloyd's Rep 582; *Deepak Fertilisers & Petrochemicals Corp Ltd v Davy McKee (London) Ltd* [1999] 1 Lloyd's Rep 387; *Stone Vickers Ltd v Appledore Ferguson Shipbuilders Ltd* [1991] 2 Lloyd's Rep 288. The appeal in *Stone Vickers* was allowed on other grounds, and the Court of Appeal therefore did not discuss the insurable interest issue [1992] 2 Lloyd's Rep 578, 585.

[61] *Feasey v Sun Life Assurance Co of Canada* [2003] Lloyd's Rep IR 637 [66].

[62] *Quadra Commodities SA v XL Insurance Co SE* [2022] EWHC 431 (Comm) [56].

[63] *Feasey v Sun Life Assurance Co of Canada* [2003] Lloyd's Rep IR 637 [66]; *The Moonacre* [1992] 2 Lloyd's Rep 501.

[64] (1866–67) LR 2 Ex 139.

for 2,000 miles over the bottom of the sea. The marine policy stated 'it is hereby understood and agreed that the policy, in addition to all perils and casualties herein specified, shall cover every risk and contingency attending the conveyance and successful laying of the cable'.

The assured shareholder had no direct interest in the cable. Later, in *Macaura v Northern Assurance Company Ltd*,[65] it was held that a shareholder had no interest in the subject matter insured owned by the company. Although *Wilson v Jones* looks similar, the difference there was that the insurance was not on the cable but on the interest which the assured had in the success of the adventure. The policy covered 'every risk and contingency attending the conveyance and successful laying of the cable'.[66]

It can further be argued that the English courts have not been in favour of a restricted interpretation of insurable interest.[67] In *Cepheus Shipping Corp v Guardian Royal Exchange Assurance Plc (The Capricorn)*[68] Mance J stated: 'If underwriters make a contract in deliberate terms which covers their assured in respect of a specific situation, a Court is likely to hesitate before accepting a defence of lack of insurable interest.'

In *Quadra Commodities SA v XL Insurance Co SE*, in his analysis of insurable interest, Butcher J[69] at first instance – upheld by the Court of Appeal[70] – took the insuring clause as his starting point: The goods were insured under the marine cargo policy and Quadra had insurable interest in the goods through its 'legal or equitable relation' to them. The judge took into consideration that at the time of the fraudulent warehouse receipts were issued, they were stored in the Elevators in Ukraine. Although the goods were unascertained, Quadra had paid for them. Butcher J was satisfied that even though there were competing interests in the goods, Quadra might benefit from the safety of that property or be prejudiced by its loss; and that benefit or prejudice arose in consequence of the contracts it had entered into and paid under.[71]

[65] [1925] AC 619. In *Kosmopoulos v Constitution Insurance C*, [1987] 1 SCR 2, Supreme Court of Canada held that Macaura should no longer be followed. The Court was of the view that the policies underlying the requirement of insurable interest generally did not require the restrictive approach to insurable interest reflected in *Macaura*. Instead, if an insured can demonstrate 'some relation to, or concern in the subject of the insurance, which relation or concern by the happening of the perils insured against may be so affected as to produce a damage, detriment, or prejudice to the person insuring', that insured should be held to have a sufficient interest.

[66] Here *Macaura v Northern Assurance Company*, Ltd [1925] AC 619 was to be distinguished, given that the subject matter insured was the property itself only, the 'timber' and a shareholder was held not to have had insurable interest in the timber which was owned by the company. Similarly, in *Sharp v Sphere Drake Insurance* (*The Moonacre*), Mr S insured the boat in his own name although the boat belonged to the company. Mr S had an insurable interest as, due to two powers of attorney, he had wide authority to enjoy and use the boat exclusively for his own purposes.

[67] *Feasey v Sun Life Assurance Co of Canada* [2003] Lloyd's Rep IR 637.

[68] [1995] 1 Lloyd's Rep 622.

[69] [2022] EWHC 431 (Comm).

[70] [2023] EWCA Civ 432.

[71] [2022] EWHC 431 (Comm) [81].

In contesting the assured's insurable interest, the insurers asserted that the cargo did not form part of a bulk which was sufficiently identified. Sir Julian Flaux C,[72] however, found this ground fundamentally unsound. It sought to impose on the relationship of assured and insurer an additional requirement beyond any authorities. Under the Sale of Goods Act 1979[73] for the buyer to obtain proprietary interest, the good must be ascertained. Sir Julian Flaux J held that for the assured to have insurable interest in goods, such an ascertainment is not a precondition. The concept of an insurable interest as between assured and insurer must not be confused with that of a proprietary interest as between buyer and seller. An insured can have an insurable interest in goods even though it has no proprietary interest.[74]

In *Quadra* Butcher J found *Cumberland Bone Company v Andes Insurance Co*[75] a persuasive authority and Sir Julian Flaux C held at the Court of Appeal that the principle established by *Cumberland Bone* should now be recognised as a principle of English law.[76] In *Cumberland Bone* the claimant had agreed to buy fish scrap from a seller, and advanced the price, but had left them in storage with the seller, unsegregated from other stock belonging to the seller. The Supreme Judicial Court of Maine held that the claimant had insurable interest in the goods although the property and risk in the goods remained with the seller. The court reiterated that it was not necessary for the claimant to hold a legal title to the property upon which the insurance is affected. Damage to the subject matter insured may prejudice either the concern the assured had in the subject matter insured or the relation to it.

It appears from *Cumberland Bone* and *Inglis v Stock* that even if property and risk have not passed, payment or part payment of the price will give the buyer an insurable interest. *Cumberland Bone* also took the interpretation of insurable interest a step further than *Inglis v Stock*[77] where the House of Lords found insurable interest in favour of the assured buyer for whom two parcels of sugar shipped on the *City of Dublin*. There were other goods on board and appropriation would take place upon arrival in England. The buyer was held to have an insurable interest because the goods were shipped at his risk. Lord Blackburn[78] said:

> I am quite unable to perceive why an undivided interest in a parcel of goods on board a ship may not be described as an interest in goods just as much as if it were an interest in every portion of the goods.

[72] [2023] EWCA Civ 432 [121].
[73] Under the Sale of Goods Act 1979, s 16: 'Subject to section 20A below, where there is a contract for the sale of unascertained goods no property in the goods is transferred to the buyer unless and until the goods are ascertained.'
[74] [2023] EWCA Civ 432 [122].
[75] 64 Me 466 (1874).
[76] [2023] EWCA Civ 432 [125].
[77] (1885) 10 App Cas 263.
[78] (1885) 10 App Cas 263, 274.

In *Quadra* no title had yet passed to the buyer when the cargo was in the Elevators as the delivery was to take place at the seaport. However, this did not prevent a ruling in Quadra's favour. The insured in *Cumberland Bone* would have been prejudiced by the loss of the fish scrap, in that if the seller had been insolvent, the assured might not have been able to recover the money he paid for it. The insured stood in a legal or equitable relation to the insurable property since it had purchased it pursuant to a sale contract and paid for it. Accordingly, any prejudice it suffered through the loss of the fish scrap arose because of that legal or equitable relation to the property. Similarly, Quadra's immediate right to possession of goods under the warehouse receipts gave rise to an insurable interest in them.[79]

9. Sue and Labour and Damages for Late Payment

When a claim is based on a fraud, investigating fraud may be a costly and lengthy exercise. The two more issues relevant to the assured's claim when fraud led to the assured's loss are the expenses that the assured incurred to prevent or minimise the loss and damages that the assured might be entitled to in case the insurer delays in indemnifying the assured's loss. The assured's claim for the former will firstly be subject to an express policy term.[80] The absence of such term, known as sue and labour clause, would mean that there is no right to recover such expenses from the insurer.[81] Secondly, the expenses must be incurred to prevent or minimise an insured risk. If the insurer agreed to cover PLOD to the cargo only, and if the expenses incurred to prevent or minimise a pure economic loss, the expenses do not fall under the sue and labour clause. The assured's recovery is not subject to its success in the attempt to prevent or minimise the loss. However, the expenses must be incurred when the danger of the risk to occur is imminent and the expenditure must be reasonable.[82] In *Quadra* the assured's loss was held to be not purely economic, it was covered under the policy for misappropriation, and the expenses incurred in the form of issuing legal notices and proceedings against the Elevators in Ukraine was recoverable. The only issue was for the assured proving that they were 'properly and reasonably incurred'.

After the addition of s 13A to the Insurance Act 2015 (IA 2015), it is open to the assured to claim damages for late payment against the insurers. It is an implied term of every contract of insurance under s 13A(1) that the insurer must pay any sums due in respect of the assured's claim within a reasonable time. Having received a claim under an insurance policy, the insurer's first step will be investigating the

[79] [2022] EWHC 431 (Comm) [88].
[80] MIA 1906, s 78.
[81] *Yorkshire Water v Sun Alliance & London Insurance* [1997] CLC 213.
[82] *Integrated Container Service v British Traders Insurance Co* [1984] 1 Lloyd's Rep 154; *Royal Boskalis Westminster v Mountain* [1997] LRLR 523.

facts to find out how the loss occurred. This is a factual investigation, and it may be lengthy especially where transnational fraud is involved. In *Quadra*, the assured notified the insurer of the loss on 14 February 2019. Proceedings against the insurers were commenced on 20 May 2020. Quadra argued that the insurer breached s 13A and therefore claimed damages for late payment. *Quadra* is significant for being the first case that applied s 13A to a claim.

Remedies (for example, damages) available for breach of the term implied by s 13A(1) are in addition to and distinct from any right to enforce payment of the sums due, and any right to interest on those sums (whether under the contract, under another enactment, at the court's discretion or otherwise).[83]

The assured bears the burden of proving that the insurer failed to make a payment under the insurance contract within a reasonable time. What is reasonable will depend on all the relevant circumstances examples of things which may need to be taken into account include the type of insurance, the size and complexity of the claim, compliance with any relevant statutory or regulatory rules or guidance, and factors outside the insurer's control.[84]

The insurer's investigation would include whether the assured's claim is supported under the terms of the policy. If so, then the insurer will determine the amount payable to the assured. If the insurer shows that there were reasonable grounds for disputing the claim, the insurer does not breach the term implied by s 13A(1) merely by failing to pay the claim while the dispute is continuing.[85]

Butcher J held that the fact that the insurers' actual conduct of the claims handling can be said to have been too slow does not naturally lead to the conclusion that the insurer failed to act within a reasonable time. The judge held that the claim was complicated by its location as the transactions involved many different countries and locations and claims under such a cover could involve various factual patterns. The size of the claim, about US$5.7 million, was substantial but not exceptional in the context of marine cargo insurance. The factors that were outside the insurers' control, such as the destruction and unavailability of evidence as to what had happened at the Elevators, necessarily lengthen the time to investigate the claim. Between the assured served its notice of loss and brough proceedings against the insurer there was about a year which, Butcher J found, was reasonable.

10. Concluding Thoughts

Whether a loss falls under the insurance contract is determined, among many other points, through the interpretation of the insuring clause under the 'objectivity principle'. Parties can only try to predict at the outset of the contract what risks might happen during the currency of the policy. When the assured suffers a loss, the way

[83] IA 2015, s 13A(5).
[84] ibid s 13A(3).
[85] ibid s 13A(4).

that the loss took place is compared with what was agreed in the insurance contract. Insurance disputes arise mostly when there is a mismatch between these two.

In the exercise of interpreting policy terms to find out their true meaning for the parties objectively, terms must not be considered in isolation from the overall structure and purpose of the policy.[86] The editors of Arnould suggest that[87] 'it has always been realised that a less meticulous regard for the strict meaning of the words used is desirable in the construction of commercial documents, such as policies of insurance'. The above cases, however, appear to have followed a more assiduous approach than the one expressed as desired by the editors whose view is likely to be shared by many.

It is hardly ever the case that an insurance contract term is tested on the ground of 'unfairness'. The Unfair Contract Terms Act 1977 does not apply to insurance contracts.[88] The justification for this exclusion is that many policy conditions are concerned with the risk run by the insurer, so that any attempt to regulate those terms would be to rewrite the basis on which the premium had been set by the insurer.[89] The Consumer Rights Act 2015 applies to most forms of consumer contracts, including insurance. However, under s 64, the main subject matter of the contract or terms that set the price (i.e., core terms) are exempt from the test of fairness if they are 'transparent and prominent'. To satisfy the transparency requirement, the term must be in plain and intelligible language. To be prominent, the term must be brought to the consumer's attention in such a way that the average consumer (who is assumed to be well informed, observant, and circumspect) would be aware of the term. The fact that a core term does not meet these requirements does not make it automatically unfair, but it exposes that term to additional scrutiny.

From the insurer's point of view, one of the reasons they are reluctant to provide cover for cargo whose existence cannot be proven is that their exposure to the risk would be unlimited: the insurer's liability is normally limited by reference to the value of existing cargo, in the absence of which there is no value to set such a limit.[90] This does not mean, however, that the insurer's liability cannot be limited in the case of insurance of a paper loss.[91] It is always open to the insurer to insert a policy limit with the aggregation wording appropriate and applicable to the nature of the loss. The issue is, whether a loss, in the absence of PLOD, is covered under the insurance contract, and if covered, how will the assured prove the loss actually suffered?

In the words of Clarke LJ in *Coven*, accepting that the policy covers a paper loss where the wording does not expressly provide so, would be transforming the insurance policy.[92] The risk involved would be nothing like the ordinary insurance

[86] *Financial Conduct Authority v Arch Insurance (UK) Ltd* [2021] UKSC 1.
[87] See [3-27].
[88] See Sch 1, para 1(a).
[89] Merkin, *Colinvaux's Law of Insurance* [3-008].
[90] Dunt (n 40).
[91] *ABN Amro Bank v Royal & Sun Alliance* [2021] EWCA Civ 1789.
[92] The court rejected the assured's claim for the same reason in *Outokumpu Stainless Limited v Axa Global Risks (UK) Limited* [2007] EWHC 2555 (Comm).

risks of something untoward happening to the goods on the voyage. In an all-risks policy, as long as the goods existed at the outset, theft through a fraud would be a fortuitous event. However, the key is the actual physical loss of the cargo.

As noted most recently in *TKC London Limited v Allianz Insurance Plc*,[93] it is most unlikely that the assured, whether business or consumer, would know the specialist insurance law principles included in this chapter. Nevertheless, their insurance contract will be subject to those principles, irrespective of whether the outcome of a dispute is, by some, found unfair for the assured. The parties' reasonable expectations at the outset of the contract might be included in the considerations that led through the interpretation of the policy terms. However, this has been observed very rarely by the English courts.[94]

As stated by Mr Salter QC,[95] the overwhelming considerations are 'the law must provide a solid, practical and predictable foundation for the resolution of disputes and the confidence necessary for an eventual recovery. … Contractual rights are to be evaluated by applying settled principles to the contract in question. Legal certainty remains paramount and gives the surest basis for resolution'.

What is the best way for the assured to deal with its insurance transactions where, no doubt, the assured may be exposed to fraud.? A clear-cut answer to this question seems to be as impossible as to predict accurately what risks may occur and in what form in the currency of the insurance policy. Although fraudsters might always be a step ahead of their victims, taking measures aiming to prevent fraud as much as possible is obviously an option to the assured cargo owner. Although the assured cannot be expected to understand the policy terms as much as an insurance expert, the more the assured has a grip on them, the more it can protect its interests. Moreover, the assured is likely to seek help from a broker in insuring the commodities. If the broker is negligent and fails to obtain the cover that the assured wished to have, there might be room to claim damages against the broker.[96] This point aside, the assured must be clear in its instructions to the broker in terms of the assured's insurance needs. A continuing communication with the broker aiming to understand the details of the insurance cover would help the assured achieving the cover the assured desired.

The meaning and significance of the words 'all risks' and the fraudulent document clause appear to be well settled. Selecting the wording that suits the assured's interest best will be the duty of the assured's broker. When the matter will ultimately be resolved through the interpretation of the policy wording, there might be room to argue against the settled meaning of the words, in the context. This will be down to the legal experts, and it remains to be seen to what extent the context will be taken into account by the court.

[93] [2020] Lloyd's Rep IR 631 [105].

[94] *Financial Conduct Authority v Arch Insurance (UK) Ltd* [2021] UKSC 1.

[95] See *TKC London Limited v Allianz Insurance Plc* [2020] Lloyd's Rep IR 631 [134], in reference to Blair, Lein, Gullifer and Fu, '"Breathing space", BIICL Concept Note 2 on the Effect of the 2020 Pandemic on Commercial Contracts' (British Institute of International and Comparative Law, May 2020) [68]–[69].

[96] *Dunlop Haywards (DHL) Ltd v Barbon Insurance Group Ltd* [2010] Lloyd's Rep IR 149.

13

Preventing Fraud on Bank Customers and Creditors

HANS TJIO*

1. Modern-day Fraud

Fraud today is different for a number of reasons. First, much of it is linked to technology. This has facilitated greater anonymity and automation in facilitating fraud. At the same time, the enhanced security of systems today, whether financial or proprietary, even if not absolute, means that, as Low has pointed out,[1] fraud will be at the end user level. This will be the focus of the first part of this chapter.

But regulatory changes have also meant that what may not have been seen as fraudulent once is now so, and vice versa. Money laundering and terrorism financing are the clearest examples of the former. Know-your-client rules are expected not just of banks but also solicitors and even real estate agents who are in a difficult position as facilitators given their lower-level involvement. Conversely, what may have been seen once as financial fraud is no longer so and this will form another focal point for this chapter. Many Commonwealth corporate law rules have been liberalised before the altar of shareholder primacy since the 1980s,[2] and this has impacted not just the corporation and its directors but also private law, especially in its effects on shareholders and third parties dealing with corporations. But the factual matrices are not that different in that the parties are the same: there is a victim, primary wrongdoer and facilitator. What has changed, however, is the *roles* that the parties play in the fraud: whilst in the past, the victim and primary wrongdoer were often connected and there would have been a relational breach that a facilitator assisted in, today, it is more likely that the victim and facilitator are linked, and we may thus expect the latter to do more to protect the former.

* I would like to thank Kanaga Dharmananda, Lan Luh Luh, Chua Rui Yuan, Walter Wan and participants at Fraud and Risk in Commercial Law Conference held in June 2023 at the NUS Faculty of Law for their invaluable comments.

[1] K F K Low, 'Confronting Cryptomania: Can Equity Tame the Blockchain?' (2020) 14 *Journal of Equity* 240, 256.

[2] R J Rhee, 'The Neoliberal Corporate Purpose of Dodge v. Ford and Shareholder Primacy: A Historical Context 1919–2019' (2023) 28 *Stanford Journal of Law, Business, and Finance* 202.

2. *Selangor Rubber Estates*: Financial and Dishonest Assistance

The case that evidences these temporal changes most clearly is *Selangor United Rubber Estates Ltd v Craddock (No 3)*[3] ('*Selangor*'). Here, District Bank was found to have knowingly assisted a breach of trust by the directors of the plaintiff company, who had used the company's funds to provide financial assistance to Craddock to purchase 79% of the plaintiff company's shares in a takeover. In a roundabout way, company money was paid by cheques drawn on the bank to WT Ltd who borrowed the money at 8% and then lent the money to Craddock at a 1% premium. As a result of Craddock having disappeared with the loan outstanding, successful claims were brought against the directors of the plaintiff company for breach of fiduciary duty, as well as against WT Ltd and the bank for dishonest assistance of those breaches, with the latter also said to be negligent in handling the plaintiff company's accounts by paying the money to WT Ltd without inquiry.

The concerns about fraudulent takeovers of cash-rich companies in the 1960s and 1970s[4] gave way to LBOs and MBOs in the 1980s with the belief that the market for corporate control would improve corporate governance.[5] There was growing faith in shareholder primacy which led to regulatory changes to permit takeovers where the bidder did not have its own resources. While the requirements of dishonest assistance have evolved,[6] more important for present purposes is the fact that the foundational prohibition against a company giving financial assistance to a share purchaser – the contravention of which was what District Bank was held to have assisted in the *Selangor* case – no longer applies to private limited companies in the UK. This is the case in many countries now, with some relaxation intruding even into the sphere of public companies, which, in Singapore for example, are now merely subject to a material prejudice test that is also of general application in Australia.[7]

But private law always tries to find a way, and the other aspect of the bank's liability in *Selangor*, based on a duty of care on the part of the bank to its corporate customer in relation to the latter's bank account, has found a new lease of life. It was largely overlooked until recently, as the focus was on restitutionary and third-party

[3] *Selangor United Rubber Estates Ltd v Craddock (No 3)* [1968] 1 WLR 1555 (Ch).

[4] A Hudson, *The Law and Regulation of Finance*, 2nd edn (London, Sweet & Maxwell, 2013) [30–35].

[5] P L Davies, *Introduction to Company Law*, 3rd edn (Oxford, Clarendon Press, 2020) 107.

[6] In particular, the mental element, which has shifted over time from a form of notice to knowledge, then dishonesty, and now possibly back to knowledge again: *Group Seven Ltd v Nasir* [2019] 3 WLR 1011; see generally, P S Davies, 'The Mental Element of Accessory Liability in Equity' (2022) 138 *LQR* 32.

[7] Respectively Companies Act 1967 (Singapore), s 76(9)(BA); Corporations Act 2001 (Cth), s 260A.

claims in equity.[8] Steyn J (as he then was) in *Barclays Bank plc v Quincecare Ltd*[9] ('*Quincecare*') reformulated the relevant principle as follows:

> In my judgment the sensible compromise, which strikes a fair balance between competing considerations, is simply to say that a banker must refrain from executing an order if and for as long as the banker is 'put on inquiry' in the sense that he has reasonable grounds (although not necessarily proof) for believing that the order is an attempt to misappropriate the funds of the company ….

Even so, the now-termed *Quincecare* duty of care remained dormant for almost 30 years until 2017 when Rose J (as she then was) applied it in *Singularis Holdings Ltd (In Official Liquidation) v Daiwa Capital Markets Europe Ltd*[10] ('*Singularis*'). It was then quickly applied in *Federal Republic of Nigeria v JP Morgan Chase Bank, NA*[11] ('*Nigeria*') (where the bank was refused reverse summary judgment) and then *Roberts v Royal Bank of Scotland plc*[12] (where the action was time barred and the bank resultingly awarded reverse summary judgment, although the court thought it was not difficult for bank customers to plead a prima facie case in this context). However, these were still orthodox cases involving the bank being in substance an accessory to a breach of duty owed by the wrongdoer to the victim. This subsequently set the stage for the argument in *Philipp v Barclays Bank*[13] ('*Philipp*') that the duty could be extended to cases where the wrongdoer is independent from or unknown to the victim but has set up a scheme which has led to the victim's will being slightly overborne. This is important as the Court of Appeal in *Philipp* noted that authorised push payment fraud had been identified as the second most prevalent financial fraud after credit card fraud.[14]

3. *Philipp* and Return to Agency

In *Philipp*, a couple lost their life savings after instructing Barclays Bank to transfer money in their account to accounts of a petroleum company in the UAE.

[8] See, eg, C Hewetson and G Mitchell QC, *Banking Litigation*, 4th edn (London, Sweet & Maxwell, 2017) Ch 1 (Deposit-Taking Liability).

[9] *Barclays Bank plc v Quincecare Ltd* [1992] 4 All ER 363 (Comm), 376–77.

[10] *Singularis Holdings Ltd (In Official Liquidation) v Daiwa Capital Markets Europe Ltd* [2017] EWHC 257 (Ch), [2017] Bus LR 1386 whose decision was upheld on first appeal in *Singularis Holdings Ltd (in Liquidation) v Daiwa Capital Markets Europe Ltd* [2018] EWCA Civ 84, [2018] 1 WLR 2777, and then on final appeal in *Singularis Holdings Ltd (in Liquidation) v Daiwa Capital Markets Europe Ltd* [2019] UKSC 50, [2020] AC 1189.

[11] *Federal Republic of Nigeria v JP Morgan Chase Bank, NA* [2019] EWHC 347 (Comm), affirmed in *JPMorgan Chase Bank, NA v Federal Republic of Nigeria* [2019] EWCA Civ 1641.

[12] [2020] EWHC 3141 (Comm).

[13] [2022] EWCA Civ 318, [2022] QB 578; noted S Booysen 'Authorised Payment Scams and the Bank's Duty of Care' [2022] *LMCLQ* 349; P Watts 'Playing the Quincecare Card' (2022) 138 *LQR* 530; RY Chua, 'The Quincecare Duty: An Unnecessary Gloss?' [2023] *JBL* 161.

[14] *Philipp (CA)*, ibid. [15].

They were advised to do this by fraudsters who convinced them that they had to transfer the funds to safe accounts to avoid fraud and were, in fact, assisting FCA investigations by doing so. While the actual facts were in dispute, particularly as to whether the bank had warned the claimants about possible risks, the Court of Appeal reversed the decision of the first instance judge[15] who had struck out the plaintiffs' claim on the basis that they were individuals who were victims of external fraud that they authorised and not corporate customers defrauded by their own agents. The Court of Appeal traced the line of cases from *Selangor* to *Singularis* and acknowledged that they had lowered expected standards of care but felt that the duty was to protect the customer and not the bank. Consequently, there was no limitation of the duty to corporate claimants only and the bank possibly owed a duty of care to the individual claimants here.

Subsequently, on final appeal to the Supreme Court,[16] it was held that the obligation of inquiry under the so-called *Quincecare* duty arose only where a bank is put on notice that an agent of its customer may be acting dishonestly when providing instructions to the bank. There was, in substance, no material difference between this obligation to exercise reasonable skill and care to verify the authenticity of the instruction and the well-established obligation to clarify where the 'customer's instruction is patently ambiguous'.[17] As such, the Supreme Court restored the first instance decision holding that the duty applied only in the context of internal, and not external, fraud.[18]

One can discern a difference between the approaches of the Court of Appeal and Supreme Court. While the Court of Appeal recognised that the duty of care was likely co-extensive with an implied term in the banker-customer contract,[19] which required the bank to observe the customer's mandate, it looked also at the fact that banks are required to have anti-money laundering procedures in place in finding that a duty could exist.[20] In contrast, Lord Leggatt was at pains to stress that private law should not overreach into areas which are more suited to regulation.[21] As the difference in opinion between the intermediate and apex court demonstrates, the relationship between private law and regulation has never been easy. In the UK, in the trial of the *Nigeria* case,[22] it was held that the *Quincecare* duty required a bank to be put on inquiry that a specific payment instruction that had been impugned might be vitiated by fraud, and not merely 'fraud in broad terms' based on historical allegations of corruption and financial crime.[23] Thus, simply because there might have been 'plainly high-risk features for the

[15] [2021] EWHC 10 (Comm). See Chua (n 13), who points out that a duty of care to ignore the customer's instructions directly contradicts the bank mandate. It is better dealt with by agency and fiduciary principles in cases of internal fraud and external fraud respectively.
[16] [2023] UKSC 25, [2023] 3 WLR 284.
[17] ibid [90]–[91].
[18] See, generally, substantially the same argument made in Chua (n 13), 167–172.
[19] *Philipp (CA)* (n 14) [37]–[38].
[20] ibid [77]–[78].
[21] *Philipp (SC)* (n 16) [22]–[24].
[22] [2022] EWHC 1447 (Comm).
[23] ibid [346]–[347].

purposes of AML and financial crime and corruption generally' was 'plainly not enough' for the bank to be put on notice of a 'serious and obvious risk of a fraud' on a particular occasion.[24] It was also held that the terms and conditions there required gross negligence as they had modified the *Quincecare* duty. Hence, it is clear now that the duty is carefully calibrated and narrowly circumscribed,[25] as demonstrated by the requirement of specificity that the red flags alleged must relate to the particular transaction involving the customer. This was consistent with pushbacks even before the Supreme Court's decision in *Philipp* in attempts to keep open the existence or applicability of the duty as a question of law that provides a filter at an earlier stage.

4. Pushback

A recent Malaysian case shows that the *Quincecare* duty does not apply to moneys borrowed from the bank but only where the bank is 'custodian' even though in *Selangor* it was seen more as the liability of a paying bank.[26] In Singapore, without referencing *Quincecare*, it was held that a bank which refused to accept its customer's deposit could not be seen to owe a duty of care as negligence just did not fit the factual matrix.[27] That may, in fact, be a problem in these cases – how to frame the action such that it is intuitive and does not lead to too much unnecessary litigation given that banks have so many different relationships with their clients, many of which are not 'custodial' in nature. Even where the *Quincecare* duty exists, the majority in the UK Supreme Court in *Stanford International Bank v HSBC plc*[28] ('*Stanford*') rejected an appeal against the striking out of a claim on the basis that the bank's customer was already insolvent by the time its account was depleted and so did not suffer an actionable loss.

Just prior to *Stanford*, in *Royal Bank of Scotland International Ltd v JP SPC 4*[29] ('*RBS*'), the Privy Council found that the duty did not extend to third party beneficiaries of a customer's account who were defrauded by the customer unless the purpose of the bank's service was to protect the third party. Here the bank customer was a company run by two fraudulent individuals who misapplied

[24] ibid [350].
[25] Booysen (n 13) 354.
[26] *Alliance Bank Malaysia Bhd v Khee San Food Industries Sdn Bhd* [2021] 12 MLJ 78.
[27] *AL Shams Global Ltd v BNP Paribas* [2018] SGHC 143, [2019] 3 SLR 1189. Previously, the Singapore Court of Appeal in *Hsu Ann Mei Amy v Oversea-Chinese Banking Corp Ltd* [2011] SGCA 3 applied Quincecare in a situation where the bank customer lacked mental capacity. In *Envy Asset Management Pte Ltd (in liquidation) v CH Biovest Pte Ltd* [2024] SGHC 46, [77] however, the judge noted that the UK Supreme Court 'undertook a root and branch re-examination of the juridical basis of the *Quincecare* duty'.
[28] [2022] UKSC 34, [2023] 2 WLR 79, Lord Sales dissented on the basis that *Sequana* sees the company representing creditor interests in insolvency; see R Y Chua, 'The Aftermath of a Ponzi Scheme' [2023] *LMCLQ* 218.
[29] *Royal Bank of Scotland International Ltd v JP SPC 4* [2022] UKPC 18, [2022] 3 WLR 261, noted A Bellas 'Royal Bank of Scotland International Ltd v JP SPC 4: Assumption of Responsibility and the Quincecare Duty' (2023) 139 *LQR* 215; K P Soh and R Tan 'The Quincecare Duty and Third-Party Beneficial Owners' [2023] *LMCLQ* 6.

monies beneficially owned by fund investors. The moneys were to be lent to a law firm but much of it went to accounts of the two fraudsters. In upholding the decision of the court below to strike out the claim against the bank, the Privy Council said that it would only be in highly exceptional situations that there would be a duty of care as it would otherwise undermine extant dishonest assistance rules.[30] It disapproved of cases suggesting a duty of care to third party non-account holders such as *Baden v Société Générale pour Favoriser le Développement du Commerce et de I'Industrie en France SA*[31] ('*Baden*') (like *Selangor* better known for accessory liability and states of knowledge) which had relied on the discredited two-stage *Anns*[32] test. It also thought[33] that Peter Gibson J in *Baden* had not identified the case as one involving economic loss and omission, where there is a duty only in more restricted circumstances. The PC ultimately used the incremental approach of *Caparo Industries plc v Dickman*[34] and the more modern doctrine of assumption of responsibility contained in the judgment of *N v Poole Borough Council*[35] and, finding none in relation to the third-party beneficiaries of the account, held that the protection offered by the *Quincecare* duty did not extend to them.

These are understandable attempts at retaining some form of control at the duty of care level. This examines the scope of duty not as a test of causation or remoteness – as a question of fact – but more of a threshold inquiry – as a matter of law.[36] It shows that using the general rubric of negligence without more may not always be the best fit here. The question, then, is how to translate a duty of inquiry from a relationship with a bank customer into negligence if inquiries are not made by the bank. This suggests some form of gatekeeper or oversight liability at a time when fraud is omnipresent but while there is some intuitive link between the duty to inquire and negligence, there are also difficulties implementing it. First, there is the overlay between contract and tort. Second, courts have generally been reticent to impose negligence liability in respect of omissions,[37] and with pure economic losses.[38] Third, it seems to apply to entities only, possibly because there are external

[30] *Royal Brunei Airlines Sdn Bhd v Tan* [1995] 2 AC 378 (PC). Although this involved authorised push payment fraud, it was held in *Tecnimont Arabia Ltd v National Westminster Bank Plc* [2022] EWHC 1172 (Comm) that the receiving bank's role is to protect rather than investigate its customers, which was here the fraudulent party. It would be anomalous if a receiving bank in such cases is not liable for knowing receipt but the paying bank could be in negligence for not protecting its customer, the defrauded party.

[31] *Baden v Société Générale pour Favoriser le Développement du Commerce et de I'Industrie en France SA* [1993] 1 WLR 509.

[32] *Anns v Merton London Borough Council* [1978] AC 728 (HL).

[33] *RBS* (n 29) [53].

[34] *Caparo Industries plc v Dickman* [1990] 2 AC 605 (HL).

[35] *N v Poole Borough Council* [2019] UKSC 25, [2020] AC 780.

[36] *Manchester Building Society v Grant Thornton UK LLP* [2021] UKSC 20, [2022] AC 783 and *Meadows v Khan* [2021] UKSC 21, [2022] AC 852, noted AC Walton 'Negligence and Scope of Duty Post *SAAMCO*: Old Ideas, New Look' [2022] *LMCLQ* 33, 38 who sees the assumption of responsibility in *South Australia Asset Management Corpn v York Montague Ltd* [1997] AC 191 as more about remoteness.

[37] *Smith v Littlewoods Organisation Ltd* [1987] AC 241 (HL), 271C. 'The most troublesome question in negligence today remains omissions liability': J Morgan 'A Riddle Wrapped in An Enigma: Assumption of Responsibility, Again' (2022) 81 *CLJ* 449, 449.

[38] *Caparo* (n 34) 621.

rules applicable to them. Fourth, even if it is in substance negligence liability, can it be better categorised given that banks have insulated themselves from liability in much of their other dealings with their customers.

The Supreme Court in *Philipp* has answered the question by re-locating the bank's duty of care within the context of agency reasoning.[39] An agent that acts dishonestly acts without authority. A bank with notice of this but who carries out the agent's instruction is in breach of its mandate with the principal/customer.[40]

5. Oversight Liability and Contextual Negligence

Recently, Loth has said that private law is a 'discourse on other discourses'.[41] While there is always an impetus to rationalise the law with heuristics,[42] such as a generalised single test of negligence, the reality is that we should still be aware of the particularised context in which liability arises. Weir has always maintained that there are different harms recognised by the tort of negligence with, in decreasing order of importance: personal injury, property damage, and economic losses.[43] It is not that the language of negligence is inappropriate but that in the case of a bank's oversight liability for economic losses it had to be properly understood or the number of cases brought to court would not subside even if they continue to be unsuccessful.

What are the important facts here that are categorisable even if they do not lead to the need for a new conceptual framework? There used to be a reluctance to find a duty of care in tort overlapping or concurrent with contractual liability.[44] This is no longer the case, although Gardner and Murphy have pointed out that we still have to be careful about the tort/contract interface given remaining contextual issues.[45] Exceptionally, though, there may be a contractual framework which is incompatible with any assumption of responsibility by the defendant.[46]

[39] *Philipp (SC)* (n 16) [97].
[40] ibid [90].
[41] M Loth, *Private Law in Context: Enriching Legal Doctrine* (Cheltenham, Edward Elgar Publishing, 2022) 136 paraphrasing JB White, *Justice as Translation, An Essay in Cultural and Legal Criticism* (Chicago, IL, University of Chicago Press, 1990) 261–62.
[42] K Amirthalingam, 'Clinical Negligence and Relational Psychiatric Injury' (2022) 138 *LQR* 370, 370 states that 'Lord Atkin used the neighbour principle as a metaphor to explain existing case law; it was not intended as a heuristic device for judicial expansion of the law of negligence'.
[43] T Weir, *Tort Law* (Oxford, Clarendon Press, 2002) 20.
[44] *Tai Hing Cotton Mill Ltd v Liu Chong Hing Bank Ltd* [1986] AC 80 (PC), 107, where Lord Scarman doubted whether 'there is anything to the advantage of the law's development in searching for a liability in tort where the parties are in a contractual relationship'.
[45] J Gardner and J Murphy, 'Concurrent Liability in Contract and Tort: A Separation Thesis' (2021) 137 *LQR* 77. See 'complete concurrence' in Australia: Y Goh and M Yip, 'Concurrent Liability in Tort and Contract: An analysis of Interplay, Intersection and Independence' (2017) 24 *Torts Law Journal* 148.
[46] *Henderson v Merrett Syndicates Ltd* [1995] 2 AC 145 (HL),196; *White v Jones* [1995] 2 AC 207 (HL), 257. Or if there are private international law considerations although strong arguments have been made against this in S Peari and M Teo, 'Justifying Concurrent Claims in Private International Law' (2023) 82 *CLJ* 138.

Specifically, the contract may exclude or limit the scope of tortious duties and obligations owed by one party to the other.[47] More likely, however, as Booysen has pointed out,[48] the bank mandate here to look after the customers' accounts delineates the scope of duty which suggests that this is a form of negligence circumscribed by contract like that observed in *Henderson v Merrett Syndicates Ltd*.[49] Indeed, Lord Leggatt in *Philipp* did not see that tort added anything to the contractual relationship here, and that the duty to exercise reasonable care was not in conflict and in fact arose from the bank mandate.[50] He referred to Lord Sumption's statement in *PT Asuransi Tugu Pratama Indonesia TBK v Citibank NA*,[51] that '(t)he law cannot coherently treat compliance with an authorised instruction as a breach of duty …',[52] then went back to reexamine various cases, including the *Selangor* decision, and stated:[53]

> The logical consequence of it is that a payment made without inquiry when the bank is on notice that the payment is being made for the signatories' own purposes is not only a breach of the bank's duty of care but is also outside the scope of its mandate.

At the same time, however, there is often no liability in the tort of negligence for omitting to do something especially where individuals are concerned. But here there is an omission in a contractual and regulatory setting where a bank was arguably tasked with protecting its customer's interest.[54] Lord Bridge in *Curran v Northern Ireland Co-ownership Housing Association*,[55] who was bound by but did not like *Anns*, thought that there was a distinction between misfeasance and nonfeasance.[56] However, Tofaris and Steel see negligence liability for omissions apposite for certain institutions like the police given their extant purposes and position, and a victim's dependence on them.[57] Some form of categorisation exists, but more is required given the width of 'assumption of responsibility'. What is it about banks that warrants opening them up to greater possible liability for omissions like the police?

[47] *JP Morgan Chase Bank v Federal Republic of Nigeria* [2019] EWCA Civ 1641 at [40]; Soh and Tan (n 29) 9.

[48] Booysen (n 13) 355. Cf Watts (n 13) and Chua (n 13).

[49] *Henderson* (n 46) 181 per Lord Goff, citing Lord Shaw in *Nocton v Lord Ashburton* [1914] AC 932 (HL), 972.

[50] *Philipp (SC)* (n 16) [34]; [63]–[66].

[51] [2023] HKCFA 3 [14], noted Jeremiah Lau, 'Limitation in Bank Fraud Claims: Effect of Account Closure' (2023) 82(2) *Cambridge Law Journal* 224.

[52] ibid [64].

[53] ibid [96].

[54] See Watts (n 13) who does not see any particular undertaking. It is argued in the next part that the special position of banks today puts them in this position.

[55] *Curran v Northern Ireland Co-ownership Housing Association* [1987] AC 718 (HL).

[56] ibid 728.

[57] S Tofaris and S Steel, 'Negligence Liability for Omissions and the Police' (2016) 75 *CLJ* 128.

6. Entities and Regulation – Failure to Prevent Duty

The late Lynn Stout[58] pointed out that entities have less of a conscience compared to humans who are prosocial creatures and are already incentivised to act well regardless of liability rules. Traditional negligence liability generally undercompensates but that has not resulted in suboptimal societal behaviour as humans take more care than legally required than, say, corporations.[59]

While Lord Templeman in *Winkworth v Edward Baron Development Co Ltd*[60] ('*Winkworth*') referred to the 'conscience of the company'[61] that was 'confided in its directors', that was to take into account the interest of creditors and not just shareholders/directors themselves when acting in a company's best interest. Micheler has argued that there is the corporate culture[62] to consider which allows an entity to do things that no person could do for herself (there may be more individual guilt there) and thereby become a 'corporation man'.[63] In any case, we shall see when examining *BTI 2014 LLC v Sequana SA* ('*Sequana*'),[64] where Lord Briggs referred to the *Winkworth* quote that, even if a company were liable, the directors that act on its behalf may not be, without something extra that suggests that the directors are assuming personal responsibility to the third party,[65] or if the directors have breached their duty to their own company. Given that personal shield, entities (and their organs) may take less care than human individuals would when acting for themselves in the same matter, which may explain why corporate purposes are struggling to find a concrete foothold to latch onto.

Banks can last in perpetuity and are more likely to be viable gatekeepers. Aside from being incorporated, given bail-in rules now, a bank cannot really be insolvent given that its debt will be swapped for equity – or even wiped clean – whenever it defaults.[66] As Jacinda Arden has pointed out, banks are public bodies exercising public functions with a social licence.[67] Given the advantages banks have, there

[58] L Stout, *Cultivating Conscience* (Princeton, Princeton University Press, 2011).

[59] ibid 174.

[60] *Winkworth v Edward Baron Development Co Ltd* [1986] 1 WLR 1512 (HL).

[61] ibid 1516.

[62] E Micheler, *Company Law – A Real Entity Theory* (Oxford, Oxford University Press, 2021). In Singapore and Australia, 'corporate culture' is formally used in legislation to determine whether the corporation should be liable for an employee's misdeeds: Securities and Futures Act 2001 (Singapore), s 236B(8)(*c*); Criminal Code Act 1995 (Australia), s 12(2)(c).

[63] Stout (n 58) 168 *et seq.*

[64] *BTI 2014 LLC v Sequana SA* [2022] UKSC 25, [2022] 3 WLR 709 [140].

[65] See, eg, *Williams v Natural Life Health Foods Ltd* [1998] 1 WLR 830 (HL), 835 holding that directors need to separately assume responsibility which should be based on objective exchanges between plaintiff and defendant. See FMB Reynolds, 'Personal Liability of Company Directors in Tort' (2003) 33 *HKLJ* 51.

[66] T Hale, 'Additional tier 1 bonds: the wiped-out debt at centre of Credit Suisse takeover', *Financial Times* (20 March 2023).

[67] 'Jacinda Ardern says banks "wrong" to take huge profits as cost-of-living crisis deepens' *The Guardian*, (9 November 2022). Available at: www.theguardian.com/world/2022/nov/08/jacinda-ardern-says-banks-wrong-to-take-huge-profits-as-cost-of-living-crisis-deepens (accessed 7 May 2023).

are usually external constraints on banks imposed by statutes, codes and guidelines that need to be internalised. Negligence as a reasonable person standard can accommodate external requirements more easily than, say, the duty of loyalty owed by a director.[68] In *Philipp*, Lord Leggatt said that:[69]

> the standard of reasonableness provides the necessary flexibility to adapt the principle to different types of commercial transaction and accommodate practices and expectations particular to a field of commerce.

The reality, though, is that, in the past, courts have been ambivalent about using external codes, and even when they are used, they have been used just as often to shield banks from liability, especially if they have their own dispute resolution mechanisms and are not amenable to private claims. Hudson has lamented that courts have not been consistent in using codes,[70] even though he feels that '[t]he regulatory context of money laundering is what is actually informing banking practice in any event'.[71] We are seeing this played out again with these bank cases, with the willingness to look cursorily at them at the summary stage to prevent a striking out action. But, at trial, like in *Nigeria*, when scrutinised more carefully, the codes are usually not seen as sufficient support for a duty of care or, more likely, any high-level standard of care. This is because, as Lord Leggatt went on to say:[72]

> Exigencies of banking practice, such as the vast number of transactions which banks process on a daily basis and the speed at which, in the interests of efficiency, most banking business is expected to be conducted, will naturally affect what reasonable skill and care requires.

The thing is that we only want an institution to do slightly more, and not to become an insurer. The idea is for someone, even while working in an entity and not likely subject to personal liability (these are not cases where first the employee is liable and the entity only vicariously so – the entity is directly responsible for an omission),[73] or even a well-written algorithm,[74] to prevent the holes in the cheese from lining up in these banking cases. Stout has suggested slightly more onerous negligence rules perhaps for corporations.[75] We are at the moment in time where this is a possibility, with numerous instances where the UK Supreme Court has expressed willingness to hear cases of holding companies being liable in negligence for damage to persons affected by its subsidiaries, although again any duty

[68] A Gold, 'The Internal Limits on Fiduciary Loyalty' (2020) 65(1) *American Journal of Jurisprudence* 65.
[69] *Philipp (SC)* (n 16) [94].
[70] Hudson (n 4) [26-23].
[71] Hudson (ibid.) [30–32].
[72] *Philipp (SC)* (n 16) [94].
[73] Weir (n 43) 21 that tort has these two devices to make a company liable as 'non-existent bodies are very good at *not* doing things, since in fact they can't do anything'.
[74] Christopher M Bruner, 'Managing Fraud Risk in the Age of AI', Chapter 3 in this volume.
[75] Stout (n 59) 172 arguing for special damages 'based entirely on concern for economic efficiency, and particularly the need to ensure that conscienceless corporations fully "internalize" the otherwise-external costs they impose on others'.

of care must be seen in context.[76] Even there, the relevance of extrinsic things like codes and public documents (which may have standard terms pushed by consumer groups) are being fought over with some leading to a possible assumption of responsibility and duty of care on the part of the parent, and others not.[77] In this regard, Europe may be leading the way as evidenced by Royal Dutch Shell's recent experience before the Dutch courts, which suggests that environmental concerns may be a different form of public negligence involving a 'standalone'[78] or 'undirected duty'[79] not owed to a neighbour but more generally.[80]

But what is anomalous is that banks have traditionally been able to protect themselves from liability in many similar and arguably more egregious situations. There has traditionally been no duty to warn customers against improvident transactions.[81] The bank mis-selling cases have also seen low level duties of care at best imposed and protection from non-reliance clauses, despite the fact that banks were proximate causes of the Global Financial Crisis. However, this also shows the contractual limitations of the negligence standard which, in *Nigeria*, was even reduced to gross negligence. It is, however, harder to craft something like non-reliance clauses in a 'custodial' relationship than in an antagonistic transactional one. Perhaps *Barclays Bank plc v O'Brien*[82] ('*O'Brien*') situations provide a closer analogy. That was seen as a priority fight that may also have had some kind of quasi-property or restitutionary basis, or even an equitable duty of care.[83]

[76] See P L Davies, 'Corporate Liability for Wrongdoing within (Foreign) Subsidiaries: Mechanisms from Corporate Law, Tort and Regulation' in *Festschrift for Sarah Worthington* (forthcoming) who argues that:

> To perform that second-stage task, the courts needed to move beyond the generalities of *Caparo* and focus directly on the characteristics of the parent/subsidiary relationships which would lead the courts to regard the imposition of a duty of care on the parent towards third parties as appropriate.

[77] Compare the first instance decision in *Okpabi v Royal Dutch Shell plc* [2017] EWHC 89 (TCC), [2017] Bus LR 1335 [95]–[96] where compliance with extrinsic material was not seen to found a duty of care with that in the Court of Appeal in *Okpabi v Royal Dutch Shell plc* [2018] EWCA Civ 191, [2018] Bus LR 1022 which placed weight on those documents whilst affirming, although both were then reversed by the Supreme Court in *HRH Emere Godwin Bebe Okpabi v Royal Dutch Shell plc* [2021] UKSC 3, [2021] 1 WLR 1294.

[78] P B Miller & AS Gold, 'Fiduciary Governance' (2015) 57 *Wm & Mary L Rev* 513, 555.

[79] S Bright and B McFarlane, 'Private Law Failings and Policy Development following the Grenfell Tower Fire' in J Gardner, A Goymour, J O'Sullivan and S Worthington (eds), *Politics, Policy and Private Law: Volume 1: Tort, Property and Equity* (Oxford: Hart Publishing, 2024).

[80] *Milieudefensie v Royal Dutch Shell plc* ECLI:NL:RBDHA:2021:5337 where Shell was ordered to reduce its emissions by 45% by 2030: B Mayer, '*Milieudefensie v Shell:* Do Oil Corporations Hold a Duty to Mitigate Climate Change?' in A Engert, L Enriques,W-G Ringe, U Varottil and T Wetzer (eds), *Business Law and the Transition to a New Zero Economy* (Beck, Hart, Nomos, 2022). This led to Shell dropping the 'Royal Dutch' prefix and moving to London, and the derivative action led by ClientEarth against its directors which failed: *ClientEarth v Shell Plc* [2023] EWHC 1137 (Ch).

[81] See, eg, *RH Deacon & Co v Varga* [1971] 1 OR 233.

[82] *Barclays Bank plc v O'Brien* [1994] 1 AC 180 (HL).

[83] C Rickett and D McLauchlan, 'Undue Influence, Financiers and Third Parties: A Doctrine in Transition or the Emergence of a New Doctrine?' [1995] *NZ Law Review* 328. See also H Tjio, 'O'Brien and Unconscionability' (1996) 113 *LQR* 10.

The goal may be just to get the bank to warn the customer. Given bank mandates, we cannot expect the bank to stop the transaction altogether as it may open itself up to countervailing contractual liability. The Supreme Court has now drawn a line in the sand, endorsing the view propounded by commentators that it is incongruous to say that a bank has agreed to be both unyieldingly obedient but also sometimes disobedient.[84] Lord Leggatt specifically addressed this when he said:[85]

> Where the bank receives a valid payment order which is clear and leaves no room for interpretation or choice about what is required in order to carry out the order, the bank's duty is simply to execute the order by making the requisite payment. The duty of care does not apply.

But if it is just about notice that triggers some precautionary warning, we needed to understand how the duty of inquiry fits into negligence liability as, like with *O'Brien*, it is likely to lead to a set of procedures that banks will have to follow. This will probably be along the lines of what the UK House of Lords did in *Royal Bank of Scotland plc v Etridge (No 2)*[86] in setting out what is expected of a bank and independent solicitor in ensuring that a surety is free of undue influence from the borrower. This has worked out even though it has never been totally clear what the source of the *O'Brien* duty is. *Philipp* has provided an agency basis for the *Quincecare* duty. Loth states that 'what matters here is that if we see private law as a kind of regulation, it is essentially a two-tier regulation; general in advance, tailor-made afterwards'.[87] The next step is perhaps a private law code even if Lord Leggatt was clearly uncomfortable with private law overreach into public regulation.[88] But formal codes are a hybrid mixture of private ordering and public regulation which often lags behind practice.[89] Courts may have to be a gap filler.

In the context of corporate liability, there is a wrong by an individual within the entity that is then attributed to the entity because there has been the necessary delegation and proper exercise of power or because of 'system intentionality'.[90] But this may not be what is happening in these bank negligence cases as it does not arise because an employee, even if senior, has carried out a negligent act which is then attributed via, eg, vicarious liability. Liability here is not derivative but direct and comes from the bank mandate with the customer which requires

[84] See Chua (n 13), 164; Watts (n 13), 531.

[85] *Philipp (SC)* (n 16) [63].

[86] [2001] UKHL 44, [2002] 2 AC 773 [120].

[87] Loth (n 41) 169.

[88] *Philipp (SC)* (n 16) [22]–[24]. At [21], Lord Leggatt stated that banks will be required to reimburse customers through regulations introduced by the Financial Services and Markets Act 2023, s 72, which will amend regulation 90 of the Payment Services Regulation. This will come into effect in 2024.

[89] R Brownsword, R A J Van Gestel and H-W Micklitz (eds), *Contract and Regulation – A Handbook on New Methods of Law Making in Private Law* (Cheltenham, Edward Elgar Publishing, 2017).

[90] R Leow, *Corporate Attribution in Private Law* (Oxford, Hart Publishing, 2022); E Bant, 'Catching the Corporate Conscience: A New Model' [2022] *LMCLQ* 468; see now, E Bant, 'Systems Intentionality: Theory and Practice' in E Bant (ed), *The Culpable Corporate Mind* (Oxford, Hart Publishing, 2023).

that the former take reasonable care to protect the latter from fraud. The entity may not have done enough given its public functions and privileged position. It is about negligence in the context of an agency relationship, public charters and codes. That may trigger a duty of inquiry to see that the bank customer is aware that its agent may be acting outside the scope of her authority before executing her order.

7. The Need for Individual Liability

What may be needed in these cases where entities have direct duties of care (as opposed to derivative liability) to third parties is for individuals within them to also be exposed to the risk of liability to incentivise them to go against a corporate culture that to various degrees requires them to focus on profits and to cut costs. The parallel in criminal or public law with failure to prevent offences[91] imposed on corporations is the senior management liability for poor supervision that we see in the UK. There is a Financial Conduct Authority and Prudential Regulatory Authority (PRA) Senior Managers and Certification Regime which sets out a responsibilities map for senior managers to assess the fitness and propriety of certain employees carrying out a 'significant harm' function. If there is a breach of responsibility within a senior manager's remit the regulator can take action against the senior manager for failing to take 'reasonable steps' to avoid a breach occurring. This regime became applicable to banks from March 2016 and other PRA firms from 2018 although doubts have been expressed whether it is working to change bank culture.[92] This is not the first time that the UK has struggled with the boundaries of corporate and individual liability to prevent moral hazard. The UK Corporate Manslaughter and Corporate Homicide Act 2007 was introduced to remove the directing mind requirement even for manslaughter to one where more generalised management failure could make the company liable. But Gower and Davies recount how 'the wheel thus came full circle'[93] when, during passing of the Act, there was debate on imposing liability not just on the company but on senior individuals within it, but this was eventually resisted by the legislature. Similarly, Hanrahan discusses how Australian law reform efforts with respect to individual liability for failure to prevent was left to the financial sector.[94] In contrast, the MAS

[91] It presently applies to bribery and tax evasion. See UK Law Commission's potential reform of corporate criminal liability for failure to prevent more generally with respect to employees and agents of company though not fraud in general at www.lawcom.gov.uk/law-commission-sets-out-options-to-government-for-reforming-how-companies-are-convicted-of-criminal-offences/ (accessed 7 May 2023).

[92] E Hickman, 'Is the Senior Managers and Certification Regime Changing Banking for Good?' (2022) 85(6) *MLR* 1440.

[93] P L Davies, *Gower and Davies, Principles of Modern Company Law*, 8th edn (London, Sweet & Maxwell, 2008) [7-32].

[94] P Hanrahan, 'Culpable Executives' in E Bant (ed), *The Culpable Corporate Mind* (London, Bloomsbury, 2023) 383.

in Singapore has consistently stated that it prefers to punish the individuals behind corporate action, although again that may only be in areas under its purview, ie finance.[95]

Within private law, however, it is clear that directors and senior management will not ordinarily be liable in negligence to third parties given that the interposition of a separate entity which they represent insulates them from any assumption of responsibility to those third parties[96] – they have to themselves be fraudulent.[97] Their duties are to the company itself, and the struggle today is to craft something which can make management internalise – or at least take account of – external rules applicable to the company. At one level it seems to work until we delve into its mechanics. What we seek to do is to make the decision-maker behave like a pro-social individual again so that this in turn feeds into corporate action.

A company could sue its directors if the company suffers a loss or is criminally liable in a way that is 'attributable' to the director. 'Stepping stone' liability in Australia has helped in having directors made liable, usually for breaches of the duty of care and to act in the best interests of the company in relation to the breach or non-compliance with other statutes by the company, often involving securities disclosure. But Langford[98] has highlighted that derivative stepping-stone liability was seen in *Cassimatis v Australian Securities and Investments Commission*[99] as merely an application of a direct statutory duty. A Singapore judge also expressed 'surprise' that defendants pleaded guilty to a breach of s 157 of the Singapore Companies Act, an earlier version of Australian legislation, that required directors to act 'honestly and use reasonable diligence', for failing to get their company to comply with the continuous disclosure rules of the exchange.[100] The fit of these more traditional directors' duties with omissions and external requirements is not always a comfortable one, especially since s 157C of the Singapore Act provides that directors can delegate and are only liable if they failed to act in good faith or to make proper inquiry where the need for inquiry is indicated by the circumstances.

It becomes even more complex if the company suffers no clear loss from breach as it is then purely about good faith compliance and faithfulness to rules. In the US,

[95] Y Yahya, 'Huge 1MDB-related fines "hurt shareholders, not those liable"' *Straits Times* 30 June 2017, quoting Ravi Menon, MD of MAS. See further RA Guttman, 'Effective Compliance Means Imposing Individual Liability' (2018) 5 *Emory Corp. Governance & Accountability* Rev 77. Contrast S W Buell, 'The Limits of Individual Prosecutions in Deterring Corporate Fraud' (2024) 59:3 *Wake Forest Law Review* (forthcoming).

[96] *Williams* (n 65).

[97] See also *Standard Chartered Bank v Pakistan National Shipping Corpn (Nos 2 and 4)* [2002] UKHL 43, [2003] 1 AC 959 [22]; and now *Sim Tee Meng v Haw Wan Sin David* [2019] SCGA 71, [2020] 1 SLR 82, *Barclay-Watt v Alpha Panareti Public Ltd* [2022] EWCA Civ 1169, [2023] 1 BCLC 240.

[98] R T Langford, 'Dystopian Accessorial Liability of the End of "Stepping Stones" As We Know It?' (2020) 37(5) *Company and Securities Law Journal* 262.

[99] *Cassimatis v Australian Securities and Investments Commission* [2020] FCAFC 52, (2020) 376 *ALR* 261, where directors were found liable in negligence to their financial advisory firm when their investment strategy led to losses to their clients and caused the firm to lose its licence.

[100] *Public Prosecutor v Ngiam Zee Moey* [2022] SGDC 115 on rule 703 of the SGX Listing Manual which has statutory backing under section 203 of the Securities and Futures Act 2001 (Singapore).

it has been said that oversight compliance duties were created by the recognition of directorial good faith and its use in *In re Caremark International* ('*Caremark*').[101] However, the duty of loyalty is usually used in the context of reducing agency costs, whereas here we may have to increase them in order to detect misconduct even at the expense of profits, which is the main reason why it is said that *Caremark* has not worked in providing a foundational duty (as opposed to what the court wanted directors to do in that specific case).[102] Instead, *Marchand v Barnhill*[103] is thought to be the first example of *Caremark* 2.0 where Leo Strine CJ in the Delaware Supreme Court said that:

> If Caremark means anything, it is that a corporate board must make a good faith effort to exercise its duty of care. A failure to make that effort constitutes a breach of duty of loyalty.

Loth (and later Wittgenstein[104]) have pointed out the limits of language, but juxtaposing good faith, care and loyalty together like this does not make it any easier to digest into something that tells directors how to balance their duties to the company, which is still mainly concerned with maximizing shareholder value, and regulatory requirements on them which may come at a cost not through breach but compliance.

While good faith has perhaps been translated into a duty to comply with external rules in the US, this requires some investment in knowing the law and the context behind the words which is not obviously captured by saying that directors have a duty of good faith (which is, on its face, subjective) to the corporation, when in the US directors can be directly accountable to shareholders.[105] In his chapter, Weiming Tan argues that the UK can learn from *Caremark*. Gold, however, asks in this context 'if the Delaware courts haven't stretched fiduciary loyalty concepts to the breaking point, even in corporate contexts where charters are a component of the parties' relation'.[106] We will see if Commonwealth law can, in fact, do better given its experiences with the duty to act bona fide in the company's interest.

8. Directors' Duties and External Purposes

The quote from *Marchand* shows the continued difficulties in weaving in external regulatory oversight duties into the relationship between a director and company, which has a major shareholder constituency to consider. In the Commonwealth,

[101] *In re Caremark International*, 698 A 2d 959 (Del Ch 1996). Gold (n 71) fn 24, discussing *In re Walt Disney Co Derivative Litigation* 907 A 2d 693 (Del Ch 2005).

[102] J Arlen, 'Evolution of Director Oversight Duties and Liability under Caremark: Using Enhanced Information-Acquisition Duties in the Public Interest' (28 August 2022). Available at https://ssrn.com/abstract=4202830 (accessed 7 May 2023).

[103] *Marchand v Barnhill* 212 A3d (Del 2019) 805, 824.

[104] Loth (n 41) 88 said that Wittgenstein was a 'philosopher born twice' and legal concepts need to be understood in context of the particular language game.

[105] R Flannigan, 'The Academic Contribution to the Shaping of American Director Fiduciary Duty' (2022) 66 *Canadian Business Law Journal* 58.

[106] Gold (n 71) 72.

the US good faith duty finds its closest analogue in the duty to act bona fide in the company's best interest.[107] In the UK, however, s 172 of the Companies Act 2006 has translated that into the duty to promote the company's success for the benefit of shareholders which has to balance the interests of the various corporate constituencies such as employees, customers and even 'the community and the environment'.[108] According to Flannigan, this may be a nominate duty,[109] not fiduciary. This explains why it can apply to non-fiduciary managers too as historically fiduciary duties were only about controlling opportunism in limited access arrangements and the good faith duty was seen as an agency add-on which applies to many other employees.[110]

With bank negligence, the duty is to the customer; we just need to understand what it has to do in light of fraud which damages the customer and it may be that not much is required given the contradictions with the bank mandate. With what we see, however, with directors' duties to comply with ESG and corporate purposes, Paul L Davies has said that we need to find:[111]

> ways of using corporate law to secure better levels of compliance with external regulation. These look like fruitful lines of enquiry, but, unfortunately, not simple ones.

Certainly, we can internalise some rules into the director-company relationship as Gold explained.[112] However, it is invariably the case that some regulations cannot fit the internal rule of law box, particularly when the cost to the company comes from compliance and not breach. More firm specific corporate law rules are needed,[113] but these are difficult to back with hard sanctions. Corporate law could mandate the specification of purposes in corporate constitutions, but Davies has further argued against them on the basis that they would be watered down in the same way company objects were in the past to avoid ultra vires transactions. Where voluntary, they have not led to the widespread use of such constitutional purposes in jurisdictions like France that introduced regulations in that regard.[114] It would be ideal if these purposes were inserted into constitutions, as s 171(a) of the Companies Act 2006 requires that directors must 'act in accordance with the

[107] D Kershaw, *The Foundations of Anglo-American Corporate Fiduciary Law* (Cambridge, Cambridge University Press, 2018) believes that there is really a great deal of convergence in Anglo-American fiduciary law even if the language used is different.

[108] Companies Act 2006 (UK), s 172(1)(d).

[109] R Flannigan, 'The Adulteration of Fiduciary Doctrine in Corporate Law' (2006) 122 *LQR* 449.

[110] ibid 457–58. The distinction between the duties of fidelity and fiduciary duties were set out by the Singapore Court of Appeal in *Smile Inc Dental Surgeons Pte Ltd v Lui Andrew Stewart* [2012] SGCA 39, [2012] 4 SLR 308 [49]–[55].

[111] P L Davies, 'The role of corporate law in corporate purpose: the British Academy Report' *ECGI Blog*. Available at: www.ecgi.global/blog/role-corporate-law-corporate-purpose-british-academy-report (accessed 7 May 2023).

[112] Gold (n 71) 69.

[113] L Anidjar, 'Corporate Law and Governance Pluralism' (2022) 35(2) *Canadian Journal of Law and Jurisprudence* 283.

[114] This is illustrated in recent amendments to Article 1835 of the French Civil Code which merely '*allows*' rather than mandates a corporation to specify its '*raison d'être*' in its articles of association.

company's constitution' and s 172(2) modifies the duty to promote the success of the company for its shareholders in cases where 'purposes of the company consist of or include purposes other than the benefit of its members' where the focus is on 'achieving those purposes'. But it will be argued in the last part that, even if not, the other half of the proper purpose rule in s 171(b) still has a part to play in coordinating the various directors' duties into something that can accommodate ESG more intuitively. However, we will first examine the difficulties of using the general s 172 company success/good faith/best interest test even in the case where the company has suffered a clear loss. This may be because on the face of it is a subjective test but may need to be understood from an objective angle to work.[115]

9. Sequana and Absent Proper Purposes

We have seen that capital maintenance rules have been pushed back for 40 years now in the case of financial assistance rules that buttressed the private law actions in *Selangor*. Those who cannot adjust suffer the most, usually employees or involuntary creditors. What remains a thorn to those desiring the frictionless movement of assets in the corporate/financial world is s 423 of the Insolvency Act 1986 which, despite the statute it is part of, is not dependent on bankruptcy and applies in the context of undervalued transactions made with the purpose of prejudicing persons with claims against the transferor. This was observed by Lord Neuberger in *Prest v Petrodel Resources Ltd*[116] as a 'specified and limited' application of the principle that 'fraud unravels everything'. US fraudulent conveyance cases in practice see a necessary purpose to defraud creditors only if it leaves the company 'insolvent or with unreasonably small capital' as that then puts assets beyond the reach of creditors.[117] Intent may otherwise be hard to prove as this is rarely 'susceptible to direct proof'.[118] However, that is not the position in the UK, where in *Sequana* the judges continued to apply it without the need to prove insolvency,[119] which is itself a difficult matter to show in practice even if not conceptually.[120]

[115] R T Langford and I M Ramsay, 'Directors' Duty to Act in the Interests of the Company: Subjective or Objective?' [2015] 2 *JBL* 173. Compare Lady Arden (at [180]) and the majority (at [232]) in *Children's Investment Fund Foundation (UK) v Attorney General* [2020] UKSC 33, [2022] AC 155. See further W M Tan, 'Negotiating New Curves Along Chancery Lane: Four More Questions on Fiduciaries' (2022) 35 *TLI* 197, 214–16.

[116] *Prest v Petrodel Resources Ltd* [2013] UKSC 34, [2013] 2 AC 415 [83], noted E Lim 'Salomon Reigns' (2013) 129 *LQR* 480, H Tjio 'Lifting the Veil on Piercing the Veil' [2014] *LMCLQ* 19.

[117] M Kahan, 'Legal Capital Rules and the Structure of Corporate Law: Some Observations on the Differences Between European and US Approaches' in Hopt and Wymeersch (eds), *Capital Markets and Company Law* (Oxford, Oxford University Press, 2003) 147. See US Bankruptcy Code, s 548(a)(1); *In re Semcrude LP* 526 BR 556 (Dist Del 2014).

[118] This is illustrated by *In re Kaiser*, 722 F 2d 1574 (2d Cir 1983).

[119] *Sequana (SC)* (n 64) Lord Reed at [61] appeared to see s 423 as an insolvency rule but compare, eg Lady Arden at [368]. See J Armour, 'Transactions Defrauding Creditors' in J Armour and H Bennett (eds), *Vulnerable Transactions in Corporate Insolvency* (Oxford, Hart Publishing, 2003) [3.1].

[120] *BNY Corporate Trustee Services Ltd v Eurosail-UK 2007-3*BL plc [2013] UKSC 28.

In *Sequana*, section 423 was used to set aside a lawful dividend paid by a company from distributable reserves to its holding company Sequana whilst having one material contingent liability. That was some ten years before the company, which was set up to meet the liability, became insolvent. However, the estimate of that liability which involved costs arising from the clean-up of a polluted river was too low and so the dividend payment was challenged as a conveyance intended to defraud creditors, including here BAT, which was to be indemnified for the clean-up costs. The dividend was ultimately set aside by the court on the basis that it was given for no consideration (clearly a transaction at an undervalue) to Sequana to set off against debts owed by it to the company and to put those assets out of the reach of the company's creditors. Unfortunately, Sequana was also bankrupt so the appeals which ultimately reached the Supreme Court, focused only on whether the directors of the company, which assigned its claims to BTI and been sold by Sequana, had breached their duties to the company.

This was held not to be so at every level as directors' duties, while owed to the company (to promote its success for the benefit of its members as a whole) under section 172(1), did not shift its focus to creditors under subsection (3) as insolvency was not 'probable'[121] or 'imminent'[122] when the dividend was paid. While much academic ink will be spilled over this, the concern with this paper is not with that *West Mercia*[123] duty but why some form of 'stepping stone' argument based on a breach of directors' duties to comply with s 423 (without asking the insolvency question) failed to launch. Indeed, Lord Briggs, with whom Lord Kitchin agreed, pointed this out as an 'irony'.[124]

The strange anomaly, as highlighted above in cases like *Selangor*, was that third-party liability in those cases was premised on there being a primary breach of duties by directors misapplying corporate assets by providing financial assistance to a purchaser for the acquisition of its shares regardless of insolvency (or perhaps loss). That capital maintenance leak seems less egregious than the breach of the fraudulent conveyance rule which directly claws back undervalued transactions with third parties. It could be because the prohibition against financial assistance is a manifestation of the proper purpose rule.[125] But that itself is linked to the wider concept of 'fraud on a power'[126] which underpins the fraudulent conveyance rule in s 423.

[121] *BTI 2014 LLC v Sequana SA* [2019] EWCA Civ 112, [2019] 1 BCLC 347 [220] per David Richards LJ.

[122] *Sequana (SC)* (n 64) [86] (Lord Reed), [186] (Lord Briggs), [243] (Lord Hodge).

[123] *West Mercia Safetywear Ltd (in liq) v Dodd* [1988] BCLC 250 (CA). In Singapore, see now *Foo Kian Beng v OP3 International Pte Ltd* [2024] SGCA 10.

[124] *Sequana (SC)* (n 64) [182]. J Armour, 'Avoidance of Transactions Fraud on Creditors at Common Law' in Armour and Bennett (eds) (n 119) [7.59-60] thought that directors could be liable in negligence (although he also discussed a breach of terms of the constitution).

[125] *Selangor* (n 4) 1575 – 'clear and not disputed that they owe a fiduciary duty to the company to apply its assets only for the purposes of the company and are therefore liable for breach of that duty'. See Davies (n 93) [10-024] and R P Austin and I M Ramsay, *Ford's Principles of Corporations Law* (17th edn, Australia: LexisNexis Butterworths, 2018) 24.670.

[126] Flannigan (n 136); *Eclairs* (SC) (n 130) [15]. In *Grand View PTC v Wong* [2022] UKPC 47, [56] Lord Richards said that there could be 'fraud' even if 'the trustee may have acted in good faith and genuinely with a view to benefiting the beneficiaries'.

In the Court of Appeal,[127] David Richards LJ (as he then was), was quite pointed in stating that section 171 of the Companies Act 2006 had not been sufficiently advanced before the judge even though it had been pleaded that it was an improper use of directors' power to pay dividends to Sequana to put Sequana's debts beyond the reach of the company's creditors. Section 171 was not discussed in any detail in the Supreme Court, but Lord Briggs discerned the general need for some impartiality as:[128]

> There is nothing inconsistent with the fiduciary nature of the directors' duty that it calls for a balancing of potentially competing interests.

Maintaining fairness amongst the shareholders is, in fact, expressly mentioned in s 172(1)(f) but it appears that too much is expected of the duty to promote the success of the company which, like the US good faith duty, may not be able to operate on its own in allowing directors to take account external concerns when it may actually damage certain shareholder interests. As with the *Quincecare* duty, we could be expecting conflicting action, which is why Lord Leggatt in *Philipp*[129] restricted the former to only instances of internal fraud where the duty remains conceptually consistent with the strict operation of the bank mandate. The chance was missed in *Sequana* to make a proper purpose argument (or even directorial negligence given the clear loss suffered by the company). But there was enough there to suggest that it could be foundational towards getting directors to act in accordance with external requirements. First, it was pointed out that s 171(a) could be used if purposes were inserted into the constitution. While this is highly unlikely, the proper purpose rule has enough in it that it could still provide the key to the incorporation of outside values. Earlier, in *Eclairs Group Ltd v JKX Oil and Gas plc* ('*Eclairs*'),[130] in what Lord Sumption saw as a 'formidable dissent' in the Court of Appeal,[131] Briggs LJ (as he then was) said:[132]

> I consider it important that the court should uphold the proper purpose principle in relation to the exercise of fiduciary powers by directors, all the more so where the power is capable of affecting, or interfering with, the constitutional balance between shareholders and directors, and between particular groups of shareholders.

Maintaining a 'fair balance', a phrase otherwise thought unsuited to private law by Lord Leggatt in *Philipp*[133] could be the additional understanding that illuminates s 171(b) which otherwise states that directors have to 'only exercise powers for the purposes for which they are conferred'. There is enough there to accommodate

[127] *Sequana (CA)* (n 121) [231]–[234].
[128] *Sequana (SC)* (n 64) [177].
[129] *Philipp (SC)* (n 16) [63]–[66]. In *Stanford* (n 28) [137], Lord Sales saw no distinction between the *Quincecare* duty and a director's *Sequana* fiduciary duty but compare Lady Rose at [34].
[130] *Eclairs Group Ltd v JKX Oil and Gas plc* [2015] UKSC 71, [2016] 1 BCLC 1, noted H Tjio, 'The Proper Purpose Rule' [2016] *LMCLQ* 176.
[131] *Eclairs (SC)*, ibid. [29].
[132] *Eclairs Group Ltd v JKX Oil and Gas plc* [2014] EWCA Civ 640, [2014] 2 BCLC 164 [122].
[133] *Philipp (SC)* (n 16) [67].

external codes given that it is about constitutionality, fairness and faithfulness to powers that are given to the power-holder.[134] And enforcing the duty is less about obtaining damages but seeing that the power is exercised properly. Thus, in *Eclairs*, for example, an action was successfully brought by shareholders to enjoin the company from suspending their votes in an AGM as the board had done so not to compel disclosure (as the relevant power was intended to) but to improperly prevent a hostile takeover.[135] But it may be that even if s 171 does not do so on its own, it can in tandem with the other duties set out in the Companies Act 2006 do enough to accommodate external purposes. It adds another dimension to fiduciary duties as its role is to 'regulate the exercise of authority'[136] rather than prevent opportunism or promote loyalty. It comes closest to the intersection between public regulation and private law.

10. Conclusion

There has been deregulation in commercial/corporate law for the past 40 years now. This has removed certain frictions that provided protection against fraud and risk, such as rules maintaining capital in a company.[137] Private law has had to respond to these changes and while it has held the fort there are clearly still difficulties that need to be resolved. We believe that the right language regarding liability must be attached to the wrongs that are seen today. Negligence law and the best interest duty may have been overworked and we should explore whether other duties, such as one to act for proper purposes, can provide a better understanding of why a bank may have to protect its bank customer against external fraud affecting her accounts[138] (negligence having been seen to contradict the customer mandate in *Philipp*) or why directors cannot deal with company assets in a way that harms its creditors (the best interest duty requiring insolvency in *Sequana*) or damages the environment (which failed on both negligence and best interest

[134] See Leow (n 90) 72 that 'for other powers, the proper purpose is likely to be what the power-holder believes to be the company's interest'.

[135] The other thing to note was that the shareholders could bring the actions personally and not derivatively through the company.

[136] R Flannigan, 'Fraud on a Power, Improper Purpose and Fiduciary Accountability' (2019) 62 *Canadian Business Law Journal* 133. It about controlling the 'abuse of power' and not 'excess of power': *Eclairs (SC)* (n 130), approved by Lord Richards in *Grand View PTC v Wong* (n 126) [55], who saw 'abuse' in the non-pejorative sense and approved the use of extrinsic materials like letters of wishes in determining the purpose of the power: [63].

[137] See T Dudycz and P Mielcarz, 'The Capital Maintenance Regime Matters for Creditors' (September 15, 2021). Available at: https://ssrn.com/abstract=3924627 (accessed 7 May 2023), for empirical evidence showing that capital maintenance rules affect a company's ability to raise debt due to the perception of its credit risk.

[138] As Lord Leggatt stated in *Philipp (SC)* (n 16) [21] banks will be required to reimburse customers through regulations introduced by the Financial Services and Markets Act 2023, s 72, which will amend regulation 90 of the Payment Services Regulation. This will come into effect in 2024.

grounds in the Shell derivative litigation[139]). It has been argued that negligence is better at incorporating external requirements or purposes but should still be understood in context. However, the best interest director duty of loyalty which may translate to one promoting the success of the company for the shareholders finds it more difficult to do so. It could do with a nudge from the proper purpose rule in a more coherent way than good faith in the US has arguably required regulatory compliance oversight on the part of boards.

[139] *ClientEarth v Shell Plc* [2023] EWHC 1137 (Ch). Some shareholders of Shell, led by ClientEarth which bought a small holding in the company (27 shares), tried to bring a derivative action to sue Shell's board to get it to adopt a more environmentally friendly strategy when the majority of shareholders already approved the existing strategy at the AGM. The derivative action, the underlying causes of which are the duties under ss 172 and 174 of the Companies Act 2006 to promote the success of the company and negligence respectively, failed on the threshold grounds that it may not have been brought in good faith nor was it prima facie to promote the success of the company as, on the face of it, ClientEarth could not show that Shell's directors had acted unreasonably.

14

Mind Your Own (Micro)Business: Fraud, Risk and Microbusinesses

DEVON AIREY AND JODI GARDNER

1. Introduction

This chapter calls for an increased focus on the inherent risks associated with operating as or contracting with a microbusiness ('MB') in the world of commercial contracting, particularly those risks related to fraudulent transactions. The lack of focus, by academia or regulators, on MBs creates a range of risks – both to the business themselves and trading with them.

First, MBs are provided with little-to-no tangible protection against larger companies despite their relative lack of expertise in purchasing products or services, high opportunity costs of time spent making such decisions, and poor bargaining power.[1] For the purposes of commercial law, both legislative and common, MBs are treated the same as larger businesses.

Secondly, MBs are increasingly vulnerable to fraud – as they tend to have limited awareness or resources to protect themselves from exploitation. The Department for Digital, Culture, Media and Sport recently reported 38% of MBs fell victim to cyber-fraud in 2021; a third of which suffered significant financial loss as a result. Despite these real concerns, 80% of MBs do not see cyber-attacks and data loss as a considerable threat to their business.[2] This lack of awareness means that they do not take steps to protect themselves and therefore remain vulnerable to these fraudulent activities.

[1] A Fletcher, A Karatzas, A Kreutzmann-Gallasch, 'Small Businesses as Consumers: Are they Sufficiently Well Protected?' (Centre for Competition Policy, 2014). *National Westminster Bank plc v Morgan* [1985] AC 686 (HL), 707–708 (Lord Scarman) who dismissed Lord Denning's view in *Lloyds Bank Ltd v Bundy* [1975] QB 326 (CA) 339).

[2] The Department for Digital, Media, Culture & Sport, *Cyber Security Breaches Survey: 2022*. Available at: https://assets.publishing.service.gov.uk/government/uploads/system/uploads/attachment_data/file/1089586/Cyber_Security_Breaches_Survey_2022_Infographic-Micro_Small_business.pdf (last accessed 30 May 2023).

The chapter has six sections. The second outlines the framework of MBs, focusing specifically on the United Kingdom (UK), Singapore and Australia. It outlines the background, regulatory environment and recent developments in MBs in the three countries, and highlights that MBs are more likely to be both victims and perpetrators of fraud in commercial transactions. The third section develops this outline by discussing how MBs fall victim to fraud in the three countries, while section four considers the rate and situations where MBs can be perpetrators of fraud – with a particular focus on COVID-19 transactions. The fifth section provides suggestions for regulatory reform in order to 'level the playing field' for MBs, both in terms of their transactions with consumers but also with other businesses. Thes sixth section concludes the chapter.

2. Show (Micro)Business: The Framework of MBs

In the UK, MBs are defined under the Companies Act 2006, s 384A as a business consisting of not more than 10 employees with a turnover of no more than £632,000. In Australia, there is no single definition of a MB. The Australian Bureau of Statistics ('ABS') defines an MB as a small business with 0–4 employees, and a small business as having 5–19 employees. In contrast, the Corporations Act 2001, s 45(2) defines a 'small proprietary company' as a company which has at least two of the following: (a) a consolidated gross operating revenue for the financial year of less than AUD10 million; (b) a value of the consolidated gross assets at the end of the financial year less than AUD 5 million; and (c) fewer than 50 employees. In Singapore, the Ministry of Trade and Industry defines SMEs (Small and Medium-sized Enterprises) as a business with an annual sales turnover of under S$100 million, or one that employs less than 200 workers.

The focus of this chapter is not to address these differences or provide a comprehensive definition of MBs that can apply globally.[3] It is important to recognise that MBs are a specific and unique type of small business that generally has the resources, skills, and knowledge more aligned with a consumer than a standard 'business' party to a transaction.

Despite their size, MBs are vital organs of the local and global economies. In the UK, there are approximately 5.3 million MBs, accounting for 95% of all businesses,[4] contributing c.£5.5 billion annually to the economy and employing one-fifth of UK workers.[5] MBs are also on the rise in Singapore. Whilst no specific

[3] We do note that there have been calls for a more robust definition of MBs to be developed and we agree with this call: see The McKell Institution, *Micro but Mighty: Magnifying Microbusinesses in Australia* (2023) (last accessed 21 August 2023) p 17.

[4] Commons Library Research Briefing, 'Business Statistics' (21 December 2021), 12. Available at: https://researchbriefings.files.parliament.uk/documents/SN06152/SN06152.pdf (last accessed 30 May 2023).

[5] ibid.

figures are currently available, SMEs in Singapore make up 99% of all enterprises and provide employment to 70% of the workforce.[6] The numbers of MBs are generally increasing year-on-year as jobseekers are drawn to the entrepreneurship, freedom and flexibility afforded by MBs compared to larger, more traditional businesses.[7] In Australia, MBs employ 2.9 million people (in a country of just under 26 million people) and generate $265 billion for the economy.[8]

Following the COVID-19 pandemic, reports of MBs as victims and perpetrators of fraud have made headlines.[9] There is limited research on the relationship between fraud and MBs from a legal and regulatory perspective. This is unfortunate. The vital role MBs play in the global economy, and the considerable size of the MB population, combined with their limited experience in fraud prevention, makes them fertile ground for fraudulent activity. Nonetheless, MBs often evade the scope of legislative or common law protections. It is beyond the scope of this paper to analyse the motivation of fraud offenders, however such fraudsters are often motivated by a mixture of economic need, created by a decline in business activity and loss of jobs, and personal greed driven by apparent opportunities to access extra capital, especially in a time of crises where there is a perceived reduction in fraud controls.[10] Additionally, fraud arises from the absence of capable guardians, who can act as an inhibiting factor in the decision to act illegally and/or dishonestly. In particular, law enforcement priorities have often excluded MBs from the scope of their supervision, concluding that such regulation presents unnecessary and burdensome 'red tape'.

In the sections that follow, this chapter shines a spotlight on MBs as both victims and perpetrators of fraud, and the legislative and regulatory environment that makes engaging with MBs a 'risky business'.

3. Risky (Micro)Business: MBs as Victims

It is a common trend in multiple countries around the world that MBs are significantly more likely to fall victims of fraudulent activities. For example, a survey and report from Xero from 2021 showed that nearly one in five Australian small businesses had been victims of 'invoice fraud' and, as a result, falsely paid out

[6] Singstat, "Enterprise by SMEs and Non-SMEs" (28 March 2023). Available at: https://tablebuilder.singstat.gov.sg/table/TS/M600981 (last accessed 30 May 2023).

[7] Office of National Statistics, 'UK Business; activity, size and location: 2021' (4 October 2021). Available at: www.ons.gov.uk/businessindustryandtrade/business/activitysizeandlocation/bulletins/ukbusinessactivitysizeandlocation/2021 (last accessed 30 May 2023).

[8] The McKell Institution, *Micro but Mighty: Magnifying Microbusinesses in Australia* (2023) 20.

[9] See, eg, Sky News, '£1.1bn of COVID small business loans identified as fraud, claims government source' (3 September 2022). Available at: https://news.sky.com/story/1-1bn-of-covid-small-business-loans-identified-as-fraud-claims-government-source-12688393 (last accessed 30 May 2023).

[10] M. Levi and R.G. Smith, *Fraud and its relationship to pandemics and economic crises: From Spanish flu to COVID-19*, Research Report 19: Australian Institute of Criminology (2021).

AUD$15,500 on average.[11] Data from Scamwatch further supported this, stating that MBs are the fastest growing scam victims in Australia, with a 130% increase in activity between 2021 and 2023. An example was provided of a farmer from Western Australia who lost over $1 million when their email account was compromised. The scammers then fraudulently updated two invoices for payments – one for grain and one for agricultural machinery – with different bank details.[12] As MBs are struggling to survive in a post pandemic cost-of-living crisis, this amount can have an overwhelming impact on their survival and longevity.

The consequences of fraud are also exceptionally severe for MBs, as they are less likely to have mechanisms in place to protect themselves and therefore more likely to have long-term detrimental impacts. For example, in 2022 the United States Securities and Exchange Commission ('SEC') reported 60 per cent of SMEs went out of business within six months of a data breach or cyber-attack.[13] The SEC commented that 'Cyber security is clearly a concern that the entire business community shares, but it represents an especially pernicious threat to smaller businesses'.[14] Despite having similar resources, knowledge and ability to protect themselves, small business fraud is three times more profitable than consumer fraud.[15] This is not, however, a new issue: in 2015 the SEC Commissioner Luis A. Aguilar issued a statement about the issues of cyber fraud and small businesses. In this he commented that SMEs 'are not just targets of cybercrime, they are its principal target'.[16]

One of the main reasons MBs are more likely to be victims of fraud is that they often do not have the size or resources to adequately protect themselves. The SEC review discovered that the smaller the business, the less they prioritise protection from fraud, particularly cyber-fraud. This means that MBs are particularly vulnerable and likely to be victims.[17] For example, the Xero survey discovered that nearly three in 10 small businesses in Australia do not spend *any* money on cyber-protection or education for their business.[18]

[11] Xero, 'Nearly one in five Australian small businesses a victim of invoice fraud', (8 November 2021). Available at: www.xero.com/au/media-releases/nearly-one-in-five-australian-small-businesses-a-victim-of-invoi/ (last accessed 30 May 2023).

[12] Australian Competition and Consumer Commission, *Targeting scams: Report of the ACCC on scams activity 2022* (April 2023). Available at: www.accc.gov.au/about-us/publications/serial-publications/targeting-scams-report-on-scams-activity/targeting-scams-report-of-the-accc-on-scams-activity-2022 (last accessed 21 August 2023) 26.

[13] MoneyBusiness, 'More than half of small businesses close after a cyber attack', (24 February 2022). Available at: www.mybusiness.com.au/resources/news/more-than-half-of-small-businesses-close-after-a-cyber-attack.

[14] ibid.

[15] Experian (2009) *Identifying Small-Business Fraud* (An Experian White Paper) p 1.

[16] Luis A Aguilar, 'The Need for Greater Focus on the Cybersecurity Challenges Facing Small and Midsize Businesses', 19 October 2015. Available at: www.sec.gov/news/statement/cybersecurity-challenges-small-midsize-businesses (last accessed 30 May 2023).

[17] ibid.

[18] Xero, 'Nearly one in five Australian small businesses a victim of invoice fraud', (8 November 2021). Available at: www.xero.com/au/media-releases/nearly-one-in-five-australian-small-businesses-a-victim-of-invoi/ (last accessed 30 May 2023).

This situation is exacerbated by the fact that fraud, particularly to small businesses, is of decreasing importance to law enforcement around the world. Nowhere is this more obvious than in the United States, where fraud is steeply rising but support from law enforcement for investigating and prosecuting fraud cases is decreasingly significantly. For example, data from the US Justice Department highlights those prosecutions of frauds against financial institutions dropped 48 per cent from 2000 to 2007.[19] This is particularly evident for MBs, as the smaller the fraud committed, the less likely that the police will investigate and, where appropriate, prosecute.[20]

4. A (Micro)Business Affair: MBs as Perpetrators and Facilitators

Frequently overlooked is the role of MBs in perpetrating and/or facilitating fraud. Three prevalent practices are discussed in this section. The first concerns material misrepresentations made by or on behalf of MBs in respect of applications for loans, credit, or grants. In this example, MBs can perpetrate and facilitate fraud by evading the controls and regulation supervising bank-to-MB or government-to-MB lending. The second example concerns instances where MBs facilitate fraud due to failings in their ability to mitigate against, for example, phishing scams or email compromise, causing loss to third parties. The third example concerns MBs as 'money mules' who, knowingly or not, allow their business account to be used by fraudsters for money-laundering purposes.

These examples expose deficiencies in the law's approach to MBs. MBs all too often fall outside the scope of legislative and regulatory provisions designed to mitigate against fraud. Despite the increasing prevalence of MB fraud, new proposals by the UK Government to combat economic crime omit MBs from their scope. This is unfortunate. While it is important that 'red tape' does not stifle the ability of MBs to conduct business, excluding them entirely enables economic harm.

4.1. MB Lending Fraud

In MB lending fraud, MBs (or individuals purporting to be MBs) make loan applications which materially misrepresent the purpose of the loan and/or the identity and nature of the business. According to a recent report, the average year-on-year increase in MB lending fraud is 14.5%, compared to 6.9% in 2021, and is estimated to represent up to 15% of overall losses sustained by lenders.[21] Two factors have

[19] Experian (2009) *Identifying Small-Business Fraud* (An Experian White Paper) p 2.
[20] ibid.
[21] LexisNexis Risk Solutions, *The State of Small Business Lending Fraud* (2023: LexisNexis).

driven this increase in fraud in recent years: first, the uptake in and emergency provision of loans as a result of recent crises (including the pandemic and cost of living), and second, the uptake in applications being made via remote channels (such as online or over the phone) as opposed to in-person.

The rise in MB lending fraud has a clear, causal relationship to the onset of the pandemic and the associated economic crisis. In the UK and Australia, reports suggest that MBs engaged in dishonest attempts to obtain government economic stimulus funding during the pandemic.[22] In Australia, the pandemic led to a substantial increase in government-support payments being made to small and MBs. The Coronavirus Economic Response Package Omnibus Act 2020 contained 16 schedules of support payments enabling MBs to claim between $20,000 and $100,000 as a cash flow boost to help them maintain operations during the pandemic.[23] Similarly, in the UK, stimulus programmes included the Bounce Back Loan Scheme. Under the scheme, eligible businesses could apply for a 100 percent, government-backed loan of up to £50,000 per business, with no interest charged or repayments during the first 12 months. By August 2020, more than 1.5 million businesses had borrowed up to £50,000 each, worth a total of £35bn.[24]

It is now believed that a proportion of these loans were provided to MBs in the UK and Australia who had dishonestly made claims outside the strict eligibility requirements.[25] According to the National Audit Office, around 11 per cent of the loans granted under the UK's Bounce Back Loan Scheme were fraudulent – equating to some £4.9 billion.[26] The scale of the fraud remains unknown.[27] The limited literature has so far identified three ways in which the material misrepresentations were perpetrated by or on behalf of MBs: MBs inflated their turnover or other requirements in order to fit the eligibility criteria and/or receive more funds; MBs made a loan application through the business and then, upon receipt, declared the company insolvent; and MBs applied to multiple lenders for a loan.

The speed and urgency with which the schemes were introduced, which led to insubstantial due diligence and regulations for approving applications, has been the primary rationale provided for this type of fraud. This appears to be only part of the problem. The inadequacy of the current law in identifying and combating fraud perpetrated by and through MBs undermines efforts to diminish the risk of economic harm. Legislative measures, both prior to and following the pandemic,

[22] ibid.

[23] Australian Treasury, Annual Report 2020–21. Available at: https://treasury.gov.au/sites/default/files/2021-10/p2021-216241-tsy-annual-report-2020-21.pdf (last accessed 30 May 2023).

[24] HM Treasury, Annual Report and Accounts 2020–21. Available at: www.gov.uk/government/publications/hm-treasury-annual-report-and-accounts-2020-to-2021 (last accessed 30 May 2023).

[25] S Browning, *Coronavirus: Business loans schemes* (House of Commons Library, 21 March 2023).

[26] ibid p 37.

[27] Browning, Coronavirus: Business loans schemes (n 25). See also HMRC, *Error and Fraud in the COVID-19 Schemes: methodology and approach (an update for 2022)*, (18 July 2022). Available at: www.gov.uk/government/publications/measuring-error-and-fraud-in-the-covid-19-schemes/error-and-fraud-in-the-covid-19-schemes-methodology-and-approach-an-update-for-2022 (last accessed 30 May 2023).

either entirely omit MBs from their scope in preventing fraud or fail to adequately recognise the part MBs play in perpetrating and facilitating fraud.

A failure to consider the role of MBs in perpetrating fraud is illustrated by the Rating (Coronavirus) and Directors Disqualification (Dissolved Companies) Act 2021 ('CDDA'), introduced in December 2021. The CDDA was introduced to prevent directors (whether naively or deliberately) dissolving their company to avoid repaying debts owed to the Bounce Back Loan Scheme. The legislation extends the Insolvency Service's powers to investigate and disqualify company directors who abuse the company dissolution process. In announcing the changes, the government emphasised that the measures would specifically 'tackle directors dissolving companies to avoid repaying Government backed loans put in place to support business during the Coronavirus pandemic'.[28] Nonetheless, the enforceability of the Insolvency Service's new measures are unlikely to have any substantive effect on MBs. Under the CDDA, s 6, the court is obliged to disqualify a director where they are found to be unfit. Although, given the company will not have become insolvent (within the meaning of the CDDA) prior to dissolution, there will be no office holder responsible for reporting on the conduct of its directors prior to dissolution. It appears, therefore, that the Insolvency Service will be heavily reliant on the creditors of a dissolved company to raise concerns regarding its directors' conduct in order to initiate their investigations. While a creditor may be able to benefit personally from any resulting compensation order, providing an incentive to participate, it is far from clear such incentives will exist for creditors of MBs – who may consider the size and limited means of the business, and the costs associated with any enforcement measures, to outweigh the value of the loan itself. In any event, the Insolvency Service's guidance 'Dissolved Company Investigations', makes clear that the primary purpose of any investigation is to protect the public or the business community, not the repayment or recovery of assets for creditors and, before it will consider bringing a case, the Insolvency Service must be satisfied the expense is justified.[29]

The pandemic also accelerated the development of, and changes in, the methods by which loan applications are made. Post-pandemic, nearly three-quarters of all loan applications are made online or by mobile. It is estimated that some 19 per cent of MB lending fraud losses are attributed to these changes, and presented further difficulties in verifying the truth of the statements made. While such fraud is clearly a result of inadequate internal controls and fraud prevention mechanisms by lenders – indeed most fraud is not caught until *after* the point

[28] HM Government, 'Crackdown on directors who dissolve companies to evade debts' (16 December 2021). Available at: www.gov.uk/government/news/crackdown-on-directors-who-dissolve-companies-to-evade-debts#:~:text=Rogue%20directors%20who%20dissolve%20their,disqualified%20from%20being%20a%20director.&text=The%20Insolvency%20Service%20has%20been,to%20avoid%20paying%20their%20liabilities (last accessed 30 May 2023).

[29] Insolvency Service, '*Dissolved Company Investigations*' (16 December 2021). Available at: www.gov.uk/government/publications/dissolved-company-investigations/dissolved-company-investigations (last accessed 30 May 2023).

of account origination (some 68 per cent of MB lending fraud),[30] it is concerning that, despite such growing practices by MBs, legislative measures nonetheless propose to *exclude* MBs from anti-fraud legislation. According to recent reports, Ministers are planning to exclude small UK businesses from measures targeting liability for businesses who 'fail to prevent fraud' contained in the Economic Crime and Corporate Transparency Bill.[31] The UK's Home Office stated that 'the offence will only apply to large companies, to avoid disproportionate burdens on SMEs and support economic growth'.[32] As discussed below, the inadequacies in the law's response reveals a key misunderstanding about the role MBs can play in perpetrating and facilitating fraud, at the expense of both consumers, businesses and the broader economy.[33]

4.2. Business Email Compromise

The current law further provides limited protection in instances where MBs *facilitate* fraud as a result of their inexperience, negligence and/or recklessness. A key concern is the rise of 'Business Email Compromise' or 'phishing' scams whereby fraudsters can infiltrate an MB's email system and impersonate the MB, directing fraudulent payments to be made. While this form of fraud arises in all businesses, MBs are prime targets due to the (often) inadequate systems in place to detect fraud and prevent cyber-security attacks. According to the Cyber Security Breaches Survey, 39 per cent of the UK's small and MBs were subject to a cyber-attack in 2022, with an average cost per attack from loss of money or data of £4,200.[34]

For example, the Western Australian farmer discussed in section 2 above, was a victim of Business Email Compromise, when their business partners paid nearly AUD $1 million to scammers who issued fake invoices as opposed to the farmer who owed the money. The current law in England, Australia and Singapore provides little guidance on who is to bear the responsibility for such fraud – the business or consumer who made the payment to the wrong account, or the MB whose email account was hacked? This presents key challenges to those transacting with MBs – particularly in relation to consumers who, like MBs, often also lack the sophistication to detect and prevent cyber-attacks. Thus far, three responses to

[30] LexisNexis Risk Solutions, *The State of Small Business Lending Fraud* (2023: LexisNexis).

[31] See, eg, 'Small UK companies set to be excluded from anti-fraud legislation' (13 March 2023). Available at: www.ft.com/content/ddbbe258-e0d2-40ad-bfd5-23b9b91cf51d (last accessed 30 May 2023).

[32] HM Government, 'Factsheet: failure to prevent fraud offence' (11 April 2023). Available at: www.gov.uk/government/publications/economic-crime-and-corporate-transparency-bill-2022-factsheets/factsheet-failure-to-prevent-fraud-offence (last accessed 30 May 2023).

[33] See also the recent comment from Cifas, the UK's leading fraud prevention service, which expressed concern at MBs' exclusion from the 'failure to prevent' fraud legislation. Available at: www.cifas.org.uk/newsroom/economic-crime-plan (last accessed 18 October 2023).

[34] HM Government, 'Cyber Security Breaches Survey 2022' (11 July 2022). Available at: www.gov.uk/government/statistics/cyber-security-breaches-survey-2022/cyber-security-breaches-survey-2022 (last accessed 30 May 2023).

determining liability have been posited and will be discussed in more detail below, but none adequately assist MBs in detecting and preventing such attacks, nor do they adequately mitigate against the harms incurred.

The first response is to consider the contractual position governing the parties. It is common ground that one of the primary purposes of a contract is the allocation of risk between contracting parties. Accordingly, in circumstances where one party has sustained a loss, any relief to be obtained may be provided for in such a contract. This response rests on two assumptions: first, that the parties have entered into a binding agreements; and second, that such an agreement contained an express or implied term allocating responsibility for the loss presented by Business Email Compromise. Finding that the parties have entered into a binding agreement is unlikely to be contentious – even for MBs and consumers, who lack the sophistication of larger commercial parties, it is common practice for contracts of goods or services to be entered into. More difficult is identifying a precise term that allocates responsibility for the loss caused by Business Email Compromise (or similar such frauds). At present, no such legislation exists which gives authority for such terms to be readily implied or incorporated. Further, it is rare for an MB contract to expressly allocate the risk arising from Business Email Compromise.

Another response the law may adopt is to determine whether the MB owes the consumer or other transacting party a duty of care to ensure that payment instructions are not altered by reason of the MB's negligence. Although such a duty is not established under the current law, parallels have been drawn with case law on cheque fraud, which state that a duty is owed by a customer to a bank when drawing on a cheque which was intercepted by a third-party fraudster. For example, in *Young v Grote*,[35] the plaintiff was a customer of the defendant bankers; on leaving home he entrusted to his wife several blank forms of cheques signed by himself desiring her to have them filled up according to the exigencies of his business. Mrs Young subsequently, for the purpose of the business, required the sum of £50 2s. 3d. and she delivered one of the cheques so signed by her husband, the plaintiff, to a clerk of the plaintiff, and asked him to fill it up with such sum. The clerk subsequently altered the cheque so it was drawn in the sum of £350 2s. 3d., presented it at the bank and absconded with the proceeds. It was held that a customer drawing a cheque owes a duty of care to the bank to take care that it cannot be altered and that, by reason of Young's negligence, he was liable for the loss suffered.

The House of Lords in *London Joint Stock Bank v Macmillan*[36] cited the duty of care established in *Young v Grote* with approval. Lord Finlay LC noted at p 810:

> 'The ground on which Young v Grote proceeded was, according to my judgment of three out of the four judges, simply this, that if a customer in drawing a cheque neglects reasonable precautions against forgery and forgery ensues, he is liable to make good the loss to the banker and the fact that a crime intervenes to cause the loss does not make it too remote … No one can be certain of preventing forgery, but it is a very simple thing

[35] *Young v Grote* (1827) 4 Bing 253.
[36] *London Joint Stock Bank v Macmillan* [1918] AC 777.

> in drawing a cheque to take reasonable and ordinary precautions against forgery. If owing to the neglect of such precautions it is put in the power of any dishonest person to increase the amount by forgery, the customer must bear the loss as between himself and the banker.'

In *Macmillan*, the respondents' firm, which had an account at the appellant bank, entrusted to a clerk the duty of filling in the cheques for signature. The clerk presented to one of the partners of the firm for signature a cheque drawn in favour of the firm or bearer. There was no sum in words written in the space provided for the writing, and there were the figures '*2.0.0*' in the space intended for figures. The partner signed the cheque. The clerk subsequently added the words '*one hundred and twenty pounds*' in the space left for the words and wrote the figures '*1*' and '*0*' respectively on each side of the figure '*2*'. The clerk presented the cheque for payment and obtained the funds out of the firm's account. It was held by the House of Lords that the bank was entitled to debit the firm's account with the full amount of the cheque.

There are, of course, differences with MBs. Most obviously, the cases concern a relationship between customer and bank, as opposed to the position between an MB and its customer. Further, it is by no means clear a court will find there to be sufficient proximity and foreseeability in an instance of Business Email Compromise, such that an MB would be deemed liable for any failure to prevent such fraud. Indeed, the law of tort has been averse to finding that omissions give rise to liability unless there is some 'special relationship' between the parties. It is not altogether certain that a relationship of MB and customer will give rise to such a relationship.

It must also be queried whether recognising such a duty will have the effect of 'opening the floodgates', and therefore be deemed undesirable. Lord Scarman in *Tai Hing Cotton Mill Ltd v Liu Chong Hing Bank Ltd*[37] rejected the notion that a duty to take reasonable care in drawing a cheque extends to a common law duty to organise one's business in such a way as to prevent fraud. In *Tai Hing*, a bookkeeper perpetrated a series of frauds on his employers. In some cases, he tricked them into signing blank or incomplete cheques which he converted and completed. There was no attempt by the company to check his activities and his frauds went undetected from approximately six years. The employers accepted responsibility for all cheques which carried genuine signatures but demanded that the three banks recredit the firm's respective accounts with the amounts paid out against the forged cheques. The bank's defence was, principally, that the frauds were occasioned by the firm's negligence in the way it conducted its business. Reversing the Hong Kong Court of Appeal's decision in favour of the banks, Lord Scarman emphasised that a customer's duty of care was confined to what could:

> '... be seen to be plainly necessary incidents of the relationship. Offered such a [current account] service, a customer must obviously take care in the way he draws his cheque, and must obviously warn his bank as soon as he knows that a forger is operating his account'.[38]

[37] *Tai Hing Cotton Mill Ltd v Liu Chong Hing Bank Ltd* [1986] AC 80.
[38] ibid 106D.

His Lordship however rejected the view that the customer's duty at common law went further than this. Accordingly, unless it can be established that there are certain '*incidents of the relationship*' which give rise to a duty of care, the courts are unlikely to hold that an MB owed its customer any duty of care to prevent the fraud.

That no duty of care is owed in such circumstances was affirmed by the English Court in *Sell Your Car with Us Ltd v Sareen* [2019] BCC 1211. Mr Sareen had sold a Maserati Levante car through the company and, under the terms of the contract, the company was obliged to pay him £51,800. A third party fraudulently intercepted the email exchanges between the company and Mr Sareen. The third party, impersonating Mr Sareen over email and telephone, induced the company to wrongly divert £30,000 to a different bank account under the control of the fraudster. The company refused to pay up and Mr Sareen served a statutory demand. The company issued an injunction to restrain the presentation of a winding-up petition. The company argued that they had a genuine counterclaim against Mr Sareen equal to the debt on the basis that: first, there was an implied term in the contract that Mr Sareen would take reasonable care over the security of his email communication which he had failed to do; secondly, there was an implied representation by Mr Sareen that he had reasonable control over the security of his emails. If he did not, it amounted to a negligent misrepresentation. The Court rejected both arguments. It held that there was no basis to imply a term as it was neither necessary nor obvious that such a term should be implied. Further, the mere agreement by Mr Sareen to accept communications by email did not imply any representation about the security of his email account or control he exercised. It represented no more than that he was contactable at that address. Even if supplying his email address did amount to a representation, there was no evidence that the company had relied upon any such representation or that any alleged representation was false at the time it was given.

The result is that MBs are not only perpetrators of but, increasingly, facilitators of cyber fraud by virtue of their flawed IT systems and/or failings to adequately prevent such attacks. The current law has no clear means by which customers of MBs can be adequately protected from such harms. Nor has the law provided clarity on how such losses should be allocated.

4.3. Money Muling

Another example of MBs facilitating fraud is the practice of 'money muling', which involves a fraudster using a third party's bank account for money laundering purposes. It takes various forms but, in the MB context, typically involves the fraudster claiming to be interested in 'investing' in the MB. Funds are paid by the fraudster into the MB's account and, over time, the MB is persuaded to transfer the funds into another (fraudulent) account. Often, MBs are unaware of their role in such money-laundering activities. For example, one former MB owner interviewed by the National Fraud Intelligence Bureau noted that they were unaware of why they had been targeted:

> 'I had a small engineering company which I was trying to get off the ground. The first contact I had was by email from an investment company in the Middle East. They said they wanted to invest some capital into my company and they had other business interests in the UK. They only transferred a few thousand pounds at a time so the bank never questioned it.'[39]

According to the National Fraud Database, in 2021 some 79,000 cases of fraud demonstrated a misuse of banking facilities, nearly three-quarters of which (72%) showed behaviours indicative of money mule activity.[40] As with loan misrepresentations and business email compromise, money muling activities have grown in prevalence since the COVID-19 pandemic and the cost-of-living crises whereby fraudsters have been known to more readily prey on an MBs' need for investment.[41]

The current law's response to money muling is a contradiction. On the one hand, MBs are portrayed as innocent victims unaware of having committed a crime and 'tricked' by a fraudsters' fake investment offer.[42] On the other hand, MB owners can face criminal sanctions for facilitating (even unwittingly) such activities.[43] At present, there appears to be no clear civil or commercial response to money muling by MBs. This is an area in urgent need of reform, as it is important to have clear guidelines on the approach to regulating these activities, specifically whether intent is necessary to be held liable for money muling.

5. Back in (Micro)Business: Levelling the Playing Field

The above sections highlight the commercial law's deficiencies in responding to the specific issues presented by MBs as victims, perpetrators, and facilitators of fraud. The law has adopted an 'all or nothing' approach: either an MB is a 'business' and bound to follow the same rules as applied to medium and large businesses, which are significantly greater in both size and sophistication, or; it

[39] Action Fraud, 'Alert: Small businesses tricked into laundering money' (18 May 2016). Available at: www.actionfraud.police.uk/alert/alert-small-businesses-tricked-into-laundering-money (last accessed 18 October 2023).

[40] Cifas, 'UK businesses under increasing attack by criminals as latest Cifas data reveals reported cases of fraud up 16%' (28 April 2022). Available at: www.cifas.org.uk/newsroom/fraudscape-2022 (last accessed 18 October 2023).

[41] See, eg, BBC, 'Money launderers 'prey on generation Covid' (10 March 2021). Available at: www.bbc.co.uk/news/business-56334862 (last accessed 18 October 2023).

[42] See, eg, Cifas 'Latest fraud statistics reveal middle-aged mules targeted by online money laundering gangs' (3 June 2021). Available at: www.cifas.org.uk/newsroom/middle-aged-mules (last accessed 22 October 2023).

[43] Such criminal sanctions are beyond the scope of this chapter. By way of a broad overview, money mules have been convicted for money-laundering offences under Part 7 of the Proceeds of Crime Act 2002 for prison sentences of up to 14 years. Available at: www.lloydsbankinggroup.com/media/press-releases/2022/lloyds-bank/money-mules-are-getting-older.html (last accessed 18 October 2023).

has opted to exclude MBs entirely from the scope of protective measures (such as anti-money laundering and economic crime legislation) in fear that this would overly-burden MBs with 'red tape'. Neither approach addresses the needs of, or risks posed by, MBs. In this final section, we provide recommendations for 'levelling the playing field'. Our recommendations are guided by two aims: the first is to provide MBs with more protection to mitigate against fraud; the second is to ensure MBs are also made accountable for their role in perpetrating and/or facilitating fraud.

5.1. Providing Additional Protection to MBs

The first recommendation is to afford MBs the same level of protection as consumers. This has already occurred in Australia with little controversy and significant popularity, but there does not seem to be the political appetite in either the UK or Singapore. The starting point is to recognise that MBs often have the same levels of knowledge, power, and resources as individual consumers. There is therefore a strong argument that they should be treated as consumers in terms of regulatory protection available. As outlined by Experian:

> 'Among fraud topics, small-business fraud and the challenges organizations face in identifying and mitigating these losses frequently are overlooked and are not well-understood. Small-business fraud is not as visible as consumer fraud because businesses often are not seen as victims in the way that consumers are. With no legislation requiring fraud to be reported and no national bodies to collate information, there is a dearth of information on which to base statistics.'[44]

As has been proposed by the Law Commission in 2005[45] and in debates surrounding the passage of the CRA,[46] MBs should be included in the statutory definition of 'consumer' under the CRA (or, in Singapore, the Consumer Protection (Fair Trading) Act).

The primary objection to such an amendment is 'floodgate concerns' – that is, a substantial increase in the number of claims regarding unfair terms.[47] This can be easily dismissed. A sufficiently tight definition of MBs should be adopted. Such a definition already exists in the Companies Act 2006, s 364A which defines an MB as consisting of not more than 10 employees and having no more than £632,000

[44] Experian (2009) *Identifying Small-Business Fraud* (An Experian White Paper) p 1.

[45] The Law Commission and the Scottish Law Commission (Law Com no 292), 'Unfair terms in contracts: Report on a reference under section 3(1)(e) of the Law Commissions Act 1965 (Cm 6464 SE/2005/13).

[46] See, eg, Department of Business, Innovation and Skills, 'Protection of small businesses when purchasing goods and services: call for evidence' (March 2015). Available at: https://assets.publishing.service.gov.uk/government/uploads/system/uploads/attachment_data/file/433139/bis-15-209-protection-of-small-businesses-when-purchasing-goods-and-services-call-for-evidence.pdf (last accessed 16 September 2021).

[47] ibid.

in turnover. This would translate to around 4.5 million MBs in the UK[48] and fewer than 300,000 in Singapore.[49] If this was considered to be too broad and increased the scope of protection beyond acceptable levels (something with which neither of the authors agree), the definition used by the Australian Bureau of Statistics – as a small business with 0–4 employees – could be utilised instead.

Regardless of which definition is used, the number of MBs will pale in comparison to the number of consumers, some 67 million in the UK[50] and 5.5 million in Singapore,[51] for whom substantial protection has already been afforded. The significant detriment to the livelihood of MBs, and in turn the economy, as well as the adoption of unfair practices by larger corporations therefore cannot be justified by 'floodgate' arguments.

Amendments to the CRA can take inspiration from the success of reforms implemented in Australia, where MBs have been recognised as deserving the same protection as consumers. The Treasury Legislation Amendment (Small Businesses and Unfair Contract Terms) Act 2015 (Cth) amended the Australian Securities and Investments Commission Act 2001 and the Competition and Consumer Act 2010 to allow smaller businesses to be included in the Australian definition of consumer. Australian MBs thereby gain access to the greater protections of consumer law when contracting on account of their weaker bargaining power. Adopting a precise definition of when a small business can rely on consumer protections, Section 12BF provides that contracts with small businesses with an upfront contract price of AUD$300,000 or less, or AUD$1 million or less[52] where the term of the contract is for more than 12 months are covered under the Act. Resultantly, small businesses benefit from enhanced protections, including a fairness test for the courts to apply to strike out unfair terms. Further, Australian law more adequately reflects the realities of B2MB contracting. It is notable that the reforms have received almost universal praise.[53]

[48] Department for Business, Energy and Industrial Strategy, 'Business Population Estimates for the UK and the Regions 2020' (8 October 2020). Available at: www.gov.uk/government/statistics/business-population-estimates-2020/business-population-estimates-for-the-uk-and-regions-2020-statistical-release-html#:~:text=Composition%20of%20the%202020%20business%20population,-The%20UK%20private&text=there%20were%20estimated%20to%20be,aside%20from%20the%20owner(s) (last accessed 30 May 2023).

[49] The exact numbers in Singapore are not known, however there were estimated to be 291,000 SMEs in Singapore in 2021; the definition of MB will be significantly more restricted than that of an SME, therefore the numbers will be notably lower than the total number of SMEs.

[50] Based on the number of adults in the UK. Office of National Statistics: 'Overview of the UK population: January 2021' (14 January 2021). Available at: www.ons.gov.uk/peoplepopulationandcommunity/populationandmigration/populationestimates/articles/overviewoftheukpopulation/january2021 (last accessed 30 May 2023).

[51] Based on the number of adults in Singapore: Statista, 'Number of adults in Singapore from 2012 to 2021'. Available at: www.statista.com/statistics/667768/number-of-adults-in-singapore-by-country/#:~:text=In%202021%2C%20there%20were%20approximately,the%20age%20of%2018%20years (last accessed 21 August 2023).

[52] Around £160,000 and £530,000 respectively.

[53] Debate has centred around whether protections for small businesses should be enhanced further, not whether they should have been introduced in the first place. See, eg, the Consumer Affairs Forum,

Such a reform would have numerous benefits. In economic terms, minimising opportunity and bargaining costs will allow MBs to grow through reduced difficulties caused by poor bargaining power. Additionally, by instilling a more 'level playing field', reform would incentivise larger businesses to be more efficient and innovative, driving productivity and GDP-per-capita.[54] In legal terms, the law will better reflect the nuances and realities of the business landscape and fulfil its stated aim of protecting against unfair terms. The reform also has the moral benefit of protecting against the increased commercialisation of individuals who, through self-employment structures such as the gig-economy, are more frequently being used as a 'means to an end'[55] and for whom the UK Supreme Court has deemed it important to protect.[56] It would also put bigger businesses and – most importantly – financial institutions 'on notice' when contracting with MBs, ensuring that they are provided with the same level of protection as individuals. This places the risk on larger institutions, which are more likely to have the safety protocols, knowledge, and resources to have protections in place preventing fraud from occurring in the first place.

As MBs are both victims and perpetrators of fraud, it could be argued that providing them with 'consumer' status is too much of a risk, as it could allow them to facilitate fraud more easily. This, we argue, is using a sledgehammer to crack a nut. As will be discussed below in section 5.3, different mechanisms can be implemented to restrict MBs ability to perpetrate fraud and to hold them to account when this occurs. We believe that, instead of removing additional protection from all MBs, an approach that aims to hold the rogue businesses to account creates a much more equitable approach. It would be inappropriate and unfair to stop all MBs receiving additional protection because of a handful of bad apples who can be dealt with by other means.

5.2. Empower MBs to Protect Themselves

The second recommendation is to empower MBs, so that they can protect themselves from fraud. One of the most significant barriers associated with this is the cost of implementing fraud protection processes. It is therefore important to both increase the resources available to MBs for fraud protection and identify ways to create 'economies of scale' for fraud prevention for MBs.[57] This should include

'Regulation Impact Statement for Decision' (2020). Available at: https://treasury.gov.au/publication/p2020-125938 (last accessed 30 May 2023).

[54] A. Fletcher, A. Karatzas and A Kreutzmann-Gallasch, 'Small Businesses as Consumers: Are they Sufficiently Well Protected?' (Centre for Competition Policy, 2014).

[55] For an excellent exploration of this see J Prassl, *Humans as a Service: The Promise and Perils of Work in the Gig Economy* (Oxford University Press, 2018).

[56] *Uber BV and others v Aslam and others* [2021] UKSC 5.

[57] Luis A Aguilar, 'The Need for Greater Focus on the Cybersecurity Challenges Facing Small and Midsize Businesses', 19 October 2015. Available at: www.sec.gov/news/statement/cybersecurity-challenges-small-midsize-businesses (last accessed 30 May 2023).

encouraging businesses to work together to identify repeat fraud offenders and to share resources for developing fraud protection processes.[58]

It is accepted that this is a difficult ask. A balance must be struck between what is realistically achievable for MBs in terms of protecting and monitoring for fraud, and what protection is necessary to ensure customers of MBs do not become victims. A starting point is to issue detailed government guidance to MBs on the standards they are expected to meet in respect of cyber-security. Government-issued 'best practices' or regulatory guidance can assist in signalling to MBs the extent of the risks faced, the actions that should be taken, and the resources available to them to consult. Unlike larger businesses, MBs often lack the expertise on how their business can be targeted. Educating MBs and providing resources to assist in bolstering their protection will help to ensure MBs can detect and prevent fraud. There are significant resources available for advising consumers on how not to avoid being victims of fraud, and similar advice and assistance should be provided specifically for MBs.

As outlined above, one of the main reasons that MBs are so frequently victims of fraud is that they lack the funds to create bespoke, tailored fraud prevention strategies in their business. Considering the growing reliance on MBs in the economic development across a number of countries *and* the devastating impact of fraudulent activities on MBs, it is important to think imaginatively about potential solutions. Creating systems where similar MBs can work together to develop and implement a fraud protection system that would be appropriate for all the businesses, but share the costs associated with its development.

5.3. Holding MBs Accountable

The third recommendation recognises that a balance needs to be struck. Where MBs are known to be perpetrators and/or facilitators of fraud, they must be held accountable. A significant weakness in anti-fraud legislation is its failure to include MBs within its scope. An oft-cited concern is burdening MBs with 'red tape'. MBs are likely to find it more difficult than larger businesses to comply with, for example, the reporting and compliance standards imposed by such legislation. This is not a reason to exclude MBs entirely from its scope. Parliament and policymakers must consider how such legislation can be tailored to the size and sophistication of the business. For example, by tempering, where necessary, the monitoring and reporting requirements for anti-money laundering and fraud legislation, or the level of sanctions for failing to comply.

To reduce and mitigate against the economic harms caused by Business Email Compromise, policymakers should consider introducing a legislative duty of care. This requires careful consideration: it would be unwelcome and cumbersome for the law to recognise a general duty of care to prevent fraud. Nonetheless, where

[58] Experian (2009) *Identifying Small-Business Fraud* (An Experian White Paper) p 2.

MBs transact with consumers and/or businesses via email and require those individuals or businesses to make payment in accordance with instructions provided by email, MBs should have a duty of care to ensure that those instructions are not intercepted by a fraudster due to the failure by the MB to detect and prevent against cyber-attacks.

Finally, lenders should strengthen internal controls when verifying loan applications made by MBs. This is particularly so where applications are made online and remotely – as has become increasingly frequent following the pandemic. Policymakers should consider regulating the checks lenders need to make in respect of customer due diligence and, where necessary, enhanced customer due diligence, before loans are granted.

6. Conclusion

Fraud is on the rise – particularly amongst MBs. This chapter has called for an increased focus on the inherent risks associated with operating as, or contracting with, MBs. The lack of focus by policymakers and academics on the relationship between fraud and MBs has created a range of risks for MBs themselves and those transacting with them. On the one hand, MBs are increasingly victim to fraud. As this chapter has shown, MBs are among the most targeted for cyber-fraud and are often ill-equipped to mitigate against such harms. Despite this, law enforcement has shown a decreasing interest in investigating and prosecuting such fraud – particularly among MBs where the losses sustained by MBs as victims of fraud are often small.

On the other hand, for certain types of fraud – such as loan fraud and Business Email Compromise – the MB population is among the main perpetrators or facilitators. The legislative and regulatory response has been the same: to exclude MBs from the scope of anti-fraud legislation and initiatives. Fears that MBs will become overburdened by 'red tape' are too simplistic. Policymakers need to adopt a more nuanced approach to anti-fraud controls, which are tailored to the size and sophistication of the business. Without this, further economic harms are inevitable.

15

Should the Delaware *Caremark* Fiduciary Duty be Part of the Corporate Governance Regime in English Law?

WEIMING TAN*

1. Introduction

It has been observed that in the modern era, instead of being reinvented from scratch, laws are being transplanted instead.[1] In the context of company law, UK judges[2] and commentators[3] have on occasions explored American law for comparison and inspiration. Within the American legal system, the Delaware courts have been particularly active in developing its corporate law jurisprudence.[4] It is therefore no surprise that scholars have sought to analyse how UK corporate law could be refined through the experience of the Delaware courts. In recent times, it has been suggested that the Delaware *Caremark* duty be transplanted into the UK system of corporate governance.[5] Nevertheless, any legal transplantation must have regard to the context of the recipient jurisdiction.[6] Drawing from lessons of

* My thanks to Hans Tjio, Lionel Smith, Peter Candy, and Mark Ortega for their valuable comments. Earlier drafts of this chapter were presented at the Cambridge Private Law Centre, and the 'Fraud and Risk in Commercial Law' Conference at NUS. My thanks to the participants of both presentations for helpful discussion. All errors are mine.

[1] M Chen-Wishart, A Loke and S Vogenauer, *Studies in the Contract Laws of Asia I: Remedies for Breach of Contract*, 1st edn (Oxford, Oxford University Press 2016) 2.

[2] See, eg, *BTI 2014 LLC v Sequana SA* [2022] UKSC 25, [2022] 3 WLR 709 [248], [263], [301], [409], [448] (Lady Arden JSC).

[3] See, eg, D Kershaw, *The Foundations of Anglo-American Corporate Fiduciary Law* (Cambridge University Press 2018), J Armour, 'Derivative Actions: A Framework For Decisions' (2019) 135 *LQR* 412.

[4] D Kershaw, *Company Law in Context: Text and Materials*, 2nd edn (Oxford University Press 2012) 213.

[5] Armour (n 3) 419; C A Witting, 'Corporate Liability: A Systems Perspective' in M Petrin and C A Witting (eds), *Research Handbook on Corporate Liability* (Edward Elgar Publishing, 2023) 42. Building on this existing work, I understand that Witting is currently developing a separate piece to further his argument that the *Caremark* duty ought to be applicable in the UK.

[6] M Chen-Wishart, 'Legal Transplant and Undue Influence: Lost in Translation or a Working Misunderstanding?' (2013) 62 *ICLQ* 1, 12.

the Delaware courts, and considering the UK Companies Act 2006 ('CA 2006') and the equity jurisprudence emanating from the English courts, it is submitted that a more nuanced and modified version of the duty should be introduced to strengthen corporate regulation in the UK.

This chapter argues it would be desirable for the English courts to recognise a fiduciary duty of active oversight owed by directors to their companies. Although fiduciary duties in English law is traditionally perceived to be 'proscriptive' in nature, it will be argued that the growing momentum of the courts to recognise fiduciary duties beyond the 'no conflict' and 'no profit' rules provides a conceptual space to potentially develop this duty of active oversight. Alternatively, Parliament could also put this duty on a statutory footing, alongside the other directors' duties found in the CA 2006. However, unlike the Delaware *Caremark* duty, liability for a breach of the proposed duty should not be predicated upon the director acting in bad faith. The case for a *Caremark*-style duty for non-directorial officers will also be explored. It is submitted that any attempt to extend such a duty to officers should be decided by Parliament instead of the courts.

The chapter proceeds as follows. After the introduction, Section 2 investigates the developments and scope of the *Caremark* duty as conceived by the Delaware courts. Section 3 then presents the case for a similar duty, in the form of a fiduciary duty of active oversight, that could be adopted by the English courts. It is submitted that the proposed duty should be enforced as a fiduciary and mandatory duty. Section 4 argues that the duty should not be subsumed under the CA 2006, s 172 while Section 5 argues that it is inadequate to enforce the duty under the CA 2006, s 174. Finally, Section 6 argues that it is plausible for Parliament to legislate an oversight duty for non-directorial officers. While Delaware law does not specify which officers are under the *Caremark* duty, it is suggested that only C-suite officers should be subject to such a duty.

2. Developments and Ambit of the *Caremark* Duty

Although the existence of the *Caremark* duty is well-recognised under Delaware law, its precise scope of application has been a matter of some ambiguity. It is therefore important to track its origins and subsequent developments. The duty was first conceived by Chancellor Allen in *In re Caremark International Derivative Litigation*,[7] where his Honour formulated and elaborated on two contexts of directorial liability.[8] The first context where liability arises was when a board of directors had made a decision that resulted in a loss because that decision was 'ill-advised or negligent'.[9] The second context where liability would arise is when the company suffered a loss that flowed from 'an unconsidered failure of the board to act in

[7] 698 A2d 959 (Del Ch 1996).
[8] ibid.
[9] ibid 967.

circumstances in which due attention would, arguably, have prevented the loss'.[10] Although two situations of liability were envisaged by Chancellor Allen, subsequent courts tend to refer to the latter situation concerning unconsidered inaction as the '*Caremark*' duty.[11] Hence, to avoid confusion, references to the *Caremark* duty in this chapter are similarly confined to liability from unconsidered inaction.

Upon closer examination of the judicial developments, it would be apparent that the *Caremark* duty itself embodies two distinct prongs. First, there is an obligation by directors to ensure that the company has in place systems of management and control that, in concept and design, are reasonably adequate for assessing operational risks ('First Prong').[12] The Delaware courts have traditionally drawn a distinction between the board failing to ensure that companies implement adequate compliance systems to *prevent violations of positive law* by the company's employees and the board's failure to *prevent excessive business risk*.[13] Although the language in *Re Caremark* was in principle wide enough to encompass both categories of risks,[14] the courts have since demonstrated that the director's *Caremark* duty is to institute systems to prevent transgressions of prevailing laws and regulations.[15] Second, even after the board of directors has installed such systems and controls, they are under a further obligation to monitor the company and its compliance with the law to prevent wrongdoing that would expose the company to liability and subsequent losses ('Second Prong').[16]

An essential aspect of the *Caremark* duty is that liability for its breach is scienter-based. Consequently, a claimant is required to prove that the defendant has acted contrary to good faith (or has acted in bad faith).[17] In relation to the First Prong of *Caremark* liability, a director would not have acted in good faith if he had 'utterly failed' to implement any reporting or information system.[18] On the second prong of *Caremark* liability, the directors will only be liable if, having implemented such a system, they had 'consciously disregarded' or 'consciously failed' to monitor or oversee its operations, thereby disabling themselves from being informed of risks requiring their attention.[19] As one would expect, the threshold for liability is therefore a very high one to surmount, with Chancellor Allen in *Re Caremark* commenting that '[t]he theory here advanced is possibly the most difficult theory in corporation law upon which a plaintiff might hope to win a judgment'.[20]

[10] ibid.
[11] *Stone v Ritter* 911 A2d 362 (Del 2006) 369 (Holland J); *Marchand v Barnhill*, 212 A3d 805 (Del 2019) 821 (Strine CJ); *Guttman v Huang*, 823 A2d 492 (Del 2003) 506 (Strine VC).
[12] *Stone*, ibid. 370.
[13] CA Williams, 'Fiduciary Duties and Corporate Climate Responsibility' (2021) 74 *Vanderbilt Law Review* 1875, 1892.
[14] *Re Caremark* (n 7) 970.
[15] *Stone* (n 11) 370 (Holland J).
[16] ibid.
[17] ibid.
[18] ibid.
[19] ibid.
[20] *Re Caremark* (n 7) 967.

Given that a lack of good faith is an integral condition for a director to be liable for breach of his *Caremark* duty, the Delaware Supreme Court in *Stone v Ritter* held that the duty should be recognised as part of the fiduciary duty of loyalty.[21] This stood in contrast with the analysis of Chancellor Allen in *Re Caremark*, where the duty was originally construed as a fiduciary duty of care.[22] This reclassification has two important consequences. Firstly, the *Caremark* duty becomes a mandatory duty. As a result, liability for its breach cannot be excluded, and directors in breach of the duty cannot be indemnified for any personal liability.[23] Secondly, directors cannot rely on the protection of the business judgment rule when claims of oversight concerns are levelled against them, unless what is being challenged involved the board's decision on how to conduct its business.[24] By contrast, a director can rely on the business judgment rule to avoid liability when the claim concerns a breach of the duty of care.[25]

In addition to directors owing the *Caremark* duty to their companies, the Delaware Court of Chancery has recently held in *Re McDonald's Corporation Stockholder Derivative Litigation* that officers do owe similar oversight duties that mirror both prongs of the *Caremark* duty, albeit that the scope of an officer's oversight duty is context-driven, and potentially narrower than that of a director's duty.[26] The duty applicable to officers will be explored further in Section 6. While the *Caremark* duty provides much critical food for thought, not every aspect of the duty should be readily transplanted into UK company law. The subsequent parts of the chapter will examine the extent to which the *Caremark* duty could be introduced into English law as part of its corporate governance regime.

3. The Proposed Fiduciary Duty of Active Oversight as a Mandatory Duty

Corporate discipline in the UK is regulated and maintained by a combination of the common law and legislation. The principal statute concerned is the CA 2006.

[21] *Stone* (n 11) 369 (Holland J).

[22] *Re Caremark* (n 7) 970.

[23] See DEL. CODE ANN. Tit. 8, § 102(b)(7) (2021) (limits to exculpation); ibid. § 145(a)–(b) (company's power to indemnify its agents limited to actions in good faith, which is part of the duty of loyalty). Section 102(b)(7) provides that the certificate of incorporation may include:

> 'A provision eliminating or limiting the personal liability of a director to the corporation or its stockholders for monetary damages for breach of fiduciary duty as a director, provided that such provision shall not eliminate or limit the liability of a director: (i) For any breach of the director's duty of loyalty to the corporation or its stockholders; (ii) for acts or omissions not in good faith or which involve intentional misconduct or a knowing violation of law; (iii) under § 174 of this title [unlawful distributions rendering the company insolvent]; or (iv) for any transaction from which the director derived an improper personal benefit.'

[24] Williams (n 13) 1892.

[25] *Aronson v Lewis*, 473 A2d 805 (Del 1984) 812 (Moore J).

[26] *In re McDonald's Corporation Stockholder Derivative Litigation*, 289 A 3d 343 (Del Ch 2023) 350 (Laster VC).

It is submitted that the UK's corporate governance regime can be further enhanced with the adoption of a *Caremark*-style duty, which this chapter refers to as the 'duty of active oversight'. Like the Delaware duty, the duty contains two distinct

> First, there is an obligation for directors to ensure that the company has in place systems of management and control that, in concept and design, are reasonably adequate for assessing the company's compliance with positive law and regulation. Second, directors are under a further obligation to monitor the company and its compliance with the law to prevent wrongdoing that would expose the company to liability and subsequent losses.

Consistent with the *Caremark* duty, the duty of active oversight will be a mandatory, fiduciary duty. However, unlike the Delaware version, the duty of active oversight should not be scienter-based, and its breach should not be conditional upon a director's lack of good faith. This will be elaborated below in Section 4 which focuses on demonstrating why the duty ought to be a *fiduciary* and *mandatory duty*.

In investigating whether the duty of active oversight should even be a legal *duty* in the first place, it is apposite to start by examining a director's undertaking to the company. In *Boardman v Phipps*, Lord Upjohn observed that one should first study the fiduciary's relationship and undertaking 'to see what duties are thereby imposed on the [fiduciary, and] to see what is the scope and ambit of the duty imposed upon him'.[27] Every fiduciary gives a specific undertaking to his principal and, as Conaglen has argued, a fiduciary is subjected to general duties that enhances the likelihood of the proper performance of that core undertaking.[28] In other words, the general duties are second-order obligations which are meaningful only through their interaction with the first-order undertakings given by the fiduciary.[29] It shall be argued that the duty of active oversight, as a second-order obligation, is necessary to enable directors to effectively fulfil their first-order directorial undertaking.

In the director's context, a person can give multiple and separate undertakings. For instance, a 'managing director' or an 'executive director' may undertake different fiduciary obligations *qua*, inter alia, director, senior manager, or agent.[30] It is therefore important to appreciate that a director can take on several legal capacities, and that a *directorial* undertaking is distinct from a *managerial* undertaking even though both roles can be fiduciary in nature.[31] To further illustrate the point, an 'independent director' or a 'non-executive director' is a directorial fiduciary but not a managerial one. As Kershaw has persuasively argued, much of the post-1970 company law jurisprudence on directors' duties, including the general duties in

[27] [1967] 2 AC 46 (HL), 127.
[28] M Conaglen, *Fiduciary Loyalty* (Hart Publishing, 2010) 32–34, 61–62.
[29] D Kershaw, 'Corporate Law's Fiduciary Personas' (2020) 136 *LQR* 454, 455.
[30] ibid 456.
[31] ibid.

the CA 2006, was developed to address the managerial fiduciary relationship.[32] Consequently, the directorial fiduciary has been obscured from vision. A managerial undertaking given by a director, or a senior manager, is a full-time positive undertaking to pursue the company's corporate purpose and interest.[33] By contrast, the directorial undertaking is a narrower and more limited one, focusing on the collective exercise of board power and responsibility for its exercise.[34] The UK Corporate Governance Code 2018 stipulates that non-executive directors should, inter alia, hold management to account – a responsibility that can be discharged by participating in the collective exercise of power on matters brought before the board, and taking responsibility for the exercise of that power.[35] Crucially, this would include the supervision of management.[36] To avoid doubt, all directors are subject to a specific *directorial* undertaking regardless of whether the person is a managing or executive director, or simply a non-executive director. A person who is a managing or executive director would have taken on an additional *managerial* undertaking. The proposed duty of active oversight is therefore a directorial duty that applies to all directors.

Central to a directorial undertaking is the ability of a director to be able to hold management to account. To do so, a director must first be apprised of the company's operations and risks before he can assess them and provide a constructive challenge to management.[37] However, non-executive directors are often faced with formidable obstacles. First, a non-executive director does not determine what issues are to be brought before the board.[38] He must necessarily rely on senior management, who has a closer working knowledge of the company's affairs. Second, it has been observed that little time is allocated to address company problems, strategising and tactics,[39] while virtually no time is made available to address liability issues unless the issue becomes unavoidable.[40] Therefore, the 'monitoring board' model has been criticised as 'inherently weak' given that non-executive directors have limited access to information, with board time and agenda being dominated by management.[41]

[32] ibid.

[33] ibid 480.

[34] ibid 456.

[35] Financial Reporting Council, *The UK Corporate Governance Code* (2018), Principle H.

[36] Kershaw (n 29) 459.

[37] Providing constructive challenge to management is part of the directorial undertaking (see *The UK Corporate Governance Code* (n 35), Principle H).

[38] Kershaw (n 29) 458.

[39] R Leblanc and J Gillies, *Inside the Boardroom: How Boards Really Work and the Coming Revolution in Corporate Governance* (Wiley, 2005) 54 (20 to 25 days per year), 55, 76 and 77 (two to three days per month); S M Bainbridge, *The New Corporate Governance in Theory and Practice* (Oxford, Oxford University Press, 2008) 199 (18 hours per month); M Petrin, 'Corporate Management in the Age of AI' (2019) *Columbia Business Law Review* 965.

[40] *In re The Boeing Co Derivative Litigation* CA No. 2019-0907-MTZ (Del Ch 2021) 40 (Zurn VC); *Marchand* (n 11) 814 (Strine CJ).

[41] J D Cox and R S Thomas, 'A Revised Monitoring Model Confronts Today's Movement Toward Managerialism' (2021) 99 *Texas LR* 1275, 1284, 1289.

While it is understandable that a company would want to focus most of the board's time on business performance and financial risks, it is equally important to ensure that a company adheres to prevailing laws and regulations. In *Ho Kang Peng v Scintronix Corp Ltd*, the Singapore Court of Appeal emphasised that the 'interests of the company' were not just 'profit maximisation by any means' and noted that a director who ran the 'unjustified risk of subjecting the company to criminal liability is not acting in the company's interests'.[42] The case involved a director giving bribes to third-party vendors, thereby potentially exposing the company to criminal wrongdoing, namely the offence of offering a bribe.[43] Although the director, who was concurrently appointed as the company's CEO, was acting in his managerial capacity, nothing should turn on this since a director, in discharging his directorial undertaking of holding management to account, must also be alive in preventing the company's executives (including himself) from violating laws and regulations. Simply put, acting in the interests of the company broadly requires all directors, including non-executive directors, to monitor for wrongdoings that might expose the company to possible criminal and regulatory sanctions.

Given that non-executive directors are often unable to determine board agenda and are not involved in the day-to-day running of the business, it is crucial that directors establish some form of reporting or information system such that the board is routinely updated on compliance matters. Relying on *ad hoc* disclosures is inadequate given that senior management may obfuscate them or derail them with matters deemed to be more pressing. Consequently, directors must have direct oversight over compliance matters and be apprised of them in a regular fashion. Subjecting directors to a duty of active oversight would not only compel them, but also enhance their ability to properly discharge their directorial undertaking of scrutinising management.

The duty of active oversight should be recognised as a *fiduciary* duty because enforcing it as such would enhance the protection of the fiduciary relationship between the director and company. In many circumstances, the primary purpose of retaining a fiduciary is to capitalise on his expertise, which in turn requires according him a certain latitude of discretion.[44] This in turn gives rise to 'knowledge' and 'power' gaps.[45] A 'knowledge' gap exists because there is an asymmetry of information of subject matter between principal and fiduciary.[46] A principal therefore has little choice but to rely on his fiduciary. In addition, a 'power' gap exists by virtue of the principal's limited ability to monitor and detect breaches by the fiduciary.[47] The vulnerabilities that a principal is exposed to is sometimes referred to as the principal-agent problem.

[42] [2014] SGCA 22; [2014] 3 SLR 329 [40] (Chao Hick Tin JA).

[43] Prevention of Corruption Act 1960 (Singapore), s 5; Bribery Act 2010 (c. 23) (UK), s 1.

[44] W Tan, 'Peering Through Equity's Prism: A Fiduciary's Duty of Care or a Fiduciary Duty of Care?' (2021) 15 *Journal of Equity* 181, 192.

[45] I Samet, 'Guarding the Fiduciary's Conscience – A Justification of a Stringent Profit-stripping Rule' (2008) 28 *OJLS* 763, 774–75.

[46] ibid 769.

[47] ibid 778.

In the agency problem, a principal is equally exposed to his fiduciary's disloyalty and mismanagement.[48] Specifically in the director's context, Mullighan J in *Duke Group v Pilmer* cited Ford's *Principles of Corporations Law* with approval:[49]

> With this power comes the opportunity for fraud and mismanagement. Anyone who entrusts their property or affairs to another person is at risk of suffering loss by the other person's wrongdoing. The shareholders of companies are often especially vulnerable, because they are frequently passive investors who do not follow the company's progress on a day-to-day basis. Their vulnerability is all the more acute if they are numerous and not organised.
>
> The law responds to the directors' position of temptation and the vulnerability of shareholders by subjecting the directors to strict fiduciary and statutory duties.[50]

To guard against a fiduciary's fraud, equity subjects him to the 'no-conflict' and 'no-profit' duties. By contrast, 'mismanagement' is broader than fraud and would include errors arising from incompetence, misjudgment and negligence. Although a non-executive director does not manage the company in a way an executive director does, he can still falter through incompetence, misjudgment or negligence, so the shorthand of 'mismanagement' shall be retained for current purposes. Therefore, just as a company is vulnerable to a director's disloyalty, it is equally vulnerable to his mismanagement.[51] In this vein, Delaware law represents a step in the right direction by enforcing fiduciary duties of loyalty and care.[52] I have argued elsewhere that a fiduciary duty of care can be defended and the arguments will not be revisited here.[53] Under English law, it is very likely that a director owes a fiduciary duty of adequate deliberation. In *Pitt v Holt*, the Supreme Court recognised this duty, and held that it applies to trustees and 'persons acting in a fiduciary capacity'.[54] In *Passport Special Opportunities Master Fund, LP v ESUN Holdings Ltd*, the Court of First Instance in the High Court of Hong Kong has already taken the step to impose this duty on directors.[55] The mischief that the fiduciary duty of adequate deliberation was intended to cure was 'mismanagement', rather than 'disloyalty'. To better prevent a director's mismanagement, the duty of active oversight should also be recognised as a fiduciary duty given the rigours and stringency of fiduciary liability and remedies.

It has been observed that the functional core of fiduciary duties is deterrence.[56] The fiduciary is incentivised to fulfil his undertaking properly by the threat of

[48] R Sitkoff, 'Other Fiduciary Duties: Implementing Loyalty and Care' in E J Criddle, P B Miller and R H Sitkoff (eds), *The Oxford Handbook of Fiduciary Law* (Oxford, Oxford University Press, 2019) 423.

[49] *Duke Group Ltd (in liq) v Pilmer* [1998] SASC 6529, (1998) 27 ACSR 1, 296 (emphasis added).

[50] HAJ Ford, *Ford's Principles of Corporations Law*, 12th edn (Chatswood, LexisNexis Butterworths, 2005) [8.010].

[51] Tan (n 44) 193.

[52] *Stone* (n 11) 369.

[53] Tan (n 44) 182.

[54] *Pitt v Holt* [2013] UKSC 26, [2013] 2 AC 108 [10] (Lord Walker JSC).

[55] [2011] HKCFI 349, [2011] 4 HKC 62 [149]–[150] (Barma J).

[56] Sitkoff (n 48) 424.

after-the-fact liability for failure to have done so. Fiduciary duties are enforced more robustly than common law duties, and the remedies are designed to tilt the scales largely in favour of the principal. For instance, while the claimant is required to prove 'but for' causation, the English courts have held that the 'reasonable foreseeability' remoteness cap does not apply in a claim for equitable compensation.[57] Whereas under both Singapore[58] and Canadian law,[59] the claimant only needs to prove breach and loss and a rebuttable presumption that the fiduciary's breach caused the loss would then arise.[60] The legal burden is then on the fiduciary to prove that the principal would have sustained the loss in spite of the breach.[61] Furthermore, it is likely that the defence of contributory negligence would not be available in resisting a claim for equitable compensation.[62] The upshot of more pro-claimant remedies would mean that it would be more difficult for a defendant-fiduciary to escape liability. Therefore, recognising a fiduciary duty of active oversight is likely to induce a director to be hypervigilant in performing his directorial undertaking of holding management to account. Section 5 below will elaborate further on why it is inadequate to merely rely on the CA 2006, s 174, which codifies the common law duty of care and skill.

In addition to being a fiduciary duty, the duty of active oversight should also be a mandatory duty. This is consistent with how the Delaware courts have enforced the *Caremark* duty. The duty ought to be mandatory given that it is central and necessary to secure the performance of a director's undertaking. A key directorial undertaking is that a director must exercise his collective power and responsibility to hold management accountable. A company is a unique legal construct. While it can have a separate legal personality, it can only function through natural persons. The day-to-day operations of the company are undertaken by management which consists of senior executives and managers. A question therefore arises: *quis custodiet ipsos custodes*?[63] The company must rely on a body to ensure that management is properly discharging its responsibilities and very often the board of directors is the more appropriate organ than the shareholders to monitor the operations of management. In effect, the directors, through their directorial undertaking, stand in the shoes of the company to ensure that management's activities operate within an accepted paradigm. If the duty of active oversight can be excluded, this would empty the directorial undertaking of one of its integral contents.

[57] *Target Holdings Ltd v Redferns (A Firm)* [1996] AC 421, 438 (Lord Browne-Wilkinson); *AIB Group (UK) plc v Mark Redler & Co Solicitors* [2014] UKSC 58, [2015] AC 1503 at [36] and [86] (Lord Toulson JSC), [92] (Lord Reed JSC). In *Swindle v Harrison* [1997] 4 All ER 705, 717–18, Hobhouse LJ extended the principle developed in *Target* to breach of fiduciary duties.

[58] *Sim Poh Ping v Winsta Holding Pte Ltd* [2020] SGCA 35, [2020] 1 SLR 1199 [240] (Andrew Phang JA).

[59] *Hodgkinson v Simms* [1994] 3 SCR 377 (SC) [76]; *Southwind v Canada* [2017] FC 906, [2017] FCJ No 966 [248].

[60] *Winsta* (n 58) [240].

[61] ibid; *Hodgkinson* (n 59) [76]; *Southwind* (n 59) [248].

[62] *Pilmer v Duke Group Ltd (in liq)* [2001] HCA 31, (2001) 207 CLR 165 [74], [127] (Kirby J).

[63] 'Who guards the guardians?'

Under Delaware law, the mandatory nature of the *Caremark* duty is a consequence of their courts reclassifying it from a fiduciary duty of care to a fiduciary duty of loyalty.[64] As argued above, a principal is equally vulnerable to both his fiduciary's disloyalty and mismanagement. It has also been argued elsewhere that fiduciary duties can consequently be categorised into 'selflessness oriented' duties and 'competence oriented' duties.[65] The former set of duties dissuades the fiduciary from betraying his principal by preferring his own or a third-party's interest, while the latter set of duties are aimed at ensuring the fiduciary discharges his responsibilities towards his principal properly and effectively. While the 'no-conflict', 'no-profit', and the duty to act in good faith,[66] would be classified as 'selflessness oriented' duties, the duty of adequate deliberation would be an example of a 'competence oriented' duty.[67] Analysed through this lens, the Delaware *Caremark* duty is an instance of a 'selflessness oriented' duty given that it embodies an obligation to act in good faith. By contrast, the proposed duty of active oversight is properly conceived to be a 'competence oriented' duty instead. As argued above, the duty should not be scienter-based and a director need not be disloyal or have acted in bad faith to be in breach of the duty. While there is force in the analysis that 'selflessness oriented' duties should form the 'irreducible core' of fiduciary obligations, the mandatory duties of one category of fiduciaries (e.g. a director) may differ from another category of fiduciary (e.g. a solicitor).[68] Simply put, while all fiduciaries share a common 'irreducible core', one fiduciary can owe more, or different, mandatory fiduciary duties from another depending on the scope and nature of their respective undertakings to their principals. Given the gravity of the duty of active oversight in securing the performance of a director's undertaking, it is apt to enforce it as a mandatory directorial duty notwithstanding that it has little to do with ensuring that a director remains selfless or loyal.

At this juncture, it is apposite to address two potential concerns in recognising a fiduciary duty of active oversight. The first concern is statutory while the second is doctrinal. One of the most noticeable changes introduced by the CA 2006 was the codification of directors' general duties in Pt 10, Ch 2. This engenders a question as to whether the Act prevents further director duties from being recognised. It is important to appreciate that the statutory duties do not displace any duties owed by directors under the common law and in equity. Although s 170(3) states that the statutory directors' duties 'have effect in place of those [common law] rules and [equitable] principles', s 170(4) also provides that these duties 'shall be interpreted and applied in the same way as common law rules or equitable principles'.

[64] *Stone* (n 11) 16.

[65] W Tan, 'Negotiating New Curves Along Chancery Lane: Four More Questions on Fiduciaries' (2022) 35 *TLI* 197, 208.

[66] In *Winsta* (n 58) [253], the Singapore Court of Appeal held that the duty to act in good faith is a core fiduciary duty.

[67] Tan (n 65) 208.

[68] ibid 209.

During the Parliamentary debates, the Solicitor-General clarified that common law rules and equitable principles remain relevant to the regulation of directors, except where they are obviously irreconcilable with the statutory statement.[69] Therefore, equity can continue to interact with, and augment, the statutory duties in the CA 2006 as long as it does not contradict the Act. Simply put, the CA 2006, Pt 10, Ch 2 is not exhaustive of directors' duties. That equity continues to co-exist alongside the CA 2006 is confirmed by post-2006 developments. For instance, in *Goldtrail Travel Ltd v Aydin*,[70] the court accepted that the claim against a director to recover misapplied company's assets need not be pleaded as a distinct breach of a particular duty with the CA 2006 even though such a claim could potentially succeed under ss 171(b), 172, and 175.

As regards the doctrinal concern, it can be questioned whether the extant nature of fiduciary obligations would pose an obstacle to the recognition of the duty of active oversight. It is often said that fiduciary duties are proscriptive, and in that sense confined to the 'no-conflict' and 'no-profit' duties.[71] Given that the duty of active oversight is clearly prescriptive, the objection is that it cannot exist as a fiduciary duty. However, although longstanding in origin, such a characterisation of fiduciary obligations is increasingly outdated, and the courts have taken modern fiduciary doctrine beyond the strictures of the 'no-conflict' and 'no-profit' duties. The duty of adequate deliberation, unanimously recognised by a panel of seven Justices in *Pitt*, is an example of a prescriptive fiduciary duty. It does not seem that this duty is confined solely to dispositive powers but also applies to administrative powers. Indeed, in *R (Palestine Solidarity Campaign Ltd) v Secretary of State for Housing, Communities and Local Government*, Lord Carnwath JSC accepted that the duties which govern the deliberative process of persons who invests for and on behalf of others are also fiduciary duties.[72] Furthermore, in *Children's Investment Fund Foundation (UK) v Attorney-General*, Lady Arden JSC held that:

> If a person is a fiduciary then, as part of his core responsibility, he must not put himself into a position where his interest and that of the beneficiary conflict ('the no-conflict principle') and he must not make a profit out of his trust ('the no-profit principle'). The fiduciary is likely to owe other fiduciary duties as well, such as the duty to act in the best interests of the person to whom the duty is owed.[73]

The fiduciary duty to act in the principal's best interests is another example of a prescriptive fiduciary duty. It is apparent that as a matter of English law, the development of fiduciary duties has been inching in the prescriptive direction. Indeed, recently in the context of bitcoin developers, Birss LJ in *Tulip Trading*

[69] HC Debs, Session 2005-06, Standing Committee D, col 536 (6 July 2006). See also, *Burns v Financial Conduct Authority* [2017] EWCA Civ 2140, [2018] 1 WLR 4161 [65] (Kitchin LJ).

[70] [2014] EWHC 1587 (Ch), [2015] 1 BCLC 89 [65] (Rose J).

[71] *Breen v Williams* [1996] HCA 57, (1996) 186 CLR 71, 92 (Dawson and Toohey JJ), 113 (Gaudron and McHugh JJ), 117 (Gummow J), *Al Nehayan v Kent* [2018] EWHC 333 (Comm) [159] (Leggatt J).

[72] [2020] UKSC 16, [2020] 1 WLR 1774 [44].

[73] [2020] UKSC 33, [2022] AC 155 [46] (emphasis added).

Ltd v Bitcoin Association For BSV reasoned that the recognition of fiduciary relationships are developed 'incrementally'[74] and that the content of fiduciary duties 'includes a duty not to act in their own self-interest and *also involves a duty to act in positive ways in certain circumstances*'.[75] Therefore, there is neither a doctrinal nor a statutory impediment to the recognition of the duty of active oversight. Just as how the *Caremark* duty was developed by the Delaware courts, the English courts are also at liberty to adopt a similar course. Even if the English courts are loath to develop such a duty for directors, a viable alternative would be for Parliament to legislate for the recognition of this duty, distinct from the existing director's duties contained in the CA 2006.[76] The analysis below will demonstrate that the duty should not be subsumed under the existing duties found in the CA 2006.

4. A *Caremark*-style Duty should not be Subsumed under CA 2006, Section 172

At first blush, one might be tempted to argue that s 172(1) CA 2006 could be an appropriate receptacle to host the *Caremark* duty. After all, both the statutory duty and the *Caremark* duty require a lack of good faith for liability to bite. Nevertheless, the weak link in both duties is precisely the need for a claimant to demonstrate that the director has failed to act in good faith (or has, in other words, acted in bad faith). This has led to a weak enforcement of both duties.[77] The proposed duty of active oversight is shorn of this scienter-based requirement to augment it with more legal muscle. Consequently, s 172(1) would no longer be a compatible provision to accommodate the duty. Furthermore, the underlying context of the s 172(1) duty differs from that of a *Caremark*-style duty. Therefore, to subsume the duty under s 172 would be akin to adding oil to water.

Firstly, the requirement that directors must fail to act in good faith for them to breach their s 172 duty significantly robs the provision of much of its enforcement potential. The problem of weak enforcement has plagued the Delaware *Caremark* duty. To prevent the duty of active oversight from becoming a paper tiger, it cannot

[74] *Tulip Trading Ltd v Bitcoin Association For BSV* [2023] EWCA Civ 83, [2023] 4 WLR 16 [71].

[75] ibid [86] (emphasis added).

[76] For example, future courts may wish to stem the further development of 'prescriptive' fiduciary duties, and revert to the 'proscriptive' orthodoxy. Alternatively, given that Parliament has intervened to codify and modify directors' duties, the courts may conclude that it would be better for Parliament to legislate for a new directorial duty instead. The duty could then be enforced in the same way as a fiduciary duty (see CA 2006, s 178(2)).

[77] *Iesni v Westrip Holdings Ltd* [2009] EWHC 2526 Ch, [2011] 1 BCLC 498 [85] (Lewison J); *Re Caremark* (n 7) 967 (Allen C).

be subsumed under s 172 insofar as breach of the statutory duty is conditioned upon a finding of bad faith. Section 172(1) provides that:

> A director of a company must act in the way he considers, in good faith, would be most likely to promote the success of the company for the benefit of its members as a whole, and in doing so have regard (amongst other matters) to–
>
> (a) the likely consequences of any decision in the long term,
> (b) the interests of the company's employees,
> (c) the need to foster the company's business relationships with suppliers, customers and others,
> (d) the impact of the company's operations on the community and the environment,
> (e) the desirability of the company maintaining a reputation for high standards of business conduct, and
> (f) the need to act fairly as between members of the company.

The duty in s 172(1) is subjective and merely requires a director to act in the way he considers, in good faith, would be most likely to promote the success of the company. This was unequivocally affirmed by Jonathan Parker J in *Regentcrest plc v Cohen*:

> The question is not whether, viewed objectively by the court, the particular act or omission which is challenged was in fact in the interests of the company; still less is the question whether the court, had it been in the position of the director at the relevant time, might have acted differently. Rather, the question is whether the director honestly believed that his act or omission was in the interests of the company. The issue is as to the director's state of mind.[78]

The recent decision of *ClientEarth v Shell Plc* is illustrative of the high hurdle to surmount in bringing a challenge under s 172(1).[79] The claimants commenced a derivative action against the directors of Shell plc in relation to their alleged failures to properly address the risks of climate change. In rejecting the s 172 claim, Trower J observed that the claimants' arguments:

> [S]eek to impose specific obligations on the Directors as to how the management of Shell's business and affairs should be conducted, notwithstanding the well-established principle that it is for directors themselves to determine (acting in good faith) how best to promote the success of a company for the benefit of its members as a whole.[80]

His Lordship went on to reaffirm that the 'weighing of all these considerations [as set out in s 172] is essentially a commercial decision, which the court is ill-equipped to take, except in a clear case'.[81] Indeed, deferring to the honest belief of directors has been the longstanding position taken by the courts in relation to the

[78] *Regentcrest plc (in liquidation) v Cohen* [2001] 2 BCLC 80 [120] (Jonathan Parker J).
[79] *ClientEarth v Shell plc* [2023] EWHC 1137 (Ch) [2023] All ER (D) 65 (May) (Trower J).
[80] ibid [19].
[81] ibid.

board's commercial decisions. As Lord Wilberforce emphasised in *Howard Smith Ltd v Ampol Petroleum Ltd*:

> There is no appeal on merits from management decisions to courts of law: nor will courts of law assume to act as a kind of supervisory board over decisions within the powers of management honestly arrived at.[82]

Therefore, unless the director's bad faith was evident, liability for breach of s 172 will not be visited upon him. Instead, a company would very often have to rely on other provisions in the CA to hold the errant director accountable. Similarly, claimants have experienced difficulty in successfully establishing their *Caremark* claims before the Delaware courts. It is well recorded that liability for breach of the duty is exceedingly difficult to establish,[83] and that these claims are 'among the hardest [for claimants] to plead successfully'.[84] A major obstacle to the successful enforcement of the *Caremark* duty is attributable to the fact that claimants must demonstrate that the director has failed to act in 'good faith'. The Delaware Supreme Court in *Stone v Ritter* neatly encapsulated the tall order that a claimant must surmount to prove the lack of good faith:

> [Directors must have] utterly failed to implement any reporting or information system or controls; or … having implemented such a system or controls, consciously failed to monitor or oversee its operations thus disabling themselves from being informed of risks or problems requiring their attention. In either case, imposition of liability requires a showing that the directors knew that they were not discharging their fiduciary obligations.[85]

In other words, a director will only be liable if he *wholly and deliberately disregarded* his undertaking to supervise the affairs of the company. One can therefore see why the Court in *Stone* reclassified the duty from one of *care* to one of *loyalty*, given that mere incompetence and negligence is insufficient to ground liability. While having no systems of control at all will attract liability, having an imperfect or even an inadequate system would generally not cross the hurdle of bad faith.[86] In *Oklahoma Firefighters Pension & Retirement System v Corbat*, it was held that the directors had not breached their *Caremark* duty even though the company was slapped with repeated fines for violations of legislations and regulations.[87] The court noted that:

> [The claimants] describes red flags placed before the directors, dating back to the financial crisis of a decade ago as well as more recently, in connection with activities of Citigroup and its subsidiaries that led to large fines levied against the bank. The

[82] [1974] 1 AC 821 (PC), 832; also *Burland v Earle* [1902] AC 83 (PC), 93 (Lord Davey).
[83] C A Hill, 'Caremark as Soft Law' (2018) 90 *Temple Law Review* 681, 682.
[84] *Re Oklahoma Firefighters Pension & Retirement System v Citigroup Inc* CA No 9587-ML (Del Ch 2014).
[85] *Stone* (n 11) (emphasis added).
[86] Hill (n 81), 682–83. See, also, *Re Caremark* (n 7), 970 (Allen C) ('Obviously the level of detail that is appropriate for such an information system is a question of business judgment.').
[87] 2017 WL 6452240 (Del Ch 2017) 5 (Glasscock VC).

> Complaint makes it reasonably conceivable that the directors, despite these red flags, failed to take actions that may have avoided loss to the company. That is not the standard, however. To my mind, the allegations of the Complaint, if true, fail to demonstrate scienter. The Complaint does not make it reasonably conceivable that the directors acted in bad faith. Therefore, the Motion to Dismiss is granted.[88]

For the duty of active oversight to escape the ill-fate of the *Caremark* duty, liability for its breach must not be conditioned upon a finding of bad faith. It suffices that the Board of Directors have failed to implement an *adequate* information or control system (First Prong) and had no *reasonable* excuse for its inaction in the face of positive law violations (Second Prong). Hence, the duty of active oversight is properly classified as a 'competence-oriented' fiduciary duty. Given that a director's bona fides is irrelevant for liability, s 172(1) is then an unsuitable host to accommodate the duty of active oversight.

In addition, it is not appropriate to subsume the duty of active oversight into the s 172(1) duty as the context in which both duties operate are materially different. The obligation imposed on a director in s 172 is 'commercial centric', where a director must, in good faith, consider the various interests of the stakeholders, and balance the short-term interests of shareholders against the long-term interests of future members.[89] On the other hand, the duty of active oversight is 'compliance centric', and demands that directors must implement system controls and be vigilant in their monitoring on management's adherence to positive laws and regulations. The consequence of this distinction lies in the way which both duties can be effectively discharged.

Under the 'commercial centric' s 172 duty, while a director must 'have regard' to a list of non-exhaustive factors such as business relationships with suppliers, customers, and the impact on the community and the environment, he will not be in breach of duty as long as he acted in good faith. In having regard to these factors, a director may have to resolve a conflict between two or more factors.[90] However, the resolution of such conflicts is a matter for the business judgment of the director.[91] Where the director has acted in good faith and has exercised reasonable care, skill, and diligence, he will not be exposed to a greater risk of liability under s 172 than he was under the common law obligation to act bona fide in the interests of the company.[92] As highlighted earlier, the courts will not second guess and intervene in the commercial decisions of directors. This deferential judicial attitude is because the statutory duty is designed to regulate a director's decision in relation to business risks and strategy.

[88] ibid.

[89] *Re Smith & Fawcett Ltd* [1942] Ch 304 (CA), 306 (Lord Greene MR); Second Savoy Hotel Investigation, Report of the Inspector (1954) HMSO.

[90] B Hannigan, *Company Law* (6th edn, Oxford University Press, 2021) [10–33].

[91] J Lowry, 'The Duty of Loyalty of Company Directors: Bridging the Accountability Gap through Efficient Disclosure' (2009) 68 *CLJ* 607, 621.

[92] A Keay, 'The Duty to Promote the Success of the Company: Is it Fit for Purpose in a Post-financial Crisis World?' in J Loughrey (ed), *Directors' Duties and Shareholder Litigation in the Wake of the Financial Crisis* (Edward Elgar Publishing, 2012).

By contrast, the duty of active oversight is not meant to regulate a director's commercial or business decisions. Instead, it is concerned with securing compliance with positive laws, and compelling directors to ensure that management operates within legally prescribed boundaries. The duty is therefore non-derogable and it is inappropriate for legal compliance to be merely a factor to be considered alongside a laundry list of factors. Under s 172, no one consideration takes precedence over another; it is up to the directors' business judgment to decide how best to take the company forward. However, ensuring legal compliance is such a paramount obligation that directors cannot negate it by subordinating it to some other stakeholder's interests. For the duty of active oversight to be subsumed into s 172, legal compliance must be a factor that is valid in its own right and cannot be negated by a director's preference to other factors. This would, in turn, trigger a philosophical shift in s 172 from the existing enlightened shareholder value approach to the pluralist approach.[93] Nevertheless, the pluralist approach has been rejected by the Company Law Review as neither workable nor desirable.[94] One of the reasons for rejection was that the pluralist approach would achieve external benefits through company law which are better served by specific legislation applicable to all businesses on issues like planning, environmental, and competition law.[95] Indeed, specific legislations pertaining to such concerns do exist dehors s 172 and securing their compliance is better done through a separate duty such as the duty of active oversight.

Before leaving the analysis between s 172 and the duty of active oversight, some mention should be made about the reporting obligations supporting s 172. More recently, all companies other than those subject to the small companies regime have to file an annual strategic report.[96] As clarified in the CA 2006, s 414C(1), the purpose of the report is 'to inform members of the company and help them assess how the directors have performed their duty under section 172'. It is now mandatory for some companies to include a s 172(1) statement as part of the report describing how the directors have had regard to the matters listed in s 172(1)(a) to (f) when performing their s 172 duty.[97] The introduction of the strategic report may make matters more transparent to the shareholders and, with this additional information, a disgruntled shareholder may be more likely to bring a derivative action against the board for breach of their s 172(1) duty. Nevertheless, a director can ultimately still avoid liability if he had considered the

[93] Company Law Review, *Strategic Framework* (1999), [5.1.12]–[5.1.13]. The pluralist approach is based on the idea that a company should serve a wider range of interests not subordinate to shareholder value but as valid in their own right. The interests of a number of constituencies should be advanced without the interests of a single constituency (shareholders) prevailing.

[94] Company Law Review, *Completing the Structure* (2000), [3.5].

[95] Company Law Review, *Developing the Framework* (2000), [3.24], see also *Strategic Framework* (1999), [5.1.25]–[5.1.29]; and HL Deb, vol 678, GC 273 (6 February 2006).

[96] For a detailed elaboration on these reporting obligations, see Hannigan (n 90) [10-35]–[10-46].

[97] CA 2006, s 414A provides that all companies except for those entitled to the small companies exception must prepare such a report.

factors in s 172(1) and made a good-faith decision in resolving any conflicts that arise. Therefore, it is difficult to see how this additional reporting requirement would improve the enforceability of s 172 or make it a more attractive candidate to accommodate the duty of active oversight.

5. A *Caremark*-style Duty is not Adequately Enforced under CA 2006, section 174

Section 174 of CA 2006 is another potential provision that one might consider appropriate to accommodate the duty of active oversight. The provision provides that:

> A director of a company must exercise reasonable care, skill and diligence.
>
> This means the care, skill and diligence that would be exercised by a reasonably diligent person with—
>
> > the general knowledge, skill and experience that may reasonably be expected of a person carrying out the functions carried out by the director in relation to the company, and
> >
> > the general *knowledge, skill and experience that the director has.*

While similarities exist between the statutory duty and the duty of active oversight, it would be preferable to recognise the latter duty independently of s 174. Crucially, the duty in s 174 is enforced as a non-fiduciary duty whereas the duty of active oversight, as argued above, should be characterised as a fiduciary duty. It is merely a reflection of the common law position in *Bristol and West Building Society v Mothew*, where it was held that the principles governing the fiduciary's duty of care mirror that of the common law and any divergence was 'merely the product of history' and presents a 'distinction without a difference'.[98] Accordingly, s 178(2) provides that s 174 is not to be enforced 'in the same way as any other fiduciary duty'. While recent authorities have cast doubts over the correctness of the *Mothew* dictum, it remains the case that the s 174 duty is enforced as a non-fiduciary duty.[99] Given the difference in the modes of enforcement, this would immediately rule out s 174 as a viable provision to accommodate the duty of active oversight. Nevertheless, even if s 178(2) were to be amended, and the s 174 duty enforced as a fiduciary one, it is submitted that there is still value in separating the statutory duty and the duty of active oversight.

While s 174 identifies the *standard* of care, skill, and diligence required of a director, it does not articulate the *content* of the duty.[100] In essence, what it provides

[98] [1998] Ch 1 (CA), 17 (Millett LJ).

[99] *AIB* (n 57) [119]; *O'Keefe v Caner* [2017] EWHC 1105 (Ch) [89]–[96] (HHJ Keyser QC); *Youyang Pty Ltd v Minter Ellison Morris Fletcher* [2003] HCA 15, (2003) 212 CLR 484 [39] (Gleeson CJ, McHugh, Gummow, Kirby and Hayne JJ).

[100] Hannigan (n 90) [11–28].

is that a director, in discharging whatever responsibilities he has, must do so with reasonable care, skill, and diligence. However, the provision does not articulate any prior actions or steps that a director must take in the first place. Simply put, the way the s 174 duty was drafted guides one to focus on the *adjective* but not the *verb*. In *ClientEarth*, Trower J, in rejecting the claimants' arguments that the directors owed specific 'incidental duties' under the s 174 duty, emphasised that '[t]he law does not superimpose on that duty more specific obligations as to what is and is not reasonable in every circumstance'.[101] A similar reasoning was deployed by the Hong Kong Court of Final Appeal in *Zhang Hong Li v DBS Bank (Hong Kong) Ltd*. Sitting in the Court of First Instance, Bharwaney J held that a 'high level supervisory duty' could be derived from Article 21(1) of the Trusts (Jersey) Law 1984 which provides that trustees should act (i) with due diligence; (ii) as would a prudent person; and (iii) to the best of the trustee's ability and skill.[102] In disagreeing with Bharwaney J, the apex court clarified that:

> The point is that the requirement that trustees 'act with due diligence, as would a prudent person, to the best of the trustee's ability and skill; and observe the utmost good faith' operates to lay down the standards which trustees must adhere to in executing their duties or in exercising their powers. It does not create free standing duties to act prudently, etc. One must first identify the duty or power executed or exercised and then assess whether the trustees have executed or exercised the same in accordance with the specified standards … Accordingly, if taking into account the effect of the anti-Bartlett provisions, any potentially relevant duty has been disapplied (so that, for instance, there is no duty to interfere or supervise management or to avoid speculative or non-diversified investments, or to preserve or enhance the value of the trust fund) the standards laid down by Art 21(1) do not come into play.[103]

In other words, Article 21(1), which is functionally identical to s 174, only spells out the standards with which a given power or duty must be exercised, but says nothing about the content and nature of any substantive duty.[104] Therefore, even if s 174 were to be enforced as a fiduciary duty, the duty of active oversight would still be necessary given that it is central in securing the proper performance of the directorial undertaking. This free-standing duty, at least in its first prong, is needed to overcome the fact that management often downplay or avoid addressing compliance risks. Even if the board were to exercise utmost care and diligence, it would nevertheless be operating on an incomplete premise, having been supplied with materials prepared by management that could potentially understate or sanitise issues of compliance.

There could be some signs that the courts might be willing to develop a free-standing duty similar to the duty of active oversight. Recently, in *Sharp v Blank*,

[101] *ClientEarth* (n 79) [20].
[102] *Zhang Hong Li v DBS Bank (Hong Kong) Ltd* [2017] HKCFI 687 [83].
[103] *Zhang Hong Li v DBS Bank (Hong Kong) Ltd* [2019] HKCFA 45, (2019) 22 HKCFAR 392 [48] (Ribeiro and Fok JJ, Lord Neuberger of Abbotsbury NPJ) (emphasis added).
[104] I Sin, 'Bartlett Duty and 'Anti-Bartlett' Clauses: Resolving Controversies' (2021) 137 *LQR* 50, 51.

Sir Alastair Norris, who accepted that devolution of labour within a business is permissible, opined that:

> [T]here is a recognised duty to monitor employees upon whom significant reliance is placed and to ensure that there are in place appropriate supervisory and review systems; and … the reliance must in the particular circumstances be consistent with the discharge of the duty of reasonable skill and care by the director.[105]

This statement must, however, be treated with caution. First, it was made in the context of delegation and supervision of managerial responsibilities. It is therefore different from the duty of active oversight insofar as this duty is concerned with securing compliance rather than business risks. Second, the judge, sitting at first instance, did not cite any authority in support of this proposition. As Hannigan observed, the jurisprudence on s 174 has largely been decided at first instance; the appellate courts have had little opportunity to examine the cases.[106] In fact, the current legal position does not seem to compel directors to take additional steps to put in place any 'supervisory and review systems'. Instead, as clarified by Jonathan Parker J in *Re Barings plc (No 5)*, it suffices that directors possess sufficient knowledge and understanding of the business and industry in which the company was operating to exercise the requisite level of supervision.[107] His Lordship went on to explain that 'if a manager does not properly understand the business which he is seeking to manage, he will be unable to take informed management decisions in relation to it'.[108] Once again, it bears repeating that the s 174 duty articulates the standard but falls short of prescribing the content of any substantive duty. However, this is not to say that the dictum in *Sharp* should not be followed. On the contrary, courts should expand on its trajectory and develop the fiduciary duty of active oversight as a distinct directorial duty to secure the company's compliance with positive law and regulations.

A further reason to recognise a separate duty of active oversight, even if the s 174 duty were to be enforced as a fiduciary duty, is that enforcing the free-standing duty sends a strong virtue signal to society of the law's commitment to institutionalise externally imposed regulatory standards within companies using targeted directorial liability. Separating the two duties has at least two implications. First, even if s 174 were to be enforced as a fiduciary duty, in effect transforming it into a fiduciary duty of care, it is unlikely to be classified as part of a director's 'irreducible core' of fiduciary obligations. As argued earlier, 'competence oriented' duties, such as the duty of care, generally do not constitute part of a fiduciary's 'irreducible core'. Consequently, even if the s 174 duty cannot be ousted altogether (given its statutory form), liability for its breach could still be limited or excluded. By contrast, it has been argued above that the fiduciary duty of active oversight, being part of a director's 'irreducible core', cannot be

105 [2019] EWHC 3096 (Ch) [628].
106 Hannigan (n 90) [11–28].
107 [1999] 1 BCLC 433 (HC), 489, aff'd [2000] 1 BCLC 523 (CA), 535.
108 ibid 528.

ousted and liability for its breach cannot also be excluded. This is consistent with Delaware law, where the fiduciary duty of care can be exculpated, whereas the *Caremark* duty can neither be exculpated nor can directors be indemnified for any personal liability.[109]

Second, the losses arising from a breach of the duty of active oversight are generally not confined to the company, and separating the two duties acknowledges this fact. A director who has made a negligent error may cause the company to incur a loss. Accordingly, the director would be liable under s 174. However, under s 174, the losses suffered are confined to the company. By contrast, losses following a breach of a *Caremark*-style duty such as the duty of active oversight often spill over to society. When a company violates regulatory standards and laws, the ramifications do adversely affect other stakeholders including its consumers. Two recent cases will be illustrated. In *Marchand v Barnhill*, the directors of a prominent ice-cream manufacturer were found liable for failures to implement systems of reporting on 'mission critical' food-safety issues. This led to multiple listeria-related deaths, the recall of all its products and the shuttering of its manufacturing plants until the issues could be addressed.[110]

Furthermore, *Re Boeing* concerned a similar fact pattern where the directors of the company consistently failed to respond to red flags despite the fact that aircraft safety was 'mission critical' to manufacturers such as Boeing.[111] As a result, two recently produced airliners crashed, all Boeing 737 MAX aircrafts were grounded worldwide and the production line was shut down.[112] Although the company's audit committee oversaw risk and compliance matters, its overwhelming focus was upon financial risks rather than safety risks. In fact, there was no nexus between internal safety reporting processes and the board. Zurn VC found that:

> Boeing's management was taking charge while the Board remained a passive recipient of updates: management would 'determine whether any action is required,' … the Board was not privy to the truth about MCAS, AOA sensor vulnerabilities, or how those issues were handled in FAA certification and pilot training.[113]

Therefore, a company's breach of compliance matters does burden society with negative externalities, so the losses suffered are neither merely pecuniary nor simply confined to the company. Recognising a distinct duty of active oversight underscores that the gravity and consequences of a compliance breach are materially different from a director's negligence *simpliciter* under s 174.

[109] *See* DEL. CODE ANN. tit. 8, § 102(b)(7) (2021) (limits to exculpation); ibid. § 145(a)–(b) (company's power to indemnify its agents limited to actions in good faith, which is part of the duty of loyalty).

[110] *Marchand* (n 11) 807 (Strine CJ).

[111] *Re Boeing* (n 40) 73.

[112] ibid 45.

[113] ibid 81.

6. A Potential *Caremark*-style Duty for Non-Directorial Officers

Most recently, in *Re McDonald's*, Laster VC of the Delaware Court of Chancery held that the *Caremark* duty extends to corporate officers in addition to the board of directors. In arriving at this position, Laster VC relied on Delaware authority that 'the fiduciary duties of officers are the same as those of directors'[114] and that officers owe 'additional duties … as agents who report to the board'.[115] He went on to explain that while 'this duty applies equally to officers, its context-driven application will differ'.[116] As such, the extent of an officer's *Caremark* duty will be limited to his area of responsibility. For example, the Chief Financial Officer is responsible for financial oversight and for establishing reasonable information systems to cover that area.[117] Nevertheless, Laster VC concluded that 'a particularly egregious red flag might require an officer to say something even if it fell outside the officer's domain' to comply with the duty.[118]

A case can be made for English law to adopt a similar position in subjecting non-directorial officers to a *Caremark*-style duty. After all, there is some force in imposing oversight obligations on officers given that '[i]n the typical corporation, it is the officers who are charged with, and responsible for, running the business of the corporation'.[119] Therefore, '[c]ompared to directors, officers have greater knowledge about and responsibility for the areas under their control' especially since they are 'full-time employees'.[120] However, the appropriate organ to extend this duty to corporate officers should be Parliament rather than the courts. First, there exists significant doctrinal differences between English and Delaware laws. Unlike Delaware law, officers and directors are not exposed to the same fiduciary duties under English law. While some officers could be managerial fiduciaries, employees are generally not regarded as fiduciaries.[121] Furthermore, even if officers are truly 'agents that report to the board', English law does not treat all 'agents' as 'fiduciaries'.[122] In fact, under Laster VC's analysis, it is not immediately apparent whether these officers are agents to the company or to the board. Second, and more importantly, subjecting non-directorial officers to personal liability for the company's losses would require careful deliberation and weighing of different commercial and policy considerations. Indeed, Laster VC acknowledged that

[114] *Gantler v Stephens* 965 A2d 695 (Del 2009), 709 (Jacobs J).
[115] *Re McDonald's* (n 26) 31.
[116] ibid 2.
[117] ibid 41.
[118] ibid 2.
[119] M W Shaner, 'The (Un)Enforcement of Corporate Officers' Duties' (2014) 48 *University of California, Davis, Law Review* 271, 285.
[120] *Re McDonald's* (n 26) 47.
[121] See, eg, *University of Nottingham v Fishel* [2000] ICR 1462 (HC), 1491E (Elias J).
[122] *Eze v Conway* [2019] EWCA Civ 88 [2019] All ER (D) 75 (Feb) [39] (Asplin LJ).

'[r]easonable minds can disagree about whether, as a matter of policy, stockholders should be able to sue to hold an officer accountable for a failure to exercise oversight'.[123] Difficult questions will need to be addressed. For example, should the officers of all companies, regardless of complexity and size, be subject to oversight duties? What level of seniority is required before officers are imposed with such duties? Should such a duty be enforced as a tortious obligation or be enforceable in the same way as any other fiduciary duty?[124] The task of grappling these difficult issues is better left for Parliament to decide.

It is suggested that Parliament could plausibly enact a provision providing that C-suite officers should owe a *Caremark*-style duty to the company. This is unlike Laster VC's approach, which does not contemplate the buck to stop at the C-suite level.[125] Nevertheless, consistent with the Delaware version, this duty is context driven and each C-suite officer is only tasked with oversight duties within his domain. For a significant number of companies, such a provision would do little to shake up the scene. In the first place, it is normal parlance for C-suite level officers, such as the CEO or the Chief Operating Officer, to be concurrently appointed on the board as 'executive directors'. Such officers will already owe the duty of active oversight *qua* directors in any event.

By contrast, in bigger corporations, it is not uncommon for the board of directors to be entirely constituted of non-executive directors, while the C-suite officers form a separate committee known as the 'Group Executive Board'. Where the board of directors consists of non-executive directors, it would be unrealistic to expect them to conceptualise reasonable information and reporting systems without management input given that they must first be apprised of the nature and nuances of the company's operations. In this regard, the C-suite officers should work in tandem with the directors in designing the systems of control. After all, a C-suite officer is the apex-level officer of his domain and would possess expert knowledge to guide the directors on the intricacies of his domain, enabling the directors to better understand the various compliance issues that require monitoring when designing the information systems. Nevertheless, as observed by Laster VC, some officers, like the CEO, have a 'company-wide remit'.[126] Such officers will attract the full panoply of the oversight duty whereas other C-suite officers will only owe these duties within their respective areas.

Given that C-suite officers invariably have a body of subordinate officers under their charge, coupled by the fact that they are the officers overseeing the day-to-day operations of the company, it is sensible for Parliament to also provide that they owe an obligation to actively monitor for legal compliance in relation to matters within their domain further to their obligation to work with the board of directors in designing the systems of control. However, each C-suite officer should only

[123] *Re McDonald's* (n 26) 34.
[124] See, eg, for directors' duties, CA 2006, s 178(2).
[125] *Re McDonald's* (n 26) 2.
[126] ibid.

monitor on matters within his remit, and Laster VC's dictum on an officer's obligation to report 'egregious red flags' outside of his domain should not be followed. It is suggested that such an extension creates more problems than solutions. For example, disputes may arise as to when a particular issue is sufficiently 'egregious' to attract liability for a non-domain officer. Furthermore, it potentially tips the scales too far in favour of accountability, with this threat of expanded liability inducing a chilling effect on officers.[127] Finally, it also introduces an unnecessary layer of enforcement given that the domain officers and the board of directors would already be subjected to their respective oversight duties. On balance, while Laster VC's dictum may be perceived as fortifying management accountability and increasing a company's or shareholders' recourse for compliance breaches, English law should be extremely circumspect in adopting it.

7. Conclusion

Comparative legal analysis often provides valuable food for thought in approaching a common legal conundrum. Through the lessons of the Delaware experience, it is desirable that a *Caremark*-style duty be introduced in UK company law in the form of a directorial duty of active oversight. Like the Delaware *Caremark* duty, this will be both a fiduciary and a mandatory duty. However, liability for its breach should not be conditioned upon a lack of good faith. In addition, it is not appropriate to subsume the duty under the CA 2006, ss 172 or 174. In addition, it is plausible to extend a *Caremark*-style duty to non-directorial officers. However, such a move will have to be initiated by Parliament instead. Ultimately, adopting duties of active oversight for directors, and plausibly for officers, is likely to enhance the UK's corporate governance regime by sharpening a company's adherence to compliance matters.

[127] The threat of liability deterring good people to serve is a concern that has been noted by M Petrin, 'Assessing Delaware's Oversight Jurisprudence: A Policy and Theory Perspective' (2010) *Virginia Law & Business Review* 433, 460–73.

16

China's Corporate Credit System and the Boundaries of Corporate Liability

VIRGINIA HARPER HO*

In recent years, governments and international organisations worldwide have been working to develop new mechanisms to improve corporate accountability in areas ranging from climate and sustainability to business and human rights. These systems supplement more traditional financial credit rating systems that also now integrate certain environmental and social factors.[1] Many of these systems rely on expanding market access to information on corporate operations and impacts.

These emerging standards and rules promise to tighten the regulatory environment for business by encouraging responsible business practice, mandating corporate climate and sustainability disclosure and raising companies' risk of liability and reputational damage if they engage in harmful business activities. Most do not regulate corporate behaviour directly but are instead disclosure-based, relying on information transparency to motivate changes in corporate behaviour indirectly. Their effectiveness as a regulatory tool depends heavily on the use of private rating systems and indices that aggregate data on a wide range of corporate sustainability and financial performance indicators so that it can be understood and used by consumers, investors, other market actors and governments. An important aspect of these new mandates is that they increasingly require companies to bear responsibility not only for their own activities, but for the conduct of affiliates and other business partners.

China is no exception. It has been working since the early 2000s and more formally since 2014 to develop a 'social credit system' – a big data-driven transparency and incentive system to promote the 'trustworthiness' of individuals, organisations and even government itself.[2] The system's potential to facilitate

* Shen Huimin and Wu Meimei provided invaluable research assistance.

[1] See, eg, 'ESG Credit Rating' (*Moody's Investors Service*). Available at: ratings.moodys.io/integration-of-esg-into-credit-risk.

[2] State Council, Notice on Issuing the Outline of Plan for Building the Social Credit System (2014–2020) [关于印发社会信用体系建设规划纲要（2014–2020 年）的通知], 14 June 2016. On the history, key elements and goals of the social credit system, see V Brussee, *Social*

large-scale social control by the Chinese party-state has raised concerns among observers, particularly as it applies to individuals.[3]

Without diminishing these concerns, the Chinese system, as applied to companies, aspires to address the regulatory enforcement and accountability challenges created by corporate groups and business networks. The system aims to aggregate information on corporate compliance and other indicia of '(un)trustworthy' business practice to encourage responsible corporate behaviour, strengthen legal compliance and combat fraud.[4] It is also intended to give consumers, investors and business partners more information on the companies they do business with. Broadly speaking, it therefore seeks to achieve many of the same public policy goals that are driving governments elsewhere to adopt corporate disclosure and due diligence regulations and which have led private standard setters and certification bodies to develop rating systems for corporate sustainability, governance and financial performance. Like the Chinese corporate credit system, many of these systems have emerged because of the complexity of corporate group structures and the limits of formal law to hold companies accountable for actions taken by related entities in a corporate enterprise. These challenges are even greater for corporate supply chains or values chains involving close business partners that are often only connected contractually without equity control.

This chapter makes two contributions. First, it offers a new comparative perspective on the Chinese corporate credit system by placing it in the context of international developments aimed at expanding corporate responsibility and accountability beyond legal compliance and across corporate groups and networks. Second, it sheds light on how the various regulations, policy documents and platforms that form the corporate credit system reach corporate groups, a topic that has not yet been the focus of prior work on China's corporate credit system.[5] China's evolving corporate credit system also offers a unique opportunity to consider the limits and potential of any data-driven system that attempts to create corporate compliance incentives and accountability mechanisms.

Credit: The Warring States of China's Emerging Data Empire (Palgrave Macmillan, 2023); Brussee traces the roots of the system back to at least 2002 and to even earlier regulatory initiatives in the 1990s. Brussee (ibid), M von Blomberg, 'The Social Credit System and China's Rule of Law' in O Everling (eds) *Social Credit Rating: Reputation und Vertrauen Beurteilen* (Springer 2020); X Dai, 'Toward A Reputation State: A Comprehensive View of China's Social Credit System Project' in Everling (ibid).

[3] A number of studies have focused on the surveillance and data aggregation aspects of the system. See generally Y J Chen, C F Lin and H W Liu, '"Rule of Trust": The Power and Perils of China's Social Credit Megaproject' [2018] 32 *Colum J Asian L* 1; Y H Lin & C Milhaupt, 'China's Corporate Social Credit System and the Dawn of Surveillance State Capitalism' (2023) *China Quarterly* 1–19.

[4] See Section 3 below.

[5] Key work on the corporate credit system includes Lin and Milhaupt (n 3); T Krause and others, 'China's Corporate Credit Reporting System: A Comparison with the United States and Germany' (2022) 17(3) *Regulation & Governance* 755.

1. Corporate Groups and Emerging Accountability Mechanisms

Governments worldwide struggle to effectively deter corporate harms, incentivise corporate compliance and encourage corporate practices that are socially beneficial. In part this is because many of the features of the corporate form, such as limited liability and separate legal identity, were designed to facilitate investment of capital at scale by shielding the corporation's shareholders from the full risk associated with corporate activity. These risk-shifting and asset-shielding features extend to corporate groups where related business entities may be owned and controlled by other legal entities or individuals. Companies also depend on key suppliers, joint venture partners, distributors and other third parties that may be considered part of a company's business network and over which they may exercise some degree of control, often through contract.[6]

Corporate groups are therefore able to shift risky, illegal, or substandard business practices to others in the corporate group or network in order to shield themselves and individual corporate directors and officers from liability. Corporate group structures may also more easily externalise costs from the company and its shareholders to creditors, potentially including tort claimants, employees, communities and even ecosystems. Harms can also be readily exported through transnational business activity, since jurisdictionally bound legal regimes have limited extraterritorial effect and companies can easily move their operations to countries with weaker legal systems, or lobby governments for less stringent regulation. Even where those directly harmed by corporate misconduct have a legal remedy, identifying (and getting jurisdiction over) the responsible persons or entities is often difficult due to the scale, complexity and opacity of corporate structures that are sometimes used intentionally to hide, shield, or diffuse the responsibility of individual or corporate actors.[7]

Formal legal mechanisms to attach liability to the corporate group or its controlling parent on an enterprise basis exist, but their effectiveness has been limited in practice. Under the common law in many jurisdictions, a parent company as shareholder may be held directly liable for corporate harms in certain

[6] Witting defines corporate networks as collaborative business relationships 'based upon contractual arrangements between independent businesses and typically are more cooperative' and do not generally have the same degree of hierarchy and control that characterise most corporate groups. C Witting, *Liability of Corporate Croups and Networks* (Cambridge University Press 2018) 39.

[7] All these problems have been widely observed. See, eg, JS Nelson, 'Paper Dragon Thieves,' [2017] 105 *Georgetown LJ* 871 (considering how individual and corporate responsibility can be intentionally partitioned to avoid criminal liability); J A Zerk, *Multinationals and Corporate Social Responsibility: Limitations and Opportunities in International Law* (Cambridge University Press 2006) (discussing the challenge of corporate accountability for human rights obligations); Witting (n 6) (focusing on involuntary creditors).

rare circumstances under corporate veil-piercing doctrines.[8] Some jurisdictions allow courts to engage more liberally in 'veil-peeking' in order to at least identify the culpable individuals and entities that may be hiding behind complex corporate structures.[9] Other approaches include principal-agent theories of vicarious liability, fiduciary duties for corporate directors and other officers,[10] contract and tort remedies, statutory creditor protections and direct statutory obligations for individuals who have authority to act on behalf the corporation.[11] In some circumstances, these may extend to controlling shareholders as well.[12] Victims of corporate harms may also assert private remedies or seek public enforcement under other regulatory regimes such as environmental protection, labour and employment law and consumer protection regimes. However, there are many procedural and practical hurdles to all these remedies where the corporate actors involved act through subsidiaries or through third parties.[13]

In response to the limits of legal remedies on the one hand and the high economic and societal impact of transnational corporate groups on the other, numerous voluntary standards, rating and certification systems and other self-regulatory initiatives have emerged. These include voluntary supply chain management and industry sourcing standards.[14] Many of these measures seek to harness the threat of reputational sanctions and market pressure to encourage companies to go beyond legal compliance and undertake positive corporate action in areas like climate mitigation, environmental protection and workforce diversity; most apply transnationally across the corporate enterprise.[15]

[8] Corporate veil-piercing was codified by statute in China's 2005 revision of its company law. See generally C Xi, 'Piercing the Corporate Veil: How Did We Get There?' (2011) *J Bus L* 413.

[9] See M Pargendler, 'Veil Peeking: The Corporation as a Nexus for Regulation' (2021) 169 U Penn LR 717 (arguing that the corporate form facilitates 'regulatory partitioning' between the entity and its shareholders and that courts can look behind the corporate veil for reasons beyond those considered in veil-piercing doctrine).

[10] See V Harper Ho, 'Board Duties: Monitoring, Risk Management & Compliance' in A Afsharipour and M Gelter (eds), *Handbook of Comparative Corporate Governance* (Edward Elgar 2021) (surveying these rules across common law and civil law jurisdictions).

[11] Courts in the United Kingdom have also recognised the possibility of direct liability of parent companies for negligent acts of their affiliates in certain cases. See V Harper Ho, G Berger-Walliser and R Chambers, 'Corporate Groups: Toward Corporate Group Accountability,' in Martin Petrin and Christian Witting (eds), *Research Handbook on Corporate Liability* (Edward Elgar 2023).

[12] E Lim, *A Case for Shareholders' Fiduciary Duties in Common Law Asia* (Cambridge University Press 2019).

[13] See Witting (n 6) above; see also (n 7) above and sources cited therein. On the jurisdictional challenges, see G Berger-Walliser, 'Reconciling Transnational Jurisdiction: A Comparative Approach to Personal Jurisdiction over Foreign Corporate Defendants in US Courts' (2018) 51 *Vanderbilt Transnational LJ* 1243.

[14] On their limits, see A S Chilton and G Sarfaty, '*The Limitations of Supply Chain Disclosure Regimes*' (2017) 53 *Stanford J International L* 1.

[15] V Harper Ho and S K Park, 'ESG Disclosure: Optimizing Private Ordering in Public Reporting' (2019) 41 *University of Pennsylvania Intl LJ* 249. Voluntary and mandatory corporate responsibility programmes abound in China as well. V Harper Ho, 'Beyond Regulation: A Comparative Look at State-Centric Corporate Social Responsibility & the Law in China' (2013) 46 *Vanderbilt Transnational LJ* 375.

Over the past decade, successive corporate scandals, economic crisis and public demand for greater corporate accountability have led globally to a visible 'hardening' of voluntary corporate accountability standards into legal mandates. Most notable are the European Union's forthcoming Corporate Sustainability Due Diligence Directive[16] and its 2022 Corporate Sustainability Reporting Directive,[17] as well as the international climate and sustainability reporting mandates introduced by the International Sustainability Standards Board (ISSB) of the IFRS Foundation in 2023.[18] In addition, an international treaty on business and human rights is under development to make enforceable corporate oversight of suppliers and other business partners with regard to human rights impacts.[19] Data produced in response to these mandates are expected to improve the quality and utility of corporate sustainability ratings and indices that have been roundly criticised in the academic literature for their lack of consistency and uncertain reliability.[20]

Many of the new measures have several common features that enable them to potentially reach more broadly than traditional regulatory tools, all of which have parallels in China's corporate credit system:

- *Enterprise- and Network-wide Scope.* A key feature of the new reporting and due diligence mandates is that they extend broadly across corporate entity boundaries. For example, the proposed business and human rights treaty and the EU's Corporate Sustainability Due Diligence Directive are expressly designed to require companies to monitor and report on relevant conduct by other companies in their supply chain.[21] Similarly, corporate climate disclosure frameworks ask companies to report information related to their 'value chains'.[22] Mandatory financial disclosure also generally applies to companies

[16] European Commission, 'Proposal for a Directive of the European Parliament and of the Council on Corporate Sustainability Due Diligence' COM (2022) 71 final.

[17] Directive of the European Parliament and of the Council amending Regulation (EU) No 537/2014, Directive 2004/109/EC, Directive 2006/43/EC and Directive 2013/34/EU, as regards corporate sustainability reporting [2022] OJ L 322/15 ('CSRD'); Commission Delegated Regulation (EU) 2023/2772 of 31 July 2023 supplementing Directive 2013/34/EU of the European Parliament and of the Council as regards sustainability reporting standards, C/2023/5303, [2023] OJ L 2023/2772.

[18] IFRS, 'S2 Climate-related Disclosures' (June 2023); IFRS, 'S1 General Requirements for Disclosure of Sustainability-related Financial Information' (June 2023).

[19] OEIWG Chairmanship, Fourth Revised Draft, Legally Binding Instrument to Regulate, in International Human Rights Law, the Activities of Transnational Corporations and Other Business Enterprises (July 2023). Available at: www.ohchr.org/sites/default/files/documents/hrbodies/hrcouncil/igwg-transcorp/session9/igwg-9th-updated-draft-lbi-clean.pdf.

[20] F Berg et al., 'Aggregate Confusion: The Divergence of ESG Ratings' (2022) 26(6) *Rev Finance* 1315. A Rzeźnik et al., 'Investor Reliance on ESG Ratings and Stock Price Performance' (2022) SAFE Working Paper No 310. Available at: papers.ssrn.com/sol3/papers.cfm?abstract_id=3801703.

[21] The EU CSRD provides for public enforcement and potential civil liability against covered companies for their own operations, those of their subsidiaries and also those with whom they expect to have a lasting relationship and that is not 'a negligible or merely ancillary part of the company's value chain': see CSRD (n 17) 17. The international climate and sustainability disclosure standards (n 18), as well as the European sustainability reporting standards (n 17), all require certain companies to report indirect greenhouse gas (GHG) emissions from their 'value chain'.

[22] Task Force on Climate-Related Financial Disclosures [TCFD], 'Final Report: Recommendations of the Task Force on Climate-Related Financial Disclosures' (2017). Available at: assets.bbhub.io/company/sites/60/2020/10/FINAL-2017-TCFD-Report-11052018.pdf.

on a consolidated basis that includes both the reporting entity and controlled affiliates. These measures are designed to encourage parent companies and business partners to actively monitor related companies.

- *Beyond Compliance to Societal Impacts.* Another key feature of international reporting and due diligence regimes, particularly in Europe, is that they seek to measure and monitor corporate performance on environmental and social matters, in addition to legal compliance.[23] Financial credit rating agencies also now include climate, sustainability and even human rights and geopolitical risks financial credit ratings for firms and investment products,[24] in addition to corporate sustainability ratings and indices that measure corporate performance across a broad range of economic, environmental and social indicators.[25]
- *Data-driven and Ratings-driven.* Another feature of international corporate financial and sustainability regimes is a focus on improving information quality and transparency. International reporting systems are designed primarily to inform markets, but for the European Union and other governments where corporate reporting is part of broader development strategies, greater access to this data may also facilitate more targeted government and public oversight of covered companies.[26]
- *Harnessing Reputation and Market Oversight.* International corporate reporting mandates, like voluntary corporate responsibility standards and programs before them, rely on reputational incentives and, in some jurisdictions, private litigation by consumers, investors and other corporate stakeholders to change corporate behaviour, remedy harms and supplement public enforcement.

Internationally, strengthening enterprise-wide accountability across corporate groups relies on an array of measures that are increasingly mandatory, extend to corporate societal impacts and facilitate data-driven incentives to varying degrees.

2. The Regulation of Corporate Groups in China

As in most jurisdictions, regulation of corporate activity in China is generally directed at the entity, not enterprise level. However, there are both regulatory and

[23] Corporate sustainability disclosure and due diligence reporting standards in Europe are the most extensive and require companies and investors to report on their own climate, sustainability and human rights impacts. See (n 18) above.

[24] See ESG Credit Rating (n 1) above.

[25] On these ratings, see sources referenced (n 20) above.

[26] The EU has developed a 'taxonomy' of sustainable activities and investments for this purpose: Council Regulation (EC) 2019/2088 on Sustainability-related Disclosures in the Financial Services Sector [2019] OJ L 317/1; Council Regulation (EC) 2020/852 on the Establishment of a Framework to Facilitate Sustainable Investment [2020] OJ L 198/3. A social taxonomy is under development: EU Platform on Sustainable Finance, 'Final Report on Social Taxonomy' (February 2022).

policy tools that seek to reach firms on an enterprise-wide basis. First, China's company law contains a statutory veil-piercing provision that can be applied within corporate groups to extend liability to a corporate parent.[27] A number of empirical studies have found that Chinese courts pierce the corporate veil within corporate groups more liberally than in many jurisdictions.[28] While it is doubtful that Chinese courts would go so far as to adopt a 'single economic entity' approach to impose liability for the group on its parent, they have been quite willing to do so in liquidation through substantive consolidation of corporate groups for the benefit of creditors, which has the same effect.[29] In addition, as in other jurisdictions, a corporate branch is not considered a separate legal entity like a subsidiary, so its liabilities will be borne by its parent unless it has the power to contract independently under its business licence.[30]

Chinese companies have also been encouraged to engage in supply chain due diligence and adopt enterprise-wide corporate responsibility practices that could extend to business networks. In 2021, the State Council released China's current National Human Rights Action Plan, which expresses China's commitment to implement the United Nations' 2030 Agenda for Sustainable Development and to promote 'responsible business conduct in supply chains'.[31] It encourages Chinese companies to 'comply with the UN Guiding Principles on Business and Human Rights in foreign trade and investment, to conduct due diligence on human rights and to fulfill their social responsibility to respect and promote human rights'.[32] As discussed below, the corporate credit system could be applied to implement these commitments.

The direct influence of the party-state in both state and private-sector firms is perhaps one of the most important levers for more directly aligning companies with central policy priorities in the Chinese system. Indeed, the Chinese Communist Party (CCP) has led the development of the social credit system itself. In the state sector, corporate accountability to advance public policy goals is further facilitated by the state's corporate governance rights as shareholder, although the separation of ownership and management control means that this alignment is

[27] PRC Company Law, art 20. See also Xi, 'Piercing the Corporate Veil: How Did We Get There?' (n 8) above.

[28] R Hui Huang, 'Piercing the Corporate Veil in China: Where Is It Now and Where Is It Heading? [2012] 60 *Am J Comp L* 743. On the application of the doctrine in China, see CHawes, A K L Lau and A Young, 'Lifting the Corporate Veil in China: Statutory Vagueness, Shareholder Ignorance and Case Precedents in a Civil Law System' [2015] 15(2) *J Corp L Stud* 341.

[29] L Xiaolin, 'Substantive Consolidation of Bankruptcy Proceedings in China: A Critical Examination' (2021) 95 *Am Bankr LJ* 537.

[30] See PRC Company Law (n 27) art 14; PRC Supreme People's Court Guiding Case No 149, *Changsha Guangda Building Decoration Co Ltd v Guangzhou Yuexiu Sub-branch of Industrial and Commercial Bank of China Co Ltd and others* [长沙广大建筑装饰有限公司诉中国工商银行股份有限公司广州粤秀支行、林传武、长沙广大建筑装饰有限公司广州分公司等第三人撤销之诉案] (recognising this principle).

[31] Information Office of the PRC State Council, National Human Rights Action Plan of China (2021–2025) (2021).

[32] ibid.

not always assured.[33] In addition, the central government through the State-owed Assets Supervision and Administration Commission (SASAC) has direct administrative oversight over 96 centrally administered state-owned enterprises (CSOEs) and administrative authority over the rest of the state sector.[34] Departmental guidance on compliance management for Chinese companies' operations abroad[35] and separate guidance encouraging corporate social responsibility by CSOEs[36] are two examples of measures that encourage these enterprises to actively monitor affiliates' operational conduct on an enterprise-wide basis. The CCP also controls executive appointments for state-sector firms and, as of 2015, requires them to establish a CCP committee.[37] Like their counterparts abroad, listed and state-sector firms must also adopt internal risk, reporting and financial controls that operate on an enterprise-wide basis.[38]

In addition to SOEs, other large firms in China have been making corporate responsibility or sustainability commitments since at least the mid-2000s that apply on an enterprise-wide basis, and listed firms, banks and other financial institutions have been encouraged or required to produce firm-wide sustainability reports since 2008.[39] For these reasons, some aspects of the corporate credit system are arguably less necessary to corporate group oversight, which may explain why publicly available corporate credit information on SOEs and other large firms is quite limited, as discussed below.

3. China's Corporate Credit System and the Bounds of Corporate 'Trustworthiness'

One of the most interesting features of the corporate credit system is that it appears intended to reach corporate groups and networks, but whether and

[33] A number of sources have identified limits to the central government's ability to exercise the high degree of control many outsiders presume. See generally C S C Hawes, *The Chinese Corporate Ecosystem* (2022). See also J Wang, *Company Law in China* (Edward Elgar 2015) 216 (noting that SOEs also suffer from a disconnect between 'strong owners, weak managers').

[34] CSOEs are owned and controlled by the central government and operated under the oversight of the State-owed Assets Supervision and Administration Commission (SASAC). For a list, see SASAC, 'Directory'. Available at: en.sasac.gov.cn/directory.html.

[35] See, eg, National Development and Reform Commission (NDRC) and others, Guidelines for Compliance Management of Enterprises' Overseas Operations (2018); NDRC, Measures for the Administration of Overseas Investment of Enterprises (2014, amended 2017).

[36] SASAC, Measures for the Compliance Management of Centrally Managed Enterprises (2018, amended 2022); SASAC, Guidelines to State-Owned Enterprises Directly Under the Central Government on Fulfilling Corporate Social Responsibilities (2007, amended 2016).

[37] L Yu-Hsin Lin and C J Milhaupt, 'Party Building or Noisy Signaling? The Contours of Political Conformity in Chinese Corporate Governance' (2021) 50(1) *J Legal Studies* 187.

[38] V Harper Ho, 'Corporate Governance as Risk Regulation in China: A Comparative View of Risk Oversight, Risk Management, and Accountability' (2012) 4 *European J Risk Regulation* 463 (discussing these rules).

[39] Government- and CCP-led policies and programs to encourage corporate social responsibility began to be introduced by several central government ministries and by a number of subnational governments around 2008. See generally Harper Ho, 'Beyond Regulation' (n 15).

how it does so is as yet unexplored. There are two key questions in this regard: (i) whether the corporate credit system applies to corporate groups on an enterprise or entity basis; and (ii) whether companies face negative credit consequences for the 'untrustworthiness' of their affiliates and business partners. To answer these questions, it is also important to examine how individual and entity-level credit consequences intersect, since overlapping ownership, board directorships, or senior management are all common means of control and connection within corporate groups and networks. Section 3.1 introduces the social credit system and Section 3.2 presents new findings on its application to corporate groups.

3.1. From Creditworthiness to Trustworthiness

China's social credit system has been described as a comprehensive, data-driven social management system of unprecedented scale and scope.[40] It is intended to apply across the whole of the society, not only to companies, but also to other organisations and to the government itself.[41] Its purpose is to deter fraud, improve legal compliance and foster integrity 'so that honesty and trustworthiness become the conscious pursuit of the entire society'.[42] More specifically, the system was developed to address the need for effective financial credit risk management systems, persistent obstacles to the enforcement of legal obligations and concerns about low morality across the society.[43] For companies, business integrity includes promoting corporate charitable contributions and other aspects of corporate responsibility.[44]

The social credit system remains under active development, as has been the case for nearly two decades.[45] Its core framework rests on policies and

[40] See von Blomberg 'The Social Credit System and China's Rule of Law' (n 2) 119.

[41] PRC Social Credit Law (consultation draft) [中华人民共和国社会信用体系建设法（向社会公开征求意见稿] (2022), arts 1–2 and preamble (stating that the '[e]stablishment of a social credit system, as used in this Law, refers to the state mobilizing and leading government, market, and all social forces' to establish creditworthiness in business, society, and government, including the judiciary, financial systems, and the institutions behind the social credit system).

[42] ibid art 50. See also Guiding Opinions of the General Office of the State Council on Accelerating the Construction of a Social Credit System and Constructing a New Credit-based Supervision Mechanism [国务院办公厅关于加快推进社会信用体系建设构建以信用为基础的新型监管机制的指导意见], No 35 (2019), art 1 (defining the social credit system as 'a new supervision system that penetrates into the whole life cycle of market participants [in order to] further regulate market order, optimize the business environment, and advance high-quality development').

[43] Brussee (n 2) 19–24.

[44] For example, China National Quality Supervision and Inspection Bureau & China National Standardization Management Committee, Index of Enterprise Credit Evaluation [企业信用评价指标] GB/T 23794-2015 (adopted 21 Sept 2015, effective 1 Jan 2016) (emphasising values, competitiveness, and social responsibility as the foundation of the enterprise social credit audit standards).

[45] Brussee (n 2) (tracing its origins to the late 1990s). See also PRC State Council, 'Guiding Opinions on Further Improving the Untrustworthy Restraint System and Establishing a Long-term Mechanism for Integrity Construction' [关于进一步完善失信约束制度构建诚信建设长效机制的指导意]见], No 49 (2020).

administrative regulations adopted under the leadership of the CCP by leading ministries, provincial-level governments, the Supreme People's Court and experience gained from a number of policy pilots in partnership with the private sector.[46] In 2022, the PRC central government proposed a draft Social Credit Law which, if adopted, would be the first national-level legislation to elevate, formalise and further align the main elements of the current system.[47]

The social credit system in fact encompasses three different types of information and multiple credit reporting systems – financial, market and public (i.e. regulatory) credit systems. The term 'social credit' is often used to refer to market and public credit, as distinct from financial credit, where market or commercial credit refers to information obtained through commercial transactions and public credit refers to information provided by regulators and other public authorities as defined in national and subnational public credit catalogues.[48] Credit information can therefore be sourced not only from financial institutions and state administrative agencies nationally, but also from commercial actors, trade and industry associations and commercial credit information providers, such as e-commerce platforms, as well as through real-time technology-driven monitoring, such as emissions monitoring or integration of video-based data.[49] However, these diverse information sources, some of which are proprietary, are not necessarily incorporated into the various central and subnational credit platforms. Primary responsibility for the development and coordination of the project rests primarily on the People's Bank of China (PBOC), which is responsible for the financial credit system and the National Development and Reform Commission (NDRC), which leads coordination of the rest of the social credit system.[50]

As shown in Table 16.1, the 'main control centre' of credit information sharing is the National Credit Information Sharing Platform (NCISP) jointly developed by the NDRC and the State Information Center (SIC), which connects over 90 central-level government departments, provincial regulators and information-sharing

[46] On these pilots and the development of the system, see von Blomberg (n 2) 124-26; Brussee (n 2).

[47] Draft PRC Social Credit Law (n 41).

[48] See, eg, Regulations of Shanghai Municipality on Social Credit [上海市社会信用条例], No 54, 2017 (1 October 2017), art 8 (defining social credit to include public credit information obtained by regulators and market (ie, commercial) credit information obtained by companies and credit service organisations based on commercial transactions and operations). The scope of public credit information is defined in the National Basic Catalogue of Public Credit Information [全国公共信用信息基础目录] (2022).

[49] European Union Chamber of Commerce in China (EuroCham), 'The Digital Hand: How China's Corporate Social Credit System Conditions Market Actors' (Beijing 2019), 14–15.

[50] Draft PRC Social Credit Law (n 41) art 4 (assigning primary responsibility to the PBOC and the NDRC), art 8 (regarding industry credit systems). See also Guiding Opinions (n 42); Draft PRC Social Credit Law (n 41).

with over 70 social credit institutions.[51] Bringing together regulatory enforcement information across departmental silos, it is intended to integrate and regulate formerly separate financial, commercial and public credit information.[52] However, integration has proven difficult even for public credit information at various levels, with far less integration of private sources of credit information and while all of the information on the NCISP is available to regulators, the NCISP itself is not accessible by the public.

A subset of this information is, however, publicly available through the national Credit China portal[53] administered by the NDRC and PBOC and the NDRC's National Center for Public Credit Information (NCPCI) platform,[54] which reports largely identical information. Credit platforms are also maintained by provincial governments, which may collect locally designated public credit information.[55] These platforms also maintain credit blacklists and links for credit repair in addition to the Supreme People's Court, which maintains blacklists on judgment enforcement. In addition, the State Administration for Market Regulation (SAMR), which is responsible for corporate registration and oversight has maintained the separate National Enterprise Credit Information Publicity System (NECIPS) since 2016.[56] Financial credit reports for companies can be obtained via the PBOC Credit Reference Centre, but these are not publicly available,[57] nor is financial credit information included in public credit reports on any of the other platforms.[58] Despite the potential for a 'unified' social credit system to emerge, the reality is instead highly fragmented.[59]

[51] SIC, 'National Credit Information Sharing Platform Project (Phase II) (Constructed by the State Information Center) Successfully Passed the Completion Acceptance' (4 Jan 2021). Available at: www.sic.gov.cn/News/603/10918.htm; 'About the National Credit Information Sharing Platform,' [全国信用信息共享平台简介]. Available at: www.ncpci.org.cn/ztzl/202010/t20201022_213912.html.

[52] On the scope of the social credit system, see general sources at (n 2) above.

[53] Credit China. See www.creditchina.gov.cn.

[54] National Centre for Public Credit Information (国家公共信用信息中心) See www.ncpci.org.cn/ztzl/202010/t20201022_213912.html.

[55] National Basic Catalogue of Public Credit Information (n 48) above, para 6.

[56] SAMR, National Enterprise Credit Information Publicity System (国家企业信用信息公示系统). See www.gsxt.gov.cn/index.html.

[57] 'Credit Reference Centre'. See www.pbccrc.org.cn/crc/zxgk/index_list_list.shtml; 'Commercial Credit Reporting'. See www.pbccrc.org.cn/crc/qyzx/listx.shtml. Corporate credit reports can be obtained from the PBOC under a service subscription, including mapping of related enterprises based on the PBOC's proprietary data mining. ibid.

[58] Financial credit reports are maintained by the PBOC but can only be obtained by the company itself or with government authorisation. Financial credit ratings are therefore not integrated into the social credit records reported on the Credit China platform.

[59] See generally Brussee (n 2).

Table 16.1 Social Credit Portals

Platform	**Authority(ies)**	**Access**	**Related Party & Key Personnel Information**	**Other Credit Information**
National Centre for Public Credit Information (国家公共信用信息中心) (NCPCI)	NDRC	Public	Legal representative only	Registration information, social credit pledges, seriously untrustworthy blacklisting, abnormal operations,[60] public credit pledges, public credit audits, judicial orders and enforcement, suggestions for improving credit status
Credit China (信用中国)	NDRC & PBOC	Public	Same as NCPCI	Same as NCPCI
National Enterprise Credit Information Publicity System（国家企业信用信息公示系统）(NECIPS)	SAMR	Public	Shareholders & capital investment, key persons without SCID List of branches and related entity names, with SCID Senior management Share transferees	Amendments to registration information, liquidation, administrative permits and penalties, abnormal operations, serious legal violations, inspections, judicial orders/agreements, security interests on property or equity, intellectual property registrations, annual reports
National Credit Information Sharing Platform	NDRC; State Information Centre	Non-public	N/A	N/A

(continued)

[60] 'Abnormal operations' refers to failure to file an annual report or filing false or misleading information. State Council, Interim Regulation on Enterprise Information Disclosure [企业信息公示暂行条例] (2014), art 17.

Table 16.1 ***(Continued)***

Platform	Authority(ies)	Access	Related Party & Key Personnel Information	Other Credit Information
PBOC Financial Credit Platform	PBOC	Non-public; accessible to regulators and to own record on application	Shareholders, related entity names, nature of relationship and SCID Major investors Senior management, with SCID Enterprises directly related to data subject Guarantors/ guarantees Debtor/creditor relationships	Current and long-term liabilities, guarantees and related payments; loans and other financing sources; public records summary on tax arrears, civil judgments and enforcement, administrative penalties, social insurance payments, licences and permits, customs inspection benefits

In order to facilitate clear identification of each 'credit subject', each legal person, whether a corporate entity or natural person, has a 'unified social credit code' (统一社会信用代码) to which its social credit report is linked across all these platforms.[61] Social credit reports for affiliates must be located by their own unique number or by name. With respect to content, each credit subject's record includes the public credit information that is legally permitted to be collected under the annually updated Catalogue of Public Credit Information, such as judgment defaults, administrative permits and inspection results and information on any breaches of the corporate registration requirements.[62]

Relevant guidance on the development of the system contemplates the potential for a comprehensive public credit assessment (公共信用) for all market participants that would be available to all regulators, trade associations and financial institutions.[63] However, there is not yet an aggregate ranking or score of this sort

[61] State Council, Notice of the State Council on Approving and Forwarding the General Plan of the National Development and Reform Commission and Other Departments on the Development of a Unified Social Credit Code System for Legal Persons and Other Organisations [国务院关于批转发展改革委等部门法人和其他组织统一社会信用代码制度建设总体方案的通知 [现行有效]], No 33, 11 June 2022.

[62] The catalogue is jointly published by the State Council and the CCP Central Committee. National Basic Catalogue of Public Credit Information (n 48) above.

[63] Guiding Opinions (n 42), art 3(6)–(7). Numerous studies on the system's evolution have identified significant technical and institutional challenges to the project. See sources cited n 5 above.

for any particular company or individual. Instead, SAMR itself, as well as several subnational credit audit systems, assign points and letter grades to classify conduct that falls within the scope of social credit measures.[64]

Like some of China's early state-led incentive systems for corporate social responsibility,[65] the corporate credit system uses a mix of carrots and sticks to promote better corporate 'trustworthiness'. Companies with strong social credit records may be eligible to participate in public procurement, be subject to less frequent inspections by enforcement authorities and enjoy other preferences, while companies designated as 'untrustworthy' may be subject to designated penalties.[66] These include a ban on public listing, restricted market access, restricted access to credit and finance and public censure.[67] 'Naming and shaming' is one of the primary tools of the social credit system and central and subnational government entities maintain various 'blacklists' for those with low 'trustworthiness' and 'redlists' for those with exemplary social credit records.[68] Market participants and trade associations are encouraged to use credit information as the basis for their own incentives and penalties depending on whether business partners or members have 'good' or 'bad' social credit, beyond traditional financial creditworthiness.[69]

A central feature of the system and one of the most controversial is the potential for joint penalties (失信联合惩戒) that are imposed by multiple regulators in the event of 'seriously untrustworthy' conduct, such as a judgment default, even if the conduct would not be within the legal authority of the regulator imposing the joint penalties; joint rewards are also permitted.[70] These rules also provide that seriously untrustworthy conduct by an entity may result in penalties against its

[64] SAMR, Opinion on Promoting Corporate Credit Risk Classification Management Guidance [市场监管总局关于推进企业信用风险分类管理进一步提升监管效能的意见 国市监信发] No 6 (13 Jan 2022). See also China Banking & Insurance Reg Commission, Banking and Insurance Institutions Corporate Governance Oversight Audit Measures [银行保险机构公司治理监管评估办法], No 199, 28 November 2022 (establishing a graded (A, B, C, D, E) ranking system); Shanghai Bureau of Ecology & Environment, Shanghai Municipal Enterprises & Institutions Ecology & Environmental Credit Audit Draft Measures [上海市企事业单位生态环境信用评价管理办法（试行）No 5 (1 August 2022) (imposing compliance-based audit grades); Lin & Milhaupt (n 3) (analyzing the Zhejiang corporate credit system).

[65] Harper Ho, 'Beyond Regulation' (n 15).

[66] As of 2022, permitted penalties are defined in an annually updated list that includes cross-references to relevant supporting legal authorities. See NDRC & PBOC, Basic Checklist of National Untrustworthy Punishment Measures [全国失信惩戒措施基础清单] (2022).

[67] Guiding Opinions (n 42), art 4(9)-(11); Draft PRC Social Credit Law (n 41).
art 90.

[68] M von Blomberg and H Yu, 'Shaming the Untrustworthy and Paths to Relief in China's Social Credit System' 49(6) *Modern China* 744 (2023). National level blacklists at present focus on judgment defaults, migrant worker wage defaults and tax evasion. 'Seriously Untrustworthy,' Credit China. Available at: www.creditchina.gov.cn.

[69] For example, see Shanghai Social Credit Regulations (n 48), arts 26–27.

[70] Guiding Opinions (n 42), para 8 ('The construction of a cross-regional, cross-industry, and cross-field joint punishment for dishonesty mechanism shall be accelerated, to fundamentally resolve the problem of repeated occurrence of dishonesty and occurrence of dishonesty in different places'). See also Guiding Opinions of the State Council on Establishing and Improving the Joint Incentive System

legal representative and other responsible persons, which is another form of joint penalty.[71]

A noteworthy feature of the corporate credit system is that it defines business 'trustworthiness' more broadly than legal compliance, reaching conduct that has historically been the subject of corporate voluntary charitable or corporate responsibility initiatives. It also includes business integrity or 'honesty,' and encompasses voluntary information parties may provide on performance of contract obligations, although reporting on private contract performance or breach is not presently required.[72] Companies are also encouraged to make voluntary 'public social credit pledges,' which are included in the public credit report and are verified by trade associations, charitable organisations, or government authorities.[73] This aspect of the CSC could be used to reward Chinese companies for the voluntary corporate responsibility commitments that many have been making under various domestic and international regimes like the UN Global Compact since the mid-2000s.[74]

Companies or individuals can request corrections to their credit record online or seek to repair their social credit by remedying the underlying behaviour, making positive social credit pledges, undergoing social credit training, or making charitable contributions.[75] Social credit blacklisting and other penalties can also be appealed through administrative reconsideration or administrative litigation against a regulatory agency,[76] though challenging social credit penalties is often difficult.[77]

for Keeping Trust and the Joint Punishment System for Dishonesty and Accelerating the Construction of Social Integrity' [国务院关于建立完善守信联合激励和失信联合惩戒制度加快推进社会诚信建设的指导意见] GuoFa No 33 (2016). Under its authority, memoranda of understanding for joint penalties and rewards have been adopted among various regulators. NDRC & 31 Departments, Joint Memorandum on Joint Penalties for Untrustworthiness and Joint Incentives for Trustworthiness [发展改革委31个部门联合发布《失信联合惩戒和守信联合激励备忘录》] (31 Aug 2017).

[71] M von Blomberg and B Ahl, 'Debating the Legality of Social Credit in China – A Review of Chinese Legal Scholarship,' manuscript (on file with author) (discussing academic criticisms by Chinese scholars of these provisions).

[72] Existing guidance and the draft Corporate Social Credit Law define performance of contract obligations as part of public credit information, but it is currently voluntary and there is no mechanism for private parties to report on contract breach outside of litigation. Guiding Opinions (n 42), art 58; Draft PRC Social Credit Law (n 41) (stating that serious contract breach should affect the credit record of the breaching party)).

[73] Guiding Opinions (n 42), art 2(1); Draft PRC Social Credit Law (n 41), art 7.

[74] On PRC corporate responsibility commitments, see Harper Ho (n 15). There is no indication from the review of public credit reports conducted in this study that this is yet being done.

[75] Guiding Opinions (n 42) paras 9, 13. See also Measures for Management of Credit Repair Following Disputes over Untrustworthy Behaviour [失信行为纠纷后的信用信息修复管理办法] (1 May 2023).

[76] Guiding Opinions (n 42), arts 4(13), 5(17); Draft PRC Social Credit Law (n 41), arts 93–100. State Council, Interim Regulation on Enterprise Information Disclosure (23 July 2014), art 21 (regarding administrative reconsideration and litigation).

[77] See von Blomberg and Yu (n 71), discussing both of these procedures and the legal obstacles to challenging social credit penalties; Brussee (n 2) 122–24.

3.2. Mapping the Reach of the Corporate Credit System

Corporate credit records are associated with the entity-level SCID, raising many interesting questions over the system's application to corporate groups. As with legal liability, there are several possibilities: (i) social credit rewards and penalties could be applied only at the level of the individual entity; (ii) the system could assign social credit rewards and penalties for corporate subsidiaries' conduct on an enterprise-wide basis to the direct shareholder (i.e. parent company) and thus directly or indirectly to the ultimate parent of the corporate group; and (iii) the social credit rewards and penalties of *any* entity in the group could affect the social credit record of all related entities, horizontally and vertically. The first approach disregards the control and coordination of the ultimate group parent but more strongly respects the autonomy and legal separateness of group affiliates. The second and third approaches would be more difficult to implement and justify legally in the absence of some degree of shareholder/affiliate control over the affiliates whose untrustworthy actions may have led to a social credit penalty. In addition, as with legal liability, credit responsibility could, in theory, rest on a parent company, affiliate, or business partner for the 'trustworthiness' of another entity based on direct or vicarious liability theories related to its own breach of a legal obligation, or its facilitation of the untrustworthy acts of another.

3.2.1. *Methodology*

To understand how the corporate credit system treats corporate groups and networks, I used a mix of documentary and case law research, as well as an inductive analysis of the content of credit reports on each of the public platforms for selected entities. The initial question to be addressed is whether corporate credit records and platforms report information on related parties, including shareholders, subsidiaries and branches. The first step in this analysis was to review the provincial- and central-level guidance, policy documents and regulations that define credit information and authorise its collection. Next, the content of blacklists, redlists and the credit reports of specific companies in the national and subnational databases were examined to determine whether such records linked to or made mention of any information concerning related entities or persons, or whether negative credit information of an affiliate or individual is reflected in the credit report of related companies.

In order to confirm what information the public can access about corporate affiliates and whether the public credit of affiliates affects the public credit report of a related entity, I reviewed central- and provincial-level blacklists and redlists and the social credit reports of a range of companies from different sectors on the Credit China, NCPCI, PBOC and SAMR platforms and on selected provincial-level platforms.[78] This search included (i) companies who were the named defendants in cases that imposed (or challenged) corporate credit penalties; (ii) several companies included on a central or subnational blacklists;[79] and (iii) several corporate groups with large listed companies and their affiliates, namely China Mobile (a healthy company) and Evergrande Group (a distressed company).

For the Evergrande Group, I also searched the credit records of key responsible persons and certain affiliates to see if they contained any reference to negative credit or untrustworthy behaviour of any other individuals or affiliates within the group. Specifically, I searched national and provincial blacklists for any records related to two key Evergrande holding companies: Evergrande Group Ltd. and Evergrande Real Estate Group Co Ltd (Evergrande Real Estate), both of which are affiliates of China Evergrande Group, which is listed on the Hong Kong stock exchange, as well as for responsible persons associated with these entities. The Evergrande Group is one of China's largest real-estate developers and is now one of the largest distressed firms in the region and the world; in fall 2023, its Chairman was detained in a criminal investigation.[80] As of mid-2023, the Group was reportedly facing over 1,000 lawsuits for claims totalling more than 350 billion yuan (USD 49 billion) as a result of defaults arising out of the group's substantial domestic and overseas debt obligations.[81] Given the significant litigation and domestic impact of Evergrande's downturn, its financial credit is clearly impaired. The public credit records of group affiliates should also include negative indicators and shed light on any enterprise-wide impacts of the poor public credit of its operating affiliates.

In addition, I reviewed cases at all court levels where the term 'social credit' (社会信用), 'corporate credit' (企业社会信用), or 'untrustworthy' (失信) was applied in combination with a broad range of terms, including 'subsidiary', 'affiliate', 'supply chain', 'due diligence', 'controlling shareholder', 'parent-subsidiary' and the like.[82] The resulting cases included tort cases alleging reputational harm or damage, administrative cases challenging the 'trustworthiness' of credit management companies or administrative agencies and cases seeks credit repair.[83]

[78] To ensure the most comprehensive review, I first selected several companies randomly from the Credit China blacklist (as of 25 May 2023) and then searched by the company's unified social credit number on the provincial social credit site for the province of its place of registration.

[79] Not all provinces publish redlists and blacklists, but several, including Guangdong (see www.credit.gd.gov.cn) and Zhejiang (credit.zj.gov.cn), do so for separate types of untrustworthy behaviour, such as tax evasion, migrant wage defaults and judgment defaults.

[80] U Dugar, 'Evergrande Chairman investigated over offshore asset transfers' *Reuters* (2 Oct 2023), Available at: www.reuters.com/world/china/evergrande-chairman-investigated-over-offshore-asset-transfers-wsj-2023-10-02/.

[81] L Liu and L Y Chen, 'Evergrande Unit Faces 1,426 Lawsuits Involving $49 Billion' *Bloomberg* (2 June 2023). Available at: www.news.bloomberglaw.com/securities-law/evergrandes-hengda-unit-is-facing-1-426-unsettled-lawsuits.

[82] Caselaw searches relied on the Beida Fabao (北大法宝) database. Additional review of cases involving corporate credit repair did not identify cases involving company attempts to repair credit of their affiliates.

[83] *Chen Liangguo v Zhengzhou Human Resources and Social Security Bureau Labor and Social Security Administration (Labor and Social Security)*, Administrative Ruling of Zhengzhou Intermediate People's

3.2.2. Findings

My review of the policies and rules governing the construction of the corporate social credit system did not identify any that authorise penalties to be imposed on a corporate 'credit subject' because of the conduct of its business partners or affiliates. As discussed below, numerous social credit policies and rules extend to individual control persons, but these provisions do not appear to apply to entities.[84] Moreover, none of the regulations and policy documents, including subnational ranking or rating systems, that define social credit information or social credit penalties bring subsidiaries or business partners within their scope, nor are companies required to disclose the identity of their key business partners under the public credit catalogue.[85]

In addition, basic information categories relevant to corporate group affiliation are limited in the public platform reports, while public credit platforms (Credit China and NCPCI) provide far more limited information on controlled affiliates, significant shareholders, or even the identity of corporate directors and supervisors, when compared to information that would be found in the annual report of a company listed on any of the Chinese stock exchanges.[86] The SAMR corporate registry reports, which exist for purposes separate from the public credit platforms, are the most comprehensive, yet even these include almost no public credit information or information on subsidiaries and other affiliates, despite this information being with the scope of SAMR reporting requirements.[87] Corporate credit information and even basic identification of shareholders and key persons is also inconsistently available on the public credit platforms, even where these categories of information are provided for. Financial credit information is not integrated into the public social credit platforms, in part due to the division of power between the PBOC and the NDRC.[88] In addition, the social credit system now protects personal financial

Court of Henan Province (2020) 01-535[陈良国诉郑州市人力资源和社会保障局劳动和社会保障行政管理(劳动、社会保障]，河南省郑州市中级人民法院行政裁定书 (2020)豫01行终535号] (rejecting allegations that the labour bureau and breached its obligation to properly record social credit information and impose joint penalties).

[84] See the discussion on shareholder attribution and control person liability below.

[85] National Basic Catalogue of Public Credit Information (n 48).

[86] The disclosure requirements for companies listed on China's stock exchanges do not currently require any reporting related to social credit.

[87] SAMR, Credit Risk Classification (n 64). SAMR records have a reporting category for this, but none of the credit records reviewed here included such information. SAMR, Regulations on the Disclosure of Enterprise Information [企业信息公示条列] (2019).

[88] Some courts have also held that because the financial credit and social credit (ie public and market credit) systems are not connected and financial credit is not publicly available, it cannot produce reputational harm. *Binzhou Dayou New Energy Development Co Ltd. v Liuzhou Bank Co, Ltd Nanning Branch and China Cinda Asset Management Co., Ltd., Civil Judgment of Binzhou Intermediate People's Court of Shandong Province* (2020), 16-2712 [滨州大有新能源开发有限公司诉柳州银行股份有限公司南宁分行、中国信达资产管理股份有限公司名誉权纠纷案，山东省滨州市中级人民法院民事判决书 (2020) 鲁16民终2712号].

information by excluding it from the definition of public or 'social' credit information that may be collected.[89]

Public credit reports on Credit China and NCPCI often indicate that entire categories of credit information, indeed, most information, is unavailable or not accessible to the public even when reporting templates indicate it should be collected. Corporate registry reports from SAMR and financial credit reports from the PBOC generally contain more detailed information on share ownership, debtor-creditor relationships, key personnel and, in fact, social credit, than is available in the social credit reports from Credit China or the NCPCI.

Finally, consistent with the findings of Krause and others, my review indicated that leading private corporate due diligence platforms generally provide much more dynamic and detailed information on corporate affiliations, related entities and key individuals than is publicly available on public credit portals.[90] Although no comprehensive analysis was done for this study, information gaps appear to be more extensive for larger companies and for state-owned enterprises. For example, the Evergrande holding companies' public credit records, include SAMR's corporate registry reports, do not give any indication of their impairment, nor do they provide information that would allow their reports to be linked to those of other affiliates or key individuals. Perhaps to protect individual privacy, the credit records for Evergrande Group and Evergrande Real Estate identify their shareholders without the SCID, which is listed as 'nonpublic' (非公示项). Beyond the corporate annual reports, there is no information on any judicial measures, administrative inspections or credit penalties, nor is there any information on related entities.

The case law research revealed a wide range of cases mentioning corporate social credit, including credit repair cases and cases involving substantive consolidation, veil-piercing and the like. However, I found no cases where one company's social credit had been attributed to or affected the social credit of a corporate affiliate or where the dispute concerned 'untrustworthy' conduct of a corporate affiliate or business partner.[91] In a number of cases, courts hesitated when requested to do so by the plaintiff if there was insufficient justification on the facts of the case to pierce the corporate veil to the affiliate.[92] In the vast majority of cases, the social

[89] See, eg, Shanghai Social Credit Regulations (n 48), art 14 (restricting collection of personal financial information without the credit subject's informed consent).

[90] Key providers include Qi Chacha (企查查), www.qichacha.com/; Tian Yan Cha (天眼查), www.tianyancha.com/; Qixin Bao (启信宝), www.qixin.com/. As of 2023, all of the main public portals and some of the subnational ones require users to create a user account using real ID information in order to obtain access.

[91] Case research is made more difficult by the fact that all cases involving companies use the term 'social credit' in reference to a litigant's unified social credit number.

[92] See, eg, *Mingming Co Ltd v Ruien Construction Co Ltd, Civil Judgment of Suzhou Intermediate People's Court of Jiangsu Province* [2018] 05-8402 (苏州市铭铭物资有限公司与苏州瑞恩建材有限公司、夏雨俊等买卖合同纠纷二审民事判决书) (2018) 苏05民终8402号 (rejecting a petition to impose joint liability on the company, its controlling shareholder and an affiliated entity based on the debtor's untrustworthiness).

credit system was not directly relevant but social credit identification (SCID) was used to confirm the identity of one of the parties to the case.[93] A search for cases referencing the supply chain or suppliers in relation to social credit or untrustworthiness also found none relevant to the question of attribution of social credit penalties among affiliates or business networks.[94] In addition, none of the 216 guiding cases issued by the Supreme People's Court, which are binding on lower courts, reference the social credit system.[95]

3.2.3. Enterprise or Network Effects?

It therefore appears that the corporate social credit system does not yet impose social credit consequences on an enterprise basis for corporate groups, nor does it at present directly reach business networks. As Table 16.1 indicates, some information on related entities, including their unified social credit codes, is available from the SAMR portal and from the PBOC, although not uniformly elsewhere. Such information could facilitate litigation against multiple related corporate entities and their key personnel, as well as horizontal and vertical attribution of social credit factors to parent and sister entities. Since all corporate credit reports are identified by SCID at the entity level, regulators could aggregate these records relatively easily in order to get a picture of enterprise-wide public credit levels, but there is currently no direct evidence that affiliate social credit performance is aggregated in this manner. Publicly available social credit reports only include the name and social credit identifier (SCID) for branches on the parent company's corporate registration, but not subsidiaries' names or SCIDs, so linking related entities' credit records is not possible using information provided on the public portals.[96] Given the limitations of the current findings, it is not clear that credit penalties for a subsidiary will affect the credit of its parent or of another affiliate.

There are, however, indications that companies' social credit may have more concrete effects on corporate groups and affiliates in the future. For example, a 2020 revision to the information disclosure rules for small- and medium-sized enterprises (SMEs) that are not listed on a stock exchange but whose securities

[93] For example, *Guangxi Shengda Construction Engineering Co., Ltd. v. Jiangxi Zhongsheng Construction Group Co, Ltd, Sales Contract Dispute, Civil Judgment of Nanning Intermediate People's Court of Guangxi Zhuang Autonomous Region* [2020] 01-1965 [广西昇达建筑工程有限公司诉江西省中盛建筑集团有限公司，买卖合同纠纷，广西壮族自治区南宁市中级人民法院民事判决书] (2020) 桂01 民终1965号 (using the SCID to facilitate determination of the contracting party).

[94] The low number of cases is not surprising. There is no supply chain due diligence mandate currently in force in China, so the application of credit penalties for supply chain conduct may lack legal basis.

[95] 'Guiding Cases [指導案列]', PRC Supreme People's Court. Available at: www.court.gov.cn/fabu-gengduo-77.html (accessed 24 November 2023). Six guiding cases involve affiliated entities, including four veil-piercing cases.

[96] Beijing Catalogue of Public Credit Information Part 2: Legal Person and Other Organization [公共信用信息目录， 第2部分：法人和其他组织], Beijing Local Standards DB11/T 467.2 (1 January 2023), para 6 (requiring identification of branches and their responsible persons, but not for subsidiaries).

are quoted for sale in over-the-counter markets defined 'material' information to include the designation of an entity and its subsidiaries as the subject of penalties for untrustworthiness.[97] No similar rules apply at present to listed companies on Chinese stock exchanges, but this example indicates how social credit penalties may interact with other regulatory regimes.

3.2.4. Shareholder Attribution and Control Person Liability.

In general, however, the corporate credit system relies heavily on penalties for individuals under the national guidelines on joint penalties, which are reflected in the credit audit systems of some subnational governments.[98] Specifically, when credit penalties are imposed for seriously untrustworthy acts by the entity itself, credit penalties may also be imposed on the entity's directors, individual shareholders or actual controllers,[99] legal representative, supervisors, and other individuals who are deemed 'responsible persons' or who exercise control over an 'untrustworthy' entity.[100] Similarly, the conduct of these key corporate personnel may affect the public credit of the entity itself such that if these individuals default on a judgment or commit other seriously 'untrustworthy' acts or have a judgment default, their conduct will lower the entity's credit grade.[101] However, the joint penalty rules that extend to shareholders of the 'untrustworthy' company appear directed solely at natural persons, not affiliated entities, and so do not appear intended to impose enterprise liability effects on corporate groups.[102] In addition, despite the clear emphasis on individual accountability for corporate wrongdoing under the social credit system, these joint penalties cannot be readily identified by the public, since none of the national platforms report individual SCIDs for shareholders or other responsible persons.

[97] National Equities Exchange and Quotations (NEEQ), Information Disclosure Rules for Companies in the National Equities Exchange and Quotations System [全国中小企业股份转让系统挂牌公司信息披露规则] (2021). Available at: www.neeq.com.cn/class_c0/200011043.html, arts 28 and art 56(14) (retaining the 2020 provisions that require immediate disclosure of defined material events).

[98] Memorandum on Joint Penalties (n 70); Draft PRC Social Credit Law (n 41), para 4 ('For dishonest persons subject to enforcement and their legal representatives, principal persons in charge, and those affecting debt performance' and the 'directly responsible personnel and actual controllers' are subject to personal penalties, such as limits on 'high-level' consumption).

[99] The Company Law defines 'actual controller' as any non-shareholder who holds actual control 'by means of investment relations, agreements or any other arrangements': PRC Company Law (n 27), art 226(3).

[100] See Guiding Opinions (n 42), art 4(12) ('The legal representative, primary person in charge, and actual controller of a market participant [subject to joint punishment for dishonesty] shall be subject to punishment for dishonesty, and the relevant dishonest acts shall be recorded in his or her personal credit records.'); Shanghai Social Credit Regulations (n 48), art 33.

[101] For example, see Zhejiang Province Five Types of Public Credit Audit Guidance [浙江省五类主体公共信用评价指引] (2020) 6–7.

[102] See the following discussion on joint penalties for individuals.

Individual social credit penalties include restrictions on high-end consumption and bans on investing in, or in some cases being employed in, a related industry.[103] Similarly, social credit penalties for entities that are designated highly untrustworthy include multi-year bans on market access to the given sector. Joint penalties for responsible persons can also have collateral effects on related entities if there is joint ownership or overlapping directors or officers, since individuals who commit major violations in certain fields may be banned from serving as a legal representative, director, supervisor, or senior manager in another company in that field.[104] Depending on the seriousness of the harm, employees or other responsible personnel may also bear social credit penalties even if they are not acting in a managerial or controlling capacity.[105]

In this regard, the corporate credit system is consistent with, and indeed is legally based on, other pre-existing regulatory regimes that extend liability for regulatory violations to control persons, the company's legal representative, or other responsible persons. These include, for instance, insider trading prohibitions, anti-money laundering rules and certain environmental regulations.[106] Some of these regimes, such as securities regulation and stock exchange listing rules, also utilise reputational sanctions against both companies and responsible officers.[107] If controlling shareholders are held liable on veil-piercing grounds for abuse of control in ways that result in a loss to the company itself, their responsible persons may also bear direct liability.[108]

3.2.5. Summary Observations

By integrating information on corporate group affiliates and related parties through entity and individual SCIDs, China's corporate credit system already has the potential to apply credit incentives on an enterprise-wide basis. Were PRC

[103] Memorandum on Joint Penalties (n 70); Draft PRC Social Credit Law (n 41), para 4 ('For dishonest persons subject to enforcement and their legal representatives, principal persons in charge, and those affecting debt performance' and the 'directly responsible personnel and actual controllers' are subject to personal penalties, such as limits on 'high-level' consumption).

[104] ibid.

[105] For example, penalties for serious production safety or food safety violations may lead to a limited-term industry ban and other social credit penalties for the 'operating unit' and their relevant employees. Memorandum on Joint Penalties (n 70).

[106] Wang (n 33), 216–19 (referencing examples). See also PRC Ministry of Ecology & Environment (MEE), Measures on the Management of Enterprise Environmental Disclosure According to Law [企业环境信息依法披露管理办法], effective 22 August 2022. Available at: www.mee.gov.cn/zcwj/zcjd/202112/t20211221_964842.shtml (establishing corporate and individual liability for disclosure violations).

[107] B L Liebman and C J Milhaupt, 'Reputational Sanctions in China's Securities Market' (2008) 108 *Colum L Rev* 929.

[108] For example, CBIRC, Measures on the Supervision of Large Shareholders of Banking and Insurance Institutions [中国银保监会关于印发银行保险机构大股东行为监管办法（试行）的通知], No 43 (14 October 2021) (imposing affirmative risk oversight and governance obligations on institutional investors).

regulators to do so, the system would reach corporate groups and networks to an extent that goes beyond even the broadest boundaries contemplated by international corporate due diligence and reporting regimes. At present, however, the public-facing corporate credit platforms are not sufficiently transparent to facilitate public oversight of corporate groups and business networks, nor indeed to help the public readily identify related parties, control relationships and corporate group structures, much less business networks. Even as designed, the system does not directly require supply chain or value chain due diligence and its opacity with respect to large, state-sector firms in practice suggests a double standard for transparency. Fragmentation among platforms and regulators impedes the system's goals to comprehensively integrate multiple public and private oversight systems. The tension between protecting private personal data and financial credit information, on the one hand and expanding access to social (i.e. market and public) credit information on the other, also points to necessary limits that will also constrain the system's ability to achieve its competing regulatory goals.

4. Corporate Trustworthiness in Comparative Context

China's corporate social credit system has high ambitions to promote corporate accountability, individual integrity and responsible business practice. In this regard, it has much in common with private and government-backed corporate reporting and due diligence regimes internationally that also seek to promote greater accountability for corporate groups by regulating information.

However, the regulatory goals of the Chinese system are more comprehensive and the role of the party-state more central than in emerging international reporting and due diligence regimes. Most critically, the corporate credit system is directed at all areas of legal compliance and public credit records, as well as much of the underlying data on which they depend, are generated by regulatory authorities rather than by companies themselves. The high degree of government control over credit information gives the party-state privileged access to comprehensive credit data, as well as the power to limit public access. This appears to be the case for public credit reporting for many of China's largest firms.

There are, of course, other critical distinctions between the corporate credit system and international corporate reporting, rating and due diligence systems that ultimately facilitate market oversight, support private standards and ratings and do not directly penalise corporate conduct as long as corporate actors comply with relevant reporting obligations. Most obviously, public enforcement and incentive mechanisms for the corporate credit system are far more expansive. For example, the joint penalty system amplifies the collateral financial, reputational and operational risks of regulatory violations.[109] The design of the system

[109] von Blomberg and Ahl (n 71).

therefore rests on incentives that go well beyond legally grounded principles of liability and attribution, creating new compliance risks for companies. Its implementation also appears to rely heavily on credit penalties for key individuals that are linked to corporate conduct and vice versa.

Examining the question of how the corporate credit system approaches corporate boundaries and whether it extends to the corporate enterprise also brings to light shared challenges of any system that seeks to define and enforce corporate accountability so extensively. For example, what should be the role of government in policing unethical, if not strictly illegal, business practice? What should be the relative role of the state and corporations (whether private or state-owned) in promoting sustainable and responsible business practice? How well will the 'credit system for the credit system' that China's system contemplates work to regulate credit information processors and providers? In other words, can it monitor the monitors?[110] These and other critical technical challenges have long plagued international financial credit systems and related corporate governance and sustainability ranking systems. They present equal obstacles to the PRC's social credit project. However, since the design of corporate compliance incentives and the particular regulatory challenges of corporate groups are universal challenges, how China's corporate social credit system evolves and how it extends to corporate groups and business networks bear watching.

[110] China's current regulations and the forthcoming Social Credit Law seek to impose obligations of this sort on social credit management agencies, all who collect and disseminate social credit data and on government itself. See (n 2) above and sources cited therein. See also Draft PRC Social Credit Law (n 41). Compare I Chiu, 'The EU Sustainable Finance Agenda: Developing Governance for Double Materiality in Sustainability Metrics' *EBOLR* (2022) 23: 87–123 (arguing for meta-regulation of rating agencies and other sustainable finance information intermediaries).

INDEX

www.ingramcontent.com/pod-product-compliance
Ingram Content Group UK Ltd.
Pitfield, Milton Keynes, MK11 3LW, UK
UKHW020231290926
15470UKWH00002B/478

9 781509 970759